To Swear Like a Sailor

Anyone could swear like a sailor! Within the larger culture, sailors had pride of place in swearing. But how they swore and the reasons for their bad language were not strictly wedded to maritime things. Instead, sailor swearing, indeed all swearing during this period, was connected to larger developments. This book traces the interaction between the maritime and mainstream worlds in the United States while examining cursing, language, logbooks, storytelling, sailor songs, reading, images, and material goods. *To Swear Like a Sailor* offers insight into the character of Jack Tar – the common seaman – and into the early republic. It illuminates the cultural connections between Great Britain and the United States and the appearance of a distinct American national identity. This book explores the emergence of sentimental notions about the common man – through the guise of the sailor – on stage, in song, in literature, and in images.

Paul A. Gilje is a George Lynn Cross Research Professor at the University of Oklahoma, Norman. His book *Liberty on the Waterfront* (2003) won the best book award from the Society for Historians of the Early American Republic. He is the author or editor of ten other books, including the most recent, *Free Trade and Sailors' Rights in the War of 1812* (2013). He has lectured throughout the United States and in Europe and has received numerous grants to support his research. In 2009–10, he served as president of the Society for Historians of the Early American Republic.

To Swear Like a Sailor

Maritime Culture in America, 1750–1850

PAUL A. GILJE
University of Oklahoma, Norman

CAMBRIDGE
UNIVERSITY PRESS

CAMBRIDGE
UNIVERSITY PRESS

32 Avenue of the Americas, New York, NY 10013-2473, USA

Cambridge University Press is part of the University of Cambridge.

It furthers the University's mission by disseminating knowledge in the pursuit of
education, learning, and research at the highest international levels of excellence.

www.cambridge.org
Information on this title: www.cambridge.org/9780521746168

© Paul A. Gilje 2016

First published 2016

Printed in the United States of America

A catalogue record for this publication is available from the British Library.

Library of Congress Cataloging in Publication Data
Gilje, Paul A., 1951– author.
To swear like a sailor : Maritime Culture in America, 1750–1850 / Paul A. Gilje,
University of Oklahoma, Norman.
pages cm
Includes bibliographical references and index.
ISBN 978-0-521-76235-9 (hardback) – ISBN 978-0-521-74616-8 (pbk.)
1. Seafaring life – United States – History – 18th century.   2. Seafaring
life – United States – History – 19th century.   3. Sailors – United
States – Social life and customs.   4. Sailors – United States – Social
conditions.   5. Sailors – Language.   I. Title.
VK23.G538   2015
387.50973'09033–dc23   2015029114

ISBN 978-0-521-76235-9 Hardback
ISBN 978-0-521-74616-8 Paperback

To my brother, Stephen Gilje
and my sister, Kathleen Gilje

Contents

Illustrations

Acknowledgments

Although most of this book has been written since 2011, some of the writing and much of the research and thinking reach back decades as I labored on earlier projects. Over the course of this time span I have incurred many debts.

It costs money to do research, especially to travel to manuscript collections. Since 2008 I have been a George Lynn Cross Research Professor at the University of Oklahoma, which carries with it an annual research account. Before this award I was fortunate to have received numerous grants from the University of Oklahoma which all told add up to many thousands of dollars. I want to thank Paul Bell and Kelly Damphousse, who have served as deans in the College of Arts and Sciences during the writing of this book. The Office of the Vice President for Research under the leadership of first Lee Williams and now Kelvin Droegemeier has been the source of several research grants. Likewise I want to acknowledge two provosts – Nancy Mergler and Kyle Harper – for their support. Kyle, who is a classicist, also provided an important Latin translation for one of the images. President David Boren has offered inspirational leadership at the University of Oklahoma for more than twenty years and deserves to be singled out for creating and sustaining an intellectual atmosphere that values research and scholarship.

Because this book builds on the research I did for my *Liberty on the Waterfront*, the same institutional support I had for that book should also be acknowledged in this one. My first forays into maritime history began during a Rockefeller Resident Fellowship at the program of Atlantic History and Culture at Johns Hopkins University in 1987–88. I continued my exploration of sailors during the spring of 1991 at the

Center for the History of Freedom, Washington University, St. Louis, under the directorship of Richard Davis. My work for *Liberty on the Waterfront* was also supported by funding from the Massachusetts Historical Society, the Peabody Essex Museum, a summer stipend from the National Endowment for the Humanities, and two grants from the Oklahoma Humanities Council. Since the publication of *Liberty on the Waterfront* in 2004, I have received additional support for research and writing. In November 2008 I spent a wonderful month gearing up to begin writing *To Swear Like a Sailor* at the C. V. Starr Center for the Study of the American Experience in Chestertown, Maryland, only to find myself immersed in another project – *Free Trade and Sailors' Rights in the War of 1812*. I owe a special thanks to Adam Goodheart for arranging my stay in Chestertown and to Jill Ogline Titus, Michael Buckley, and Jennifer Emily for facilitating my work at the Starr Center. As I explain in the introduction to *Free Trade and Sailors' Rights in the War of 1812*, that book was supposed to be a chapter in this one but grew into a project all its own. After finishing this side project in 2011, I returned to my original plan of action and was able to complete a draft of *To Swear Like a Sailor* by the summer of 2014. I was particularly fortunate not to have a teaching assignment in the spring of 2014 and was able to focus all of my efforts on writing as a research associate at the McNeil Center for Early American Studies in Philadelphia. I thank Dan Richter for this opportunity and cherish my time working in that hotbed of scholarly activity surrounded by so many young and incredibly active minds. I especially appreciate the friendship of Katy Hemphill, my officemate, and Brenna O'Rourke Holland, whose office was across the hall. I also want to thank Amy Baxter Bellamy and Barbara Natello for everything they did to make my sojourn at the McNeil Center so pleasant and easy. I would also like to thank John Dixon for reading the chapter on logbooks and Alp Atay for assistance in running down some of the sources on Hugh Calhoun.

All researchers owe a great deal to librarians and libraries. The University of Oklahoma Library has been a refuge and incredible resource for me ever since I arrived on campus in 1980. My small library study has provided me with the space to research and write. And the staff of the library has always been helpful in the extreme, especially the interlibrary loan office and Laurie Scrivener, the history librarian. Beyond the confines of my own institution I am grateful for the assistance of the wonderful staffs at the following repositories: the Beinecke Rare Book and Manuscript Library at Yale University, Center for Maine

History, Connecticut Historical Society, the G. W. Blunt White Library at Mystic Seaport, the Historical Society of Pennsylvania, the Kendall Whaling Museum, the Library of Congress, the Marblehead Historical Society, the Maryland Historical Society, the Massachusetts Historical Society, the Mariners' Museum, the Nantucket Historical Association, the National Archives in New York and Washington, DC, the New Bedford Free Public Library, the New Hampshire Historical Society, the New-York Historical Society, the New York Public Library, the Old Dartmouth Historical Society at the New Bedford Whaling Museum, the Newport Historical Society, the Phillips Library at the Peabody Essex Museum, the Providence Public Library, and the Rhode Island Historical Society. Since I visited some of these libraries two decades ago, some of the staff have moved on or retired, while others have continued to render wonderful service to new generations of scholars. Whether they are still in the same institutions or not, I would like to single out a number of individuals who have been particularly helpful to me, and to especially thank a few people whose guidance in their archives was invaluable, including Paul O'Pecko, Chris White, and Kelly Drake at Mystic Seaport, Conrad Wright and Peter Drummey at the Massachusetts Historical Society, Michael P. Dyer at the Kendall (now part of the New Bedford Whaling Museum), Betsy Lowenstein at the Nantucket Historical Association, Tina Furtado at the New Bedford Free Public Library, Judith Downey at the New Bedford Whaling Museum, Rick Stattler at the Rhode Island Historical Society, Rick Sanger at the Providence Public Library, and William T. La Moy, Kathy Flynn, Charity Galbreath, and Irene Axelrod at the Phillips Library. I want to acknowledge the assistance I received in working on the images from Anna J. Clutterbuck-Cook, Massachusetts Historical Society; Louisa Alger Watrous, Mystic Seaport; Mark D. Procknik, New Bedford Whaling Museum; Nicole Joniec, Library Company; Jackie Penny, American Antiquarian Society; Peter Harrington, curator, Anne S. K. Brown Military Collection, Brown University Library; J. D. Kay, Rhode Island Historical Society; and Kristen McDonald and Susan Chase Jones, Yale University Library.

I wrote the original draft of the first chapter long before completing the rest of this book. I therefore had the opportunity to present it in a number of public forums. Needless to say there was always an audience for an academic paper on swearing and plenty of questions that have helped me to refine and rethink my argument. The first time I "swore like a sailor" at an academic conference – at least from a podium – was at the 2003

Organization of American Historians conference in Memphis, Tennessee. I also presented "To Swear Like a Sailor: Cursing in the American Age of Sail," as a Presidential Lecture at Old Dominion University as well as at Carleton College, Northfield, Minnesota; the McNeil Center for Early American Studies at the University of Pennsylvania, Philadelphia, Pennsylvania; and the Phi Alpha Theta Oklahoma Regional Conference, Cameron University, Lawton, Oklahoma. In addition, under the title "'The Worst and Most Profane Language I Have Ever Heard from Mortal Lips,'" I offered my ideas on cursing at the C. V. Starr Center and Washington College, Chestertown, Maryland; the John Carter Brown Library, Brown University, Providence, Rhode Island; the Glasgow Maritime Geographies Conference, University of Glasgow, Glasgow, UK; Warwick University, Coventry, UK; and East Anglia University, Norwich, UK. I have also presented an overview of my work to the staff at Mystic Seaport Research Library and Museum Collections and at the Phillips Library at the Peabody Essex Museum, Salem, Massachusetts.

Beyond swearing in public, I have had too many private conversations about my research and writing to be able to recount them all. But I would especially like to thank the late Bill Pencak for his long friendship and support. Among the many other people with whom I have discussed this work I would like to single out Lisa Norling, Frank Cogliano, Simon Newman, John Brooke, Alan Taylor, Peter Onuf, Dan Richter, Serena Zabin, and Myra Glenn. My colleagues at the University of Oklahoma have always been supportive, especially Robert Griswold and James Hart, who have served as the chairs of the department. Cathy Kelly, Rachel Shelden, David Wrobel, Jennifer Davis, and Kevin Butterfield have been particularly helpful. Josh Piker and Fay Yarbrough (who have left the University of Oklahoma for greener pastures) also should be singled out. I have discussed my work with several graduate students, past and present, including Robyn Davis, Dan Moy, Bethany Mowry, Bryan Nies, Heather Walser, Billy Smith, Patrick Bottiger, and Bryan Rindfleisch. The staff of the history department – Barbara Million, Christa Seerdof, Janie Adkins, and Bobby Collins – have been wonderful over the years. I have shared some of my ideas about cursing with my noontime running group in Norman: Fred Carr, Dave Sabatini, and Randy Kolar. At Cambridge University Press I truly appreciate the support of my good friend and editor, Lew Bateman.

I have been fortunate in having a great family. I dedicate this book to my brother, Stephen Gilje, and my sister, Kathleen Gilje. They have known me all my life and I must confess that as we were growing up they occasionally made me swear. But they have always loved, watched out for, and supported their younger brother. I owe more to them than they can ever imagine. I have two exceptional children – Erik and Karin – who have started their own careers and their own families and two great children-in-law, Beth Gilje and Joshua Hignight. My life has also been brightened by the arrival of my granddaughter, Rachel Brooklyn Gilje, as I was working on this book. My greatest blessing remains my wife, Ann. As a scholar I have occasionally stumbled upon a passage that speaks to me directly across the ages. The reader will find one such passage in this book in a line of poetry from the logbook of Thomas Nicolson. "Amazing was thy love! God of my life / Hannah thou gavest me for a partner! Wife!" After more than forty years of marriage I understand Nicolson's gratitude. I close these acknowledgments with a slight altera-tion to Nicolson's words: "Amazing was thy love! God of my life / Ann thou gavest me for a partner! Wife!"

Abbreviations

Libraries and Museums

AAS	American Antiquarian Society, Worcester, Massachusetts
Beinecke	Yale Collection of Western Americana. Beinecke Rare Book and Manuscript Room, Yale University, New Haven, Connecticut
CHS	Connecticut Historical Society, Hartford, Connecticut
HSP	Historical Society of Pennsylvania, Philadelphia, Pennsylvania
LC	Library of Congress, Washington, DC
MdHS	Maryland Historical Society, Baltimore, Maryland
MeHS	Maine Historical Society, Portland, Maine
MHS	Massachusetts Historical Society, Boston, Massachusetts
MM	The Mariners' Museum Library, Newport News, Virginia
Mystic	G. W. Blunt White Library, Mystic Seaport, Mystic, Connecticut
NA	National Archives, Washington, DC
N-YHS	New-York Historical Society, New York, New York
NBWM	New Bedford Whaling Museum, New Bedford, Massachusetts
NHS	Newport Historical Society, Newport, Rhode Island
NMM	National Maritime Museum, Greenwich, United Kingdom
ODHS	Old Dartmouth Historical Society (now part of NBWM)
PEM	Phillips Library, Peabody Essex Museum, Salem, Massachusetts

PPL   Nicholson Whaling Collection, Providence Public Library,
     Providence, Rhode Island
RIHS Rhode Island Historical Society, Providence, Rhode Island
UCSB University of California, Santa Barbara, Santa Barbara,
     California

Journals

EIHC *Essex Institute Historical Collections*
JER   *Journal of the Early Republic*
WMQ *William and Mary Quarterly*

Introduction

America began as a maritime nation. Before expansion across a continent and the mythology of the western frontier captured imaginations, Americans traversed the deep Atlantic, and were entranced by the oceanic eastern frontier. Before settlement and urbanization scarred the landscape, commerce and the specter of the seascape transfixed the nation. Before Americans proclaimed their mastery of industrial technology, they built incredible sailing machines that spread across the globe. Americans have all but forgotten their maritime origins.

To Swear Like a Sailor seeks to resuscitate that memory by exploring the intimate connections between maritime and mainstream cultures. In *Liberty on the Waterfront* I traced the impact of the age of revolution (1750–1850) on the people of the American waterfront, examining how their world was and was not changed by the ideals of liberty and equality.[1] When I finished that book, I wished to study further certain issues and questions concerning how to decipher the diverse sources I had been examining. I therefore started writing *To Swear Like a Sailor* as a series of semiautonomous essays on how historians can gain insight into the world of Jack Tar – the deepwater sailor – through creative reading of the types of documents at our disposal. If the chapters in this book began as semiautonomous, they have not remained that way. This book has become more than a study of the methodologies in "reading" maritime culture. As I wrote chapter after chapter I came to realize that, although there is much that is unique and peculiar to the world of Jack Tar, the bigger story was that despite many differences, maritime culture was merely one component of a larger Anglo-American culture coated with saltwater. Perhaps this relationship is most evident in material not in this book. When I started to write about the political slogan "Free Trade and Sailors' Rights," I discovered that I had so much to say that it quickly ballooned into a book on its own. That work centers on the welding of Enlightenment ideas about political economy espoused by many of the Revolution's leaders – the Founding Fathers – with the practical concerns of personal freedom by common seamen – the Jack Tars – in one catchphrase that emerged at the beginning of the War of 1812.[2] If this connection is evident in a maritime motto used in politics in a discussion not included in this volume, it can also be seen in the chapters that are. Moreover, the relationship between mainstream and maritime culture demonstrated both change and continuity over time that manifested itself in several different areas, including ideas about gender and class, the movement toward American independence, the democratization of society, and the alterations in the cultural landscape and seascape that accompanied the shift from Enlightened rationalism to Romantic sentimentalism.

Scholars, of course, have examined the maritime world and noted its role in early American history. Several of these historians have illuminated a complex nautical heritage and emphasized the variety of experiences of the men who went to sea. Some sailors were fishermen who repeatedly sailed from the same port and were closely connected to the land-based community. Others became whalers who journeyed to distant oceans for years at a time. Still others became itinerant seamen with no single base of operations. Some sailors cruised aboard coastal vessels; others served on privateers and naval ships in times of war. Any given seaman might engage in one or more of these activities. Each of these experiences also entailed an array of labor conditions dependent on ship category and crew size. The nature of maritime activity changed over time in the period under consideration in this book. Indeed, compounding distinctions in blue-water navigation was the growth of brown-water navigation on rivers and bays in the nineteenth century as well as on the proliferating canals that began to crisscross the nation in the 1820s and 1830s, and the emergence of a separate shipping industry on the Great Lakes. Deepwater vessels became larger and more complex, trade routes expanded, and voyages lengthened. Moreover, race and place of origin had an impact on what it meant to be a sailor. Although I have often relied on and have been informed by the work of the historians who have amplified these distinctions, and while I appreciate the important variations of the maritime experience, my book focuses on a larger, overarching cultural nautical world centered mainly on blue-water sailors involved in long distance coastal or cross-ocean voyages. The aim here is to articulate a generic American maritime culture – identified with the ubiquitous Jack Tar – and trace how this world reflected, intersected, and interacted with the rest of society.[3]

I have also been influenced by several other important currents of scholarship on the American Revolution and the early republic. I began my career with an interest in what in the 1960s and 1970s was called the "new social history." This field sought to extend our understanding of the past by looking at those individuals – poor people, women, African Americans, and Native Americans – who had been previously ignored in the traditional story of the big shots. As a graduate student in the 1970s I eagerly embraced this field and wrote about riots. Since that time I have remained committed to the study of the "inarticulate" – a term sometimes used to describe the subjects of the "new social history" – as any perusal of this book and of my previous publications will show.[4]

Building on this work, in the 1990s and early 2000s scholars extended the interest in the inarticulate to politics. Crucial to this development has been consideration of the public sphere. Jurgen Habermas originally defined the public sphere as the expansion of the discussion of politics and ideas to a larger public comprised mainly of the rising middle class in the eighteenth century through print in books, pamphlets, and newspapers. Historians of Revolutionary America have taken this concept and applied it to a wide array of expressions of political culture and to groups beyond the middle class, including lower-class males, women, and African Americans. Even if I do not focus on politics, the chapters in this book discuss the interactions between the maritime and mainstream cultures through language, ideas, behavior, the printed word, images, and material goods that were connected to the public sphere.[5]

Similarly, recent decades have seen an explosion of scholarship in the burgeoning field of Atlantic history which centers on the interconnectedness between the shores washed by the waters of the Atlantic. These historians emphasize cross-oceanic networks and view the Atlantic as a highway that transmitted ideas, goods, and people. Atlantic history is more transnational than national and encompasses both the age of exploration and the age of revolution. As a field, Atlantic history has forced scholars to rethink a host of relationships and allows us to approach the past with a new understanding reaching beyond borders and incorporating politics, economics, ideology, migrations (especially the slave trade), and even the environment. Any study of sailors in the 1750 to 1850 period by definition is in part Atlantic history and must touch on most, if not all, of the key areas of the subject. But many of the characters I have studied not only sailed the Atlantic, they also entered the Pacific,

Indian, and Arctic Oceans. As they traveled the seven seas, they brought with them their cultural baggage and brought back experiences that ran the gamut from the mundane to the exotic. The insights of Atlantic history have helped me to understand that experience, but I also recognize that what I have written is part national history, part Atlantic history, and part global history.[6]

This book, which focuses on the era in which what became the United States moved from a colonial to an independent status, demonstrates the "postcolonial" nature of American culture and the subsequent emergence of an American nationalism during the early republic. Despite the creation of the United States, as the postcolonial studies tell us, there remained a heavy reliance on British culture and taste. My research demonstrates that this colonial dependence continued in expressions of maritime culture. Informed by this scholarship, I will draw connections between the British antecedents of American cultural forms when necessary, and trace the emerging cultural independence that accompanied both the democratization of society and a shift from the reason of the Enlightenment to the sentimentality and passion of Romanticism.[7]

I have written a cultural history that relies heavily on a careful dissecting and reading of evidence. This approach has led me to venture into areas where I was not always comfortable, confident, or perhaps even competent. I know that much of what I have written delves into areas of expertise, like literary and critical studies, as well as the history of language, reading, books, songs, and art, where I am barely a novice. As much as possible I strove to learn something about each of these areas. But I also wanted to push on, write this book, and put my ideas down on paper. To those experts whose territory I have trampled on I ask some tolerance. I seek to establish no imperial claims. Instead, like so many of the sailors I write about, I hope only to sail upon distant seas, write about my impressions, and then report back to others all the wondrous and interesting sights.[8]

I begin my analysis with swearing. Perhaps, given the title of this book, I do not need to comment about my use of certain words. Yet I feel compelled to point out that I use some language that only a few decades ago would have been unprintable, and that even today I am personally uncomfortable using in public. Considering the nature of the subject, I believe that relying on dash marks or writing around such words is inappropriate. So reader be forewarned: you will see some swear words in this book. But also be apprized that whenever I use these words I do so within an "academic" context.

As it turns out, anyone could swear like a sailor. Within the larger culture sailors may have had pride of place in swearing. But how they swore and the reasons for the bad language they used were not strictly wedded to things maritime. Instead, sailor swearing, indeed all swearing during this period, was connected to larger developments within mainstream culture. What, then, did it mean to swear like a sailor? Put simply, it was to call someone a "damned son of a bitch." Today, we recognize many different severe swear words. No doubt, as the dictionary tells us, much of that foul language existed in previous centuries. Why would sailors fight over being called a "damned son of a bitch?" The answer is twofold. First, "damn" was a strong word in the eighteenth and nineteenth centuries that was tantamount to taking the name of the Lord in vain. Second, "son of a bitch" had a gendered meaning that struck the American seafaring male to his very core – insulting his mother, as well as all that she represented. The potency of this phrase emerged out of changing ideas about class and gender, and the profanity that came to predominate in the forecastle both reflected and affected the profanity the rest of society used.

If anyone could swear like a sailor, was there anything different about the language of Jack Tar? Absolutely. Seamen did have a special argot which became stereotyped over time. Jack Tar emerged as a persona for the generic sailor in the eighteenth century in England, crossed the Atlantic during the colonial period, and was adopted by the newly independent United States. On stage and in the popular press, Jack Tar became a stock figure in mainstream culture and his language could be enjoyed and understood by many people in the rest of society. In the years before the Civil War the dulcet sounds of the sailor were written into literature as they appeared in the exaggerated expressions of fictional characters like Dick Fid in James Fenimore Cooper's *Red Rover* and the maritime preacher, Father Mapple, in Herman Melville's *Moby Dick*. Other published sources, even those written by sailors, may have played up the language for effect. Unpublished journals and letters sometimes contained "sailor language," but often did not. We will never know how much of this sailor language reflected the spoken word and how much reflected the medium. Jack Tar used two types of language. One can be found in the colorful maritime metaphors in the novels of Cooper and Melville; the other was the technical language of the sea which gave birth to those metaphors. Sailors relied on both to set themselves apart from the rest of the culture and to also demonstrate their own expertise. When sailors used the technical language of the sea in their writing, they offered

a testimony to their authenticity as seamen writers. Taking that technical language and applying it in metaphors extended that statement of
authenticity to the point of exaggeration. By the early nineteenth century
sailors recognized that their language had to fulfill a stereotype if they
were to be believable as seamen. But this language was intelligible to the
rest of society. Because America was a maritime nation, references to the
parts of a ship which we cannot understand were comprehensible to a
people who lived almost within hailing distance of the sea.

We will also examine a specific maritime artifact – the logbook. The
logbook had nautical origins: it was a means of recording speed, location,
and direction that assisted in navigation. It emerged as an invaluable aid
to the mariner as he left the close confines of sailing in sight of land and
ventured into deep water and across oceans. Indeed, the logbook became
a tool of empire, contributing to the success of European overseas ventures. Gradually, however, it emerged as something beyond a recitation
of wind, wave, and weather. It also became the sailor's memory tool. As
more and more sailors kept sea journals, and as more and more logbooks
began to contain personal commentary, logbooks became a way of looking at the world. The idea of thinking about life as some great sea journey
did not begin with logbooks. But the logbook helped to give shape to the
idea – an idea that became increasingly important in the democratized,
sentimental, and Romantic world of the nineteenth century. Ultimately a
host of American authors, giant literary figures as well as impoverished
chroniclers of a hard life at sea and ashore, brought the logbook of memory into mainstream culture.

Logbooks might have been a way to remember and order a story, but
the art of the story went beyond the logbook. Our discussion of spinning yarns examines both the etymology of this wonderfully evocative
nautical phrase and the role of storytelling in maritime and mainstream
culture. Sailors have always told stories. The nature of their occupation,
which sent them across the ocean to face storms, combat pirates, visit
distant places, and encounter a host of adventures, lent itself to storytelling. Moreover, seamen honed the skill of storytelling into an art form
during long night watches, or in taverns, or in any spare moment that
might occur at sea or on land. At some point in the late eighteenth or
early nineteenth century sailors began to label this art form "spinning
yarns," a notion connected to one of the menial tasks seamen had to
labor on aboard ship. The metaphor of twisting fibers together to form a
longer skein of rope seemed to fit the way sailors told their stories, offering little bits and pieces of information that tied together and formed a

larger narrative. Eventually, through a convoluted passage into the criminal underworld and banishment to Botany Bay, the phrase worked its way into print. By the 1830s it had become a standard part of the published lexicon embraced by Jack Tar and the rest of society. Indeed, the yarn-spinning sailor emerged as a powerful representative of the folklore that became such a central part of the Romantic era. Sailors told all sorts of stories while spinning yarns, and like the logbook, this form of nautical narrative seeped into literature. Before Herman Melville wrote a single novel, he practiced his storytelling skills by spinning yarns.

Connected to storytelling is the ability to sing. Ballads about seamen have a long tradition in Anglo-American culture. A huge body of literature exists on songs used by sailors. Much of it is on songs and shanties from the second half of the nineteenth century. Antecedents, however, reach back at least to the seventeenth century in an English ballad tradition that expressed key ideas about the seaman as a defender of the nation and as a purveyor of commerce. These ballads cast a popular image of the mariner as the jolly jack who caroused ashore, but could also show him forming more meaningful land-based attachments. These themes were carried over into the eighteenth century as reflected in song and on stage. The sailor became a standard character of the period's theater in both England and America. This importance was connected to the rise of nationalism in the United Kingdom and in the United States. In Great Britain the sailor came to stand for the ability of the British people to prevent invasion and to establish an overseas empire. This image and this sense of nationalism were transferred to the colonies and then the United States. The common seaman became increasingly important to American identity in the 1790s and early 1800s. But who was this American Jack Tar? The answer goes to the heart of the sailor's self-identification. These popular tunes, often borrowed directly from the British and then adapted to the American setting, were important to seamen. Sailor music went beyond patriotism and nationalism. Used for both work and entertainment, the themes of this music also included sex, sentimental images of women, pirates, and shipwrecks. Although a persistent thread connected these songs through the centuries, by the antebellum era the raunchiest lyrics were largely relegated to the emerging category of work songs we call shanties.

Reading, too, was important to the sailor. And what he read was not all that different from what the rest of society read. Sailors loved stories about pirates. But so did most everyone else. *The Pirates Own Book*, which first appeared in 1837, was immensely popular even as it was condemned by some as frivolous and dangerous because it seemed to idealize the life of the pirate. *The Pirates Own Book* built on a long tradition of sea stories and was part of a larger print revolution based on spreading literacy, changes in publishing technology, enhanced illustration, and new methods of marketing. Sailors, like landsmen and landswomen, read a wide variety of books. Indeed, seamen even read literature written by and about women. Religious groups also took advantage of the print revolution to reach and to reform seamen. In short, we will explore what sailors read, ranging from the outrageous to the quotidian. Our aim will be to gain insight into the worldview of sailors, as well as to examine the intersection between that worldview and the rest of society.

The tar-stained images of seamen are an important component of this analysis and reinforce the interconnections between what happened on land and what occurred at sea. We will begin with the image of sailors in the popular media in the eighteenth century and trace a shift from portraying the sailor as something of a buffoon and clown, as appeared in British caricatures during the Anglo-French wars, to emerging as a proud symbol of the American nation. We will then turn to an examination of images created by sailors. Seamen accepted the new vision of the sailor in the nineteenth century and used that image when depicting themselves for others. But when it came to a sailor's personal art in his journals or on his body a mariner was more interested in noting the world around him or the world he left behind. In this context pictures of his ship were more important than portrayals of himself or other seamen. When it came to crafting scrimshaw or other material goods he might create images of the ideal sailor because he frequently made these goods for others, and for domestic use at home.

Packing and unpacking a sea chest forms a convenient way to summarize the interaction between maritime and mainstream culture. Although the size of the sea chest might vary and some of the goods kept in its confines changed over time, this physical object reminds us of the continuity of Jack Tar's world. Contained within the wooden walls of this box were all of the mariner's personal possessions, ranging from the clothes he wore to everything he held precious. The sea chest accompanied the sailor as he traveled across the wide ocean, and returned with him when he came back home. This connection between land and water that the sea chest represented reveals how in the great age of sail America was truly a maritime nation.

1

To Swear Like a Sailor

Simeon Crowell went to sea sometime in the mid-1790s before he was twenty years old. He sailed first in a New England fishing fleet. Brought up in a Christian home by a widowed mother, Crowell liked to read the Bible and could recite many of its stories from memory. Aboard a fishing schooner on the Grand Banks, however, it was difficult to hold to one's convictions. The other seamen swore constantly, and gradually Crowell began to join them. By his third season on the Banks, Crowell had become an expert in bad language and thought that he might have astonished even some of the old salts with his "wicked conversation" and the many "carnal songs" with which he "diverted the crew at times." Enjoying the attention and respect he gained, Crowell continued to entertain the crew. Sometimes he recited stories from the Bible – especially from the spicier Old Testament. Other times he sang carnal songs, cursed, and swore.[1]

Unfortunately, Crowell related his experience after he had a religious conversion. As a respected land-based Christian, Crowell was not about to commit sinful utterance to ink and paper. We are left to wonder about the content of the carnal songs and the exact words that comprised "wicked conversation" aboard a fishing schooner on the Grand Banks in the 1790s. Crowell's reluctance was not unusual. We can search journal after journal, and logbook after logbook, and stumble across only a few moments when the oral culture of Jack Tar's cursing was written down. All too often what we get are references to the act of swearing, without the choice words mentioned. During one mutiny on the American privateer *Tyrannicide* in January 1777 the captain reported that the crew gave him "much ill Language."[2] When Charles Tyng first went to sea in the early nineteenth century, he "listened with horror to the profane language of the sailors" and was so distressed that "the idea that I was to be a companion with such creatures perfectly shocked" him.[3] Aboard the USS *Peacock* in 1827 men were punished with the lash for "disrespectful language" and "slandering some of the crew."[4] In the 1840s Samuel Chase admitted in his journal to using profane language on a whaling cruise to the Indian Ocean, saying that he was relying on such language more than in the previous fifteen years. But he did not really put any of this profanity in writing. In fact, he would not even write out that one of his crewmates slipped on his "a –."[5] Aboard a merchant ship in 1846 two sailors ignored their captain's orders and used "very insulting language."[6] And an argument between two sailors aboard a whaleship in the Pacific was merely described as the two sailors exchanging "some jaw."[7] In none of these cases do we get specifics. Occasionally, however, manuscript and even printed sources fill in the missing words and allow us to see what "ill Language" may have looked like. This chapter represents a brief look at when the oral and written cultures of swearing intersect. Having identified this "jaw," we can explore some of its hidden meaning.

Before we look at this bad language, we must be aware that cursing in the age of sail might not be quite as awful and "R" rated as we might think. Swearing is a culturally conditioned practice. Different cultures use different swear words. Sometimes swearing and cursing focus on genitalia, sometimes on bodily excretions, sometimes on sexual acts, sometimes on a person's origins, and sometimes on God or gods. A few cultures, as is true for many Native American societies, have no cursing. In the Icelandic movie called *The Sea*, characters, like an aged grandmother, would use crass language in Icelandic that would state "By the Devil" or the "hell with you." Such phrases, however, did not carry enough shock value when put into current English, so the translators who wrote the subtitles inserted the most vulgar of English profanity instead, having the grandmother using the word "fuck." Only with this shift in vocabulary could the dark humor of the scene in Icelandic be fully conveyed for an English-speaking audience.[8]

The nature of swearing and cursing varies between cultures and shifts over time within specific cultures and languages. Scholars have noted that before the modern age, defined by the beginning of the Renaissance, Europeans more often swore *by* things, rather than *at* things. Thus in ancient times Greeks and Romans swore with "by Zeus" or "by Athena," rather than focusing their epithets at specific individuals. In the medieval era, swearing by God or some saint predominated. During the Renaissance, this practice changed as human beings became the object of profanity. There were two other key developments during the Renaissance in swearing in the English language. First there was a shift from religious to secular swearing, and then there was the rise of censorship. The two were not unrelated. During Elizabethan times, there was a good deal of swearing, including by Queen Elizabeth, who was reported to have "never spared an oath in public speech or in private conversation when she thought it added energy to either." In the seventeenth century, largely in response to the Reformation and the rise of Puritanism, censorship began to limit swearing – at least in print and on the stage. In reaction to the censorship, authors and playwrights had characters swear to pagan deities and use minced oaths where two words were slurred into each other like "sblood," which was short for the blood of Christ – a phrase that would have taken the name of the Lord in vain. Some clever writers used evasions and euphemisms to get around the censors.[9] William Shakespeare was particularly good at this. In *Much Ado About Nothing* Shakespeare has Beatrice declare: "With a good leg and a good foot, uncle, and money enough in his purse, such a man would win any woman in the world, if 'a could get her good will."[10] This somewhat bewildering comment contains at least three coded words: "leg" stood in for penis; "foot" represented the French "foutre," which is the same as "fuck"; "will" equals sexual appetite, as in he had his way with her. However, during the Stuart Restoration in the late seventeenth century, and in reaction against Puritanism, there was a more open outburst of swearing again. Some of the raunchiest printed comments in English, at least before the twentieth century, appeared in the second half of the seventeenth century. John Wilmot, Earl of Rochester, was especially obscene in his Restoration poetry. He wrote the following lines:

> So a proud Bitch does lead about
> Of humble Currs the Amorous Rout
> Who most obsequiously do hunt
> The savory scent of salt swoln Cunt.

In the eighteenth century Samuel Johnson declared that his greatest pleasure in life was first "fucking and second was drinking," and "wondered why there [were] not more drunkards, for all could drink though all could not fuck."[11] At the same time, however, profanity began to disappear from mainstream printed sources. In 1721 Nathaniel Bailey defined "fuck" in his *Universal Etymological Dictionary*, but Samuel Johnson did not list the word when he published *A Dictionary of the English Language* in 1755.[12] By the nineteenth century, profanity was relegated to special dictionaries. The first edition of the *Oxford English Dictionary* excluded the worst vulgarity (recent editions are more inclusive). In the twentieth century profanity made a comeback in both written and oral forms. Recognizing that profanity is not a constant opens up new areas of inquiry and allows us to understand how the past differed from the present. We thereby not only gain new insight into a world we have lost, but we might also be able to better comprehend some crucial moments of the past.

Son of a Bitch

What, then, did it mean to swear like a sailor in the American age of sail? Reading sailors' journals and ship logs can sometimes be tedious work, as they often are little more than a compilation of wind, wave, and weather. If you are lucky, a sailor might describe some aspect of his work, and if you are really lucky, the sailor might describe conflict at sea. Occasionally the journal keeper might even scribble down the words and phrases he heard aboard ship. Nathaniel Sexton Morgan wrote about several incidents between the captain and the crew from a whaling voyage in 1849 and 1850, including some verbal exchanges. Morgan piques our interest when he proclaimed of one tete a tete that the captain used "the worst and most profane language I have ever heard from mortal lips." Morgan then continued, "He thinks nothing of calling a man a d–n w – s ghost – or wh – s pup – or son of a b–h and like elegant expressions – even in the presence of his wife." Morgan later quoted the captain as calling a boat-steerer, who had returned drunk and disorderly from a liberty ashore, "a dam piratical son of a bitch."[13]

Was that it? Was calling a person a son of a bitch swearing like a sailor? To our more modern ear the phrase "son of a bitch" is not particularly offensive. Certainly children have heard worse nearly every day in schoolyards and on school buses for decades. Moreover, "bitch" has become so common that it is repeated on primetime television almost every night. We might dismiss this "discovery" as the mere reflection of a prudish sailor who was too tight-laced even to write out the phrase in his own private journal, except that we can find the same phrase in other sources, and seldom see anything stronger (by our standards).

Let us turn to a few more examples. The first example comes from before the Revolutionary War and is found in a captain's journal and represents little more than venting some anger. Aboard the *General Wolfe* in 1767 a robbery occurred of a purse belonging to Captain Hodges.

Although angered by the theft, the captain believed that there was not much he could do about the "son of a bitch" except to call on God to "damn and blast him to hell."[14] The second example is from the nineteenth century and led to a fight. John Dunford, a cooper aboard the whaleship *Brooklyn*, refused to let his captain borrow one of his tools. The captain called Dunford "a damned liar." The cooper declared he was not. The captain then berated Dunford again, calling him "a damned lying son of a bitch, that he was anything but a man, if he was a man he would give him a damned good thrashing." Dunford, who must have been short, said that he believed that he was a man, "what little there was of him." The captain merely repeated himself, calling Dunford "a damned lying good for nothing son of a bitch," and then jumped the cooper, tugging his beard and pulling fistfuls of hair off of his face. Dunford grabbed the captain as the two tumbled to the deck together.[15] Example three is another fight between a sailor and a captain. In this case the sailor was an Englishman working aboard an American ship in the Atlantic in 1847. The conflict erupted when Joshua Last was slushing the main mast in a heavy wind. On a calm day this was a tiresome task. In rough weather it was irksome and dangerous. Last came down from the mast and asked for a rope to hook up a gantling as a safety harness. The mate told him to just go up and finish the job. Last grumbled a little bit, something one of his shipmates said was normal for a sailor and should not have been a problem because Last started to go back to his work. But the captain heard the muttering and told the mate that he should have given Last a "licking." The captain then turned and said that Last should not have responded to the mate with so much "cheek." Working himself into a rage, the captain then grabbed Last by the shoulders. Last retorted, fearing a lashing, "Is this the way you do [things] in American ships?" The captain replied, "Yes, you son of a bitch, I'll murder you." He then took him into the cabin for a flogging.[16]

Similar examples could be cited from other incidents. During a mutiny aboard the whaleship *Israel* in 1841, one sailor turned to the captain and called him "a damned old son of a bitch & whores pimp," shaking a fist in his face. To show that he truly meant the threat, he continued by telling the captain that his age and grey hairs would not protect him.[17] In another case involving the mistreatment of a seaman, the captain accosted a sailor for staying in the forecastle after being called to duty: "Ain't you going on deck, you son of a bitch?" and then hit him over the head three times and threw him in irons.[18] In a confrontation aboard the *Lorena* before the ship even left New York harbor, one of the more contentious sailors turned to

an officer and said "he should like to have the son of the bitch ashore."
This comment led to a scuffle and the arrest of the crew for instigating a
revolt. Orrin Day, the second mate of the *N. W. Bridge*, had a confrontation with sailor Noel Brooks in Havana harbor in 1856. Brooks "began
to curse and swear" and when asked what was the matter, declared that
it was none of Day's "damn business." Day replied that "if he gave such
answers" he "would come up and heave him off the yard." Brooks was
nonplused and retorted, "if you come up here or any other son of a bitch
he would split him down." When Day started to climb up, Brooks threw
something that hit the mate in the head. And in 1842 aboard the *Courier*,
Mate Addison Grindell grabbed John Gilbert and said, "you black son
of a bitch, you go on shore without liberty."[19] Finally, there is the mutiny
of the *Holkar* in the West Indies in 1818. Several members of the crew
assaulted the first mate during his watch at night. When one crew member,
who was reluctant to join the rebellion, questioned the attack, the mutiny
leader told him, "You son of a bitch, if you say a word, I will knock your
brains out." After the mutineers killed the captain and mate, they attacked
a passenger, who was also a ship captain, saying, "let us go down and kill
that damned privateer son of a bitch."[20]

Even more surprising about the evidence for this language is that several uses of this profanity, like the last one, appeared in print in the early
nineteenth century. Soloman Sanborn provided a few examples of cursing
in his published memoir of his life in the American navy. When an officer
ordered a man to be punished, he said, "Go aft to the main mast, you d–n
son of a b–h!" One drunken boatswain, who was not American born,
called Lieutenant Tilton "a d–d ignorant Yankee son of a –" and concluded by cursing the flag " ... and every son of a b–h that was in favor
of it."[21] Tiphys Aegyptus quoted a midshipman cursing: "Haul away,
God d – n you; pull away, you d–d sons of b–s."[22] F. P. Torrey cites two
examples of the use of the word "bitch." First, an officer called a sailor a
"damned Irish son of a b –h," to which the man replied that he was "no
son of a b–h," a response that earned him sixty lashes. In the second, during an argument between a ship owner and a sailor, the ship owner told
the sailor he was an "American son of a b–h."[23]

If calling someone a "damned son of a bitch" was fighting words and
the worst language a sailor ever heard in the nineteenth century, then it
is incumbent upon scholars to figure out how and why this was so. Ever
since Clifford Geertz used "thick description" to decode "a wink" and
examine other cultures, and historians like Robert Darnton unraveled
the hidden meanings of events like a cat massacre by eighteenth-century

Parisian apprentices, scholars have sought to go beyond the surface of actions and words to uncover their deeper meanings.[24] In the same spirit, we will dissect the phrase "damn son of a bitch" in an effort to plumb its resonance for the late eighteenth and early nineteenth centuries. We will begin by looking at the significance of "damn," especially for the nineteenth century. "Damn" was often used by itself, sometimes it appeared with other words, and occasionally it was strung along with the strongest of language as in "damn son of a bitch." We will then turn to "son of a bitch" and explore its literal meaning by talking about the place of dogs, and particularly bitches as a canine category, and then look at the inner meaning of the phrase by examining the gendered implications of the term. Having discussed "the worst language" sailors used during the late eighteenth and early nineteenth centuries, we then will look at a larger historical perspective by considering some of the other profanity that was available to sailors, but not used extensively. Finally, we will turn to one example demonstrating the relationship in cursing between mainstream and maritime society and gain insight into how the nature of changes in cursing over time can affect the way we think about history.

Damn

Most, but not all, of the examples listed earlier in this chapter repeat the word "damn" as a part of the profane phrase. Even more so than with the word "bitch," "damn" has lost its more horrific connotations. If some of us prefer to use the less offensive "darn" or "drat," few of us would look askance at someone exclaiming "damn" as they hit their finger with a hammer, or who merely wanted to express their ire or disappointment. When we place the phrase in its historical context, however, its meaning becomes more severe. The word "damn" derives from the Latin "damnare," which means to inflict loss on or to condemn. It is most usually associated with the phrase "God damn," which asked that a person experience loss, and invoked the power of the Almighty to do so. The history of the word reached back to at least the time of Joan of Arc, who referred to the English soldiers as "Goddem" because of their frequent use of the phrase. However, it did not appear in print until the end of the seventeenth century. By the eighteenth century the word was ubiquitous in Anglo-American oral culture.[25]

The word "damn" violated two interrelated religious taboos. First, the phrase was associated with the sin of taking the Lord's name in vain. Second, the prolific use of "damn" could be seen as placing oneself on the same level as the Lord because only God had the power to condemn someone to hell, and to damn. Often, these two sins were joined in the barrage of cursing. Richard Gatewood, a supercargo aboard the *Flying Fish* in 1815, believed his captain was "a good fellow at bottom" but he "damns his Eyes & everybody's limbs & souls too hard." The implication here was that the captain was guilty of claiming equality with God. Worse, he also took the name of the Lord in vain. The captain singled out the black steward for abuse, and "once told him to take Jesus Christ's head to cover a flour barrel," which Gatewood believed was "Shameful" and somehow reflected that he "Don't love his wife enough."[26] To capriciously call on God to condemn someone was seen as an especially nefarious action by any would-be evangelical. As one sailor in a New York prayer meeting explained, "I profaned the name of God without any remorse of conscience ... I have often called on God to damn my body and my soul, yards and sails, rigging and blocks, everything below and aloft, the ship and my shipmates." This Christian sailor could only exclaim, "O! It fills me with horror when I reflect on what I have said, and what I have done."[27] Mariner Simeon Crowell copied a song called *The Sailor's Folly* into his commonplace book that played on the word "damn" and the sense of power embedded in the idea of a sailor's swearing:

> When first the sailor comes on Board
> He dams all hands at every word
> He thinks to make himself a man
> At Every word he gives a dam
>
> But o how Shameful must it be
> To Sin at Such a great Degree
> When he is out of Harbour gone
> He swears by god from night to morn

God's judgment, however, was only a strong gust of wind away. The lyrics continued:

> But when the heavenly gaile doth Blow
> The Ship is tosled to and froe
> He crys for Mercy Mercy God
> Help me now O help me God

The sailor nonetheless returned to his folly:

> But when the storm is gone and past
> He swears again in heavy Blast
> And still goes on from Sin to Sin
> Now owns the god that rescued him.[28]

Most Christian sailors, however, did not see the humor in this behavior. One evangelical seaman warned in the religious publication *Sailor's Magazine*: "Shipmates! If ye dishonour God's holy name by the employing it in cursing, and swearing, and damning, instead of praying," then "God will hold you guilty; he will call you to account for this great sin in the day of judgement; and his terrible wrath will smite you." Like Crowell's poem, the sailor reminded the reader of God's awesomeness: "And is not the Almighty to be feared? If he can dash you by his hurricane upon the rocks, or whelm you in the deep, or send you a wanderer on the ocean, in a leaky boat, without bread or water; can he not in the future cause the tempest of his vengeance to 'steal you away,' and cause you also to feel the gnawings of that 'worm which never dies'?"[29]

Crowell's poem and the rants of evangelical converts suggest that even for the most persistent swearer, under a thin veneer of a seasoned salt's profanity, was a deeper religiosity that surfaced in moments of crisis. There was an old saying that the only time to worry in a storm at sea was when the sailors stopped cursing and began praying. It is far too easy to miss the importance of religion for many sailors, and hence not understand the full significance of using "damn." Even before the efforts of evangelicals to bring religion to the waterfront after the War of 1812, many of the young men who went to sea, like Simeon Crowell, had religious backgrounds. Some of these individuals, unlike Crowell, never abandoned their Bible. Others rejected religion. For both groups of men, the use of "damn" at every turn was significant. For the good Christian it was a reminder of the powers of Satan and the evil that surrounded all humans. For the hard-talking swearer it was a purposeful refutation of mainstream society and an assertion of his maritime identity. By uttering "damn," a sailor intentionally took the name of the Lord in vain. He thereby proclaimed his command of his own destiny and a liberty from shore-side attachments and the norms of mainstream society. But, as Crowell suggested, when faced with meeting his maker, he was quick to seek amends.[30]

Sailors often used "damn" on its own, without following it with "son of a bitch." During the Revolutionary War, Francis Boardman complained of his treatment after being captured at sea by the British, declaring "I Received [sic] arouf [sic] treatment from that Damn'd Raskel John Linzey Capt of the *Falcon*."[31] Sargent S. Day's journal, while occasionally giving a nod to God and the role of Providence in his voyages, was packed with "damns" as he sailed a merchant vessel to the far Pacific and back in the 1840s. Neither the men of the crew nor the other ship officers could meet Day's standards of work. On October 18, 1846, he complained: "No head aloft & nothing done right – for my part I am sick of such second mates & damn'd foolish work." A few months later, when the crew had more trouble with the rigging, Day lamented: "Oh such Officers I'll be damned if they are fit to be trusted with the deck in a Lake. The sooner we get rid of one another the better." A month later he complained that they "make a damn'd humbug of everything." Another time he confessed, "I am getting tired, discouraged, & unhappy – making everybody else so on board. I am so much damn'd & reputation, Name & Character Gone Gone Gone Gone." A few months more and he was again venting in his journal about the mates and the rigging: "that is What I call a dam smart job of Work & that is the way all other work is done here[.] Another regular damn'd humbug & blasted old Maid[.] dam such folks on board Ship[.]"[32] Sailor and author William Leggett used the word "damn" in his writing as a sign of nautical authenticity. In his short story "Merry Terry" he had Merry say "Damn the Captain" when he first heard of the Captain's plot to abduct Merry's betrothed. In another portion of the same tale the phrase "damn my chain-plates" also appeared. In "Fire and Water" Leggett relied on the same phrase as an exclamation. In "Brought to the Gangway" the word "damn" or its variant was used twice. The first time it occurred was when a boatswain told a sailor who was to be whipped that he was going to use the "damn cats" on him – referring to the cat-o'-nine-tails. In a more comical scene, Leggett had the clerk, who had been elevated to ship chaplain, say "Damnation purser" as he was trying to get dressed to preach five minutes later.[33] Even the imprecations of mutineers and murderers might be limited to damnation. In testimony concerning a mutiny in 1816, John Williams reported that one of the plotters told him, "If you are a man, will you join us and take the vessel from the officers? We are determined to bear this ill usage no longer. They are a set of damned rascals, and we will heave them overboard."[34] Williams eventually joined the other crew members and took the ship, which had $40,000 in cash on board, killing the captain and officers. In short, we cannot underestimate the force of using "damn" as a mode of swearing in the American age of sail.

Beyond the uttering of "damn" with "son of a bitch," a few other maritime terms – "piratical" and "privateer" – were coupled with "the worst and most profane language" sailors used. Although some scholars have suggested that turning "pirate" represented a class-conscious rejection of capitalism that many common seamen eagerly embraced, most Jack Tars looked at piracy as something loathsome and despicable. From the perspective of ordinary sailors, pirates were brutish individuals who cared little about life and who cut themselves off entirely from the rest of society. Many sailors may have come from a plebeian world that often rejected mainstream values; for most seamen, pirates went too far and were generally detested.[35] This view of piracy was especially true in the early nineteenth century when high-seas bandits often represented an alien culture or seemed especially onerous in their violent behavior. For Americans in the 1790s and early 1800s the most notorious pirates came from the North African coast and were Muslims who enslaved captured seamen.[36] In the 1820s, 1830s, and 1840s, piracy became a problem in the far-off waters of the Pacific where Chinese and Malay corsairs raided American shipping and were known for ruthlessly murdering their victims. Likewise, a wave of piracy, often under the guise of privateering for Latin American states fighting for independence (hence the derogatory reference to "privateering" by a mutineer who was himself committing an act of piracy), spread across the West Indies in the 1810s and 1820s. These cutthroats were noted for adhering to the notion that "dead men tell no tales" and often killed the seamen they captured to hide the fact that they had slipped across the thin line between privateering and piracy. In other words, to call someone a "damned pirate" was to assert that the individual had an alliance with the devil.[37]

The word "rascal" was also used frequently with "damn." Like "pirate" and "privateer," it was a degrading word. "Rascal," however, had many different meanings, including "the rabble of an army, or of the populace," especially "persons of the lowest class." Often it was used to identify "a low, mean, unprincipled or dishonest fellow; a rogue, knave, scamp." Its origins have a resonance, as we shall see, not very different from "bitch." The word derived from the French "racialle," meaning "of uncertain origin." In addition, it was also used to label inferior animals, especially deer, but also occasionally dogs as in the 1576 quotation "Curres of the Mongrell and Rascall sort." Its appearance with "damn" in lieu of "son of a bitch" thus had a logic that we might miss without knowing where the word came from.[38]

Bitch

If sailors used "damn" with some regularity, and added a few choice epithets to spice up the insult, to combine it with "son of a bitch" was to conjure up a more potent linguistic profanity. The immediate definition for "bitch" is "the correct term for a female dog and usually an insult when applied to a female human, of obscure origin, possibly related to the Latin *bestia* (beast)." The word "bitch" as an insult goes back several centuries. The phrase "biche-sone" appeared in 1330 and Shakespeare used a variant of "son of a bitch" in *King Lear*. He has Kent berate Oswald, saying that he was, among other things, "nothing but the composition of a knave, beggar, coward, pandar, and the son and heir of a mongrel bitch."[39] We have already seen the Earl of Rochester use the word, along with what we would consider as even more offensive language. By the eighteenth century "bitch" had become a loaded term. Francis Grose defined "bitch" in 1785 in his *A Classical Dictionary of the Vulgar Tongue* as "a she dog, or dogress" and then went on to explain that the word was "the most offensive appellation that can be given to an English woman, even more provoking than that of whore" since the "regular Bilingsgate or St Gile's answers, 'I may be a whore, but can't be a bitch.'"[40] While perhaps common even in eighteenth-century literature – Henry Fielding used "bitch" in *Tom Jones* – by the early nineteenth century the word had become increasingly pejorative. In particular the word became associated with a dog in heat. Therefore to call a woman a bitch was to imply something more lewd than a prostitute, as Grose indicated: a bitch was a woman whose animal sexual instincts compelled her to take on any and every available male. By the end of the eighteenth century the word began to drop out of English literature and the *Oxford English Dictionary*, prepared at the height of the Victorian era, did not cite a usage of the term after 1833.[41]

But if we can trace the history of the use of the word "bitch" to its insidious meaning in the late eighteenth and early nineteenth centuries, we are still left with some questions. Why was it that these words were considered "the worst and most profane language ... ever heard from mortal lips?" Why was it that this phrase became fighting words and the kind of language with which a common sailor might challenge the dictatorship of the quarterdeck, or that a ship's officer might use to put Jack Tar in his place? And what does this phrase teach us about maritime culture and about popular culture in general? The answers to these questions are multifaceted and connected to developing ideas about dogs as pets and as animals, and, even more important, to ideas about gender.

The relationship between man and dog deserves its own history and we can only briefly touch on it here. Dogs were one of the first domesticated animals and served a variety of functions in work and war. Known as man's best friend, dogs have been esteemed for both their utility and their companionship. So it is somewhat puzzling that dogs could be linked with derogatory language. In Old English comparing someone to a canine, with the word "hound," had been used as an insult by 1000. The term "dog" as a slur appeared as early as 1325. The "dog" metaphor for subhuman behavior continued thereafter. Yet in Elizabethan times the phrase "son of a whore" was considered the most grievous aspersion, not "son of a bitch." We need therefore to ask what was happening to the relationship between man and dog in the eighteenth and nineteenth centuries to help create this change. Humans had long sought to breed dogs, as they bred other animals, to emphasize certain characteristics. Those who raised sheep, for instance, strove to develop dogs adroit at herding. In the early modern period aristocrats also took to creating special breeds of dogs. Out of this effort came different strains of canines: some were trained for the hunt, which was the special province of the elite; some were used for blood sports like bull baiting; others became pets and were intended merely as ornaments. Royalty took the lead in the development of dogs as pets. In the seventeenth century the Stuarts had an affinity for spaniels. At the end of the eighteenth century Queen Charlotte popularized the Pomeranian and even had Thomas Gainsborough paint her portrait with her favorite dog. In a society with limited resources only aristocrats could afford to feed specialized animals that had no daily work function. Yet the common folk were loath to give up their own relationship with dogs as they moved from the countryside into town environments. Urban plebeians therefore continued to keep dogs around them. These animals, however, were seldom tied up or confined to any property boundary. Instead, they were allowed to roam the streets scavenging for food in garbage or wherever. In short, dogs were ubiquitous on the urban scene. We can get some sense of this by looking at eighteenth-century depictions of American towns. In the forefront of Paul Revere's famous engraving of the Boston Massacre, for instance, appears a dog of questionable lineage watching the soldiers fire into the crowd. On one level, dogs, along with pigs, helped to keep the otherwise refuse-strewn streets and lanes clean. On another level, the dogs were often scrawny, ill-kept, flea-ridden, and unsightly. They would also fornicate openly and frequently. In an odd way, then, the aristocrats had developed one type of animal that reflected their own sensibilities and breeding, while the plebs had their mongrel canines that, from the aristocratic point of view, reflected the coarse breeding of the lower classes.[42]

Enter into the picture the rise of the middle class. Richard Bushman and other scholars have demonstrated that throughout the eighteenth century and into the nineteenth century, the middle class sought to copy the refinement of the aristocracy in housing, consumer goods, and gentility, creating their own special identity.[43] Among the other attributes of the aristocracy that the middle class mimicked was the need for a domesticated pet – the well-bred dog. In fact, by the second half of the nineteenth century the dog had become so embraced, both literally and figuratively, by the middle class that the canine pet had come to be seen as almost essential to the bringing up of the proper middle-class child. Thomas Wentworth Higginson wrote in 1887: "A dog is of itself a liberal education, with its example of fidelity, unwearied society, cheerful sympathy, and love stronger than death."[44] Thorstein Veblin, however, may have come closer to the truth for the middle class when he wrote that dogs are "an item of expense" that "commonly serves no industrial purpose." The "commercial value of the canine monstrosities … rests on their high cost of production, and their value to their owners lies chiefly in their utility as items of conspicuous consumption."[45] If the aristocracy tolerated the mongrel canines that littered the streets with the same equanimity they tolerated the "swinish multitude" of the lower classes, the urban middle class viewed the unchecked dogs roaming the streets as threats to their own class identity and to a new urban order. In the early nineteenth century several American municipalities passed licensing laws that set annual fees at anywhere from one dollar to three dollars in order to control the "mischievous and noxious animals."[46] Because an average workman earned only about a dollar a day, a member of the middle class might be able to afford the fee, but a poorer person could not. All dogs were also supposed to be kept on a leash. This provision, too, created hardships for the poor because they would now have to feed their dogs rather than let them scavenge for sustenance. In New York City, this law led to a series of riots during which crowds assaulted dog catchers who in 1811 collected and killed more than two thousand animals. As one opponent of the law explained, the measure would "prevent entirely the keeping of dogs in the city" and ignored "the kind of attachment which a master indulges toward his favorite Dog." From this perspective, the city magistrates were meddling "with a kind of liberty" that the common folk believed was their right.[47]

What do these developments concerning dogs have to do with the phrase "son of a bitch"? As the middle class began to distance its fine pets from the dogs that roamed the streets, the status of the lowly bred animals, who were seen as carriers of disease and inappropriate denizens of the new urban environment, declined. Any phrase that associated an individual with those animals therefore became inimical. To say that someone worked like a dog or was buried like a dog was to indicate that they were not being treated as a human or as a Christian. As early as 1669 a captain referred to one of his mutinous crew as "no more mate than a dog."[48] In the late eighteenth and early nineteenth centuries, even calling someone a cur was seen as an insult and led to more than one duel among the American elite. But "son of a bitch" freighted even heavier rhetorical baggage. It was also a direct reference to the sexual behavior of dogs in the streets and an attack on one's origins and mother. This association can be seen in several of the examples cited earlier in this chapter: "a damned old son of a bitch & whores pimp" and "a d–n w – s ghost – or wh – s pup – or son of a b–h." Both phrases relate the word "bitch" to prostitution and the second phrase makes the dog connection explicit. In fact, calling a woman a bitch was dehumanizing and associated her sexual activity with bestial behavior.

The use of nationality in some of the "bitch" quotations might also be seen as a comment on degenerate origins. In an ethnocentric era, connecting an individual with another nationality was labeling that person both alien and almost subhuman. This connection is easy to see when an officer aboard the USS *Ohio* called one sailor a "damned Irish son of a b –h" in an era when the Irish were hardly considered white. The same ethnocentric strains appeared from a British perspective when Englishmen used phrases like "American son of a b–h" and "a d–d ignorant Yankee son of a –."[49] Likewise, racial distinctions were important in references like "you black son of a bitch."

Gender and Sentimentalization

As significant as the history of canines is to the potency of the term "bitch," the gender implications are even more important. The chronology of the phrase "you son of a bitch" as "the worst and most profane language ... ever heard from mortal lips" is crucial in understanding the role of gender in cursing. Thomas Laqueur argues that both sex and gender are culturally defined. Scientific explanations of sex reflected basic cultural assumptions. Beginning with the Greeks, sex was defined in terms of a one-sex model, a belief that there was no essential difference between men and women. From this perspective a woman was a less perfect version of a man, with the vagina being nothing more than an inward-turned penis and the ovaries being internal testicles. This view of sex meant that both men and women could experience passion

and orgasm. Starting with the scientific revolution that accompanied the
Enlightenment and accelerated in the age of revolution, a two-sex model
emerged that set women off as sexually different from men. Within this
new view women's sex organs were identified as uniquely female and
not inversions of male organs. The two-sex approach also had broad
implications for understanding the place of women in the culture.
Women were no longer to be seen as passionate; instead, they were to
be morally responsible for themselves and for men. Women could also
be seen as unequal and not a part of the political world because their
different organs made them both inferior in terms of participation in the
public and superior in that their passionlessness became a sign of civilization and separated them from common beasts. Laqueur explained
that, "as biologically defined beings," passionless women "possessed to
an extraordinary degree, far more than men, the capacity to control the
bestial, irrational, and potentially destructive fury of sexual pleasure."
Women therefore became both the physical and cultural progenitors
of civilization. Laqueur argues that within the two-sex model women
might still experience the physical reaction of orgasm – sensitivity in the
clitoris and even the vagina – without feeling anything. This lack of pleasure came from civilization, which separated mankind from the "scenes
and habits of disgusting obscenity among those barbarous people whose
propensities are unrestrained by mental cultivation." In short, women
became the special repositories of civilization by not indulging in sexual
passion during intercourse. By implication, any woman who was not
passionless, indeed, any woman whose passion was unrestrained, like a
bitch-dog in heat, was barbaric, threatening to civilization, and almost
subhuman.[50]

Thus "bitch" emerged as truly a fighting word just as attitudes toward
sex were undergoing a significant transformation from the age of Defoe
to the age of Victorianism. In the mid-eighteenth century there was an
openness about sex that had disappeared by the mid-nineteenth century
in mainstream Anglo-American culture. Much of the burden of this shift
fell on the shoulders of women. In 1750 most Anglo-Americans accepted
women of all classes as sexual beings; by 1850 Anglo-Americans viewed
respectable women as divorced from sexuality. Wanton sexuality became
confined to the lower classes. In the eighteenth century books like *Moll
Flanders* and *Tom Jones* displayed both men and women of different
classes embracing their sexual identity. By the mid-nineteenth century,
women in literature – for example, in *Little Women* – seldom seemed
interested in sex. And when women did engage in sexual activity, as in

FIGURE 1.1. **"The Sailors Farewell,"** by Henry Hudson, November 5, 1785. In the eighteenth century attitudes towards sexuality were unrestrained as appears in this depiction of the classic story of the sailor leaving his love ashore. The sailor and his sweetheart visually demonstrate their affection with an embrace. The sailor has one foot on the boat and the other ashore, suggesting an amorphous boundary between life at sea and life at home. Photograph by National Maritime Museum, Greenwich, UK, Courtesy of The Image Works.

The Scarlet Letter, not only was the sex not in the text, but the overall personal cost for illicit behavior was terrifyingly high.[51]

This shift can be seen even on the waterfront in the depictions of the sailors' farewell, a popular tune in both centuries that was used as the basis of a number of prints in Great Britain and North America.[52] In one British eighteenth-century print the women are portrayed as sexual beings whose desire can be read in their body language. The closer female leans into a sailor boarding a boat about to take him to sea. His finger is on her chin and she looks lovingly and longingly at her man. She is a mother, whose children are by her feet and whose presence testifies to the fact that the couple have had a sexual relationship. In the background is another couple having just broken their parting embrace. The details of the other couple are more difficult to make out, but again there is strong sexual

FIGURE 1.2. **"The Sailors Adieu,"** Lithograph by Baille and Sowle, ca 1845. In the nineteenth century sexuality was restrained. In contrast to the eighteenth-century portrayal of relationships between men and women, in this nineteenth-lithograph the physical contact is out of sight with only the fingers of the woman's hand appearing over the sailor's shoulder. The scene, too, suggests a greater separation between the distant ship and the domestic sphere ashore. Courtesy of the New Bedford Whaling Museum, New Bedford, Massachusetts.

electricity passing between the two as can be seen in the body language and dress of the woman displaying cleavage discernable at a distance. In contrast is the mid-nineteenth-century print called – more romantically – "The Sailor's Adieu." Here a sailor has one arm around the waist of his sweetheart, but this signal of affection is hidden. Instead, we see his other arm pointing, hat in hand, to the call of his ship in the harbor. Despite the closeness of the two figures, there is a formality between the two and no children, as she stands before a house – the scene of her domesticity – and he before his ship. Perhaps the woman's toe peeking out from the bottom of her dress was a nineteenth-century code for a more physical relationship. The fact that this message had to be coded in and of itself speaks to the stiffness and passionlessness of the woman. We can imagine a romantic attachment between the two, and even love, but sex seems absent from the relationship. Although the word "bitch" carried negative connotations before 1750, different ideas about the sexuality of women freighted the term with much greater meaning by 1850.[53]

The association between the word "bitch" and an understanding of sexuality and gender were also connected to the increased sentimentalization in nineteenth-century American culture that worked its way from the mainstream culture into the forecastle and the American maritime world. Within this sentimentalization was a greater emphasis on the shore-side attachments between sailors at sea and women on shore. Here the two illustrations of the sailor's farewell are instructive. In the eighteenth-century picture the couple parts on the waterfront, suggesting a more permeable boundary between life at sea and life ashore. In the nineteenth-century sailor's adieu, the fact that the "parting" occurs in front of the house, with the shore in the distant background, demonstrates both a separation between life at sea and ashore and the pull of hearth and home. Regardless of their differences, both prints bare testimony to the salience of all things maritime to the larger culture.

In some instances the sentimentality focused on sweethearts and wives. However, because most seamen were young, their first line of attachment was to the mother who gave them birth. This sentimentalized relationship appeared repeatedly in story and song. Charles Tyng remembered how on his first voyage he would fall into a deep sleep and dream of his mother, and William Henry Allen sketched mother-like figures in his journal from his first voyage as a young midshipman in 1800.[54] William Torrey recalled that as soon as he began his first voyage "Then the joys of home, a mother's kind care, and a sister's fond love rushed upon my mind and I half regretted the step I had taken."[55] For many sailors in the mid-nineteenth century, the mother became a hallowed and revered figure who should not be sullied. To call a man "a son of a bitch" was to assail his mother directly, bringing into doubt his own origin. Every Jack Tar knew women along the waterfront who slept with men for money – that was bad enough – but in the nineteenth century a "bitch" was a woman in perpetual heat whose animal instincts demanded sex with every man who came along. Equally important, sailors, regardless of their often reckless behavior, clung to certain notions of propriety. Ashore sailors easily fell into rounds of drunkenness and were more than willing to patronize prostitutes, but they also claimed a special role as the protectors of womanhood. To be a true man meant that a sailor had to protect women – particularly the sanctity of motherhood. The phrase "son of a bitch," then, was a challenge to both motherhood and manhood. Such a challenge not only could lead to fisticuffs, but was also the type of phrase a mutineer would use to intimidate anyone who stood in his way.[56]

Maritime culture, however, was nothing if not full of contradictions. While on one hand we can see how the new sentimentalism of the middle class reached into the forecastle and added special meaning to the phrase "son of a bitch," this language also served as a refutation of that middle-class culture. In other words, by uttering "son of a bitch," a sailor, or any working man, denigrated the object of his wrath, and also the family values represented by the pet dogs the middle class so eagerly embraced. Although the word "bitch" could still be used in its technical sense as a female dog, few middle-class Americans in the nineteenth century would have been comfortable referring to the female dog cuddled and adored by the family's children as a bitch. So by using this phrase the sailor was proclaiming his manly allegiance to a world alien to that middle-class experience.

Implications

So far we have emphasized the maritime context of cursing. But was this bad language limited to sailors? The answer is a qualified no. For many of the same reasons discussed so far, "You damn son of a bitch" reached beyond the forecastle and became the epitome of profanity in the young United States. Often, when males, especially young adult males, congregated away from family and away from women, swearing proliferated. This was as true for the English "Goddems" fighting Joan of Arc as it was for George Washington's Continentals. During the Revolutionary War cursing may have expanded but was usually limited to "damn." Anthony Wayne, who had begun life in humble circumstances, was infamous for his "damns." Lieutenant Ebenezer Elmer reported that when Wayne found no sentries posted "he damned all of our souls to hell." "You damn son of a bitch," however, also made its appearance, ordinarily in a more extreme context. In short, the rationale that made "You damn son of a bitch" so potent among sailors, meant that during the same period it came to be the most serious swearing among other American groups. In November 1777, Sergeant Thompson shoved Private William Howell into line when he had stepped out of place during a drill. Howell called the sergeant "a Chuckleheaded Son of a bitch." However, after greater discipline had been established in the Continental Army, Charles Royster argues, a recalcitrant private might use the less offensive "Damn your orders, sir."[57]

Like the maritime culture that is the focus of this study, cursing had a special appeal on the frontier where a rough masculine culture predominated. At a house raising in New Londonderry, Pennsylvania in 1744, two men competed for placing notched logs the fastest. After finishing the two quarreled and called each other "a lying son of a Bitch." Similarly during the Pennsylvania/Maryland border difficulties in 1736 the Pennsylvania officials arrested Thomas Cressap, who used "Oaths and Imprecations," calling the sheriff and company, "'Damn'd Scotch Irish Sons of Bitches, and the Proprietor and people of Pennsylvania Dam'd Quakering Dogs and Rogues.'" Cressap also wondered why the men "wou'd ffight for a parcell of Damn'd Quakering Sons of Bitches."[58] A Native American warrior used the phrase during the War of 1812 as he kicked the body of an American prisoner whom the Indians had just burned.[59] As European Americans moved westward during the nineteenth century they brought the phrase with them and in the early twentieth century H. L. Mencken called "son-of-a-bitch" the "maiden-of-all-work" in American profanity.[60]

Yet, because maritime culture embraced cursing with a distinct gusto, and because it retained its mostly young male cast in peace and war, swearing and cursing became the particular province of the sailor. John Adams noted the prolific cursing and swearing among sailors, declaring during one of his voyages in the Revolutionary War that "The Practice of Profane Cursing and Swearing, So Silly as well as detestable, prevails in a most abominable Degree. – it is indulged and connived at by officers, and practiced to in such a Manner that there is no Kind of Check against it."[61] As we have seen, some aspects of maritime culture were important in developing and sustaining cursing, and that made swearing into a maritime art form. Swearing was something sailors took pride in. To curse and swear was a part of what made a man a sailor. Samuel Leech explained this sense of identity by proclaiming that "fancy swearing and drinking" were "necessary accomplishments of a genuine man-of-wars-man."[62] Young sailors like Simeon Crowell learned to swear while aboard ship and did so to assert their membership in the group. By taking on the attributes of bad language a sailor joined a distinct class of laborers in the maritime world. That identity rejected many mainstream values by taking the name of the Lord in vain and using "the worst and most profane language ... ever heard from mortal lips." Others might curse and swear, but the liberty of the waterfront enjoyed by sailors and their own maritime culture gave the phrase "to swear like a sailor" a resonance that rebounded throughout society. Other members of the working class understood that going to sea offered a special license to resort to bad language.

If profanity made a man a sailor, it also made a sailor a man. The strong sense of manhood, including the act of protecting women, that became crucial to Jack Tar's identity in the American age of sail permeated his use of swearing. As Simeon Crowell explained in his *The Sailor's Folly*, the sailor "thinks to make himself a man / At Every word he gives a dam." Repeatedly the issue of manhood and cursing went hand in hand. The mutineer turned to his shipmates and asked, "If you are a man, will you join us and take the vessel from the officers? We are determined to bear this ill usage no longer. They are a set of damned rascals, and we will heave them overboard." Besides cursing him, John Dunford's captain centered his verbal abuse on Dunford's manhood by declaring him "a damned lying son of a bitch, that he was anything but a man, if he was a man he would give him a damned good thrashing." Sargent S. Day connected his swearing to manhood when he referred to his mates' work as "Another regular damn'd humbug & blasted old Maid[.]" Swearing became a special badge of identity as both sailor and man in the all-male fraternity of the forecastle.[63]

To gain a better insight into the type of maritime swearing that came into prominence during the late eighteenth and early nineteenth centuries, and its relationship to manhood, we should spend some time looking at alternative words. "Damn son of a bitch" replaced another term – "bugger" – which was a powerful swear word in the Anglo-American maritime community of the eighteenth century and continued to hold sway in the British world after American independence.

The word "bugger" was probably the most significant swear word for Anglo-American sailors before 1800. In the twenty-first century the word "bugger" appears quaint and Americans do not use it frequently. We almost forget that it means "one who practices sodomy" and was once considered a vile epithet by Anglo-Americans. "Bugger" derived from the French "Bougre," "a Bulgarian," which referred to heretics in the fourteenth century. Because religious deviancy was often coupled in popular minds with sexual deviance, by the sixteenth century a sexual meaning related to sodomy had been added to the term. The *Oxford English Dictionary* lists the word as first used as an insult in 1719 and probably by that time "bugger" had become an important maritime curse.[64] We know that the British Navy severely punished buggery during this period. But because it was a frequently punished act, we also know that it must have occurred with some regularity. In the freewheeling sexual world of Defoe, there may have been a wider practice among sailors of homosexual activity than in other periods. With examples of sodomy in evidence, calling a man a bugger threatened an exposure that would bring official sanction and possible capital punishment, and challenged a heterosexual identity of manhood.[65]

The American situation was different. There are several examples of American seamen uttering or commenting on being called bugger, usually in complaints about the use of the word by the British. During the Revolutionary War, Christopher Hawkins reported that the only curse that British officers would flog a man for was "damn'd saucey bo-g-r." When Hawkins bragged of the American victory at Saratoga several British sailors insulted him with the word.[66] In the 1790s and early 1800s impressed American seamen complained about similar ill usage. Several impressed Americans had their Fourth of July celebration aboard a British man-of-war disturbed when a British-born seaman called them "you d–d yankee buggers." Joshua Penny was so upset by this interruption of their singing "Hail Columbia, happy land" that he started a fight with the man.[67] But by the beginning of the nineteenth century, "bugger" had started to lose some of its punch for Americans. Young Joseph Ward found his first experience at sea surprising in 1809. In part he was amazed by how much work he had to do, but he was also shocked by the living and eating conditions and the language he heard. In particular he was cursed at and referred to as "bugger."[68] Only occasionally does the word appear in any violent confrontations, like the one Penny described. As late as 1820, one captain, angered that some of the crew had been drinking while working in the rigging, cursed one of the inebriated sailors with "Dam Bugger you are Drunk now." After using this expression, the captain and the mate beat two of the intoxicated seamen senseless.[69] In another instance Charles Tyng reported how he and another captain from Marblehead attended a revival meeting in Nantucket where their misbehavior brought condemnation from the preacher. In response the other captain retorted, "Go to hell yourself, you bugger."[70] Putting these handful of exceptions aside, for the most part, after 1815 "bugger" had lost its bite as a swear word among Americans and, like Joseph Ward, most sailors might not like the word but were not about to start a fight because of it.

This development was related to sexual practices and ideals of manhood. The little evidence for homosexuality in American maritime culture from the Revolution and after indicates that Jack Tar frowned upon homosexual activity. Nathaniel Fanning, an American naval officer during the Revolutionary War, violently and indignantly resisted the sodomite advances of a German colonel with whom he was sharing a bed.[71] Josiah Cobb commented during his stay in Dartmoor Prison during the War of 1812 that the "unpardonable sin" – sodomy – "was but seldom done" even by the most "depraved" prisoners. He believed that "there had been but two or three instances of this heinous sin being committed, on account of the serious penalty immediately following the conviction of the offender."[72] Aboard the USS *Congress* from 1845 to 1848 there were probably only three cases of punished homosexual activity, which the ship's books described simply as "scandalous conduct." The exact nature of that conduct is not delineated, yet given the other offenses listed – insubordination, fighting, smuggling liquor, and drunkenness – the reader is left to suspect some sexual act.[73] F. P. Torrey explained that two men – a Swede and a black man – were sent home from a cruise on an American warship for "a crime hardly ever committed, and as the officers of the ship would not disgrace the criminal calendar trying them, I will not sully this page by describing it; but it would have been as well to make an example of the wretches."[74] Margaret Creighton found reference to only three cases of homosexual activity in more than one thousand whaling logbooks and journals. In other words, American sailors, as we move into the nineteenth century, did not have as much need to distinguish their sense of manhood from sodomite behavior. As a result, buggery became less a concern among American sailors and lost some of its stridency as a means of deprecation.[75]

If "bugger" seemed to be losing its potency in the nineteenth century, and "son of a bitch" gained in importance, what might we say about the word that today is the most frequently used profanity – "fuck"? This word is defined as the act of copulating, but is also commonly used today as an adjective for almost anything. The word "fuck" has a long history. Its first known printed usage is 1503, but it probably appeared earlier. The word's etymology is unclear. It might be related to the French "foutre," or German "ficken" ("to strike"), or it might come from old Norse "fukja," "to drive." It was printable in the eighteenth century, but began to disappear from the pages of books in the nineteenth century and was only liberated from the confines of oral culture, or pornographic fringes of the print culture, in the twentieth century.[76]

Did eighteenth- and nineteenth-century sailors often use "fuck"? We can never answer this question for certain. Some sailors knew the word and it had some currency on the vulgar edges of society. In Forton Prison during the American Revolutionary War, Timothy Connor copied only two ribald songs into his journal that used the word. In one example he used dashes and in the other he spelled it out. Thus on May 30, 1778, he wrote the following lines:

> There in old Mother Jenkins he ow'd a dam spite
> He oft times fuck't the old whore in the Night
> And because she denied him a shove on the grass
> It's good as his word he got flames to her A–e.[77]

There are a few other appearances of "fuck" at the end of the eighteenth century that help us to understand the context in which Connor used "fuck't." These examples show the word applied as a crude descriptive term for fornication. The infamous John Wilkes, sometime member of Parliament and later mayor of London, was attacked by his political enemies in the 1760s not only for publishing the North Briton No. 45 critical of George III and the Earl of Bute, but also for printing the obscene "Essay on Women," a parody of Alexander Pope's "Essay on Man." This work had the following lines: "life can little more supply/ Than just a few good fucks and then we die."[78] In 1776 *The Frisky Songster* contained a number of risqué verses, but only once, and then with ellipses, used "f–d." The same book, however, used "sh–t," "a–s," "sl–t," and "c–t," with the same or even more frequency.[79] Similarly, Connor copied "fuck't" twice in his journal in 1778, but it was only one of many vulgar words in the song. In fact, Connor thought so little of the word, or "dam" for that matter, that he copied its spelling down without any ellipses, while writing the word "arse" as "A–e."

Some aspects of oral culture we will never know as we cannot turn our ears to the past and must depend on the written word. The *Oxford English Dictionary* does not list "fuck" as a personal insult until the twentieth century. Several scholars of profanity have linked the current prominence of "fuck" to the experience of the two World Wars. Even as late as 1944 H. L. Mencken could write, "The talk of the American soldiers in the present war seems to be full of obscenity, but it is all based upon one or two four-letter words and their derivatives, and there is little true profanity in it."[80] The word "fuck" refers to sexual intercourse.

Before the Victorian era, Americans in general viewed sex with less prudishness and more openness than we would think. In fact, given the limited living spaces most Americans experienced as they grew up, sexual behavior between two humans was perceived as natural and a part of daily life. Referring to the act of fornication in coarse language would not be as appealing an insult to use, nor as powerful a weapon, as referring to one's origins or declaring that an individual's mother behaved like a female dog in heat. Till proven otherwise, we must conclude that American Jack Tars in the age of sail knew of our crudest profanity, used it occasionally, recognized its coarseness, but that they considered it no big deal.

"To swear like a sailor" could thus have different meanings within different contexts. However, one thing is clear. Sailors viewed swearing as an art form that helped to define their own maritime identity. The words that they chose, words that we may not find all that offensive, therefore, offer us an opportunity to begin to read their culture and understand how different their world was from our world today.

That said, one of those differences was the constant interaction between sea-based and land-based society. The significance of the changing vocabulary of cursing reaches beyond the waterline and can have an impact on our understanding of the past. Let us return to the Boston Massacre. March 5, 1770, has come to represent a signal episode in the unraveling of the imperial relationship between Great Britain and its colonies in the 1760s and 1770s. For weeks tension had built up around the waterfront of Boston as British soldiers, both on and off duty, confronted Boston's workingmen. Many of those Bostonians earned their livings on the docks or at sea. Three of the five colonial fatalities from the massacre had clear nautical connections. This encounter, mentioned and illustrated in almost every American history textbook, is a well-known dramatic moment in the creation of the American people. To this day the exact sequence of events precipitating the violence remains immersed in contradictory evidence. However, we can read the testimony of the later trial and see the crescendo of emotion building toward violence. In one of the street fights shortly before the fatal encounter on King Street, British soldiers accosted some apprentices and journeymen by asking "Where are the sons of bitches" who had fought with the soldiers earlier. A few minutes later on King Street, one barber's boy in the Boston crowd was shoved to the ground by a soldier. He then turned to the crowd and said, "this is the son of a bitch that knocked me down." These words made the blood boil on both sides.

No one knows if Captain Preston gave the order to fire, or if the first soldier's gun went off accidently. We do know one thing, however. Amid the shouting and clamor of the riot we call the Boston Massacre one phrase was heard the instant before the bullets began to fly. Someone in the crowd had cried out, *"Damn you, you rascals; fire. You dare not, fire. Fire and be damned."* With each side calling the other sons of bitches, these were fighting words indeed.[81]

2

The Language of Jack Tar

"Avast, ye mateys! Let me spin ye a yarn." Did sailors really talk like that? What was the language of Jack Tar in the age of sail? And how peculiar of an argot was it? Did it have a special vocabulary and intonation? Was it comprehensible to others? Or was it a secret mode of communication whose meanings were open only to those who served in the forecastle? The answers to these questions must be tentative, complex, and in many ways unsatisfactory: real Jack Tars, it seems, may have selected when and where they were going to use their maritime vocabulary. Tentative, because unfortunately we will never know how sailors truly spoke. As Leigh Eric Schmidt explains in a somewhat different context, "The voices of the past are especially lost to us. The world of unrecorded sounds is irreclaimable, so the disjunctions that separate our ears from what people heard in the past are doubly profound." It is left to the historian to "act as a kind of necromancer" to reconstruct those voices and conjure up lost language.[1] Complex, because we need to separate our own modern reactions to that language from the reactions of contemporaries. What is strange and alien to us may not have been as strange and alien to the landsman in the age of sail – an age when the United States was truly a maritime nation. During that period the majority of Americans lived close to saltwater, many young men served some time at sea as sailors, and at least until the 1830s the most efficient mode of transportation was by ship. That world, in other words, knew and understood sailors and their language in a way we with our land-based mindset can only imagine. Moreover, both the British and the Americans praised the sailor for defending the nation in times of war and for carrying commerce in times of peace. Heralded in song and portrayed on stage, the honest Jack Tar became a familiar figure.[2] Given this popularity, the written medium with which we as historians must work to make our magic and reconstruct the language of Jack Tar – novels, magazines, newspapers, journals, log-books, and letters – sends mixed messages. On one hand are stereotypes of the language in literature as expressed in the exaggerated exclamations of fictional characters like Dick Fid in James Fenimore Cooper's *Red Rover* or maritime preacher Father Mapple in Herman Melville's *Moby Dick*. On the other, Jack Tar could write in a more straightforward manner without nautical trappings in published and unpublished sources. And although our final answer to the question of what was the language of Jack Tar must be unsatisfactory – because in the end our magic will not work and we will never definitely determine if and how often sailors used the language we read in Cooper, Melville, and the popular press – at least the process of looking at the seaman's idiom will bring us nearer to the dulcet sounds of the sailor and the dialog between the world of Jack Tar and the larger American culture that surrounded and embraced him.[3]

Cooper and Melville

We can begin to gain insight into the language of Jack Tar by taking a closer look at Cooper's character Dick Fid. Although Long Tom Coffin, who also spoke in nautical metaphors, may well be "second only to Natty Bumppo as Cooper's most enduring fictional figure in the nineteenth century," Dick Fid's comic function placed him closer to the familiar stereotype portrayed on the nineteenth-century American stage. Fid was loyal (to friends) and argumentative (to everyone), uneducated (he was illiterate) and knowledgeable (about ships), and strong of character (he will do right in the end) while weak (he could be easily tricked, especially when drinking).[4] From the moment he was introduced in *Red Rover*, Cooper's wildly popular novel about a pirate during the French and Indian War, we know that Fid and his black companion, Scipio Africanus, were true sailors because they were "dressed in the plain, weather soiled, and tarred habiliments of common seamen, bearing about their persons the other never-failing evidences of their peculiar profession." Fid's opening comments combined maritime language as metaphor with an expert knowledge of seamanship. Describing the location of a ship anchored outside the inner harbor of Newport, Rhode Island, Fid declared: "This is a pretty bight of a basin, Guinea [his black friend Scip], ... and a spot is it, that a man who lay on a lee-shore without sticks, might be glad to see his craft in! Now do I call myself something of a seaman, and yet I cannot weather upon the philosophy of that fellow, in keeping his ship in the outer harbor, when he might warp her into this mill-pond, in half an hour. It gives his boats hard duty, dusky S'ip –, and that I call making foul weather fair!" This short passage is packed with nautical phrases, with some of the meanings obvious and others more obscure. A "bight of a basin" makes sense as a geographical description because "bight" is any bend in the shoreline, but it made special sense to a sailor who would use the same term to describe the bend in a rope. The phrase "a man on a lee-shore without sticks" refers to an individual aboard a vessel without masts ("sticks") and sails in the dangerous position of being driven by wind, tide, and current toward land ("a lee-shore"). The combination of the words "weather upon the philosophy" might be more difficult for a landsman to comprehend. Fid here uses the nautical term "weather," meaning to sail to the windward of either a land mass or a ship to get clear of the object. To "weather upon the philosophy," then, would be to figure out – get clear of – the reasoning behind placing the ship in the outer harbor. The words "warp her into this mill-pond" combined the nautical term "warp," which was to move a ship along by using boats to tow an anchor ahead and then hauling on ropes to bring the ship forward, with a standard phrase for a placid body of water ("mill pond"). Sailors referred to any difficult task as "hard duty," and Fid here expressed concern for the poor seamen who would have to row the ship's boats to the shore. To make "foul weather fair" referred to Fid's belief that the captain of the ship seemed to think that its vulnerable position in the outer harbor ("foul weather") was really a good anchorage (fair weather).[5]

We can only guess how many of these metaphors would be obvious to readers in the 1820s. Cooper, however, knew the language of the sea, having served as a midshipman in his youth, owned a vessel as an adult, and crossed the Atlantic several times. Equally important, as a popular author he also knew that too many obscure references would have limited his audience. For Cooper the language of Jack Tar formed a bond between sailors, but his playfulness with that language in his sea novels also allowed him to build a bond with his readers. That bond can be seen in the interaction with another set of characters in a running joke in *Red Rover*. Early in the book the hero of the story, Henry Wilder (alias Henry Ark, alias Henry De Lacey – Cooper loved hidden identities), met with the pirate Red Rover (who also, as it turns out, is Henry's uncle) disguised as a lawyer while still in Newport. Although Wilder did not immediately see through the disguise deep enough to discern that he had met the Red Rover, he quickly recognized that this lawyer in a green suit knew more about the sea than he pretended. This knowledge began to build a connection between them that only solidified when they overheard a conversation between Gertrude (Wilder's love interest in the story), Mrs. Wyllys (Gertrude's governess and, in another case of hidden identity, Wilder's long-lost mother), and the widow of Admiral de Lacey (Gertrude's aunt), when the latter asserted what she thought was her own command of nautical language. The overconfident admiral's widow declared that "we wives of sailors only, among our sex, can lay claim to any real knowledge of the noble profession." She then quoted her late husband, who evidently enjoyed having fun at the expense of his spouse. "What natural object is there or can there be … finer than a stately ship, born down with by its canvass, breasting the billows with … its taff-rail ploughing the main, and its cut-water gliding after like a sinuous serpent … ". Wyllys, who had nautical knowledge, saw right through the phrase, which placed the bow at the stern and the stern at the bow (the taffrail was the aftermost rail on the end of a ship and the cut-water was the foremost edge of a ship where the bow met the sea). Wyllys thought the phrase reflected "the waggery of his [the late admiral's] vocation," and the laughter of Wilder and the Red Rover, who had been hiding in an old mill, almost gave away their position. The widow's sincere gaff in quoting her husband, however, demonstrated the importance of maritime language to Cooper and his readers – he returned to the "taffrail plough-ing the main" phrase several times. On the very next page the widow de Lacey repeated herself: "A charming object is a vessel cutting the waves with her taffrail, and chasing her wake on the trackless waters." The Red Rover, still disguised as the barrister, completely let down his landsman veil when he used the phrase as a joke to Wilder: "What spectacle … can be finer than a noble ship, stemming the waves with her taffrail and chasing her wake, like a racer on the course!" Which Wilder answered by stating, "Leaving the 'bone in her mouth' under her stern, as a lighthouse for all that come after" (another one of the widow's ludicrous nautical-isms). The joke also helped to move Cooper's plot along when Wilder, who was an undercover British officer supposed to help capture the Red Rover, later approached a disguised pirate ship (the vessel Fid saw in the outer harbor) and responded to a guard's hail by declaring that he was "Cutting the waves with my taffrail." This answer confused the watch-man, but was a signal the Red Rover immediately recognized. The joke, of course, would not be a joke at all if Cooper's readers were as ignorant of the language of Jack Tar as the admiral's widow.[6]

Nautical metaphors were a more serious means of communication to American readers in Herman Melville's description of Father Mapple's sermon in *Moby Dick*. Based in large part on a real-life Methodist preacher who had been a sailor – Father Taylor or Edmund Thompson Taylor – Father Mapple climbs up a rope ladder, "like those used in mounting a ship from a boat from at sea," into the bow-shaped pulpit of the New Bedford Bethel Society to deliver a fire-and-brimstone sermon on the book of Jonah. Mapple addressed his congregation as "shipmates" and began his sermon by reminding his listeners that the book of Jonah contained only "four chapters – four yarns" and was "one of the smallest strands in the mighty cable of the Scriptures." Having referred to each chapter in Jonah as a yarn – the sailor word for a story – and the entire Bible as like a ship's cable with each book a link in a greater chain that anchored the soul, Mapple continued with a tale that spoke directly to the whalemen: "Yet what depths of the soul does Jonah's deep sea-line sound! ... How billow-like and boisterously grand! We feel the floods surging over us; we sound with him to the kelpy bottom of the waters; sea-weed and all the slime of the sea is about us." What followed was a reiteration of the story of Jonah, whose flaunting of God's plan and fate of being swallowed by a giant fish presaged the future disaster facing the *Pequod* and its crew. Seamen knew this book of the Bible well because maritime superstition continued to identify every mishap aboard a ship as caused by a modern-day Jonah. Mapple's retelling of the story, however, had a special appeal as his conclusion, also packed with maritime references, demonstrated: "But oh! Shipmates! On the starboard [right] hand of every woe, there is sure delight.... Is not the main-truck [a fixture at the top of the highest mast] higher than the kelson [fore and aft timbers parallel to the keel on the bottom of the ship] low.... Delight is to him whose strong arms yet support him, when the ship of this base treacherous world has gone down beneath him.... Delight – top-gallant [the highest of sails] delight is to him, who acknowledges no law or lord, but the Lord his God.... Delight is to him, whom all the waves of the billows [swells] of the seas of the boisterous mob can never shake from this unsure Keel [the structural beam around which the ship is built] of the Ages." Although there is no denying the lyrical power of Melville's words, without some knowledge of the ship, without some awareness of the maritime metaphors, and without some fluency in the language of Jack Tar, these passages lose some of their potency and could even border on the meaningless.[7]

Cooper and Melville relied on the language of Jack Tar for several reasons. It was colorful. Cooper created characters like Dick Fid and Long Tom Coffin who used words borrowed from their maritime experience, and relied on such language in his own romanticized description of the sea. As Wilder took a ship out of Newport harbor: "Every thing being set to advantage, alow and aloft [referring to the sails high and low on the masts], and the ship brought close upon the wind [sailing with the sails pulled taut to gain speed], his [Wilder's] eye scanned each yard [the cross-poles from which sails hung] and sail from the truck [a piece of conical wood used at the top of the mast] to the hull [the body of the ship itself], concluding by casting a glance along the outer side of the vessel in order to see that not even the smallest rope was in the water to impede her progress." Then once out in open water Cooper described the ship in prose that bordered on poetry: "As the air fell upon the distended and balanced sails, the ship bowed to the welcome guest, and then rising gracefully from its low inclination, the breeze was heard singing, through the maze of rigging, the music that is so grateful to a seaman's ear. The inspiring sounds and the freshness of the peculiar air, gave additional energy to the movements of the men." This poetic prose still contained some shipboard vocabulary: "The anchor stowed, the ship cast, the lighter sails set, the courses had fallen, and bows of the Caroline were throwing the spray before her, ere ten minutes had gone by."[8] The combination of this special lexicon with lyrical descriptions of the sea had a powerful attraction for readers in the first half of the nineteenth century. Melville opened *Moby Dick* with a nod to this romance of the sea by describing "the crowds of water-gazers" along the New York waterfront. "Posted like silent sentinels" there stood "thousands upon thousands of mortal men fixed on ocean reveries." These "Inlanders," Melville jested, "must get just as nigh the water as they possibly can without falling in." Despite this mocking tone, Melville understood, as the success of his *Typee* and *Omoo* attested, saltwater represented a path to the exotic, a way to reach other worlds, an avenue to adventure. Using the technical language of the ship, drawing nautical metaphors, having characters utter phrases packed with maritime allusions, were ways to bring the reader out on the ocean that pulled on them like "the magnetic virtue of the needles of the compasses" aboard every ship.[9]

The language of Jack Tar was also a testimony to authenticity. Jack Tar used two types of language. One was the maritime metaphor that appeared in Cooper and Melville's novels; the other was the technical language of the sea that gave birth to those metaphors. Ships were complicated pieces of machinery with thousands of moveable parts. Each of those parts had a special name and knowledge of those parts was crucial to the efficient operation of the ship and essential to survival on the tempestuous ocean. Almost every greenhorn on his first voyage experienced a frightening baptism under fire in this specialized technical language. Richard Henry Dana Jr. noted the "unintelligible orders" the mate issued during his first storm at sea. As Herman Melville explained in his *Redburn*, "sailors have their own names, even for things that are familiar ashore; and if you call a thing by its shore name, you are laughed at for an ignoramus and a land-lubber." Beyond remembering that a pail was really a bucket, there were also "an infinite number of totally new names of new things to learn." Complaining of the complex technical language of the rigging, Melville explained: "Now the very smallest of these ropes has its own proper name, and many of them are very lengthy, like the names of young royal princes, such as *the starboard-main-top-gallant-bow-line*, or the *larboard-fore-top-sail-clue-line*."[10] Melville might lampoon these detailed labels for what initially seemed to be only ropes, but knowing which line to tighten and which line to loosen could mean the difference between life and death at sea. Hauling on the wrong line could send a piece of the ship's machinery – a block, a tackle, a yard, a sail – smacking into a shipmate or even capsize the vessel. Some of this basic vocabulary might be found in specialized dictionaries like William Falconer's *An Universal Dictionary of the Marine …*, but it was the experience on a ship that taught the true meaning of these terms.[11] Cooper wrote his first nautical novel because he believed that English authors employed incorrect detail in their descriptions of ships. Using his own experience at sea, he wanted to get the ropes right and offer a more accurate picture of the maritime world. Within this context Long Tom Coffin and Dick Fid offered Cooper an opportunity to demonstrate his acquaintance with Jack Tar and his language. Melville, too, was interested in having his readers acknowledge his command of the maritime lexicon and was probably glad to hear a critic proclaim *Typee* "one of the most interesting, amusing, and original books of adventure" that he had read, and that it was "by an American sailor."[12] When authors like Cooper and Melville used the technical language of the sea in their writing, they offered testimony to their authenticity as writers. Indeed, sailor authors – and both Cooper and Melville spent some time at sea – recognized that their language had to fulfill a stereotype if they were to be believable as sailors.

Jack Tar's language was also familiar. Readers would not need bracketed explanations, which after all interrupt the flow of the phrase, for words like "cut-water" and "taffrail," just like anyone today would not need an explanation for using the less poetic airplane metaphors of cockpit and tail fin for front and back. That familiarity was based on personal experience, as well as on a tradition of using sailor language on stage and in print. Long before the mid-nineteenth century Jack Tar had become a stock character whose special language was defined, parodied, and publicized.

The Anglo-American Stereotype

Jack Tar began as an Englishman. He appeared on stage, in literature, and in prints during the eighteenth century. The actual name Jack Tar fused two popular references to the regular sailor. Jack started as a nickname for a person named John, was early generalized as a label for any common man, and by the seventeenth century was sometimes used as a familiar appellation for a seaman. The word "tar" refers to the black, sticky substance used ubiquitously on a ship to waterproof materials, including canvas. Like Jack, by the end of the seventeenth century "tar" became a moniker for the British sailor. By the early eighteenth century the two nicknames were combined into one – Jack Tar – although both continued to be used separately, and offered a first and last name to the anonymous common seaman.[13] Jack Tar could be used either in the generic sense, as in "he was a jack tar," or as a specific pseudonym. English newspapers first began referring to Jack Tar in the 1720s, and he performed as a character on the London stage doing a hornpipe as early as 1740. Seamen themselves seem to have welcomed the nickname. In 1741 one London paper published a list of grievances from British naval seamen signed, in good sailor style, "Stem to Stern, Jack Tar."[14]

By 1750, the character Jack Tar, with or without the name, had emerged in print and on the stage. Novelist Tobias Smollett's most famous sailor was Tom Bowling. Although a lieutenant in the navy, Bowling was a crudely hewn character who quickly came to represent the average British seaman. What made Smollett's Bowling so memorable was his pose as an "honest tar" and his salty language. In his very first appearance in *Roderick Random* Bowling warned a young gentleman threatening to assault him: "Lookee, you lubberly son of a w–e, if you come athwart me, 'ware your ginger-bread-work. – I'll foul your quarter, d–n me." Translation: Look out, oaf – sailors usually used "lubber" in relation to awkward behavior at sea, as in landlubber – your mother worked in the sex trade (son of a w–e is obviously son of a whore), if you come any closer (athwart ships was to come along side of a ship), watch out for your pretty ass (ships with fancy carvings for decoration on the stern had gingerbread work), I'll slap you on your backside (a ship fouled another ship by running into it, and the quarter was the last fourth of the ship's side). Bowling's earthiness and forthright ability to cut to the quick, despite, or perhaps because of, the maritime metaphors had a certain attractiveness. It also built on a long literary practice of having common folk characters, hayseed farmers, bumbling soldiers, and drunken sailors, act as a foil for the main characters in a story and offer some comic relief.[15]

During the second half of the eighteenth century songwriters, building on a long-standing ballad tradition, as well as artists, shifted the focus on sailors directly to the forecastle and provided an increasingly sympathetic portrayal of Jack Tar. The timing of this development was crucial. The common sailor garnered so much popular attention in an eighteenth century during which international commerce, overseas empire, and a deepwater policy that depended on a navy for protection of the British Isles solidified the maritime character of the Anglo-American world.[16] Isaac Bickerstaff's operetta *Thomas and Sally* may be so saccharine in its tone that it is almost impossible to take seriously today. But the public and the Jack Tars who packed the theaters adored both the plot line and the words. The story depicts an evil squire about to force his sexual intentions on young Sally when Thomas the sailor returns and declares, in good mariner language:

> What's this I see? may I believe my eyes.
> A pirate just about to board my prize?
> 'Tis well I this way chanc'd my course to steer
> *Sal!* What's the matter?

Thomas then tells the squire to "Tack about, and bear away" and threatens him with violence. Of course the squire backs off and in the last scene Thomas and Sally are about to marry at a church and are surrounded by sailors singing the chorus:

> Ye *British* youths, be brave, you'll find
> The *British* virgins will be kind;
> Protect their beauty from alarms
> And they'll repay you with its charms.

This short production was played over and over again and contributed to the basis of two of the most indelible stock images of maritime

FIGURE 2.1. **"Sailors Drinking the Tunbridge Waters,"** Thomas Rowlandson, 1815. In the late eighteenth and early nineteenth centuries, Thomas Rowlandson and other artists perfected the caricature, mocking all elements of British society. The sailor became a favorite subject for these caricatures, often portraying Jack Tar with flush cheeks and a bulbous-nose from imbibing alcohol. Inevitably sailors were cast in comical roles such as the seamen visiting the Tunbridge spa perplexed at the strange concoction – water – the young maid innocently offers them. Courtesy of The Lewis Walpole Library, Yale University, New Haven, Connecticut.

iconography in the age of sail: the pictures of the sailor's return, and, perhaps even more important, the sailor's farewell (at the end of the operetta Thomas is ready to go to sea again to defend the nation).[17]

However sympathetic these prints of sailors departing and returning may appear, British artists produced a host of stereotypes of more comical Jack Tars. "Sailors Drinking the Tunbridge Waters" by Thomas Rowlandson depicted red-cheeked and bulbous-nosed sailors perplexed by the taste of the water from the spa. Reputed for their intemperance, these sailors clearly would have preferred to imbibe more potent liquids than the salubrious nonalcoholic libations of Tunbridge. In the same vein, Thomas Tegg's "Jack in a White Squall, Amongst Breakers – on the Lee Shore of St. Catherine's" has a poor bewildered tar at the end of a spree on land, emptying his pockets, unable to pay two women whose demands

FIGURE 2.2. "Jack in a White Squall, Amongst Breakers – on the Lee Shore of St. Catherine's," Thomas Tegg, 1811, Reproduction Number: LC-USZ62-20409. In this comic scene the sailor has spent all of his money, and like the mariner upon the ocean is in danger of being "shipwrecked" by the onslaught of the white breakers, the tavern women, who want him to pay his bill. Courtesy of the Library of Congress, Washington, D. C.

were turning violent. One termagant was about to hit him over the head with a fiddle as another shoved the bill in his direction. The farcical nature of these prints should not mislead us. Imbedded in such portraits was a certain affection for these well-meaning Jack Tars. We get a better sense of the combination of humor and sympathy in Rowlandson's "The Last Jig, or, Adieu to Old England," showing a group of sailors in a waterfront public house dancing, drinking, and cavorting. Despite the burlesque appearance of some of the characters in the print, including the central figure of the Jack Tar dancing, there is a certain dapperness to the sailor's step and bearing as he holds his hand over his head and has his arm tucked behind his back.[18]

Although he could write lyrics that might apply to all of these prints, Charles Dibden extended this sympathetic portrait of the British sailor and thereby further popularized the patriotic image of Jack Tar. In 1789 Dibden borrowed Smollett's character Tom Bowling for a song

FIGURE 2.3. **"The Last Jig, or, Adieu to Old England,"** Thomas Rowlandson and Thomas Tegg, 1818. This tavern scene in a waterfront neighborhood in London centers on a sailor and a woman dancing. The dancing seamen is both dapper and comical, while the other mariners are either engaged in promiscuous behavior with women or drinking. Courtesy of Anne S. K. Brown Military Collection, Brown University Library, Providence, Rhode Island.

that captured the essence of the ultimate seaman sacrificing all to do his duty:

> Here, a sheer hulk, lies poor Tom Bowling,
>   The darling of our crew:
> No more he'll hear the tempest howling,
>   For death has brought him to;
> His form was of the manliest beauty,
>   His heart was kind and soft,
> Faithful below, he did his duty,
>   but now he has gone aloft.[19]

This Tom Bowling, unlike the officer in *Roderick Random*, was a regular sailor – he did his duty "below," referring to below decks, which is where common seamen served. Dibden, as well as others writing about the sea, could not resist the nautical metaphor, describing Bowling's corpse as a "sheer hulk" (remnants of a ship), his death having "brought him to" (stopping a ship) and then having Bowling sent aloft (high in the rigging) to heaven. Likewise, Dibden packed his most popular tune, "Poor Jack," with nautical vocabulary, using words like "lubbers" and "swabs" in the very first line. Many of the contrived sailor names in Dibden's work – Ben Backstay, Jack Ratlin, Jack Junk, Ben Block, and especially Tom Bowling (sometimes Tom Bowline) – joined Jack Tar and became pseudonyms for the common sailor. Jack Tar, however, was the only proper name applied in the generic sense: sailors were Jack Tars, not Tom Bowlings. Dibden's seamen may have been caricatures – Tom Bowling's heart belonged to his Poll (girlfriend), his rhino (money) to his shipmates, and his life to King George – they also were seen to have feelings. It was possible to think that sailors had mothers, sisters, and even sweethearts. This sympathetic portrait of seamen as people with shore-side connections fighting on the high seas to protect king and country helped to make Jack Tar an important symbol of the British nation even while retaining some of his comical and less appealing trappings.[20]

Not surprisingly, given his nautical roots and the shared Anglo-American culture of the eighteenth century, Jack Tar and his various aliases crossed the Atlantic. As early as 1741 the *Boston Evening Post* published a poem that referred to Jack Tar. In 1760 another Boston paper printed a letter signed by Jack Tar complaining against the press gangs in the city. This sailor used just enough nautical references to assert his maritime authenticity. Tom Bowline made an appearance in 1773 in Newport urging the "sons of Neptune" (another cognomen for common seamen) to oppose the landing of tea and "preventing the pestilential commodity from being parbuckled on shore."[21] One indication of the popularity of these nicknames is that John Adams used "Jack Tar" at least twice in the prerevolutionary period, although for the status-conscious Adams it was more a pejorative than an endearing term. In 1763 Adams wrote a letter to Jonathan Sewall decrying Sewall's willingness to become a "hireling Scribbler," who had "prostitutest thine Head, thine Heart," in support of partisan causes. Searching for more invective to trash Sewall as an unthinking agent of others, he charged that "thou art a silly, undistinguishing Jack Tar, on board the ship, who never lookest into the Right and the Wrong the True or the false, but eer fightest valiantly, whenever the Master gives a dram and pointeth out an Antagonist." The diatribe by Adams gave the sailor little credit and even belittled Jack Tar's patriotism. Adams repeated this dismissive view of sailors in his more famous Jack Tar reference when he, in "plain English," referred to the crowd at the Boston Massacre as "a motley rabble of saucy boys, negroes and molattoes, Irish teagues and out landish jack tarrs." From his perspective, as was clear in the 1763 letter, common seamen were unthinking, acted at the behest of others, and were the stuff out of which mobs were made.[22]

What Adams did not understand was that the sailors in the crowd who had confronted the British soldiers on King Street on March 5, 1770, *did* think for themselves. These seamen and waterfront workers joined the mobs during the Stamp Act tumult, continued to demonstrate and riot throughout the 1760s and 1770s, and helped to propel the colonies toward rebellion. The Sons of Neptune were thus central to the origins of the American Revolution. Further sacrifices during the War for Independence in the navy or as privateersmen elevated Jack Tar in the mind of the general public. In the 1780s and 1790s sailors became increasingly important as the men who sailed the ships necessary for American commerce. This economic function became even more vital after war broke out between Great Britain and France in 1793 and the United States emerged as the most important neutral carrier in the world. Sailors also defended the young republic in the Quasi War against France and in the conflicts with Tripoli and other Barbary states. Seizure of American ships and impressment of American seamen became central issues in the two decades leading up to the War of 1812. Taking all of these developments together, it became possible to declare that the lowly American sailor had rights and was a citizen equal to merchants, lawyers, and legislators.[23]

At the same time Jack Tar became a symbol for the nation defending and carrying commerce, he persisted as something of a comic figure. The comical, or perhaps we should say farcical, sailor appeared in newspapers and almanacs in short anecdotes that might best be called Jack Tar jokes. Although these reports ridiculed the sailor, he remained a sympathetic figure whose antics contained a critical edge and a not-so-hidden message. As one editor explained, "The race of sailors" was "eccentric." "Like other arts, that of navigation possesses a number of technical terms peculiar to itself. The sailor forms these into a language, and introduces them without hesitation into all companies, on all occasions, and generally, with brilliant success, as nautical expressions are pointed, humorous and easily adapted to the situations of common life."[24] One vignette described a sailor driving a horse-chair furiously down a street and accidently running over a news hawker who had been shouting "Bloody news! – bloody news!" to get people to buy the latest edition. The poor newsboy was left cut to pieces and bleeding. Some "gentlemen" stopped the sailor and were about "to chastise him" when the tar "bawled out, – 'D'ye see, gentlemen, d–m his eyes, he hollowed bloody news and had none, – now he may cry out bloody news, 'till his heart akes, and ne'er tell a word of a lie neither!"[25] This story may have made the sailor buffoon-like, but it also criticized the print media for over-hyping the news. Although it did not use much sailor language, it did have the sailor offer an oath and speak in an unrefined lampoon that contrasted the coarse sailor with the dignified gentlemen. Other Jack Tar jokes rely more on a nautical lexicon. A humorous description of an incident in the summer of 1784 made fun of the sailor ashore who had too much to drink, while offering a critique of women's fashion that indicated Jack Tar had little tolerance for the trappings of aristocracy. A "blunt groggy Jack Tar was doubling the corner of a street, the wind then at N. W. he ran foul of a lady with her calash round her head." Stunned by the woman's head scarf (calash), which followed the high style of the day and covered an oversized wig, the tar "immediately hailed her, and desired to know who was her milaner [milliner]." The woman told him that it was none of his business. Unfazed by this rejection, the sailor replied, "true, madam, … but methinks she has made a d-mn–le mistake in taking the dimensions of your hull, for your main top gallant royal balloon is too taunt; and by G–d, if you don't keep a steady helm you will turn keel up in a jiffin [jiffy?]."[26] The elaborate clothing and headdresses of "ladies" served as the butt of several Jack Tar jokes.[27] Sailors also objected to exaggerated religious pretensions. When amid the paroxysms of religious fervor one minister exclaimed, "*you are agoing! You are sinking! fast sinking!*" a pragmatic sailor "honestly replied, '*Well then, why don't you heave out the* LONG BOAT?'" This pointed barb implied that rather than exhorting sinners, the preacher should be doing something practical to save them. The "honest Jack Tar" – and many of these news items used the word "honest" as an adjective for the sailor – may have been a fool, but like the court jester in Shakespeare plays, he was not just jesting. Instead, his comments revealed a just jest.[28]

Americanization

These Jack Tar jokes often had British origins. Despite independence, Americans continued to borrow many of their ideas about sailors from the British, especially in the 1790s and early 1800s with the expansion of the American merchant marine and the creation of the U.S. Navy. This cultural mimesis can be seen in the frequent use of British music and stage productions in the United States. Bickerstaff's *Thomas and Sally* was published in Philadelphia as early as 1791 and it was performed in theaters throughout the American nation.[29] Because of the popularity of common sailors, the portrayal of jolly tars singing about their life on sea and ashore had a general appeal, but the plot line in which Thomas foiled the squire's evil intentions and won his Sally's hand had a special attraction for egalitarian American theatergoers, who applauded the common man's triumph over the landed aristocracy. Starting in the mid-1790s stage managers repeatedly produced a similar operetta by British lyricist J. C. Cross called *The Purse, or the Benevolent Tar*. The original lyrics, however, had to be altered for American audiences. In Cross's version Will Steady, who has returned from his Algerian captivity – a subject near and dear to Americans in the 1790s – found the local baron attempting to take sexual advantage of Will's wife. Explaining his Algerian captivity, Will proclaimed "a British sailor loves *native freedom* too well, ever to willingly let a *foreigner* interfere with it" and that "Had but a score our countrymen" been on board when the Algerians attacked they never would have captured the vessel because "an *Englishman* never *strikes* his *colours*, while he's able to *strike* another *stroke*." The American publication of the same work altered these words: "a benevolent sailor loves *universal freedom* too well, ever to willingly let *slaves* interfere with it" and "Had but a score of our old messmates been on board" the ship the Algerians would not have captured it because "*a true-bred Tar* never *strikes* his *colours*, while he is able to *strike* another *stroke*." Even this doctored version may not have gone far enough for Americans. In nearly every city the musical was produced under the title *The Purse, or American Tar*. The published lyrics of this retitled work have not come to light, but we can well imagine the word "American" replacing "benevolent" in the text as well as the title.[30]

By the early 1800s Jack Tar's American credentials were secure. In 1802 Washington Irving wrote a critical review of a comic opera called *The Tripolitan Prize; or an American Tar on an English Coast*. Irving's Jonathan Oldstyle ripped into the contrived plot and overacting, but not even his wit and sarcasm could hide the popularity of this melodrama. During the play the American captain appealed to his son, who wanted to stay in England because of his affection for a young woman, by declaring, "What! an American desert his duty!" To Irving's apparent disgust, this exclamation brought three cheers from the gallery. Having paused for this response, the captain continued, "impossible – American tars forever!! True blue will never stain!! &c. &c." At which point, Irving lamented there was "a continual thundering among the gods."[31]

This Americanization of Jack Tar helped to bring the sailor into politics. The use of Jack Tar, Tom Bowling, and other pseudonyms as pen names became a common practice as a means to reach out to ordinary people in the heated political atmosphere of the early republic. The authorship of these letters, essays, and news items is not important in this discussion. Some of these commentaries may have been written by real sailors. Many probably were not. Regardless of the maritime origins of this work, the use of the language of Jack Tar testifies to the American public's attraction to and familiarity with the sailor idiom. As we have seen, the persona of the political Jack Tar and his various alteregos had appeared occasionally in Great Britain and colonial America. This trend continued into the 1780s. In a few instances Jack Tar could be used as a political slur.[32] In other instances he was an individual with his own political opinion. Tom Bowling, for example, signed a letter packed with nautical metaphors about divisions between the states under the Articles of Confederation. This supposed common seaman explained how the nation began under bright auspices with the "American fleet" putting "to sea with a fair wind and glorious prospect of a successful voyage." Soon disputes broke out with "officers and a part of the crew refusing to obey the directions of the admiral and commodores." After rehearsing the errors of several of the ships (individual states), Bowling cautioned that "the natural enemies of the American fleet" were "watching every manauvre" hoping for a shipwreck so they could take advantage of the situation. In 1789 Jack Tar debuted in a less flattering role in a dialog with a merchant discussing the issue of discrimination – the policy of charging some nations higher duties and tonnage fees to convince them to open trade with the United States. In this case the author portrayed Jack Tar as a comical figure complaining about the proposed higher duty on imported rum.[33]

In the mid-1790s, the common sailor and his specialized vocabulary began to appear with greater frequency in letters, essays, and reports featuring Jack Tar, Tom Bowling, and a host of new cognomens with maritime roots. Like the emergence of Jack Tar in the mid-eighteenth century, the timing of the common sailor's entry into political debates should not be surprising. During the 1790s American commerce expanded rapidly and the United States created a navy. Threats to the American merchant marine from the Barbary states, the British, and the French brought sailors into popular focus just as the ideal of equality was spreading throughout the Atlantic world. All common men were becoming politically important, including Jack Tar. In an odd twist of a long literary tradition using

common folk for comic relief, the sailor (as well as his farmer and tradesman counterparts) began to be taken more seriously. Late in 1793 Jack
Mizen – a fictional nautical character who danced a hornpipe in 1787 on
the same stage on which Tom Bowling sang – joined his messmates Tom
Bowlin (aka Tom Bowling), Dick Shroud, and Will Anchor in writing a
letter "to the *Federal Fleet*, now riding in Congress Bay." They claimed
to support the Constitution but were concerned with the customs duties
they had to pay on their private ventures (small investments in goods that
sailors carried on a voyage), which they thought were being "*squandered
among a set of lounging* ship cousins, *that are living in the* cabins *and the*
state-rooms, *while we honest fellows are standing watch and watch on
deck to earn our small pittance.*" In particular they thought that the current Indian war in Ohio wasted money when a small fraction of that sum
could be used to free American sailors held in Algiers. Jack Mizen was
not interested only in protecting seamen. He had republican sympathies
evident in his support of the French Revolution and the French minister
to the United States (Edmond Genêt); he requested that the government
repay the French loan from the American Revolution and decried the
"round robin *signed by the officers in the cabin against the captain of
the* GENET" – a round robin was a written agreement among mutineers
in which all names would be signed in a circle to ensure no one person
was singled out as the leader.[34] Jack Mizen and Tom Bowling (spelled
correctly this time) entered electoral politics in Boston the next year.
Mizen wrote praising Bowling for orchestrating a "general rendevous" –
recruiting stations for the navy – to support a republican candidate,
probably Charles Jarvis. After "returning from the ship Faneuil [Faneuil
Hall] ... He hailed us as ship mates, as we came on board and having
a can of grog, he drank success and long life to his worthy Lieutenant
[Jarvis]," whom he wanted promoted to captain. In the fall Bowling
issued a call – the newspaper piece began "HALLOO! Ship-Mates!" –
that made this support explicit as Jarvis, a state assemblyman, challenged
Fisher Ames for a seat in Congress. Bowling said that Jarvis, who was
a doctor, was "an intrepid officer and sailor's firm friend" who was as
"good a seaman as ever step'd between stem and stern." Jarvis "would
do credit to the fleet" and was "ready to stand his watch." This support
brought Tom Bowling criticism from Ned Halyard (another invented
nautical name) who attacked Bowling as "some land-lubber, who never
mounted a wave of old Neptune." Halyard went on to defend Ames,
who was as arch a Federalist as can be imagined, because "He has frequently called all hands on board the good ship Congress, GEORGE

WASHINGTON, commander, to consult on means to make us seamen happy and flourishing."[35]

Halyard's attack on Bowling indicates that as the political divisions between the Federalist Party and the Republican Party developed, both sides were willing to use Jack Tar and his idiom for their own purposes. A Tom Bowling supported "our old First-Mate, JOHN ADAMS," for the command of the "Federal ship" in 1796 because he "has kept the log," while "fair weather, favourable winds, twenty-five dollars a month, good provisions, and plenty of grog and tobacco, have been the seaman's luck and cheer."[36] Four years later another Tom Bowling called for his messmates to vote for Thomas Jefferson because the nation had lost its way, "that we were wrong in our *latitude* – that we were out in our *reckoning* – that many of our pilots could not take an accurate *observation* ...." On election day "the genuine Tars will come forward, and put the ship in sailing trim." Bowling promised, "When we *make land*," with the election of Jefferson, "I will address you again. The Log-Book will be worth reading."[37] In the years after 1800 this contest to speak for and to speak as Jack Tar continued. Federalist outrage at Republican rhetoric against the British impressment of American seamen only intensified as the Republicans unsuccessfully sought to use commerce to gain concessions concerning both sailors' rights and free trade in the years leading to the War of 1812.[38]

Of course Jack Tar's persona was not the only pen name partisans adopted in this era. Publishing under an assumed identity was commonplace in the eighteenth and early nineteenth centuries. Essayists in Great Britain had done so, and so had their colonial counterparts. In the years leading up to the American Revolution both supporters and opponents of resistance to British imperial measures relied on pseudonyms, usually based on the classics. This practice continued after independence, as the authorship of the Federalist Papers under the name Publius demonstrated. Antifederalists, too, wrote using similar Classical identities – Cato, Brutus, and others.[39] Jack Tar was not even unique in representing the lower classes. Many eighteenth-century writers, influenced by the emphasis on nature and reason in the Enlightenment, had assumed the pose of the humble farmer. Lawyer and planter John Dickinson signed his classic essays against British imperial impositions the "Pennsylvania Farmer." New York Anglican minister and Loyalist Jonathan Sewall attacked the actions of the Continental Congress under the guise of a Westchester farmer. And J. Hector St. John de Crevecoeur posed as the simple farmer John in his sweeping examination of American society in the 1780s.[40] With the rise of the common man as part of the American Revolution other groups were brought into the political arena. Artisans like Paul Revere became politically important and the eighteenth-century term for a man who labored with his hands – "mechanic" – underwent a metamorphosis from a slur word to a symbol of pride: "By hammer and hand all arts do stand" became the mechanics' rallying cry. Because many artisans helped to lead the revolutionary movement, "mechanic" became another popular way of signing an essay.[41]

Jack Tar, Tom Bowling, Jack Mizen, and the similar maritime-sounding names that appeared in American sources after the Revolution were thus not in themselves singular. Other pen names, both Classical and common, abounded. For our purposes it is not so much the signature of the sailor that counted. Rather, it was that these articles, as well as the stage productions, could use a nautical argot appreciated and understood by the public at large.

By the 1820s, 1830s, and 1840s, as we have seen in Cooper's *Red Rover* and Melville's *Moby Dick*, the language of Jack Tar had been set. It continued in song and stage, the printing and reprinting of Jack Tar jokes, more lengthy sailor anecdotes, and the occasional political commentary during the Jacksonian era. Tunes like *Poor Jack* sustained their popularity during the antebellum period and *Tom Bowling* was a favorite with Henry David Thoreau.[42] Stage productions featuring sailors and Jack Tar's hornpipe dance continued to be performed. In the 1830s the American Theater produced a "Nautical Melo-Drama called Tom Bowline" and in 1840 the Walnut Street Theater concluded the evening's entertainment with two new maritime pieces called *The Landsharks and Seagulls* and *Jack Tar Ashore*.[43] Jokes using the jolly sailor to criticize the larger society abounded. In a pithy 1844 commentary on politics several newspapers reported that "a jolly jack-tar, was rolling" along a Boston street when he heard that the Democrats had nominated James Polk and George Dallas. The sailor responded: "'Pork and Dollars? ... that's the ticket; *something to eat and money in the pocket.*'"[44] Given the special place of sailors in the popular culture, there were often anecdotes about Jack Tars and their peculiar language. In 1829 newspapers published a humorous description of a militia muster in which Bill Bobstay called the captain a "lobster faced landlubber!" and threatened that if the officer "come athwart my bows, I'll cut your hawser," asserting that the captain had never been "o'sight of land in your life, you fresh water land crab – you snapping turtle of a mill pond; d'ye spose I'll close up the hatchway of my mouth? If I do may old Davy Jones sink me in his locker."[45]

Jack Halyard, yet another invented nautical name, became a character in a popular children's book in the 1820s.[46] Over the years there had been a number of Buntlines – Ben, Bob, Harry, Jack, and Barney – on the stage and in the newspapers, but the most famous member of this fictional clan appeared in the mid-1840s when sensationalist writer Edward Zane Carroll Judson Jr., having spent some time at sea, took the pen name Ned Buntline in his sea stories and tales of adventure in the West.[47] Jack Tar and his shipmates did not shy away from political commentary either. Tom Starboard supported the Democrats in an 1838 election and hoped that "our good ship's company" would "steer clear" from "Banks," using a pun on the nautical word for an underwater hazard like a sandbar – banks – while referencing the controversy in the 1830s over monetary institutions – again banks – that many believed threatened the ship of state.[48] In 1844 Bob Backstay was a Whig who supported Henry Clay for "*Commodore of the United States fleet*" because he knew "every rope in the ship, and can judge well when to *make sail* and when to *shorten sail* – can tell how the cargo should be stowed, and how to manage a ship in all weathers."[49] Through this repetition in song, stage, print, and politics the language of Jack Tar became standardized and stereotyped. It almost did not matter what the sailor really sounded like. What mattered was what people, even the common seaman himself, thought he sounded like.

Image and Reality

Disentangling the sailor from the language of Jack Tar is difficult. Many common seamen began to think that they had to speak like the caricature of Jack Tar if they were to be believable. Perhaps at times they were even fooling themselves. Sailors in the first half of the nineteenth century published a host of personal narratives that have formed a rich resource mined by historians exploring the American maritime world. Some of these books offered readers and historians exactly what they expected – the jolly tar effusively sharing his colorful language.[50] In these narratives sailors ashore who were drinking and whoring "were on a cruise" or "raising a breeze"; they did not simply have a drink, they "spliced the main brace"; and if they became intoxicated they were "three sheets to the wind."[51] Friends were "shipmates," implying that they had sailed together on the same ship; close friends were "messmates," men who sailed together and prepared and ate food together. Both terms could be implied in the shorthand "mate" or "matey." Body parts, too, had special names: a hand became a "flipper." As he was returning from a long voyage, George Edward Clark cautioned, "Ah, Jack Tar, you don't know how many hands are waiting to grasp your tar-stained, hardened flipper that now rests on the rail."[52] The human body could be called a "hulk" or a "craft," and the left and right sides became larboard and starboard, as Josiah Cobb's comical description of his first night after capture by the British in the War of 1812 made clear. Thrown into the dark cable tier, the front part of a ship where ropes and anchor chains were stored and where prisoners of war would be kept, the men had difficulty finding any comfortable spot. "Whereaway, shipmate, and what cheer?" called one sailor to a friend. "Hard wedged in between the layers of the cable close upon a lee shore" was the response. "If my old hulk isn't hogged [having the ship's keel warped so that its front and back were lower than the middle] by the morning, it will be no fault of the breakers underneath, which are doing their best to loosen the joints of my back bone, … How gets you on, brother shipmate." The second sailor fared no better: "Bravely, bravely, Jim, my boy; but have a hard time of it, to find out the soft parts of the cable for my old craft to rest upon. If the rope ever part, it will be where it is chaffed by my starboard hip, which has now become so dull with its tough job," that he wanted to shift his position to have the "larboard one to bear upon the same spot."[53]

The conviction that sailors had their own language helps to explain the sermons of Father Taylor, the model for Melville's Father Mapple. Born in 1793, Taylor went to sea as a boy. He had his conversion experience in Boston in 1811, but continued as a sailor for several more years, was captured by the British during the War of 1812, and experienced the ordeal of Dartmoor as a prisoner of war. After the Treaty of Ghent he sought to make a living on land and held prayer meetings in his own house. Eventually he became a fulltime Methodist minister, preaching to Boston's maritime workers. But his eloquent fervor attracted national attention. His sermons would be "majestic and picturesque," while being "Colloquial in a severe sense." Above all, Taylor gained renown for his "allusions to Ships and the Ocean and Sailors' lives of unrivalled [sic] power and life-likeness." Recalling his first religious experience Taylor described how he "put in" to church out of curiosity and seeing "the port was full," in his words, "I up helm, unfurled topsail, and made for the gallery; entered safely, doffed cap or pennant, and scud under bare poles to the corner pew. There I hove to, and came to anchor." The minister's words had a powerful effect on Taylor, who later reported in his best seaman's idiom: "Pretty soon he unfurled the mainsail, raised the topsail, run up the pennants to free breeze; and I tell you, the old ship Gospel never sailed more prosperously." With the "salt spray" flying "in every direction," especially down Taylor's cheeks, "Satan had to strike sail; his guns were dismounted or spiked; his various light crafts, by which he led sinners captive, were all beached; and the Captain of the Lord's host rode forth conquering and to conquer." In a maritime culture and language stereotyped by Dibden and Bickerstaff, amplified for decades on stage and in print, Taylor's sermons brought thousands of seamen into his chapel. This religious theater, as Melville's Father Mapple attested, had an appeal that reached beyond the waterfront. Poet Walt Whitman, as well as many other landsmen, eagerly attended Taylor's performances. "[A]mong all the brilliant lights of bar and stage I have heard in my time," Whitman explained, "I never had anything in the way of vocal utterance to shake me through and through, and become fixed, with its accompaniments, in my memory, like those prayers and sermons – like Father Taylor's personal electricity."[54]

Whatever the popularity of the stereotypical sailor lexicon, however much some sailors may have found it personally appealing, often the sailor in print balanced some of the language of Jack Tar against a greater dose of everyday English. Samuel Leech could pursue a nautical metaphor if he wanted. Captured on the HMS *Macedonian*, this young British tar sought to join the U.S. Navy. First, however, he had to undergo an interrogation by an American officer who questioned Leech's false claim about being born in Philadelphia. Unable to identify some streets in the City of Brotherly Love, Leech admitted that "My colors, which had fallen to half-mast before, were now fairly struck." When asked about the British naval buttons on his jacket, he knew his game was up: "This was a shot which raked me fore and aft. I hauled down my colors and stood silent." Despite the reliance on the naval metaphor on this page, Leech wrote most of the rest of the book in good clear English with little of the usual sailor jargon.[55] J. Ross Browne wrote without much maritime vocabulary when in narrative mode, but broke into standard Jack Tar lingo, with phrases like "splice the main brace" and "shiver me if I've ever been athwart such a craft, shipmates" when creating dialog for his seamen.[56] Many other narratives contained some technical language of the sea but little of the stereotypical maritime metaphors. Tiphys Aegyptus, who was not born in the United States and had joined the American navy in part to learn the English language, used a few nautical terms to describe sailing and referred to the men he served with as "ship mates," but he otherwise wrote in clear sophisticated prose in his pamphlet outlining a series of complaints about the treatment of sailors in the navy.[57]

Gurdon L. Allyn wrote in unvarnished language but had to rely on his maritime vocabulary in some of his descriptions of a ship at sea. During one storm, for instance, he wrote, "Not being able to lay to we scud under a very little sail."[58] Christopher Hawkins described the waves in one storm as breaking over the taffrail and used similar nautical terms, like having "our close reefed top sails set" in a technical sense. Otherwise, like Leech, Aegyptus, and Allyn, his prose was not particularly salty.[59]

In a few instances Jack Tar's language was almost untainted by nautical references. In 1755, in one of the earliest published dialogs involving the Jack Tar character, there was a supposed conversation between "Monsieur Baboon, a *French* Dancing Master," and "Jack Tar, an English Sailor." As the exaggerated comments by "Monsieur Baboon" attested, this anonymous author did not shy away from absurd caricatures in depicting language. In this pamphlet, however, Jack Tar was a straight-talking Englishman whose "good heart" and "good spirits" contrasted with the Frenchman, who admitted "me be ver phlegmatique, and ver melancholique, because of de times." In response to this absurd parody of Frenchified English, the British seaman spoke clearly and directly. Moreover, the author had this sailor declare that he had "a right of claim to the illustrious name of *Jack Tar*" because he "had the honour, many years to serve his most excellent majesty King *George*, in the sublime station of a fore-mast man." Despite this humble persona, the author avoided almost all nautical metaphors in Jack Tar's speech. In fact, this common seaman had an uncommon command of language, telling Monsieur Baboon that his "grand Monarque" had "in every instance since the late peace, trifled, and prevaricated with our good and gracious sovereign king *George*, (whom God long preserve) and the *British* nation, in a manner unbecoming the royal style and dignity." The author of this "Humorous and Diverting" dialog may not have been a foremast hand. But that is beside the point. This publication indicates that just as the image of the caricature of Jack Tar and his plethora of sea-talk was taking shape, it was possible to depict Jack Tar speaking plain English without any nautical babble.[60]

Perhaps this type of publication would have been more difficult to produce after 1755 when the multitude of stories and songs of exaggerated Jack Tars gained in popularity. Straight-talking sailors, however, might still be found well into the nineteenth century. In 1836 "Jack Tar" signed published letters opposing the New York port tax on seamen to support the marine hospital. In lucid and deliberative prose, with nary a "mate" or "lubber" mentioned, the author referred to the heritage of the American Revolution and cited the Constitution. This cultivated tar ended his first essay with a flurry of polished language: "It thus appears that contrary to the usages of government, a particular class of men is taxed in an odious and unusual form (a capitation tax) and are subject to a double burden, being assessed as citizens, and assessed as *sailors*."[61] "JACK TAR" quoted the Constitution in the second essay before moving on to general principles. "In a free government it is essential that the laws should operate equally upon all, and the burdens of the State should be so distributed among the people that no hardship may be borne by one to which the others are not subject." Paraphrasing Andrew Jackson's Bank Veto message, the writer reminded readers, "The president has said, that the benefits of government, like the dews from Heaven, should descend equally upon all. This sentiment was commended to the perusal of the Regency [the group in the Democratic Party in New York that controlled state government] by a JACK TAR." Maybe this "JACK TAR" was not a Jack Tar after all. Certainly his command of English, if we assume a common sailor could not write in this high style and with this vocabulary, would suggest otherwise. The subject matter and the passion about an issue that affected only seamen indicates this assumption is wrongheaded. Moreover, if we have no absolute proof of the nautical roots of this "JACK TAR," we also have no proof as to the actual authorship of the myriad of essays published under the signature of other Jack Tars, Tom Bowlings, or Jack Mizens. All could have been fabrications.[62]

The selectivity in the use of language by Jack Tar can be seen in one important subset of the American maritime world – the African American sailor. Many blacks served as seamen during the early republic. Cooper's *Red Rover* wrote this fact into fiction with the creation of Scipio Africanus – Scip – as Fid's boon companion, even if Scip's color prevented them from being messmates. Scip may have been an even more knowledgeable seaman than Fid, but unlike Fid he generally kept his mouth shut. When he did speak, Cooper had Scip combine Jack Tar's technical language with black dialect. "Em got a stream down, and all a rest of he anchor stowed … S'pose he jam he helm hard-a-port, Misser Harry, and take on he larboard bow, what you t'ink make him kick and gallop about!" Other writers, like William Leggett followed suit.[63] Black sailors, however, could write, and, we suspect, speak differently. Olaudah Equiano claimed to be born in Africa and enslaved as a young boy. He served for decades as a seaman in the British navy and on merchant vessels in the West Indies and colonial North America. His prose reveals no hint of the burlesque tar although he did use "avast" in its technical sense, as well as other maritime words in discussing the sailing of the ship. Even the passages he wrote as dialog contained no hint of either sailor or black dialect. Indeed, in one exchange over the right of his master to sell him after years of service in the British navy, the merchant captain who had purchased Equiano told him that he "talked too much English."[64] Equiano's purpose in writing his life story in the 1780s was the same as waterfront worker Frederick Douglass's purpose in writing his narrative in the 1840s. Both men wanted to demonstrate their intelligence as articulate spokesmen for their race and the cause of abolition.[65] Venture Smith, an enslaved African who gained his freedom and earned his living in part as a sailor in and around Long Island Sound, wrote a less overtly abolitionist narrative of his life. His prose is lucid without either the black dialect of Scip or the sailor's idiom.[66]

African American sailors, however, could employ Jack Tar's language if they thought it was useful to them. In the 1820s black seamen confronted new regulations in slave states that threatened to imprison them if they came ashore when their ships entered Southern ports. Beginning with South Carolina, Southern legislatures wrote these so-called Negro Seamen's Acts to prevent the spread of information about emancipation both in the North and in the West Indies for fear such knowledge would encourage slave rebellions. Blacks and their abolitionist allies saw these laws as a violation of African American rights and citizenship.[67] William P. Powell, an African American who ran a reform boarding house for black seamen in New York, published a short dialog between black sailors attacking these detested laws. The names of the sailors were predictably maritime – Mr. Spunyarn, Tom Handy, and Jack Haulyard – and their conversation was sprinkled with the language of Jack Tar. All three men had a few leisure minutes on their watch having adjusted the rigging after tacking the ship. When Spunyarn offered a salute touting the central political slogan from the War of 1812, "Success to Free Trade and Sailors' rights," Jack Haulyard objected in good nautical style, "Avast, there Matey; better belay that." Here the sailor idiom combined with the shipboard setting to underscore the message that blacks had "sacrificed their lives on their country's altar" to secure "every American citizen rights, privileges, and immunities, which, alas, the colored sailors do not now enjoy!" As these quotations demonstrate, Powell utilized both sailor language and clear, even stirring, English.[68]

Black Jacks could also speak – or be reported as speaking – without any reliance on nautical jargon. Early in 1842 New York African American seamen held a public meeting to petition against the hated

Southern laws. Two black sailors who had been held captive in Dartmoor
Prison addressed the crowd. One declared that "when war broke out with
England, this country looked around for strength," and recruited white
and black sailors. "After suffering for my country" in Dartmoor "it is too
hard to be arrested, denied all the rights of citizenship, and thrown into
a common jail, merely because my skin is black." Another Dartmoor sur-
vivor described his incarceration in a Southern port. Sometime thereafter
he joined the U.S. Navy and was asked to be a gun captain. He accepted
this responsibility, but also told his lieutenant that it was not right, "in
times of peace, I'm nothing but a poor black nigger, and wherever I go,
they ask me for my *free papers*," but on a warship no one asks for those
papers, and a black man will "do to fight as well as a white man." As is
true with every other printed source, we might question the authenticity
of these words. Perhaps the reporter cleaned up the language of these two
Jack Tars who were described as having "the peculiar swing of the body
that belongs" to sailors. However, taking the various sources of African
American sailors together, as well as the sources by white seamen, we can
at least begin to question the universality of the language of Jack Tar and
realize that sailors, and those who spoke in the persona of sailors, might
have a utilitarian approach to their vocabulary.[69]

That sailors might chose when and where they wanted to use the language of Jack Tar helps to explain why the maritime metaphor did not
appear frequently when sailors put pen to paper in personal correspondence. These sources might have a mixture of regular and sailor English.
A letter written by the captain of the *Tuscaloosa* to the ship's owner
was largely in clear declarative prose, but when he reported the illness
of one seaman, the captain turned to his nautical lexicon to joke about
the man's medical condition. The captain explained that one seaman was
at present "hove too," and unable to work because he has "a *foul bottom*" (a ship with barnacles on its hull was said to have a foul bottom).
Although in some instances sailors used the same phrase for venereal
disease, in this case it probably meant severe diarrhea – the captain noted
it was "a complaint that sailors is apt to have in N.[ew] Bedford owing
to *muddy water*," too much drink and high living.[70] Often letters and
manuscripts of a more personal nature written by seamen do not differ
from similar material produced by non-sailors in the period. Caleb Foote
could use the technical language of the sea when reporting the fall of a
seaman from the rigging, but his letters to his wife were clear of maritime metaphors and even eloquent in their use of regular prose. When he
was a British prisoner during the Revolutionary War, a despondent Foote

began one letter to his "*Most Affectionate Friend*" (his wife) with "I take this opportunity to write you a few lines to acquaint you of my welfare, which is very poor at present for here we lie in prison, in a languishing condition and upon very short allowance, surrounded by tyrants, and with no expectation of being redeemed at present."[71] These words were not the babbling effusions of Dick Fid or any of the various stage Jack Tars. Less heartrending, although often with the same sense of loneliness and homesickness, are the letters from whalemen and sailors found in a variety of different libraries. These letters often do little more than chronicle activities like where the seaman has been or report on friends and relatives, just the sort of material that might be in letters exchanged by anyone. Sometimes there might be some ship vocabulary as a matter of description. Even when the author of the letter tells a story, seldom did the writer resort to the language of Jack Tar.[72]

Who, then, is the real Jack Tar? Is he the buffoon? Is he the joker with the just jest? Is he the happy-go-lucky, jolly tar? Is he the despondent Caleb Foote? Is he the serious individual who might write and speak in a manner similar to anyone else in that world? Although we will never truly know the answer to these questions, we can conclude that he was a little of each of these and that at times he chose one persona and then another.

Cooper and Melville used the language of Jack Tar to demonstrate their familiarity with the maritime world. That language represented a longer development that transformed a clown-like, lower-class character in the guise of the common seaman, through portrayals on stage, in song, and in print, into a national symbol. This development began in Great Britain and continued in the new United States in the celebration of Jack Tar, Tom Bowling, and other fictitious sailor identities. In the process the progenitors of the stereotypical Jack Tar, whether professional writers or the seamen themselves, used a technical maritime vocabulary to fabricate metaphors to mold a stylized and specialized nautical argot. Although this language of Jack Tar seemed to set maritime culture off from mainstream culture, the distance between the two was not as great as we might imagine because so many land-based people would be conversant with the technical lexicon of the sea through personal experience in the forecastle, as travelers, or through expressions in theaters or in print. Sailors might use this language themselves, but often did so when it suited them. There are plenty of examples in print and in manuscript where seamen wrote in a plain style ungarnished with maritime metaphors. Popular culture created an image of Jack Tar, and some sailors may have sought to live up to that image. How many and how often they did so we will never know. No matter what magic we attempt as historians in bringing the past to the present, when reaching across the centuries we remain largely confined to the written word. Careful reading of that written word suggests that Jack Tar's language did not so much represent vast distinctions between the maritime and mainstream cultures; rather the two interacted and fed off of one another. What we see, and not hear, was a language of Jack Tar reflected in both the maritime and land-based worlds. Ultimately there is no potion we can brew, no spell we can cast, no conjuring trick that can bring back the actual sounds of the past. By examining the language of Jack Tar, however, we can see the interaction between the cultural landscape and the cultural seascape of the early American republic.

3

The Logbook of Memory

Wind, wave, and weather. Read any logbook from the great age of American sail and you are likely to see merely a dry record of a ship's journey. And yet, as any researcher into maritime history can tell you, amid the constant litany of the direction of the wind, the course of the ship upon the ocean, and the atmospheric conditions that could bless or bedevil a ship, appear occasional vignettes into life and work at sea. Put a pen into a man's hands poised over paper and there is no telling what he might write or draw. Most often he only did what was required – a simple chronicle of progress at sea. But he might also record the punishment meted out to a sailor who balked at climbing into the rigging during a storm. Or copy a few words of a favorite song he heard during the dogwatch that evening. Or comment on that strange ship on the horizon that he thought was a pirate. Or sketch some landfall to help him remember how the shoreline looked for the next time he navigated upon those waters. Scholars have used this additional information to explore shipboard experiences. This chapter is less concerned with describing that life at sea than examining how logbooks speak to us across time, became the metaphor for the sailor's life, and ultimately contributed to mainstream culture in the development of American literature.

Whatever the logbook's distant impact beyond the confines of a ship, the idea of maintaining an official record of a voyage had its greatest impact on the world of the common sailor. As an important navigational aid, logbooks were expected to be accurate. For the sailor, then, the logbook not only measured a ship's progress, but its veracity became a testimony to truth. James Fenimore Cooper has Tom Coffin affirm in *The Pilot* that he had killed more than 100 whales in his lifetime by declaring,

"It's no bragging, sir, to speak a log-book truth!"[1] In addition, in both physical and mental terms the logbook became an instrument of memory. The logbook itself was a written record of a voyage, but it also reflected a certain view of time and place that gave shape to a narrative form. Like the memory palace constructed in the mind of Matteo Ricci where fragments of information were lodged in each room that could be recalled by merely visualizing the chamber, a sailor remembered every ocean journey in relationship to specific times and places, even across the vast expanse of the trackless sea.[2] The sailor's memory palace did not have rooms; instead, the pieces of the sailor's life were marked by the ships he sailed and his ports of destination. When two old shipmates met in a tavern they did not just reminiscence and catch up with each other's lives. Instead, they "began to compare reckoning and," metaphorically speaking, "read over log-books" to rehearse the saga of their voyages.[3] Real logbooks occasionally show this "memory palace" in action. Joseph P. Clifford, for example, wrote a "Chronological Memoranda" at the beginning of a logbook listing every voyage he took, beginning as a "foremast Jack" in 1815 to commanding his own vessels in 1830.[4] We can also see this memory tool at work in James Fenimore Cooper's *Ned Myers; or Life before the Mast*. Although the author of the Leatherstocking novels may have embellished some of the language and, as he himself admitted, provided additional background, the basic tale belonged to Ned Myers, who demonstrated a remarkable capacity to recall more than seventy voyages covering decades of experience. Cooper has Myers explain, "this is literally my own story, logged by my old shipmate."[5]

This use of memory also meant that sailors looked at time as linear and not, as so many who were wedded to the rhythm of agriculture, as seasonal. The logbook, like the trip it chronicled, had a beginning, a middle, and an end. Equally important, that journey took the sailor someplace with every point along the way plotted by each day, if not each hour. This approach to life as a voyage became an important part of the sailor's mind-set. The conjunction between time and place mattered as the logbook shaded into the seaman's journal in the late eighteenth and early nineteenth centuries. In turn, the sailor's journal merged with the autobiography, the travel story, and the captivity narrative. Ultimately, this format worked its way into American literature through the guise of Richard Henry Dana Jr.'s *Two Years before the Mast*, and Herman Melville's fiction. Encouraged by these examples, some sailors put their own humble stories – their logbooks of memory – into print.[6]

What is a Logbook?

Fundamentally, a logbook was a navigational aid that kept track of a ship's location by noting its speed and direction. One eighteenth-century navigation manual explained, "a Journal, or Sea-Reckoning" – as the author called a logbook – "is a punctual writing down every Day (in a Book fit for that Purpose) the Course, Distance, Difference of Latitude, and Departure the Ship hath made, what Latitude and Longitude she is in; and also the Wind, Weather, with all Accidents and occurrences that happen."[7] The name "logbook" derived from the fact that in the age of sail mariners measured a ship's speed with a log-line, which was a knotted rope with a weighted piece of wood, a log-chip, that was tossed over the side. The log-chip then floated along the surface of the water while the ship continued to be driven by the wind in its sails. As the rope tied to the log-chip ran out, the knots, which were spaced at forty-seven feet and three-inch intervals, were counted. The total number of knots passed in twenty-eight seconds, as measured by a log-glass, indicated the total number of knots (or nautical miles of 6,080 feet) traveled per hour. On deck a ship's officer recorded the hour-by-hour readings, or sometimes readings every two hours, on a log-board, which was a piece of slate written on with chalk. At some regular point every twenty-four hours, usually at noon, which was when the day at sea was officially counted, this information would be written permanently into the logbook, noting the total distance traveled. There was plenty of room for error, given the role of currents and the direction and force of the wind. However, along with knowing the latitude and longitude of the last landfall and compass readings for direction, a skilled navigator could use trigonometry to determine the location of a ship that was out of sight of land. These computations formed the basis of navigating by dead reckoning.[8]

Logbooks have a history reaching back at least to the sixteenth century and were increasingly useful in the age of exploration and the development of European overseas enterprise. Indeed, because logbooks were so crucial to navigation out of sight of land, in many ways they can be considered vital instruments of empire. Working out the speed of a ship and maintaining a logbook, however, could be irksome, so navigation manuals began to make recommendations for format as well as to provide tables to aid in calculations. William Bourne's 1574 *A Regiment for the Sea* offered the earliest English description of the use of a log-line and advised keeping track of the log-line readings in a book. Seventeenth-century navigation manuals offered instructions on the best way to keep a logbook by drawing columns with the hour, day, and month, along with reports on wind conditions and distance run, as well as location in latitude and longitude.[9] By the mid-eighteenth century the instructions on maintaining a logbook had become more elaborate, including sample logbooks with explanations of the process of calculating and recording the appropriate information. James Atkinson argued in his *Epitome of the Art of Navigation* that a ship's position should be "*summarily comprehended in a new Form of keeping a* Sea-Reckoning *or* Journal, *wherein the* Log-Book *and* Journal *in Words at Length, and Tabular in Figures, are kept together in one Book.*" This practice "*will be no small Satisfaction to those concerned in* Ships *and* Goods, *nor a little Augmentation to the* Mariner's Credit *and* Reputation." Atkinson believed that keeping a logbook "(under God)" preserved "a Ship, and all in it" and prevented the loss of "divers rich Ships, and many dear Lives, and thence the impoverishing of several Families." Everyone, therefore, who navigated ships "to remote Places" with "so great a Trust as Mens Lives and Estates ... reposed in them" needed to keep "an exact *Journal*" so that "they may not only bear the Name of *Navigators*, but thereby prove themselves deservedly worthy of the Title of *Compleat Artists*."[10]

The British and American navies wrote regulations concerning logbooks. The British navy insisted that its officers keep a logbook in 1730, issuing instructions in 1731 stipulating that from the moment the captain stepped aboard ship he was "to keep a Journal, according to the Form set down ... and to be careful to note therein all Occurences, viz. Place where the ship is at Noon; changes of Wind and Weather; Salutes, with the Reasons thereof; Remarks on Unknown Places; and in general, every Circumstance that concerns the Ship, her Stores, and Provisions." After six months the admiralty expected him to submit "a Copy of his Journal for the said Time," to the government.[11] Later naval instructions made the sailing master (an officer who specialized in navigation) responsible for the logbook.[12] In 1802 the young American navy issued regulations for a uniform method of keeping logbooks and even required the captain to examine the journals and logbooks of all of his subordinate officers to incorporate any information "which may contribute to the improvement of Geography" or comments about "currents, tides, and winds" into the ship's official logbook.[13] By 1818 the logbook's role as the record of an American warship had become more elaborate. The logbook remained the ultimate responsibility of the captain, who was expected to list even the ship's provisions in it. In addition, each lieutenant was "to see that every occurrence worthy of notice" during his watch was "properly entered on the log board" and hence eventually transmitted into the log-book. As in the British navy, the sailing master had immediate control of the logbook and had to deliver it to the captain every six months for transmittal to the secretary of the navy.[14]

No such rules bound American merchant, whaling, and fishing vessels. Instead, by tradition the logbook had become another navigational tool, akin to having a compass and quadrant, to ensure a safe passage. By the mid-eighteenth century keeping a logbook was simply good navigational practice. Indeed, logbooks became so common that when Congress wrote its first maritime regulations they were hardly mentioned. The 1789 Navigation Act outlined a host of documents for every ship, including a ship registry to demonstrate ownership, a manifest detailing its cargo, and articles of agreement indicating the conditions of employment for the crew. But there was not a word about a logbook. In 1790 Congress wrote a statute concerning the recruitment of seamen that did refer to logbooks, but only in terms that assumed every ship had one. The law stipulated that whenever a sailor was absent without leave in violation of the articles of agreement, the officer in charge of the logbook was supposed to note the date the sailor left the ship.[15] Nathaniel Bowditch, following a pattern his English predecessors had set, included instructions for a method of keeping a logbook in his 1802 edition of *The New American Practical Navigator*, and a sample logbook on a run from Boston to Madeira.[16] As Richard Henry Dana Jr. explained in the mid-nineteenth century, "it is the custom for each officer at the end of his watch to enter upon the log-slate ... the courses, distances, wind and weather during his watch, and anything worthy of note that may have occurred." Following a tradition that reached back at least to the eighteenth century, Dana also advised that it was then the chief mate's duty, with the concurrence of the ship's captain, to record those details in the logbook.[17]

Although navigational manuals in the eighteenth and nineteenth centuries indicated that the first mate was responsible for the logbook, that was not always the case. Many captains apparently insisted on maintaining their own logbooks. In a few instances the same volume included a log from a cruise where an individual maintained the navigational record of one ship as a mate, and then a log he kept as captain on the same or another ship.[18] On some ships both the mate and the captain kept logs and discrepancies between the two could cause insurance problems if any claims were made at a later date. In one controversy a captain refused to let his first mate see his own log to check the disposition of the sails after the leaky ship had to return to port.[19] Others aboard ship might also be responsible for the log including the second mate, a supercargo, or ship's clerk. Difficulties in identifying a logbook's keeper are compounded by the overlap in format between a ship's log and a sailor's journal. Moreover, many logbooks did not indicate who wrote the daily entries.

Logbooks came in a variety of shapes and sizes. Some were smaller than this page and less than a quarter of an inch thick. Many were in large folios as big as an oversized coffee-table book, but with many more pages. Often, especially in the eighteenth century, they were simply bound in canvas, with the pages tied together with string. The tiny logbook Samuel Tillinghast kept in 1750 fits this description and even has stitching around the edges of the canvas cover.[20] There were also huge logbooks in canvas covers like the one mate William Brown kept on a trip to Havana from Salem in 1808.[21] Later in the eighteenth century and into the nineteenth century, more logbooks were leather bound. As suggested in the navigational manuals, the pages generally followed a set format, with lines drawn to delineate the day, time, direction, weather conditions, and an additional space for remarks. This last section might contain comments about the setting of the sails and work the crew had done. On July 1, 1818, the first mate of the *Neva* briefly described the wind and weather as mild and then reported that "the watch [was] picking oakum at meridian," a tedious task of taking loose fiber from old rope and preparing it for caulking the ship, which was done when no more pressing job was available for the crew. Nine days later, however, the log keeper described a more strenuous day of labor when the first mate wrote that "all hands employed in shifting the fore top Sails and getting the jolly boat in on deck."[22]

There were variations on how the page was organized. In a few instances, these differences would appear in the same volume, and sometimes even on the same voyage.[23] Whalers often kept the navigational information in a log to a minimum, especially while on whaling grounds when the actual location of the ship was less important than the hunting of whales. Merchantmen, too, could record only a minimum of navigational information. The log of the *Acastus*, sailing from Philadelphia to the Indian Ocean, merely had a line devoted to each day that noted little more than the wind, weather, and location.[24] This truncated record keeping was unusual for merchant ships in the early nineteenth century and most logs contained greater detail. The logbook of the brig *Catherine* in 1809 was typical and followed the pattern suggested in the navigational guidebooks with hand-drawn columns on the page for the hour, set every two hours, listing the speed under the heading K for knots, followed by a column with an HK at the top to indicate half-knots. Additional columns noted the course of the ship, distance traveled, and the direction of the winds. A large area to the right of the page, which overlapped all of the bi-hourly readings, contained remarks briefly describing the weather, the tacking of the ship, and similar sailing occurrences. There were two days on each page. At the bottom of each day's hourly entries was a space for stating the day's progress, the course of the ship, the distance traveled, and the days at sea. This summary also listed the ship's location at the end of the day (remember the day at sea changed at noon) with two columns for indicating latitude, one based on observation and the other based on reckoning from the information in the log. An additional column had the deviation (departure) between the two. There was also space for writing down the longitude of the ship.[25] By the end of the eighteenth century entrepreneurial printers produced leather-bound books with the columns labeled and pre-drawn, creating the opportunity for even greater standardization.[26] These printed pages followed formats similar to the one drawn in the *Catherine*, ordinarily dividing each page into two halves to fit two days with columns and headings for the logbook information. They might also feature an advertisement on the inside cover like the one that appears in the log of the *Henry Eubank* in 1834, that reads "Seamen's journal sold at stationers in Boston."[27] Henry Whipple in Salem provided a title page that announced that the logbook could be purchased at his own bookstore and the lottery office at Franklin Place.[28] Despite the availability of printed formats, as late as 1850 some logbooks had been purchased with blank pages with the log keeper ruling in his own lines.

We can discuss the shape, size, and format of logbooks because American libraries and archives contain thousands of these records. There are at least five thousand logbooks and journals from the whaling industry held by a wide variety of institutions. The Phillips Library of the Peabody Essex Museum alone has more than three thousand logbooks, mostly from merchant ships.[29] Why does this massive archival resource exist?

Because the logbook was a navigational tool central to sailing in the correct direction and informing the captain of the location of the ship, during every voyage the logbook needed to be maintained and protected. The canvas and leather covers offered some of that protection, as did the care and storage of the logbook when not in use. The paper in all of the logbooks – at least in all of the logbooks that have survived – was of high

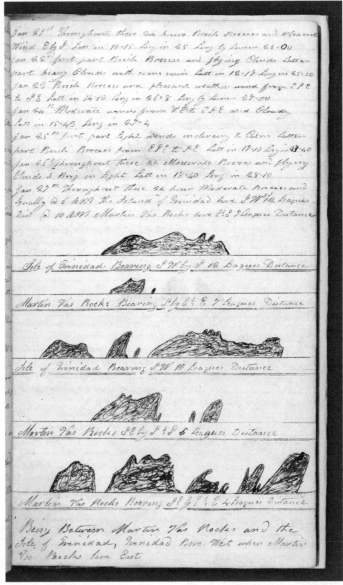

FIGURE 3.1. **Log of the *Acastus*,** kept by Francis A. Burnham, 1817, Barker-Edes-Noyes Papers, Ms N-1800. Although Francis Burnham's logbook for the *Acastus* had only a line or two devoted to each day and noted little more than the wind, weather and location, Boardman also included a series of profiles to help identify landfalls in the future. Courtesy of the Collection of the Massachusetts Historical Society, Boston, Massachusetts.

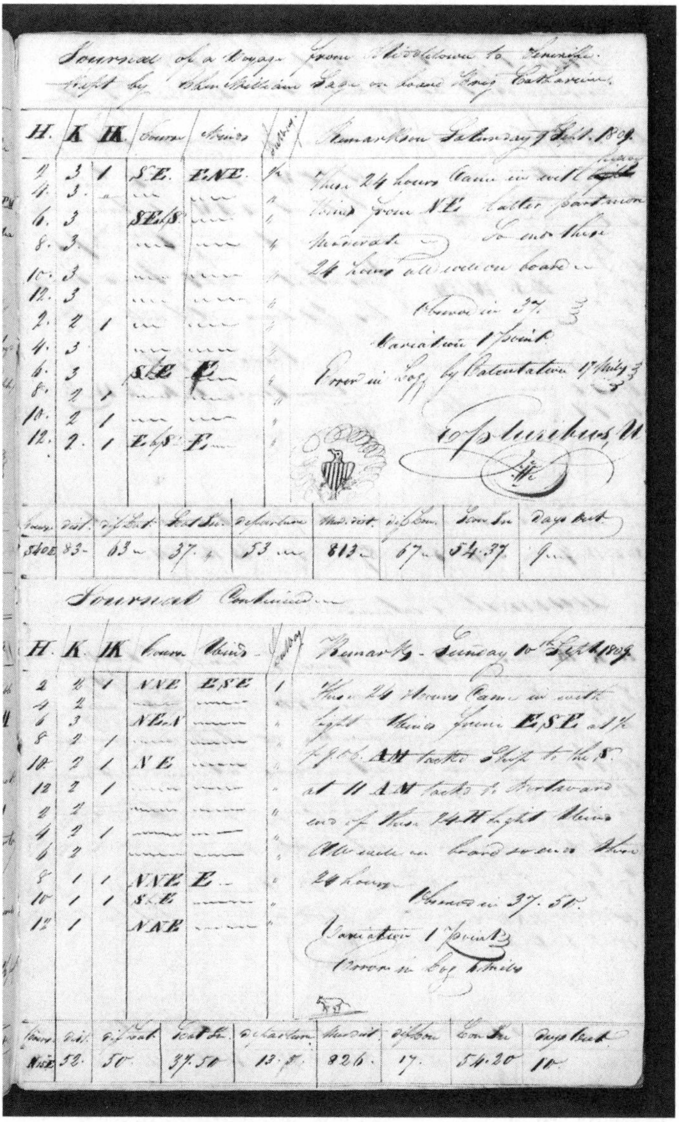

FIGURE 3.2. **Log of the *Catherine*,** kept by Ebenezer William Sage, 1809, Ebenezer William Sage Papers, Ms N-856. The log of the *Catherine* was typical for a logbook with hand-drawn lines, with entries for two days to each page. On the left hand the day is divided into twelve two hour segments with the speed listed for every two hours. Next are columns with the course and wind direction. The large area to the right of the page contains remarks concerning the weather, the tacking of the ship and similar sailing occurrences. Across the bottom of the daily entry is a summary of the ship's distance traveled and location at the noon hour. This page is somewhat unusual since it contains two small images: an emblem of the US on one day, and some sort of animal on the second day. Courtesy of the Collection of the Massachusetts Historical Society, Boston, Massachusetts.

quality so that the log could withstand the onslaught of wind and waves that often beset a ship. But problems arose. Ships, of course, were always in motion. Any unexpected wave might jeopardize the daily entries. First mate Thomas Wilson Ross explained the dark ink stain on the page for November 5, 1832, in the log of the ship *Lotos* by noting that "While writing in this days work a sea struck her [the ship], a lee lurch followed like any that my self, Book, inkstand, went tumbling to Leeward, the effects may be [evident?] on the book."[30] This mishap shows the difficulty of keeping the logbook in a world surrounded by water. Reading some of the sagas chronicled in the logbooks, with storms that lasted for months and the trials and tribulations created by war, reveals just how amazing it is that so many logbooks have survived.

The voyages of the *Dispatch Packet* from Salem to the West Indies in 1820–21 and of the ship *Prince Ferdinand* in 1759 reveal the trauma a ship and its logbook might experience from nature. Stuck by a hurricane on its return trip, "sea mountains" surrounded the *Dispatch Packet* for almost a month, stoving in the cabin (smashing in of its wooden walls), knocking the ship on its beam ends (turned over so that the ship's deck was almost vertical with the sea), and leaving the vessel dismasted. Short on food and water, the ship limped back to the West Indies (it never returned to its home port) after ninety-eight days at sea. Somehow, however, the log survived to be copied and a transcript placed in the Massachusetts Historical Society.[31] During its winter transatlantic passage, the ship *Prince Ferdinand* was also assaulted by storms. The stark description of one day's events, filled with the technical language of the ship, offers dramatic testimony of the ordeal:

Feb. 12, 1759: "This 24 Hours a Violent Hurricane from the WNW with a Dismal high sea, at 2 P. M.: as we were scudding under bare poles the ship brocht too, finding the scudding Dangerous, Lay her too under a Double reeft Mizzen the Gale still Increasing with great Violence the ship lay down with much water on her decks sent two hands up in the Maintop to cut away the Main top mast: they cut away the top sail yard which very providentially swong by the Lifts in upon Deck w[h]ere we Secured him [them?]: the Gale so hard & the weather Extreme cold the men were so numbed they could not handle any thing to cut away the top mast and with great difficulty gott down on deck again at 4 P. M.: the Gale still increasing the seas now Mountain high & the Ship intierly to the Mercy of them, unable any Longer to hold her sides up to it, having lain down with three Sheets of water on Deck. the sea making a breach over her for the Preservation of our Lives came to a Resolution to cut away the fore mast: which we Effected with it went all the Riggin: the foresail, foretopsail, maintopmast, staysail, Middle staysail: on which she rited & became more Lively. The Gale still Increasing: but in the Mercies of God we had hopes having a tite Ship att 10 P. M. the gale was at the height."

We can only imagine the terror that day. However, thanks to the seamanship of a few unnamed sailors the ship remained afloat with much of its masts, yards, and rigging cut away to ensure that the vessel would not be cast to the bottom of the sea in the fierce and unrelenting wind. The storm persisted and a few days later a wave broke over the back of the ship, saturating everything in the cabin. Yet somehow both the ship and its logbook made it to port.[32]

Man-made problems, especially the vicissitudes of war, could also threaten the logbook. We may never know the full history of the log Francis Boardman kept on multiple voyages before, during, and after the Revolutionary War. Captured aboard the sloop *Adventure* in early 1776 off the North Carolina coast, Boardman was held for eight weeks on British ships and put on half allowance. The British looked upon him with "Disdain Spite & malis [*sic*]" and threw him into irons after three of his men managed to swim ashore when the ship was in a river near Cape Fear. After his release from this close confinement, Boardman and a British sailor slipped off the ship and somehow made it ashore. Boardman does not explain if he swam or stole a boat, nor does he indicate whether he carried his logbook with him during this escapade. For the rest of the war, the book remains silent, although Boardman went on other cruises as an officer and was even captured a second time. In all likelihood he had left the logbook on board the British ship when he escaped and some kindhearted officer miraculously returned it to him in Salem at the end of the war. With some pages still empty, Boardman wrote an account of his escape and then simply took the volume with him on his first peacetime journey in 1783 to once again record the details of wind, wave, and weather.[33] David Chever, the clerk who kept the log on the private armed ship *John* in the War of 1812, was not so lucky. Sailing on a cruise that lasted less than two months, he left a final entry that reads: "All hands [sent] to quarters expecting an action in a short time." As it turned out, the *John* lost the ensuing battle with the British and sixteen days later, having refused to have his leg amputated, Chever died from his wounds. Yet the log survived. In 1899 a nephew wrote a note about Chever's tragic demise that remains with the log today.[34]

Although most logbooks chronicle more mundane experiences, the fact that we have these stories attests to their significance to the log keepers and their families. There were several reasons for this importance. As suggested in the ordeal of the *Dispatch Packet*, which was condemned as a wreck after it returned to the West Indies, the logbook bore testimony to the efforts to save the ship. Richard Henry Dana Jr. explained in his *Seaman's Friend* that logbooks were a legal record and therefore might be used as evidence in a judicial process. The logbook was so sacrosanct for the lawyer Dana that he wrote that "nothing should be entered [into the logbook] which the mate would not be willing to adhere to in a court of justice."[35] Long before Dana made this observation, log keepers were aware of the legal nature of their logs: in 1808 mate William Brown wrote a sworn affidavit at the end of the logbook of the *Agnes* stating that he was the one who wrote the log and that no one dictated any part of it to him.[36] Logbooks were even sent through the mail at great expense to be used as evidence in court proceedings.[37] The log of the *Prince Ferdinand* reveals another important reason for holding on to the volume after reaching port; as explained in the earlier British navigational manuals, logbooks also aided in evaluating the captain and crew's role in the success or failure of the merchant's venture. Most logbooks, however, never made it to the courtroom, and soon after the completion of the voyage the logbook became superfluous to the merchant. Yet many captains and mates tenaciously clung to their logbooks.

The patched-together chronicle of Francis Boardman's logbook, which recorded one cruise in 1776 and then was used for another in 1783, suggests an additional reason for keeping possession of a logbook: it cost money to buy the book and the empty pages still had value. Paper was an expensive commodity and any frugal captain or mate wanted to make the best of his investment. Many logbooks, like Boardman's, therefore chronicle multiple voyages, even on different vessels. The leather-bound log of the *Acastus* also contained the logs of the *Laurel* in 1815–16, the *Three Sisters* in 1821, and the *Fenwick* in 1822.[38] Enos Field reused his logbook on several vessels from 1811 to 1813, and recorded his log in Spanish when serving in a Spanish ship.[39] Sometimes the logs from a new journey would begin on the very next page after the end of the previous one. At other times a few empty pages set off the next ship's record. The owners of some logbooks, like in the log of the *China* in the 1830s, simply flipped the book over to start the next log from what had been the end of the book.[40] Multiple voyage logs could be in the same ship, or as we have seen, in different vessels. The log of the *Commodore Perry* chronicled three trips in that ship and one aboard the *Mary* during the 1820s.[41] Logbooks also changed hands. The logbook of the *Three Sisters* in 1789 and 1790 had originally been the logbook of a British ship that Americans captured in 1776. The book, however, was not simply the plunder of war – the original British owner retained possession of the book during part of his imprisonment, using it as a private journal to copy letters, record songs, and make notes on his experience. It also returned to Great Britain with the original owner when he was exchanged five months after his capture. More than a decade later, the volume found itself on an American ship on its way to China, and in a different handwriting, was once again registering the daily progress of a ship as a logbook.[42] The logbook of the *America*, a merchant ship sailing in the 1820s, was used by a new owner on a different ship a quarter of a century later.[43] Logbooks could be combined from different ships at a later date. Someone sewed the smaller log of the schooner *Hawke* from 1778 into the larger logbooks of the *Remembergrace* and *William*. Whether these books were joined by the keeper Thomas Nicolson, a descendant, or a later librarian, remains unclear.[44]

If using the empty pages in a logbook provided a practical reason for not discarding it upon returning to a home port, the log keeper might also have emotional reasons for preserving his navigational record as a ship's officer. Throughout America's great age of sail, hundreds of thousands of young men went to sea. Only a few sailors worked their way through the ranks. Ordinarily these men would have a modicum of education and both leadership and intellectual abilities. Whether through strong-arm tactics or the power of personality, a ship's officer had to be able to exert his authority. He also had to demonstrate his intelligence in navigating and handling a ship. Even the simplest schooner was a complicated machine, and a three-masted square rigger would have dozens of sails and hundreds of ropes, each of which needed to be adjusted under the officer's supervision. It took a complete knowledge of every component of a vessel, from the deepest compartment of the hold to the uppermost mast, to ensure that everything remained shipshape and in optimum operational condition. And, as even a brief perusal of almost any logbook suggests, calculating a location on the open expanse of the ocean was no easy task. The best and brightest sailors would move through the ranks quickly, and a young man could become a captain in his early twenties. Most officers, however, would reach command of a ship in their late twenties and continue going to sea into their forties.[45] For these individuals the logbook was a testament to the command of their craft. Once the pages of any one volume were filled, many a ship's officer would be loath to discard such a record. Perhaps equally important, the logbook documented where he had traveled and what he had done in the peak years of his maturity. Despite the often monotonous litany of wind, wave, and weather in every logbook, hidden in its pages were the memories of the severe challenges met and conquered. The passage quoted from the

Prince Ferdinand indicates how searing those experiences could be. No doubt many logbooks have disappeared, ending up in a garbage heap or as fodder for a fire. Thousands were kept and handed on to the next generation.

The relatives and descendants of the logbook keepers were thus left a powerful legacy. What those descendants did with that legacy could vary widely. Heirs to these keepsakes from the seafarers in their family might have tossed the dusty old volumes chronicling long-ago voyages as soon as they could. Over the generations, some logbooks disintegrated from lack of care or fell to new uses. Empty pages remained valuable and old logbooks were good for practicing penmanship or as a sketchbook for a clumsy child's pencil.[46] A few logbooks became scrapbooks with newspaper and magazine articles pasted over the entries.[47] Many families, however, would cherish the memory of their sea captain forebears and hold on to the keepsake of their parents', grandparents', or great grandparents' experiences. David Chever's nephew must have felt this way when he wrote his note of how his uncle died during the War of 1812. By the late nineteenth century, the image of the wooden ship propelled only by the power of the wind and guided by the skill of man, in an age of steam and iron, conjured romantic notions of a life at sea in an age gone by. Logbooks as a tangible reminder of that image often remained sacrosanct and were passed from one generation to the next.

Logbooks also became collector items for individuals and libraries. Businessman Paul C. Nicholson began to buy old books about the sea and other maritime memorabilia in 1920. Soon he started to purchase logbooks from whaleships. By the 1930s Nicholson had centered his collection on whaling logbooks. Nicholson's logbook library continued to grow until it reached 836 manuscript logbooks, journals, and account books, which he bequeathed to the Providence Public Library in 1956. His decision to place these prized possessions in a safe repository where the books could be preserved created an important cache for scholarly use. Other libraries also developed a huge store of logbooks, particularly in specialized institutions devoted to American maritime history. Several more traditional historical societies, as well as smaller regional historical associations, also have significant collections of logbooks. Perhaps the reason for the centrality of the logbooks to the collections of these libraries was that the volumes had survived. But, like the family and collectors who owned the logbooks before, the romance of the sea helped. The archive of logbooks exists in part because scanning even the most mundane entries fires our imagination with clipper ships upon the high seas.

Stories like the ones imbedded into the logbooks of the *Dispatch Packet*, the *Prince Ferdinand*, the *Adventure*, and the *John*, whose purpose was originally to serve as a navigational aid, demonstrate how these logbooks survived trials created by nature and man, and suggests why the original owners, their descendants, collectors, and libraries have held on to them. For historians the logbook remains an unparalleled source for understanding what it was like to plough the ocean blue. For all of us, logbooks play to our romantic notions of the great age of sail. Answering the simple question of what is a logbook might begin with how the log evolved as a means of helping a mariner locate his ship when out of sight of land. But to truly understand how Jack Tar speaks to us through this unique source we must also examine how the logbook was more than a navigational tool and became a journal that at times revealed life and death at sea.

The Logbook as Journal

The content of the logbooks varied dramatically, depending on the preferences of the person writing. Logbooks could begin and end with elaborate or prosaic pronouncements. Robert Emery commenced his record of the voyage of the *Hannah and Elizabeth* in 1798 with a flourish and a nod to the Creator: "Journal of an intended Passage by God's Permission on board the Good Ship Hannah and Elizabeth Robt Emery master from the port of Charleston south Carolina towards Copenhagen in Denmark. May God grant a safe speedy & prosperous Voyage. Amen."[48] William Bedlow started his log with a simple description of the voyage: "A Journal on Board the ship Prince Ferdinand From New York to Bristol Jany. The 24th 1759."[49] Many logbooks merely had the ship's name and the headings for each column of information. The conclusion of a voyage likewise might simply end with the last entry at sea or a celebratory statement marking the completion of the journey. Upon arriving in port safely, Lot Stetson offered a drink to his men, writing in the log: "Att: 6 of the Clock this morning we made Barbadoes all hands are well on Borde Boys make a can of flip hear is Love to wives an sweat hart mate hear it goes."[50] The log keeper of the ship *Prince Ferdinand*, which was so beset by storms in its transatlantic crossing in 1759, noted upon arrival in Bristol: "Praise be to the Almighty God for his Mercy in bringing us to our Desired Port."[51]

The remarks section of a log was supposed to be limited to descriptions of the work sailors did on board, or special notes about wind, wave, and weather. Log keepers also might indicate the number of sails loosened to the wind. Some log keepers, however, wrote personal observations as well. Amid the normal recital of wind, wave, and weather, and while cruising on a calm sea in the West Indies, the log keeper aboard the brigantine *Sally* wrote on June 4, 1792: "May the [days] of my future life Be as the Sea on which I now fl[o]at, mild and Serene, as though no rude Tempest had 'er disturbed it."[52] The first mate of the *St. Paul* facetiously asked on May 27, 1839, shortly after beginning a long voyage from Salem to Manila: "Who would not be a sailor? Who would not sell a farm and go to sea? To be away from home, Society, Friends, and Acquaintances, and be confined to a floating prison for 10 to 12 months and then to return home for as many day[s] just long enough to make it unpleasant." After several more days sharing his depressed spirits with the log, and after repeated days of wet and foggy weather, the sky cleared and the log keeper could exclaim, "I am well contented and highly pleased with the Ship and heartily glad that I came in her as I hope to have a pleasant and [illegible] voyage." Despite the fine weather, he remained a little homesick. Two days later the log reports, "The sea is as smooth as a mill pond. And the ship is slipping through the water about 9 knots. Sunday at Sea, on such a day as this, is Sunday indeed, with nothing to divert the attention the mind naturally diverts to home until one almost imagines themselves there."[53] The log keeper of the *William Henry* was even more melancholy on his long journey to China in 1789, writing that "there is such a sameness & the same tegious [tedious] recurrence to Nautical observations that I am obliged to Really [rally] all my little philosophy to drive off the Hypocondriac, which hovers about me." On a different ship a few years later, but using the same book as his log, this sailor wrote: "Long passage dark Gloomy weather very unpropitious, the Blue Devils hover round."[54]

Logbooks might also have commentary on interpersonal relationships aboard ship. On his first whaling voyage as captain, Benjamin Neal chronicled his trouble in controlling the crew, unwittingly suggesting that he might not have been ready to assume the responsibilities of command. Neal wrote on February 25, 1839, that the whole crew came aft and wanted to know when he was going to put into some port, threatening to stop work if he did not do so soon. Cruising in the Indian Ocean, Neal thought it was too hot to head for a nearby port. The next day the situation became even more tense when Neal heard of "an agreement between some of my men not to report a whale" if they saw one. Although disgusted with his crew and concerned with his failure to capture many whales, Neal relented and sailed to Fort Dauphin in Madagascar. There his discipline problems only intensified as the crew fell into drinking and debauchery. As Neal exclaimed on March 8: "the crew are worse than the devil could wish them to be they sent aft to night to know if I would sleep on shore to let the women come on board this of course I refused." He also noted that on the previous night "there was a complete hell on board" because several men were "beastly drunk and made noise enough to have confused the worst Brothel." Many a captain at this point would have resorted to strong-arm tactics. Neal, however, confessed that he was afraid to strike any of his men, believing that if he hit anyone or used harsh measures "it would have bin a fin handle [something to grab him by] for them in Salem" and lead to legal action. Neal must have negotiated with the crew – a few days later he admitted that "Last night slept on shore let the Girls come on board for the purpose of keeping the crew quiet this is hard but I am forced to do it." This surrender did not work because the men wanted "the girls" on board the next night and they combined to refuse to do any work as Neal tried to prepare the ship to leave port. When the beleaguered captain finally managed to get the vessel to sea on March 13, eight men still would not work, and Neal had to watch the forecastle to make sure that these men did not damage anything. Rather than continuing the voyage under these circumstances, Neal headed the ship back to Salem with his hold only partially filled with whale oil. Although this type of documentation of conflict between captain and crew is rare in logbooks, it appears often enough to provide a rich source for scholars of maritime history, and reflects how a logbook could also be used as a journal to record daily activities and personal feelings.[55]

However, even stark entries could hint at the daily drama aboard ship and the thin line between life and death at sea. On June 23, 1816, Daniel Benjamin wrote that a Spanish sailor had fallen from the main yard and that the crew had "hove the ship too as soon as possible" and got the launch ready to be lowered. However, it "being very dark and a heavy sea going," the captain "did not think it prudent to risk the lives of any in the boat."[56] With these terse comments we are left to imagine the unnamed Spanish sailor's terror as he sank beneath the swelling waves. We are left wondering what the rest of the crew thought of the captain who dared not risk their lives to rescue a shipmate. Less lethal, but also reflecting the hardships Jack Tar faced, are the occasional references to impressment. Holton J. Breed was outraged when the British searched his ship and seized goods and impressed some of the crew who were "free born sons of liberty."[57] The men aboard the sloop *Remembergrace* in 1769 were luckier. When the captain heard that a British tender was taking men into the British navy off the coast of New England, he allowed several of the crew to go ashore to avoid the press gang.[58]

Beyond the comments in the remarks section, a logbook could contain a wide range of material within the confines of its cover. The sloop *Industry* sailed from Newport, Rhode Island, to Jamaica in the spring of 1767. While at sea the log keeper limited himself to the standard wind, wave, and weather observations, but while in port, because there were no navigational requirements, he followed more of a diary format, noting the day's activities.[59] The pages of a logbook might have important notes and information related to the ship. Captain Jonathan Colesworthy started his logbook in 1800 with a statement of the ship's dimensions, a list of the cargo, and a copy of his sailing orders before beginning his chronicle of the day's sailing progress and remarks on the day's events.[60] To commemorate the arrival of the new year Holton J. Breed also wrote his ship's dimensions following the log entry of December 31, 1804, almost five months after leaving port.[61] Sometimes there would be a list of the ship's crew, and there might even be accounts of payments to the ship's seamen, especially on long voyages, where advances would be made in foreign ports and the sailors would need to purchase personal supplies from the ship's stores.[62] At the back of the logbook of the privateer *America* is a list of marines and of the crew, divided into watches with each man's station at the guns and his assigned position when changing sails.[63] Logbooks also might have pages devoted to mathematical calculations, or notes on the art of navigation.[64] The mate of the *Matsey* wrote out instructions on how to find the departure in latitude in his logbook, and drew a compass with degrees and direction indicators, as well as an illustration of a Davis quadrant, highlighting the horizon vane, the shade vane, and the sight vane (the lines of sight used to measure the altitude of a celestial body – the sun or moon – that helps to locate the ship's latitude).[65] Other illustrations and even some physical objects glued to a page might appear in a logbook (for a full discussion of pictures drawn in logbooks, see Chapter 6). Mate J. Wiley seems to have bought some sketches of junks and fish in China and pasted the exotic images into his logbook.[66] Among the oddest objects found in a logbook are the wings of flying fish pressed into its pages.[67]

Perhaps the most interesting material in logbooks is the ephemera that occasionally fills what otherwise might have been empty pages. Paper was expensive in the age of sail and a rare commodity while at sea. Logbook keepers used any extra space for all kinds of purposes. At the end of the 1764 log of the *Exchange* are several pages of remedies for various

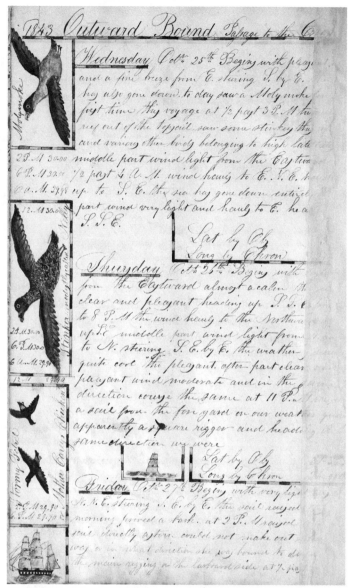

FIGURE 3.3. **Log of the *Emiline*,** kept by Washington Fosdick, 1843–44, ODHS Log147. Washington Fosdick kept a record of his whaling voyage in the 1840s that was a cross between a logbook and a journal. Instead of dividing the page with lines and providing columns with bi-hourly information, he writes daily entries. However, he also notes the ship's progress which was taken from the official log or the log board itself. Fosdick draws seabirds, and two small pictures of ships, one with the sails showing above the horizon, the other of a ship from a broadside view. The original illustrations are in color. Courtesy of the New Bedford Whaling Museum, New Bedford, Massachusetts.

ailments, such as corns, problems with teeth and gums, "Burgundied," dropsy, infection, spleen, and the like. There are also instructions on how to tan a hide.[68] Holton J. Breed wrote a list of the books he owned, along with the price he paid for them, on the last page of his logbook.[69] Sometimes the extraneous information in a logbook was added years after the voyage. The log of the *Nancy* from 1811 has shoemaking accounts from 1826, suggesting a change in occupation of seaman Seth Barlow.[70]

Religious material might also be copied into a logbook. At the end of one logbook from 1769 appears several passages of religious verse "composed a few Days before receiving the Sacrament," concluding with:

> Prepare me for that awfull hour
> When dust to dust shall fall;
> And let my Soul oh; gracious pow'r
> With joy await thy call.

The author offered eight pages of commentary about religion inspired by reading passages in the Bible, describing an austere and unforgiving God, but also suggesting that redemption was possible.[71] Thomas Nicolson wrote poems squeezed between the logs of two voyages and at the back of his logbook. In one poem he praised the Lord for providing him with such a wonderful wife: "Amazing was thy love! God of my life / Hannah thou gavest me for a partner! Wife!"[72] The bits and pieces of religious poetry found in logbooks often focused on how sailors at sea depended on God to protect them when they were most vulnerable. As his ship approached land in foul weather, and after being away from New York for seventeen months, Seth Barlow wrote:

> A leaky Ship in a distant Shore
> A Stormy Nite through thunderous roar
> The Listening blazen from pole Poseiden
> White foaming waves across us roll
> The raging Winds Are Whistling loud
> With floods of rain From every Cloud
> All those Contend. – To Make it his own.
> That we depend upon God alone.[73]

Logbook keepers, of course, also copied less serious poems and songs. Peter Pease used the same volume as a logbook for multiple voyages in the 1760s and 1770s. Although the opening pages of the book included some Bible verses and several religious poems, a series of more common and even bawdy verses showed up at the end of the logbook, written by Pease and others. These include *The Recruiting Sergeants Recitation*, which ensured any enlistee would soon find a sweetheart attracted by the sound of the drum and the uniform of the soldier. Standard maritime folk songs also appear, such as *William Was a Youthful Lover* (labeled *The Female Lieutenant; Or, Faithless Lover Rewarded* in the log) and *Ladies of Spain*. One song described a nubile servant maid as having "Two white Breasts, [that] hang so Low Like Two White hills covered with Snow." Several logs have similar songs and poems.[74]

Taken together, the personal remarks and the wide-ranging ephemera copied into logbooks suggest that these volumes became more than a navigational aid – they were also introspective testimonials that expressed private thoughts. These personal observations appeared in logbooks as early as the mid-eighteenth century. But they seem to increase by the close of the eighteenth century and the opening of the nineteenth century. This development probably reflected the expansion of the American merchant marine and the lengthening voyages as Americans extended commercial connections across the globe. The growth of the whaling industry in the United States, with cruises lasting several years, also contributed to the increased commentary in logbooks. At the same time that logbook keepers were personalizing their daily entries and filling empty pages with extraneous material, more and more common seamen began to keep their own journals, often borrowing their format from logbooks.

The Journal as Logbook

If logbooks blended into personal journals, then journals and diaries written at sea blended into logbooks. The official logbook was not the only record kept by those who went to sea. A wide array of individuals – naval officers, doctors, passengers, mates, regular seamen, and some women – might be found aboard ship scribbling away each day. Whatever the reason for keeping these records, the form and the content in such personal diaries and journals were similar to the basic logbook. Because these volumes are difficult to distinguish from logbooks, and cover the same sort of information, many libraries simply catalog all such sea journals under the general rubric of logbook. The various journals of Doctor Benjamin Carter aboard the *Ann and Hope* around 1800 are listed as logbooks by the Rhode Island Historical Society.[75] The library at Mystic Seaport labeled William Leeds' record of his first voyage aboard a whaleship in 1843–44 as a logbook and the Phillips Library of the Peabody Essex Museum in Salem catalogued a journal kept by two common sailors in the 1840s as the "Logbook of the *Ann Parry*."[76] These institutions should not be faulted for this blurring in the distinction between logbook and journal because the two types of books looked so much alike and, from the point of view of most researchers, both sets of records contained the same kind of information concerning the location of the ship and shipboard experiences. The fact that both logbooks and diaries could also begin with the word "journal" further complicates the issue. Moreover, the distinction between logbook and personal journal became increasingly hazy moving from the eighteenth to the nineteenth century, just as more logbooks contained more and more personal information, and just as a larger number of logbooks and diaries were being produced. To more fully understand the confused boundary between the diary and the logbook we need to examine the larger context of the diary or journal as a literary form.

Daily records "of events and transactions," the *Oxford English Dictionary* definition for "diary," have an ancient lineage. Both "diary" and "journal" trace their etymology to words connected to "day": "diary" comes from the Latin *diār-um* for daily allowance, while journal derives from Old French *journal* (with variant spellings) meaning daily, and itself is a Frenchified form of the Latin *diurnus*, of the day. As a practice the keeping of diaries reached back millennia and began to take its current form during the Italian Renaissance. In English "diary" and "journal" appeared as early as the sixteenth century in their modern usage. For our purposes, however, it is important to note that the diary emerged in the seventeenth and eighteenth centuries as a means of self-expression with increasing frequency.[77]

There were many different reasons for keeping diaries. Among the elite it was a way of offering personal reflection and recording political commentary. The diary of Samuel Pepys remains one of the best sources on the restoration of the Stuart monarchy in England, while the journal of William Maclay is our most detailed account of the first two years of the U.S. Senate.[78] Steven Kagle's examination of early American diary literature identifies several different categories for the personal journal. The spiritual diary, centered on the religious experience of the writer, expressed both religious doubt and conviction as well as chronicling the effort to encourage others to pursue a religious life. Travel diaries traced a physical journey across space, as well as a cultural journey from one geographical region to another. These works also contained useful information about the places visited and compared them, either implicitly or explicitly, with the writers' own homes. Other diaries centered on romance and courtship, confiding trials and tribulations as well as the

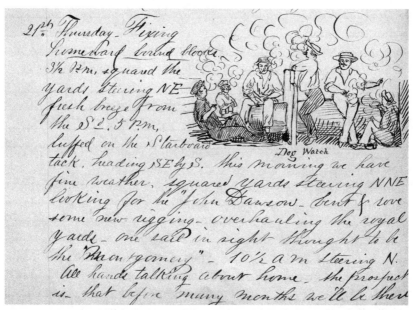

FIGURE 3.4. **Log of the *Clara Bell*** kept by Robert Weir, 1856, Log 164. Robert Weir combined information about the ship's sailing typical of logbooks with more narrative fare. He also provided a wonderful series of pictures of sailors aboard ship. Few logbooks had this kind of depiction of daily life and few sailors demonstrated the ability to draw as effectively as Robert Weir. Equally important, this illustration demonstrates how sailors could integrate their drawing into the body of their written comments. Courtesy of Mystic Seaport, G. W. Blunt White Library, Mystic, Connecticut.

intimate feelings of the heart. Equally emotional could be the wrenching experience of war noted in a journal. Each of these categories reflected a stage of life or a set of circumstances that had a time limit. Kagle also offered a more comprehensive category of journal that would cover larger chunks of time spanning most of the diarist's life. These life diaries, such as the multiyear personal ruminations of John Adams, could contain elements of each of these categories, transcending any one of them.[79]

Few maritime journals were life diaries, but many of them included material from one or more of the categories Kagle outlined. Religious concerns appeared in the journal of the brig *Nancy* on a whaling voyage in the 1780s when the writer offered the following prayer on the new year: "Thus ends the year 1785 all well on board. Thanks be to god who has thus preserved me these sixteen months since I have Left my Family and Friends, hoping that in my absence they have been protected by his kind providence and Carried through the Troubles and Fatigues that attend this Life."[80] The anonymous sailor who wrote a journal of a voyage to the South Atlantic whaling grounds greeted the new year of 1830 with similar sentiments: "So bless god to think that he has let me live another year, and will praise him & bless him if he will let me See the end of another one," but then launched into a religious discussion about aging and the difficulties of life that covered more than two pages.[81] Almost by definition every maritime journal was a travel diary. Commentary about different ports and different cultures abound, usually cast in negative hues. After setting sail from Manila, Eleazer Elderkin complained that they had "lain in that Damn'd ugly hole [Manila] near fifty days." He thought the place unhealthy and described the inhabitants as dark complexioned with straight hair and flat noses. Elderkin also complained of the low morality of the inhabitants. Not only were they "much addicted to Gaming – and smoking," but the "Chief part of the Handsome females" loved intrigue. Indeed, he confided, "they are very fond of Making Assignations with Americans – and for a trifle an Officer on board a Vessel may have one while he stays in harbour."[82] Courtship, as opposed to more base sexual references, might also appear, but seldom was it the main focus of a maritime journal. Elderkin began his record of his voyage to the East Indies in 1796–98 by writing on the inside cover: "Miss Mary Cushman Chief Ornament of Her Sex, Miss Catherine Forester of Lively Witt – Distinguish'd Beauty – Large Fortune – and an Honour to the Female Work," but seldom mentioned either of these young women again.[83] John Remington Congdon, however, kept his journal explicitly to amuse Cynthia, his future wife, and packed it with sentimental references of his love. (In turn, Cynthia kept her own journal of life in East Greenwich, Rhode Island, while John was at sea.)[84] Wartime experiences appeared in many sailor journals. One of the diaries Kagle discussed was written by Charles Herbert, captured at sea and sent to Mill Prison in England.[85] The unidentified writer of the "Journal Kept on Board the Ship *General Hancock*" during the Revolutionary War mainly listed sightings and captures, but also penned a detailed description of a brutal yet successful battle at sea with a British ship.[86]

What made sea journals and diaries stand out, however, was not how they might be similar to land-based personal daily records, but how they appeared so similar to logbooks in content. Indeed in some instances, as we have already seen, logbooks became journals and journals became logbooks, depending on circumstances. During the War of 1812, Captain Jeduthan Upton Jr. maintained his journal as a logbook of the privateer

Polly until the ship was captured on December 23, 1812. At that point the same volume became a personal journal recording his experiences as a prisoner of war.[87] But even those volumes intended as a diary look and feel like a logbook. Supercargo Sam Winchester kept a journal of his voyage to India in 1809–10 that reads like a wind, wave, and weather log, interspersed, like many a logbook, with commentary about life at sea.[88] Midshipman Thomas J. Harris on the USS *Peacock* from 1824 to 1827 kept a journal that was a detailed log. At sea he used a standard log form with columns and each page representing a day. All twenty-four hours were listed with the distance covered, course, and winds. The bottom of the page noted latitude and longitude. There was also a summary of the daily activity that included sails set and work done. Yet like any good daily journal or diary, and many logbooks, there was plenty of other material. On July 25, 1826, for example, Harris wrote some wonderfully salacious detail of the ship's visit to Nukaviah in the Marquesas Islands in the Pacific Ocean. "I have forgotten to mention," exclaimed the young midshipman, "that we received a visit of a different kind last evening, from 18 to 20 young females of 14 or 16 years of age, who swam off to the ship completely naked, except a small sprig of orange tree drawn round their middle to conceal that part of the body which decency required to be covered." This Edenic fig leaf, the astonished Harris wrote, "was only temporary ... until they received a better one from the person who had them in keeping for the night. A silk Handkerchief or a yard of Linen was as valuable a present as they expected to receive."[89]

As these examples of the various sea journals suggest, and as noted at the beginning of this discussion, a wide array of individuals kept a record of their time aboard ships. Sea officers wrote personal journals for a variety of reasons. Louis Brantz kept a logbook while he was captain of the brigantine *Equality* sailing to the Indian Ocean, but continued to maintain a daily record once he left the ship and later became a passenger aboard another vessel.[90] A young officer on the merchant ship *Talma* proclaimed that he wrote his journal for his own amusement, although he often complained his mood was low and that he was attacked by "Mr. Bluedemon." He also pined for a young woman named Katie he wanted to marry.[91] Second mate Alfred Terry aboard the whaler *Vesper* maintained his journal for a year and a half with log-like data and personal commentary. Terry does not explain his reason for writing his daily entries, but his emphasis on the wind, wave, and weather and the work done aboard ship suggests that he may have been preparing himself for the day he would be promoted to first officer and take responsibility for the ship's official log.[92] Likewise, Thomas Delano, who was neither the captain nor the mate aboard the *Herald*, maintained a log-like journal probably for practice since he shifted page organization for his entries in mid-voyage.[93] Similar concern with preparing for advancement explains many of the journals written by naval officers. As we have seen, naval regulations assumed that each officer had his own logbook or journal that the captain had to examine. No doubt this regulation encouraged even the most junior of officers in the navy, the midshipmen, to maintain journals. Midshipman Alexander S. Wadsworth kept a journal aboard the USS *Constitution* and the USS *President* that had little more than wind, wave, and weather.[94] In 1821 midshipman James Freeman Curtis quickly found copying out of the official logbook "tedious" and decided "only to make general observations as to time & place may present." Although, he wrote some passages in a more narrative style, he frequently fell back to standard logbook fare when the ship was at sea. After he joined the merchant marine as an officer he kept a more regular logbook.[95] This flitting between personal journal and logbook was not unusual for naval officers. The unnamed journal keeper on the brig USS *Porpoise* on the Wilkes expedition in the late 1830s repeatedly moved between the two formats, hoping to chronicle what was recognized at the time as an important scientific expedition.[96] Other naval officer journals were almost indistinguishable from an official logbook.[97]

For supercargoes, clerks, physicians, and passengers the journal may have been a way to fill time aboard ship. Although most merchants relied on their captains for the business end of a voyage, they occasionally appointed special agents – supercargoes – as their representatives during the voyage. As such, supercargoes had little to do at sea and had plenty of time to note their experiences in journals. They were often not interested in the navigational aspects of sailing. Usually with little previous maritime experience, their journals were often a hybrid between a diary and logbook.[98] Clerks were occasionally sent out on ships to gain some deepwater experience before advancing in a mercantile house and had few responsibilities while at sea. Complaining of "the monotony & dullness, of a long voyage," Thomas W. Abbott commented on the books he read and described the games he played with the two other clerks on their passage to China.[99] Physicians served in the navy and occasionally were hired for long voyages on merchant ships and whalers. Benjamin Carter aboard the *Ann and Hope* bound for China was a ship's doctor for a crew of more than sixty men during the Quasi War crisis with

France, while Theodore Lewis was the ship's surgeon on an Indian Ocean cruise on the whaleship *Atlantic* in the 1830s. The journals of both physicians had typical logbook information as well as additional commentary. Indeed, Lewis's daily entries often ran on for pages, indicating that he had time to spare. Passengers, too, could use a journal as a means to bide away the time.[100] On his first Atlantic crossing, John Adams did not copy the information from the logboard, but he did record wind and weather and made comments about his maritime experience.[101] Other passengers on different voyages, like preacher George Denham off to the gold fields of California in 1849, sometimes recorded longitude and latitude from the logboard, and sometimes did not.[102] A. B. Mayhew, who may have had a nautical background since he noted the sails spread aloft and the work done by the crew, kept a better sea record of his trip to California aboard the *Alexander Coffin*.[103]

In the nineteenth century more and more common seamen kept their own journals. Literacy had little to do with this increased journal keeping. Sailors may have been slightly less literate in the eighteenth century than in the nineteenth century, but most American sailors in both periods could probably read and write.[104] Instead, the increase in journals by common seamen had other causes. In part this development reflected the expansion of the American navy, merchant marine, and whaling industry. More American ships sailing the seven seas meant that there were more common seamen to write journals. In 1790 approximately 20,000 men served in the merchant service and as fishermen in the United States. There was no navy and most merchant vessels sailed on relatively short voyages to the West Indies or across the Atlantic to Europe. Fishermen remained close to home, seldom venturing beyond the Grand Banks. Whaleships cruised further into the Atlantic, but not until 1791 did the first American whaleship enter the Pacific. By 1850 well more than 100,000 men worked on American ships.[105] The U.S. Navy, created in 1794, in 1850 had squadrons stationed around the world including the East Indies. A seaman aboard an American warship might chalk up tens of thousands of miles: Midshipman Thomas J. Harris "logged" more than 70,000 miles in almost three years at sea.[106] American merchant ships could be found in every ocean and hundreds of whaleships scoured the seas in pursuit of the leviathan. Longer voyages meant more time at sea and away from a home port. Although sailors aboard merchant ships worked especially hard because high wages meant that captains kept crew size to a minimum, longer voyages had larger crews and increased the possibility of providing time for seamen to keep a journal. Aboard whalers where the size of the crew was more than ample to sail the ship – much of the labor was for the catching and processing of whales – there would be long periods between whaling grounds with little to do.

Time and numbers alone, however, do not account for the increase of sea journals kept by regular sailors. Larger trends in society, especially the rise of equality, also played a role. We can see this egalitarianism in comments that bristled over the poor treatment of sailors. William Wilson's journal on the whaleship *Cavalier* is packed with descriptions about confrontations between the crew and its officers, and he complained that he was being treated like "a dog – a slave, at the beck and call of an ignorant course tyrannical brutish coward." Other journals written by sailors echoed these comments.[107] Whatever the explicit expressions of equality and for the rights of men, the new age of democracy placed an emphasis on individualism: what common seamen had to say in their sea journals had become significant even if it reflected only their day-to-day experiences. When sailors claimed to be writing for themselves, many were merely posing – they ultimately believed that what they had to say as common seamen was important enough to gain a larger audience. One self-absorbed tar, having already said he was writing solely for his own enjoyment, revealed this interest in a larger audience by commenting that if anyone did see his journal he hoped that the reader would not be too critical and that somewhere in his pages there might be some information or idea that was new and worthwhile. The contents of the journal reinforced this impression. For example, the author – and we should call him an author – suggested that the ship's rules for the forecastle "might not be uninteresting" to the "landsman." Later in the journal, this articulate Jack broke away from the logbook and the diary format and penned sections under chapter headings like "A Strange Sail," "Dull Times," and "The Race."[108] In short, the tone of the commentary in most of these personal records suggests that as an individual the writer believed his thoughts mattered and the words he penned should someday be read by others.

Connected to the new emphasis on the individual we can see another important development in American culture – an intensification of a sentimentality that grew out of the Romantic era. Material about love and sentimentality appeared before 1800. But it was limited and not nearly as intense as occurred in the nineteenth century.[109] Even the logbook/journal itself could become the object of this sentimentality. The logbook of the whaling ship *Halcyon* by Captain William George Bailey became a journal after his shipwreck off the Australian coast. Amid several sentimental verses was an ode to the special role of the journal/logbook as a chronicle of the voyage and shipwreck:

> This book contains the story of its life
> And journeys made upon the trackless seas
> I tell of calms and elemental strife
> Of rushing winds and of the foaming breeze
>
> It tells of scenes upon the vast domaine
> Ruled by old Neptune its eternal king
> Of water spouting rising but to rain
> In scattered drops which form the sea and spring
>
> Much it records of oceans monster slain
> By brave New Englanders sons adventurous crew
> Who breast the seas and cross the lashing main
> Thus forced to bid their friends a long adieu
>
> And more anon I glean when I peruse
> These faithful pages. Here records the flash
> The thunders roar are chronicled defused
> In simple narrative also the Halogens crash
>
> The Halcyon anchored on Australia's coast
> Within a bay she thought herself secur
> Three chains she broke and then she soon was lost
> For naught against the howling blast is sure
>
> Oh how I envy thee thy bright career
> O how I long to go where thou hast been
> And see the green isles rise all bright and clear
> Upon the smooth sea as thou hast seen.[110]

A key element of this sentimentality, implied in Bailey's description of storm and shipwreck, was portraying the romantic draw of the ocean. This type of sentimentality appeared repeatedly in the first half of the nineteenth century despite a recognition of the harsh reality of a life at sea. The contrast between the romantic image and the hard life at sea became a trope itself that rather than diminish the romanticism of the sea actually enhanced it. Thus, William Silver declared, after more than thirty months at sea, that "I am heart sick of this voyage, it has bin a protracted disagreeable unprofitable dirty voyage, and to me I am afraid it will be the blindest eror [*sic*] of my whole life." A few weeks later he wrote a poem that closed:

> Our canvass is spread to the breeze
> our signals are waving in the wind
> Love I am hurried away to the seas
> an emblem of love fare you well.[111]

On the last day of 1849, whale man William H. Wilson expressed this same duality: "The life of a sailor in its best light, is hard and unsocial," and then quickly added, "The *Sea*, the dark blue sea, has its fascination, and its hails like the abandoned female is overlooked."[112] Midshipman Lucius M. Mason expressed similar conflicting emotions: "as I climbed up into the rigging, and looked out over the heavy sea as it rolled towards us with the cold wind, rain & hail beating in my face; I thought of the sentiment, happiness, & pleasure of going to sea, of being on the boundless Ocean, that element, which is so often made the subject, of the beautiful song or Poetry." And then he immediately corrected himself by declaring, "but never was a more erroneous idea entertained, for no life can a man lead, whereas he sees more hardships – & privations."[113]

Sailors in the nineteenth century could also wax eloquent about sentimental values of hearth and home. Silver penned some truly saccharine lines about a lock of hair:

> Yes lady I will keep thy prise
> and place it next my breast [the word "heart" is crossed out]
> there it shall lie to still the sighs
> that now disturb its rest
> O it will bear a magic charm
> dispelling clouds of care
> and as I feel a peaceful calm
> I'll keep the lock of hair.[114]

John Baker copied an *Address to Young Men* that compared the "permanent pleasures" of marriage to the fugitive and insincere joys of "lawless connection." After drawing out this contrast for several stanzas, Baker concluded: "If ye ask me from whence my felicity flows / My answer is short – from a wife" because "we find ourselves happy from morning to night" and "By our mutual endeavours to please."[115] Aboard the whaleship *Arab*, Captain Ephraim Harding repeatedly expressed his longing for his wife and child. Concerned about not capturing many whales after seventy days at sea, Harding pondered over "how much different I shall spend these winter months to those I spent one year ago." Now he was "wraped up with Care anxiety and troubles of the Seafaring life" while then he was "seated by my fireside with my Wife and Child who would be ready to take an Equal share of all my troubles and sympathise with me in all my misfortune in life."[116]

An indirect result of this sentimentality, especially a concern for family and the development of the companionate marriage, was the growing presence of women who were eager to share those "troubles" by going to sea with their husbands. Although many women had been passengers before, and some women even traveled aboard British and American warships during the eighteenth and early nineteenth centuries as wives of sailors and petty officers, not until the middle of the nineteenth century do we find a number of sea journals written by women. Usually these journals were kept by the wives of captains on long voyages or whaleships. Cynthia Congdon, for instance, kept a diary while her husband was at sea as a second mate and then mate. She continued the journal later after she joined him aboard ship when he served as captain.[117] Most of these diaries, however, fall into the same pattern of sea journals kept by men: a notation of latitude and longitude taken from the ship's log, weather conditions, sightings of ships, a report of the work done, and, if aboard a whaler, an indication of the quarry chased and killed. As one scholar who has written about the subject has noted with some frustration, "Scarcely an explicit thought or emotion, much less one of interest, causes a ripple in the flat narrative and descriptive surface."[118] Yet amid all of this plain recounting of life at sea, as with the male-authored journals, there appears some more useful information. Mary Brewster's published journals were typical. Some days she provided little more than the ship's log. On others she skipped noting longitude and latitude and focused on her own life aboard ship with more personal and religious reflections.[119]

Whether written by a man or a woman, or from the quarterdeck or the forecastle, by the mid-nineteenth century the sea diary looked much like the logbook. Amid the wind, wave, and weather record came more personal commentary that reflected a sentimental emphasis on the individual and the democratization of American society that celebrated even the common man's thoughts and opinions. These journals often reflected a self-conscious belief that what the author had to say was important for others to read. Although many of the lives written into these works were destined for obscurity, others did wend their way into print. In 1829 a critic in the *American Quarterly* complained about this development: "Authorship and travelling are all the fashion. Sailors wash the tar from their hands and write verses in their log-books; midshipmen indite their own adventures; and naval commanders, not content with discovering countries and winning battles, steer boldly into the ocean of literature."[120] Whether the critic approved, however, did not matter. The sea journal was becoming literature.

Becoming Literature

The publication of *Two Years before the Mast* by Richard Henry Dana Jr. marked a sea change in American literature. Books about the sea, especially the novels of James Fenimore Cooper, and books about common seamen had appeared before Dana. But Dana transformed sea literature and the way Americans viewed the life of Jack Tar. After Dana came a wave of new publications about life at sea and the world of the common seaman that ultimately saw its greatest expression in the works of Herman Melville. The writings of Cooper, Dana, Melville, and others derived only a part of their power from the logbook/journal. Melding with the linear format of the logbook were other types of literature including the captivity narrative, the travel tale, and the autobiography. Regardless of the complex origins of the rise of America's first great literature in the Romantic era, the logbook not only served as a metaphor for the sailor's life that was central to the worldview of Jack Tar, but also entered the mainstream culture.

Dana began *Two Years before the Mast* by looking over his shoulder at the influence of James Fenimore Cooper and his sea novels, asserting that his own book would be different because it would provide a "*voice from the forecastle.*" Cooper had himself revolutionized sea writing by fusing his technical expertise, based on his maritime service on ships, with the ocean as a backdrop for a romance between elite characters. As Dana noted, plenty of "stories of sea-life [were] written" in Cooper's wake. But Dana believed that they were "written by persons who have gained their experience as naval officers, or passengers" and not "intended to be taken as a narrative of facts."[121] Cooper's early sea novels focused on the quarterdeck and featured common seamen only as secondary characters. Sometimes he used Jack Tars for comic relief. Dick Fid in *Red Rover*, like many of the common folk in a Shakespeare play, appears as a caricature who struts across the stage – or "rolling along the deck." All too easily fooled, despite his seamanship, Fid cannot be taken seriously. At other times the characters appear as an ideal type whose command of all things nautical made them the Leatherstockings of the ocean. Tom Coffin of the *Pilot* was serious and whenever there was a crisis at sea, Coffin appeared with a steady hand. Ultimately, however, Coffin was too wooden, too unhuman to be fully believable. We do not see much of the lives of real sailors in Cooper's early work.[122]

Despite his own elite background, Dana self-consciously wrote his book in an effort "to present the life of the common sailor at sea as it really is – the light and the dark together." Dana thought that the only other book about regular sailors prior to his work was Nathaniel Ames's *Mariners Sketches* published in 1830.[123] This conclusion was not quite true. Ames, who like Dana was a member of a prominent Massachusetts family, wrote two additional books about life at sea. His *Nautical Reminiscences* appeared in 1832 and like his first book it was a rambling collection of comments and observations about the life of the common seaman. Ames's third work was largely a self-professed series of fictional stories. Although none of these books follows a logbook format and all lack a narrative flow, Ames was clever, could turn a phrase, and offered vital insight into the world of the common sailor. Having gone to sea for more than one voyage, Ames knew Jack Tar better than Dana, even if there was little that was lyrical about his prose and the books did not have a wide readership.[124]

However, Ames was not alone as a precursor to Dana. Common seamen had written numerous tales of shipwreck, piracy, and especially of captivity by native peoples, or by the British (either with press gangs or imprisonment during war). Some of these used the logbook/journal format, and some did not. Among the shipwreck narratives none was more riveting – and disturbing because it featured cannibalism – than the saga of Owen Chase aboard the whaleship *Essex* when it was rammed and sunk by a whale. Herman Melville later used this story as the basis of his classic *Moby Dick*. Although Chase was the first officer of the *Essex*, he had worked his way into that position having first sailed as a common sailor on previous voyages. Chase probably had help in writing his *Narrative of the Most Extraordinary and Distressing Shipwreck of the Whale-Ship Essex*, but the day-by-day account was based on a log he kept aboard the whaleboat he commanded as it made its way from the wreck to the coast of South America. His story may not have provided much insight into the daily grind of life at sea, but it did reveal the dangers every seaman faced when he sailed upon the ocean.[125]

Pirate tales, especially those told after the pirate was convicted and sentenced to death, sometimes revealed remarkable detail about life at sea. Although the actual author of such publications may not have been the sailor himself, whoever wrote down the story sought to trace how the common sailor turned pirate – something Dana pointed out was all too easy if a sailor were to resist forcefully the officers of a ship. The pirate confession thereby demonstrated how the sailor narrator tapped into his logbook memory and could recall almost every voyage and port he had visited. The confession of John Williams in 1819 offers a good example of how this form of popular literature could reveal a common seaman's life course. Williams remembered each voyage with great clarity, indicating the name of the ship, its captain, what ports he stopped in, and even the wages he was paid. Perhaps some of his stories were embellished or even made up. However, the broad outlines ring true. For our purposes these works demonstrate that other publications were in print before *Two Years before the Mast* that often followed the narrative format of the logbook and detailed the life and even the work of Jack Tar.[126]

Even more revealing of Jack Tar's experiences before Dana were the publications depicting sailors held in bondage as captives in distant lands, as prisoners of war, or as impressed seamen. Scholars of captivity narratives focus most of their attention on the stories of people seized by North American Indians. However, the genre really included captives held against their will in a wide variety of circumstances.[127] *A Narrative of the Mutiny on Board the Whaleship Globe*, by William Lay and Cyrus M. Hussey, was both a story of piracy – by definition a mutiny during which the ship is seized is piracy – and a captivity tale because after the sailors took control of the ship they traveled to a South Pacific island and became prisoners of the local population. Not surprisingly, sections of the book covering the post-mutiny voyage read like a logbook.[128] Common seamen also related their experiences when seized by ships from the Barbary states of North Africa. John Foss chronicled his capture, offering a heartrending account of his life as an Algerian slave. Both before his capture and after his release several years later, Foss relied on a logbook format to describe his time at sea, while he provided a more general description of his life in Algiers. William Ray was a marine on the USS *Philadelphia* when it grounded and surrendered off Tripoli. Ray was highly critical of his treatment aboard a frigate in the U.S. Navy, making serving on the ship sound like a form of captivity. He then shifted to a day-by-day chronicle of his wretched experiences as a prisoner in Tripoli.[129] Stories of being held as a British prisoner of war and of impressment often blended into one another. Two of the earliest accounts of this combined experience were written by John Blatchford and Joshua Davis. Both men were captured during the Revolutionary War and either by choice or by coercion, or some combination, were compelled to serve in the British armed services. Blatchford's saga in particular demonstrates the power of a sailor's memory to reconstruct a series of voyages under several flags.[130] The early nineteenth century brought an ever-growing interest in the common man and especially the common seaman. This development led to an increase in the number of publications describing sailors suffering during the Revolutionary War, experiencing the ordeal of impressment, and then as the War of 1812 came to a close, witnessing the horror of the Dartmoor Massacre when British soldiers fired into a huddled mass of boisterous sailor prisoners of war in a compound in southwest England.[131]

The logbook provided the basic narrative framework for many of these pre-Dana works, as well as for *Two Years before the Mast*. Although Dana only occasionally noted the daily record of latitude and longitude typical of the logbook, the overall structure of the book follows the sea journal's chronological format. Dana claimed that the book was "written out from a journal which I kept at the time, and from notes which I made of most of the events as they happened." As it turns out, this assertion was only partially correct. Dana's detailed log of events, along with other memorabilia from the voyage, was lost when his sea chest disappeared from the docks upon Dana's return to Boston in 1836. The only written record Dana had to go on was a smaller notebook and letters he had sent home while he was away. However, like many a sailor, Dana could recall in great detail his daily routine using the memory tool of noting the ship he sailed on, the ports he stopped at, the ships sighted on an otherwise empty ocean, and even the storms at sea.[132]

From the very first pages Dana used his memory to trace how he as a landsman turned into a sailor. Dana began his tale in self-mocking terms, asserting that before boarding the brig *Pilgrim* he had donned sailor's clothing and imagined that he might "pass very well for a jack tar" and supposed he looked "as salt as Neptune himself." He quickly admitted, though, that a seasoned eye would know better and recognize him as a landsman. "A sailor has a peculiar cut to his clothes, and a way of wearing them which a green hand can never get." More, his pale complexion and smooth hands distinguished him from a "regular *salt*." At sea Dana the greenhorn underwent a metamorphosis. The first few days he struggled with seasickness and "unintelligible orders" cast in the argot of shipboard life. Somehow he managed during his first storm to climb into the rigging "to reef the topsails" – literally a gut-retching experience for Dana as he clung desperately to the yard and vomited up the contents of his stomach. Dana felt whole again only after he began a seaman's diet of "salt beef and sea bread." By the time the *Pilgrim* reached Cape Horn, Dana felt sure enough of himself as a sailor that he joined the most experienced seaman on the ship to furl the jib-sail (in non-nautical terms: the triangular sail in front of the first mast that is attached to the long pole projecting from the ship) at the onset of a storm. As the ship bobbed up and down, the two men were twice plunged to their chins in icy water and thrown high in the sky afterward. Having successfully completed their work, Dana bragged, they "were not a little pleased to find all was snug" and the ship safe amid the tempest. Despite such feats of seamanship, Dana did not make the final transformation into a regular tar until he had reached the Pacific. As the scion of an elite Boston family, Dana had been granted the privilege of bunking in the steerage, away from the rest of the crew in the forecastle. The young mariner came to regret this separation and petitioned the captain to move in with the rest of the crew. "No man can be a sailor, or know what sailors are, unless he has lived in the forecastle with them – turned in and out with them, eaten of their dish, and drank of their cup." After this move, Dana felt like a real sailor and could, upon his return, speak for Jack Tar.[133]

Giving voice to common seamen at the height of the age of Jackson when the entire nation seemed to be heralding the triumph of the common man, was one of the reasons for the great success of *Two Years before the Mast*. As Dana eloquently explained, "We must come down from our heights, and leave our straight paths, for the byways and low places of life, if we would learn truths by strong contrasts." Dana's seamen were perpetually set to work. There was no idle time at sea. Whether laboring at the constant maintenance of sails and rigging, working at "small stuffs" like making spun-yarn, or the persistent "tarring, greasing, oiling, varnishing, painting, scrapping, and scrubbing," a sailor toiled "more regularly" than convicts at a state prison. Dana also provided a riveting depiction of the arbitrary nature of the captain's authority to use corporal punishment by reminding his readers that sailors were men: "A man – a human being, made in God's likeness – fastened up and flogged like a beast! A man, too, whom I had lived with and eaten with for months, and almost knew as well as a brother." Although many reviewers believed that Dana wrote this passage as a call for the abolition of the lash, Dana, who supported the officers' right to limited corporal punishment, was only trying to show the humanity of sailors confronting the inhumanity of some officers.[134]

The details of work and the ordeal of punishment demonstrate another big draw of Dana's book that had a huge influence on the literature of the sea: like many of the logbooks and journals discussed earlier (some of which were modeled on Dana's book) there was a contrast between romantic descriptions of life at sea and a biting reality that never quite managed to dispel the magical draw of the ocean. This contrast appeared throughout *Two Years before the Mast*. On the very first day of the voyage Dana, with Boston fading in the distance, "felt for the first time the perfect silence of the sea" and fell into a reverie of how the "beauty of the sea, the bright stars, and the clouds driven swiftly over them" reminded him of all he was leaving behind – a nostalgia that he confessed gave him some pleasure. Such dreams, however, "were soon put to flight by an order from the officer to trim the yards." At the end of the narrative Dana asserted that he was sure his readers would now be convinced "that the sailor has no romance in his every-day life to sustain him, but that it is very much the same plain, matter-of-fact drudgery and hardship, which would be experienced on shore." But the poetry of Dana's prose stood out. As one critic noted, Dana failed in his aim at dissuading the young romantic from going to sea, and capitalizing on a phrase Dana himself used, the critic wrote that Dana "told his story too well. He has made the witchery of the sea more witchery than ever" regardless of the ordeal of Cape Horn and the brutality of the lash.[135]

In that witchery – in the spell cast by his own narrative – Dana further propelled the common seaman into a direction in literature that the logbook and published stories about Jack Tar had been heading for decades. After *Two Years before the Mast* there was a huge outpouring of books by and about common seamen. Although a few of these books may have been works of fiction, most were based on true experiences.[136] Some were reminiscences reminding readers of the sacrifices American tars made during the Revolution and the War of 1812. Others were explicitly reformist, calling on sailors to turn to religion or for society to ameliorate the condition of seamen. Others were simply rambling tales of misadventure intended to play on the imagination and the voyeurism of the reader. Often these books were some combination of all three. Regardless of the intent of the author the influence of the logbook and of Dana is unmistakable.[137] George Lightcraft, who went to sea for more than twenty years, used the word "logbook" in his title, *Scraps from the Log Book of George Lightcraft*, as a testament to the veracity of his part religious tract, part adventure tale.[138] Although Josiah Cobb centered his reminiscence mainly on his experience as a prisoner during the War of 1812, especially the stirring events at Dartmoor, he entitled his book *A Green Hand's First Cruise, Roughed out from the Log-Book of Memory*. Cobb's preface elaborated on the relationship between memory and the logbook by asserting that his story was "recorded" in his log – his memory – "for however mutilated by time," it was "his only guide." Explaining his methodology further, Cobb cautioned that

"Narratives, like campaigns, should be recorded, as the narrator saw the events which produced them, not altogether from the reports he gathers after those events have transpired."[139] It is this type of narration that had helped Dana's *Two Years before the Mast* come alive and that became imbedded in almost every book written by and about common seamen thereafter.

Much of this literature had the same tension between the romantic vision of the sea and the harsh reality of life aboard a ship that permeated Dana's writing. Lightcraft, for example, decried the "heartless men" who took advantage of sailors ashore and the brutality of captains at sea, but he could also wax eloquent about sunrises and sunsets.[140] Jacob Hazen patterned his *Five Years before the Mast* after Dana's book in his title and by opening the description of his first voyage with the same sort of melancholy and almost poetic reflections about leaving friends, followed by his seasickness and struggles during his first storm at sea. Like most of these stories about life in the forecastle, Hazen explained that the "youthful mind" might "imagine to itself something pleasing and romantic in the routine of ocean life," but experience on "Blue water ... told a different tale," and that "a sailor's life" was "one of hardship and privation." As if to belie this nod to reality, in exaggerated prose a few pages later he described the phosphorescent lights that sometimes appear at night on the sea. This flickering illumination is a natural phenomenon that struck Hazen with "astonishment and wonder," as he mutely watched "the progress of the changing colors, until at last the whole scene, as far as the eye could penetrate along the horizon, presented an ocean of rolling and burning lava. The wind still increasing, the caps of the waves shot up into the air like flames of fire, while the myriads of particles of spray darted from them, shone with a splendor equal to the sparks of a fiery furnace."[141] These passages played on the emotions of armchair sailors. Some seamen's books were more restrained in their flights of fancy and stuck more closely to the message that life at sea was hard. Charles Nordhoff's account of his service on a man-of-war in the 1850s revealed life in the navy as rough, exploitive, and not the romantic paradise he had envisioned it (although the illustrations in a later edition counteracted this impression). James Fenimore Cooper's foray into the life of a common seaman based on the experiences of Ned Myers, written in part to demonstrate a new empathy for the regular sailor, told a similar tale.[142]

If the logbook helped to shape the form of these narratives and served as a metaphor for both the life and the memory of the sailor, these works reflected other emerging trends in American literature as well. We have already seen the importance of the captivity narrative in the pre–*Two Years before the Mast* literature of the common seaman. This genre remained crucial to sailor memoirs, not just in terms of having the subject trapped in exotic locales by local natives, but also in terms of simply being trapped at sea aboard a ship for long stretches of time. Hazen found the work of hunting whales "incessant" and viewed service on an American ship "as an absolute prison."[143] Many of these books also reflected the growing interest in the travel tale in depicting far-off and exotic places. Sailor authors often felt compelled to describe the bizarre scenes and different cultures that they visited as they ploughed the seven seas. William Meacham Murrell spent several pages describing Muscat and the entire Arabian peninsula, with its torrid climate, which was "excessively hot and dry," and its soil, which was "in many parts ... nothing more than immense sands, which when agitated, roll like the troubled ocean, and bury whole caravans in their course."[144] The first half of the nineteenth century saw a blossoming of the autobiography, especially after the popularization of Ben Franklin's published life story in the 1790s and early 1800s. The increased interest in personal improvement and the emotional journey of self-reflection of an individual of the Romantic era further enhanced this trend. Many of the narratives by reformed drunkards fit this model of the autobiography.[145]

All of these developments came together in the work of Herman Melville. *Typee*, Melville's first book, combined a captivity tale with travel literature describing the exotic world of the Typees in the Marquesas Islands in the South Pacific. This book only briefly covered the life of the sailor. When Melville continued his story in *Omoo*, his second book, he wrote about another South Pacific island, Tahiti. However, he also expanded on the life of a common seaman in the whaling industry, provided more information on the hardships of sailors, and even detailed a near-mutiny.[146] The quasi-autobiographical *White-Jacket* and *Redburn* unveiled Jack Tar's world more fully. *Redburn* traced Melville's first voyage across the Atlantic. Although the main character, the youthful Redburn, went for a jaunt on land in England, the heart of the book was the saltwater experience of a green hand learning the ropes. *White-Jacket* chronicled Melville's fourteen-month trek home from the Pacific on an American warship. However many detours he took as he expanded on the inner tensions of the forecastle and the gun deck or lamented the cruelty of the quarterdeck, central to both books was the narrative format of the log and nautical journal. For Melville life was like any sea voyage, and his book was a ship's log tracing the course of that voyage. "As a MAN-OF-WAR that sails through the sea, so this earth sails through the air. We mortals are all on board a fast-sailing, never-sinking, world-frigate." God was not only the shipwright, he was also "the Lord High Admiral." This odyssey had a beginning because "The port we sail from is forever astern." The end came with death. "And though far out of sight of land, for ages and ages we continue to sail with sealed orders, and our last destination remains a secret to ourselves and our officers; yet our final haven was predestined ere we slipped from the stocks of Creation."[147] Without ever providing longitude and latitude, Melville's great masterpiece, *Moby Dick*, traced a mystical quest in pursuit of the white whale. Like many whaleships, the *Pequod* did not keep a careful log and so seldom was the log-line used that it became rotten and broke when finally cast into the sea. No matter, for the ship continued on its tragic course with its progress solely "determined by Ahab's level log and line" – the inner demon that drove Ahab and his ship to destruction.[148]

The churning of many currents produced the powerful stream of America's first great literature. The Romantic movement with its concern with the awesome unpredictability of nature may claim pride of place among those currents. The sense of being trapped in a world not of your own choosing (the captivity narrative), interest in exotic cultures (travel literature), and the introspection of the individual and concern with self-improvement (the autobiography) were also important. Added to this mix was the lowly logbook. Perhaps Herman Melville did not need the logbook to convince him to portray life as a chronological journey marked by geographical or even psychological coordinates. Yet given the long history of the logbook and the emergence of a literature by and about the simple Jack Tar, the influence is clear. Logbooks began as a navigational tool as sailors crept gingerly out of sight of land. When Europeans created overseas empires and extended their commerce across the globe, the practice of keeping a logbook became regularized. But not so regular that logbook keepers did not use its pages for other purposes, offering comments, reflections, drawings, poetry, and songs. By the end of the eighteenth century writing in a logbook had bled into maintaining a nautical journal prized by its sailor owner. A new interest in the common man convinced some seamen to publish their stories based on their journals, or based on recollections etched into their memories as firmly as if they had been written into a logbook. In the process the logbook, either in terms of an internal memory or an external record of events, became a metaphor for truth. Richard Henry Dana Jr. was not the first sailor to publish a chronicle of his maritime experience, but he did popularize the genre. Melville took the sea-tale to magisterial heights. The logbook of memory remained central to the world of Jack Tar, but it had also embedded itself in American culture.

4

Spinning Yarns

Sailors really did spin yarns. Storytelling was an important art form for seamen who took great pride in their ability to weave together an elaborate tale in the quiet moments of a watch late at night or within the confines of the forecastle. Many a sailor would then repeat these stories on shore in taverns to anyone who would listen or in more domestic settings among family and friends. Unlike the logbook, the yarn did not have to accurately represent the truth. The whole point of a yarn was to sail along the borders of the factual and the fanciful. Like the language of Jack Tar itself, spinning yarns was an oral art form largely lost to historians dependent on the written word. But also like the sailor's special lexicon – and yarns contain more than their share of nauticalisms – we can gain some idea of the content of yarns from sailors who recorded such stories in their personal journals or in the great wave of books by common seamen that appeared in the first half of the nineteenth century. How and why those tales became recorded as spinning yarns is a yarn unto itself.

Tracing the history of the phrase "spinning yarns" demonstrates an odd give and take between maritime and mainstream sources. There can be little doubt that sailors created the metaphor "spinning yarns" for their storytelling, but the actual phrase seeped into print in the autobiography of a British criminal. Whatever the first published appearance of the phrase, it quickly became applied largely to the world of Jack Tar. Even if the authors who first wrote about old salts spinning yarns were British and did so for notions born out of the nationalism and the Romanticism of the early nineteenth century, and even if many of them had little deepwater experience, the phrase soon appeared in the United

States and returned to its maritime spawning ground, developing an even more special meaning for seamen. In the 1830s sailors began to use the phrase "spinning yarns" in their own published narratives and to mention it in private manuscripts. By the 1840s Jack Tar's art of the yarn appeared in two vastly contrasting types of literature represented by Ned Buntline and Herman Melville. Buntline's writing appealed to a more plebeian audience, but probably had a greater readership at the time with its saccharine prose, predictable plots, and sensationalism. Melville brought the yarn into the heart of a great American intellectual tradition with work that has become the epitome of American Romanticism. Combined, Buntline and Melville helped to demonstrate that before the Civil War America was a maritime nation.[1]

Origins

The etymology of the phrase "spinning yarns" is relatively recent. Sailors had been telling tales since time immemorial, and we can only assume that they referred to relating their fanciful stories as spinning yarns long before these words appeared in print. The exact origin of the phrase "spinning yarns" remains conjectural, but it most likely reflected a metaphor derived from the making of a special rope called "spun-yarn" aboard ships. In the early nineteenth century the phrase moved from the ship's deck to the British underworld from where it first worked its way into publication. During the 1820s several British writers picked up the term, possibly from the underworld, but more likely because of its widespread occurrence in the maritime vocabulary. By the 1830s American authors had started to use the phrase and soon enough American sailors began to refer to "spinning yarns" in print and even in their unpublished journals. We may never know when the first American Jack Tar referred to his ability to tell a story as spinning a yarn. But by following the spread of that phrase in the first half of the nineteenth century we can pursue its trajectory from the language of Jack Tar to the British criminal underworld, to the Anglo-American mainstream culture, and back again to the language of Jack Tar.

The *Oxford English Dictionary* dates the first published reference of "spinning a yarn" to 1819 and a work by James Hardy Vaux, a British criminal sentenced to transportation for life to Australia.[2] Vaux was a repeat offender (the life sentence was his second transportation to New South Wales) who found himself confined to hard labor for breaking the law in Australia. During that period of close confinement he claimed at last to have seen the evil of his ways, although he would later be pardoned and escape to Ireland where he was again caught breaking the law and sent to Australia for a third and final time. As a testimony of his desire to follow the straight and narrow he wrote a memoir of his criminal exploits in which he used the technical language of the underworld. To help his readers with this vocabulary Vaux added a glossary of terms at the end of his manuscript that included "yarn spinning." Vaux believed the term was created by what he called the "flash-people," individuals who affected "any peculiar habit," such "as swearing, dressing in a particular manner, taking snuff," in order to call attention to themselves. Telling "their various adventures, exploits, and escapes to each other" was a practice that was "most common and gratifying, among persons in confinement or exile, to enliven a dull hour, and probably excite a secret hope of one day enjoying a repetition of their former pleasures." Vaux did not admit it, but he and his flash cohorts had probably borrowed yarn spinning from the maritime world. The swindlers, pickpockets, and low-lifes of the flash culture often interacted with sailors while ashore and many of them spent some time at sea. Vaux himself had been forced to serve before the mast and every transported criminal spent months aboard the ships that brought them to their exile in Australia.[3]

The likely seafaring origins of the term become clear when we take a closer look at the word "yarn" itself, which is of more ancient lineage than the phrase "spinning yarns," and is an Anglo-Saxon term for spun fiber of any kind that went back at least a millennium. While retaining its original textile meaning, "yarn" developed a more nautical connection during the sixteenth and seventeenth centuries when it was applied to the netting used by fishermen and then in rope-making as one of the threads out of which a rope was composed or even all of the threads of a rope collectively. It is probably in this rope-making usage that it became applied to the telling of tales by sailors. As we have already seen, Jack Tar was more than capable of taking the words used for his daily tasks and applying them in creative metaphors. Although rope-making was a specialized waterfront occupation, crews aboard ships manufactured spun-yarn – a chord made out of two ropes twisted together. The spun-yarn was ubiquitous on a ship and had many uses. As William Falconer explained in his *Universal Dictionary of the Marine* the spun-yarn "is employed for several purposes; particularly to fasten one rope to another, to seize block-strops to the shrouds, and to *serve* ropes which are liable to be chafed by rubbing against another, &c." Before a merchant ship sailed owners purchased "old junk" – threads, pieces of string, and leftover rope – which sailors had to untangle and roll up into balls during the voyage. These bits were twisted together with a spun-yarn winch comprised of a wheel and a spindle, making the spun-yarn, which was then tarred.[4] Richard Henry Dana Jr. noted that the spun-yarn winch could "be heard constantly going on deck in pleasant weather" and would employ three sailors "drawing and knotting yarns, and making spun-yarn."[5] A boy might be used to pull the spun-yarn along the deck, but the other two seamen would be stationed near the winch. This labor kept the hands busy, but left the mind free. With at least two men set to the tedious labor close together, we can well imagine that they began to talk to each other, relating their life adventures, and, being the creative sort, pushing the boundaries of the believable. Sailors also, no doubt, might chuckle at how nicely the metaphor of spinning yarn fit into the telling of tales as they intertwined different elements of their stories, twisted and turned the truth, until the entire production was strung out before their listeners like the spun-yarn on which they toiled.

When and where yarn spinning as a labor activity first underwent the metamorphosis that led to the spinning of yarns as storytelling is lost to us. Even if it had not appeared in print, the phrase was a common idiom long before Vaux recorded it in Australia. After the publication of Vaux's glossary, the phrase "spinning a yarn" began to be repeated with some regularity first in British sources and then in the American print media.[6] But it did so not in relation to Vaux's flash culture. Rather, reflecting its nautical roots, spinning a yarn was portrayed as a part of the maritime idiom. It is hard to imagine that Vaux's relatively obscure book, and the minor role spinning yarns played in it, led to the spread of the phrase in Anglo-American published sources. Instead, the expression must have already been in circulation within the maritime world and maybe even in mainstream society. However familiar it may have been, having a sailor spinning a yarn quickly became a trope that fulfilled several literary functions.

Most of the early references to sailor yarns in the 1820s appeared in British stories told by Greenwich pensioners – men who had served in the British navy and who were either too old or too injured to work and who therefore were housed and supported by the government in Greenwich Hospital along the Thames River outside London. The historical moment for the emergence of spinning yarns in print was important. The struggles with Revolutionary and Napoleonic France cast a long shadow over postwar Great Britain as that nation became a dominant economic and political power with a global empire. For much of the second half of the eighteenth century the British had trumpeted the role of their seamen in defending the nation and the tales of Greenwich pensioners spinning their yarns became a means of keeping alive the memory of the sacrifice of the common sailor. One pensioner, who had lost an eye and a limb in the service of the king, rehearsed the story of his shipmate William, who had been about to return to his wife, Nancy, and baby after a shipwreck – a variation of the standard musical theater sailor's return – only to be impressed. Women were often aboard larger British warships and, so the tale went, his wife and child joined him in his majesty's navy. During a battle with the French the women went below decks to tend the wounded, and after two hours of fighting, during which "William was the first in every danger," this intrepid, impressed tar was severely injured and his mangled body brought below. There he expired before his beloved Nancy with her name on his lips. The yarn, of course, at this point stretched the tale almost to the unbelievable. Nancy, with her babe in her arms, fainted across her dead husband's body, and then, "oh mysterious providence! at that very moment, while senseless and inanimate ... a ball entered through the vessel's side – it pierced her bosom!" This yarn tugged on the heartstrings while offering a stirring testament to the sacrifices seamen and their families had made for king and country.[7]

Beyond highlighting the British seaman as a hero who helped to save the empire, the sailor spinning a yarn also fit into larger cultural developments. Using a sailor's yarn as the medium through which to relate a maritime story provided a supposed note of legitimacy to a publication. With the rise of Romanticism in the early nineteenth century came a new interest in common people on both sides of the Atlantic, and having a seaman rehearse his often wondrous adventures made a nautical story seem more authentic. One British writer went so far as to dismiss the hack productions of the Jack Tar on stage, by declaring, "Away with all the fine poetry that Horse-marines are made to sing, by chivalrous bards, when lying on imaginary decks, beneath imaginary moonlight, on a voyage to the continent of nowhere." These tunes were nothing more than "Brown soap-bubbles ... blown from the pipe of [a] poet, for his own delight, and that of other grown-up children." The author continued by denigrating higher forms of literature: "Dang to your Spenserian stanza – your octo syllabics – your longs and shorts; your heroics and blank verse." Instead of such formal styles, "give us Jack himself, putting his quid in his tobacco pouch above the dexter or sinister jaw, and lolling on a coil of cable – give us Jack, we say, spinning a long yarn, faster than any backward pedestrian, in the walk of a rope-work, and interlarding

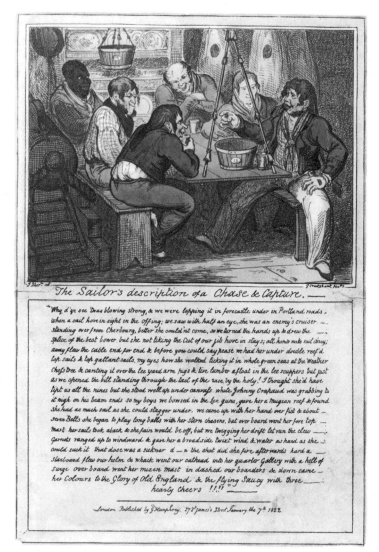

FIGURE 4.1. "The Sailor's Description of a Chase & Capture," George Cruikshank (London: Published by G Humphrey, 1822). Reproduction Number: LC-USZ62-44035. Sailors often spun yarns aboard ship. This English illustration includes five messmates listening to a story as well as the text of the story written out in the language of Jack Tar. Courtesy of the Library of Congress, Washington, D.C.

his narrative with 'old familiar phrases,' redolent of pitch and salt-petre, and of all the composite fumèe of the ancient sea." This author who called for "a ship that you can smell in a dark night," and whose reference to a rope-walk was suggestive of the origins of spinning yarns, was more interested in the imagined persona of the sailor as a common man than either the Jack Tar of the stage or the real seaman.[8]

Romanticism emphasized the unpredictability of nature and expressed concern for a fast-disappearing traditional folk culture. For many authors the sailor's yarn became a quaint vestige of an old-fashioned means of oral communication in a world increasingly marked by the spread of print and fraught with economic and social change. The sailor as both a representative of the common man and as a creature close to nature made spinning yarns by seamen a special form of storytelling. Again, the stereotypical sailor was more important than the real thing. From this perspective the seaman could be portrayed as lacking guile and being fond of "veering and hauling" to get around some difficulty. There was no need for a more industrial straight path. Instead, a story, like the mariner himself, had to bend itself to the fickle currents of nature. Using the nautical lexicon popular with seamen and with those who wrote about the seaman, a sailor's yarn could be compared to "a ship's course in working to windward," which tacked back and forth "in order to weather her object indirectly, and fetch her port in the end." Such a narrative "may make twenty digressions, and fly off in chase of every strange sail heaving in sight, no sooner has he 'run em down,' then he will 'close haul his wind,' and resume his original course."[9] Richard Henry Dana Jr. recalled one captain who visited his ship and, "with but little intermission," kept his yarn going longer than four hours, ranting "all about himself, and the Peruvian government, and the Dublin frigate, and Lord James Townshend, and President Jackson, and the ship Ann M'Kim of Baltimore." The yarn only ended when the wind picked up and the captain had to return to his ship and continue his voyage.[10]

The special role of the sailor as narrator within the larger Romantic movement can be seen in Samuel Taylor Coleridge's "Rime of the Ancient Mariner." Written in 1798 before "spinning a yarn" entered mainstream vocabulary, the potent imagery of this mystical tale centered on the ancient mariner telling of the tragedy of his voyage after he killed an albatross. In 1820, shortly after the metaphor of spinning yarns appeared in print, one critic was unimpressed with the poem and thought Coleridge's opening description of the ancient mariner – who was nothing but an old tar – stopping a gentleman going to a wedding was improbable. He dismissed Coleridge's lines describing the old sailor's wondrous story as what "sailors generally denominate 'a long yarn.'" This criticism rejected as unbelievable what had been Coleridge's point in using the ancient mariner in the first place: Coleridge had an ancient mariner tell this story of the supernatural upon the ocean deep to add authenticity and to demonstrate the helplessness of all men before the powerful and unpredictable forces of nature.[11]

American authors copied the British in using the sailor's yarn as a literary device and then made it their own. As with so much in the culture of the early republic, Americans followed the British in both form and function. Similar to the stories of the Greenwich pensioner, American yarn spinning was a way to remember how important Jack Tar was to the United States. In one "Forecastle yarn" a boatswain's mate named Bob O'Neal tells the story of his experience aboard the USS *President* when the British captured the frigate on January 16, 1815. Stephen Decatur plays a role in this tale, but the heart of the yarn is on the experience of the common seamen who worked feverishly to escape the blockading British squadron and then fought bravely against overwhelming odds. Like the British yarn of the old Greenwich pensioner, O'Neal's story portrayed the sacrifice of maritime families as well as those of the sailors. After the *President* surrendered, the yarn spinner met Harry Brown, a fellow topman who had his scalp torn up by a musket ball. Brown, knowing he was going to die from his wounds, asked O'Neal to take a gold chain he wore and give it to his wife – an obligation O'Neal says he fulfilled "according to orders." The yarn did not end with the capture of the *President* because there was more to tell about the spirit of the American Jack Tar. O'Neal went on to describe the ordeal of imprisonment and how the American crew had been denied food and drink for almost two days until he went to the sergeant of the guard to request some sustenance. The officer of the deck granted the Americans some bread and water, and then provided O'Neal with a meal of fresh beef and potatoes as well as a half-pint of grog for being such "a whole-souled fellow."[12]

More important than this patriotic message was the significance of having a sailor spin a yarn as a Romantic literary device. Authors in Great Britain had emphasized the folk identity of their ancient mariners and Greenwich pensioners in the spirit of the nineteenth-century Romantic movement. For Americans in the age of Jackson, the persona of the common man not only placed the sea story in the same intellectual tradition, but also trumpeted the common man's authority in an era that heralded the common man. If British authors could prefer the language of an old salt over the popular stage or even a "Spencerian stanza," Americans could compare a sailor's yarn to great literature. Samuel Leech loved the tall tales of Dick Dickinson and thought of him as "a sort of off-hand novelist" because "all he cared for was *effect*, and where truth failed him, fiction generously loaned her services." Dick's yarns may not have been as "interesting as the thousand-and-one stories in the Arabian Knights Entertainments," but they were "at least as true to nature, and, in respect to its humor, might be compared to some of the sayings of that illustrious personage, Sancho Panza, the renowned squire of the immortal Don Quixote."[13] Another sailor believed that "Shakespeare would have recognized some of these" story tellers "as his kindred, and they him as a relation."[14] Writers made clear that it was the seaman's experience that provided him with his authority. The author of one ghost story has his yarn spinner declare, "I have lived a long while, and sailed the blue water long enough to know something of these things" – of apparitions of the dead seen aboard ships. For these old tars book learning was irrelevant. What counted was their years before the mast. As one sailor narrator reminded his listeners, he could tell what he saw when he was young, "and though every sea I've seen had washed my heart, it wouldn't have taken that out."[15]

The romantic setting on the broad sea was crucial to the author dependent on a yarn spinner. Following a model the British frequently used, American writers set the mood for these tales by describing the "immense folds of spotless canvass … spread" before a fair wind driving the ship across a peaceful ocean which glistened "in the moonbeams, and ever and anon, crimsoned with the phosphoretic illumination of the ocean." This imaginary scene etched in extravagant prose had "the sailors lay around in groups, dreaming, either sleeping or waking," of returning home. Against this background some old salt "having taken a fresh quid [piece of tobacco] and worked up his reckoning," would begin his yarn.[16] Perhaps one of the best known of these yarn-spinning authors was William Leggett, who had served as a midshipman in the American navy for four years during the 1820s. Historians have largely focused on Leggett's career as a Jacksonian journalist and free trade advocate in the 1830s, but he also used his maritime experience to write fiction. He had a yarn-spinning sailor narrate one of the stories in *Tales and Sketches by a Country Schoolmaster*, while his *Naval Histories*, a collection of magazine articles that he published as a book in 1834, was nothing more than a series of yarns.[17] A literary notice in the *Ladies Companion* explained, "The author [of *Naval Histories*] is himself a sailor and spins a yarn with unusual force," such that, "We do not think any nautical romancer, could have done the thing better."[18] Leggett wrote with a strong emphasis on nature and passion typical of the Romantic movement. In "Merry Terry," using the persona of an old salt to tell his tale to midshipmen, Leggett described how a young officer rescued his betrothed from the evil intentions of his captain only to have the captain, the officer, and the young woman all die in the ensuing scuffle.[19]

Yarns also became a way to describe and categorize the old salt. Leggett explained in his "Merry Terry," Jack Palmer, the yarn spinner of the tale, "was an old sea-dog, and a clever fellow, that is to say in the Yankee sense of the word. He had seen all sorts of service, and knew all sorts of stories, which were perhaps not the less amusing for the nautical phraseology."[20] When one author asked the "boatswain's-mate" for a yarn, the seaman "wanted no better fun, so, without wasting breath in a lubberly parley, he began."[21] A supposed passenger who published a pirate story claimed he would spend evenings during a voyage to the West Indies "listening to those '*Yarns*' which the sons of Neptune are so famous for spinning."[22] As Enoch Cobb Wines, who served as a schoolmaster for midshipmen on the *Constellation*, explained, "There is no amusement of which sailors are more fond than that of spinning yarns and by dint of practice they acquire a facility in doing it, which is really astonishing." Because of their "habit of exaggerating on all subjects," many seamen made up "their stories as they go along" and "You must generally set down one half of what an old tar tells you for sober truth, to a love of the marvellous, and a disposition to excite wonder."[23]

If gentleman authors might create seaman characters spinning yarns, by the 1830s, 1840s, and beyond, the notion of spinning yarns gained popularity among sailors themselves. William Leggett really did go to sea, even if it was as a midshipman.[24] Naval officer William Reynolds also commented on the vital role of yarn spinning to while away "moments that would otherwise have been dull enough." He found such tales "marvelous and made truth stranger than fiction."[25] Average Jack Tars also adopted the phrase "spinning a yarn." When seaman Nathaniel Ames wrote his third book he called it *An Old Sailor's Yarns*.[26] Looking back over his thirty years of experience at sea, Samuel Leech fondly remembered "spinning yarns" and viewed them as great "intellectual time-killers," even if he believed they "were by no means favorable in their moral effects on the listener" because they "generally consisted in fictitious adventures on the sea and on the shore, plentifully interlarded in their recital with profane oaths and licentious allusions." Providing manuscript evidence

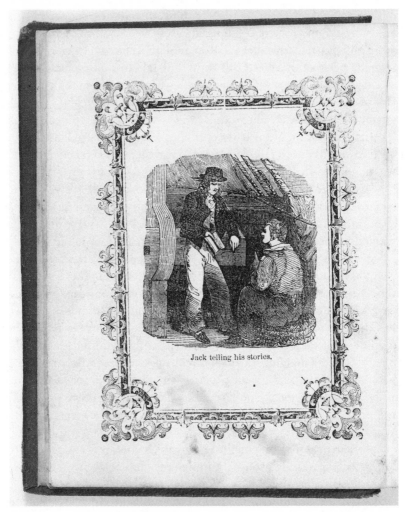

FIGURE 4.2. "**Jack Telling His Stories**," in Francis C. Woodwoth, *Jack Mason, The Old Sailor* (New York: Clark, Austin & Smith, 1855). By the mid nineteenth century the mariner spinning a yarn became a trope that appeared in a host of books. In this illustration we see two seamen on deck in standard sailor garb, exchanging stories. Courtesy of the American Antiquarian Society, Worcester, Massachusetts.

that sailors did spin yarns on quiet nights described by so many authors, whale man Nathaniel Sexton Morgan confided in his personal journal that during the "Latter part of the watch some rather tough and amusing yarns were got off, which I should like to remember."[27] Other seamen made similar comments concerning the importance of yarn spinning both aboard ship and on shore. One sailor reported that because seamen traveled the whole world there was a great deal to be learned from the sailor's yarn, although he also noted that the ship captain issued a regulation that there should be "no long yarns while at work" to make sure the men stayed on task.[28] William Clarke could even note how yarn spinning fired the imaginations of young people and misrepresented life at sea: "Some of our 'green horns' looks truly pitiful, this [serving as a seaman] was nothing what they fancied in their dreams of sea life in their puerile days after listening to the yarn of some old 'tar.' "[29]

Even if sailors did not always refer to the phrase "spinning yarns," they emphasized the importance of storytelling to Jack Tar. Naval surgeon Edward Cutbush made this point early in the nineteenth century when he commented that "There is scarcely a ship, without a happy Ned or happy Jack to enliven the evening watch by some facetious story."[30] Recalling his capture by the British during the War of 1812, privateersman Josiah Cobb wrote that the American crew spent the first hours of the night aboard one of his majesty's men-of-war as prisoners storytelling or singing. This storytelling became even more essential once the sailors were sent to the dismal compound at Dartmoor in southwest England. Cobb explained that "many of the lagging hours of each day were occupied, to enliven our feelings and dissipate the ennui, which was ever getting the upper-hand of the desponding, by tales, stories, and narratives." This activity was so important to these prisoners of war that they made anyone in their mess serve an extra turn as cook if he would not spin a yarn.[31]

In all likelihood the phrase "spinning a yarn" began as a creative metaphor in some sailor's mind as a wonderful way to describe Jack Tar's ability to tell stories. That phrase was picked up by the underworld – James Hardy Vaux's flash culture – and appeared in print in the glossary of terms that accompanied the memoir of Vaux's life of crime. Whether because of this book's publication, or because of the widespread use of the phrase within the maritime world, British writers started to rely on it to remind readers of the sacrifices British seamen made in the French wars and as a means of asserting an authentic voice for common folk in romantic tales of the sea. American writers picked up the phrase and applied it in their sea stories. When sailors began to publish accounts of their own lives they, too, called on the metaphor. Whatever the exact origin of the phrase, however, it was used by aspiring authors from all social strata; as common seamen sought to describe

their world to the rest of society they felt compelled to explain that storytelling, whether it was called spinning a yarn or not, was an essential
element of Anglo-American maritime culture.

Why Spin a Yarn?

The significance of yarn spinning went beyond the role of storytelling as a
means to fill empty hours of a late watch, the boredom of a long voyage,
or the isolation of being held captive. The stories themselves were significant. First, spinning yarns was a means of building bonds among sailors.
By sharing one's life story, however embellished, strangers cast together in
the forecastle and compelled to work together became shipmates. Second,
a well-spun yarn gained a sailor prestige and esteem. By telling a tale that
was both persuasive and pushed the boundaries of the believable, a sailor
earned respect aboard ship. Third, there was often a moral to the tale
that inculcated a set of values: being true to one's shipmates, outlining the
appropriate authority of the quarterdeck, and the difficulty of maintaining
relationships at sea and ashore. As such, yarns were a rite of passage, a
means whereby the greenhorn learned what it meant to be a sailor. Finally,
yarns were just fun and provided sailors with an opportunity to embellish the truth, invent fantasies, and express suppressed desires in tales of
romance, pirates, and ghosts. Here wondrous adventures across the seven
seas as well as the supernatural came into play.

To understand why sailors spun yarns we need to examine the content of these stories. But as with the language of Jack Tar, we are hand-
icapped in not being able to hear the words of the seamen ourselves.
Instead, we must look at the tales as they are recorded on paper – a filter
that makes this enterprise all the more complicated because of the way
"spinning a yarn" entered the world of print. Distinguishing authentic
sailor yarns from those created by non-sailor authors is not easy, making
the genuineness of many of the yarns that appeared in magazines and
books beginning in the 1820s and 1830s difficult to determine. Did a real
Greenwich pensioner narrate the story of William and Nancy dying in a
fight against the French, or did some writer make it up? Did Midshipman
William Leggett hear the sad tale of Merry Terry aboard ship, or did
aspiring writer William Leggett fabricate this young hero and conjure the
yarn-spinning Jack Palmer out of his own imagination to help provide
the right mood for his short story? The literary device of having a sailor
spin a yarn as a means to tell a story became so popular that regular
sailor authors relied on it. George Little, a seaman who had worked his

way to captain, included several yarns in the two books he wrote about his twenty years at sea. J. Ross Browne, who served aboard a whaler but who later became a travel writer and journalist, sprinkled his *Etchings of a Whaling Cruise* with several yarns he claimed to have heard during his voyage. Even the unpublished manuscript journal of Hugh Calhoun written while in the American navy contains a succession of yarns, some of which he reported had been told to him aboard ship, others of which were recitations of his own experiences. Drawing too fine a distinction concerning the origins of a yarn may be impossible. Yet some distinctions can be drawn. Based on those distinctions, the following account of the reasons behind spinning yarns relies largely on the yarns written by men who had actually gone to sea.[32]

Spinning yarns formed bonds among seamen as shipmates. The life of a sailor took many twists and turns. Some mariners might go to sea with people they knew on land or from previous voyages, especially if they sailed from smaller ports. Many other sailors entered the forecastle a stranger to the rest of the crew.[33] This last situation could create tension because there was limited individual space aboard every ship, whether a merchant vessel, a whaler, or a man-of-war. Close quarters was the order of the day. Spinning a yarn offered an opportunity to break down boundaries, open oneself up, and yet, because a yarn could stretch the truth, not reveal everything about the inner person. George Little described the special friendship he developed with Jack Sawyer, who "was as true-hearted a sailor as ever floated upon the ocean." When Little promised to teach Sawyer to read, Sawyer in return offered to spin a long yarn about his life story and his experience of being captured by the British during the Revolutionary War and then being forced to serve in the British navy. Looking back at his days before the mast, Little fondly remembered his "old messmate" and how the two of them "spun out many long yarns in the foretop."[34] In his second book Little described the friendship between a boatswain's mate and a young sailor based in large part on the spinning of yarns. The youth told a romantic tale of lost love ashore, while the boatswain's mate "would spin a yarn of combined fleets, forming a line, battles fought, or the indissoluble friendship of true seamen." So grateful was the young sailor for these diversions that he "would grasp the hand of the" boatswain and exclaim, "'You are my true messmate, my friend, my noble friend.'" Yarns also tied groups of seamen together as evidenced by a ghost tale a popular crew member told on the same ship. Many descriptions of yarn spinning depict knots of sailors gathered around an experienced old salt, with some of the younger seamen offering tobacco and even grog to encourage the storyteller.[35] As we have already seen in Josiah Cobb's discussion of storytelling at Dartmoor, yarn spinning was also important to sailors when they were confined as prisoners of war.

Spinning a yarn was a means of gaining respect. Samuel Leech noted that the talent of spinning good yarns was highly prized in a man-of-war.[36] When someone called for a yarn, several of J. Ross Browne's ship-mates encouraged Ned Harrison, a famed storyteller, by announcing that "Nobody can spin a yarn like Ned Harrison" and urging, "That's a fine fellow, Ned." In the yarn "Bob Grimsley's Ghost," Ned lived up to his reputation by relating such a terrifying tale of murder and apparitions of the dead that the crew expected to see a ghost the rest of the night.[37] The sense of respect for a talented yarn spinner can be seen in Henry James Mercier's description of the beginning of Bill Garnet's yarn. During the dogwatch in the evening "a crowd was huddled together" around "Bill Garnet and two or three others famous for 'spinning twisters,'" urging them with sundry promises and entreaties to commence a narration of the wild and the wonderful." Of course, after some mock protests, and after a "half-a-dozen hands at the same time" offered to fulfill his oblig-atory request for "a chew of tobacco" to "moisten" his "mouth a little," Garnet began to spin his yarn.[38]

Yarn spinning taught seamen lessons about their world. Sailors were superstitious, but behind the ghost tale was often a not-so-hidden mes-sage. As one sailor explained, spirits "sometimes appeared with horrid visage and menacing countenance, at the bed-side of a cruel captain; and above all to the false hearted Tar, who cruelly deserted his too credulous Poll, who drowned herself in despair. The common sailor often tells such stories, … which are generally ended with a good moral sentiment of the punishment of cruelty and treachery; and the reward of the kind hearted and humane."[39] Ned Harrison's "Bob Grimsley's Ghost," similar to Leggett's "Merry Terry," began with shipboard tensions over the affec-tions of a young woman. In both stories the individual with the higher status, the captain in "Merry Terry" and Rockford, the mate, in "Bob Grimsley's Ghost," loses out in the competition for the heart of a young woman to the sailor with lower status – Terry was a senior midshipman and Grimsley just a regular member of the crew. Listeners, of course, would identify with Terry and Grimsley in both stories because they were prime seamen. Grimsley "was a brave, generous, and manly fellow" and "A better sailor never put his weight on a brace." Indeed, "Jovial in his disposition, free, cheerful, and intelligent," Grimsley "was the life and soul of the whole crew." Rockford did not directly abuse his power over Grimsley on the voyage, but he did plot the sailor's demise with a Spanish seaman on the ship. Revealing some of the ethnic prejudice typical of American seamen in the antebellum period, Grimsley said that the Spaniard had a criminal past. He had served aboard a Portuguese slaver at a time when the international slave trade had been banned by both the United States and Great Britain, and was a criminal who had committed piracy. The Spaniard agreed to kill Grimsley for Rockford, stabbing the honest mariner and casting him overboard in a storm. Then, fearing that Rockford's conscience would lead him to admit the evil deed, the Spaniard posed as Grimsley's ghost and killed the mate. The Spaniard confessed everything before he died of a fever near the end of the voyage. The tragic message was clear: jealousies disrupt the functioning of a ship and treachery gets punished in the end. "Bob Grimsley's Ghost" was a story about the competition for the affections of a young woman, as well as about the importance of maintaining the proper bounds of authority aboard ship. Rockford may not have directly abused his power, but he did use his role as mate to persuade the Spaniard to murder Grimsley. In fact, this indirect abuse of authority made his actions even more treacherous and a violation of the bonds that were supposed to exist aboard a ship.[40]

Henry James Mercier offered additional insight into the nature of shipboard relationships in an ironic tale about friendship in "Pat Bradley's Yarn." Bradley began by describing his fast friendship with Dick Fisher, an eighteen-year-old seaman he met on a merchant ship who was "as stout, active, and handsome a young fellow as you'd see here and there in a crowd." Bradley told his listeners, "him and I got pretty *thick* on the passage, being both in one watch, and finally we got to be regular *chummies*." Bradley goes on to explain how Fisher twice saved his life. On their first voyage together the two seamen were working in the rigging at the onset of a storm when Bradley was smacked in the head by a loose sail and tossed into the sea. Barely conscious and too weak to swim, Bradley gave himself "up for lost." But Fisher had jumped into the tempestuous ocean after him and kept him afloat until the jolly boat could be launched and collect them. On their next voyage together to the West Indies, Bradley caught a fever while in port and Fisher stayed by his side and nursed him back to health. As Bradley explained, "don't blame me then if I say, after these proofs of kindness, that I loved him; aye, better than I ever loved the brother that was brought up in infancy with me." During their passage to New Orleans, Bradley heard the cook and the steward – both Spaniards as it turns out – plotting to steal the specie on board once they arrived in port. Bradley warned the captain, who did not believe him. Convinced that the plot was for real, Bradley armed himself the first night they were in New Orleans. Sure enough the two Spaniards and a half a dozen ruffians broke into the captain's cabin. Hearing the scuffle, Bradley came running to the scene and helped to drive the pirates off. As he headed back to the deck to give further alarm he saw a "tall powerful looking man, armed with a knife" blocking his exit. Believing that his life was in jeopardy, Bradley fired a pistol and "the ball whizzed through" the man's brain. The rest of the pirates escaped. When the remaining crew were able to strike a light they looked at "the wretch" Bradley had shot. Bradley then exclaimed: "I perceived before me, to my horror and astonishment, the corpse of my best and dearest friend, poor Fisher: – Yes, shipmates, it was him; and I whose life he had perilled[*sic*] his own to preserve, was the means of sending him to a bloody grave." This story was a pointed reminder that in the flotsam-and-jetsam life of the sailor, the ties that could bind shipmates formed quickly when one's life literally could hang by a thread – or at least a rope. But however deep those ties could reach, in the mobile world of maritime labor where workers came from all walks of life and from many countries, you could never know if the man with whom you became "chummie," and you considered closer than the brother with whom you were "brought up in infancy," was nothing more than a cutthroat and pirate.[41]

Ghosts and the supernatural filled the sailor's yarn. Such stories appealed to mariners, who were notoriously superstitious.[42] George Edward Clark repeated a yarn about finding the apparition of a man on the jib-boom on a night "darker than a stack of black cats." When the mate tried to strike at the man with a piece of wood he disappeared into thin air.[43] Mercier also retold a yarn of an apparition in the upper rigging. In this case it was of a sailor who had been knocked overboard by the mate. On the next night that same mate climbed up to the yard. There was a flash of light as bright "as if it was wrapped in flames" that revealed the ghost-like figure enveloping the mate with "a fiend-like grasp." Then, "all was dark as the grave, and a heavy plunge in the water with a faint struggle, told but too plainly the fate of this cruel blasphemous wretch" – the mate.[44] Charles Nordhoff had one yarn spinner tell the story of the barque *Sunderland* with a crew of rough-speaking sailors, one of whom had sworn that he would rather have "Jemmy Squarefoot" – a nineteenth-century term for some sort of goblin – take him "to perdition" than allow the rest of the crew to shave him during a Neptune ceremony for crossing the Equator. No sooner had he uttered the words than his body started to wriggle with convulsions and some invisible force dragged him off his sea chest, up to the deck, and then off the ship. The sailor mysteriously was returned a week later, tossed onto the rigging leeward of the foremast. The man never told the crew of his experience, but he came back changed: "From being a noisy, violent fellow, always ready to quarrel," he became quiet and soft spoken and never uttered a curse or swear word.[45] Hugh Calhoun wrote in his journal a yarn entitled "The Sea Demon" that he must have spun a number of times. Calhoun described a dark ship spotted off Cape Horn that had a bell pealing with "the deep intonations of a death knell." When the first lieutenant and a handpicked boat crew boarded the ship to investigate, they found no one on board and a line attached to the clapper running into the sea. The sailors hauled the rope in, which ran for hundreds of fathoms, only to find a bloated corpse attached with "numerous stabs upon the body." At that moment "The bell commenced tolling with fearful rapidity; shrieks unearthily filled the air." The lieutenant cried out, "Cut, Cut, for Gods sake." With the line severed, the body sank back into the deep. Suddenly "sweet music was wafted upon their senses, they listened as entranced." Recognizing that something was amiss, the lieutenant ordered the men back to their boat. No sooner had the men gotten clear of the mysterious vessel, than the demon ship sank.[46]

The best yarns, as Calhoun's tale suggested, often bordered on the fantastic. J. Ross Browne's "John Tabor's Ride" not only pushed the boundaries of credulity, it also aptly demonstrated why sailors spun yarns. Tabor was a true whale man from Taborstown, Massachusetts. Having been put ashore in a hospital at Algoa Bay, South Africa, for drinking too much alcohol, Tabor described waking up and walking down to the beach, where he saw an aged seaman who recruited him to hunt a giant whale offshore. After the old man had harpooned the whale, the two of them jumped atop their prey, abandoning their boat. Then came a ride for the ages as the whale sped off, past Cape Town, St. Helena, Cape Hatteras, and Nantucket with the two whalemen hanging on for dear life. The whale came ashore at Taborstown, where it was temporarily halted by smacking into the town pump, sending Tabor and his companion helter-skelter to the ground. A legion of Captain Tabor's living in Taborstown then added their harpoons to the side of the whale, but to little effect. Tabor and the old seaman jumped aboard again and off they went, faster than a steamship or a locomotive, across Massachusetts, over the Alleghenies, into the Ohio River, and then down the Mississippi. The ride continued to South America, over the Andes, past Hawaii, China, the Straits of Malacca, and across the Indian Ocean and back to the beach at

JOHN TABOR'S RIDE.

FIGURE 4.3. "**John Tabor's Ride,**" J. Ross Browne, *Etchings of a Whaling Cruise …* (New York: Harper & Brothers, 1846). Like many sailors who wrote of their experiences at sea, J. Ross Browne imbedded a series of yarns into his work, including John Tabor's Ride. Browne has his shipmate John Tabor relate a whale of a tale. Tabor was recovering from alcohol abuse on shore in southern Africa when he joined an old seaman to harpoon a whale and then jumped on the back of the great leviathan for a trip around the world. This engraving was so popular that it even appeared in an almanac. Courtesy of the Collection of the Massachusetts Historical Society, Boston, Massachusetts.

Algoa Bay, where they were tossed ashore. Knocked unconscious, Tabor awoke in his hospital bed. After Tabor told him his tale, Browne asked him if the strange ride was nothing but a dream. Tabor responded: "I could easily have supposed it as all a dream," but "The old man, with the same supernatural glare" was standing beside his bed when he awoke. When Tabor tried to grab for the old man, he receded from him. Tabor pursued the apparition, but he could never catch it. After Tabor returned to the hospital the man followed him. And, even though Tabor shut the door in the old man's face, the ancient whaler just passed right through it. Nor, Tabor claimed, was the old man a one-time hallucination created by a fever because whenever he had too much to drink the old man reappeared "as a kind of punishment" for his sins. That very night while lying in bed Tabor heard the old man approach and hiss, "D'ye want to get clear of me?" When Tabor replied, "'Fore God, I do," the man replied,

"Swear, then, this night, that you'll never taste another drop of grog."
A promise that Tabor said he "hadn't the resolution" to make, although
Browne reported that the next night Tabor "made a solemn vow to
abstain from rum." Of course, this tall tale was too fabulous to be true.
Tabor, however, did not fully concede that point. His story brought the
listener into his world and however strange the yarn appeared, he made
it almost believable. Tabor began by describing how the crew had smug-
gled liquor on board his whaleship, with the men drinking so much that
they fell into a "helpless ... condition," compelling the captain to put into
Algoa Bay so they could recover. While such a breach of discipline would
have been unusual, it was believable. Once ashore Tabor gained access
to "a fresh supply of liquor" and within a week he "was laid up with a
fever in consequence of" his "deep potations." Although this drinking to
excess may have shown a weakness, it was a weakness that every seaman
could understand and sympathize with and thereby built a bond between
the storyteller and his listeners. Gradually Tabor stretched and twisted
his yarn to the improbable. Walking down to the beach, putting his ear
to the sand to listen for the breaching of a whale, even meeting the old
seaman dressed in "a tremendous sou-wester, a greasy duck jacket, and a
pair of well-tarred trowsers" provided detail with which seamen aboard
a whaler would be all too familiar. Only after Tabor and the old man
had struck the whale with their harpoon and jumped onto his back did
the tale become truly marvelous. By then the listeners, like Tabor himself, were hanging on for the bizarre ride across the globe. The details
of that journey demonstrated that Tabor was an experienced seaman,
one whose knowledge of geography spoke to his years sailing the seven
seas and even traversing some of the continents. Browne complimented
the lyrical nature of Tabor's tales by asserting "though he never made
use of a poetical word; though he had never read a line of real poetry"
he "had a thorough appreciation ... of the poetry of *incident*, and could
throw the true poetic mantle over the most ordinary narrations by the
very simplicity and natural energy of his narratives." Had he been educated and preserved "the freshness of his language ..., few men would
have ranked higher in the literary world." Tabor played a huge role in
Browne's *Etchings of a Whaling Cruise* as the oldest and most regarded
of seamen. Serving as a boatsteerer, a highly skilled job on any whaleship,
Tabor was "a man 'whose like I ne'er shall look upon again.'" Tabor
"had spent twenty years of his life at sea, and had seen a great deal of
the world, and experienced many hard rubs in the whaling business." As
demonstrated in his yarn, "There was scarcely an island in the Pacific

Ocean that he had not visited; and few were those whose minds were better stored with plain, matter-of-fact knowledge than John's." Generous and stouthearted, Tabor "had all those blunt, manly qualities that characterize the genuine son of Neptune." As seaman and yarn spinner Tabor earned the respect of his shipmates. His one great flaw, not surprisingly for a Jack Tar portrayed as a stereotype, was his fondness for alcohol. And here is where his ride on the back of a whale came into play. Like many yarns, this one had a moral: the evils of liquor.[47]

Book-Length Yarns

Browne's *Etchings of a Whaling Cruise* represented a hybrid form of literature: it was part logbook, part journal, part travelogue, part adventure tale, and part a spun yarn that happened to contain other spun yarns. As we have seen in our discussion of logbooks, volumes authored by common men began to appear with greater frequency during the early republic era. There were plenty of such books from all walks of life. However, perhaps because of the great adventures and exotic locations, the sailor's yarn as a book seemed to have a special place in this emerging literature.[48] This development began before the phrase "spinning yarns" ever entered print. Sailor writers recording specific experiences often told incredible stories, such as in the captivity of John Blatchford or the desperate survival tale of Owen Chase, that may not have had any ghost-like apparitions, but often contained details that were almost unbelievable. Such published tales were really extended yarns. Once Richard Henry Dana Jr. opened the floodgates, leading to an outpouring of publications by common seamen, the number of book-length yarns increased. We can see the affinity between the published stories tracing the sailor's experience at sea and the verbal recitation of a sailor's spun yarn in reminiscences like those of Ebenezer Fox, who claimed that he wrote down his story of the American Revolution because a cough prevented him from relating his narrative orally to his grandchildren. The ability of a sailor to spin a book-length yarn became an intrinsic part of both lowbrow and highbrow American culture in the works of Ned Buntline and Herman Melville.[49]

The *Narrative of the Remarkable Occurrences in the Life of John Blatchford* represents an early example in the United States of the spun yarn of a common seaman that had made its way into print. No author was named, although the title page indicates that the tale was "Taken from his [Blatchford's] own mouth." Blatchford was from Cape Ann,

Massachusetts, and was "a poor man with a wife and two children" employed in fishing and sailing in coastal vessels in New England at the time of the publication of his story. The book was in the first person as if Blatchford was spinning his own yarn. He related a tale of sacrifice and hardship experienced during the Revolutionary War, and his story was popular enough to be republished several times during the early national period both as a separate book and as extracts in newspapers.[50] As the title of this short book proclaimed, John Blatchford's experiences were remarkable. Going to sea as a fifteen-year-old cabin boy in 1777 aboard the Massachusetts ship *Hancock*, he became a prisoner of war when his vessel was captured a month after it left port. Over the next six years he underwent an odyssey in which he attempted to escape several times and he served under six different flags. Even if this ordeal was a bit extreme, elements of the story reflected the experience of other common seamen during the war. Blatchford's narrative, however, contained a tinge of the exotic that stretched the yarn to the realm of the unbelievable. Among the litany of Blatchford's tribulations and adventures was a stint in the East Indies, where the British sent him to serve in a garrison on the island of Sumatra. After he and two other American prisoners refused to do their duty as British soldiers they were punished by being forced to work in the pepper fields. The three Americans then attempted to escape, were caught, and sentenced to death because they had killed one of the sepoys sent after them. Blatchford and one of the other young sailors had their sentences commuted to 800 lashes and the third was executed. When Blatchford and his remaining companion recovered from their corporal punishment they escaped again into the Sumatran wilderness. This time they were not recaptured, but Blatchford's companion perished from eating poisonous fruit. Here is where the story pressed on the edges of belief. We might accept that Blatchford had hallucinations concerning his home and that he would even hear his mother's voice calling him. But he also claimed that a "small dog" that "came fawning round" and followed him was really a young lion, whose lioness parent soon appeared only to feed its cub and leave Blatchford unmolested. If the recitation of weeks of wandering in a wilderness with limited food and drink and this near-death experience with a lion were not enough to excite the interest of the reader, and stretch the boundaries of our imaginations, Blatchford also declared that "a monstrous large tiger" approached him one day. To save himself Blatchford raised his arms "and hollowed very loud," scaring the tiger into running back into the woods. Just as incredible was the end of Blatchford's escapade in Sumatra when he stumbled across "a Female

Indian" fishing at a brook who had "no other dress on than that which mother nature affords impartially to all her children, except a small cloth which she wore round her waist." This shy young woman guided the bedraggled and desperate Blatchford back to her village, and from there he eventually managed to reach a Dutch settlement. Blatchford's saga continued after he left the Sumatran jungle until he eventually returned to Cape Ann in May 1783.[51]

In the context of understanding the development of spinning yarns in American culture, Blatchford's *Narrative of the Remarkable Occurrences* – not necessarily the experiences reported, but the relation of those experiences – represents a signpost: some of the first book-length sailor yarns in the United States were printed as a testimony of the ordeal of Jack Tar in defense of the new nation.[52] Within this context some American seamen published their stories of imprisonment during the Revolutionary War, the Barbary wars, and the War of 1812. During the opening decade of the nineteenth century, especially after the *Chesapeake* Affair, when the British precipitated a diplomatic crisis by firing on an American warship and forcefully removing four sailors they claimed were deserters, impressment also became an important story line in these publications. After the Treaty of Ghent in 1814 ended the second Anglo-American war, and as literature by and about common men became increasingly prominent, sailor yarns about imprisonment and impressment only became more frequent.[53]

If patriotism was central to the publication of many sailor yarns in the early republic, so too were more traditional maritime tales of adventure and survival against the frightful forces of nature. Blatchford added a component of this struggle against the elements in his journey through the jungle and his confrontation with a lion and a tiger in Sumatra. Other book-length yarns centered more directly on the perils sailors faced at sea. None was more startling than the sensational tale of Owen Chase aboard the whaleship *Essex* that appeared in print in 1821. Struck by a whale, the *Essex* sank in the far Pacific Ocean in 1819. The crew managed to save some provisions, but found themselves forced to sail four thousand miles in flimsy whaleboats to reach civilization. Chase, who was the first officer of the *Essex*, published a harrowing account of death and survival that included cannibalism as the men ate a shipmate who had perished from thirst and hunger. The book was probably written by someone other than Chase, but was based on his journal and his telling of the tale. The language of the publication was not the standard Jack Tar jargon of the stereotypical yarn. Instead, it assumed a more formal, matter-of-fact tone that had an especially chilling effect when discussing the gruesome aspects of the narrative. Chase related that when one man had died, "after reflecting on the subject all night," he addressed his two remaining comrades "on the painful subject of keeping the body for food!!" The passages that followed may have been statements of fact, but were so spine tingling that the reader probably wished that they had been made up. "[W]e set to work as fast as we were able to prepare it [the corpse] so as to prevent its spoiling. We separated his limbs from his body, and cut all the flesh from the bones; after which, we opened the body [and] took out the heart." They then "commenced to satisfy the immediate craving of nature from the heart, which we eagerly devoured" and hung up the strips of flesh cut from the body to be preserved by drying them in the sun. Without the ghosts and apparitions that packed so many sailor yarns, Chase's true story contained an unimaginable horror that made the reader almost not want to believe the tale.[54]

Other mariners confronted both natural and man-made dangers that provided great material for book-length yarns. Several seamen told tales of survival. Samuel Swett wrote about how his ship sprung a leak that grew so bad in a storm that the ship foundered and sank. Sixteen survivors piled into the longboat and suffered eighteen days on the open sea before another vessel rescued them. Charles H. Barnard related how during a sealing voyage to the South Atlantic he and four other crew members were left on an uninhabited island in the Falklands to lead a Crusoe-like life after the British seized his ship during the War of 1812. A few of these stories had an incredibly broad readership. The antislavery message in James Riley's *An Authentic Narrative of the Loss of the American Brig Commerce* made it a favorite with many readers, including Abraham Lincoln. As with other patriotic book-length yarns, captivity played a major role in these publications. This theme also appeared in stories about mutineers and pirates. When William Lay and Cyrus M. Hussey published their story of the mutiny on the whaleship *Globe* they described multiple captivities. First they felt trapped and coerced by the mutineers who killed all but one of the ship's officers. Then, after the mutineers sailed to a South Pacific Island, they were enslaved by the natives. Barnabas Lincoln and his crew were captured by pirates in the West Indies in 1821 and were held prisoner for a couple of weeks before the pirates marooned them on a deserted island.[55] Black sailors also published what might be considered book-length yarns about captivity. Perhaps the most famous of these books was Olaudah Equiano's story of his sojourn from African captive to West Indies slave to British subject and free man. This tale, centered on Equiano's experience as a seaman, can be seen as a yarn that hid the truth about some aspects of his life.[56] Less noted, and perhaps extending and twisting the facts even further, was the printed yarn of the illiterate mulatto Robert Adams, who was shipwrecked off the coast of western Africa and held in slavery for three years. Adams claimed to have visited the fabled Timbuktu during his captivity and that he had a love affair with his master's wife.[57]

Many of these stories appeared before the phrase "spinning yarns" entered into print and before Richard Henry Dana Jr. awakened greater popular interest in the common seaman. Once yarn spinning became a genre unto itself in the United States, and once Dana had published *Two Years before the Mast*, even more book-length yarns appeared. During the 1830s and 1840s, encouraged by these developments and the metamorphosis of the logbook into life stories about Jack Tar, sailors wrote of their experiences in the patriotic defense of the nation, and as common sailors who had a right to share their yarns as seamen and as citizens. It was within this context that Ebenezer Fox's cough convinced him to record his adventures during the Revolutionary War and detail what life and death was like aboard the prison ship *Jersey* in New York Harbor.[58] Tiphys Aegyptus called several of his stories about abuse in the American navy "yarns" in a book written as an American citizen who hoped to see the nation's "institutions honored and respected ... and the broad wings of her eagle flapping in triumph over every nation."[59] In *Ned Myers, or a Life before the Mast*, a collaborative work between James Fenimore Cooper and an old salt he knew in his youth, Ned Myers referred to the famous novelist as his "ship-mate, who is logging this yarn," combining the idea that a sailor's story reflected both the logbook of memory and the spinning of a yarn.[60]

The spinning of yarns spread beyond maritime literature and became popularized in the lowbrow stories and cheap novels of Ned Buntline. The details of the early life of Ned Buntline – really Ned Judson – remain somewhat vague and depend largely on his own often exaggerated prose. Born in upstate New York, Judson moved with his family to Philadelphia, where he later ran away to sea. After several voyages on merchant vessels, Judson joined the navy and eventually earned a midshipman's berth, hoping to gain more experiences that could fuel his desire to pursue a career as a writer. His first story, "The Captain's Pig," was rejected by *Knickerbocker* magazine and was self-published. Because Judson was still in the navy and the story amusingly recounted how he had stolen a pig from the captain's table for the midshipmen's mess, he created a nautical pseudonym to hide his identity. Obviously pleased with the cognomen, Judson retained the pen name after he left the navy in 1844 and began publishing his own periodical, *Ned Buntline's Magazine.* That enterprise was short-lived, but he also started to write essays for *Knickerbocker* and soon earned a reputation as a writer of sensational articles and dime novels. By the fall of 1845 *Knickerbocker* had agreed to publish sections of Buntline's supposed autobiography, appropriately entitled "Ned Buntline's Life-Yarn." Embellished with purple prose, Buntline explained that at age eleven he had refused to train as a lawyer as his father had insisted and ran off to sea by jumping aboard a ship just as it was departing Race Street Wharf. Quickly winning over the captain with his pluck and determination, within days Ned "learned to furl the royal" – the highest of sails – and even "take 'a trick at the helm,' " skills that took full grown men months, if not years, of training to gain. This imaginative "Life-Yarn" of adventures in which young Buntline took the lead, from falling in love with a thirteen-year-old girl in Cuba whose "little figure was full and perfect" to rescuing attractive women from a shipwreck on the high seas. The "Life-Yarn" subsequently appeared in book form in 1849. In the meantime Buntline began publishing a series of sea stories that would include *The Last of the Buccaneers: A Yarn of the Eighteenth Century.* His early work, and his pen name, reflected his maritime experience, but he eventually moved on to other topics as well, especially urban crime and the Wild West. Indeed, he became famous for his exposé of the New York underworld and as one of America's leading Western writers. He also became a promoter of Wild West shows. Whether writing about escapades on the high seas, the grit of Five Points, or the romance of the far West, he kept the literary quality of his work the same: sensational tales laden with saccharine prose and one-dimensional characters that were immensely popular and earned him a fortune.[61] Mark Twain described Buntline's writing as "wordy, windy, flowery 'eloquence,' romanticism, sentimentality – all imitated from Sir Walter [Scott], and sufficiently badly done, too – innocent travesties of his style and methods." Unlike the forthright Ned Buntline of the Life-Yarn, the real Ned Buntline was a scoundrel who had almost been lynched for an affair with a married woman in Nashville, sent to prison for leading the deadly Astor Place Riot, a proponent of the Know Nothing Party in the 1850s, an unscrupulous businessman, and a polygamist. Regardless of his unsavoriness and shortcomings as an author, his work helped to sustain the importance of spinning yarns in the lowest levels of mainstream culture.[62]

In contrast to the banal work of Ned Buntline was the magisterial prose of Herman Melville. Both authors broke into the New York literary scene at about the same time and both authors began their careers as sailors spinning yarns in print. Although Melville was not above using popular sensationalism as he sought to appeal to what he himself called "my ruthless democracy on all sides," he refused to pursue the nativist working-class popularity Buntline craved. As Buntline led the mob at Astor Place attempting to purge English actor Charles Macready from the American stage, Melville was signing a petition insisting on the right to allow Macready to perform.[63] Regardless of this upper-class cosmopolitanism, Melville was fully aware of the importance of yarns both in their oral and written forms. In *White-Jacket* the boatswain was called "Old Yarn" and Melville recounted his fondness for listening to yarns in the main-top at night. The mean-spirited Henry Jackson in *Redburn* told grisly stories "full of piracies, plagues, and poisonings."[64] Melville first spun his yarns in the forecastle, and his tale of his experience on Typee, with its intense sexual implications, ensured the interest of his listeners. That same ability to spin a yarn of life among the South Sea islanders convinced his family and friends to urge him to write down his yarn and publish the story of his adventures. The success of that first effort in *Typee: A Peep at Polynesian Life during a Four Month Residence in a Valley in the Marquesas* led to a succession of books built around his maritime experience.[65] Melville, however, did not rely solely on his own yarns. He often took stories by other sailors and integrated them into his novels. His book on Revolutionary sailor Israel Potter was roughly based on the seaman's published yarn, but pushed it to extremes, having Potter forced to change ships and change sides several times for reasons beyond his own control. As Melville cleverly explained: "Thus repeatedly and rapidly were the fortunes of our wanderer planted, torn up, transplanted, and dropped again, hither and thither, according as the Supreme Disposer of sailors and soldiers saw fit to appoint." Melville twisted Potter's already hard to believe yarn of suffering during the Revolutionary War, followed by forty years of poverty in London, even further. The focus of the story, as was true with every good yarn, was on the years of action and Melville gave short shrift to the long post-war exile. Even when he only briefly touched upon those years, Melville did so with the choice of language of a gifted storyteller. "For the most part, what befell Israel" – here Melville pursued a wonderful play on the sailor's real name – "during his forty years' wanderings in the London deserts, surpassed the forty years in the natural wilderness of the outcast

Hebrews under Moses."[66] Melville's greatest masterpiece, *Moby Dick*, also was based on other writers' yarns. The story of "Mocha Dick: or the White Whale of the Pacific" first appeared in *Knickerbocker* in 1839. The author, J. N. Reynolds, was a newspaper editor and would-be explorer with some experience at sea, but not as a common sailor. Most of "Mocha Dick" was spun as a yarn by the mate of a whaler Reynolds met off the coast of Chile. The ensuing narrative is breathtaking with its reference to "a sort of superstitious dread of Mocha Dick, from the exaggerated stories of that prodigy" because "in many a tough yarn" the mate had heard that the white leviathan was "some ferocious fiend of the deep," rather "than a regular-built legitimate whale!" In Reynold's story, the whalers finally kill their quarry. Melville, of course, reverses the order of things in the most fantastic of all yarns and, using Owen Chase's narrative of the attack of a whale on the *Essex*, has Moby Dick ram the *Pequod*, drowning all the crew but Ishmael.[67]

The spinning of yarns began on the deck of a ship sometime before 1819, entered the British underworld, spread to mainstream Anglo-American culture during the Romantic era, and returned to Jack Tar in countless sailor narratives. Whether written by an author pretending to be a mariner, a sailor himself, or an ex-sailor turned professional writer, the expression "spinning a yarn" became imbedded in American print culture. The prolific writing of Ned Buntline and Herman Melville – one representing a lower form of popular hack writing and the other reflecting the highest form of literary expression – adds one more twist to our tale of spinning yarns, ensuring that the tradition of telling both real and imagined stories of adventures on the ocean deep reached into the late nineteenth century and down to the present day.

5

Songs of the Sailorman

Along with spinning yarns, sailors loved to sing. When Herman Melville decided to portray the ideal seaman as an "upright barbarian," as close to nature as Adam in the Garden of Eden, Billy Budd, besides being "Invariably a proficient in his calling" and regardless of the fact that he could not read, was a great singer, "and like the illiterate nightingale [he] was sometimes the composer of his own song."[1] For Melville, and for many sailors, skill as a seaman went hand in hand with skill in music. Just as with spinning yarns, having the talent to carry and create a tune garnered respect among the men who went to sea. Whether on the deck during the dogwatch, idle moments in the forecastle, ashore in taverns, in theaters, or even in the streets, sailors enjoyed the pleasures of song. Samuel Leech described the musical celebrity of two British seamen during his service aboard the HMS *Macedonian*. The first was a crew member who was "quite popular" with his shipmates "for his lively disposition and his talents as a comic singer, which last gift is always prized in a man of war." The second was called "happy Jack" and visited the frigate while it was in port. As soon as this jovial sailor came aboard, the crew ran toward him. "Every voice was hushed, all work was brought to a stand still" as the men listened "to his unequalled performances."[2] Another measure of music's importance to mariners is the number of songs found written in journals and logbooks kept at sea and elsewhere.[3] Privateersman Timothy Connor wrote down more than fifty songs in a notebook while held as a prisoner of war during the American Revolution.[4] Among the seamen in Dartmoor Prison in the War of 1812 "Music was a favourite amusement." The sailors "met at one another's mess tables with their instruments and note books, and could easily wear away a few hours each day, which otherwise would have hung heavily upon them."[5] Sailor songs ran the gamut from the sentimental to the sensational and from true love to the bawdy. On the sentimental side, a favorite theme was that of distressed lovers separated by the man going to sea, but sailors also sang about family and an idealized vision of home. On the sensational side, songs described the perils of prostitution, drinking, forced recruitment, and oppression at sea, as well as battles, shipwrecks, storms, and pirates. Combining the sentimental and the sensational were songs that trumpeted national identity.[6] In many ways the content of sailor songs was similar to the content of spun yarns. This similarity makes sense: for centuries, if not millennia, humans have used music as a memory device and as a convenient way to transmit information. Both the spinning of yarns and the songs of the sailorman reflect ancient methods of oral communication that pose problems to the historian bound by the written text.

If anything, the story of the sailor's music, and how it was transmitted into print and manuscript, is even more complex than the story of the written record of spinning yarns, revealing a give and take between mainstream and maritime culture. Mariners have probably sung of their exploits since the first humans ventured from land on hollowed-out logs. The earliest entry in *The Oxford Book of Sea Songs* chronicles a tale from the fourteenth century with lyrics that were recorded by 1562 and published by 1609.[7] But we do not know who first thought of the song – a landsman or a seaman. Although we can identify the composers of some of the music in the eighteenth and nineteenth centuries, we cannot determine the provenance in all cases. Moreover, maritime music became extremely popular with landsmen who wrote street ballads and produced songs for the theater. The land-based and professional origin of these art songs, as opposed to folk songs created by common people, did not preclude the sailor from making them his own even as he changed, altered, amended, or misremembered the words. So as with the spinning of yarns we have a legacy of folk traditions being taken up by professional writers whose work was in turn embraced, and sometimes not embraced, by real seamen who all the while may still have been active inventing their own music. Complicating this tale of the songs of the sailorman is the issue of nationality. Like the polyglot crews of the Atlantic world, the sources of this music were multinational even as the lyrics often struck a nationalist chord. Whatever the complex international origins of maritime music we will focus mainly on the Anglo-American world, examining the interconnectedness in song between Great Britain and America.

To disentangle this skein of twisted threads of composition and content, we will trace the development of sea songs from when they first appeared in print in the sixteenth century until the latter days of sail in the mid-nineteenth century. Some of these tunes were folks songs devised by men who had gone to sea. Others were art songs written by professionals. Our analysis will suggest that such distinctions are sometimes difficult to sustain. Rather than looking for a pure form of sea songs, we shall consider the art and folk songs together. We will begin with the early sea ballads of the seventeenth century and find that whatever the source of the songs, they established a set of themes in content that would remain in place for centuries: the articulation of a special status for the common seaman within society and within the nation. We will then examine the Anglo-American nautical music of the eighteenth century to trace the continuation and elaboration of the earlier pattern, especially as it related to the development of the British empire and the independence of the United States. The same patterns of celebrating the sailor's personal and national triumphs and tragedies persisted during the early years of the American republic. After the War of 1812, Americans continued to assert their sense of patriotism, but perhaps with a little less stridency. More importantly, the cross-Atlantic currents in the songs of the sailorman performed on stage and aboard ship continued in terms of the content and music within both the maritime and the mainstream worlds. That said, during the antebellum period – some call it the heyday of sailor song – a further distinction can be made concerning nautical music. Shanties, or work songs, developed as a separate identifiable genre.[8]

English Ballads and Sea Songs

Written by professional composers and by professional seamen, the early English maritime ballads covered a variety of topics and themes that would appear in later sailor songs and marked the beginnings of a distinct genre that asserted a special place for the seaman. On one level the confessions of love, the separation of sweethearts, the jilted maidens, the cross-dressing, the perilous vicissitudes of life, the criminal activity, the disguised and not-so-disguised bawdy lyrics, the sexual prowess of males and females, the cuckolding, and even the contributions to the larger nation appeared in ballads not devoted to the seaman. But each of these categories, especially the last, applied to the tar with particular meaning. As Great Britain came to depend on its seamen even more in the eighteenth century, and as the image of Jack Tar began to emerge and gain in importance with the expansion of the British Empire, the songs of the sailorman helped to facilitate the ongoing interaction between the maritime and mainstream cultures.

The earliest published sailor songs appeared in the seventeenth century as broadsheet ballads printed on a single page. Traditionally, ballads, or "stories in song," had been learned simply by listening. Beginning in the sixteenth century such ballads made their way into print and ballad writers began to embellish, alter, and even create new lyrics and music. These compositions thus represented a combination of folk and art songs. *Lustily, Lustily*, appeared in a play in 1576 and may have derived from a tune actually sung by sailors. At the same time some would-be professional writers hoped to earn a living producing ballads. Three of the four extant ballads commemorating the English victory against the Spanish Armada were written by the same landsman. During the seventeenth century the broadsheet ballad became ubiquitous in England, sold by hawkers in the street, plastered on tavern walls, and heard almost anywhere.[9]

Although all the early broadside ballads, whether they covered maritime subjects or not, had similar themes, songs centered on sailors had developed a special status connected to the nature of the maritime trade. For example, the young farmer boy or craftsman could just as easily proclaim his love for a young woman, or leave the girl standing at the altar, but he was not ordinarily drawn from the hearth by his profession like a mariner. An early rendition of the sailor's adieu, *The Sailor's Departure from his Dearest Love*, opened with the line "Now I am bound to the Seas, and from my love must part," and has the refrain

> *Remember me on shore,*
> *as I the[e] on the main,*
> *So keep my love in store,*
> *til I return again.*

The song, which is set as a duet, continued with the sailor describing the dangers of the deep and how "Of life no man is sure, while Seas raging last." He went on to promise her in a series of inversions, similar to *The World Turned Upside Down* ballad, that he would remain true to his love or the entire world would turn topsy-turvy:

> The fish shall seem to flye,
> yea Birds to fishes turn,
> The Sea be ever dry,
> and fire cease to burn:
> When I prove false to thee,
> shall these things come to pass.

The maiden replied in a similar vein and concluded the ballad with

> Farewell to thee sweet-heart,
>   That now to Sea art gone,
> With great grief I part,
>   To Lovers best tis known.

Because the sailor was intrinsically mobile, he became a natural subject for a song lamenting the separation of lovers. Moreover, his occupation provided a series of readymade images – like "while raging seas last" – that dramatized that separation.[10]

The sailor's ability to escape to the sea also made it easy to cast him as a cad who jilted his lover. Mariners thus became notorious for not keeping their promises and breaking hearts in the process. Even if such songs centered on the women left ashore, the idea that the girl left behind pined for the absent sailor appealed to those on land and those at sea. *The Perjured Sayler* described how a seaman won his way into the favor of "a young maid of Greenwich," despite her protestations, and then refused to see her when he returned from his next voyage.[11] Lovesick, she died at the end of the ballad. In *The Laundry-Maids Lamentation for the Loss of Her Seaman* a young woman struggled with the idea of killing herself and her baby after being forsaken by her sailor lover and then hearing the news of his death at sea. She looked on the "The Watry Region" as her "delight, since there he lost his life," and thought about throwing herself into the ocean with her child and having her soul search for her drowned lover, declaring, "I'll be his Comrade soon this night, / since I cannot be his Wife." This ballad concluded with ambiguity. The laundry maid imagined that when she found her dead lover she would ask him why he had left her and "his pretty little Swain." The ballad did not have a happy ending. Instead, she expected him to stand silent upon which she would "give him gentle Kisses three, and wring him by the hands."[12]

The mariner returning to the sea provided the context for the development of another plot line that became popular in sailor songs – the woman who disguised herself as a man to follow her lover – for which the ship seemed particularly suited. Such stories had been long a part of the English stage; William Shakespeare wrote several plays where women characters wore men's clothing. It was possible to portray women disguised as a tradesman, a servant, or a soldier. But because England was surrounded by water, the maritime setting fit the ballads nicely. The forecastle also had a hyper-masculine homo-social culture that added to the tension in the ballad and such songs offered a safe avenue to express male-to-male sexual attraction. Similar lyrics would be repeated throughout the age of sail and beyond. *The She Mariner's Misfortune* left the sexual innuendo to the imagination and centered on the dangers sailors confronted on the high seas. The ballad began with a seaman who was about to leave "a Maiden pretty" for a voyage, promising that he would marry her when he returned. The young woman, however, insisted that she would go with him to be his "Mesmate" and share in every hardship. He finally agreed to this proposition:

> By joynt consent, to Sea they went
> to satisfy her hearts desire
> This was not known, to any one
> for she was drest in man's attire.

At sea she exhibited bravery and learned navigation, but during a storm the two lovers were swept overboard. Despite the sailor's best efforts to swim with his lover on his back, they were about to drown when they were saved by a passing ship. Unfortunately, the ship was from Algeria and took the two into captivity. The maid continued in disguise and only confessed the truth when brought before the local ruler, who rewarded her "constancy" by returning both of them to England.[13] *The Maiden Sailor* had a similar opening, with the maiden dressing as a sailor and getting pressed into the navy as she sought to follow her love in the wars. Her motivation was less to be with him and more "So that she, might serve the King as well as he." This ballad also had increased sexual content with one "sailor bold" believing that she was not just "a very pritty Colliers Lad," but a young woman. The sailor decided to make a sexual advance on "this young Damsel" and "strove to feel her knee" to which "she would not agree." Having been found out, she revealed her sexual identity to the captain, who then sent her home to her native town, which just happened to be "Maiden-Head."[14] A somewhat later ballad played even more explicitly to the homoerotic when a Bristol merchant's daughter followed her ship carpenter sweetheart into the navy, keeping her true identity from her lover. Having "passed for a seaman brave" aboard ship, her "pretty fingers long and strait" soon earned her a berth as "the surgeons mate." When the "pretty surgeons mate" attended to the ship carpenter after he was wounded in a battle, the sexual tension became palpable. The balladeer explained that the ship carpenter still did not recognize his true love:

> She cur[e]d him in a little space,
> He often gazd upon her face;

> Surgeon, said he, such eyes as thine
> Did formerly my heart entwine:
>
> If ever I live to go on shore,
> and she be dead whom I adore,
> I will thy true companion be,
> And neer forsake thy company.

Even if the pledge of being the surgeon's "true companion" was not an explicit homosexual promise, the ship carpenter then proclaimed a complete abandonment of women.

> If she be dead this will I do,
> To the female sex Ill bid adieu,
> And neer will marry for her sake,
> But to the sea myself betake.

Before the ship returned to port, the female surgeon in disguise revealed her true identity to the ship carpenter. The two were married and lived happily ever after.[15]

Although anyone could face trials, the mariner's occupation left him especially vulnerable to hardships. As the special genre of maritime ballads developed during the seventeenth century, this aspect of life at sea became the focus of several songs. The experience of the couple in *The She Mariner's Misfortune* touched on two central topics that appeared in the songs of the sailorman: shipwreck and captivity. Shipwreck ballads became a mainstay of sailor songs. One strain of this music was an elaboration on the parting lovers theme with the sailor heading out to sea where he loses his life. Many of these ballads have the woman dying upon hearing the news of the loss of her love at sea.[16] Other shipwreck ballads, like a song describing the *Benjamin*'s destruction as it entered Plymouth harbor, were more straightforward descriptions of maritime disasters.[17] The Barbary captivity ballad about Vincent Jukes is an instructive example of the relationship between the sea-based and land-based origins of maritime ballads. Jukes used his captivity for personal advancement by converting to Islam and became himself a corsair. Eventually he and three other renegades took over a ship and sailed to England with their fortunes assured. Upon his return, Jukes visited London taverns bragging about his Barbary escapades only to find that his tale had quickly been reshaped into a broadsheet ballad. Oddly, the positive twist to the Jukes ballad and the experience of the she-mariner were not untypical in songs about Barbary captivity. Rather than focus on the horrors of enslavement, these songs, and scores of others like them, emphasized the ability to escape and even profit from the experience.[18]

Land-based criminals or quasi criminals could be the subject of a ballad, but seaborne criminals seemed to have had a special attraction. Early pirate songs, a form of ballad that had a long lineage, tended to have mixed messages: sometimes they made the pirate's life appealing and sometimes they had the pirate's career end in capture and execution. Perhaps this ambiguity reflected the hazy boundary between licit and illicit maritime raiding in the fifteenth and sixteenth centuries where one nation's adventurer was another nation's buccaneer, especially in the distant waters of the West and East Indies. Or perhaps the more positive portrayals of piracy spoke to the attraction and sympathy some common seamen might have had for men who willingly flouted authority and took to free booting, while the more negative portrayals addressed the common sailor's fear of cutthroats who were violent and who had severed connections with shore-side attachments. As we will also see in our discussion of reading, both the attraction and repulsion to piracy remained a part of Anglo-American maritime and mainstream culture well into the nineteenth century. *Andrew Bardeen*, which can be linked to several other early pirate songs, ends on an antiauthoritarian note with the pirate ordering his captive to go back to the king and tell him, "If he can reign king over all dry land, / I can reign king o'er the sea." The popular ballad rehearsing the career of Captain Ward is more ambiguous in its message. On one hand, the song portrayed Ward as a successful pirate who had amassed great riches and a palace in Tunis; on the other hand, "This wicked-gotten treasure / Doth him but little pleasure" because he wasted his money "In drunkenness and lechery, / Filthy sins of sodomy." Whatever the attraction or repulsion of pirates like Ward or Captain Avery (authorities never captured the latter) may have had for regular mariners, some of the most popular pirate ballads made clear that the gallows awaited men who broke the laws of man and God. One version of the often sung *Captain Kidd's Farewell to the Seas* ends:

> Take a warning now by me, for I must die, for I must die
> Take warning now by me, and shun bad company,
> Lest you come to hell with me, for I must die.[19]

The sailor's travails abroad and pirate fantasies furnished opportunities to create lyrics that might seem to set him apart from other Englishmen. We must, however, remember that England was a maritime nation and as such these lyrics had a special appeal to many within the larger society.

That same connection between land-based and sea-based culture can be seen in the use of nautical double entendre with sexual content, although we might assume that the use of the tar's peculiar nautical vocabulary hid such lewdness. As we have seen in our discussion of the language of Jack Tar, the familiarity of so many people ashore with that special language meant that veiling ribaldry with the maritime vocabulary would have provided only a thin disguise. Moreover, even if ballads of all stripes could be bawdy, given the seaman's reputation for misbehavior ashore, Jack Tar's language seemed especially suited to the risqué. Perhaps no ballad better represents the use of the sailor lexicon to provide a transparent veil to hide salaciousness than *An Excellent New Song, Entitled a Hot Engagement between a French Privateer and an English Fire-Ship*, which described what superficially appeared to be a sea battle. Anyone who understood the language of Jack Tar would have known better. On the surface the naval engagement makes no sense because fireships would ordinarily be used in fleet actions where the sacrifice of one vessel might lead to the destruction of several enemy ships close together. It would be a waste of resources to launch a fireship in an attack against a single naval vessel, and even more so against a privateer. Moreover, as the lyrics demonstrate, in this supposed episode it was the French privateer ship which was the aggressor. The apocryphal battle therefore had other purposes: to present a bawdy ballad disguised as a celebration of English maritime prowess. The ballad began with an assertion of a sexually vulnerable female identity: "I'm a Prize for a Captain to fall on, / My Name is Sea faring Kate." And then goes on to suggest a curvaceous profile: "My Sails they are Top and Top Gallon. A Friggot that's of the First Rate." Sailors often described the bust of a woman in reference to the sails high up in the rigging, and a frigate was considered a sleek and well-proportioned ship. (Note, too, that using a first-rate frigate as a fireship against a privateer makes no naval sense.) Having thus informed any listener with a modicum of sailor vocabulary that the English ship was a metaphor for a woman, the balladeer identifies the French privateer as a male with a phallic reference: "On his Mid Ship he had a good Cannon, / which was all the great Guns he had." With the identity of the cast in this sexual encounter clarified, the action commenced:

> His Main Yard he hoisted and Steered
> his Course; and gave me a Broad Side:
> My Poop and my Starn Port Sneered
> betwixt the Wind, Water and Tide.

The verse uses two phallic symbols, the main yard and the single-gun broadside (from a naval point of view, a broadside should have entailed multiple guns) to describe how the Frenchman made Kate shift ("sheer" is a nautical term for deviating a ship's course) her buttocks because the poop and stern-port represented the top and the bottom of the ship's backside. "Betwixt Wind, Water and Tide" was a standard phrase for the middle of the ship's hull and suggested a sexual approach. Redundancy only added to the bawdy humor. If the listener had not picked up on the song's real intent, the balladeer quickly became more explicit:

> Still under his Lee I did hover,
> With all the force I could afford
> But as he had been a rank Rover
> he briskly did lay me on Board.
>
> He looked for some hidden Treasure,
> And fell to his doing of Feats,
> But found me a Fire-Ship of pleasure
> When he enter'd the mouth of the straights.

Kate thus described her resistance and then the Frenchman's discovery of "a Fire-Ship of pleasure" as he consummated the encounter by entering "the mouth of the straights" – Kate's vagina. The would-be conquering Frenchman, however, soon found that he had taken on more than he could handle, as Kate explained "Our Frigats were foul [nautical phrase for entangled] of each other, / And could not get off, or ride to," and that "But ne'er was a poor Dog in a Blanket / So tossed as was Monsieur." The Frenchman soon had enough of this encounter, but Kate was not finished with him.

> No near than his Course he still steered
> And clap'd his hand down to his Sword
> But as his Love tackle he cleard
> I brought down his Main Top by the Board.

In other words, the French privateer attempted to withdraw only to be forcefully brought back into Kate's embrace.

> Then he feared to burn a Sea martyr,
> For my Gun-room was all in a Fire;
> And I blew up my second Quarter
> just as he was about to retire.

Having reached the climax in this "battle," the French ship, which should have been completely destroyed had this been a real sea engagement, manages at last to withdraw, with Kate reporting she had used the poor man up: "I burn his Main Yard at a venter / So that he will press me no more."[20]

Although the description of this encounter from the female perspective may have been atypical, bawdy songs using maritime metaphors could also portray the English sailor as a hyper-sexually attractive male. Again, other ballads might have carried similar messages about other professions, but the tar's language and reputation set the sailor apart. In *Buxom Joan of Lymas's Love to a Jolly Tar*, several suitors sought to marry "buxom Joan." While the soldier, tailor, and tinker all proffered their love, the sly sailor bided his time, waiting for an opportunity to make his move.

> And just e'en as he meant, Sir,
> To Logger-heads they went, Sir
> And then he let fly at her,
> A shot 'twixt wind and water,
> Which won [this fair Maid's heart].

In other words, as the three other suitors began arguing, the sailor, using the "shot twixt wind and water" reference, had sexual relations with "Buxom Joan." Having experienced the sailor's sexual prowess, "Buxom Joan's" heart was his. The following stanzas had each of the suitors in turn threaten the sailor to no avail. In a series of metaphors the sailor continued to satisfy Joan, while the other suitors were in a bluster and stammer. The soldier challenged the sailor to a duel. The sailor's response was continued sexual activity:

> But he aboard his Pinace [Joan],
> Ne'er fear'd the Bully's menace,
> But lustily he ply'd, Sir,
> Against both wind and tide, Sir.

The tailor threatened to cut off his "ears" with his "shears." Unmoved by this threat, the sailor simply laughed at "Bodkin's bombast," and using a phallic reference (needle) to the tailor's trade, the persistent seaman

> Still pointing right his needle,
> He launch'd into the middle;
> She tost and heav'd; he drove.

Then when the "Man of Metal / Began to beat his Kettle" and threatened to "thump" both the sailor and his "doxy," using yet another phallic reference (rudder) the ballad explains:

> But still the merry Sailer
> Defy'd Buff, Brass and Tailor
> Whilst, in h[is] jolly mood, her

> He manag'd with his rudder,
> And right his course did stear.[21]

Another common theme in bawdy ballads was the cuckolded husband. Nobles, tradesmen, and farmers might have wives who cheated on them, but the fact that the sailor's employment compelled him to leave his wife at home made him particularly vulnerable to this situation. Again, a theme that could be applied generally to all of society had a special poignancy in the maritime context. These songs also addressed a sad truth for the waterfront community and would be repeated throughout the age of sail. In one ballad "A Seamans Wife" seduced her tenant, a shoemaker, offering him not only sexual access, but also clothes and money while her husband sought his fortune upon the ocean.[22] In another ballad several seamen's wives go out together to drink punch and make merry. There was no explicit reference to sexual activity during their visit to the tavern, but the final line declared that when the husbands returned after enduring "the worst Toy'l that e're was bourn," they would be "forc'd to Drink out of a Horn." The last phrase was more than a neat rhyme; it also referred to a pair of horns, the traditional symbol of a cuckold.[23] Even if the woman abandoned the sailor for the arms of another, the original attraction could return when the mariner came back from his voyages. In one ballad a woman promised herself to a seaman, but he was pressed into the navy before they could wed. She waited for three years and then heard news that he had died. The young woman then married a carpenter and had three children before the sailor returned. With her original love entreating her, and also telling her of the vast fortune he had earned, she at last relented, and abandoned her husband and three children. Upon hearing of this desertion the husband hanged himself and the children were orphaned.[24]

Many ballads described the consequences of frequenting taverns and brothels; but the seaman's lifestyle seemed to make him especially susceptible to this form of bad behavior. The lyrics of *Farewell to Graves-end* warned seamen against visiting prostitutes in a playful style that had a mixed message. On one hand was the description of a succession of girls willing "to please men in the Bed" and "kiss and play, both night and day." On the other hand was the problem that once the sailor spent his money, the girls lost interest. "And when your money doth fall short, / shel say tis time to go." The ballad concluded:

> He that is wise, let him despise,
> such wenches as are there,

> And you that had your pockets pickt
> I hope will have a care:
> And come no more, upon that Shore,
> where you were served so,
> Be your own friend, and leave Graves-end.[25]

The Seaman's Frolick: Or a Cooler for the Captain had the same whimsical tone with a more serious outcome. While in Plymouth harbor the ship's crew reported that "Our Captain did a small pinnace board." The word "pinnace," as the next few lines made clear, referred to a young woman: "She did abide him many a shot ... Before the upper hand he got" and then "but under deck she prov'd too hot." The entire experience "prov'd to him a sad mishap / For by report he got a clap." The final lines of the ballad offered advice, urging "brave Seamen all beware / How you meddle with such ware," and suggested that "When as you desire to range / Cast Anchor in no harbor strange."[26]

All of the themes in the ballads considered so far could have been sung about the lives of landsmen as well: lovers parting for reasons beyond their control; a man jilting an innocent young woman; females wearing male disguises; men and women facing disasters and captivity (Barbary raiders attacked the English coast); criminal activity; ribaldry and double entendre; cheating husbands and wives; and the dangers of brothels and taverns. Yet because England was a maritime nation, and because there was something about the mariner's occupation that left him particularly susceptible or vulnerable to each of these experiences, the nautical context made the songs popular within the larger culture and contributed to the image and status of Jack Tar. That said, beyond the rollicking and frolicking sailor, another key element emerged in the maritime ballads of the seventeenth century.

However bawdy and comical some sailor songs might get, with the expansion of overseas commerce and the development of an English empire abroad, sailors also began to earn pride of place and gain praise for their role in larger geopolitical developments. These songs of the sea defined a special place for mariners within the nation that must have appealed to seamen. One song featured a young woman trying to convince her mother to allow her to marry a sailor. The mother, no doubt thinking of all those ballads describing sailors leaving guileless young girls abandoned on the docks, or the women who lost their lovers to the violence of the sea, at first refused her consent. But the daughter insisted, asserting that sailors were "valient stout and brave" who served as "Strong Bulwarks to their native Isle, / the Kingdom to support and save." Seamen also were central to the economy:

> The Merchants Trade wou'd soon go down,
>   and many Callings more beside,
> If famous Seamen of Renown,
>   left sailing the main Ocean wide.

Ultimately the daughter persuaded her mother, who concluded:

> Now Daughter dear, I needs must own,
>   your Arguments has conquer'd me,
> They are the Supporters to the Throne,
>   and do defend our Liberty.[27]

Several ballads highlighted the mariner's role in sustaining the nation's commerce. *Neptune's Raging Fury* detailed how the sailor faced the dangers upon the ocean to bring spices back from the Indies and wine from Spain and France for landsmen to enjoy. Like the song with the young woman trying to persuade her mother to allow her to marry a sailor, other ballads described the seaman's role in both commerce and in the defense of the nation.[28]

The tar's special role as the protector of England – a country separated from most of its enemies by water – appeared in songs throughout the second half of the seventeenth century. Many of these ballads were sentimental portrayals of parting lovers. The mariner would proclaim that he had to fight the enemies of the king, while the maiden would seek to persuade him to remain home. Ultimately the protests were to no avail, as the sailor explained in *The Dover Lovers*: "Time draws on a kindly Spring, / And I must go to serve the King" and "Honor calls, I must away, / Yet love bids me for to stay."[29] Occasionally the maid encouraged her love to leave:

> I am a Damsel which doth part
>   with my Love for a season,
> And yet am pleased to the Heart,
>   since 'tis no more than reason,
> That he right valiantly shou'd fight,
>   upon the vast wide Ocean,
> For to maintain King *William*'s Right,
>   and raise his own promotion.[30]

A few of these ballads also had the young woman declare her willingness to dress as a sailor and join her love, only to be told that "Thy soft and

tender milk-white Hand, Seamen's labor cannot do."[31] Other patriotic
ballads did not mention sweethearts and simply emphasized the navy's
importance in protecting both the nation and the Protestant succession.
After William of Orange became king in 1689 one ballad called on sailors
to fight for the new monarch to ensure "The Total Destruction of Popery
in this Reformed Land."

> Come brave noble hearted Sea-men,
>   let us all with Courage stand,
> To maintain our Natives free men,
>   in this Ancient Christian Land;
> That *Rome* never may enslave us,
>   by their crafty Villainy;
> We'll not do as they would have us.
> *But will pull down Popery.*[32]

Not all of these songs about the contribution of sailors to the nation were
positive. *The Sea-Martyrs* complained that the sailor was not rewarded
for his sacrifices and that the families of mariners were mistreated.[33]

Few such protest songs have survived. More typical was the undiluted
patriotism of ballads that trumpeted England's maritime triumphs. There
may be only four extant copies of ballads celebrating the defeat of the
Spanish Armada, but the Stationary Registry recorded twenty-four such
ballads at the time. Other major battles were also remembered through
song. Commemorating the combined Dutch and English destruction of
sixteen French ships in 1692, ensuring the crown for William of Orange
and preventing a Jacobite invasion, *The Sea Fight in 92* had a last
stanza that began with a pun: "For evermore adieu, thou royal dazzling
Sun," – on one hand, the word "sun" referred to Louis XIV of France,
the self-proclaimed Sun King, and, on the other, it referred to the son
of James II, the supposed Catholic heir to the British throne. The final
three lines asserted loyalty to the new king and offered a paean to the
common sailor:

> Enough thou mighty god of war,
> Now we sing: "Bless the king,"
> Let us drink to every English tar.

In a ballad almost any battle could be lionized and pumped up into a victory. *The Famous Fight at Malago* was not really famous and was nothing more than a raid by five or six ships on the Spanish port of Malaga in
1656, but the ballad was reprinted several times over the course of fifty
years and was sung for many years thereafter.[34]

The Elevation of Jack Tar

As we have seen in the emergence of the language of Jack Tar, by the mid-eighteenth century the common seaman had come in for special praise in the Anglo-American world as defenders of the island nation and its empire and as the workforce that extended commerce across the globe. The ballads of the seventeenth century had set the pattern for this development, which professional and folk songwriters continued and expanded. Indeed, in the second half of the eighteenth century, and within the context of the wars for empire, this music helped to define what it meant to be English on both sides of the Atlantic. The American Revolution broke the Anglo-American empire in two. The new American nation borrowed and built on the Anglo-American tradition in song on stage and in the forecastle. Americans, both common seamen and common folk, sang many of the same ballads that had been in circulation for at least a century. But they also began to develop their own patriotic maritime tunes, often adapted from British music. By the 1790s two interlaced musical traditions had developed. The British enriched and enhanced the maritime music during the French Revolutionary and Napoleonic Wars; the Americans countered with a patriotic music of their own. Aboard ship and on shore, however, a full panoply of song might be found echoing the themes repeated from the seventeenth-century ballads.

Several maritime songs came to define the British nation and its relationship with the common seaman in the mid-eighteenth century. First among these was *Rule Britannia*, written by Thomas Augustine Arne in 1740 as part of a masque to celebrate the Hanoverian succession at the residence of Frederick, the Prince of Wales. Performed in London in 1745, the song became incredibly popular. The words proclaimed a God-given heritage of freedom blessed with commerce and had a refrain that praised the navy: "Rule, Britannia! Britannia, rule the waves; Britons never shall be slaves!" If *Rule Britannia* was a favorite of the nation in general, then *Heart of Oak* was the favorite of sailors and became something of an unofficial anthem for the British navy. Like *Rule Britannia*, *Heart of Oak* was professionally written for the stage. First performed in 1759, its verses touted the role of sailors in protecting the island of Britain from invasion and its chorus spoke directly to the quality of men in His Majesty's Navy as ready and steady.[35] When Samuel Leech served on the HMS *Macedonian* during the War of 1812 the tune was played to beat the men to quarters in preparation for battle.[36] Less well known, but used repeatedly by naval ships going into action, was *Britons, Strike Home!* which was originally written in 1695 and had as its only lyrics "Britons, strike home! revenge your country's wrongs! / Fight! and record yourselves in Druids' songs!"[37]

Besides music that elaborated on the patriotic tunes inherited from the seventeenth and early eighteenth centuries, a host of new ballads appeared that continued the tradition of featuring the life and travails of Jack Tar. These songs, along with the ballads created earlier, either with the original text or with additions and emendations, were sung both at sea and on land. Like many of the seventeenth-century ballads some of these centered on the separation of lovers; others recounted how the sailor was betrayed by his supposed sweetheart while he was at sea. Representing an interesting twist on the cross-dressing female who joined the navy to follow her lover was *William Taylor*. When "At last the wind blew open her waistcoat, / And exposed her milk-white breast" the female character dressed as a sailor told the captain she had followed her lover, William Taylor, who had been pressed into the navy. The captain replied that the sailor she sought had taken another as his wife. Enraged, the woman "called for her sword and pistol" and "shot sweet William Taylor / With his bride at his right hand." Reiterations of this song would appear for generations thereafter.[38] In the tragic tune known as *The Gosport Tragedy* a sailor got a young maid pregnant only to lure her out to a moor and kill her. However, there was no escape from this crime; at sea the ghost of the dead woman haunted his ship until he confessed his guilt as he was about to die. More ribald tunes also appeared. In one song the captain of the ship began having sexual relations with the wife of one of his sailors only to have the sailor sneak into the bedroom while the captain was sexually preoccupied, steal the captain's uniform, and in disguise go to the captain's house to have his way with the captain's wife in turn. Another song described the hordes of women who streamed aboard naval ships in port and the riotous scenes of sexual activity that followed.[39] One tune was a cautionary tale to "You jolly young Sailors that loves to delight / In Whoring and Drinking both Day and Night" and described how a mariner was robbed by a prostitute, stripped of his clothes, and left in bed with another prostitute who had died from venereal disease.[40] Mid-eighteenth-century ballads could have more serious cautions. In one song a young sailor detailed all the activity, down to the cutting away of masts and rigging, in a vain effort to prevent a shipwreck. The last two stanzas recorded the result:

> The seas they roard like mountains high
> Which staved our boat in pieces small

Of all our lofty standing masts,
  Our fore-mast top stood and that was all:

Now to conclude and make an end,
  I wish I had known as much before,
  I would have chose some other trade,
    And livd contented on the shore.[41]

This type of music crossed the Atlantic. Francis Boardman, who sailed out of Salem, Massachusetts, copied *The Gosport Tragedy* in his logbook, and similar ballads appeared in other maritime journals. The lyrics to the tragedy *William Taylor* appeared in a logbook on a ship out of Boston in 1771, and in a journal kept aboard a Fairhaven whaler in 1817–19.[42] This music, too, was popular in port cities. *Buxom Joan of Lymas's Love to a Jolly Tar* was sung in Philadelphia before the Revolutionary War.[43]

It is against this background of a long history of sailor ballads with a wide variety of messages and the elevation of Jack Tar as a patriotic symbol that we can view American maritime music during the Revolutionary War. Following the pattern of British nationalism was music focused on military prowess and a sense of a separate identity for Americans. However, for common seamen the wide range of sea ballads that had been popular for at least a century retained its appeal.

The American patriotic music contained a potent political message that transcended both sea and land. A few American maritime ballads touted the achievements of naval heroes like John Paul Jones and John Manly.[44] More likely, however, patriotic music focused on land-based achievements and even rhetorical attacks on the king. John Palmer, a seaman who served on privateers during the Revolution, jotted down the words to a song about Bunker Hill. He also noted lyrics that asserted that King George was a tyrant and decried the activities of British officials while praising George Washington: "But Washington shall be the toaste / Grate Washington that gards our Host / from British Rage and Tyranny."[45] Similarly, when Joshua Davis celebrated his twenty-first birthday chained as a captive on a British holding ship in Spithead, he drank a bottle of gin and proudly sang a tune with the refrain "Huzza, huzza, huzza, huzza, for *war* and *Washington*." Although these patriotic songs represented only a small proportion of the music of the American sailor during the Revolutionary War, their political meaning was apparent to both sides. After hearing Davis's song the master-of-arms told the young American, "you d–d rascal, how dare you sing such a rebel song on board of his majesty's ship? If I hear you sing that song again, I will gag you."[46] American prisoners of war often challenged their captors through music. Christopher Hawkins remembered the first night of his captivity aboard a British warship when 200 prisoners crowded into the cable tier sang a number of "patriotic songs." He did not recall the lyrics, but he bragged that their "poetry ... was of the most cutting sarcasm upon the british and their unhallowed cause." The refrain of one song, "For America and all her sons forever will shine," were words that "grated upon the ears of our humane captors in a manner less acceptable than the thunder of heaven." The British threatened to fire on the prisoners if they did not quiet down, to which the American tars retorted, "Fire and be dam'd." The British did not shoot anyone that evening. By the second night the severity of the prisoners' situation dampened spirits and curtailed any further "hilarity."[47] Once at their final prison destination, however, Americans could still taunt the British with song. Aboard the prison hulk *Jersey* in New York harbor the persistent singing of patriotic tunes on the Fourth of July, even after the men had been locked below decks, led to a bloody confrontation where the British used cutlasses to injure several Americans. At Mill Prison in Plymouth, Charles Herbert reported that one night the prisoners were singing and laughing so much that the British became concerned and sent one man to the black hole – solitary confinement – as punishment and threatened to place the rest of the men on half allowance if they persisted in their boisterous behavior.[48]

Whatever the patriotic message of many of these tunes, sailors could just as easily sing apolitical ballads. Herbert did not detail what lyrics the men used, or if the British guards objected to the noise or to the message. In all likelihood, it was a combination of the two. Besides the two patriotic songs, Palmer recorded several other lyrics that fit the general long-standing tenor of seafaring ballads. There were several romantic songs, including one about a young man leaving his love to go fight in the wars. He also wrote down a song about the dangers of the sea:

> from bounding billows flight in motion
> When the Distant Whirlwind Strife
> to the tempest trouble ocean
> Where the seas Contend with Skies.[49]

Timothy Connor's notebook from Mill Prison provides an excellent sampling of the type of songs available to seamen, and prisoners in particular, during the Revolutionary War. We cannot be sure about his reasons or his methodology, but from the context of the manuscript it appears that some of the lyrics were written with broadsheet music in hand (the copy

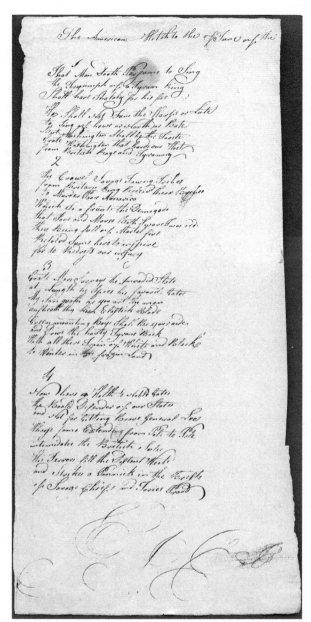

FIGURE 5.1. **"The Americans,"** Coll. 53, Folder 5, Box 1, John Palmer Papers, 1776–86. However dependent on Anglo-American traditions for music, American seamen could also be stridently patriotic. John Palmer served on privateers during the Revolutionary War and recorded a number of different songs in his journal. Some were standard sailor fare, others asserted an American national identity. In this song, called "the Americans", the lyrics decry King George as a tyrant and praise Washington and other American military leaders. Courtesy of Mystic Seaport, G. W. Blunt White Library, Mystic Connecticut.

is clean and neat) and some were composed from memory (with the transcription less precise). Regardless of how Connor kept his notebook, the songs offer a unique archive. Only a handful of the lyrics was patriotically American. *An American New Song* recounted some of the steps in the imperial crisis, especially the Stamp Act and the Tea Act, as examples of British attempts to enslave Americans. The ballad also recited the brave stand of American patriots at Bunker Hill, and resounded with a call for unity and asked the heavens to "protect our love the Sons of Liberty."[50] Yet, oddly, several songs expressed a prewar Anglo-American patriotism touting victories during the French and Indian War, and a few even discussed the Revolutionary War from the British perspective. One sea song described a naval action off the coast of Spain in 1757 and another discussed Highlanders going off to fight the Americans for their king.[51] There were also a few antiwar songs. *The Widow's Lamentation for the Loss of Her Husband in America* began with:

> All true hearted Britons that passing along
> I would have you draw near and attend to my song
> O what terrible news do we hear every day
> Of the lives that are lost in North America.

The lyrics went on to describe fathers and sons killing one another, portraying the conflict as a civil war.[52] The vast majority of Connor's songs dealt with sexual relationships typical of the Anglo-American ballad tradition. Some of these were sentimental, describing parting lovers and even cross-dressing females who sought to join their sweethearts in battle. Driven insane by the loss of her beau, "a lovly Maiden" asked, "Why did my dear jewel cross the ocean / Tost up and down the raging main," and exclaimed:

> See bloddy flags and streamers flying
> Why don't you hear my silent call;
> Now by the Spanish balls he lies dying,
> O don't you hear him expiring call![53]

Many were bawdy, even raunchy. We have already seen in our earlier discussion of swearing that Connor was one of the few sailors to write down the word "fuck." The two songs with that word were part of a host of other ballads he transcribed that described sexual encounters with varying degrees of specificity. *A Tar's Song* has a mariner meet a woman on the street and then engage in sexual intercourse in her chambers, a process described with nautical metaphors such as he "boarded her" and "entered her cabin" so that he could "plum her depth." In short, whatever the nationalist feelings of the American seamen during the Revolutionary War, they sang many of the same songs Anglo-Americans had been singing for more than a century.[54]

In the years after the independence of the United States the British continued to emphasize their Jack Tars' special role in defending the nation. After the French Revolutionary and Napoleonic Wars broke out in the 1790s the British government provided an annual subsidy to songwriter Charles Dibden as he churned out one sea ballad after another. Although Dibden wrote other music, he gained his greatest renown for his maritime work. His appeal remained broad, including audiences of seamen and landsmen. Some of this music emphasized the stereotypical jolly tar. As *Jack in His Element* sang:

> I sails the seas from end to end,
> And leads a joyous life,
> In every mess I find a friend
> In every port a wife.[55]

Dibden, however, often portrayed this lighthearted seaman as always ready and willing to do his duty. The *True English Sailor* began with a carefree "Jack" dancing and singing, making promises "to his lass he'll ne'er fail her," but heading off to sea once his money was spent. This happy-go-lucky approach to life, however, did not affect the sailor's skill at sea: when confronted by a storm "Jack is found working and singing"; and when faced with an enemy ship he would "with broadside and broadside regale her." Ultimately it was his character that made the British Jack Tar an emblem for a nation:

> Tho' careless and headlong, if danger should press,
> And rank'd 'mongst the free list of rovers,
> Yet he'll melt into tears at a tale of distress,
> And prove the most constant of lovers.
>
> To rancour unknown, to no passion a slave
> Nor unmanly, nor mean, nor a railer;
> He's gentle as mercy, as fortitude brave –
> And this is a true English Sailor.[56]

Dibden's work was only a part of a much larger output of British patriotic maritime music during the 1790s and early 1800s. As in the past, individual naval triumphs were celebrated in song. *A New Song on the Total Defeat of the French Fleet* commemorated Horatio Nelson's victory at the Battle of the Nile, and *Nelson's Death and Victory* combined the jubilation in the defeat of the French at Trafalgar with a sense of tragedy in the loss of Nelson in battle:

> Huzza, valiant seamen, huzza, we've gained the day,
> Though lost a bold commander who on the deck did lay;
> With joy we've gained the victory,
> Before me dead I now do see.
> "I die in peace, bless God" said he,
> "The victory is won."

Many of these songs were popular on land and at sea and entered oral tradition. They would be sung long after the events the lyrics described.[57]

Although sailors would join in patriotic tunes with enthusiasm, other maritime songs criticized the treatment of seamen in the British navy. Similar ballads had appeared earlier, but the ideology of the age of revolution provided an additional edge to this music. Some of these songs complained of the impress, others lamented the lack of provision for sailor wives, still others decried the exploitation and treatment of mariners aboard His Majesty's ships. Just as Dibden and others hailed the sacrifices of Jack Tar in defense of the nation, some of those same sailors continued to make their own protest music. The great mutinies of 1797 in Spithead and the Nore led to the creation of many such songs. The lyrics of one of these tunes challenged the celebrationist propaganda of the era:

> If liberty be ours, oh say
> Why are not all protected?
> Why is the hand of ruffian sway
> 'Gainst seamen thus directed?
> Is this your proof of British rights?
> Is this rewarding bravery?
> Oh shame to boast your tar's exploits,
> Then doom those tars to slavery.

A song about the sufferings of Richard Parker's widow – Parker had been executed for leading the mutiny at the Nore – remained a favorite with sailors. The lyrics explained how the widow had to steal Parker's body from its shameful grave between high and low tide and provide it with a proper burial. The song ended with a statement that "Although my Parker was hung for mutiny there were worse men in the wars than he" – a not too subtle reminder of those who abused the common seamen – and offered a plea to the listener to "look on me with an eye of pity, for it is now my only claim." Other protest songs were not directly connected to

events in 1797. *Distressed Men of War* appeared during a brief hiatus
in the conflict with Napoleon Bonaparte in 1802, and outlined some of
the problems of demobilization: the purser and the steward might live
off the gains they had made from shortened rations to the seamen, but
the average Jack would be unemployed and have to become a highway
robber.[58] The context of these songs suggests a maritime origin, although
such protest ballads also appealed to common folk. During this period
many Englishmen were attracted to the revolutionary ideals of liberty. In
1798 officials found two sailors with a copy of a radical songster packed
with pro-French and pro-liberty music. Only one of the songs was maritime in context, which was a parody of *Rule Britannia* that had as its
refrain: "View Britannia, Britannia view the waves, / On which thy darling sons are *slaves!*"[59]

These protest ballads were only a small part of the British musical legacy from the French Revolutionary and Napoleonic Wars. Dibden tunes
playing to the sentimental in songs like *Tom Bowling*, harping on the
frivolous in *Jack in His Element*, or heralding the sacrifices and character of British seamen in *The True English Sailor*, were more important.
Along with the similar lyrics by other composers and songs that trumpeted British victories at sea, they added to an Anglo-American maritime
ballad tradition that had first appeared in print in the seventeenth century. Those older tunes often persisted alongside these newer iterations
of the same themes.

American Legacy

Aboard ships at sea, in taverns, in theaters, and in the streets echoes of
this British music could be heard in the newly independent United States.
There had been some nautical patriotic music during the Revolutionary
War, but not until the 1790s did Americans build and expand on the
Anglo-American musical and theatrical legacy to help create their own
national identity. The timing of this development was crucial. During the
1790s American sailors became increasingly vital to the new republic.
Commerce expanded rapidly as the United States emerged as the greatest
neutral carrier in the world. In the late 1790s the navy became central
to American identity in the Quasi War with France. Experiences in the
opening decade of the nineteenth century only reinforced this development in the conflict with Tripoli and with further commercial impositions
by France and Great Britain. The forced recruitment of American seamen into the British navy through impressment also enhanced national

interest in Jack Tar. It was in these years that maritime patriotic songs appeared in large numbers and several publishers printed songsters packed with nationalist music as well as pirated (printing without authorization) British songs about the life of Jack Tar at sea and on shore. The War of 1812 marked a high water in the ongoing assertion of a strident nationalism in maritime music even as older patterns of borrowing persisted in both the patriotic and non-patriotic songs of the sailorman.[60]

The British influence on American music can be seen in the popularity of Charles Dibden, whose lyrics were sung in theaters, were printed in newspapers, and were sold as individual broadsheets or as a part of larger collections. Sometimes the publisher acknowledged the British character of the sailor in the songs. One editor noted "the genius of Dibden, to divert the reader" by his ability to summarize "the practical philosophy of a British tar, his frankness, his simplicity, his glee, and his very stubbornness."[61] In songsters published around 1800 music written by Dibden and other British composers appeared without attribution and was mixed in with more blatantly American tunes. No doubt many Americans recognized the British origins of *The Sailor's Journal* or *The Flowing Can*, which had the words "A Sailor's life is a life of woe" that was "Bless'd with a smiling can of grog." But because these songs were not specifically identified as British, it was easy to assume that the words applied to American seamen, many of whom packed the theater during the performances.[62] Whether he intended it or not, besides sentimentalizing and personalizing the image of Jack Tar, several of Dibden's works had democratic overtones. Most American imprints of *Tom Bowling* contained a verse that offered the somber reminder that death was a great equalizer, dispatching both "Kings and Tars."[63]

The American patriotic music also borrowed heavily from the British. *Rise Columbia* spoke directly to American republican values, but was patterned after *Rule Britannia*: it heralded freedom in the United States, while its refrain announced the new nation as a great maritime power.

> Rise Columbia! Brave and free!
> Thy thunder when in Battle hurl'd
> Shall rule the billows of the sea.
> And bid defiance to the world.[64]

Susanna Rowson's career spanned both sides of the Atlantic as an actress, as an author, and as a composer. Written in Philadelphia, the main stanza of her *The Sailor's Landlady* followed British practice of celebrating the extremes of the jolly tar's life, emphasizing how the tar faced tempests at

FIGURE 5.2. "Wives & Sweethearts or, Saturday Night," 1792, Isaiah Thomas Broadside Ballads Project. Great Britain and the United States shared many elements of their maritime culture, including sailor songs. This print depicts seamen aboard a ship toasting their sweethearts and wives. Surrounding the illustration are stanzas of a Charles Dibden song. Although published in England, the print was probably purchased in Boston. Courtesy of the American Antiquarian Society, Worcester, Massachusetts.

sea and engaged in sprees ashore. Yet even these otherwise frivolous lyrics had a chorus with a resounding praise for "America, commerce, and freedom."[65] The British influence can also be seen in Rowson's patriotic songs in support of the American navy. She created at least three versions of a song commemorating the defeat of the *L'Insurgente* by Thomas Truxton in the USS *Constellation*. In one she opened with a declaration that freedom's banner defied "each foe whom her rights would invade" and that "Columbia's brave sons swore those rights to maintain." In another she had the sailors sing that having left their sweethearts and wives, "Each jolly Tar a volunteer, Resolv'd" to clear the American coast of French privateers "or die in the *Constellation*." In the third she lauded the bravery of Truxton and "his jovial hands" for protecting commerce.[66] Stage managers pandered to this patriotism. To celebrate the completion of the super frigate, the USS *Constitution*, John Hodgkinson produced a special "Musical Piece" called "The Launch, or Huzza for the Constitution" that played in late 1797 and in 1798 "to overflowing houses" in Boston. "The piece," newspapers reported, "is said to contain a great diversity of national character" and "will afford the lovers of national sentiment a well timed and high seasoned entertainment."[67]

Both the British influence and the interest in the common sailor continued during the opening decade of the nineteenth century and into the War of 1812, playing themselves out in song and on the stage, where American mariners, just as British seamen in their own country, were held up as defenders of the nation and as the labor force vital to commerce. Several issues kept the American tar in the public eye. The war with Tripoli that began in 1801 filled the newspapers with stories about the navy and its seamen, especially after the capture of the USS *Philadelphia* and imprisonment of 300 American mariners. The burning of the *Philadelphia* by Stephen Decatur and prolonged fighting off Tripoli enhanced the reputation of the navy and its seamen. Francis Scott Key wrote a song remarkably similar to his later *Star Spangled Banner*, joining the Revolutionary heroes with the heroes who fought against Tripoli.[68] The persistent threats to the ideal of free trade by both the French and the British strengthened concern with commerce and the men who worked American ships. When the Republicans around the nation's capital celebrated the Fourth of July in 1807, one of their toasts was to commerce, followed by the song *To America, Commerce and Freedom*.[69] Nothing, however, riveted popular attention on mariners more than the issue of impressment. During their wars with the French in the 1790s and early 1800s the British impressed thousands of American seamen into His Majesty's Navy in complete disregard of the flag of the United States. On the same day that Virginians toasted commerce, celebrants in Westchester County, New York, drank to "*The infant navy of the U. S. – May it soon be able to protect our seamen,*" followed by a song entitled the "*Jolly Tar.*"[70] When William Duane published the *American Republican Harmonist* in 1803, stuffed with Republican partisan lyrics, several songs touted the importance of commerce, bemoaned British trade impositions, and complained of the "groans of our impressed seamen." Duane even printed a parody of *Rule Britannia* that declared that "Columbia ever shall be free" and proudly called on listeners to "View Columbia, view the waves," followed by a derisive "And think on Britain's conquer'd slaves."[71] Joining the issue of free trade and the need to protect the sailor, *The Highway of Nations* in 1810 requested that the "jolly tar, the ocean to repair," so that

> By the mouths of our cannon in thunder declare,
> > That we scorn to be slaves, and will die for our freedom.
> > Then our commerce again,
> > Shall swarm o'er the main,
> No foe shall molest, and no tyrant restrain;
> For sooner our blood shall encrimson the waves,
> Than we'll barter our rights and consent to be slaves.[72]

The appearance of this music on stage and in print attests to its popularity with Americans on land. Evidence from journals and logbooks also demonstrated its popularity with the object of all this affection – the American Jack Tar. Benjamin Carter, who served as a physician on a voyage to China in 1799–1800, noted the musical scores of more than twenty songs. Some of these he may have written from memory, others were probably heard aboard ship. He noted the music for patriotic tunes like *Washington's March*, *Hail Columbia*, and *Adams and Liberty*. This last song defended commerce and had American "cannon declare the free charter of trade." Although these songs might identify Carter as a Federalist, he also recorded more republican music such as *Liberty Hall*, the *Marseillaise*, and *Carmagnole*.[73] Charles P. Clinton copied the lyrics to *Adams and Liberty* in his journal during a voyage to the Pacific in the opening decade of the nineteenth century.[74] With his spelling indicating that he probably remembered the words from oral renditions, seaman Joshua Gott's commonplace book contained several songs. *A Song for Liberty* began:

> In Libertys care, Now we are bent for to join
> Come Loss of a bumper of noble good wine

In a tost to that brave and magnaminas [magnanimous?] son
The bravest of heroes the good Washington

Gott also included the words to *Burgoyns Defeat*.[75] After the British seized the *Prudent* in the Indian Ocean in 1804 the logbook keeper wrote a few lines from one of the most popular American patriotic tunes: "Yankee doodle had a Wife She was hard of hearing / he put a Swivel on her Back and sent him a privateering."[76] John Baker also used *Yankee Doodle* for political commentary and wrote down a song complaining of the Embargo restrictions.[77] While celebrating Christmas in prison in Tripoli the common seamen sang patriotic songs. One directly addressed their plight, proclaiming that on Barbary's remote "pirate coast" American sailors had been enslaved by "a miscreant host," were denied "the rights of man," and had to say "Adieu" to "blest Liberty!"[78]

If American sailors were familiar with patriotic and political music, they also knew many more songs that reflected the rich Anglo-American ballad heritage. The variety of these tunes is astounding. John Baker transcribed a series of romantic songs that pulled on current and more distant British sources. His *Address to Young Men* had recently appeared in a Scottish magazine as *The Married Man*. He also noted the ballad *Mary's Dream*, a Scottish tune written more than a quarter of a century earlier. Reaching back even further in time, under the heading "Song by Waller," Baker copied the words from the seventeenth-century poem "Go Lovely Rose."[79] The back of a logbook kept in 1789 and 1790 had several songs scribbled in it, ranging from lines supposedly *printed in the year* one thousand" under the heading "Fragments of ancient Ballads from the *Salem Gazette*," to a song written by John Wilmot, Earl of Rochester, in the seventeenth century, to lyrics about earlier British naval triumphs, and to tunes by Thomas Arne and Charles Dibden about the life of Jack Tar.[80] Charles Clinton also recorded a few Dibden songs. He included other British lyrics as well, such as *Hood Triumphant*, with the opening lines "Come all ye loyal Britons," commemorating Admiral Samuel Hood's destruction of the French fleet at Toulon in 1793.[81] Probably dating from the Revolutionary War, *The Rochester Lass* was about an English sailor pressed into the British Navy to fight against the "rebels."[82] Some of this music had a peculiar Anglo-American bent. There were several versions of the ballad *Pretty Sally*. Each contrasted a poor suitor's efforts to woo Sally, who was pretty and rich. In an English rendition, the suitor was a sailor from Dover; Clinton's version featured "a young sailor from Boston."[83] Similarly Clinton also remembered the words to a song

FIGURE 5.3. **Music from Log of the *Ann and Hope*,** kept by Benjamin Carter, 1799–1800, Ink on Manuscript, Ship's Log Collection Ms 828 B1 F5, Rhi X17 1905. Some men who went to sea copied the words of their favorite songs. Benjamin Carter, who served as a physician on a voyage to China in 1799–1800, included in his journal the musical scores of over twenty songs. On this page he noted tunes to both whimsical and martial music. Courtesy of Rhode Island Historical Society, Providence, Rhode Island.

by Michael Arne, Thomas Arne's son, composed several decades earlier, that was popular on both sides of the Atlantic: in England it was known by its first line, "Come loose every sail to the breeze," but in the United States it was called *Homeward Bound*.[84] The sources of several songs in Clinton's journal are harder to detect. *The Poor Cabin Boy* might be of American origin – the cabin boy returned to Boston after a shipwreck. It, too, though, might be a transplant with American singers inserting Boston for an English seaport. As was true with earlier maritime ballads, bawdy themes remained popular. In the lyrics of a song set in the English countryside, a seventeen-year-old farmer's daughter related a story of how she went to find a ghost on the road to London only to be met by a young "swain" named Colin.

> Says he my Dear girl what Disturbs so your mind
> i told him i come this damned Ghost for to find
> then he kissed my lips and hugged me so Close
> And then touched me with something he said was the Ghost

The young maid returned home and did not tell her parents anything about the encounter, but she must have enjoyed meeting with the supernatural: "To Each Evening when Dark[,] stead of my tea & toast / I skipt down the Lane & i Lay Collins Ghost."[85]

Regardless of the popularity of this non-patriotic music at sea and on land, we should not discount the significance of nationalist maritime songs, especially in moments of international crisis. During the War of 1812 patriotic maritime music became even more important. Much to the surprise of many Republican leaders, the war quickly devolved into a disaster for the army. In comparison, the early months of the war saw a series of brilliant American victories at sea. As the conflict dragged on, and at best became a stalemate on land, several naval triumphs still occurred, even if they were somewhat less frequent. Moreover, within the continent of North America two of the most significant victories occurred on freshwater in fleet actions on Lake Erie (1813) and Lake Champlain (1814). In short, if Americans were going to sing about their military prowess they almost had to center their attention on the navy.[86] Nearly every victory at sea was quickly followed with public celebrations punctuated by song. After the USS *Constitution* sank the HMS *Guerriere* Bostonians held a public dinner for Captain Isaac Hull and his officers that included "An original song to the tune 'Ye mariners of England.'"[87] New Yorkers invited the entire crew of the USS *United States* to a dinner held in their honor to commemorate the capture of the HMS *Macedonian*. It, too, featured a new song, the *Yankee Frolic*, which opened by challenging Great Britain's naval prowess:

> No more of your blathering nonsense
>   'Bout the Nelsons of Johnny Bull;
> I'll sing you a song 'pon my conscience,
>   'Bout Jones, Decatur, and Hull.[88]

Several theaters also celebrated the naval success. In early September 1812 artist, playwright, and composer William Dunlap added verses on Hull's victory to his *Yankee Chronology*, originally written for the Fourth of July earlier that year. He also expanded the title to *Yankee Chronology and Huzza for the Constitution*. The July Fourth version had described feats of American valor in the Revolutionary War. In anticipation of similar success the chorus had declared, "Then Huzza! for the sons of Columbia so free! / They are lords of the soil – they'll be lords of the sea!" Isaac Hull had confirmed the veracity of the last part of that chorus, even if his uncle's surrender of Detroit appeared to deny the first.[89] A later rendition, written by someone in Boston, changed the title again, substituting "Huzza for the American Navy!" for "Huzza for the Constitution," with more new verses describing victories by the USS *Wasp*, the USS *Peacock*, the USS *United States*, and the USS *Constitution* a second time (over the HMS *Java*).[90] Dunlap also produced a short "musical interlude" recounting the arrival of the news of Hull's victory in New York under the title *Yankee Chronology* that included its namesake song, as well as *The Freedom of the Seas* and *Yankee Tars*. This skit and song were performed repeatedly in theaters in several cities throughout the United States.[91] *Yankee Chronology* was only one of many tunes reported in the newspapers inspired by the success of the American navy. Moreover, publishers printed special songsters packed with naval patriotic lyrics.[92]

However patriotic and even jingoistic this music appeared, much of it relied on the Anglo-American ballad tradition. This relationship should not be surprising considering that another patriotic anthem from this era – *The Star Spangled Banner* – used music from an English drinking song. Maritime tunes often had both American and British roots. Numerous verses were added to *Yankee Doodle* and several songs with that tune – which probably was originally British – were written about American tars.

> The British long have rul'd the seas,
>   With haughty gasconading,
> And chaunting songs, their feats to praise
>   While others they're degrading.

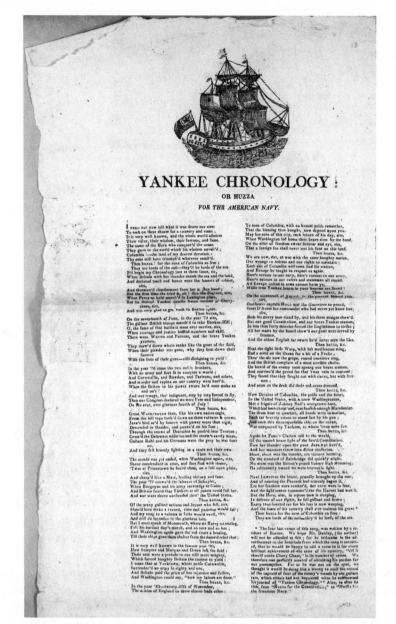

FIGURE 5.4. "Yankee Chronology, or Huzza for the American Navy, Songs, Ballads, &c. In Three Volumes. Purchased from a Ballad Printer and Seller in Boston," 1811–18. During the War of 1812 Americans printed numerous broadsheet ballads celebrating American naval prowess. William Dunlap's *Yankee Chronology* began as a song to celebrate the Fourth of July at the opening of the war, predicting great victories on land and sea. The army however, experienced one disaster after another, while the navy won a series of victories. Later iterations of the song, including this one printed in Boston, rehearsed American triumphs on land in the Revolution and then focused on American maritime prowess in the War of 1812. Courtesy of the American Antiquarian Society, Worcester, Massachusetts.

> Yankee doodle, fire away,
> > Cannon, loud as thunder,
> From brave DECATUR, JONES AND HULL,
> > Makes Johnny Bull knock under.

Other songs built on the heritage of the American Revolution: *Hull's Naval Victory* had as its tune *Paul Jones Victory*. The British musical influence, especially the long shadow of Charles Dibden, remained powerful. A song about Perry's victory on Lake Erie was based on Dibden's *Abraham Newland*.[93] A ballad called *Saturday Night at Sea* opened with two stanzas stolen directly from Dibden's *Sweethearts and Wives*. Instead of following Dibden's lead and sentimentally discussing both the sailors' ships and the loved ones they left behind, the lyrics proclaimed the heroic achievements of the "brave Yankee tars." Dibden ended his ballad with the sailors having finished their can of grog and heading for their hammocks. The American lyrics had a more rousing conclusion and called on the nation to unite "and rally round the standard of *Free Trade and Sailors' Rights*."[94] Edward C. Holland insisted that any similarity between the chorus in his *Rise Columbia Brave and Free* and the chorus of another American song, *Rise Columbia*, was coincidental. However, he ignored the connection that both songs may have had to *Rule Britannia*.[95] Few patriotic tunes had as strong a connection to the Anglo-American ballad tradition as *John Bull & Brother Jonathan, or the Seven Naval Victories*, which billed itself as "*A new song to an old tune*." With the refrain of "Derry, down," it was one of several ditties bragging of American naval prowess during the War of 1812 that used the same refrain and harked back to a seventeenth-century English ballad. "Derry, down's" lineage could be traced from its first appearance in print in the 1680s through eighteenth-century Britain, across the Atlantic to colonial America, and into the Revolutionary War. This music appeared repeatedly in the early republic, sometimes with political meaning and sometimes not. Having gone through countless reiterations and additional verses, it was almost to be expected that some wits would rely on it to brag about American naval success.[96]

Whatever its origins, if American patriotic naval music was popular on land, it was even more popular with sailors because it carried a personal and potent message: this war was being fought for them. Robert Stevenson Coffin made this connection explicit in a song he wrote while a prisoner of war that called for American tars to be free "To traverse the sea."[97] Just as had their fathers, American sailors like Coffin turned to music as a pastime and as a form of resistance when they had been incarcerated by the British.[98] After being captured by one of His Majesty's ships, Josiah Cobb's shipmates spent the evenings in storytelling and singing. At first, "The singing was made up of such songs as seamen generally have by heart, and can rattle off from memory; in general, detailing sea adventures, with a sprinkling of some love affair, ... and enough of the superstitious to insure their belief." When the privateersmen began to sing about American victories, British sailors attempted to drown them out with songs of their own navy's success.[99] Alden White kept a notebook aboard a prison ship in 1813 with handwriting exercises, poems, songs, and stories. The songs ranged from sentimental ditties with some sexual innuendo to military and patriotic songs like *Major Andre* and *Decatur's Victory*. He also composed some lyrics of his own.[100] American prisoners of war occasionally engaged in musical exhibitions, especially on holidays. Aboard the prison-ship *Crown Prince* in the Thames River, Americans opened their celebration of the Fourth of July in 1813 with *Yankee Doodle* and ended it with a series of songs including *The Impressment of an American Sailor Boy*. This last tune "drew tears from the eyes of our generous hearted sailors" and subsequently found its way onto a broadsheet in New York City.[101] Dartmoor prisoners commemorated Washington's birthday in 1814 with "Fifes, flutes, bugles, trumpets, violins, and clarionets, of all sizes and keys, played to perfection, Hail Columbia, Yankee Doodle, and Washington's March" in a procession that passed through various parts of the prison. A dinner was followed by a song written especially for the occasion.[102] Prisoners also created lyrics for political purposes to ridicule Americans who volunteered for the British navy and to decry the failure of Reuben Beasley, the American agent in Great Britain during the war, for his supposed refusal to provide more relief for the men. This music contributed to the growing tension that erupted into the so-called Dartmoor Massacre when British troops fired at American sailor prisoners of war on April 6, 1815.[103] Of course sailors who had not been captured also sang patriotic music. While the USS *Essex* and the HMS *Phoebe* lay at anchor near each other in neutral Valparaiso, seamen aboard both ships regaled each other with nationalist songs in the buildup to their dramatic battle on March 28, 1814.[104]

Published and unpublished sources before 1815 demonstrated that American maritime music included songs that spoke to a nationalist identity in the United States and songs that described the hardships on land and at sea faced by Jack Tar. Both types of music derived from an older transatlantic Anglo-American ballad tradition. As one mariner explained: "The two great ruling passions among the British sailors and the American Sailors" were the same, "*love of their country*, and *love of the fair sex*," and "these two subjects alone entered into all of their songs." Although the non-patriotic music covered more than just romance, this statement captured an essential truth. Americans were also aware of the connection of their songs to British music. The same sailor explained that the British tar sang of "the victories of Benbow, How, Jervase and Nelson," while American seamen sang "the same songs, only substituting the names of Preble, Hull, Decatur and Bainbridge, Perry and Macdonough." He continued: "Our men parodied all the English national songs. '*Rule Britannia, rule the waves*,' was '*Rule Columbia*,' &c. '*God save great George, our King*,' was sung by our boys, '*God save great Madison*.'"[105] Both British and American patriotic music fit into the Anglo-American ballad tradition. As far back as the seventeenth century ballads had trumpeted the sailor as a defender of the British nation and as an agent of empire in transporting goods across the wide ocean. As can be seen in the work of Charles Dibden and others, these themes became especially important in Great Britain during the French Revolutionary and Napoleonic Wars as Jack Tar was elevated to the status of a national icon. The music that appeared in the new United States transposed these same ideas onto the American scene, only with an additional emphasis on liberty and free trade. All of this maritime music appealed to those who remained at home as well as to those who plied the ocean waves. Although on balance the patriotic music pales in volume to the more mundane and varied songs about the world of Jack Tar, both derived from the same Anglo-American ballad tradition. Moreover, however frequently sailors may have sung romantic or bawdy tunes, the patriotic maritime music became especially prominent in moments of crisis such as the Quasi War, the conflict with Tripoli, the problems with commerce and impressment, and, most strikingly, the War of 1812.

The Heyday of Sailor Song

The pattern of American maritime music established before 1815 persisted throughout the antebellum period. What some observers might call the heyday of sailor song merely extended and adjusted the music that had appeared in print during the seventeenth century, was elaborated on in the British empire of the eighteenth century, and was inherited by the new American nation.[106] Based on a well-worn Anglo-American ballad tradition, the songs of the sailorman continued to help define national identity, while they articulated a nautical culture cherished by those at sea and those who remained ashore. There was, however, at least one significant change concerning maritime music during this period. The use of shanties – work songs seamen created to organize heavy tasks that necessitated coordination – increased. Moreover, we can begin to draw some distinctions between shanties on one hand, and the popular stage-produced maritime music and forebitters – forecastle songs composed and sung by sailors at sea – on the other. Although all of this music had pre-1815 antecedents, shanties, reminiscent of some earlier ballads, often were bawdy and spoke more directly to the hard life of the mariner at sea and on land. Stage songs and forebitters, like many other earlier ballads, tended to be more sentimental in the antebellum era. This distinction may have been the result of the changing attitudes toward women and sexuality in the nineteenth century. Sailors who might shout out all kinds of salacious comments while working aboard ship may have been reluctant to write those words down in a record that might later be seen by loved ones at home. By the same token, noting bawdy lyrics in a journal or performing them on stage became increasingly unlikely in an age we call Victorian. This distinction may also help us to understand why there is a difference in the nature of the sources between shanties and the other forms of maritime music. Manuscripts with work songs are scarce and we must rely on memory and oral renditions in the twentieth century to study shanties. In contrast, because of the logbook's changing nature, we can find many forebitters copied into the growing number of journals kept during the pre–Civil War era. Likewise, while a huge repertoire of all kinds of music was produced at this time, lyrics with nautical themes continued to be printed in songsters and performed on stage. In short, whatever the differences within the forms of maritime music, sea-based and shore-side interest in sailor songs remained acute and may have actually increased with the rise of the age of Romanticism.

Shanties were an important component of the songs of the sailor-man and during the American antebellum period their use seems to have expanded rapidly. These work songs had a long history and were mentioned as early as the fifteenth century. Thereafter the evidence is scanty, but in all likelihood singing accompanied group work aboard Anglo-American ships. Shanteyman Stan Hugill argued that the British navy did not allow shanties during its wars with France in the eighteenth and nineteenth centuries. It is unclear if the new U.S. Navy had a similar policy after it was established. Whatever the official naval regulations, few commentators mentioned shanties until the 1830s. By then they seem to have become widespread. Richard Henry Dana Jr. remembered almost a dozen "songs for capstan and falls," as he called shanties. In his wake several other first-person accounts mentioned this rhythmic work music. As Dana explained, "A song is as necessary to sailors as drum and fife to a soldier. They can't pull in time, or pull with a will, without it."[107]

If mariners really could not "pull in time with a will, without it," why did the shanty take so long to become a regular part of the American maritime experience? One explanation can be found in the changing nature of the shipping industry. Before 1815 American merchant ships were relatively small. After 1815, with the development of the Baltimore clipper, ships grew in size with huge spreads of canvas. This meant more backbreaking toil, increased use of man-driven machinery to move and adjust sails and rigging, and a greater demand for coordinated labor. The length of voyages also made a difference. After 1815 more American ships began to scour the globe in pursuit of goods and markets. One aspect of this development was the China trade. Another was a voyage like Dana's to California. Still another was the growth of the whaling industry. All three of these examples called for larger ships, more time at sea, and bigger crews. As Dana made clear, the labor did not end on these cruises once the ship reached its destination. Indeed, some of the hardest work would be in preparing and loading hides (in Dana's case), or in killing and processing whales for the men who hunted the leviathan of the seas. But even in ships involved in the China trade the labor could be intense: many of the ships in this commerce had to first obtain goods for exchange, and this often entailed work like killing seals for their skins on distant coasts. All of these endeavors meant hauling and lifting, as well as manning huge sailing ships with attendant additional labor concerning the rigging and sails. Under these conditions the shanty became almost essential.[108]

Dana was not only one of the first sailor writers to mention shanties – although not by name – he also suggested how and why Americans began using these work songs. Shortly after his arrival in California he compared the crew of an American ship to an Italian one they encountered. The Italian ship had three times the men of an American crew for a ship of the same size. Yet because the Italians were inefficient in working their vessel they took twice as long as they should have to get under way. There was one area, however, where the Italians outdid the Yankee tars: "lightening their labors in the boats by their songs." Dana blamed this difference on the fact that "Americans are a time and money saving people" who had not "as a nation learned that music may be 'turned to account.'" On the far Californian coast some Americans, however, did learn this lesson. Before the year had passed, Dana and his shipmates were heaving and hauling to music as they loaded hides with a "chorus [that] seemed almost to raise the decks of the ship." Once he saw they had worn out their songs by repetition, Dana was glad when another American ship joined them and they learned more shanties from the new arrivals, who used "their boat-songs" to keep time with their oars. Rejuvenated with novel lyrics, Dana believed that "this timely reinforcement of songs hastened our work several days." In other words, Dana described for us a part of the process whereby the shanty spread: American seamen learned the value of the shanty from others and from each other.[109]

Seamen did not have to brave Cape Horn and go to California to learn about work songs. They could find examples of this use of music much closer to home. Both free and slave African Americans used song while they labored. The call and response of the shanty and many of its rhythms were similar to these work songs. Anglo-American sailors in the eighteenth century, and earlier, would have been familiar with slave music because many British and American ships were involved in the slave trade or brought goods in and out of the colonies in the West Indies, where the vast majority of the population was enslaved. Moreover, slavery existed in all of the British North American colonies before the Revolutionary War, continued after the war in the United States in the South, and even persisted well into the nineteenth century in several Northern states. In each of these areas, black slaves interacted with sailors in port by laboring along the docks loading and unloading ships. There were also slaves, as well as free blacks, who served as sailors on British and American ships during this period. After the Revolution the number of free blacks in the Anglo-American maritime labor force increased dramatically with slaves the British had freed during the war, with emancipated African Americans from Northern states, and even with manumitted blacks and escaped slaves from the South. There was thus ample opportunity for white seamen to hear slave work songs before the great spread of the shanty. In all probability Anglo-American merchant seamen had borrowed from free and enslaved black work songs before 1815. The years between the American Revolution and 1815 may well have been a gestation period as thousands of newly freed African Americans joined the merchant marine of both the United States and Great Britain, bringing with them their tradition of work songs that seemed to explode onto the Anglo-American maritime scene in the decades after the War of 1812.[110] Naval surgeon Augustus A. Adee made these connections explicit in 1840 in a letter to his wife when he described the crew hauling his grounded ship off a sand bar "singing the various songs in vogue among negroes and merchant sailors and which you hear about the wharves in New York when they are employed in taking in or discharging cargoes."[111]

Whatever the influence of the changes in shipping practices and the presence of African American seamen on the spread of shanties in the antebellum period, this music did draw on older British and American sources that included earlier work songs, as well as traditional folk music. As a part of the British heritage, many of the shanty tunes had an Irish flavor and shantymen might even imitate an Irish brogue as they sang the stanzas between the choruses and timed the hauling and pulling. This connection appeared in *We're All Bound to Go*, with music that was Irish in origin and words that discussed the Irish immigrant experience in the 1840s. Some versions of the popular *Leave Her Johnny, Leave Her* were so Irish that they sounded almost like a jig. Scottish music also influenced sailor work songs. *Hieland Laddie* had a title suggestive of its source and derived its tune from march and dance melodies from Scotland. A few shanties were reminiscent of earlier English ballads. The lyrics of *A Rovin* described a progression of advances of a seaman on a young woman that was similar to lines in Thomas Heywood's *Rape of Lucrece* from the seventeenth century, and a series of ballads that followed after. Other English songs could also be used as shanties. *Spanish Ladies* appeared in the eighteenth century as a British naval song and was adapted as a sailor work song in the nineteenth century. Shanties could have more recent and American sources. *Shenandoah* was a land-based American folk song of obscure origin that wended its way into the merchant marine to provide rhythmic coordination for heavy work aboard ships.[112]

Most shanties centered on either sexual activity or the mariners' trials and tribulations on land and at sea. In fact, Stan Hugill repeatedly admitted that he avoided the more vulgar language in the shanties he published.[113] Besides containing language Hugill believed unprintable in the 1960s, like earlier Anglo-American bawdy ballads, shanties frequently described women with ship metaphors and depended on sexual innuendo. In *Roll, Boys Roll!* the shantyman called out that Miss Lucy Loo was "lovely up aloft, an' she's lovely down below," and in a crude double entendre asked the captain, "how do yer stow yer cargo?" – a reference to the labor of the crew and, as the answer and context made clear, sexual relations with Miss Lucy Loo. The captain responded: "Some I stow for'ard, boys, an' some I stow arter." There was even a shanty called *The Fire Ship*, a much amended version of the seventeenth-century ballad, that included the lines "I handled her, I dangled her, an' found to my surprise, / She wuz nothin' but a fire ship, rigged up in disguise."[114] Drinking alcohol was also a major theme for shanties as in *Drunken Sailor* and *Whiskey Johnny*, with lines like "What shall we do wi' a drunken sailor" and "Whiskey is the life of man."[115] Combining sex and drink often led to the exploitation of seamen, and a host of shanties narrated the woes of sailors awakening after imbibing too much and having an amorous encounter only to find their pockets empty, or worse, gone because their clothes had been stolen. As *The New York Gals* cautioned:

> Now all ye bully sailormen,
> Take warnin' when ashore,
> Or else ye'll meet some charmin' gal
> Who's nothing but a whore.
>
> Yer hard-earned cash will disappear,
> Your rig an' boots as well,
> For Yankee gals are tougher than
> The other side o' Hell!

But even this poor sailor who had to leave lodgings "With a flour barrel for a suit" might have been better off than the seaman who awoke after a night of debauchery aboard a ship heading for a port on the other side of the world.[116]

This work music did not have to be bawdy or describe a sailor's bad habits. Shanties also dealt with shipboard experiences. *The Bosun's Alphabet* wound its way through every letter of the alphabet with each line a lesson in seamanship: "A is for the anchor ... B is for the bowsprit ...."[117] Some shanties simply focused on the task at hand with a few nonsense lines thrown in:

> Haul on the bowline, Kitty is my darlin',
> Haul on the bowline, Kitty lives in Liverpool,
> Haul on the bowline, the old man is growlin',
> Haul on the bowline, it's a far cry from payday,
> Haul on the bowline, so early in the morning.[118]

Many of the shipboard shanties dealt with the hard usage of the crew by officers. In *Leave Her, Johnny Leave Her*, sung as a ship was returning to port, the verses complained about the captain and mate, lambasted the food, decried the ship's sailing qualities, and even lamented the bad weather. All of these trials made for hard work and a long voyage.[119] Although the majority of shanties followed the more bawdy and rough course inherited from the Anglo-American ballad tradition, a few shanties were sentimental and nationalistic. The romantic-sounding *Shenandoah* addressed the issue of westward expansion and the longing for a return to an idealized valley in western Virginia: "Oh Shenandoah I long to hear you, / Way hay, you rolling river." Some versions centered on the love for a Native American woman; others were about any woman the singer cared to bring into the lyrics.[120] Blatant patriotism can be found in songs about the Mexican-American War, like *Santiana*, which declared that "Santiana was a damn fine man" and then used a nice nautical reference to declare, "Till he fouled hawse with Old Uncle Sam."[121]

If some shanties were not bawdy or focused on the sailor's abuse of alcohol, then the reverse was also true: some forecastle and stage songs had sexual or course content. In Thomas Delano's journal kept on a number of voyages from 1817 to 1819 are several songs with suggestive content. One began:

> I Am A young Virgin just born and bread
> And I have as Curious A Maiden head
> As ever a young man took in hand
> besides I have forty pounds in land.

This young woman was then courted by a host of different tradesmen, ultimately choosing a sailor, saying, "Tis him is [has] my heart and my maidenhead to boot."[122] Other songs with sexually suggestive material were written into journals, and some described the abuse of sailors on shore and aboard ship. Likewise, several forebitters referred to the sailors' fondness for drink.[123] Antebellum stage songs relied more on suggestion in dealing with sexual themes. Occasionally songs performed in theaters described how ladies of the evening took advantage of drunken sailors.[124]

While shanties emphasized the risqué, excessive drinking, and the hard life of seamen, and some forebitters and stage songs included the same themes, during the antebellum era most forecastle and professionally produced songs, paralleling themes developed in popular music in general, were more sentimental. That sentimentality could be expressed either in emphasizing romantic attachments with women, or in idealizing the life of the sailor and the majesty of the ocean.[125]

Reaching back to story lines repeated for centuries, many of the forecastle and stage songs often centered on the sailor and his sweetheart separating upon his departure or reuniting upon his return. In *The Captain Calls All Hands* the female character asked her sailor love why he had to go "fighting with strangers" in war and implored him to remain "at home free from all dangers." Of course he left to do his duty and the disconsolate young woman threw herself on the ground crying. Many of these songs were bittersweet and dripping with sentiment. It is hard to imagine more saccharine lyrics than those in *The Sequel to Will Watch* that described the parting of "Brave Will" from his beloved Susan as he left to fight in the navy.

> 'Twas her hand tied his handkerchief when they last parted
> 'Twas her bosom pressed his as they stood on the beach
> 'Twas his lips that kissed off the fond tear that started
> And did for his Susan each blessing beseech.

When "Will" died in battle his Susan "Heaved a sigh and turned pale." Soon she expired from grief so that they could share a grave "held sacred and dear by the crew" and upon which "the moonbeams enclouded / Is a tear drop for Will and his Susan so [true]." In *Bright Phoebe* a sailor returned to find "Death had my dear companion slain," leaving him "foresaken and forelorn." In the conclusion the sailor blamed himself for his loss because he had abandoned Phoebe to go to sea. *The Dark-Eyed Sailor* had a more pleasant ending but was just as sentimental. A mariner invited "a comely young lady fair" to join him in a walk. She declined and said that her dark-eyed sailor had left three years before and that she would not be with any other man. Although she had harsh words for this brash seaman, she also offered him a coin to drink to the health of her William. As it turned out, the rake was really William in disguise. He revealed himself and they lived happily ever after "in a cottage neat by the river side." The song ended with a moral for young women: "So girls prove true while your lovers are away / For a cloudy morning oft brings a pleasant day."[126]

Forecastle and stage songs could also sentimentally revel in life at sea and brag about the tar's occupation. In 1847 a mariner recorded a paean to the sailor's life that began with:

> The sea the sea the open sea
> The blue the fresh the ever free
> Without a mark without a bound
> It runneth the earth's wide regions round
> It plays with clouds and mocks the skys
> Or like a cradled creature lies.

The ballad continued by proclaiming that the sailor "never was on dull tame shore / But what I loved the great sea more," and concluded that after fifty years as a mariner the singer hoped that "death when ever it comes for me / Must come on the deep and boundless sea." Several songs detailed the nature of the whaling enterprise in stirring words. Proud of their occupation, mariners disparaged other trades. All the farmer knew how to do, explained one song, was cut grass and weeds, "While we long jack hearts of gold / plow the ocean through." The farmers took their suppers "And into bed they do crawl / While we long jack hearts of gold / Stand many a bitter squall." The song portrayed sailors as real men who were attractive to "pretty damsels," especially because seamen brought home gold and silver "and will make our courtships flourish." Reminiscent of another seventeenth-century song, two versions of *The Tarry Trousers* from the 1840s featured a dialogue in which a mother tried to dissuade a daughter from marrying a sailor. One version has the mother tell the daughter that "sailors are given to roaming" and "will leave you brokenhearted." The other was more explicit about the sailor's shortcomings, exclaiming that seamen "do curse and swear" and waste their money, "First to an ale house then to a whore." The daughter countered by proclaiming that sailors were men of honor who "weather the wind and storm / To keep our country safe from harm." The first version concluded with the young woman running off to be with her love, while the second had the mother admit that most mariners "Are a noble set of nice young men." In both, the final portrait of seamen is positive.[127]

Sailors would appreciate the daughter's defense of her sweetheart because it carried a patriotic message. Several forecastle songs were blatantly nationalistic, although perhaps without the same fervor as had appeared during the War of 1812. That conflict remained important, however, as a symbol of the sailor's support for the nation. *Ye Parliament of England* rehearsed the maritime causes of the War of 1812:

> You first confined our commerce,
>   And said our ships shan't trade
> You next impressed our seamen,
>   And used them as your slaves.

The lyrics also recounted the naval victories of the war. Other songs, like *The Constitution and Guerriere*, relayed the story of single ship-to-ship battles. In 1838 one sailor noted the words to a song commemorating Thomas MacDonough's victory over a British fleet on Lake Champlain. There were also songs celebrating the Revolutionary War and the exploits of John Paul Jones.[128] More general songs trumpeting the American tar were popular. In his book about his experience on a cruise to the Pacific aboard the USS *Constitution*, Henry Mercier described an evening of song that ended with a new iteration of the tune *Yankee Doodle* that one of the more experienced seamen declared he had composed himself "in the top the other day." Under the title *Every Inch a Yankee* the lyrics touted the American tar's seamanship "to reef, or loose, or furl" because in these "little *sailor moves*, He's Every inch a Yankee." This performance was met with applause from the "delighted auditors."[129]

Such lyrics touched on the sentimental. The same could be said for many of the pirate songs from this era. Both Herman Melville and Richard Henry Dana Jr. commented on the popularity of pirate songs among sailors. In *Redburn* Melville described a broadside street hawker along the Liverpool wharves who "was full of adventures, and abounded in terrific stories of pirates and sea murders," while Dana recalled the dogwatch aboard ship when the men gathered on deck "and sung sea songs, and those ballads of pirates and highwaymen, which sailors delight in."[130] Older ballads about pirates continued the mixed message of a life of piracy. George Little reported that on a return voyage from the Pacific, one of his shipmates sang more than twenty verses of the famous pirate song "My name is Captain Kid," much to the satisfaction of the forecastle.[131] Parlor and stage songs, printed and performed for popular consumption and copied into sailor journals in the 1830s and 1840s, like *The Pirate of the Isles*, *The Demon of the Sea*, and *The Rover of the Sea*, had more romanticized portrayals of piracy. The last of these songs had a story line that harked back to the sixteenth century and bid defiance to both the law and nature with lines like "I fear not the monarch I heed not the law" and "With Lightenings above us and darkness below / Through the wide waste of waters right onward we go."[132]

As we have already seen, forecastle songs were often connected to the Anglo-American ballad tradition. Indeed, even though *Every Inch a Sailor* had been written in the tops of the USS *Constitution*, it depended on the tune of *Yankee Doodle* for its melody. Sailors not only applied new lyrics to older music, they also continued to sing traditional ballads, even if they were incomplete or somewhat altered. Among the lyrics Thomas Delano jotted down in his journal were several stanzas of the song about the widow of mutineer Richard Parker. He also copied the story of the cross-dressing young woman searching for William Taylor. Calling the song *Sweet William*, Delano's lyrics were less tragic: after the woman's identity was revealed the captain merely told her that William Taylor was on the shore. There was no mention of another woman or a murder. A copy of *The Nobleman's Daughter* found on the *Walter Scott* was nothing more than a new rendition of *The Bristol Bridegroom* from the early eighteenth century, and a seaman noted *Pretty Sally* in his journal in 1845. Sailors also sang plenty of art songs.[133] Mercier copied the eighteenth-century *The Girl I Left Behind* in his rollicking reminiscence of his time aboard the USS *Constitution*.[134] Gale Huntington's collection of songs found in logbooks and journals has an entire section called "Parlor Songs that Went to Sea" packed with land-based written music with maritime themes. Charles Dibden and other British composers were also represented on American sailing ships in the antebellum period. As late as 1847 a sailor copied the words to Dibden's *Blow High Blow Low* into his songbook aboard the *Cortes*.[135] Among the songs Dana mentioned by name was "Poor Tom Bowling." Dana claimed that "all those classical songs of the sea, still held their places." He also asserted that the sailors "were very proud" of more modern tunes they had "picked up at theatres," including those "of a little more genteel cast."[136]

Jack Tar remained a huge fan of those theaters while in port and was interested in all kinds of entertainment from Shakespearean plays to circus riders. He also greatly enjoyed watching himself being portrayed either with comic overtones or in a more sympathetic light. In 1830 a Baltimore newspaper advertised *The Humorous, Sentimental & Naval Songster* as if the two apparently opposite qualities were related when it came to maritime music.[137] At about the same time a New York theater had on its playbill "a very laughable Farce" advertising George Alexander Stevens' "description of a Storm" with the performer "in the dress and character of a shipwrecked sailor, with an appropriate scene, ship in distress, &c."[138] A decade later the Bowery Theater featured a production with the character Harry Darling, "A Yankee sailor, full of frolic."[139] The stage also portrayed the sailor in a more serious and sentimental manner. *Black Eyed Susan* may have been written by English composer John Gay in the early eighteenth century, but it became one of the most popular songs in the American antebellum theater and was performed countless times to great applause. The lyrics restated an often-repeated maritime tale of a young woman separated from her sailor beau as he headed off to war. She visited him just as the ship was about to sail, and the song ends with a true sailor's goodbye:

> They kiss'd, she sigh'd, he hung his head;
> Her less'ning boat unwilling rows to land:
> Adieu! she cries; and wav'd her lily hand.[140]

In 1817, when British singer Charles Incledon failed to perform *Black Eyed Susan*, his signature song, a riot broke out in New York even though Incledon had already sung *Hail Columbia*. By 1829 American stage managers even created an entire melodrama around the song's plot line.[141]

Although mainstream society might laugh at the comic sailor's antics, the sentimental portrait of the seaman was probably more popular, especially because the interest in the unpredictable forces of nature that marked the Romantic era made the seaman an attractive figure. Few people faced the awesomeness of nature with greater aplomb and frequency. The idea that the sailor constantly confronted the unknown added poignancy to the well-worn ballads centered on the sailor's farewell, like *Black Eyed Susan* and a host of others. In 1838 American professional writer Epes Sargent, whose father was a sea captain, wrote *A Life on the Ocean Wave*, which became popular with American and British seamen and appeared repeatedly on stage. It embraced a fearsome nature with confidence:

> The land is no longer in view,
> The clouds have begun to frown;
> But with a stout vessel and crew,
> We'll say, Let the storm come down![142]

Tom Bowling also continued in its popularity on land. It was performed in theaters well into the 1840s and its wistful lyrics about the death of a true seaman whose soul had "gone aloft" may have been why the great transcendentalist Henry David Thoreau sang it so many times for guests at his Concord home.[143]

Looking across the broad sweep of the songs of the sailorman we can see certain persistent patterns. First, subjects ranged from the sentimental to the sensational, and from the highly romantic to the raunchy. Together, these disparate themes combined to form an Anglo-American maritime ballad tradition. Second, there was a give and take between the mainstream and maritime cultures that blurred the distinction between the art song composed by professional land-based musicians and the folk song produced by sailors at sea. Mariners embraced both types of music, adjusting and revising them over time. Third, the image of Jack Tar retained a special identity in the Anglo-American world. Ballads about seamen reflected only one component of a huge musical tradition. Many of the themes in nautical lyrics appeared elsewhere. But the seaman earned pride of place in Great Britain and the United States in war and commerce. Facing dangers from enemies abroad and the forces of nature upon the ocean added luster to Jack's character. Because his occupation compelled him to leave home, the sailor's farewell to his sweetheart became a stock storyline for separated lovers, while his misbehavior ashore allowed him to be the subject of sexual misadventures. Fourth, we can separate our analysis of the songs of the sailorman into roughly four chronological sections. Indeed, in many ways, in an odd comparison for this popular music, the history of the Anglo-American maritime ballad tradition has a structure similar to a classical symphony with four movements that were variations on a theme with each movement somewhat distinct, but with the essential tone and composition the same. The first movement appeared in the printed ballads of the seventeenth and early eighteenth centuries that established the basic character of this tradition with a mixture of folk and art music and touching on almost all of the same themes that would be repeated in later eras. The second movement emerged around the middle of the eighteenth century in the elevation of Jack Tar as a symbol of the British nation, a symbol that American revolutionaries made their own. The third movement saw the further emphasis on the importance of the sailor in Great Britain and separately in the United States, culminating in the War of 1812 (for Americans). In the final movement, the sailor as patriot became somewhat less important and the strains of the music may have become a little more distinct. Although many of the ideas and sometimes even the words of the shanty, the forebitter, and the nautical stage song fit into the long Anglo-American ballad tradition, the themes expressed in that tradition began to take two different paths: one, more coarse and sexually oriented, appeared more frequently in shanties; the other more refined, maudlin, and even patriotic, appeared in forecastle and stage songs.

6

The Pirates Own Book

Scattered about the New Orleans courtroom were pistols, gunpowder, "a colossal bowie-knife," and a dark blue flag with death's head and "marrowless crossbones." Amid this pirate paraphernalia, and almost as damning as evidence, was a copy of the most popular compendium of stories of murder, mayhem, and robbery on the high seas in the antebellum era – *The Pirates Own Book*.[1] How many pirates may have actually owned *The Pirates Own Book* we will never know. We do know that this oddly named tome entertained plenty of regular seamen and landsmen in the nineteenth century. As such, it can stand as a symbol for the kind of sea literature that was popular in the age of sail and serves as an entree into our examination of Jack Tar's reading. Sold for a dollar, *The Pirates Own Book* was initially published in 1837 and quickly went through five printings for a total of 6,000 copies in its first year. Over the next twenty-five years *The Pirates Own Book* appeared in at least eight other editions. It was one of several similar books, including Charles Johnson's a century old *A General History of the Pirates*, in circulation at the time. It also represented a revolution in printing that occurred between 1750 and 1850. Several editions of Johnson's book had appeared in the eighteenth century, but only the transformations in the book industry, with cheaper paper manufacturing, automating some aspects of printing and book production, and aggressive marketing, allowed works like *The Pirates Own Book* to reach larger audiences. Hand in hand with these developments was a growing interest in sensational works of all kinds, the development of the novel, the availability of other print material, and the proliferation of religious publications.[2] *The Pirates Own Book*, much of which had been "pirated" from Johnson, became so popular because it combined stories of sixteenth- and seventeenth-century sea rovers with tales about early nineteenth-century pirates. Relatively inexpensive, the book was richly illustrated with detailed images of walking the plank, drinking, ravaging, robbing, and murdering. It also depicted the execution and decapitation of pirates. The material package of this book, a product of changes in print production, carried powerful and contradictory messages to the reader.[3]

Sailors were ready to take advantage of the revolution in print. In the late eighteenth century the literacy rate for American sailors was around 75 percent and increased thereafter: in the 1830s about nine out of ten sailors aboard the USS *Potomac* were literate.[4] Moreover, because mariners journeyed so far from home their lives had already expanded beyond the immediate community, and it was relatively easy for them to imagine the different worlds portrayed in travel works and fiction.[5] The sailor's own life story, too, always had the potential for danger and adventure, crucial components in both novels and the burgeoning sensationalist literature. Mariners also had opportunities for reading. During the Revolutionary War Charles Herbert noted how the seamen held in Mill Prison had access to newspapers, pamphlets, and other reading matter and how he bought a Bible. He also indicated that newspapers were read out loud so that even the illiterate would have access to their content.[6] Men at sea also had time to read. In the 1830s William McNally served on an American warship with hundreds of men. Naval discipline may have meant keeping the crew as busy as possible, but the sheer number of sailors aboard ship allowed for leisure time when not on watch. Long voyages, too, were conducive to reading. Richard Henry Dana Jr. was on a merchant vessel dispatched for years to the California coast. He described several scenarios where he read by himself, including those times when he was off duty and on Sundays. He also pored over books during the months he was on shore.[7] Likewise, men aboard whaleships would have spare time to read between cruising grounds when they were not catching whales. Even on merchant vessels with smaller crews during shorter voyages in the Atlantic or to the West Indies, sailors had opportunity to pick up a book. Redburn, Herman Melville's fabricated alter ego in his novel of his first voyage, was able to read books in his bunk during his watch below.[8]

We know the most about sailors reading after 1800. Before this date only a handful of seamen recorded their reading habits. After that date, many more seamen provide us a record of what they read. There are several reasons for this change in documentation. In part, it was a function of the revolution in print that began in the late eighteenth century and then took off in the early nineteenth century. As we have seen in the example of American prisoners of war, seamen could and did read before 1800. Additional evidence suggests that many sailors read the Bible and other works. In all likelihood, however, more sailors began reading after 1800 and read more broadly. One aspect of the print revolution was a change from reading intensively – going over the same books repeatedly – to reading extensively – picking up one book after another. In addition, the production of increased print matter meant more material was available for reading. Sailors also became authors during the print revolution. Famous writers like Richard Henry Dana Jr. and Herman Melville, as well as less well-known seamen like Nathaniel Ames and Ned Myers, offered testimony concerning their reading experiences. The changing nature of the logbook, which became increasingly like a personal journal that might list or mention books that were read, also affected the evidence we have to examine reading patterns.[9]

Jack Tar had an open mind when it came to print. Mariners relished extravagant tales of pirates, as well as stories about mutiny, captivity, and shipwreck. Technically any major crime at sea was piracy. Books like *The Pirates Own Book*, then, covered some mutinies. But other mutinies not usually considered piracy, such as the saga of Captain William Bligh and the *Bounty*, were also popular. Whether enslaved by Barbary corsairs, seized by natives from distant lands, or impressed and imprisoned by the British, the captivity ordeal of Jack Tars whose freedom had been curtailed also became standard reading. As with piracy, an almost separate industry developed of narratives about shipwreck that chronicled horrendous tales of death and sometimes equally horrible stories of survival. In short, disaster sold. Sailors read about other subjects beyond those that recorded the dangers of the ocean wave. Seaman author Nathaniel Ames wrote that "sailors universally are extremely fond of reading and are far better judges of books than they are allowed credit for."[10] Mariners devoured books from the highest forms of literature to the lowest sensationalist publications. They read novels, hack literature, lurid stories, travel narratives, political tracts, technical manuals, and religious books. Herman Melville suggested the span of this contrast when he referred to reading in his *Redburn*. The main character of the novel – Redburn – attempted to plough his way through Adam Smith's *Wealth of Nations*, but found it so dry and dull that "the very leaves smelt of saw-dust." Fortunately for this young tar, he was not the only reader on board: he borrowed two books from a shipmate – one "an account of Shipwrecks and Disasters at Sea" and the other, which Melville remembered seeing in several book stalls around Fulton Market, called *Delirium Tremens*. He also commented that the African American steward owned a copy of the Bible and had read Susanna Rowson's sentimental *Charlotte Temple* and George Walker's gothic *Three Spaniards*. Available, then, on this voyage, was one of the most sophisticated tomes on political economy produced in the eighteenth century, two novels popular with the Anglo-American middle class written around 1800, a sensationalized volume on disasters at sea, a medical study on a subject of concern to many sailors after binge drinking while in port, and of course, the Bible.[11] We can glean further insight into the books available to sailors at sea from Melville's *White-Jacket*, a work based on his experience in the American navy. Melville poked fun at the volumes in the man-of-war library as inappropriate for the common seaman, finding Machiavelli's *Art of War* "very dry fighting," John Locke's essays "miserable reading at sea," a book of sermons "the best reading for divines, indeed, but with little relish for a main-top-man," and a "fine treatise on rhetoric" with "nothing to say about nautical phrases." But because they were available, he and other seamen probably read these books. The ship's library, however, was a good source for travel narratives, which Melville enjoyed. As he had on his first voyage, Melville augmented his reading by borrowing books from other crew members. Here again the range of material was staggering, including Thomas Moore's poem "Loves of the Angels" and "a Negro Song-book," which Melville admitted reflected the vulgar tastes of the owner. Other sailors aboard the warship "were diligent readers, though their studies did not lie in the way of belles-lettres." They had visited the book stalls along the waterfront and their favorite authors were "slightly physiological in their nature" – by which we may assume their books were somewhat risqué. The fact that a book market stood near the docks speaks volumes for the mariner's interest in reading, and for the aggressive marketing techniques of the nineteenth century, even if many of those books, in the words of reformers, were "the scum of 'polite literature'" that filled "the imagination with scenes of debauchery and blood." Melville, of course, consumed that scum: in 1841 he read a book on a whale sinking a ship, and later used it as the basis for one of the greatest pieces of literature ever produced in the English language.[12]

There is no question that reading was important to sailors during the revolution in print. This chapter will explore the attraction of the vast array of material perused by seamen, not only examining what the sailor read but also suggesting how and why the mariner read. We will begin this study of sailor reading by turning to publications on the dangers of going to sea, and then move on to literature more generally. We will also discuss the sailor's interest in instructional and technical works, especially on travel, history, news, and navigation. Finally we will explore the impact of religion on the sailor's reading. Seamen benefited from the revolution in print and took advantage of the great variety of reading material that became available in the nineteenth century. There was thus little difference between what seamen and landsmen read. Indeed, even the literature written explicitly about maritime experiences found an audience on terra firma. Countless landsmen read about pirates and the perils of the deep while seamen read about life ashore.

Pirates, Captivity, and Shipwreck

Jack Tar loved to read pirate tales and stories about shipwreck and captivity. For men whose work often left them on the brink of disaster this may seem peculiar. After all, why read about all of the things that could go wrong aboard a ship? What was so engaging about being reminded of the risks every seaman faced? And yet there was something tantalizing about accounts of danger and destruction. Even if there was overlap in stories about piracy, shipwreck, and captivity, and many a narrative encompassed all three, we can draw distinctions in the nature of these tales. Each category of story was both attractive and repulsive to the common seaman, but for somewhat different reasons. Piracy represented an escape from the normal boundaries of shipboard behavior while it simultaneously threatened death at the hands of cutthroats and criminals. Shipwrecks were instructive on how to handle adversity and served as examples of how terribly things could go wrong. Captivity might lead to redemption or simply be a tale of woe and suffering. The tensions between the fantastic and the fearsome within each subject, although slightly varied, help to explain why such stories were so interesting to readers, whether they be at sea or ashore. These disaster tales had long been the subject of ballads, sailor yarns, and even books. The print revolution provided even more published stories of seaborne adventures and catastrophes and made them available to readers aboard ships or on shore.

As we have already seen, one of the most popular volumes in the sailor's library was *The Pirates Own Book*. Although several other similar books were in circulation at the time, *The Pirates Own Book* stands out. Some commentators believed that it had an evil effect on its readers. There were reports that it influenced the so-called mutineers on the USS *Somers*. After that mutiny controversy newspapers decried *The Pirates Own Book* as a "trashy and exaggerated" fiction that had "magnified scoundrels into heros, and imparted a false charm to ruffians of the very worst class." One reformer described the book as a part of the "corrupt literature of the sea," and another considered it a book "of the worst description" sold by street hawkers along the docks.[13] The book, however, appeared in regular bookstores from Kalamazoo to Charleston and from Boston to St. Louis and many places in between. Sometimes newspapers advertised this "trashy and exaggerated" fiction separately; it could just as easily be listed along with more sober fare, including the Bible.[14] Compiled by Charles Ellms, a Boston stationer and book entrepreneur, *The Pirates Own Book* was little more than a conglomeration of other publications, especially Johnson's *A General History of the Pirates*. But *The Pirates Own Book* also contained updates on more recent high-seas depredations such as those conducted by Jean Lafitte in the Gulf of Mexico and by other West Indies buccaneers in the 1820s, as well as descriptions of the French attack on Algiers and the American assault on Quallah Battoo in Sumatra. Like many publications of the era, its derivative nature was not a problem. American printers cared little about English copyrights and were equally unconcerned with recreating the original very carefully. Although many passages were plagiarized word for word, others were simply paraphrased.[15] The material also did not have a logical organization. Chapters followed pell-mell one after another without any sense of chronology. Despite the concerns with the book's effect, there was also no clear message about the nature of piracy: sometimes the pirates escaped and sometimes they were executed. Representative of this admixture were the illustrations that were such a prominent feature of the book. The first edition had on the title page an engraving with the caption "Gibbs carrying the Dutch girl on board" that has the poor young woman being lifted out of a longboat by a dapper-looking Charles Gibbs. The text accompanying the illustration stated that after watching her parents murdered the "wretched daughter was spared for the most nefarious purposes" and was later poisoned so she could not testify about her ordeal.[16] The title page of another of the early editions depicted a pirate and a topless native woman with the heading, "Piratical station – Isle of Madagascar." These suggestive images played to the sexual fantasies of many readers. Pictures also displayed sailors drinking, burying treasure, and ravishing women. Different illustrations, however, carried harsher messages about piracy for readers, such as brutal acts of violence, a depiction of executed

Captain William Kidd hanging in chains at an entrance to a harbor, and a picture of the head of the "daring ruffian" Vincent Benevides on a pole and a vulture about to pick out his brains. Captured in this confused message was the contrast between being attracted to the liberty from constraints the life of a freebooter offered and the repulsion to the violence and horror of the world of a criminal.[17]

The Pirates Own Book could not have been published without the revolution in print and had not other books about piracy abounded, ranging from huge compendiums like Ellms's tome to pamphlets about specific incidents. The proliferation of these other pirate publications reflected the spread of print culture. The previous work on pirates, especially Charles Johnson's early eighteenth-century *A General History of the Pirates*, was important and was copied by Ellms and many others. With easier and cheaper printing available, pirate books could multiply rapidly. In 1825 one edition based on Johnson's "history" appeared with a section added about Commodore David Porter's activities against pirates in the West Indies. Another was published in Hartford in 1829 that was small enough to fit into a pocket – a size that would be easy for any sailor to keep in his sea chest. A third edition appeared with a slightly different title in 1836 with Porter's exploits and an account of the recent trial of the men who committed piracy against the brig *Mexican*.[18] Stories like this last one were often lifted from pamphlets and small books on specific cases of piracy – printers produced several versions of the trial of the culprits who attacked the *Mexican*.[19] Pamphlet-like publications on other pirate trials also appeared. Much of this material was typical of the dying criminal confession chap book where the condemned offered advice not to follow their evil ways and described crimes in enough detail to ensure some guilty pleasure by voyeuristic readers.[20] Stories by victims were also published and copied into the bigger books. *The Pirates Own Book* repeated the *Narrative of the Capture, and Sufferings and Escape of Capt. Barnabas Lincoln and His Crew* almost verbatim.[21]

An additional, but central component of the genre of sea-based crime were stories about female pirates. *A General History of the Pirates* included biographies of Anne Bonny and Mary Read, who had joined pirate crews in the early eighteenth century. Their basic stories were repeated in *The Pirates Own Book* and similar publications. These tales, like the ballads of women who went to sea disguised as men, offered a titillating sexual slant to the standard pirate tale. That Anne Bonny had initially made sexual advances to the handsome Mary Read, both in disguise as men, only offered further interest to "the odd Incidents of their

THE

PIRATES OWN BOOK,

OR

AUTHENTIC NARRATIVES

OF THE

LIVES, EXPLOITS, AND EXECUTIONS OF THE MOST CELEBRATED

SEA ROBBERS.

Gibbs carrying the Dutch Girl on board.

WITH

HISTORICAL SKETCHES

OF THE

Joassamee, Spanish, Ladrone, West India,
Malay, and Algerine Pirates.

NEW YORK:

PUBLISHED BY A. & C. B. EDWARDS,

NO. 3, PARK ROW.

PHILADELPHIA:

THOMAS, COWPERTHWAIT, & CO.,

NO. 253, MARKET STREET.

1840

FIGURE 6.1. "Gibbs Carrying the Dutch Girl on Board," *The Pirates Own Book, or Authentic Narratives of the Lives, Exploits, and Executions of the Most Celebrated Sea Robbers ...* (New York: A. and C. B. Edwards, 1840). The compendium of pirate stories put together by Charles Ellms gained notoriety because it seemed to celebrate cutthroats, murderers, and thieves on the high seas. Foremost among contemporary hero/villains was the pirate Charles Gibbs who supposedly saved a Dutch girl from the clutches of his crew, only to have his own way with her, and then, to insure she could never testify against him, allowed her to be killed. This image, which appeared on the title page of many editions shows a dapper Gibbs swooping the Dutch girl into his arms. Courtesy of the American Antiquarian Society, Worcester, Massachusetts.

189

FIGURE 6.2. **"Piratical Station – Isle of Madagascar,"** *The Pirates Own Book, or Authentic Narratives of the Lives, Exploits, and Executions of the Most Celebrated Sea Robbers....* (Philadelphia: Thomas Cowperthwiat & Co., 1839). An 1839 edition of *The Pirates Own Book* placed this image of a pirate in Madagascar on the title page. Like the illustration of the pirate Gibbs and the Dutch girl, the engraving suggested that pirates enjoyed a world of sexual fantasy denied to mainstream society. Courtesy of the American Antiquarian Society, Worcester, Massachusetts.

The head of Benevides stuck on a pole. p. 188.

FIGURE 6.3. "**The Head of Benevides Stuck on a Pole,**" *The Pirates Own Book, or Authentic Narratives of the Lives, Exploits, and Executions of the Most Celebrated Sea Robbers* … (New York: A. and C. B. Edwards, 1840). The stories and illustrations in *The Pirates Own Book* sent contradictory messages. On the one hand the life of a buccaneer could appear attractive, on the other, it could lead to a gruesome death as depicted by the head of Benevides on pike with a vulture about to pick out his brains. Courtesy of the American Antiquarian Society, Worcester, Massachusetts.

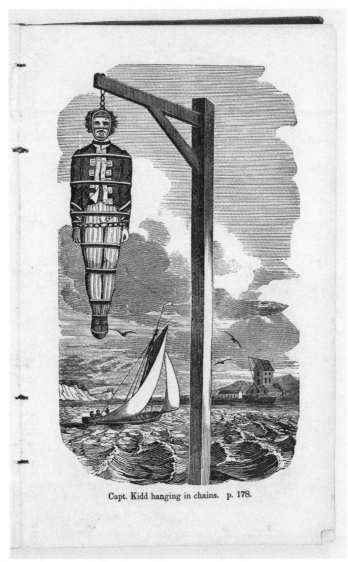

Capt. Kidd hanging in chains. p. 178.

FIGURE 6.4. **"Capt. Kidd Hanging in Chains,"** *The Pirates Own Book, or Authentic Narratives of the Lives, Exploits, and Executions of the Most Celebrated Sea Robbers ...* (New York: A. and C. B. Edwards, 1840). Celebrated in song and story, Captain William Kidd was executed in 1701. The multi-versed ballad about Kidd concludes with his death. As depicted in this illustration, whatever glory might be won by a pirate, his end was often inglorious. Great Britain frequently left executed bodies of pirates in chains at the entrances to harbors as a reminder to seamen of the fate that might befall them if they crossed over into piracy. Courtesy of the American Antiquarian Society, Worcester, Massachusetts.

rambling lives" so that the reader might think "the whole Story no better than a Novel or Romance." Even if we cannot be sure of the details of their lives, Bonny and Read were real people. Publications about fictional or quasi-fictional women pirates were also popular. The story of Alwilda, a fifth-century Scandinavian princess turned pirate, somehow captured the imaginations of many seamen and the picture of this mythical heroine found in *The Pirates Own Book* became the basis for several etchings on scrimshaw.[22] Alwilda also served as the model for the lead character in *Fanny Campbell, the Female Pirate Captain: A Tale of the Revolution*, a connection made clear in an illustration in an 1845 edition based on *The Pirates Own Book*. This popular tale had its heroine dress as a man to go to sea to rescue William, her true love who had been imprisoned in Cuba as a pirate. The complicated plot had many twists and turns, and was packed with digressive yarns. Campbell led a mutiny, rescued her sweetheart, and revealed her true identity, upon which William exclaimed, "I cannot believe that a female, a mere girl of but twenty years, could accomplish what thou hast done." After some further trials and tribulations Fanny and William live happily ever after: their piracy turned out to be nothing more than raiding the British during the American War for Independence without a privateering commission.[23]

Piracy was not an abstract to Jack Tar – it remained a very real threat to seamen throughout the age of sail – and yet pirate stories were popular with sailors. For most sailors piracy meant cutting off all land-based connections and turning to a violent and brutal existence. Aboard the whaleship *Globe*, for example, several of the men were aghast at the mutiny and bloodshed that went with it. Most sailors looked at pirates as almost a breed apart. Either they were criminals who cared little for the normal bounds of civilization, or they were foreigners who came from an alien culture. For much of the period of this study Anglo-Americans considered the depredations by the Barbary states as acts of piracy. A few Anglo-Americans who were captured by the North Africans "turned Turk," converted to Islam, and became "pirates" by serving on Barbary ships. Most refused to do so. Barnabas Lincoln claimed that the polyglot crew who captured his ship in the West Indies was composed of Portuguese, French, and Spaniards.[24] In the far Pacific Malay and Chinese pirates also raided American shipping in the early nineteenth century. The U.S. Navy attacked Quallah Battoo in Sumatra in 1832 and 1839 after locals had massacred Americans aboard merchant vessels.[25] In short, however much sailors might pore over their own copies of *The Pirates Own Book*, most did not intend to become pirates. Instead, perhaps in part because they had read so many pirate stories, they understood that in certain seas a strange sail on the horizon might bring death and destruction.[26]

Of course, some Americans did become pirates. They probably did not do so because of the books that they read. Before the War of 1812, Jean and Pierre Lafitte had established themselves in the swamps near New Orleans as a base for slave smuggling and piracy at a time when this region was a borderland between the United States and the Spanish empire. The identity of many of the men who worked with them remains unknown, but no doubt the multinational cast of pirates included Americans. We cannot be sure of their motivation. They were probably most interested in the profits offered by smuggling goods obtained through illicit activity. When the United States strengthened its control of Louisiana the Lafittes moved to the Texas gulf coast to continue their operations until the American navy drove them away in 1821. By that time Lafitte claimed to be operating as a privateer for Colombia as it was fighting for its independence from Spain. During the Latin American wars of independence new nations like Colombia commissioned privateers to attack Spanish shipping. A number of Americans had a direct hand in this activity. Baltimore merchants, who had developed a specialty in privateering during the War of 1812, refitted many of the same vessels as Latin American privateers. As these fast-sailing ships headed out of Chesapeake Bay, they were often manned by American seamen who had been privateers during the War of 1812. Charles Gibbs, a notorious pirate executed in 1831, did not sail from Baltimore, but he did join a Latin American privateer that turned to piracy. Like the vessel Gibbs was on, several of the privateers began to raid indiscriminately. Hezikiah Niles chronicled a little more than three thousand incidents of piracy between 1815 and 1824 in the West Indies. The attraction for cutthroats like Gibbs was not an egalitarian atmosphere, nor a romanticized image found in a book. Instead, it was the quick cash that could be earned as an outlaw of the sea.[27]

Mutiny, which was really a form of piracy, was also of interest to readers. For more than a century almost every sailor knew of the story of the *Bounty*, attracted perhaps because a few of the mutineers escaped the long arm of the British royal navy and because of the Edenic South Pacific setting of the tale. Captain William Bligh's account of the mutiny and his subsequent ordeal in a longboat was published in Philadelphia in 1790. Both British and American publications on the subject continued to appear for decades, especially after the discovery of the escaped mutineers' fate on Pitcairn Island. There was even a stage production of the story in the 1830s.[28] Likewise, reports of the great mutinies of the British navy in 1797 were printed in the United States and in publications and newspapers intermittently thereafter. Some editors condemned the mutinies at Spithead and the Nore, and aboard the HMS *Hermione*. Others viewed them as actions in the defense of the rights of man.[29] The shipboard trial and execution of a midshipman and two seamen supposedly involved in a mutiny plot on the USS *Somers* in 1842 also was controversial. James Fenimore Cooper was outraged by what he saw as arbitrary action by Captain Alexander Slidell Mackenzie. Others defended Mackenzie.[30] Smaller mutinies on merchant ships and whalers gained notoriety. At least three booklets were published on the trial of the men who mutinied on the schooner *Plattsburg* in 1816. These seamen sailed to Norway and divided the cash aboard the ship, pocketing $3,000 each. However, they soon began to argue and one man betrayed the others to the Danish authorities. After two years the U.S. Navy transported the "pirates" to Boston for a sensational trial in front of a courtroom jammed with 600 onlookers.[31] Equally spectacular was the story of the mutiny aboard the whaleship *Globe* in 1824. In this case the mutineers brutally murdered all but one of the officers, and then, perhaps inspired by the *Bounty* story, they sailed their ship to the Mulgrave Islands off the northern coast of Australia. The remaining officer recaptured the ship with the help of some of the crew and sailed to South America. In the meantime the Mulgraves turned out not to be a South Sea paradise for the mutineers, who were soon killed by the natives. Two seamen who had not supported the mutiny, and who had been enslaved by the locals, survived this ordeal.[32] The infamous pirate Charles Gibbs was involved in at least two mutinies. One occurred while Gibbs served on a Colombian privateer, after which he sailed as a pirate on a ship that followed the policy "dead men tell no tales." He drifted back into the regular merchant service and was on the brig *Vineyard* sailing from New Orleans to Philadelphia when he and the rest of the crew murdered the captain and officers. The pirates headed to Long Island, where they scuttled the ship and landed in small boats with $50,000 in specie. Once ashore, however, one of the men spoke to the authorities and turned them in.[33]

Many of the shorter publications were less ambiguous and condemned both piracy and mutiny without any qualification. The portrayal of pirates in the account by merchant captain Barnabas Lincoln was anything but flattering. The sea raiders were incredibly filthy and profane and their appearance was terrifying, "wearing black whiskers and long beards, the receptacles of dirt and vermin."[34] Passenger Lucretia Parker, who considered herself fortunate to have escaped "ruin" by a pirate captain with "hellish designs," described how the cutthroats massacred most of the crew with "the ferocity of cannibals" while their "yells, oaths, and imprecations, made them more resemble demons than human beings." When the captain pleaded for mercy by reminding the murderers that he had a wife and children, the entreaty was in vain because "his appeal was to monsters possessing hearts callous to the feelings of humanity!" Her virtue, and probably her life, was saved by the timely arrival of a British warship.[35]

Typical of the gallows confessional genre, many of the pre-execution statements made the moral issue explicit. Thomas Winslow, who had been convicted of piracy along with Charles Gibbs, explained that he hoped his confession "might meet the eye of some giddy and thoughtless youths who are in the daily habit of committing trifling sins, which magnify as they increase in age, for the want of due reflection on the awful consequences that ultimately follow."[36] One of the reports on the *Plattsburg* pirate trial condemned the action as driven by "a thirst after gain, and the principle of AVARICE" at which "the good, the virtuous and the amiable will always point the finger of scorn." For this writer there was no glory in piracy, only depravity and bloodshed that led to "three innocent men" being murdered by "sanguinary assassins." This report ended with a poem that offered words of advice:

> Let our youth by them take warning;
>   Shun the path those murd'rers trod –
> Lest, they should be by virtue scorning,
>   Call'd to the awful bar of God.[37]

There were those who suggested that mutinies, just like in the case of the *Bounty* and the British fleet, were the result of abuse and poor treatment. William McNally wrote that officers sometimes made "a vessel a perfect hell," leaving seamen little alternative "but to suffer the caprices, whims, and tyranny in silence for a long voyage, or else do a deed that will bring them to the scaffold, or haunt them to their grave." Having read about a mutiny on the *Braganza*, McNally quoted the last words of Cornelius Tunis Wilhelms before his execution: "that they (The crew) were obliged to do it; the master treated them so badly, that he should go." McNally admitted that "There is nothing to palliate the crime of piracy; but certainly every means should be used to have the cause removed." Demonstrating an awareness of several mutiny and piracy publications, McNally believed that most of "the mutinies, piracies, and murders that have been committed on board of our merchant vessels" had been "for revenge for injuries, and bad treatment." This was true, he argued, for the *Globe* and the *Braganza*, although perhaps not for the *Vineyard*, where the motives were selfish and mercenary. Richard Henry Dana Jr. agreed with these sentiments. After witnessing a flogging he exclaimed, "what is there for sailors to do? If they resist, it is mutiny; and if they succeed, and take the vessel, it is piracy." In his concluding chapter Dana noted that on long voyages "outrageous cruelty" can occur unnoticed by the courts back in the United States, often leading to "mutiny and piracy, – stripe for stripe, and blood for blood."[38]

Captivity, like piracy and mutiny, became a prominent subject of sailor reading. The timing of the publication of sailor captivity stories, however, resulted as much from political developments as the print revolution. Some of the most popular American stories about captivity involved the conflicts with Great Britain. In the 1790s and the years immediately before the War of 1812 one form of captivity – impressment – garnered the most attention as British forced recruitment became a major political and diplomatic issue. Impressment emerged as politically important after 1794, yet personal impressment narratives did not really proliferate until after the *Chesapeake* affair in 1807, when the HMS *Leopard* stopped an American warship and forcefully seized four British deserters who had joined the American navy. Intensified newspaper coverage of impressment cases followed accompanied by a handful of book-like publications.[39] The War of 1812 brought even greater concern for maritime affairs and increased interest in another form of British captivity – the experience of Americans held as prisoners of war. Despite the success of the United States on the high seas, thousands of Americans were captured by the British, and their ordeal, culminating in the tragedy of the Dartmoor massacre, led to a host of publications at the end of the war. As the print revolution made book production cheaper and easier in the 1820s and 1830s, and as the democratization of American society created greater interest in the lives of common folk, more and more stories of individual sailor captives appeared. Previously only a few narratives of the experience with imprisonment during the Revolutionary War surfaced. Now scores of seamen related their ordeal of impressment and imprisonment in both British-American wars.[40]

Many captivity stories overlapped with tales of piracy, especially when it came to being taken by Barbary corsairs. Anglo-Americans in the age of sail viewed the North African nations as rogue states whose seamen were nothing more than pirates who captured shipping illegally and enslaved passengers and crew. The stories of some of these "white slaves" found their way into print as early as the 1580s, and thus predated the more famous Indian captivity narratives that have become such a highly studied area of American literature. Although the subject was a part of the Anglo-American popular ballad tradition, only about fifteen printed prose narratives survive from the seventeenth and first half of the eighteenth centuries.[41] Diplomatic problems between the United States and the Barbary states that began in the 1780s combined with the changes in print culture led to an increase in the pace of publication: between 1785 and 1815 the Barbary powers collectively held approximately 700 Americans as prisoners/slaves and there were at least a dozen fictional and nonfictional accounts published on their experience.[42] Some of the sailor narratives were written as warnings to other seamen about the perils of Barbary captivity; most of these publications had a broad appeal because of the threat to the freedom of American citizens and the disruption of American commerce.[43] John Foss, whose report of his life as a slave in Algiers appeared in 1798, explained that he wrote his account to show Americans "the hardships and sufferings of their unfortunate fellow countrymen" who had fallen "into the hands of the Algerines."[44] James Riley's *Authentic Narrative of the Loss of the American Brig Commerce* was one of the best-selling books in the nineteenth century. This saga of a shipwreck and enslavement in North Africa had all the stock concerns of any captivity narrative: great suffering, testing one's commitment to God, and final redemption. But it also offered an antislavery message that gained in popularity in the years before the Civil War.[45]

Riley's book was about both shipwreck and captivity, reminding us that natural disasters upon the ocean were a regular subject of maritime reading. The shipwreck counterpart to *The Pirates Own Book* was Charles Ellms's own *Shipwrecks and Disasters at Sea, or Historical Narratives of the Most Noted Calamities and Providential Deliverances from Fire and Famine on the Ocean. With a Sketch of the Various Expedients for Preserving the Life of Mariners by the Aid of Life Boats, Life Preservers, &c.*[46] Like his pirate book produced about the same time, this volume was derivative of earlier publications, and, as was true with *The Pirates Own Book*, Ellms's shipwreck anthology had a series of spectacular engravings. Ellms borrowed the opening sixteen words of his long title from an 1812 Scottish publication.[47] But his most important source for shipwreck narratives, and the source for many of the other shipwreck books published in the nineteenth century, was a work by British naval officer Archibald Duncan, *The Mariner's Chronicle; Being a Collection of the Most Interesting Narratives of Shipwrecks, Fires, Famines, and Other Calamities* ... Duncan's multivolume collection first appeared in 1804 in London and was reprinted as early as 1806 in the United States.[48] As was true with many publications "pirated" from British printers and published in the United States, *The Mariner's Chronicle* underwent significant alterations in various editions. A single-volume *Mariner's Chronicle* produced in New Haven in 1834 used several of Duncan's shipwreck narratives, but also contained chapters on American naval victories in the War of 1812, piracy, Captain Kidd's buried treasure, and the outrages of the Malays at Quallah Battoo.[49] Both Ellms's work and the later American *Mariner's Chronicle* added recent disasters, such as steamboat explosions, to the spectacular stories of lives lost and saved on the high seas that had appeared in Duncan's earlier book. All of these shipwreck anthologies retold chilling tales of storms, sharks, and months adrift in open boats. These narratives of death and survival described men who became so thirsty they drank saltwater, urine, and even blood from deceased shipmates. Starving shipwrecked sailors ate uncooked rotting provisions, barnacles, and even each other. If the survivors made it to land they often faced hostile natives and were hundreds of miles from help. They might clamor out of the ocean and up onto rocks only to die of exposure. Icebergs and frostbite also took their toll. Small ships disappeared into the sea and whole fleets were destroyed with the loss of 20,000 men.[50]

Also like *The Pirates Own Book*, most of these anthologies had one story following after another with no consistent theme and no relation to chronology. Duncan claimed that his collection of shipwreck tales would appeal to several groups. Because humans "sympathize with victims of misfortune" the general reader would find the stories interesting, especially considering the importance of sailors to the British nation. As he explained, "The fate of the adventurous seamen, undauntedly bidding defiance to his country's foes, or engaged in the peaceful pursuits of trade – in both cases equally exposed to the multiple perils of the ocean – cannot be indifferent to those who remain at home, enjoying that security, and those conveniences which his exertion so materially contribute to procure." He also believed that "the juvenile reader" would learn about other nations and all readers would gain insight into humanity in the face of adversity. Sailors, "for whose benefit this work is particularly designed," would learn through "the examples of fortitude, courage, and constancy" how to behave when disaster struck. There was also a religious lesson: at times a seaman might have to resign himself patiently to

FIGURE 6.5. **"The Sailor Boy."** Sailors often copied favorite engravings and used them as a subject for their scrimshaw. As in *The Pirates Own Book*, Charles Ellms used illustrations to make his *Shipwrecks and Disasters at Sea, or Historical Narratives of the Most Noted Calamities ...* (Boston: S. N. Dickinson, 1836) attractive to readers. The fact that a whaleman relied on the sentimental portrayal of a sailor boy from the front of the book, with the quote from Romantic poet Lord Byron included, stands as testimony of the popularity of stories about shipwrecks to the men who went to sea. Courtesy of Mystic Seaport, #1974.691, Mystic Connecticut.

the will of God. Whatever Duncan's intention, the actual stories did not always have these effects. Some chapters offered testimony on the importance of discipline and organization in the face of disaster. Others seemed to have the opposite meaning. Duncan, followed by Ellms and almost every other shipwreck book, retold the stories of the East-Indiaman *Grosvenor* and the HMS *Centaur*. Wrecked on the coast of Africa in 1782, many of the men from the *Grosvenor* made it to shore, only to perish after discipline broke down and most of the crew abandoned the officers. These men ignored the idea that "Concord is always strength; the contrary, even in the happiest circumstances, is weakness and ruin." The concluding comments noted that the crew's "desire of gratifying a rebellious and turbulent spirit, at a time when it can be done with impunity," and refusal to follow orders led to disaster on shore after the shipwreck. The point that the author of the original narrative hoped "to impress on the minds of the seamen" was that "their only hope" in a shipwreck "must depend upon obedience." The story of the *Centaur* offered a different lesson when the captain admitted that, confronted with his ship sinking, "There appeared not more than a moment for consideration": he could "remain and perish with the ship's company," or he could save his own life. Even if not explicitly stated, the fact that "The love of life prevailed" suggested that officers could not always be trusted.[51]

The shipwreck anthologies incorporated stories that had been published separately. Ellms printed a full text of Riley's popular story of the shipwreck of the *Commerce*. R. Thomas's *Interesting and Authentic Narratives of the Most Remarkable Shipwrecks*, a rival to Ellms's book, had a brief recap of the destruction of the *Essex* in an attack by a whale that led to the horrific survival tale of sailing thousands of miles in flimsy whaleboats to the coast of Chile. Thomas also retold one of the most sensational survival stories of the early nineteenth century. In this saga Ann Saunders was a young woman who "had more strength in her calamity than most men." The vessel was wrecked in a storm and floated around the Atlantic for months before it was rescued. In the meantime the survivors had little to eat or drink on the disabled ship and had to resort to cannibalism. Saunders "performed the duty of cutting up and cleaning the dead bodies, keeping two knives for the purpose in her monkey jacket." When her own fiancé expired she grabbed a cup and slit "her late intended husband's throat and drank the blood!" She insisted that "she had the greatest right to it," and when a scuffle ensued "the heroine got the better of her adversary, and then let him drink one cup to her two." This kind of fantastic and sordid detail sold these survival stories to readers of all kinds.[52]

The literature on pirates, captivity, and shipwrecks that was produced as a result of the print revolution had a broad appeal. Sailors really did read these books. But so did many others. Josiah Cobb, a Boston apprentice who joined a privateer during the War of 1812, reported his infatuation with piracy and the sea before the war. As a youth he played at being the pirate, especially Captain Kidd, "whose history in song I had made my study" and even in his apprenticeship, his "mind was ever after boats, sea songs, narratives, and the like." The war with Great Britain only encouraged this attraction: "Now my whole readings were of naval armaments, manouvres, tactics – battles and escapes – boat duty, rowing guard, cutting out, – booming guns, long toms, – pink-em-well, cut and slash, blood and carnage."[53] Out of work shoemaker Jacob Hazen had read Cooper's *Red Rover* and other sea tales and, oddly, after seeing a pirate hanged in Philadelphia in 1837 he decided "Crusoe like" to seek his fortune by going to sea.[54] *The Pirates Own Book* remained popular throughout the nineteenth century.[55] There was even an almanac printed with the title *The Tragical cale[ndar] and Pirates Own Almanac, 1846*. The cover picture depicted pirates with a black flag – an illustration from *The Pirates Own Book*. On the back was an engraving of the massacre on the *Mexican* and a brief story about what happened on board the vessel. Inside there was nothing about piracy or about sailing. It was a standard almanac with the usual information about the sun rising and setting, zodiac symbols, and detailed descriptions of various illnesses. On the top of every other page were engravings of farm work. This calendar was not for sailors, who after all moved around too much for these charts on the sun rising and setting to be of much help. Instead, it was for farmers with pirates as an added attraction.[56] Captivity and shipwreck had an equally wide readership. Riley's *Authentic Narrative of the Loss of the American Brig Commerce* went through multiple editions and sold as many as a million copies in the nineteenth century.[57] Herman Melville was a huge fan of all types of maritime literature, both when he went to sea and when he became an author. He mentioned the "Pirates Own" in *Redburn*, based his *Israel Potter* on a captivity narrative, and used the destruction of the *Essex* in his *Moby Dick*.[58] Edgar Allan Poe relied on shipwreck narratives for background to his frightening *The Narrative of Gordon Pym of Nantucket*.[59] Printer Joseph Buckingham remembered that his seafaring brother had returned to Boston with copies of *The History of the Pirates* and *Robinson Crusoe*, testifying to the fact that both landsmen and seamen were familiar with these books.[60]

Beyond Disaster

Beyond stories about disaster, sailors benefited from the print revolution and read a wide range of material. Some of the books represented high culture; others reflected more plebeian tastes. Some were for education and information; others were purely for amusement. Holton J. Breed itemized his library and the price he paid for each volume in the back of his logbook.

Morses Geography 2 Volums	$6.00
Goldsmiths anamated Nature	$8.00
Walshes arthimetic	$1.50
American Coast Pilot	$.75
Driches Dictionary	$3.00
Johnson's Dictionary	$1.00
Bowditch Navigation	$6.50
Bible	$1.00
Fishers Companion	$1.25
Telemachuses travels	$1.40
The Gide to helth	$1.40
Nautical almanack	$1.20
A prair Book	$.50
Sparman's voyage 2 volums	$2.00
Gentle Mans pocket Library	$1.10
Eloisa 3 volumes	$2.00
Dodsleys poems	$1.75
Pilgrims progress	$1.00
Thom Jones	$1.50
the Spectator	$1.00
the Lover's instruction	$.25
To Love	$1.25

Although there was no book of piracy here, Breed's eclectic collection included novels, travel books, technical works, advice manuals, religious tracts, and the Bible. Breed owned both the risqué *Tom Jones* by Daniel Defoe, and the religious *Pilgrim's Progress* by John Bunyan, "A prair Book," and a work with the tantalizing title of "the Lover's instruction." Except perhaps for the volumes concerning navigation, this list could just as easily have been written by a landsman as by a seaman.[61] Breed's log-book catalogue is a little unusual for a mariner, however, because he listed the price he paid for each book, indicating a significant total investment of more than $40 and suggesting that he was concerned with his personal library as a material object. Most sailors were less possessive about their books. As Richard Henry Dana Jr. explained, trading of books was "a practice very common among ships in foreign ports, by which you get rid of the books you have read and re-read, and a supply of new ones in their stead, and Jack is not very nice as to their comparative value."[62]

What mattered to a mariner was not the book as object, rather he was interested in the subject and its entertainment value. James C. Osborn, the second mate on the whaleship *Charles W. Morgan*, did not identify which books he owned. Instead, he recorded in his logbook the books he read on a voyage to the Pacific in the 1840s, which ran the gamut from novels, to travel narratives, to temperance tracts.[63] J. Ross Browne read and reread the books available during his cruise on a whaleship. The cooper's "stock of literature consisted of a temperance book, a few Mormon tracts, and Lady Dacre's Diary of a Chaperon." Another sailor had "a Bible; another, the first volume of Cooper's Pilot; a third, the Songster's own Book; a fourth, the Complete Letter Writer; and a fifth claimed, as his total literary stock, a copy of the Flash newspaper, published in New York, in which he cut a conspicuous figure as the 'Lady's Fancy Man.' "[64] Scholars have chronicled the libraries available to Melville while he was at sea. When Melville joined the whaler the *Charles and Henry* in the Pacific in 1843 it had a well-stocked chest of books on board: W. S. Cardell, *Jack Halyard*; Walter Colton, *Visit to Constantinople and Athens*; Horace Holden, *Shipwreck on a Desert Islands: A Narrative of the Shipwreck, Captivity, and Sufferings of Horace Holden and Benj. H. Nute* … ; John H. Amory, *The Young Rover*; Frederick Marryat, *Poor Jack*; and the *Child's Robinson Crusoe*. There were also other non-adventure books on board, including several religious and moral tales. The frigate USS *United States* had an even longer list of books available. In short, in the first half of the nineteenth century sailors read novels, sensationalist literature, newspapers, histories, geographies, travelogues, navigational and technical works, scientific texts, and self-help guides that were products of the print revolution.[65]

Perhaps we might be surprised to find so many novels read by sailors. This form of literature emerged in the eighteenth century in accounts of fictional lives of several characters over space and time. Dependent on the imagination, the novel as a genre had a limited readership before 1800. After that date the publication of novels exploded in Great Britain and the United States as a reflection of shifting literary tastes and innovations in printing. By the 1830s it was possible to count the number of book runs of some novels in the tens of thousands. Novels were often associated with the middle class, especially middle-class women, and concerns with sentimentality during the rise of Romanticism in the nineteenth century. Yet sailors read these books. Mariners may have had a special appreciation for this form of literature because of their own experience in travel and because of their logbook mentality: novels depended on the ability to relate stories across time and space, a concept that sailors could understand all too well. Novels also reflected the many intellectual cross-currents of the age of revolution, with some writers clinging nostalgically to the past and others embracing the new social relations of the future. Sailors confound our expectations and read books carrying both radical and conservative messages. They read a full spectrum of novels, ranging from books about women, to stories about life at sea, to standard fiction on land-based themes. This wide array of novel reading calls for further explanation.

Why, for instance, would men coated in tar or knee deep in whale blubber read novels like Samuel Richardson's *Pamela* and Rowson's *Charlotte Temple* centered on female decisions about sex, marriage, family, and children? As Cathy Davidson argues, novels about women were "dedicated to the proposition that women's experience was worthy of detailed, sympathetic, and thoughtful attention."[66] Would mariners like Osborn who had read a copy of *Pamela* on the *Charles W. Morgan* and the black steward in *Redburn* who had read *Charlotte Temple* agree? There can be no definitive answers to this question because neither Osborn nor Melville's black steward explained their reading choices. But we can offer a few conjectures. The fact that these books were immensely popular at the time may alone explain why some seamen read them. But there may be other reasons for sailors' interest in novels about women. Female-centered novels were packed with implicit sexual tension that might attract a male reader in the all-male environment of the ship. More importantly, seamen might have appreciated the radical subversive aspects of such novels. These books revolved around individual sensation and experience of seemingly powerless people – in the case of *Pamela* and *Charlotte Temple*, women – and thereby challenged patriarchal and religious authority. To men who were also frequently considered powerless themselves, this message may have had some appeal.[67]

While sailors read books prominently featuring women, they read many more novels on maritime subjects. Like women reading novels about women, seamen reading books about seamen brought the daily concerns of powerless people – mariners – front and center even if the lead character was not a common Jack Tar. Daniel Defoe's *Robinson Crusoe* was one of the most popular novels in the maritime community – as well as in mainstream society. Seamen repeatedly mentioned this classic tale of shipwreck. They thought of the book whenever they passed anywhere near Juan Fernandez Island where Alexander Selkirk, the character on whom the novel was based, had been marooned. After rounding the Horn and entering the Pacific Ocean, Richard Henry Dana Jr. wrote back home that he had been to Robinson Crusoe's island. And in 1850 passenger John K. Barker on his way to California noted in his journal that the ship had passed Juan Fernandez Island, or "Robinson Crusoe's Island."[68] Crusoe was no common seaman. Even when he ran from home as a youth he did not sail before the mast. When shipwrecked on his famous island, Crusoe was a supercargo – a shipping agent for the merchant owners of the vessel. The story itself is moralistic and argues that man should be content with his life. Crusoe, born to a middling and comfortable status, did not accept his social station and suffered as a result. On one voyage he was captured by corsairs from Salee on the Barbary Coast, but managed to escape after a few years of slavery. The shipwreck in the South Seas was worse and he lived for twenty-eight years in isolation. However, he did more than survive on the island. He demonstrated the importance of self-reliance, hard work, persistence, and the providence of God.[69]

While the prominence of those values in the book assured a wide readership for the novel among the burgeoning middle class, sailors may have read the book more as a testimony to the dangers they faced from captivity and shipwreck. This relationship helps to explain why some seamen mentioned the book when they faced imprisonment or talked about sailors being marooned on a desert island. One prisoner during the War of 1812 alluded to *Robinson Crusoe* when he said that he would rather be left alone on an island and be "tormented with Alexander Selkirk's reflections whilst on Juan Fernandez" than suffer the mistreatment he experienced while being held captive on a British ship. Josiah Cobb remarked that when he first arrived in Dartmoor, he had as little to guide him in the pandemonium as did Robinson Crusoe on a desolate island, except, unlike Crusoe, "instead of being 'lord of all we surveyed,' we were more like (not in cooing meekness, but in forlornness,) the dove sent forth from the ark." When Joshua Penny escaped his British captors at Cape Town and hid on Table Mountain he described his life in Crusoe-like terms. Defoe's book was so familiar that when J. Ross Browne had Bill Mann spin a yarn about a sailor abandoned on an island, he referred to Crusoe.[70] Whatever the rationale behind the book's popularity, it was reprinted time and again in Great Britain and the United States. These many different publishers produced multiple versions of the book with altered wording, pruning, additions, and changes. The connection between sailor tales of calamity and Defoe's great novel was made explicit by none other than Charles Ellms, who published a fully illustrated compendium of exotic travel, shipwreck, and marooning narratives under the title *Robinson Crusoe's Own Book*.[71]

Mariners read many sea novels other than the various versions of *Robinson Crusoe*. There had long been a popular interest in sea fiction that had been brought into the eighteenth century by Defoe. Indeed, Defoe also wrote a pirate novel, *The Life, Adventures, and Piracies of the Famous Captain Singleton*.[72] In the 1740s and 1750s Tobias Smollett had caricaturized sailors in some of his fiction, especially *Roderick Random*. That stereotype, as we have seen, was crucial in molding popular images of Jack Tar. William Falconer's *The Shipwreck*, an epic poem first published in 1762, evoked sympathy for mariners facing dangers at sea, especially because Falconer had served aboard ships and his description of a storm at sea had a tinge of reality about it. We do not know how far this literature reached into the forecastle. But around the end of the eighteenth century, just as publications became increasingly available to broader audiences, we can begin to get a better sense of the extent of its popularity. Archibald Duncan was impressed enough with Falconer to open his shipwreck compendium with lines from Falconer's poem.[73] In 1798 Samuel Taylor Coleridge was hugely successful in his portrayal of "the Ancient Mariner" and his horrific experience on the ocean after killing an albatross. Lord Byron penned a very popular sentimentalized poem about a pirate in *The Corsair*. These long poems set the stage for Walter Scott's novel *The Pirate*, which was read on both sides of the Atlantic and which Dana mentioned seeing on the Californian coast.[74]

It is against this background that James Fenimore Cooper wrote his *Red Rover*. Scott's novel had not been technical enough for Cooper, who decided that someone needed to write about the sea who, like Falconer, actually knew the ropes. Cooper's first effort was *The Pilot*, which was a disguised story of John Paul Jones in the Revolutionary War. Believing that he had not fully succeeded in writing a sea tale in *The Pilot* as most of the action in the novel took place on land, Cooper wrote *The Red Rover*. Cooper's Red Rover turned to piracy in the 1750s as the only way to strike a blow against a tyrannical British government. That the Red Rover and the hero of the tale, who was a British officer sent under cover to capture the corsair, not only protected the heroine on the pirate ship but later fought for the Americans during the Revolution somehow absolved both men of being true pirates or anything like cutthroats despite having sailed under the "bloody flag."[75] Cooper continued to write nautical fiction, as well as a history of American naval prowess. In 1839 the American naval department issued a list of books for its warships that included Cooper's *History of the Navy of the United States of America*, *The Red Rover*, *The Pilot*, and a third sea novel, *The Water Witch*.[76]

Cooper's success, especially with *The Red Rover*, led to the proliferation of other novels that celebrated life at sea. British writer and naval captain Frederick Marryat enjoyed great popularity in both the forecastle and the drawing room. A copy of Marryat's *Poor Jack* was on Melville's *Charles and Henry*. This book was the story of a youth growing up on the London waterfront who experienced a series of misadventures before obtaining wealth through marriage and patronage.[77] The fact that Marryat had a conservative and hierarchical worldview did not seem to bother his sailor readers. Osborn read nearly two dozen Marryat volumes and Henry James Mercier created a comic dialogue in verse of a sailor "literary group" discussing Marryat novels including *Mr. Midshipman Easy*. This last book was probably Marryat's most popular work and is a rollicking parody on equality in which the main character, Jack Easy, became a midshipman in his majesty's navy because he was convinced that the sea would make all men equal. Four years in the king's service persuaded him to abandon the rights of man and espouse authority. Marryat's novels thus had a British context and aristocratic message.[78] Another sea novel on Osborn's list, Joseph C. Hart's *Miriam Coffin*, was thoroughly American and heralded the common seaman who worked in the whaling industry. Herman Melville read this book and relied on it for his description of Nantucket in *Moby Dick*. Although much of the book centered on the overreaching ambitions of Miriam Coffin, the wife of a Quaker merchant, it also provided great detail on the whaling process and even had a whale in its death throes destroy a ship. Most importantly, *Miriam Coffin* offered a paean to American ingenuity and the American seaman. Maritime readers no doubt relished the portrayal of the Nantucket whale men as "a bold and hardy race of men; in danger, cool, collected, and adventurous," who seldom indulged "in the vices or evil propensities of the common sailor," while "possessing all his generous and manly qualities, tempered with correct notions of economy and of the true obligations of society."[79]

If Cooper's sea novels spurred the pens of several authors to create additional sea fiction, then Richard Henry Dana Jr.'s *Two Years before the Mast* encouraged other men, especially common seamen, to write nonfictional accounts of life at sea. Here we see the twin effects of the democratization of society and the changes in print culture. Dana's book had an incredible reach. J. Ross Browne, who consciously modeled *Etchings of a Whaling Cruise* on Dana's work, found a copy of *Two Years before the Mast* in Madagascar. He also reported that he had heard many sailors speak highly of Dana's book.[80] Dana's impact on a flurry of sailor narratives after him can be seen in some of the titles seamen chose for their books. Listed in ascending order of time at sea there were: Jacob Hazen, *Five Years before the Mast*; George Edward Clark, *Seven Years a Sailor's Life*; Nicholas Peter Isaacs, *Twenty Years before the Mast*; George Little, *Life on the Ocean; or Twenty Years at Sea*; Samuel Leech, *Thirty Years from Home, or A Voice from the Main Deck*; and of course Cooper's *Ned Myers, a Life before the Mast*.[81] The audience for these books, was, as Hazen explained, the "general reader." But he and the other sailor authors probably assumed that their shipmates would see their books, especially because several of these sailor narratives had a reformist message attempting to convince the reader to learn by the authors' own mistakes concerning drinking and hard living.

We would expect sailors to read fiction and nonfiction about life at sea. But they also read land-based novels. As was true of maritime fiction, there were a surprising number of British and American novels aboard ships with a conservative orientation. Osborn's reading list contained Cooper's leatherstocking *The Pathfinder* and his fictional account of Columbus's discovery of America, *Mercedes of Castile*. Cooper, as we have seen, was also a favorite of the American navy, which included *Homeward Bound* in its recommended list. Despite his Jacksonian proclivities, Cooper was a social conservative, a position that was evident in his description of relations between the quarterdeck and the forecastle in his sea fiction, as well as in his portrayal of frontier society. His antidemocratic inclinations were especially evident in works like *Homeward Bound*.[82] Sailors read other novels by conservative authors. Osborn read Washington Irving's *Bracebridge Hall*, which was really just a series of stories that idealized the lives of English aristocrats, and British conservative Samuel Warren's *Ten Thousand a-Year* about a social upstart attempting to gain control over land owned by a virtuous aristocrat.[83] Even Redburn's black steward had read a work by George Walker, an earlier conservative writer in Great Britain.[84] Sailors also enjoyed the works of Edward Bulwer-Lytton, whose first novel, *Pelham*, mentioned by name by Osborn, was both a critique of aristocratic dandyism and an affirmation of the aristocrat's role in British society.[85]

Mariners read novels and other books by individuals with more liberal sympathies. Osborn's list included *Elizabeth De Bruce*, which was a book written by a woman, Christian Isobel Johnstone, about another woman, the wife of Robert I of Scotland, in a historical novel. Besides writing a story that subtly challenged the authority of the British empire with its assertion of Scottish nationalism, Johnstone was a reformer who supported antislavery movements, temperance, education, and moral training.[86] Sailors were interested, too, in more radical writers like William Godwin, a leading English Jacobin in the 1790s who had married Mary Wollstonecraft and pursued anarchic principles that called for a utilitarian distribution of property.[87] Ned Myers mentioned the most famous radical of Godwin's generation, Thomas Paine, in his reminiscences, confiding that he had abandoned the Bible and morality once a steward had lent him some of Paine's deist writings. A captain of a small sloop remembered arguing with his mate in 1802 about the "Blasphemous writings of Tom Paine."[88]

When it came to "sensational" literature, mariners did not limit themselves to works by radicals like Tom Paine, or the "trash made for seamen" about piracy, shipwrecks, and captivity. They also read "trash" written about land-based subjects. Some of these books were relatively mild. *The Female Wanderer* by Cordelia Stark, among the books read by Osborn, played to a popular artifice seen in maritime sources such as *Fanny Campbell, The Female Pirate Captain* and numerous ballads – the heroine dressed as a man to follow her beau when her father refused to countenance their marriage. After a series of adventures on land, she and her true love marry.[89] Other books offered intense social criticism and harsh portraits of urban life like Eugene Sue's *Mysteries of Paris*. Religious reformers identified this novel as "of the worst description" because of its explicit portrayal of the urban underworld.[90] One writer in the *Sailor's Magazine* complained that seamen "read licentious tales and demoralizing novels, hundreds of which are daily offered for sale among them."[91] Whatever the strength and weaknesses of Sue's writing, his popularity gave birth to a whole genre of books that quickly degenerated into little more than sensationalist exposés of crime and prostitution in the city like Ned Buntline's *The Mysteries and Miseries of New York* and George Lippard's *Quaker City, or The Monks of Monk Hall: A Romance of Philadelphia Life, Mystery and Crime*. There is no direct evidence that sailors read either of these two books, despite the fact that Buntline had been a seaman and adopted a maritime pen name. We do know from Browne that at least one sailor had a copy of the *Flash* magazine, which used the same transparent reformist veneer to discuss sexual activity, prostitution, and gambling in New York.[92]

Regular newspapers and more mainstream magazines were very important to sailors, especially when they were held in captivity or were far from home. Charles Herbert reported that the British attempted to prevent prisoners of war during the Revolution from obtaining newspapers. Despite this effort, the American captives in Great Britain eagerly read about the events of the war, such as the American victory at Trenton and the raid on the British coast by John Paul Jones. Herbert was particularly excited to have a copy of the London *Evening Post* in prison because it contained a "burlesque on the [British] ministry, very severe."[93] Newspapers were available to the men held in Dartmoor during the War of 1812. Some sailors pooled their resources to subscribe to British newspapers like the *Statesman*, the *Star*, *Bell's Weekly Messenger*, and the *Whig*. The prisoners would also occasionally get to read William Cobbet's *Political Register*, and the anti-American London *Times*. The British would purposely show the prisoners antiwar American papers like the *Federal Republican* and Boston Federalist papers, which angered the sailors. The men held in prison ships in Jamaica even produced their own newspapers.[94] Mariners in the nineteenth century read a number of different magazines. Besides sensationalist journals like the *Flash*, seamen had access to more wholesome fare. Many scrimshanders – men who etched ink into whale teeth or whale bone – copied their pictures from *Godey's Ladies Book* or *Harper's Weekly*, testifying to the presence of these journals on their ships.[95] During long voyages sailors read and reread newspapers whenever they could. Even the advertisements were repeatedly perused. As Richard Henry Dana Jr. explained: "there is nothing in a strange land like a newspaper from home." Newspapers were almost preferable to a letter from relatives because a newspaper "carries you back to the spot better than anything else. It is almost equal to *clairvoyance*. The names of the streets, with the things advertised, is almost as good as seeing the signs." Reading the story about the graduation of his college friends from Harvard brought the ceremony so much to life that he could see in his mind's eye as the graduates crossed the stage on the very day that "their classmate was walking up and down [a] California beach with a hide upon his head." Dana spent a week poring over these papers every watch below, making "sure there could be nothing in them that had escaped" his attention.[96]

Newspapers from home may have riveted the mariner's attention on local affairs, but sailors were also interested in the world around them and had access to history, geography, and travel books. Many of the volumes the American navy sent to warships in 1839 were history books ranging from Edward Gibbon's *Decline and Fall of the Roman Empire*, which originally appeared in 1776, to the first volumes of George Bancroft's *A History of the United States*, which started publication in 1834.[97] Among the books that William McNally read were "Gibbon's decline and fall of the Roman Empire, Botta's History of the United States, and life of Washington, [and] Irving's Columbus."⁹⁸ Besides history, sailors read about geography. Breed listed two volumes of "Morses Geography." These books reflected a growing interest in geography as a subject that helped to define the reader's place in a larger world and that fostered an American national identity.⁹⁹ Examining exotic and distant cultures contributed to this national enterprise. Several of the books the American navy distributed were travelogues. Osborn read travel narratives such as Michael J. Quin's *A Steam Voyage down the Danube*, *Travels in Egypt and Arabia*, and "Travels in Egypt and Nubia Felix." The subjects of these works were exotic locations that Americans would not ordinarily visit.¹⁰⁰ Osborn also read Benjamin Morrell's *A Narrative of Four Voyages*, which added a more practical purpose to its travelogue. Seeing himself as something of an explorer – Morrell claimed to be the first American to sail below the Antarctic Circle – he described the coasts of South America, the western shore of North America, countless Pacific Islands, and the East Indies. For the sailor this information was of more than passing interest; it could also help him navigate in distant waters.¹⁰¹

Of course sailors had access to works that explicitly helped them in navigation. During the eighteenth century several books were published that allowed mariners to determine their latitude and longitude by using a table that could be compared with observations made with navigational instruments of the angles on lunar measurements. This type of navigation entailed complicated trigonometry and was not foolproof. At the beginning of the nineteenth century Nathaniel Bowditch recalculated these tables and published them in his *New American Practical Navigator*. This book then became a standard resource. Indeed, the U.S. government still publishes a navigational aid based on Bowditch's original work. Bowditch did more than produce tables; he also offered instruction in trigonometry and provided a host of other material on navigating in general.¹⁰² It is not a surprise therefore that Breed had Bowditch among his possessions, that the navy supplied copies to its ships, and that Dana studied Bowditch during his two years before the mast. Oddly, Osborn does not report reading the book during his whaling voyage to the Pacific, but as second mate he was expected to learn navigation and therefore almost certainly used the book. Many other technical books were available to sailors. Breed paid seventy-five cents for *The American Coast Pilot*. This book outlined sailing directions for entering ports in the United States.¹⁰³ There were also instruction manuals on seamanship describing and illustrating the proper layout of rigging, knots, blocks, tackles, and masts.[104] William Falconer prepared an English marine dictionary that became a standard work defining the many technical terms on the ship. As with other publications, American printers produced their own variations of this volume without worrying about copyright issues.[105] Booksellers pasted advertisements for "Atlases, Pilots, & Charts for the navigating of every sea" as well as "Nautical Books of every Description" in blank logbooks and journals sold to seamen.[106] After returning to Boston and becoming a lawyer, Richard Henry Dana Jr. offered his own "Treatise on Practical Seamanship" that was a comprehensive guidebook covering the proper food to be served on ships, instructions on sailing a ship, a dictionary of sea terms, the duties of different ranks aboard ships, and the legal obligations and liabilities of seamen and ship owners.[107]

The same interest in the world and concern with the practice of navigation and seamanship convinced sailors to read scientific texts. The most expensive item on Breed's catalogue of books was "Goldsmiths anamated Nature," which cost more than half a month's wages for the common seaman. We can assume that this prized possession was Oliver Goldsmith's encyclopedic *An History of the Earth and Animated Nature*, which was originally published in eight volumes in 1774 and subsequently republished many times. In true Enlightenment style, Goldsmith had set out to summarize all knowledge on the natural world. He had a section on geology, discussing earthquakes, volcanoes, rivers, and oceans. But most of his work was devoted to biology, with information on species of fish, birds, insects, reptiles, mammals, and humans. Although Goldsmith's opus was a popularized form of science and even something of a hack job, these volumes provided a great resource for men who literally traversed the globe.[108] Sailors read other scientific surveys. Mercier jokingly remarked that a cook on his warship checked out an essay on conchology from his warship's library and that "a light hearted *harum-scarum* fore-topman" borrowed a copy of John Mason Good's *The Book of Nature* "to edify himself and the worthies of the larboard gangway."[109] Osborn also read this last book, which touched on some of the same geologic and biologic information as Goldsmith, but spent more time exploring the uniqueness of human beings in areas like instinct, sensation, and intelligence.[110] Both multivolume collections had practical applications for men at sea. It is more difficult to imagine why Osborn, and we can only assume other seamen on the whaler *Charles W. Morgan*, read Richard Reece's *The Lady's Medical Guide*. The book was a clearly written discussion of the

"*Causes, Prevention, and Mode of Treatment of the Diseases to Which Females Are Particularly Subject*," meaning it covered problems with the menstrual cycle and pregnancy, and even discussed ways of determining virginity in a woman. Perhaps this detail offered some voyeuristic pleasure to men isolated from women for so many months at sea. In the eighteenth century young men used illustrated books on female anatomy as a form of pornography. But there were no illustrations in Reece's book and no obsession with monstrosity as appeared in these earlier works.[111] More likely, Osborn and others read this layman's medical text pragmatically and in the same vein that they read Goldsmith and Good. Only in this case the practical knowledge gained was not about the world seen from a ship, but of the female reproduction system that would be useful to men who were either married or intended to marry. This interpretation is supported by the location of the item on Osborn's list following a book called *Husband's Duty to Wife*.[112]

The identity of *Husband's Duty to Wife* remains unclear. It might be a poem from the early eighteenth century or it might be a book outlining the proper modes of behavior. Breed, Osborn, and other sailors read self-help texts, such as temperance tracts and conduct manuals, on board, with titles like "Tracks on Disapation," and "Health Advisor." Breed owned a copy of *The Gentleman's Pocket Library*, which was a collection of conduct books with titles like "The Principles of Politeness," "The Economy of Human Life," and "The Polite Philosopher." It also included Benjamin Franklin's "The Way to Wealth."[113] Osborn read William A. Alcott's *The Young Man's Guide*. Like the selections in *The Gentleman's Pocket Library*, this book articulated a set of middle-class values that seemed to be the very antithesis of life as a sailor, decrying drink, gambling, and bad company. It even condemned the theater as immoral and considered tobacco a poison.[114]

This survey of reading by sailors indicates that seamen, like their land-based cousins, fully participated in a revolution both in the production and in the consumption of books. Mariners did not limit their reading to maritime subjects. The same popular novels, regardless of their political orientation, that people would read in their parlors would also be read in the forecastle. Many seamen were so curious about the world around them that they felt compelled to study works in history, geography, and science. Self-improvement, a central theme in many novels from the era, was also important to maritime readers. The message of reform in some novels and the self-help literature was even more prominent in the religious publications prepared for seamen.

Religion

Any discussion of religious reading by sailors must begin with the Bible. This book had long been essential for every literate person in the Anglo-American world. Indeed, the main reason for many people to learn how to read was to study the Bible. The Bible therefore figured prominently in the lives of seamen in the eighteenth and nineteenth centuries. The rise of evangelical religion and the explosion of print culture in the nineteenth century led to efforts to distribute even more Bibles to sailors. It also fostered an expansion of other literature to convince mariners to turn to religion. As a result reformers published Bibles, religious books, hymnals, magazines, and tracts in an effort to appeal to seamen.[115]

Given the prominence of the Bible in the Protestant Anglo-American world it is not surprising to discover evidence of sailors reading the Bible in the eighteenth century. What was unusual were the conditions and some of the reasons for reading the "Good Book." Obviously some sailors read the Bible for religious purposes. As a prisoner of war during the Revolution Charles Herbert bought a small pocket Bible for three shillings and six pence. This purchase marked a significant investment for a seaman held captive by the British, and the size of the book suggests his intent to carry it with him so that he could read and study it whenever he desired.[116] Andrew Sherburne had been a sailor during the Revolutionary War, gave up his life at sea in 1785, and in 1789 had a religious experience as a result of reading the Bible. Many years later Sherburne recounted how the Bible awakened him to God and hoped others would follow.[117] Oddly, the Bible could be used for purposes that were not religious. A seaman might pick up a Bible simply out of boredom. On a voyage to China in the late 1790s Eleazer Elderkin relied on his Bible to fill some of his spare time.[118] Even more unexpected was the reason Simeon Crowell shared certain passages from the Old Testament with his shipmates aboard a fishing vessel on the Grand Banks in the 1790s. Crowell, who had grown up in a religious family and had read the Bible carefully, recited for his illiterate shipmates the tribulations of Job, the history of Susanna, the destruction of Bel, and the killing of the Babylonian dragon mainly for their entertainment value. As Crowell explained, almost in the same breath that he would regale his shipmates with Bible stories, he sang carnal songs and exhibited his expertise in swearing and cursing. This context suggests that although for religious commentators the book of Job revealed that man's love of God should be unconditional, Crowell recounted Job's suffering in fun, perhaps because an upright and once prosperous man was forced to undergo one horrendous experience after another. Likewise, we can only imagine the embellishment Crowell added in describing the beautiful Susanna naked in her bath being observed by two older men who then tried to pressure her to have sex with them. In the book of Daniel the tales about the destruction of Bel and the killing of the dragon were intended to reinforce the importance of monotheism and the rejection of false idols. These hard-working, impoverished fishermen apparently delighted in hearing how trickster priests used a secret passage to gain access to food left for the god of Bel, were then out-tricked themselves, and punished for their deception. Crowell's shipmates must have enjoyed hearing how Daniel slew a dragon worshiped by the Babylonians by feeding him food that caused him to explode.[119]

There was a similar mixture of motives for reading the Bible after 1800. Before Ned Myers became religious, he recalled that earlier in his sailing career he read the "sacred book for amusement, and not for light." He was only interested in the "narratives, such as those of Sampson and Goliath" and he so enjoyed "The history of Jonah and the whale" that he read it "at least twenty times." However much he read his Bible, he had to confess that he could not "remember that the morality, or thought, or devotion of a single passage ever struck" him at the time.[120] Other seamen were familiar with the Bible and used biblical stories as a way to express themselves. A prison ship could be compared to "Noah's ark capsized" and the "din of noise" and "confusion of tongues" among the prisoners of war was the same as with the "Tower of Babel."[121] Like Eleazer Elderkin in the 1790s, sometimes mariners opened their Bibles out of sheer boredom. One seaman in the 1840s commented that all hands were "deeply engaged in studying their bibles." This activity seemed strange to the sailor. He jokingly remarked that if the men continued their Bible study the entire crew would get to Fiddler's Green – a mythical sailors' afterlife "in which wine, women, and song figure prominently." Two weeks later the seaman explained that tedium was the real reason for all this apparent religious interest and that there was "nothing to do but read our bibles. Everyone has read everything else on the ship. They have almost memorized it by heart." They had also told each other everything that had happened in their lives over the past ten years. In frustration he exclaimed, "so we are read out and talked out – it is time to go home."[122] Some seamen may have owned a Bible and not used it just as many land-based Americans kept a Bible in their homes as a mere token without giving the book much thought. Sailors could also open their Bibles for religious reasons. George Little noted that after the death of a ship-mate most of the crew became more religious and spent time reading the Bible.[123] In the summer of 1827 a wave of strong religious feeling swept through the USS *Constitution* and several men began reading the Bible.[124] Ned Myers also claimed that his sobriety and religious conversion were influenced by a Bible.[125]

Although Myers later returned to alcohol and died a few years after Cooper recorded his autobiography, the religious reading experience of this man who worked most of his life before the mast is instructive and reveals the extent to which the print revolution affected religious pub-lications.[126] Myers owned at least three Bibles. He bought the first copy earlier in his career and, as we have seen, used it mainly for his read-ing amusement. He must have lost this Bible at some point, because in the later stages of his life at sea, and as he was struck deathly ill in the Dutch East Indies, he sought to procure another one. As he explained, "My two great desires," as he lay in the forecastle suffering from a fever with one of his legs shriveled to half its size, "were to get to the hospital and to procure a bible." Before being sent ashore at Batavia to fulfill the first "desire," he heard that one of his shipmates had a Bible that "lay untouched in the bottom of his chest, sailor-fashion." Myers offered to trade a shirt for the Bible, but the man, showing the usual generosity typical of seamen, refused any payment. Myers reciprocated by forc-ing the shirt on him as a keepsake of their friendship. Myers obtained the third Bible toward the end of his convalescence on Java. Shortly before he was about to return to the sea, a Christian black – possibly from Africa – who had housed him after his release from the hospital insisted that Myers accept a large English Bible that also had "prayers for seamen bound in it" and was "a sort of English prayer-book." If the third Bible had come from England, the second Bible probably had been printed by the American Bible Society, an organization dedicated to dis-tributing Bibles established in 1816.[127] Throughout the antebellum era the American Bible Society printed Bibles that would be purchased by auxiliary organizations and then sold or distributed to different groups, including seamen. For example, the Boston Seamen's Friend Society dis-tributed 750 Bibles in 1846, 382 Bibles in 1848, and 249 Bibles in 1849. These handouts were just a drop in the bucket compared to the millions of Bibles placed into the hands of sinners in the backwoods, in the cities, and aboard ships by the American Bible Society before 1850.[128] Religious reformers viewed the Bible as the word of God and believed that as such it was the best means to reach the unconverted, yet as a book the Bible was huge and relatively expensive. The American Bible Society managed to reduce costs by using the most modern printing techniques and setting type as few times as possible. Even at sixty cents a copy, considering the numbers involved, the overall expense was formidable. Reformers therefore produced other kinds of religious printed material – books, hymnals, magazines, and tracts. Myers had access to each of these forms of religious literature.[129]

During his physical ordeal and religious odyssey in the Dutch East Indies, Myers combined his study of the Bible with a reading of *Pilgrim's Progress*, which had been given to him by a Christian Lascar – a sailor from India or the East Indies. This late seventeenth-century book written by John Bunyan chronicled the religious journey of its main character as he confronted difficulties in the real world on his way toward salvation and heaven. Myers considered the book "second only to the bible" as a guide to religion. He explained that "it enabled me to understand and to apply a vast deal that I found in the word of God" and offered him hope because he now understood that Christ had died for him. He decided that if "the thief on the cross could be saved, even one as wicked as I had only to repent and believe, to share in the Redeemer's mercy." *Pilgrim's Progress* was also among Breed's possessions, had been read by Crowell as a young man, and was one of several religious books in the portable library given to ships by the American Seamen's Friend Society (a reform group dedicated to bringing religion to sailors). The age of the book did not seem to affect its timeliness for Myers or those who sought to extend religion to seamen. During the antebellum period reformers encouraged the reading of several older books like Richard Baxter's *A Call to the Unconverted* and *The Saint's Everlasting Rest*, Joseph Alleine's *Alarm to the Unconverted Sinners*, John Flavel's *Touchstone of Sincerity*, and Philip Doddridge's *Rise and Progress of Religion in the Soul*. Only the last book, which Myers had exchanged with his black host in Java for his own copy of *Pilgrim's Progress*, had been written in the eighteenth century. The other volumes were all products of the seventeenth century. The American Tract Society, a reform group organized to produce and distribute religious books and pamphlets, printed these works in New York and either gave them away or sold them for as little as twelve and a half cents. One reformer explained, "Send Baxter, and Doddridge, and Bunyan to sea; and their triumph on sea shall equal, if not exceed their success on land."[130]

As Myers struggled with illness and found his way to religion, the same Lascar who presented Myers with Bunyan's book also gave him a hymnal. This collection of religious songs had a profound effect on the ailing tar, especially because, as Myers exclaimed, one of the first hymns he read "was written by a man who had been a sailor like myself, and one who had been almost as wicked as myself, but has since done a vast deal of good, by means of precept and example." Unfortunately for us, Myers did not identify which hymnal he read. Such hymnals, however, became powerful instruments in bringing religion to the masses during the antebellum era. A seaman reported that the Bible, Baxter's *Saint's Rest*, and a hymnal were all that were needed to open his heart to God. Perhaps the most successful of these hymnals was put together by Joshua Leavitt. His *Christian Lyre* sold 18,000 copies in its first year, and was reissued in twenty-six editions during the 1830s with more than 50,000 copies in circulation. Leavitt was a prominent evangelical who was the first secretary of the American Seamen's Friend Society, and later was a leading abolitionist. Leavitt also edited the *Sailor's Magazine* for more than forty years.[131]

Myers did not report reading any religious magazines while in Java, but he did read them earlier when he had gone to the Sailor's Retreat in Staten Island to dry out from his alcohol abuse. In 1821 the *Christian Herald*, a general reform magazine published in New York, became the *Christian Herald and Seaman's Magazine*. The resulting bifurcated journal was mainly geared toward reporting on reform activities across the nation, including a special section on seamen.[132] In 1828 merchants, sea captains, and evangelical reformers joined together in New York to form the American Seaman's Friend Society, which began publishing the *Sailors' Magazine* that December. Like the maritime half of its *Christian Herald and Seaman's Magazine* predecessor, the *Sailors' Magazine* reported on efforts to reform seamen and religious meetings, but it also had conversion narratives, sermons, and poetry. More relevant for the sailor, the magazine had material directly of interest to mariners. One of the first issues summarized Kent's legal commentaries on the duties and obligations of seamen, and in 1837 there was an illustrated article on the Seaman's Retreat visited by Myers. If a sailor found such reading dry, even though it was intended to inform him of his rights and provide him with practical information, there were short stories in the section called "The Cabin Boy's Locker" that were more entertaining. The *Sailors' Magazine* also contained sensational fare such as reports of shipwrecks and even piracy: in 1831 the *Sailors' Magazine* published the dying confession of pirate Charles Gibbs. Even though seaman Nathaniel Ames dismissed this publication in his nautical reminiscences as "silly" and "juvenile," this was probably the periodical Myers had read in the Sailors' Retreat and plenty of seamen enjoyed its articles.[133]

During his spiritual journey in Java, in addition to the Bible, religious books, hymnals, and magazines, Myers read several tracts given to him by an American carpenter who had brought them from the United States.[134] Reformers hoped that these pamphlet-like publications, often only four to eight pages long, would be appropriate reading matter for the unconverted. Tracts could also be geared toward specific audiences. Relatively cheap to produce, tracts were written with clear and direct language: they needed to be "short," "interesting," "pungent," and "unassuming." As Jedidiah Morse, a leader in the New England Tract Society, explained, "There must be something to allure the listless to read, and this can only be done by blending entertainment with instruction."[135] Tracts were to be a first step in the conversion process. Once readers came to understand the importance of religion, they would recognize the need to study the word of God in the Bible. The *Dialogue between Two Seamen after a Storm* offers wonderful insight into how a tract was supposed to operate. In a nod to the sensationalist literature it was intended to counteract, the tract had a hint of the disaster tale because it recorded a conversation between two mariners after a ship survived a storm. Tom, the sinner, had been terrified during the night. Believing that the ship would sink, he had been afraid that the entire crew would go to "Davy Jones's Locker" and that he would end up in hell. Jack's reaction was entirely different. He was a true Christian and was "quite happy" during the tempest "and resigned to whatever might befal" him, because he knew God was "a present help in time of trouble." Jack's confidence came from reading the Bible, which showed him "the way of true happiness and solid peace." An astonished Tom listened as Jack relied on a host of nautical metaphors to explain how the Bible was really a chart to be used to navigate around the "shoals" of "temptation," including intemperance, whore mongering, and Sabbath breaking. Impressed with these arguments, Tom declared he would buy a Bible as soon as they returned to port. This, of course, was exactly the reaction the reformers wanted every reader to have. Religion, however, could never wait. Jack therefore offered to lend his own Bible to Tom and told him that he could read it in moments when he was not on watch. Reformers, however, did not want people to read the Bible casually or for amusement. So Jack also instructed Tom that he needed to read the Bible carefully, telling him "you must pray over it, that the Lord would enlighten your mind by his Holy Spirit, without which it will be as a sealed book to you."[136]

Tracts like the *Dialogue between Two Seamen after a Storm*, which had first been printed in Great Britain, began to appear in the United States in the early nineteenth century. Both British and American reformers published tracts as a way of reaching a vast audience. Americans organized a number of tract societies in the first two decades of the nineteenth century and formed the American Tract Society in 1825. During the antebellum era the American Tract Society became a publishing powerhouse that produced millions of tracts distributed throughout the nation. This effort grew directly out of the reformist plan to compete with the sentimental, sensational, and salacious material churned out by commercial presses. Reformers believed that many of the popular books had been published at the instigation of Satan "in the cause of error and licentiousness." "Bad Books" were like drinking alcohol: both were a "*poison*" that intoxicates – "one the mind, the other the body; the thirst for each increases by being fed, and is never satisfied; both ruin – one the intellect, the other the health, and together, the soul." This evil literature encompassed more than *The Pirates Own Book*, Tom Paine's deist works, and the novels of Eugene Sue. It extended to all fiction. Novels enfeebled the intellect, compelling the reader to become "the mere slave of feeling, and his intellect languishes amidst the sickly sentimentalism, the dreamy extravagance, of the romantic world." Reformers saw themselves in a war of print and believed that the best way to win that war was to provide the same kind of excitement found in the more profane literature, while ensuring their publications had a definite religious slant.[137]

Evangelical reformers neither won nor lost that war, but by engaging in the combat over print they, too, participated in a great transformation in book culture. Print entrepreneurs like Charles Ellms with his *The Pirates Own Book*, authors like James Fenimore Cooper with his novel *The Red Rover*, and organizations like the American Bible Society with its mountains of Bibles all contributed to the revolution in print. This revolution was multifaceted, encompassing writing, paper making, printing, publishing, and marketing. All of that effort would have been for naught if there was not also a revolution in reading. In the eighteenth century sailors were well placed to participate in this revolution because many were already literate. Their travel allowed them to imagine a world beyond their own immediate experience, a vital component in compelling an individual to open a book of fiction. And their life at sea exposed them to occasional peril and adventure, the material for many a good story, while it was also often marked by hard work and boredom that furnished both the interest and opportunity for reading. Sailors eagerly embraced the revolutions in print and reading that exploded upon the scene after 1800. They devoured books about disaster at sea, pirates, and captivity, read a wide array of novels, sensational stories, educational material, technical works, and self-help guides, as well as Bibles, religious books, and reformist tracts. Some even became authors themselves, offering their life stories to the general public or, as in the case of Herman Melville, producing great works of literature. Although some of this print material may have been created specifically for a maritime audience, most of it was also perused by those in mainstream society. Cooper wrote more books about the sea than novels centered on the frontier, and Melville's tales of a tropical paradise and sailing in the South Pacific in *Typee* and *Omoo* were immensely popular. Many a youth who might never go to sea eagerly read Ellms's heavily illustrated publications. A landlocked Abraham Lincoln considered James Riley's captivity narrative one of his favorite books, and Henry David Thoreau mentioned Riley in his *Cape Cod*.[138] Seamen and landsmen alike read many of the same stories, whether they were sensational accounts about pirates or serious discussions of religion. *The Pirates Own Book* was thus not really the pirates' own book, nor even the sailors' own book. Instead, it was everyone's own book.

7

Tar-Stained Images

Although not every image of the sailor, or created by him, was tar-stained, emphasizing the relationship between this gooey dark substance and pictures of the seaman serves as an appropriate heading for this chapter. As we have already seen, sailors were identified with tar. Almost everything they touched dripped with tar. They worked with tar daily, coating much of the ship in the ubiquitous material. Mariners also covered their broad-brimmed flat straw hats with tar. This sailor cap, often referred to as a tarpaulin, usually had a riband wrapped around it with a tail at the back end, and became as identifiable with the maritime world in the first half of the nineteenth century as the cowboy hat would become identifiable with the Wild West later in American history.[1] What we do not see was that tar often covered more than the sailor's hat. Mariners understood the waterproof qualities of this resin produced by burning pine at high temperatures and coated their duck trousers and their jackets with it. They also took pride in their "sea tan" – a combination of exposure to the sun and the tar that had worked its way into their skin.[2] On some level any artist who drew a picture of a mariner in the age of sail had to either include some of that tar or purposefully exclude it. Likewise, a seaman who picked up a pen or began to work with a whale's tooth or wood to create a material object probably had to scrape the tar from his fingers first. This chapter explores the images portraying sailors, the images created by sailors, and the images in sailors' minds – images that on one level or another were stained with tar. We will begin with an examination of how the rest of society imagined the mariner, tracing the emergence of Jack Tar as a powerful pictorial symbol of the American nation in the early nineteenth century. The second half of this chapter focuses on the art of the sailor, exploring when and how sailors embraced that image. Although sailors accepted the depiction of themselves as contributors to the nation's well-being, and could use that image when creating objects for others, when it came to personal artistic expressions they were more interested in their ships, the world around them, and the world they left behind.[3]

The tar-stained image of the sailor changed over time. In the eighteenth century few artists bothered with portraying the seaman with any seriousness; by the mid-nineteenth century in the great era of the common man it was possible to center artwork around Jack Tar. Of the legions of portraits painted of the well-to-do in Great Britain and North America in the eighteenth century there might be a few successful sea captains and merchants. It was even possible that some exceptional character with maritime experience, like ex-slave and abolitionist Olaudah Equiano, might have his likeness captured by an artist. Occasionally, too, a sailor might appear in the background of a painting with a larger historical theme. But seldom was there a finely crafted portrait of Jack Tar decked out in his distinctive dress. That said, several British artists, in part inspired by the role of sailors in the defense of the nation during the wars of empire, limned cartoon-like figures that made fun of the stereotypical seaman. We will begin our examination of images of sailors with these British caricatures because, like so much in the culture of the new nation, wherever the British went Americans were bound to follow. That influence appeared in contrasting political engravings in the opening decade of the nineteenth century. The Federalists closely mimicked their English cousins and did not take seamen too seriously. Republicans were more willing to view seamen as citizens. Together, the American caricatures sought to capture the sailor as he was seen by the rest of the world. Ultimately the more serious republican image won out. As was true in our discussion of language and literature, the sailor came increasingly to reflect a more romanticized ideal – one centered on his role in commerce and the defense of the nation.

Sailors themselves turned to a variety of genres to create both pictures and material objects. Seamen relied on traditional artist tools, like pen and paper, to draw the world around them. Mariners also worked with wood, bone, and whale's teeth as a medium, to craft objects for either display or use. They engaged in body art, puncturing and inking their skin with distinctive forms. The illustrations that appear in the logbooks and journals reflected the interests of the sailor. Prominent among these images were drawings of the ships they sailed. Seamen also noted distinctive fauna, places, and people. We can gain some insight into how the sailor viewed the world by the way he depicted his ship and the many profiles of landfalls that fill logbooks. A seaman drew his own ship in two dimensions as if he were on land or on another vessel, but represented the profile of landfalls as if he were looking out from the sea toward terra firma. Rarely did sailors draw the deck and their daily labor, although whalers did picture the hunt of the great leviathan. If seamen could still laugh at their own image and portray it in comic relief, they took their economic and patriotic roles seriously. We can see this attitude most clearly when they engaged in art, like scrimshaw, intended for others. Scrimshaw, however, also demonstrated a close connection between the sailor's life and the world he left behind him – many of the objects were created for domestic consumption for family in the United States. Likewise, when the art was personal, as in the marks they imprinted on their skin, mariners tended to create images nearer and dearer to their own concerns: often tattoos were names and initials of themselves and loved ones.

Imagining Jack Tar

There was a shift in popular images of the common sailor during the age of sail. For much of the eighteenth century it was all too easy to present Jack Tar in caricature as a lower-class buffoon more interested in satiating his immediate senses than in behaving with decorum and assuming his equal status as a citizen. By the mid-nineteenth century most American images of the common seaman depicted him as a citizen sailor who was a manly defender of the nation and a contributor to commercial welfare.

Despite a few sympathetic portrayals of common seamen in prints like "A Sailor's Farewell" or in the background of a battle scene centered on a naval hero like Horatio Nelson, for the most part British artists mocked the sailor during the French Revolutionary and Napoleonic Wars.[4] If this depiction of a cartoon-like character did not quite fit the published rhetoric praising the British sailor as a defender of the nation, it appeared even more incongruous in the United States as many Americans had come to see the mariner as a symbol for their republic. Federalists and Republicans, however, differed in how they imagined Jack Tar. Republicans saw seamen as valuable citizens who had rights that needed to be protected. Federalists had a more cynical view. They claimed that Republicans did not understand mariners and that they, especially the many merchants who interacted with seamen on a daily basis, did. During the years leading up to the War of 1812, Federalists and Republicans not only battled one another at the polls and in Congress, but also fought over who was best able to speak for the common seaman. Because Republicans denounced impressment so vehemently they had an edge in this contest. After the War of 1812 the Republican image of the sailor became more refined, especially when represented as a symbol of the nation as in John Archibald Woodside's "We Owe Allegiance to No Crown."[5] Although it was still possible occasionally to depict sailors in a more comical mode, the overall trend was to take the mariner seriously. This development was a result of the democratization of American society that swept the nation during the early republic. The rise of the common man spread into the ocean and included the rise of the common seaman. As we have already seen, accompanying these changes was a revolution in print that made it easier to reproduce engravings in books and elsewhere and led to the proliferation of images of all kinds. Within this context it became possible to portray James Fenimore Cooper's comic Dick Fid as a heroic figure and to depict the death of his Scipio Africanus in epic tones.

The image of the sailor as buffoon was a legacy of British caricatures. From the mid-eighteenth century to the early nineteenth century several British artists, led by William Hogarth, provided harsh portrayals of life among all levels of society. Some of these caricatures parodied the common seaman. We can see the impact of these denigrating images during the American Revolution when it almost did not matter which side the sailor chose: British prints offered exaggerated portrayals of mariners whether in support of or in opposition to the Revolution. The well-known print "Bostonians Paying the Excise-man" lampooned the resistance movement and conflated the opposition to the Stamp Act, with the Boston Tea Party, the use of the liberty tree, and tarring and feathering of customs officials – all separate activities that occurred over almost a decade. Reprinted today in nearly every illustrated textbook, often overlooked is that the nastiest person in the crowd was a sailor in the foreground. Yet his exaggerated fiendish and threatening demeanor was only a little less frightening than the caricatured British sailors taunting revolutionaries in a cage hanging from a liberty tree in a print by the same engraver called "Bostonians in Distress."[6] In the 1790s and early 1800s British artists replaced these sinister sailors with cartoon-like mariners. These Jack Tars were both likeable and comical, as we have seen in "Sailors Drinking the Tunbridge Waters" by Thomas Rowlandson and Thomas Tegg's "Jack in a White Squall, amongst Breakers – on the Lee Shore of St. Catherine's."[7]

On one hand, it would be easy to dismiss these caricatures as banal attempts to make fun of an element of the underclass; on the other, they reflected a popular interest in mariners and a certain affection for Jack Tar. After all, no printer would have bothered with publishing any of these engravings if they did not sell. We can assume that few seamen had the wherewithal or the inclination to purchase these prints themselves. Instead, the caricature engravings were likely bought by the burgeoning commercial middle class who understood the special role the sailor played in defending and extending the British overseas empire. Equally important, however cartoon-like and burlesque, these prints offered a personal view of the sailor and recorded aspects of his life that might have been otherwise lost to us. Few seamen visually recorded life on and between the decks. Although most of the sailor caricatures mocked the sailor's frolics ashore, British artists occasionally depicted the mariner on board ship during work and leisure. Thus we get to see British tars sitting on their sea chests on a gun deck smoking and drinking grog and depictions of the frolics between decks while in port. There are also comical engravings of daily life at sea as well as during battle.[8] Some lifelike engravings cast the sailor in a more heroic and positive light. A series of four illustrations in 1798 depicted sailors in port, in a storm, manning a gun during battle, and returning at peace. The men in these prints are serious and determined defenders of the nation.[9] Likewise, the engravings of the "Sailor's Farewell," a popular theme that appeared in several variations during the eighteenth century, could depict Jack in an attractive likeness. Overall, however, the comic image predominated.

The influence of the British cartoon-caricatures can be seen in two Federalist broadsides drawn by American-born James Akin. The first mocked congressional attempts to aid sailors in 1806 using a style similar to Rowlandson and Tegg. Irate over the recent impressment of American seamen by the British navy, Republican Senator Robert Wright of Maryland proposed a draconian bill that declared impressment the equivalent of piracy and asserted that seamen had the right to use lethal force in opposing British efforts to compel them into his majesty's navy. Indeed, any sailor who engaged in such resistance was to be awarded $200 by the federal government. This measure also would have had the United States retaliate against corporal and capital punishment inflicted on American seamen in the British navy by imposing similar punishments on British subjects. Finally, the law would have given each impressed sailor $60 a month, "as an indemnification for his slavery," to be paid by the British or exacted from the seizure of British property. This compensation was five times the normal monthly wage for a seaman. The legislation was unworkable and had the United States attempted to implement the measure, it would have quickly led to war with Great Britain. Fortunately the act was tabled pending the outcome of the negotiations by James Monroe and William Pinkney in London. As a statement of Republican support of impressed seamen, however, the law spoke volumes.[10] Federalists were aghast at the proposal and believed it represented the ignorance of the Republicans on all things maritime. As the *Hampshire Federalist* explained, "our State Pilots" – the Jefferson administration – "like landsmen in a squall, do nothing but bellow and curse. They know not one rope from another, nor appear to have the least knowledge of the trim of the ship." Wright's bill was nothing less than a "*Farce*" proposed by "the democratic *Wronghead* from Maryland" and "the most stupidly blind can readily perceive the dreadful consequences to our defenseless commerce and seamen, which must result from any attempt to put it in execution."[11]

Based on the Federalist understanding of the mariner's pursuit of self-interest, James Akin engraved a broadside that extended the criticism of Wright's bill. "A Bug-a-boo to frighten John Bull, or the Wright mode for kicking up a Bubbery for 200 Dollars Bounty and 60 dollars a month, with other important Perquisites!" depicted two ships in a British port: one was a British warship and the other was an American merchantman derisively named "Wright of Maryland." As a British longboat approached, the seamen aboard the American vessel engaged in several activities in response to Wright's anti-impressment law. One seaman, in an effort to collect his $200 bounty, fired a gun at the British longboat. The man at the extreme right of the picture explained this action by declaring to the British, "You'd best make no difficulty with my people, for there is a bill before Congress to shoot every Englishman at 200$ pr head." One of the bubbles has a sailor insult and mock the British officer by swearing, "Damn you majesty & your furbill'd [a pleated border of a petticoat] hat." If some of the men were venting their animosity against the royal navy, others were seeking the main chance. One seaman had jumped into the water and was swimming to the longboat, hoping to be impressed and thereby earn his $60 a month. Three others appeared ready to follow; two were on the side of the ship and the third was being held back by another seaman, possibly a mate, who was reminding him that if he joined the British he would cut his ties to his family – in this case, his sister – back home. These men, however, remain focused on the huge windfall they expected from Congress. In the background is a black seaman, probably a cook, who is apparently confused about the law and somehow thought he would get $200 from Congress. The captain of the

American ship is coatless, having just emerged from his cabin, and can be identified by his white linen shirt. He raises an iron pot as if to clobber someone and utters one word, "Rascals," aimed at the members of his crew who are on the verge of deserting. The British for their part are baffled by all of this commotion. The officer at the back of the longboat is indignant that the Americans had dared to fire on "His Majesty's Barge." Draped over the side of the longboat is a British seaman, either dead or wounded, while one of his shipmates calls out for the Americans not to fire on them. A third British seaman offers a helping hand to the American in the water, while a fourth confesses that he wishes Great Britain had a Congress to hand out some dollars. All told, this engraving was not a flattering portrayal of the American Jack Tar. He appeared interested in only one thing – money – and cared little about his home and his nation. This visual representation of these seamen, while not completely grotesque, was not complimentary: the sailors look more like the exaggerated caricatures of Rowlandson and Tegg than depictions of national heroes. Moreover, the overall impression of the scene is chaotic and disorganized with seamen facing several different directions and speaking at cross purposes.[12]

A few months later Akin created a second print featuring sailors to blast Jeffersonian maritime policy. It, too, portrayed Jack Tar in caricature. This gruesome picture might almost be viewed as anti-British because it depicted the corpse of an American sailor – John Pierce – on the bottom, while portraying an imaginary set of hangings of other American sailors and a royal navy captain on the top. In actuality this print was a critique of the Jeffersonian failure to maintain the navy and its inability to protect commerce. Akin executed the print in the wake of Pierce's murder by the British navy off the coast of New York. The British had stationed several ships just outside the harbor to search American vessels that might have traded with Napoleonic France and its allies in violation of his majesty's most recent Orders in Council – rules that inhibited trade with Britain's enemies. Whenever an American ship failed to heave to and allow a search, the British would fire a shot across the vessel's bow. One such shot sailed past the brig *Polly* and smacked into John Pierce at the wheel on the sloop *Richard*. This "accident" created an uproar across the nation. A mob in New York City seized supplies destined for the British and distributed them to the poor, mass meetings occurred protesting the outrage, and a huge public funeral procession for Pierce marched through the streets. Republican and Federalist newspapers throughout the United States decried this "atrocity," although the Federalists focused as much

FIGURE 7.1. **"A Bug-a-boo to frighten John Bull, or the Wright mode for kicking up a Bubbery ...,"** James Akin [1806], Charles Peirce Collection. Some American artists copied the British style of caricature in their depiction of sailors. In 1806 Republicans proposed legislation in Congress that would have rewarded sailors for resisting impressment. This Federalist lampoon of the proposed law suggested that American Jack Tars would simply use the law to pursue the main chance and seek impressment by jumping ship. Courtesy of the American Antiquarian Society, Worcester, Massachusetts.

on the inadequacy of the Republican policy that allowed the tragedy to take place as they did on British actions.[13]

It is in the context of this Federalist criticism that we need to examine Akin's engraving. This busy print can be divided into two parts. The upper half is a close copy of a British print from 1802 that was sympathetic to the common seaman and criticized the class bias of the British judicial system.[14] Akin's print had other purposes. On the top is a huge "Dearborn's Patent" scale showing a rough balance between two sets of fictional executions: the hanged and hooded corpse of Henry Whitby, who as captain of the HMS *Leander* was responsible for Pierce's death, on one side, and the hooded bodies of fourteen American seamen on the other.[15] The message here does not reflect the earlier British composition and may not be immediately apparent. The placards on the wall between the two sides of the scale, however, help to clarify matters by referencing a series of public meetings triggered by the killing of Pierce. Examination of the proceedings of those meetings reveals a contrast between Republican and Federalist responses to the crisis. The top tier of notices advertises various Republican gatherings in New York that decried the incident and called for revenge. The top left placard refers to the committee that arranged the funeral for Pierce. Its announcement was inflammatory, but did not advocate direct violence.[16] The wording of the call for the Tammany meeting was somewhat stronger, urging the members of this political society, which met in Indian costume, to keep their tomahawks sharpened and ready for action. The Tammany resolutions declared that all who were "still engaged in such acts of piracy ... deserve the execration of every American."[17] The grand jury report, the final Republican notice, indicted Whitby for murder and thus threatened the British officer with the hanging portrayed in the engraving.[18] The lower tier of placards articulated the Federalist position. Like the Republicans, the Federalists were outraged by the British action, but also viewed it as an accident that was bound to occur given Republican policies. The deposition of Jesse Pierce, who was captain of the sloop in which his brother John was killed, is matter-of-fact and makes clear that, although the British fired across the bows of American ships a number of times, the *Leander* had not intentionally killed anyone.[19] The meeting at the Tontine Coffee House announced in the middle placard was not a Republican meeting despite Akin's label. Instead it was held by Federalists, or as they called themselves in a rhetorical effort not to cede the "republican" mantle to their opponents, "Federal Republicans." Like the Republicans, the Federalists declared the "murder" of Pierce "an act that excites our detestation and abhorrence." But they also denounced "an administration which consents to pay money to avoid foreign insolence, or to prevent the violation of national rights [the reference is probably to the treaty with Tripoli in 1805 and even the Louisiana Purchase in 1803], while it sells and dismantles its naval force, instead of encreasing and preserving it for the defense of our ports and commerce, prostrates national honor, endangers the public safety, and invites both injustice and insult."[20] The seamen's meeting advertised in the bill closest to the hanged sailors, which has the word "Proceedings" in bold, also expressed the Federalist position. The Federalists claimed, as we have noted in our discussion of the first Akin print, that they understood sailors and were in the best position to speak for the mariners. The headline for the report of that meeting was "HUZZA for the Jack Tars of New York!" Although described as "a numerous and respectable meeting of American seamen," it was chaired by a ship captain and probably attended mainly by other ship's captains. The opening resolution lamented that the money paid "for the wild lands of Louisiana, would have been better applied in building SEVENTY FOUR GUN SHIPS," while the second resolution blamed the failure to protect American shipping from seizure and American seamen from impressment on "the cowardice of our government." The rest of the resolutions directly blamed the death of John Pierce on this "want of protection." They also declared the Federalists the true friends of the American seamen and urged the president to spend more time defending the honor of the nation than in his so-called scientific exploits like "stuffing Raccoon Skins and dissecting new discovered animals."[21] The top half of the print therefore offers a contrast between the Federalists and the Republicans, with the Federalists wanting to be proactive by strengthening the navy to protect both commerce and seamen, while the Republicans were reactive to British outrages, threatening legal prosecution that would lead to the hanging of the British officer in command of the *Leander*. This execution, the Federalist Akin believed, would force the British to retaliate and lead to the deaths of many more common Jack Tars.

The bottom half of the print has the same basic message, but was centered more directly around the dead body of Pierce in front of a crowd. The maimed and bloodied corpse is being carried on a stretcher by two men. The first, who has his back to us, is obviously a sailor, perhaps an officer, with a high tarpaulin hat and a blue waist jacket.[22] The second is probably a merchant wearing a long coat with matching pants and ruffled collar. The message here is that both the merchant and the seaman lament

FIGURE 7.2. **"The Bloody Arena,"** James Akin [1806], Charles Peirce Collection. Both Federalists and Republicans were distressed when John Pierce, an American seaman, was accidentally killed by a stray British cannon ball fired outside of New York harbor. The Republicans organized a massive public funeral for Pierce and wanted to prosecute the officer in command of the British ship. The top half of Akin's caricature of the event is taken directly from a British print published a few years earlier. The overall message of Akin's print, including the depiction of the common sailor, was that the Republican call for justice was overstated, and that the real problem was Thomas Jefferson (Jefferson is depicted with red hair and on the bottom right of the print) and his failure to protect American shipping. Courtesy of the American Antiquarian Society, Worcester, Massachusetts.

the loss of Pierce's life. There are also three neatly dressed women in the front of the crowd mourning the death of Pierce, suggesting his connection to the land-based community. More important are the three men who have bubbles above them expressing their opinions. In the middle is a tall gentleman with red hair and a long face who resembles a young Thomas Jefferson. Oddly, he mouths a Federalist position, asking if the nation needed more proof that it "<u>must</u> adopt speedy and energetic measures to avoid outrageous insult" – a position Jefferson had taken during the 1780s in response to Algerian attacks on American commerce.[23] The two other bubbles belong to seamen and both swear like a sailor. This language is intended to capture the salt of the seaman's expression and as a means by which the caricaturist can demean the message being transmitted. The sailor in the middle of the crowd with a waist jacket, tarpaulin hat, and pudgy face reminiscent of British caricatures is American and calls out to his "fellow Citizens." This republican phrase resonated with the memory of the French Revolution and the violence it entailed. He holds a cudgel and with a finger on the same hand points to the body of Whitby dangling from the end of a noose. The cudgel, it should be noted, was a symbol dripping with irony: it was a tool of the mob, as well as the standard weapon of every press gang.[24] This Jack Tar who simultaneously represented the mob behind him and the impressment they opposed, continues by declaring in real fighting words, "there's the way these murderous sons of Bitches should swing; & I hope you will <u>exact</u> of <u>Government</u> full satisfaction for the Blood of Pierce." The mariner all the way to right is British. We know his nationality because of the queue dangling from the back of his tarpaulin – a hairstyle that by the beginning of the nineteenth century was more associated with seamen from Great Britain than the United States. His language and message also give him away, beginning with "I say Jack," and using the word "buggers," a phrase seldom uttered by American seamen and prevalent in the British Navy. He looks at the fourteen hanging seamen and declares, "what a d– n'd fine haul we'd had could we but string the b-gg–rs up after that fashion," to the obvious befuddlement of his nearest listener. He also stands off to the side, faces a different direction from the rest of the crowd, and is the handsomest sailor in the print. Just in case the overall message of the engraving was lost in the confusion of the picture, the artist offered the following inscription at the very bottom: "Independentiam Vestram Veneramini, vet omnis Natio vos Concacabit ad tibitum. Submitted to the opinions of every descendant of 1776 by their friend and Countryman James Akin." The Latin disguises a crude message while simultaneously indicating an effort to appeal to an upper-class and educated audience. Despite being transcribed incorrectly, the phrase can be roughly translated as, "You revere your independence but every nation will shit on you as they please."[25]

Akin had contempt for the Jeffersonians and feared that the seamen in the crowd would blindly follow the Republican lead. He therefore did not portray sailors in a flattering manner in the illustration and used the same British cartoon-like style as in his earlier print. We see a nice mixture of striped and non-striped pants, shirts, waist jackets, and neckerchiefs of sailor clothing for eight of the fourteen hanged seamen. But because their heads are covered with an execution hood, we have no idea of what their faces looked like or their personality. It is almost as if Akin were just as happy to portray these mariners as nonentities. Likewise, the seamen in the crowd are largely indistinct. We know that the people in the back were sailors only because their telltale tarpaulin hats appear above the mass of the crowd. The swearing pudgy sailor in the middle is anything but attractive, and his shipmates to the right and left are only a little less distorted. Unlike the seamen aboard the "Wright of Maryland," most of the men in the crowd face the same direction. This unity of purpose represents more a mob mentality than a thoughtful and reasoned objective. As was true in his earlier print attacking Wright's impressment bill, Akin is afraid that the Republican position and the mariner reaction would only lead to the escalation of conflict and possible war with Great Britain. The Federalists may have believed that they understood the sailor better than their Republican rivals, but that sailor was certainly not their equal and was best portrayed as self-seeking, impulsive, unthinking, and something of a buffoon.

Although Republican William Charles began his career as an artist in Great Britain, and his work reflected this experience, his "The Tory Editor and His Apes Giving Their Pitiful Advice to the American Sailors" was entirely different in its portrayal of seamen. In 1808 Federalists were busy attacking what they perceived as another inane law: the Embargo of 1807 that shut off almost all foreign trade and put seamen out of work. The Republicans had enacted this legislation in response to the British attack on the USS *Chesapeake*, continued impositions on American trade, and impressment. The Federalists considered the embargo ridiculous because it destroyed commerce and, as the so-called Federalist editor explained in the print, threatened war. This bedraggled character with torn clothing, a haggard look, and a miniature frame, supported by the monkey-like other

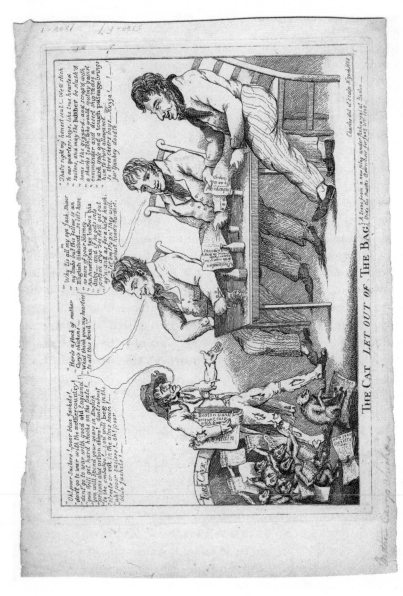

FIGURE 7.3. "The Cat Let Out of the Bag," by William Charles, 1808. In his print in support of the Embargo of 1807, Republican artist William Charles offers a sympathetic portrait of the American Jack Tar who, in good sailor language, defends Jefferson's effort to punish both the English and the French by stopping all American trade. Here, one Federalist editor appears small and bedraggled and is followed apishly by a host of other Federalist editors emerging from the Tory cave. Courtesy of the Library Company of Philadelphia, Philadelphia, Pennsylvania.

editors emerging from the "Tory Cave," addresses himself to three neatly dressed seamen who are proportionally much larger. This difference in size was not accidental or the result of poor technique: the sailors are larger because they are truer men than any Federalist polemicist. Although there are bottles and glasses on the table, the size of these objects does not imply any excessive drinking. Instead the three mariners sit calmly with an air of intelligence about them. Two of the seamen have papers in their hands – a copy of the latest British Order in Council and a copy of the Jeffersonian Embargo Act. They look nothing like the perplexed, slobbering, and feckless tars in so many British prints, or the self-serving sailors aboard the "Wright of Maryland," or the pudgy swearer in Akin's Pierce print. Charles knew how to draw more farcical seamen. Before he came to the United States he produced some sailor caricatures, and during the War of 1812 he made a number of anti-British prints denigrating "John Bull," usually portrayed by a figure with a man's body dressed as a seaman with a bull's head, but in at least one case he depicted John Bull as a sailor with a complete human form and a head that could have been just as easily a cartoon-like sailor drawn by any British artist.[26]

Charles belittled the Federalist effort to appeal to the mariners with even more vehemence than Akin had mocked Jeffersonian policies. Repeating arguments made by the Federalist politicians, and "aped" in Federalist newspapers across the nation, the editor of the *Boston Gazette* warns the "poor Sailors" not to go to "war with good old England." If they did, all they would get from this effort would be "hard knocks on the pate!" and years in English prisons. The Federalist editor also urges the men not to support the Embargo, otherwise they would have to "beg in the streets or rot in the alms house!" These well-informed seamen respond in the language of Jack Tar. The first sailor asks his shipmates, "what think you my [read me] hearties" about "this scud [foam from an ocean wave driven by the wind]."[27] The second dismisses the Federalist warnings with a "shiver my limbs" and a declaration that if they get into prison, "An American tar knows his duty" and would escape. The third concludes: "That's right my honest soul! – We'll stick to our quarters, boys, like true hearted sailors, and may the lubber be slush'd home to the gizzard, and scrap'd with a shark's tooth, who would mutiny gainst commander and desert ship cause a hard gale and a tough passage brings him to short allowance." In other words, they intended to remain loyal Republicans despite the difficult times and reduced pay and food. Anyone who opposed Jefferson was a traitor and deserter who deserved to have his stomach (gizzard) greased (slushed) and scraped. Here the three seamen all had the same message verbally and with unified body language. In contrast to Akin's first 1806 print where the sailors were divided and were twisted every which way, or his second 1806 print where most of the seamen are part of a faceless crowd, Charles's Jack Tars agree with each other and face the same direction. The confusion in Akin's print is in the jumble of small "Apes" holding their newspapers helter-skelter with limbs and bodies akimbo.[28]

Unlike in Great Britain at this time, there were few caricatures of sailors in America. Other images, however, appeared that emphasized a positive and sympathetic portrayal of Jack Tar. An 1805 engraving by none other than James Akin had good-looking mariners. Serving as the cover for the song "Sailors Glee" with a caption reading, "SINGING, LAUGHING, DANCING, QUAFFING, BOTH CHERRILY AND MERRILY AND ALL FOR THE SAKE OF HIS GIRL ASHORE," the picture has a neatly accoutered and proportioned seaman, with perhaps a little flush in his cheeks, dancing with a nicely attired woman. In the background one shipmate fiddles and two others drink beside another well-dressed woman. The room has a table and benches with three portraits of ships and a clock on the walls. This illustration is a far cry from British caricatures of seamen dancing and drinking with heavy and full-busted women bulging out of their dresses. Perhaps Americans were prudish; more likely they were less willing to see sailors cast in foolish ribaldry.[29]

In the years after the War of 1812 the popular image of the American sailor became more stylized and romanticized as the memory of his defense of the nation became embedded into popular consciousness.[30] John Archibald Woodside's "We Owe Allegiance to No Crown" epitomizes this vision of the American sailor. In a dramatic shift in composition, at the center of the painting is a well-proportioned seaman with white pants, short-waisted dark blue naval jacket, and tarpaulin cap in one hand and a flagpole and American banner in the other. The bare head has curly black hair and long sideburns similar to some of the more caricaturized mariners in Charles's print, and a hairstyle popular throughout the United States. Here is a handsome sailor. Underfoot is a broken crown and scepter with an unshackled chain lying nearby. Hovering over a low-lying cloud is a female figure of liberty holding a Phrygian – liberty – cap on a pole, about to place a victory wreath on the uncovered head of the heroic Jack Tar. The sailor stands on a rock with a harbor, a ship, and a lighthouse in the distance. The ship, which has a patch of clear blue sky above, represents both the defense of the nation and the spread of commerce, while the lighthouse symbolizes the role of the government that constructed such beacons to guide ships safely to port.[31]

FIGURE 7.4. **"Sailors Glee,"** James Akin, (Newburyport: James Akin, 1805), Charles Peirce Collection. Music and dancing connected life aboard ship and life ashore as suggested in this James Akin print. A couple dances in the middle of the room with other sailors playing instruments. The room is decorated with pictures of ships. Jack Tar dancing the hornpipe became a standard maritime image in taverns and on stage. Courtesy of the American Antiquarian Society, Worcester, Massachusetts.

In the years to come the sailor did not need props like the figure of "Liberty" as he appeared in the new democratic media. In 1836 *Naval Magazine* published an illustrated essay that captured the new vision of Jack Tar. "There stands the outer man of Brown," proclaimed the author, "Boatswain's Mate, in the United States Navy! – a perfect specimen of a true American Seaman." "A Brother Cruiser" drew an explicit comparison between the engraved image of George Brown to "shore folk" who "when they become rich enough to think of *family portraits*, get themselves depicted upon canvass, sitting in an easy chair, looking wondrous wise, with the dexter hand grappling a gaudily-bound volume." In contrast, Brown "planks it in a woodcut, and stand at his quarters, with his hand on a volume" – a cannon – "that, erewhile, proudly proclaimed the honour and glory of his country." Using several nautical metaphors, the author continued, "survey the man from truck to keelson, take all his bearings, and say – could manhood be better personified?" Brown was "a hearty, able-bodied, American seaman. One, whose very look indicates a love of enterprise, firmness of purpose, and a reckless daring that would command the attention of any man." Wrapped into this illustration was the ideal American sailor "who never forgets the proud circumstances of his birth right." The article with the engraving was reprinted in a family magazine and so striking was the image that Fitch W. Taylor used it with the caption "American Tar" in 1842 in the second edition (and subsequent editions) of his *A Voyage Round the World....* This Boatswain's Mate was a far cry from the rollicking puffy seamen of British caricature.[32]

The same type of sailor who was in the Woodside print and in the George Brown engraving appeared in other images of the mariner. By the antebellum period the sailor's farewell and sailor's return had been stock subjects of maritime art for almost a century. Although some of the depictions of the sailor in these earlier images could be sympathetic, by the antebellum period the seaman in the American versions of these representations was no jolly jack. He was instead a serious and manly figure who was sentimentally attached to his sweetheart back home. Likewise, the seamen portrayed coming ashore on "The American Seamen's Friend Society Certificate" are shown as honest, well-dressed, and well-behaved men.[33] The mariner who appeared in Edward Hazen, *The Panorama of the Professions* in 1836, which valorized almost all laborers, depicted a sailor about to go to sea with one foot in a boat taking a navigational instrument from a man on shore. This seaman and the two others in the illustration are serious men and mariners.[34] Edward Clay's cartoon, depicting the dire effects of the Panic of 1837, has portraits of several down-on-their-luck

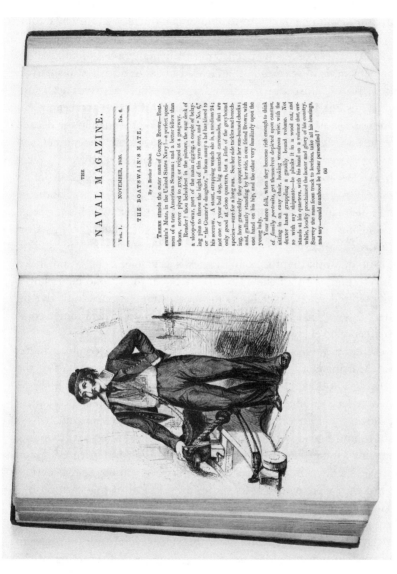

FIGURE 7.5. "The Boatswain's Mate," *Naval Magazine*, 1 (November 1836). The *Naval Magazine* published a description of Bosun George Brown depicting him as the ultimate seaman and a masculine ideal, it included an engraving of Brown, with tarpaulin hat, waist jacket, embroidered shirt, flared out bell bottom pants, and bosun whistle. This illustration stands in marked contrast with the buffoon-like British and American caricatures of the early nineteenth century. Courtesy of the American Antiquarian Society, Worcester, Massachusetts.

characters, including a barefoot seaman in the middle of the print. He stands with folded arms and tarpaulin hat sitting on the back of his head with a dejected look on his face. But unlike the Loco-Foco politician on the left, he is not drunk, nor is he misbehaving. Instead he looks every inch a man despite his inability to find employment.[35] Even when common seamen were not the focal point of the composition they now were portrayed in a serious manner reflecting their manhood and citizenship. Similar depictions of seamen had appeared in some British prints earlier. But those British illustrations centered on the officer as naval hero supported by his hearty tars. In the United States during the antebellum era the common seaman had equal billing with his commander. In the decade before the Civil War, Alonzo Chappel captured two dramatic moments in the early history of the American navy with his portrayal of the "Saving of Stephen Decatur by Reuben James" and his "Death of Captain James Lawrence." In both the centerpiece is a famous officer. But in both the common seaman has an important role. In the first, which represents a battle against Tripoli in 1804, an injured Reuben James stoops over Decatur as an "Algerine" is about to strike at the officer with his sword. There is no question that the young James is as gallant as his commander, who is wrestling with an enemy on the deck. In the second engraving a mortally wounded Lawrence utters his famous injunction, "don't give up the ship," as he is being carried below deck by manly and determined common seamen who share in the martyred officer's glory.[36]

Of course it was still possible to use Jack Tar as a comical figure. Hawser Martingdale's *Tales of the Ocean* was another product of the print revolution that relied heavily on engraved illustrations. The book itself was a compendium of maritime stories ranging from an account of impressment to pirate tales. Several chapters described sailor misbehavior ashore and had numerous pictures of foolish-looking tars drinking and dancing ashore. These illustrations, as well as several pictures of men at sea, were drawn in a different style from the earlier British caricatures, but they were every bit as burlesque. Typical of this cartoon-like approach was the depiction of a Neptune ceremony during the crossing of the Equator. With a well-dressed gentleman – either an officer or a passenger – watching the scene from the side, several smirking, simian sailors torment a blindfolded neophyte during his first crossing of the line. One man holds a razor and a large brush to lather the victim with a mixture that might consist of tar, chicken droppings, and saltwater. Other seamen spray the unfortunate greenhorn with buckets of water. All of this activity was under the direction of a tar wearing the accouterments

FIGURE 7.6. **"Father Neptune Crossing the Line,"** Hawser Martingdale, *Tales of the Ocean, and Essays for the Forecastle* ... (New York: John Slater, 1840). However esteemed the American sailor became, it was still possible in the mid nineteenth century to offer a more comical portrayal of Jack Tar. In this illustration we see rowdy seamen celebrating the crossing of the equator by abusing one of their shipmates with less than attractive glee on their faces. Courtesy of the New Bedford Whaling Museum, New Bedford, Massachusetts.

of Neptune. The vicious smirks on the celebrants' faces convey a mixed message. Martingdale claimed he had a reformist intent and that he believed that his stories would convince sailors to mend their ways. Like many such books, there was a double edge to recounting and illustrating tales of excess. On one hand, the author may have thought to gain readers interested in vicariously experiencing this misbehavior, while on the other, he hoped to simultaneously expose and denigrate it. In this last sense there may have been a subtle reason for portraying thoughtless and almost sadistic seamen in these illustrations – it made their foolhardiness all the more evident. Reinforcing this interpretation was the inclusion in the book of more serious illustrations with sailors in the midst of fighting or dealing with shipwrecks.[37]

So striking was the change in the image of Jack Tar, that by the eve of the Civil War an artist could portray James Fenimore Cooper's comic characters in *The Red Rover* in stirring fashion. As early as 1836 a set of cutouts intended for children included a dapper-looking Dick Fid with a trim figure, long sideburns, and a proper sailor outfit. This image is nothing like the well-meaning, lower-class dimwit of Cooper's prose. More surprising than this handsome paper doll of a Fid was the appearance of both Fid and Scipio Africanus in the black shipmate's famous death

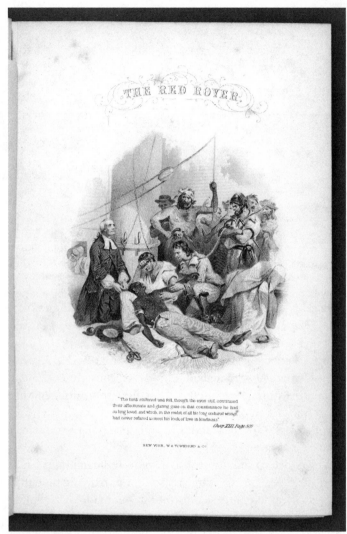

FIGURE 7.7. **"Death of S'ip,"** J. Fenimore Cooper, *The Red Rover, A Tale* (New York: W. A. Townsend, 1859). Perhaps one of the most dramatic depictions of the ideal of the respected seaman appeared in the engraving of Sip's death in the 1859 edition of the *Red Rover*. Although the standing seamen were pirates, Sip and Dick Fid, characters Cooper included for comical relief, look truly noble. Courtesy of the Collection of the Massachusetts Historical, Boston, Massachusetts.

scene in an illustration from an 1859 edition of *The Red Rover*. The setting mimics the classic portrayal of the death of General James Wolfe by Benjamin West. The expiring Scip lays sprawled out with his head in the lap of a distraught Dick Fid. In his grief Fid is handsome, manly, and seamanlike. Copying West's famous picture, various other individuals, kneeling and standing, encircle the mortally wounded black seaman. As the nation was about to be torn apart over the issue of slavery, this was a powerful statement concerning blacks that would have been unimaginable in the eighteenth century.[38]

Thanks in large part to scholars like Jeff Bolster, we know that seamen like Scip were not projections of James Fenimore Cooper's imagination.[39] Many black mariners sailed aboard Anglo-American sailing ships, and they often appeared in depictions of seamen, usually in the background and seldom in flattering poses. Several British caricaturists had blacks in their engravings. Thomas Tegg's "A Milling Match between Decks" shows two sailors, one white and one black, tied to a chest on a gun deck about to engage in a fistfight with a crowd looking on.[40] George Cruikshank portrayed blacks sometimes as cooks or waiters for officers and sometimes as part of a crowd of seamen. Blacks appeared in prints from his Midshipman Blockhead series, including a servant in "Mr. B. On the Middle Watch." There is also a black seaman working with three other sailors at a windless in his "Lacing in Style," depicting a midshipman having his corset tightened.[41] Occasionally a black seaman was himself the subject of the work of art. In the early nineteenth century at least two British artists painted Billy Waters, a black man who had probably been born a slave in North America and who served in His Majesty's navy until he lost his leg after falling from a yardarm.[42] American artists, too, might have blacks in their paintings of sailors. During the eighteenth century John Singleton Copley included a black man in the small boat in "Watson and the Shark." Several historical paintings from the nineteenth century included black seamen, although often inconspicuously. Look carefully at the famous painting by Emmanuel Leutze of George Washington crossing the Delaware and you will find a black sailor manning an oar. Similarly there was an African American seaman in the background of William Henry Powell's painting of Oliver Hazard Perry's boat in the Battle of Lake Erie. There were even a few portraits of black seamen like Captain Absalom Boston. All in all, however, there were only a handful of images where an African American was the center of attention.[43]

As surprising as these images of black seamen may be, it is the transformation from the Hogarthian clown – like "Sailors Drinking the

Tunbridge Waters" – to the citizen-sailor – like the boatswain's mate George Brown – that is critical for this analysis. Brown's clothes and tarred hat, "highly varnished, with a profusion of riband," may have distinguished him as a seaman, but the overall transformation that this image represented reached beyond the world of Jack Tar. The subject was not some rich merchant; instead, it was a humble seaman. The medium was not a canvas portrait; instead, it was a woodcut engraving in a popular magazine. But the subject could have been any common man – artisan or yeoman farmer – and the medium any product of the print revolution. Etched into the contours of this engraving, and in many of the portrayals of Jack Tar in the antebellum era, was a democratized American culture that embraced the common seaman, tarred hat and all.

The Art of the Sailor

In the nineteenth century sailors accepted the patriotic and manly portrayal of themselves as seamen. Yet their own art did not necessarily revolve around it. At times mariners created images similar to George Brown the Boatswain's Mate and seamen occasionally drew pictures of themselves or their messmates. They also might fashion images with patriotic themes. However, for the most part they were more concerned with other objects as the focus of their art. Although the subject of that art depended in part on the medium, Jack Tar was most interested in creating images of his ship, of the experiences on his voyage, and of his memory of home. Thus the sailor's art combined interests at sea and on land. By examining the art of the sailor – in pictures, in scrimshaw, in handicraft, and in tattoos – we will not only gain greater insight into the nautical world, but we will once again see the interaction between the mainstream and maritime cultures.

Only a handful of the many pictures seamen drew in their logbooks and journals depict people, and many of these do not portray sailors themselves. Perhaps this relative absence of seaman portraits reflected the technical difficulty in drawing the human form. The crude nature of some of the pictures of people in sailor journals seems to substantiate this conclusion. The sketch of a side profile of a sailor standing on the dock found in the journal of William Alfred Allen is out of proportion. The head and nose are too large, the feet are too small, and the single arm at the side of the body is misaligned. The bulge for the buttocks is also a bit low. Despite all of these difficulties in execution, the tarpaulin cap, kerchief, and the beard all denote the seaman-like qualities of the subject.

The "Sketch of three sailors, one drinking and two smoking" found in the Peabody Essex Collections is only a little better. The faces are indistinct, and the arms again malapportioned, but the sailor clothes are drawn with greater precession with broad-bottomed white trousers, and neat waist or monkey jackets sporting buttons and anchors on the collars. And, of course, the men wore telltale kerchiefs and tarpaulin hats.[44] Indeed, in the nineteenth century even when sailors are drawn as stick figures from a distance tarpaulin hats were ever present. Seamen artists recognized these caps as the ubiquitous symbol of their profession. A few sailors exhibited talent as figurative artists. David M. Bryant drew several wonderful sketches of seamen in the log of the *Tartar*, including an interior of the captain's cabin with three men sitting at a table drinking, and of a man at the ship's wheel. There is also a marvelous portrait of the African American cook standing in the doorway of the cookhouse with a boat on deck to the right and a mast to the left. Bryant took his drawing seriously – he devoted pages of the log to practice studies of the cook and the heads of other people.[45] Robert Weir's sketches of life aboard a whaleship in the 1850s also demonstrate artistic talent.[46]

Other sailors drew pictures similar to those by Bryant and Weir, but seamen tended to concentrate on the ship as a whole rather than its occupants, deck, or interior. There were limitations on how most artists depicted the entire vessel. Only a few seamen artists attempted to draw a ship from the front or back, or, more challenging, from an angle. When they did so, the artists captured a ship with its sails full of wind and, especially with the angled view, provided a sense of a vessel's motion. This approach also demanded of the artist a sense of perspective and depth that was difficult to achieve. There is a beautiful sketch of a full-rigged ship sailing at an angle toward the artist with a whale in the background in a journal kept aboard the *Alexander Coffin* in 1849 and a frontal view of a ship in the journal of John Perry on the whaling ship *Niger* in the 1840s.[47] A pen and watercolor study of a ship painted with all sail spread to the wind appears in the log of the *Lucy Ann*.[48] The majority of ship pictures, however, were from the side and in two dimensions. Despite this restraint these drawings and paintings were often spectacular and demonstrated Jack Tar's emotional attachment to his ship. The pencil sketches themselves are often impressive, but the watercolors are truly inspiring regardless of the broadside view. The artist painstakingly recorded the sleek lines of the vessel, the rigging with its ropes running in multiple directions, and layer upon layer of sails reaching to the sky. Occasionally the artist sought to capture his ship confronting the elements. One artist

FIGURE 7.8. **"Ship Arab,"** Log of the *Arab*, kept by Ephraim Harding, 1842–45, ODHS Log 435A. Mariners often drew pictures of their ships. This illustration, the original is in watercolor, is a wonderful example of a standard depiction. Sailors tended to draw their ships with a broadside view as if they were looking at the vessel from the shore or another ship. Courtesy of the New Bedford Whaling Museum, New Bedford, Massachusetts.

portrayed the *Columbia* in a gale off the Marquesas with the vessel listing to one side amid high waves and flapping sails.[49] A passenger who probably had maritime experience drew two pictures of the *Amelia* anchored near Cape Horn. One shows the vessel with a spanker and jib sail for stability pulling on an anchor with foaming breakers all around. The second watercolor has the vessel still clinging to its anchor, but now under bare poles – no sails aloft – surrounded by rocks and a threatening lee shore only a short distance away. If the anchor cable were to give, or the anchor to drag, everyone would perish. Despite the obvious action in both pictures, the view was still two-dimensional and from the side.[50] It was as if it were almost inconceivable to the mariner to portray his ship from the deck – the view that the sailor lived with day in and day out. Instead, the sailor artist had to imagine what the ship looked like from a distance. Of course the seaman had seen the ship from that distance, but probably not while he was drawing and certainly not in the action scenes of the *Columbia* and the *Amelia*. These ship portraits were also idealized: many do not have human figures and almost none depict the normal clutter on the deck. Despite the technical nautical knowledge and shipboard experience of the artist, logbook drawings – some merely scribbled in the margins and others filling an entire page – followed many of the standard conventions of land-based ship portraits in the same era. In short, when the mariner thought about his ship he viewed it in his mind's eye the way someone else would view it from another ship or from shore.[51]

Sailor artists did not forget about the work on the ocean. Whale men in particular recorded their efforts at killing the leviathan of the seas. At its most simple level, logbook keepers drew an outline of a whale or used a whale stamp on the day's entry to indicate the capture of a whale and sometimes recorded the number of barrels of oil obtained. Failed efforts at harpooning their quarry might be noted as well, with an image of the back half of the whale vertical on the page signaling that the whale had dove into the deep beyond reach. There were also more elaborate drawings of the whale hunt. Usually the whale men artists provided a broadside sketch of the ship surrounded by sperm whales and boats launched. The seamen were nothing more than stick figures sporting tarpaulin hats. Often there was a certain primitivism to the drawings and a failure to get the proportional size of the ship, the whale, and the whaleboats correct. Regardless of the artist's technical ability, the key to almost all of these sketches was action. The whaleboats approach their quarry; in the bows are harpoonists ready to strike, with whales spouting, diving, and in some instances lashing out at the hunters. The most dramatic scenes depict a whale ramming or biting a boat, tossing the men into the water. An illustration from the *Arab* shows one man struggling in the water and another clambering back into the boat after they had been knocked overboard by their prey.[52] A sketch in the logbook of the *Niger* has the whaleboat moving in to kill an expiring whale on its back. This situation was fraught with danger because in its death throes the whale might snap its flukes unexpectedly, destroying the whaleboat and drowning the crew.[53]

Seamen could also record their work experiences in just the sailing of a ship with drawings. In the 1770s Nicholas Pocock, a British officer and later landscape artist, sketched the sails of his vessel for each day, showing how they looked when the wind came from different directions.[54] Francis Barrett mocked a green hand's first experience furling sails on a yardarm in a small sketch, depicting four stick figures in the rigging – at least two with tarpaulin hats – and a fifth clinging to the main mast declaring, "O dear – O dear, save me I Shameless." Another seamen squeezed a tiny illustration into his journal of an officer flogging a man.[55] On the inside cover of his journal Sargent S. Day drew a picture of a man clinging to a mast with a pole for one hand. One of the entries in the log suggested an explanation for this peculiar illustration: "mast Painted but making a long lumber job of it."[56] In a rare deck view sketch, Alexander P. Cornell drew seamen in the navy manning a capstan to heave up an anchor.[57] This picture, however, appeared in a journal kept while Cornell was on a whaler. Of course, other exceptions to the lack of deck views of work include the pictures of the man at the wheel and the cook on the *Tartar* and the illustrations in the logbook Robert Weir kept on the *Clara Bell*.[58]

Sailor artists were also intrigued with oceanic fauna. Mariners drew images of sea creatures as seen from the deck, with only portions of the body breaking the surface.[59] The standard depiction of a whale was the spermaceti and its rounded forehead. Whalers, however, hunted many varieties of cetaceans and became experts in their differences. In his journal John F. Martin drew six different kinds of large sea mammals. Although an individual could capture only glimpses of the leviathans in the water when they breached, the whaler got to know his prey intimately during the hunt and as the huge mammal was brought to the side of the ship and sliced piece by piece so that the blubber could be boiled into oil and stowed in barrels. Fish also were of interest to seamen as objects of curiosity. Even more so than the sea mammals, who had to surface to get some air, fish in the sea might be hidden from those on a ship. Any fish that found itself on deck, sometimes as a result of fishing and sometimes by accident – as in being washed aboard by a wave – piqued the sailor's interest. Sometimes a journal keeper etched in a small picture of a fish and other times he filled in an entire page with several species. Birds were of importance to sailors because sighting certain birds could be a clue that land was near. Washington Fosdick aboard the schooner *Emiline* drew pictures of a variety of birds in the margins of his journal, including an albatross, a gooney bird, and two "Cape Pigeons or Speckled Haglets" (a petrel seen only in the southern oceans).[60]

The strange people of distant places also found their way into illustrated logbooks. Like the readers of Melville's *Typee* and *Omoo*, perhaps the most interesting part of the world to American seamen, at least in the nineteenth century, was the South Pacific. The natives of the islands intrigued sailors with their nakedness and a setting that seemed akin to paradise. Several men on Charles Wilkes' great exploration expedition kept records of the voyage. Seaman Joseph G. Clark drew excellent color pictures of topless native princesses in Tahiti. The women held bunches of cocoanuts, were stoutly built with large bare breasts, and their arms and legs were tattooed. Oddly, their female attendants wore more clothing. Clark added the following description in his journal a few days later: "The females of the common people dress in a piece of tape or cotton cloth, wrapped around the waist and over the body from that part as low as the ankles, leaving the breast, and shoulders bare, in this they take great pride, especially the young ones who have plump breasts."[61] This was the type of detail sailors relished. The strange appearance of the men, too, was noteworthy. The log of the *Lucy Ann* had an illustration of a Samoan male in a grass skirt paddling a canoe. Mariners also sketched other parts of the world. The keeper of the logbook of the *Neva* drew pictures of palm trees and local fishing prows in the East Indies. Midshipman Lucius M. Mason visited the Indian Ocean in the USS *Constitution* in the 1840s and drew pictures of native huts and canoes. Another seaman drew a likeness, with top hat and parasol, of "his Excellency Governor Tom of Annaboa" (Annobon, an Atlantic island off the coast of equatorial Africa) with top hat and parasol, while the log of the USS *Shark* contains a small picture of a hut in Africa.[62]

This type of drawing of exotic people and locales was relatively rare in logbooks and journals. More frequent were profiles and landscapes of bays and harbors. Sailors drew these sketches for several reasons. Occasionally a sailor filled his logbook with information about a foreign locale and drew a profile as a supplement to this description. When the *Arab* visited Johanna, now known as Anjouan in the Comoro Islands in the Indian Ocean, Captain Ephraim Harding commented about the inhabitants and filled a page with a sketch of how the island looked from the deck of his ship. Sometimes the strange contour of the land itself was so intriguing that the seaman artist felt compelled to draw its outline. Harding sketched a picture of the flat-topped outlines of Table Mountain hovering over the settlement at Cape Town, as did a seaman on a voyage in 1789–90. Icebergs, although an impermanent feature of the seascape, might also become the subject of a drawing. More often the mariner had pragmatic concerns and was interested in noting landfalls to aid in navigation: drawing the profile of the land as seen from the sea would help the next time he approached the same coast. As the brig *America* neared the English Channel in 1824, its logbook keeper drew an outline of the Isle of Ushant off the coast of Brittany. The next day the same journal writer provided a sketch of the coast of France near Brest, and a few days later he drew a picture of the white cliffs of Dover and Dover Castle. Some log keepers sketched profiles of the same land from different directions. Several log keepers drew remote locations like the volcanic island of Tristan Da Cunha in the South Atlantic or the Prince Edward Islands in the South Indian Ocean because they were vital landmarks in an otherwise trackless sea. The log of the *Alexander Coffin* has a sketch of Cape

Horn, with the notation of its bearing and distance, crucial information for anyone who sailed the treacherous waters at the southern tip of South America between the Atlantic and Pacific Oceans.[63]

These profile sketches were numerous and help us to understand the practice of navigation in the age of sail. Navigation was not an exact science in this era and, as we have already discussed, logbooks were navigational instruments crucial to sailing by dead reckoning. By noting the profile of a landfall a mariner could quickly recognize where he was and then make corrections to his calculations of latitude and longitude, assuming he knew the coordinates of that landfall. He would also be able to determine, if he was familiar with the waters, what he should do to keep the ship safe as it neared land. Much of what Ned Buntline wrote about his first seagoing voyage was sheer balderdash. But he really did have maritime experience, and he got at least one thing right. As his ship approached Cuba the captain asked the lookout what land he saw. The response was, "It looks to be a long black rock, Sir, half covered with surf, and right in the middle of the rock there seems to be something white. It looks like a hole through which one can see the foam from the other side." This was the kind of landmark every navigator who had made the run from the United States to Cuba knew by heart, and Buntline's captain immediately responded that "'it is the east end of Abaco, and that's the 'Hole in the Wall.'" He then predicted accurately that they would be in Havana in sixty hours.[64] This type of navigation, almost by the seat of the captain's pants, was normal. Noting wind, speed, current, and direction were important when out of sight of land, as was using more complicated instruments to make intricate calculations on latitude and longitude. But seeing a black rock with a hole in it allowed for a more precise location. This knowledge came from experience that might be reinforced by drawing a profile in a logbook. Published books also offered printed descriptions of landfalls. Although there were some books with charts available, the early versions of the main published navigational aid for the United States – *Blunt's American Coast Pilot* – had only verbal directions for entering the harbors of North America. There were no maps![65]

The profiles, combined with verbal descriptions of landfalls in *Blunt's American Coast Pilot*, also offer a clue into how most sailors viewed the world around them. What counted was what their eye could see. When we look at the ocean we ordinarily stand on land and peer into the distant horizon. Sailors stood on the deck of a ship, or aloft on the masthead, and looked either at an open sea that engulfed them or toward land. Without that landfall, or more specifically, without an identifiable landmark – mountain, lighthouse, steeple, or distinctive rock – there was no sure way to determine location. At sea maps had limited use because often the mariner could only guess at where he was. Even along a coast, maps were not as helpful as a profile because the bird's-eye view of bays and inlets on a map was not the same as what could be seen from the ship. Sailors, therefore, did not necessarily project their image of land onto a map to locate themselves. In fact, few logbooks have maps drawn in them. Sometimes there might be an angled view of the shoreline that combined a profile with a map, but seldom did a sailor draw a two-dimensional map. Maps, of course, had long existed. But purchasing maps could be expensive, especially before the breakthroughs in engraving that occurred in the nineteenth century. There were also collections of maps. As early as the sixteenth century publishers printed large compilations of maps known as waggoners. But these quickly became too big and costly. The British Admiralty ordered its own waggoner that was published in 1780. The "huge folio volumes" had 257 North American charts and colored engravings of New York Harbor.[66] The navy might be able to afford these books, but merchants would be more sparing. Did a captain on a trading voyage really need a map to tell him where he was on a route that he had sailed repeatedly? The logbook recorded his progress on the voyage and the landfall – the dark rock with a hole in it – would tell him more precisely where he was. And if he was less familiar with the coast he could open his handy copy of *Blunt's*, or some other navigating aid, and match the description to what he saw. To help him in the future he might sketch the profile of land in his logbook. When ships began to take longer voyages, and when printing and engraving costs decreased, maps and charts became more plentiful. Nautical booksellers frequently advertised maps in the nineteenth century. But the ship's-eye view and the importance of profiles remained.

Besides the many sketches of ships, sea fauna, native people, distant locations, and profiles that filled logbooks and journals, sailors also drew images that reminded them of home. Some logbooks have actual pictures of their houses. In at least one case the picture was drawn by the journal keeper's spouse after the seaman had returned. The last page of the logbook of the *Hippomenes* has a little sketch of a church with a steeple. While Joseph Peters was on board a whaleship in the late 1840s, he drew a stylized picture of flowers in a vase that has the air of domesticity about it. There are also some sketches of people who reminded the mariner of home, including portraits of women. Midshipman William Henry Allen penciled in the outlines of a matronly looking woman as he pined for home while serving aboard the USS *George Washington* in 1800. Usually these pictures depict women in nice dresses like those that appeared in the log of the *Angler*. However, Alfred Terry drew a topless woman who almost looks like a South Sea islander on the opening page of his whaling journal with the woman's name and New York address, indicating she might have been a prostitute. Terry's drawing is unusual. More typical was the illustration in a Valentine poem written for a sweetheart with a man in a sailor outfit politely holding the hand of a nicely attired woman.[67]

Creating patriotic images was also a way to remember home. Several sailors drew pictures of eagles and American flags.[68] In 1816 one logbook was illustrated with a picture of some cannon with a ribbon draped over them and the phrase "We have met the Enemy and they are ours."[69] International conflicts encouraged pictorial expressions of patriotism among seamen. Prisoners of war during the War of 1812 engaged in artistic activities. Some of the men aboard the prison ship *Vestal* in Barbados made carvings on cocoanut shells that poked fun at the British navy. One prisoner "engraved under the bottom, the English Lion conching to the American Eagle, and round its sides different flowers, fruits, trees, &c."[70] Prisoners drew pictures of the unique round shape of the Dartmoor compound in southwest England. After the Dartmoor massacre on April 6, 1815, the American seamen became especially vehement in their hatred for Great Britain and ardent in their patriotism. Painters and sculptors produced memorabilia of the tragedy. When the men finally marched out of captivity and toward boats that would return them to the United States, they did so under a banner produced especially for the occasion. The standard was white and was painted with "the representation of a tomb, with the Goddess of Liberty leaning on it, and a murdered sailor lying by its side, and a label over it in large capital letters, '*Columbia weeps, and we remember*.'" The banner also listed the names of the men killed in the massacre and had an inscription condemning the prison's British commandant. The sailors hoped to carry the banner home to show "a just resentment for the execrable deed, which it recorded, and a just respect for the sufferers."[71]

The artwork of the prisoners of war, as well as all the images that appear in logbooks and journals, demonstrates that there was a direct relationship between the reason for the creation of images and their subject and nature. The Dartmoor prisoners made memorabilia of their ordeal, including their banner, to commemorate the dead, excoriate the British, and assert their patriotism. Seamen dwelled upon the image of their ships as a means of declaring their affection for these wind-driven machines. They seldom portrayed themselves on deck or at mundane tasks because they had little interest in these functions. However, they depicted the whale hunt because it was a great dramatic moment when they put their lives on the line as they sought to gain a livelihood. Likewise Jack noted the natural wonders and exotic people and places as a means to remember these experiences. Mariners etched profiles of shorelines as a navigational aid and also because it was the way they saw the world. In most instances logbooks and journals were kept for personal reasons. The object of the art was focused inward and was mainly for the consumption of the artist. When it came to other mediums of art created for other purposes, the subject matter shifted.

The function of scrimshaw, the use of whale teeth and whale bone to fashion an image or to make an object, was more outward looking because the object was usually produced for others. The earliest American scrimshaw appeared in the second half of the eighteenth century, but not until the first half of the nineteenth century, just as the whaling industry in the United States really took off, did scrimshaw expand as a special art form. Some scrimshanders may have engaged in the art merely out of boredom, but most scrimshaw was intended for sale, for trade, or as a gift to others. In particular, based on the nature of the objects and the predominate designs, scrimshaw was generally made for loved ones back home. There are several different types of scrimshaw. First there are the inked etchings of whales' teeth (or occasionally walrus tusks). Usually a scrimshaw artist either traced a design from an engraving in a book or magazine, or drew a design himself. He would then cut that outline into the tooth or bone and fill it in with ink. The second type of scrimshaw would place similar designs on busks – a flexible piece of whalebone inserted into a corset to help mold a woman's shape. The third type of scrimshaw could be either ornamental or functional and would be a product constructed using several pieces of whalebone without necessarily having an inked design.[72]

Scrimshaw motifs were both similar and dissimilar to the kinds of pictures found in logbooks and journals. Not surprisingly, ships appear on many pieces of scrimshaw. Sometimes the scrimshander drew the picture of his own vessel as a means to commemorate the voyage. In 1829 Frederick Myrick etched a picture of the whaleship *Susan* off the coast of Japan under partial sail with a whale tied up alongside on one half of the tooth, and on the other the *Susan* under full sail, homeward bound.[73] As was true with some logbook drawings, sailors liked to depict the capture of whales on their scrimshaw.[74] They also placed their ship in specific locals either in distant ports, like in China or the South Pacific, or their home port.[75] Unlike the journal illustrations, scrimshanders created many patriotic scenes. One artist in the 1830s drew a broadside view of the whaleship *Mechanic* in the middle third of a whale's tooth, with the name of the ship and captain on the bottom surrounded by a circular sawtooth border with a banner on top stating, "Forget Me Not." The upper third has a parcel of flags, including the American and British, with a drum and cannon in the middle and a victory wreath above. The bottom third has two female figures representing justice, blindfolded with a scale in one hand and a sword in another, and liberty, sitting holding a pole with a Phrygian cap on top. The placement of both the American and British flags probably heralded the peace between the two nations that followed the War of 1812.[76] Other patriotic scrimshaw etchings exhibited less equanimity and celebrated American naval victories. Sailor artists often designed scrimshaw in pairs. One scrimshander portrayed the elaborate fleet action of the Battle of Lake Erie on one tooth and the Battle of Lake Champlain on the other. A different artist used Abel Bowen's engraving in *The Naval Monument* as the basis in depicting the USS *Constitution*'s victory over the HMS *Java* and the USS *Peacock*'s triumph over the HMS *Epervier*.[77]

There are more pictures of people in scrimshaw than in the logbooks either drawn freehand or copied from prints. Women were especially prominent as the subject of the scrimshander's art. There are a few examples of partially clad women or women engaged in sexual activity. Topless natives also appear on some scrimshaw. But these are rare. Either not many seamen bothered with promiscuous subjects, or the risqué scrimshaw has not survived. Most likely, given the dependence on printed images as a starting point, and also the purpose of the scrimshaw as a gift, there probably were not many such pictures in the first place. There were also scenes of women dressed as men based on prints of characters found in popular books, such as Fanny Campbell, the female pirate.[78] Far more common than racy themes or women donning men's clothes were carefully crafted images dressed in the height of Victorian fashion often, but not always, taken from magazines like *Godey's Ladies Book* or *Harper's Weekly*. Created by hardworking whale men these pictures were probably intended as a gift to a mother, a sweetheart, or a wife back in the United States and reflected an ideal to which these working-class women could only begin to aspire. Regardless of how much or how little the image matched the reality of the females in a whale man's family, these subjects represented a sentimentality that became increasingly

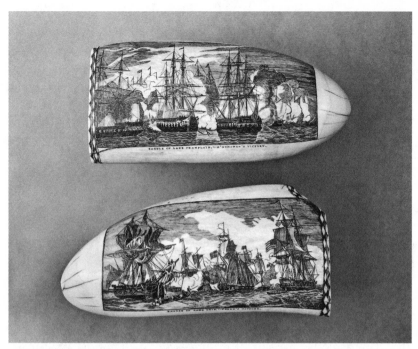

FIGURE 7.9. **Scrimshaw.** Patriotic scrimshaw celebrated American naval victories, especially those that occurred during the War of 1812. The scrimshander of this pair of etched whales tooth depicted the two great fresh water fleet actions of the War of 1812: the Battle of Lake Erie and the Battle of Lake Champlain. The images were probably traced from a book on American naval triumphs. Courtesy of Mystic Seaport, #1941.412, Mystic Connecticut.

central in the nineteenth century.[79] Indeed, there were also portrayals of men and women together in domestic tranquility, as well as depictions of other sentimental themes like homes, churches, and flowers produced by men who were not only stained by tar, but often dripping with whale grease.[80]

Another popular subject of the scrimshander was the idealized Jack Tar, replete with broad-bottomed pants, striped shirt, waist jacket, kerchief sportily worn around the neck, and tarpaulin hat. In other words, the same kind of seaman who appeared in the Woodside painting and the print of George Brown, the Boatswain's Mate – images almost absent from the journals and logbooks. The sailor may not have had much interest in drawing this idealized mariner in his journal, but when he was creating art for the consumption of others, especially loved ones at home, he eagerly embraced the popularized image of himself as a vital part of the nation. Often these sailor portraits had a patriotic theme, with the seaman holding a flag in some proximity to a female symbol of liberty. The Nantucket Historical Association has a set of engraved whale's teeth that paired the image of the sailor with the image of the goddess liberty. The sailor is dressed in his standard outfit with an anchor on one side and a shield displaying the stars and stripes on the other. An eagle is perched over his shoulder holding a streamer with the slogan "Free Trade and Sailors Rights" on it. Surrounding the entire piece is a series of geometric designs and on the top is a small image of a ship. The female liberty is dressed in clothes typical of a woman in the early nineteenth century and has almost identical surroundings as in the sailor piece. The main difference is that her eagle's streamer proclaimed, "Virtue, Liberty, and Independence."[81] Many of the depictions of the manly Jack Tar show him in domestic scenes with his family or in some iteration of the "sailor's return."[82] Occasionally seamen could mock themselves as in "Jack Contending for the Motto" that has a bottle of grog, a mermaid, and an anchor between two gruff-looking seamen with an eagle on top carrying a banner proclaiming, "Free Trade and Sailors' Rights."[83]

A whale's tooth was only one platform for scrimshaw. Other parts of the whale and other parts of sea mammals were used for the whale man's art. Both the walrus tusk and the busk (made of whalebone or baleen) were longer than the biggest of whale's teeth. The artist might use this larger "canvas" to provide a complex scene of whaling or visiting a foreign port. More often both the tusks and the busks would have a series of images one on top of another to tell a story or just to allow the artist a chance to offer several portraits simultaneously.[84] The busk, which was about a foot long and an inch wide, was an important medium for the scrimshander because he was creating an object that would literally outline a woman's figure when it was inserted in the front of a corset, providing additional shape and support. The themes of these intimate gifts would be relatively sanitary and included ships, whaling scenes, ports of call, fancily dressed women, domestic portraits, flowers, and the idealized Jack Tar. Busks were tokens of affection: they were a symbol that the sailor had thought about his wife or sweetheart back home while he was away, and, because they were worn close to the heart, the wife or sweetheart would in turn remember the sailor when he had headed back to sea. Although there was no set pattern of illustration, at least one busk copied the image of George Brown, the Boatswain's Mate. Many others featured a stylized portrait of seamen, with tarpaulin hat, a ship, and a woman in full Victorian regalia. Sometimes the sailor and woman would be in an embrace, holding hands, or just near each other. Other images might be added, like a picture of the homestead, an anchor, a flower, and maybe some words. One scrimshander added the following verse that explained both the practical and emotional function of the busk:

> Rest on the bossum of the fair
> And softly whisper Peace
> Bid every sorrow, every care
> And dark foreboding cease.
>
> In many a gale
> Has been this whale
> In which this bone did rest
> His time is past
> His bone at last
> Must now support thy breast
>
> From rocks and
> Sands and danger far
> May God protect
> the Yankee tar.[85]

Busks could have patriotic themes, with eagles, flags, and depictions of liberty. Many were simply embellished with geometric or flower designs.[86]

The busk was only one of several objects seamen made for use back in the United States. Scrimshanders made domestic tools out of whalebone and ivory. Swifts were elaborate expandable yarn holders for women who knitted and did not necessarily have a man around whose hands could hold the yarn. Likewise, sailors crafted pie crimpers, pastry tools, rolling pins, clothespins, pestles, knitting needles, clock displays, boxes, salt shakers, toys, toothpicks, and similar objects. Most of these goods did not have drawings or etchings, but the complex construction, carving, and inlays took patience and artistic talent.[87]

Sailor craftsmen worked with other mediums as well, using a variety of materials to make a host of decorative and practical items. A fancy game box made of bone by prisoners of war during the War of 1812 might not be very pragmatic within the dismal confines of Dartmoor, but as a specialty item to be sold to the local populace to raise money for extra food, it made a great deal of sense. Straw boxes were also woven in Dartmoor. Perhaps the most interesting products of prisoner craftsmen were the bone ship models. A prisoner would clean all the bones in the meat provided in his meals (which was not that much), shape them into boards, and then build, plank by plank, model ships, complete with masts, yardarms, and rigging. Aboard ship seamen decorated their sea chests with pictures

FIGURE 7.10. **Busk.** Perhaps one of the most intimate gifts a sailor could offer his wife or sweetheart was a busk, a decorated thin piece of whalebone that was inserted down the middle of a corset to mold a woman's body to an ideal shape. The busk illustrated here combined a nautical theme featuring a ship, the man's world, with arrangements of flower, suggesting the domestic world of women. Courtesy of Mystic Seaport, #1941.613, Mystic Connecticut.

and made ditty boxes for their small tools and needles and thread essential to repair the wear and tear of their clothing. That same needle and thread, and the nimble fingers that had mastered them, could be turned to decorations on sea bags (in which sailors kept their possessions) and on clothing. Men in the navy created elaborate embroidered designs of patriotic icons like eagles and the stars and stripes and intermingled them with nautical symbols like the anchor. Sailors took great pride in making knots and would sometimes create displays with different types of knots. They also used this talent to fashion macramé items, like ladies' purses. At sea, these mariners did not care that such crafts might appear feminine – they had gained these skills as a matter of course and then applied them to an artistic endeavor that also filled empty hours. A few sailors made pictures of ships out of paper cutouts.[88]

Another maritime art form favored by about 10 percent of sailors for both personal use and public display was the tattoo. The Polynesian word "tattoo" was introduced into the English language in the eighteenth century after Captain James Cook visited the South Pacific and commented on the elaborate inked skin designs of the Tahitians and other South Sea islanders. Seamen had been marking their own skin with pinpricks filled with ink and gunpowder long before then. Indeed, not until well into the nineteenth century was the word "tattoo" applied to this form of personal scarification among mariners. The marking of skin with ink was performed by sailors on other sailors; there were no professional tattoo parlors in the first half of the nineteenth century. The process was similar to making scrimshaw. On one China voyage in 1817, Charles Tyng commented that a man called Braddock Black tattooed most of the crew. Black had learned the process of skin marking while a prisoner of war in Dartmoor. "His instrument was three common sewing needles fastened round a pointed stick, the points being a little separated from one another, and a small saucer with a little ink mixed with water. He would dip the needles in to the saucer and commence pricking just raising the skin, not bringing blood, on the letters or figures previously marked out with ink." Although later in life Tyng was embarrassed by these "impressions," he offered a detailed description of his tattoos: "I had letters, anchors, hearts, on my hands and arms, and a fancy double heart with C. T. in one, and S. H. in the other, red roses between, each heart pierced with cupid's dart, the red showing the drops of blood from the wound. This was on the left arm. On the right was a pricked cross, with the Saviour nailed to it, and red showing the wounds in the hands, feet, and side, an anchor and a large letter T. On the back of my left hand was an anchor and on my middle finger was a heart representing a ring."[89] These multiple images were not unusual for seamen who marked their skin in this era. Detailed studies of tattooing in the early republic based on protection certificates and prisoner of war records indicate that the most frequent designs were initials and that many seamen marked their bodies with symbols of their occupation, like Tyng's anchor (sailors also displayed ships and mermaids on their skin). Reminders of loved ones back home, such as Tyng's, were also prevalent in this art form. Religious symbols were somewhat more rare. Missing from Tyng's litany of indelible patterns on his skin were patriotic symbols like flags and eagles, which appeared on just under 10 percent of all tattooed men. There were almost no images of Jack Tar himself in sailor tattoos.[90]

The art of the sailor was diverse and appeared in many different mediums: drawings, scrimshaw, material objects, and tattoos. In the nineteenth century the sailor may have embraced the idea that he was vital to the commerce and to the defense of the nation, as depicted in the Woodside painting and the engraving of the Boatswain's Mate, George Brown, but he only used images reflecting that political persona if it suited his purposes. When he crafted objects for other people, especially loved ones back home, a seaman might depict the stereotypical tar as a proud mariner sporting a tarpaulin hat. Yet he had greater interest in his ship, the world around him, and the memory of his life back home. The more personal the medium, whether it be his private journal or his own skin, the more likely he was to express his true inner self. However the rest of society imagined Jack, and there was a major transformation in how the sailor was depicted as we move from the eighteenth century to the nineteenth century, and however much the mariner may have accepted his new heroic status, ultimately the art of the sailor reflected his own interests and concerns and marked another bridge between maritime and mainstream culture.

Epilogue: The Sea Chest

The sea chest represented the sailor's world ashore and his world afloat. Wrapped in the confines of this wooden box were his material possessions and many of his hopes and dreams. Packed with personal and pragmatic goods, the sea chest accompanied Jack Tar as he sailed the seven seas. But the same possessions that he carried with him tied the sailor to land. Tracing the personal items a sailor brought with him aboard ship, and then the items he returned with at the end of a voyage, we will again be reminded that America was once a maritime nation. Of course, not every sailor who went to sea had a chest. Seamen, especially those on smaller vessels and in the navy, often used a canvas bag to collect their belongings. That said, many mariners had sea chests. Ishmael's isolation from the rest of the world in Herman Melville's *Moby Dick* is in part symbolized by the fact that he stuffed his clothes into a carpet bag and not a sea chest, or even a sailor's canvas bag.[1] When a young man began his maritime career, one of the first things he purchased was a sea chest. As a mere boy of fourteen, Charles Tyng went to sea in 1815 with a sea chest that would accompany him throughout his early years as a mariner. In his reminiscence of his experiences Tyng took pride that the same chest was "in the garret of the old house as a memorial" to his sailor's life.[2] In 1849 Samuel Wood signed on for a thirty-month whaling cruise and spent fifteen dollars on a sea chest and some clothes.[3] Sea chests varied in size and shape, ranging from as little as thirty inches wide by a foot high and a foot deep to almost four feet wide by nearly two feet high and deep.[4] The larger chests were probably used in the nineteenth century during longer voyages and aboard whaleships. The chests were not simply rectangular boxes; many were trapezoid prisms with the bottom wider than the top. Whatever the shape and size, or whatever the nature of the container that held the seaman's belongings, the sea chest remains a useful symbol to represent the maritime connections to the sea and to the land.[5]

As we have seen, sailors decorated material goods like the sea chest. Sea chests might have carvings or painted initials, and sometimes displayed pictures on the inside or outside of ships and other objects near and dear to the seaman. The fact that sailors used illustrations of ships on their chests should not be surprising. Such images played a prominent role in the maritime culture, appearing repeatedly in personal journals and logbooks, and were projected onto scrimshaw. Jack Tar also took pride in his handiwork in creating beckets – the handles for the chest – out of knotted rope. Canvas bags could have painted initials or pictures and might display elaborate embroidery of emblems and items that the seaman treasured. John S. Misroon had such a bag when he became a midshipman in 1824 and decorated it with stars and anchors. He also did extensive macramé work for the rope handle.[6]

Sea chests were versatile. Because sea chests were an individual's personal property, at the beginning of a voyage a mariner would place his chest on the bunk he claimed, staking out his territory.[7] The forecastle held little furniture, so sea chests doubled as chairs and tables. On prison ships sailors arranged their chests so as to create a space shared with messmates. Aboard the prison hulk *Jersey* thefts were so common that each mess had one man use the chests as a bed to prevent anyone from stealing their meager property at night.[8] Whatever their uses, the most vital function of the sea chests was as a carrier of the sailors' belongings. Sailors viewed their chests as sacrosanct, almost to the point that they worshiped them and all that was inside. To commemorate that special relationship sailors would put aside time on Sundays to overhaul their chests, examining each item, washing and mending their clothes, and repacking everything. Many sailors mentioned this Sabbath ritual. One mariner described this process as "taking a sailor's pleasure." Another confided in his journal: "Sunday at Sea! All the good folks at home at meeting – where I should like to be myself, but as I cannot be there, I employ myself during the forenoon, it being my watch below, in overhauling my Chest and reading."[9] Although sailors usually locked their chests, there was little privacy aboard a ship, including the sea chest. Shipmates often rifled through each other's belongings whether they were welcome or not, helping themselves to hidden food and drink. A sailor returned to his chest to take a swig from his secret bottle of gin,

only to find the liquid replaced with a saltier undrinkable substance –
urine.[10] Sailors could become defensive about their chests, especially if
the captain sought to open them. One captain's insistence on searching
his crew's chests for hidden alcohol almost triggered a mutiny. The mate
entered the forecastle with a crowbar to force open the lids. Suspecting
something was amiss, the crew left off work and descended from the rigging into the forecastle with the intent to "put a stop to his proceedings."
The men asked the mate if anything had been reported stolen. The mate
replied no, but that the captain had ordered him to search for grog and
to dump it overboard. Hearing that, two men said, "O, if that be all,"
and opened their chests (the locks had already been destroyed), and said,
"here is ours, the rest may do as they please." The others also opened
their chests and said they had no grog. The mate, however, insisted
"upon having their contents bundled out, in short, to have their chests
turned bottom up." The men refused to do this, saying that "their chests
were their own, and there was no grog in them, they would not have
their clothes turned topsy-turvy." On deck the mate might have swung
the crowbar at some of them, but in the forecastle, on the sailors' turf
and in close quarters, he decided to believe "them sincere." The captain,
however, demanded the search continue even though he had to flog two
men before he could do so.[11]

The sea chest was also a way to bind men to employment. One of the
many means by which the landlord "trapped" the sailor was by holding
on to the sea chest and what little property the sailor owned. As Jack
came ashore at the end of a voyage, boardinghouse keepers would bribe
carters to take the sailor's sea chest to their establishments, knowing that
once they had possession of this property, the mariner was bound to
follow. Some landlords were not above going through the sea chest to
seize anything of value before sending the seaman on his next voyage.
After the sailor had spent his money and prepared – or was prepared by
the landlord – to head off to sea, he had to take stock of his possessions
and pack his all into his sea chest. The obliging landlord then made sure
that the sailor had the right clothing and anything else the mariner might
need, including the sea chest itself. The landlord, who usually negotiated
the seaman's next voyage, would hire a carter with a wheelbarrow to
carry the chest to the waiting ship. All of these costs, as well as the last
expenditures of a spree ashore, would allow the landlord to lay claim to
the month's advance on wages typical of the Articles of Agreement – the
ship's labor contract – that the sailor signed. Often mariners complained
of the landlord's charges. But to lug one's own chest was not going in

proper sailor style. Moreover, purchasing some of the same goods aboard ship could be even more expensive. Once the chest was placed on the bunk in the forecastle, the seaman was tied to the ship. If he attempted to break his bargain and not sail with the ship he would forfeit the chest and its contents. The same was true when in other ports. Plenty of seamen "jumped" ship and broke their contracts, but when they did so, they lost the bedding, clothes, and sea chest left in the forecastle. The selling of the contents of a sea chest became a final ritual commemorating the death of a sailor aboard ship. After the burial at sea, the men would haul the chest on deck and then auction off each item with the intent of sending the money raised to the dead man's family. Although sailors were superstitious about wearing these clothes, this sale also became an effective way to distribute used goods among the crew. It was also a last rite that connected the sailor at sea to his family on land.[12]

Sea chests were an everyday object to Jack Tar, seamlessly integrated into the way he described life on a ship. George Little has one of his shipmates spin a yarn packed with the language of Jack Tar with the ever-present sea chest as a backdrop: "Sailors, as well as landsmen, will have to heave in stays and stand on tother tack, so as to get clear of the shoals of destruction that lays near grog harbour, and swearing rocks, and cape frolic" and "he must obey the orders of this book (clapping his flipper on a Bible that lay on a chest)."[13] With less sailor-like rhetorical flourish, although still using some nautical jargon, John Hoxse described going "below" during a storm. Having spent seven hours lashed to the helm (to ensure that heavy waves would not toss him from the wheel and cost him control of the ship), he began eating because he was famished after his long watch on deck. He then reported, "I was sitting on a chest, at my repast, and the first thing I knew, I found myself thrown into the lee birth, with two or three chests top of me."[14] On several occasions Ned Myers described sailors entering and leaving a ship. The only property each seaman took with him was his sea chest and its contents.[15]

Within the sea chest the most important possessions for the sailor were his clothes. The mariner's clothes set him apart. This distinction was as true in 1750 as in 1850. Look at any illustration from this period and you can quickly identify Jack Tar by his waist or monkey jacket, neck handkerchief, and long pants. Richard Henry Dana Jr. described the ideal seaman as wearing "a well-varnished black tarpaulin stuck upon the back of his head; his long locks coming down almost to his eyes; his white duck trowsers and shirt; blue jacket; and black kerchief, tied loosely round his neck."[16] This outfit underwent some alterations over the decades. In the mid-eighteenth century some seamen wore petticoat trousers that looked something like baggy culottes, but by 1800 most sailors wore full-length pants made out of duck, an inexpensive canvas material, that swelled out at the bottom. The pants might be vertically striped; usually they were either blue or white. The shirts came in several colors, sometimes in checkers, but often had horizontal stripes – seldom did you see a sailor wear both striped pants and a striped shirt. Charles Tyng offered a description of his new sailor clothes when he first went to sea. At a slop shop he procured "a couple suits of sailor's clothes, some checkered shirts &c." along with a woolen sailor's cap. He also had a sailor's jacket cut at the waist. However, when he put the hat on and wore a ruffled shirt, because his checkered ones were not ready, and "paraded the streets," some boys mocked him by shouting, "A fresh water sailor, a fresh water sailor." Tyng quickly realized that his "want of a checkered shirt" left him vulnerable to derision because his ruffled "shirt appeared ridiculous over my sailor's jacket."[17] Tyng did not pack any cold weather gear because he would not need it. Within the sea chest, however, most mariners would have heavier jackets and clothes for the harsh conditions encountered in frigid climes. Herman Melville's "White Jacket" stood out on an American naval ship because his coat was not waterproof and looked like a burial shroud. Richard Henry Dana Jr. described in detail how he and the rest of the crew opened their chests as they prepared for a passage around Cape Horn, mending their heavier jackets and coating a set of clothing with tar for waterproofing, knowing that during the tumultuous passage they would be confronted with huge waves sweeping across the deck and torrents of freezing rain and snow.[18] Folded carefully into the recesses of the sailor's locker would be his best outfit to be worn when he came ashore on liberty or at the end of the voyage. Sailors sometimes embroidered elaborate nautical designs on these outfits.[19] Seamen also took pride in having decorative buttons, especially for their shore clothes. Christopher Hawkins wore buttons proclaiming "Liberty and property," a point of contention when the British captured him during the Revolutionary War.[20] There were also varieties of head gear, including, as Tyng noted, wool caps. Early in the period the shape of more regular hats could vary, but after independence American sailors preferred to don a broad-rimmed straw cap covered in tar – the tarpaulin hat.[21]

However much a sailor's clothes appeared distinctive, several factors connected those clothes to the shore. First, the fabrics and the garments were produced on land. Within the Anglo-American context reaching back to the seventeenth century, large contracts to supply the British navy and army with standardized clothing laid the foundation for the infrastructure of the readymade garment industry in Great Britain. This in turn contributed significantly to the expansion of textile production in the eighteenth and early nineteenth centuries.[22] In the United States sailor slops remained a central component of textile production and the garment industry: Brooks Brothers began as a store close to the wharves that specialized in low-end sailor outfitting in early nineteenth-century New York.[23] Second, there were similarities between the clothing worn by sailors and by workers ashore. In seaports many of the tradesmen in maritime industries such as shipbuilding, sail making, and the like had at one point in their lives been seamen and often wore sailor-like clothing. As a young apprentice sailmaker in New York City, Stephen Allen remembered British press gangs chasing him during the Revolutionary War when he was mistaken for a seaman because of his duck canvas pants and monkey jacket.[24] In the early nineteenth century more and more Americans from all social classes wore short jackets cut at the waist typical of the working class.[25] Despite these similarities, sailor clothes remained distinctive. The material used for most sailor clothes was coarser and cheaper than what the captain or rich landsmen wore. In 1773 an advertisement stated that a runaway convict laborer had stolen some sailor shirts made of osnaburg – denoting low-quality linen – and a white shirt belonging to the captain. In the eighteenth century white linen would be an expensive and high-quality textile. Common sailors also preferred stripes and checkers, rather than white or solid colors.[26]

A seaman would keep grooming materials like combs, razors, and scissors in his sea chest. A mariner might even make these objects himself, crafting combs out of whalebone or attaching the blade of a razor to hand-carved ivory. Hairstyles were important. In the eighteenth century members of the gentry distinguished themselves by wearing wigs. No common sailor duffed a peruke – it would have been presumptuous, unseamanlike, and awkward. A British seaman took pride in his queue – the long pigtail that dangled from the back of his head that was frequently held into place with dried eel skin. This hairstyle, however, was merely an exaggerated statement and a nautical version of the queue the more affluent wore. On American ships in the nineteenth century the pigtail was considered too British and too old-fashioned. Many sailors, however, still wore their hair long, allowing it to dangle loosely on their shoulders. Increasingly in the nineteenth century American seamen cut their hair shorter in a manner similar to the way all classes wore it. The Republican print by William Charles depicting three seamen rejecting the Federalist appeal to oppose the embargo shows them with the latest style of short hair with long sideburns and the forelock swept to the front. Some seamen still wore their hair longer. In the late 1840s a sailor lamented when one of his prankster shipmates cut off one of his ringlets as he slept. Beards, too, became fashionable in the antebellum period and identified as sailor-like, especially with the upper lip shaved.[27]

As we have seen, sailors loved music. Not only would they occasionally note favorite lyrics in their journals, but they would also keep various instruments among their prize possessions in the sea chest. Perhaps two of the most common instruments for the regular seaman would be the fiddle and the flute that could be played in idle moments in the forecastle or occasionally during the dogwatch on deck. Harmonicas were also popular, in part because of their size. Few seamen would take an accordion or squeeze box to sea, despite the general association of these instruments with sailors, because they were expensive and fared poorly in the salt air aboard ship. Officers might have larger and more costly instruments for their entertainment. Aboard naval vessels a bosun might buy and keep his own whistle, but the ship would provide the drums used to beat the men to quarters. Likewise, larger naval vessels might even have had a band with talented musicians recruited from among the crew to play for official occasions. It is unlikely that the larger musical instruments – drums, trumpets, and similar brass instruments – would be owned by individual seamen and kept in their chests, although some seamen had such instruments with them in Dartmoor.[28] The music produced by and for seamen aboard ship might also lead to dancing, a skill that was both prized and competitive among mariners. This music and dancing marked a crucial connection between ship and shore as suggested in the Akin print "Sailors Glee" displaying a couple dancing and sailors with a fiddle and a flute, as well as in the repeated appearance of performers "decked out" like a "Jolly Jack Tar" doing the hornpipe on the stage in the eighteenth and nineteenth centuries.[29]

Sea chests were the repositories of personal items. A sailor would keep important papers, like his protection certificate asserting his nationality, as well as money in his chest.[30] As we have seen during the early republic and antebellum periods a great many American seamen could read and write. Sailors held on to letters from family and loved ones, reading them over and over again, and then carefully returning them to the safety of the sea chest. Some sailors so prized any letter that on a long voyage they bought them from less sentimental or more impoverished tars, even though they were not the original addressee. So, too, many a

Jack Tar recorded his experiences at sea in his own journal, which he kept tucked into a corner of his sea chest. As a prisoner of war during the revolution, Charles Herbert hid his journal in a false bottom in his chest.[31] However profane a sailor might become, he usually revered the Bible held in his sea chest. Samuel Leech wrote that he often "perused the Bible and prayer book which my mother had wisely placed in my chest, on the eve of my departure." He also noted that in something of a contradiction she had "inappropriately" left him a pack of cards as well.[32] Sailors kept their personal libraries in their sea chests, with volumes ranging from the sensational *The Pirates Own Book* to more religious fare. A tar might hold on to the oddest bits of reading material. One sailor made some purchases in a store that were wrapped in paper. Finding the paper contained some hymns, the sailor carefully preserved the sheets and brought them with him when he went back to sea.[33] Among the items Charles Tyng stuffed into his chest were a new pair of shoes, some pocket handkerchiefs, a jackknife, a tin pot, and a make-shift pillow made from an old piece of stair carpet with some strong cotton sewed around it.[34] Seamen kept personal tools and their ditty bags with a sewing kit in their chests.[35] The captain and mates, as well as regular mariners, would store their navigational instruments in their chests. After the capture of the *Hancock* during the Revolutionary War, the British searched the chests belonging to the officers and took "all the mathematical instruments such as quadrants, scales, dividers, together with all books, journals, &c. useful to navigation."[36] The Algerians who boarded the *Polly* during their depredations in 1793 "broke open all the Trunks, and Chests, there were on board, and," according to John Foss, "plundered all our bedding, clothing, books, Charts, Quadrants, and every moveable article."[37]

A highly prized item almost every Jack stored in his chest was his supply of tobacco. Ashore many sailors preferred to smoke cigars as long as they could afford them. A boardinghouse keeper in 1850 listed "sundry cigars" on his bill for a sailor and charged $1.81, or as much as a skilled carpenter earned in a day.[38] At sea a sailor might stick a wad of tobacco in his mouth at almost any time while working. Smoking a pipe demanded leisure time below deck, during the dogwatch in the evening, late at night, or a Sunday when there was little labor to perform. Amid the other smells that assaulted the nostrils in a crowded forecastle the strong "aroma" of tobacco was always present. Sailors relished their tobacco almost as much as their grog ration. George Little reported that he had "seen an old sailor overhaul his chest three times in the course of one day in search of tobacco." On long voyages when the supply ran low, sailors would sell tobacco to one another at exorbitant prices, which could lead to arguments and fighting. The shrewd merchant would make sure that there was a supply of tobacco on board that the captain could sell to the crew to make additional profit.[39]

A sailor's tobacco might be kept in a special box given as a present by a loved one as celebrated in Charles Dibden's song "The Token," in which this memento helped to sustain a mariner through trials and tribulations at sea. Such gifts were pregnant with meaning for the seaman and could include anything from a lock of hair, a letter, a Bible, a special book, or even a miniature picture. As the sailor headed across the broad ocean he kept within the confines of the sea chest any number of talismans that tied him to shore and enabled him to remember those he left behind.[40]

Upon his return a mariner brought a wide array of goods home with him. Among these possessions were the gifts intended for loved ones. The scrimshander would stow the products he made during his years on a whaleship: keepsakes like etched whales' teeth, as well as personal and practical items like busks for women's corsets, swifts to hold yarn, crimpers for pies, boxes for ornament, and many other objects made of whale teeth and bone. Exotic silks and porcelains purchased in distant ports would also be held in the sea chest. In addition, sailors stored goods they hoped to sell at a profit. Aboard merchant vessels seamen would sometimes be allowed a "privilege" or "venture" to carry a certain amount of freight to trade or sell upon returning to port. Even if a mariner did not have this "privilege" as a part of his contract, some high-value goods might have been small enough to keep in his chest or bag. These items could be sold in a foreign port or after returning home.[41] John D. Symonds sent a letter to his "affectionate brothers" from Havana to tell them that he had sold some shoes for them for $10.50 (close to a month's wages for a mariner).[42] George Little secured his "Canton adventure" in his chest.[43] After returning to New York City in 1821 from a trip to East Asia, Thomas Gregory wrote to his family in Marblehead that he was sending them some goods he had purchased during the trip. This entrepreneurial activity could also entail smuggling and illegal trade.[44] New York customs collector David Gelston wrote to the secretary of the treasury that several of the seamen aboard the USS *Peacock* had been caught smuggling items captured during a cruise at the end of the War of 1812. These men had hid their contraband in their bags and even their handkerchiefs.[45] Sailors visiting the Pacific Northwest in 1805 traded cartridges with Native Americans for tails made of fur. When the captain found out about this illicit activity he "flew as a flash with the fury of a tiger and the spirit of his mother with all vengeance upon the people." He ordered a search of the seamen's chests and found 112 tails and other items owned by six of the crew.[46] Sometimes sailors kept objects that were nothing more than odd ephemera. Several seamen inserted the "wings" of flying fish into their journals, which were in turn put in their chests. Midshipman William Reynolds obtained the remains of rare animals, a South Sea hook, and a Feejee comb while on the Wilkes expedition.[47] William Clarke plucked a flower from Napoleon's grave on distant St. Helena and also collected some feathers from rare Pacific Island birds.[48]

The sea chest tied the sailor to the land as well as the ocean. As should be evident in this discussion, many of the areas explored in this book can be related to the sea chest. Although swearing and the language of Jack Tar are not directly connected to the sea chest, the conflict over what might have been hidden within its confines might lead to a spate of cursing by both the captain and the crew. Mariners spoke of the sea chest as a natural part of their world. Those crucial tools of memory, the logbook and journal, were often found within the sea chest. Exotic goods hidden in the depths of a chest might trigger a yarn spinner to begin a long tale of his adventures and exploits. Songsters, sheets with ballads, and even old scraps of paper printed with hymns would be kept safely in a sea chest. Among the hidden treasures of the sea chest would be a Bible and the books a sailor owned. Many of the objects and images a seaman created were stored in his private locker. While images of Jack Tar reflected the special outfit he wore and the sailor's clothes helped to mold his nautical identity, those same garments linked him to the land: the clothes themselves were made on shore, were not that different from what some landsmen wore, and among the most prized of these garments were his finest outfit to be worn in port. The sea chest as an object was portable and therefore helped Jack Tar venture out upon the ocean. But it also contained memories of home that ultimately brought him back to land.

Herman Melville reminds us of the symbolic importance of the sea chest. Melville's use of the sea chest in *Moby Dick* was deliberate and dramatic. After the first lowering of the boats to hunt whales, and after his boat crew had been tossed into the water in a brush with death that presaged the tragic end of the *Pequod*, Ishmael decided to write a last will and testimony. Securing this document in the confines of a sea chest offered Ishmael a new lease on life. As Melville has his narrator explain: "I survived myself; my death and burial were locked up in my chest. I looked around me tranquilly and contentedly, like a quiet ghost with a clean conscience sitting inside the bars of a snug family vault." Here the safety of the sea chest comforted an Ishmael who had just confronted his own mortality.[49]

The sea chest was too powerful a symbol not to use again. When Queequeg, Ishmael's South Sea companion and friend, was struck with a fever and thought he was going to die he requested that the carpenter make a "canoe" like those wooden boxes in which the men in Nantucket were buried. At this moment Queequeg's thoughts returned to the land of his birth and his traditional notions of an afterlife. This canoe-coffin was to carry his corpse to "the starry archipelagoes" – islands in the sky where he believed his people came to their final resting place. The canoe represented Queequeg's life at sea, the coffin a return to land. Queequeg, however, survived his sickness and "With a wild whimsiness" used the coffin for a sea chest. He emptied all of his clothes into the coffin and "set them in order there." Like his Anglo-American shipmates, Queequeg then decorated this box, spending hours upon hours "carving the lid with all manner of grotesque drawings; and it seemed that hereby he was striving, in his rude way, to copy parts of the twisted tattooing on his body." Because Queequeg's body art had been the work of "a departed prophet and seer" from the Pacific Islands, "those hieroglyphic marks, had written out on his body a complete theory of the heavens and the earth, and a mystical treatise on the art of attaining truth," even though neither Queequeg nor anyone else on the *Pequod* could discern their meaning. This sea chest brought land and sea and all the universe together. Queequeg's hidden message and the magic of his engravings provided an appropriate ending for Melville's epic: the canoe-coffin–sea chest that had connected even the "pagan" Queequeg to the islands of his birth became the "life-buoy" that saved Ishmael from the vortex of the sinking *Pequod* and allowed him to return to terra firma.[50]

Appendix: A Note on Logbooks and Journals Kept at Sea

As explained in the text, the boundary between a logbook and a journal kept at sea was often ambiguous. The notes in this volume therefore use a consistent form of citation regardless of how the logbooks might be catalogued in the different repositories visited during the course of my research. In each case, however, the notes contain enough unique information to lead a subsequent researcher to the same manuscript source.

More than 250 logs of separate sea voyages were examined during the course of the research for this book. Although some of the voyages chronicled appeared within the confines of the same cover, each voyage is listed as a separate log. Research in these logbooks was not random. Instead, using catalog entries, citations by other scholars, and other means, I strove to identify those logbooks which might contain more than the basic wind, wave, and weather routine. I therefore purposefully looked for logbooks that described conflict and contained commentary, poems, songs, illustrations, and other ephemera. I also sought logbooks and journals that reflected different sizes and styles of ships. That said, I read through some more basic logbooks as a control to ensure that I understood the full gamut of what was and was not in a logbook. I was equally concerned with examining logbooks that came from a variety of libraries, that reflected different kinds of ships and voyages, and that were chronologically spread throughout the 1750 to 1850 period. I conducted most of this research over two decades, visiting numerous libraries that contained logbooks, and examined the vast majority of logbooks in manuscript form. Given the nature of my analysis, the ability to physically see and touch these logbooks was essential. I did examine some of the logbooks in microfilm and most recently I have looked at a few logbooks online, thanks to the digitizing of the entire Nicholson Whaling Collection of logbooks at the Providence Public Library and a partial digitization of the logbooks at the G.W. Blunt Library, Mystic Seaport Museum, Mystic, Connecticut.

Examination of the list of the logbooks in the bibliography reveals the following information. The majority of logbooks studied were in five libraries: the Phillips Library at the Peabody Essex Museum (51); the Massachusetts Historical Society (45); G. W. Blunt Library at Mystic Seaport (45); the Providence Public Library (20), and the New Bedford Whaling Museum (18). The rest came from fifteen other institutions. There were logbooks from 126 merchant vessels (including two vessels going to California in the Gold Rush), thirty-seven naval ships, nineteen privateers, fifty-seven whalers, and two sealers. Of the identifiable logbook/journal keepers sixty were captains, forty-four were mates or second mates, and at least twenty-three were seamen (there were also three carpenters and coopers and some of those listed as named were also probably seamen). Among the smaller groups represented, five were doctors, seven were supercargoes, four were clerks, six were passengers, and one was the son of the captain. Although I strove for a chronological balance in my research, I examined more logbooks in some decades than others. I read ten logbooks from before 1760 (nine were in the 1750s); fourteen from the 1760s; twenty-six from the 1770s; twenty-one from the 1780s; fourteen from the 1790s; twenty-five from the 1800s; forty-one from the 1810s; twenty-eight from the 1820s; thirty-nine from the 1830s; thirty-nine from the 1840s; and two from the 1850s.

Notes

Introduction

1. Paul A. Gilje, *Liberty on the Waterfront: American Maritime Culture in the Age of Revolution* (Philadelphia: University of Pennsylvania Press, 2004).
2. Paul A. Gilje, *Free Trade and Sailors' Rights in the War of 1812* (New York: Cambridge University Press, 2013).
3. This note, and the subsequent historiographical notes in the Introduction, cite only a few of the more important works in the fields mentioned in the text. Daniel Vickers, *Farmers and Fishermen: Two Centuries of Work in Essex County, Massachusetts, 1630–1850* (Chapel Hill: University of North Carolina Press, 1994); Vickers with Vince Walsh, *Young Men and the Sea: Yankee Seafarers in the Age of Sail* (New Haven, CT: Yale University Press, 2005); Vickers, "Beyond Jack Tar," *WMQ*, 3rd ser., 50 (1993): 418–24; W. Jeffrey Bolster, *Black Jacks: African American Seamen in the Age of Sail* (Cambridge, MA: Harvard University Press, 1997); Bolster, *The Mortal Sea: Fishing the Atlantic in the Age of Sail* (Cambridge, MA: Harvard University Press, 2014); Alex Roland, et al., *The Way of the Ship: America's Maritime History Reenvisioned, 1600–2000* (Hoboken, NJ: John Wiley & Sons, 2008); David S. Cecelski, *The Waterman's Song: Slavery and Freedom in Maritime North Carolina* (Chapel Hill: University of North Carolina Press, 2001); Christopher P. Magra, *The Fisherman's Cause: Atlantic Commerce and Maritime Dimensions of the American Revolution* (Cambridge: Cambridge University Press, 2009); Michael J. Jarvis, *In the Eye of All Trade: Bermuda, Bermudians, and the Maritime Atlantic World, 1680–1783* (Chapel Hill: University of North Carolina Press, 2010).
4. For examples of the "new social history" most relevant to this study, see Jesse Lemisch, "The American Revolution Seen from the Bottom Up," in Barton J. Bernstein, ed., *Towards a New Past: Dissenting Essays in American History* (New York: Pantheon, 1968), 3–45; Lemisch, "Jack Tar in the Streets: Merchant Seamen in the Politics of Revolutionary America," *WMQ*,

3rd ser., 25 (1968): 371–407; and Lemisch, *Jack Tar vs. John Bull: The Role of New York's Seamen in Precipitating the Revolution* (New York: Garland Publishing, 1997); Gary B. Nash, *The Urban Crucible: Social Change, Political Consciousness, and the Origins of the American Revolution* (Cambridge, MA: Harvard University Press, 1979). For my work on riots, see Paul A. Gilje, *The Road to Mobocracy: Popular Disorder in New York City, 1763–1834* (Chapel Hill: University of North Carolina Press, 1987).

5. Although influenced by this work, I do not refer to the public sphere within the book itself. John L. Brooke, "Consent, Civil Society, and the Public Sphere in the Age of Revolution and the Early Republic," in Jeffrey L. Pasley, et al., eds., *Beyond the Founders: New Approaches to the Political History of the Early American Republic* (Chapel Hill: University of North Carolina Press, 2004), 207–50; Brooke, "On the Edges of the Public Sphere," *WMQ*, 3rd ser., 62 (2005): 93–98; Brooke, "Reason and Passion in the Public Sphere: Habermas and the Cultural Historians," *Journal of Interdisciplinary History*, 29 (1998): 43–67; David Waldstreicher, *In the Midst of Perpetual Fetes: The Making of American Nationalism, 1776–1820* (Chapel Hill: University of North Carolina Press, 1997). See also Ruth H. Bloch, "Inside and Outside the Public Sphere," *WMQ*, 3rd ser., 62 (2005): 99–106.

6. Bernard Bailyn, *Atlantic History: Concept and Contours* (Cambridge, MA: Harvard University Press, 2005); Alison Games, "Atlantic History: Definitions, Challenges, and Opportunities," *American Historical Review*, 111 (2006): 741–57; Elizabeth Mancke and Carole Shammas, eds., *The Creation of the British Atlantic World* (Baltimore, MD: Johns Hopkins University Press, 2005). For a different approach to Atlantic history, see W. Jeffrey Bolster, "Putting the Ocean in Atlantic History: Maritime Communities and Marine Ecology in the Northwest Atlantic, 1500–1800," *American Historical Review*, 113 (2008): 19–47.

7. Paul Giles, *Transatlantic Insurrections: British Culture and the Formation of American Literature, 1730–1860* (Philadelphia: University of Pennsylvania Press, 2001); Sam W. Haynes, *Unfinished Revolution: The Early American Republic in a British World* (Charlottesville: University of Virginia Press, 2010); Kariann Akemi Yokota, *Unbecoming British: How Revolutionary America Became a Postcolonial Nation* (New York: Oxford University Press, 2011). See also the roundtable in the *William and Mary Quarterly* in response to Jack P. Greene, "Colonial History and National History: Reflections on a Continuing Problem," *WMQ*, 3rd ser., 64 (2007): 235–50; David Armitage, "From Colonial History to Postcolonial History: A Turn Too Far?" ibid.: 251–54; Eliga H. Gould, "The Question of Home Rule," ibid.: 255–58; Adam Rothman, "Beware the Weak State," ibid.: 271–74; Robin Einhorn, "The Nation Is Already There," ibid.: 275–80. On nationalism, see Benedict Anderson, *Imagined Communities: Reflections on the Origin and Spread of Nationalism*, rev. ed. (London: Verso, 1991); Linda Colley, *Britons: Forging the Nation, 1707–1837* (New Haven, CT: Yale University Press, 1992); Waldstreicher, *In the Midst of Perpetual Fetes*.

8. For relevant literary and critical studies of this period, see Cathy N. Davidson, *Revolution and the Word: The Rise of the Novel in America* (New York:

Oxford University Press, 1986); David S. Shields, *Civil Tongues and Polite Letters in British America* (Chapel Hill: University of North Carolina Press, 1997); Trish Loughran, *The Republic in Print: Print Culture in the Age of U.S. Nation Building, 1770–1780* (New York: Columbia University Press, 2007); Michael Warner, *The Letters of the Republic: Publication and the Public Sphere in Eighteenth-Century America* (Cambridge, MA: Harvard University Press, 1990). See also Philip F. Gura, "Early American Literature at the New Century," *WMQ*, 3rd ser., 57 (2000): 599–620. For language, see Greg Dening, *Mr. Bligh's Bad Language: Passion, Power, and Theatre on the Bounty* (Cambridge: Cambridge University Press, 1994); Daniel T. Rogers, *Contested Truths: Keywords in American Politics since Independence* (New York: Basic Books, 1987). For books and reading, see Eve Tavor Bannet, *Transatlantic Stories and the History of Reading, 1720–1810: Migrant Fictions* (Cambridge: Cambridge University Press, 2011); Roger Chartier, *The Order of Books: Readers, Authors, and Libraries in Europe between the Fourteenth and Eighteenth Centuries*, Lydia G. Cochrane, trans. (Stanford, CA: Stanford University Press, 1994); William J. Gilmore, *Reading Becomes a Necessity of Life: Material and Cultural Life in Rural New England, 1780–1835* (Knoxville: University of Tennessee Press, 1989); Robert A. Gross and Mary Kelley, eds., *An Extensive Republic: Print, Culture, and Society in the New Nation* (Chapel Hill: University of North Carolina Press, 2010); David D. Hall, *Cultures of Print: Essays in the History of the Book* (Amherst: University of Massachusetts Press, 1996); David Paul Nord, *Faith in Reading: Religious Publishing and the Birth of Mass Media in America* (New York: Oxford University Press, 2004). For songs, see Roy Palmer, ed., *The Oxford Book of Sea Songs* (Oxford: Oxford University Press, 1986); David Proctor, *Music of the Sea* (London: HMSO in association with the National Maritime Museum, 1992); Matthew Gelbart, *The Invention of "Folk Music" and "Art Music": Emerging Categories from Ossian to Wagner* (Cambridge: Cambridge University Press, 2007). For art, see Elizabeth Johns, *American Genre Painting: The Politics of Everyday Life* (New Haven, CT: Yale University Press, 1991); Margaretta M. Lovell, *Art in a Season of Revolution: Painters, Artisans, and Patrons in Early America* (Philadelphia: University of Pennsylvania Press, 2005).

1. To Swear Like a Sailor

1. Simeon Crowell, "Commonplace Book of Simeon Crowell," 1818–46, Ms, MHS.
2. William Bell Clark, et al., eds., Vols. 1–, *Naval Documents of the American Revolution* (Washington, DC: U.S. Government, 1964–), 7: 1004–05. See also Log of the *Tyrannicide*, kept by John Fiske, 1776–77, AAS.
3. Charles Tyng, *Before the Wind: The Memoir of an American Sea Captain, 1808–1833*, Susan Fels, ed. (New York: Penguin, 1999), 17.
4. Log of the *Peacock*, kept by Thomas J. Harris, 1824–27, LC.
5. Log of the *Arab*, kept by Samuel W. Chase, 1842–45, Series 1, Vol. 1, Maritime Records, Coll. 949, MeHS.

6. Log of the *Santiago*, 1846, Coll. 238, Vol. 21, William Goddard Papers, Mystic.

7. Log of the *Vesper*, kept by Alfred Terry, 1846–48, Log 955, Mystic.

8. *The Sea*, directed by Baltasar Kormákur (2002).

9. Geoffrey Hughes, *Swearing: A Social History of Foul Language, Oaths and Profanity in English* (Oxford: Blackwell, 1991), 55–125. Quoted in ibid., 103.

10. Ibid., 107–08. The quotation is from William Shakespeare, *Much Ado About Nothing*, II, i.

11. Hughes, *Swearing*, 139–41, 144.

12. Edward L. Battistella, *Bad Language: Are Some Words Better than Others?* (New York: Oxford University Press, 2005), 80.

13. Log of the *Hannibal*, kept by Nathaniel Sexton Morgan, 1849–50, Log 862, Mystic.

14. Cited in Daniel Vickers with Vince Walsh, *Young Men and the Sea: Yankee Seafarers in the Age of Sail* (New Haven, CT: Yale University Press, 2005), 65.

15. *Brooklyn* (ship) Ms, Manuscript Legal Documents, 1846–48, relating to the case of *John C. Dunford, Cooper v. Samuel Jeffrey, Master of the* Brooklyn, Mystic.

16. *Last v. Porter*, 1847, Box 1, No. 730, Dana Legal Papers, AAS.

17. Log of the *Israel*, 1841–42, Log 90, Mystic.

18. *U.S. v. Sturges*, nd, Box 2, no. 822, Dana Legal Papers, AAS.

19. The last three cases are quoted from Matthew Taylor Raffety, *The Republic Afloat: Law, Honor and Citizenship in Maritime America* (Chicago, IL: University of Chicago Press, 2013), 2, 142–43, 186.

20. *Concord New-Hampshire Patriot and State Gazette*, May 17, 1824.

21. Solomon H. Sanborn, *An Exposition of Official Tyranny in the United States Navy* (New York: no pub., 1841), 24–25, 28.

22. Typhus Aegyptus, *The Navy's Friend, or Reminiscences of the Navy ...* (Baltimore, MD: Printed for the Author, 1843), 25.

23. F. P. Torrey, *Journal of the Cruise of the United States Ship Ohio ...* (Boston, MA: Samuel N. Dickinson, 1841), 23, 39.

24. Clifford Geertz, *The Interpretation of Cultures: Selected Essays* (New York: Basic Books, 1973); Robert Darnton, *The Great Cat Massacre and Other Episodes in French Cultural History* (New York: Vintage Books, 1984).

25. Ashley Montagu, *The Anatomy of Swearing* (Philadelphia: University of Pennsylvania Press, 1967), 278–99.

26. Log of the *Flying Fish*, kept by Richard Gatewood, 1815, Logbook 097, MM.

27. *Christian Herald and Seaman's Magazine*, 9 (Dec. 21, 1822): 473.

28. Dated 1801. Crowell, "Commonplace Book," Ms, MHS.

29. *Sailor's Magazine*, 12 (Jan. 1840): 149.

30. For a further exploration of the idea of sailor's liberty, see Paul A. Gilje, *Liberty on the Waterfront: American Maritime Culture in the Age of Revolution* (Philadelphia: University of Pennsylvania Press, 2004). For a discussion of sailor religion, see Christopher P. Magra, "Faith at Sea: Exploring Maritime Religiosity in the Eighteenth Century," *International Journal of Maritime History*, 19 (2007): 87–106.

31. Log of the *Adventure*, kept by Francis Boardman, 1776, Log 1774A, PEM.

32. Log of the *Chilo*, kept by Sargent S. Day, 1846–47, Log 1846C, PEM.
33. William Leggett, *Naval Stories* (New York: G. & C. & H. Carvill, 1834), 72, 77, 132, 162, 171.
34. *Lives and Confessions of John Williams, Francis Frederick, John P. Rog, and Peter Peterson* ... (Boston, MA: J. T. Buckingham, 1819).
35. For an elaboration of this view of piracy, see Gilje, *Liberty on the Waterfront*, 90–91. The anticapitalist argument is articulated by Marcus Rediker, *Between the Devil and the Deep Blue Sea: Merchant Seamen, Pirates, and the Anglo-American Maritime World, 1700–1750* (New York: Cambridge University Press, 1987), 254–87; Rediker, "'Under the Banner of King Death': The Social World of Anglo-American Pirates, 1716–1726," *WMQ*, 3rd ser., 38 (1981): 203–27; Rediker, *Villains of All Nations: Atlantic Pirates in the Golden Age* (Boston, MA: Beacon Press, 2004).
36. Americans called the sea-raiders from the Barbary states "pirates," reflecting their belief in the lack of legitimacy behind the North Africans' actions. The Barbary states, however, technically acted under the umbrella of a declaration of war. The label "pirates" thus reflects more European-American prejudices than reality. For overviews of these conflicts, see Robert J. Allison, *The Crescent Obscured: The United States and the Muslim World, 1776–1815* (Chicago, IL: University of Chicago Press, 1995); Frank Lambert, *The Barbary Wars: American Independence in the Atlantic World* (New York: Hill and Wang, 2005).
37. For nineteenth-century sources on piracy in the West Indies and the East Indies, see *Dying Declaration of Nicholas Fernandez* ... (New York: George Lambert, 1830); *The History of the Bloody Exploits of the Most Noted Pirates* ... (Hartford, CT: Silas Andrus, 1850); *The Pirates Own Book, or Authentic Narratives of the Lives, Exploits, and Executions of the Most Celebrated Sea Robbers.* (Salem, MA: Marine Research Society, 1924; orig. pub. Boston, 1837). All page references are to this edition. For a fuller discussion of *The Pirates Own Book* and citation to multiple editions, see Chapter 6.
38. *Oxford English Dictionary*, 2nd ed., s.v. "rascal."
39. Hughes, *Swearing*, 106–12. Quotation from *King Lear*, II, ii.
40. Francis Grose, *A Classical Dictionary of the Vulgar Tongue* (London: S. Hooper, 1785).
41. Hugh Rawson, *Wicked Words: A Treasury of Curses, Insults, Put-Downs, and Other Formerly Unprintable Terms from Anglo-Saxon Times to the Present* (New York: Crown Publishers, 1989), 43–45. The second edition of the *Oxford English Dictionary* lists several twentieth-century citations, beginning in 1904. *Oxford English Dictionary*, 2nd ed., s.v. "bitch."
42. For dog history, see Jon T. Coleman, "'Two by Two': Bringing Animals into American History," *Reviews in American History*, 33 (2005): 481–92; Mark Derr, *A Dog's History of America: How Our Best Friend Explored, Conquered, and Settled a Continent* (New York: North Point Press, 2004); Jennifer Mason, *Civilized Creatures: Urban Animals, Sentimental Culture, and American Literature, 1850–1900* (Baltimore, MD: Johns Hopkins University Press, 2005); Katherine C. Grier, "Animal House: Pet Keeping in

Urban and Suburban Households in the Northeast, 1850–1900," in *New England Creatures, 1400–1900: The Dublin Seminar for New England Folklife Annual Proceedings*, 1992, 18 (1993): 109–29.

43. Richard L. Bushman, *The Refinement of America: Persons, Houses, Cities* (New York: Knopf, 1992).

44. Quoted in Mason, *Civilized Creatures*, 14.

45. Thorstein Veblen, *The Theory of the Leisure Class: An Economic Study of Institutions* (New York: New American Library, 1953; orig. pub. 1899), 103.

46. *Newport Mercury*, January 23, 1798; *Providence Gazette*, April 23, 1803; *New York Republican Watch-Tower*, June, 1, 1805; *Wilmington (Delaware) American Watchman*, November 18, 1809, May 4, 1811; *Salem Essex Register*, February 20, 1811; *New York Columbian*, April 5, 1811; *Trenton Federalist*, April 15, 1811.

47. *New York American Citizen*, July 13, 1810. See also Paul A. Gilje, *The Road to Mobocracy: Popular Disorder in New York City, 1763–1834* (Chapel Hill: University of North Carolina Press, 1987), 224–27.

48. For nineteenth-century examples of these comparisons, see Christopher Clark, *The Roots of Rural Capitalism: Western Massachusetts, 1780–1860* (Ithaca, NY: Cornell University Press, 1990), 258; and Tyng, *Before the Wind*, 244. For the 1669 quote, see Vickers with Walsh, *Young Men and the Sea*, 55–56.

49. Torrey, *Journal of the Cruise*, 22–23, 39–44; Sanborn, *An Exposition of Official Tyranny*, 28.

50. The analysis in this paragraph builds on my reading of Thomas Laqueur, *Making Sex: Body and Gender from the Greeks to Freud* (Cambridge, MA: Harvard University Press, 1990). For quotations, see ibid., 150, 189.

51. Daniel Defoe, *Moll Flanders, An Authoritative Text: Backgrounds and Sources; Criticism*, Edward Kelly, ed. (New York: Norton, 1973; orig. pub. 1722); Henry Fielding, *Tom Jones, An Authoritative Text: Contemporary Reactions; Criticism*, Sheridan Warner Baker, ed. (New York: Norton, 1973; orig. pub. 1749); Louisa May Alcott, *Little Women*, James Prunier, ill. (New York: Viking, 1996; orig. pub. 1868–69); Nathaniel Hawthorne, *The Scarlet Letter* (New York: Vintage, 1990; orig. pub. 1850). For a discussion of this transformation in broad context, see Laqueur, *Making Sex*. For a detailed discussion of this transformation in one city – Philadelphia – see Clare A. Lyons, *Sex among the Rabble: An Intimate History of Gender and Power in the Age of Revolution, Philadelphia, 1730–1830* (Chapel Hill: University of North Carolina Press, 2006). See also Ruth H. Bloch, "Changing Conceptions of Sexuality and Romance in Eighteenth-Century America," WMQ, 3rd ser., 60 (2003): 13–42; Susan Juster, *Disorderly Women: Sexual Politics and Evangelicalism in Revolutionary New England* (Ithaca, NY: Cornell University Press, 1994); Susan E. Klepp. *Revolutionary Conceptions: Women, Fertility, and Family Limitation in America, 1760–1820* (Chapel Hill: University of North Carolina Press, 2009).

52. [Isaac Bickerstaff], *Thomas and Sally; or the Sailor's Return …* (Dublin: Sarah Cotter, [1761]); [Bickerstaff], *Thomas and Sally: or, the Sailor's Return …* (Philadelphia, PA: Henry Taylor, 1791).

53. "The Sailors Farewell," by Henry Hudson, November 5, 1785, Photograph by National Maritime Museum, Greenwich, UK, Courtesy of The Image Works; "The Sailor's Adieu," Lithograph by Baille and Sowle, ca. 1845, Courtesy of the New Bedford Whaling Museum, New Bedford, Massachusetts.

54. Tyng, *Before the Wind*, 22; William Henry Allen, Journal of the *George Washington* (1800), Huntington Library. See also *Christian Herald and Seaman's Magazine*, 9 (Oct. 5, 1822), 319–20.

55. William Torrey, *Torrey's Narrative* ... (Boston, MA: A. J. Wright, 1848), 33.

56. For further examination of these ideas, see Gilje, *Liberty on the Waterfront*, 33–65. See also Margaret S. Creighton, *Rites and Passages: The Experience of American Whaling, 1830–1870* (New York: Cambridge University Press, 1995); Lisa Norling, *Captain Ahab Had a Wife: New England Women and the Whalefishery, 1720–1870* (Chapel Hill: University of North Carolina Press, 2000).

57. Quoted in Charles Royster, *A Revolutionary People at War: The Continental Army and American Character, 1775–1783* (Chapel Hill: University of North Carolina Press, 1979), 76, 216. For Royster's other references to swearing, see ibid., 28, 42, 77, 93–96. See also Richard M. Kethcum, *Saratoga: Turning Point of America's Revolutionary War* (New York: Henry Holt and Company, 1997), 82, 211; Ketchum, *Victory at Yorktown: The Campaign that Won the Revolution* (New York: Henry Holt & Company, 2004), 9, 11, 12; Alfred F. Young, *Masquerade: The Life and Times of Deborah Sampson, Continental Soldier* (New York: Random House, 2004), 161; Frederick Elkin, "The Soldier's Language," *American Journal of Sociology*, 51 (1946): 414–22.

58. Patrick Griffin, *The People with No Name: Ireland's Ulster Scots, America's Scots Irish, and the Creation of a British Atlantic World, 1689–1764* (Princeton, NJ: Princeton University Press, 2001), 111, 138.

59. *New York Statesmen*, April 2, 1813.

60. Hughes, *Swearing*, 168.

61. Clark, et al., eds., *Naval Documents of the American Revolution*, 11: 434.

62. Samuel Leech, *A Voice from the Main Deck: Being a Record of the Thirty Years' Adventures of Samuel Leech*, Michael J. Crawford, ed. (Annapolis, MD: Naval Institute Press, 1999; orig. pub. 1843), 36.

63. Crowell, "Commonplace Book," Ms, MHS; *Lives and Confessions of John Williams*; *Brooklyn* (ship) Ms, Manuscript Legal Documents, 1846–48, relating to the case of *John C. Dunford, Cooper v. Samuel Jeffrey, Master of the* Brooklyn, Mystic; Log of the *Chilo*, kept by G. I. Day, 1846–47, Log 1846C, PEM.

64. Hughes, *Swearing*, 129. *Oxford English Dictionary*, 2nd ed., s. v. "bugger."

65. Arthur N. Gilbert, "Buggery and the British Navy, 1700–1861," *Journal of Social History*, 10 (1976): 72–98.

66. Christopher Hawkins, *The Adventures of Christopher Hawkins* ... (New York: Privately Printed, 1864), 39.

67. Joshua Penny, *The Life and Adventures of Joshua Penny* ... (New York: Alden Spooner, 1815), 29–30.

68. Log of the *President Adams*, kept by Joseph Ward, 1809, AAS.

69. Memorandum of ..., Jan. 22, 1820, St. Salvadore, aboard the *Rosenew* [?], Folder 1, Box 1, Andrew Dunlap Papers, PEM.

70. Tyng, *Before the Wind*, 162.

71. Nathaniel Fanning, *Narrative of the Adventures of an American Navy Officer* ... (New York: Printed for the Author, 1806), 251–52.

72. [Josiah Cobb], *A Green Hand's First Cruise, Roughed Out from the Log-Book of Memory* ..., 2 vols. (Baltimore, MD: Cushing & Brother, 1841), 2: 246.

73. There was a fourth case in which only one individual was charged in early December, 1845. "Discipline and Minor Delinquencies: Record of Punishments, U.S. Frigate *Congress*, 1845–48," Box 283, RG 45, Naval Records Collection, NA. Christopher McKee mentions a case of homosexuality concerning an officer. He also asserts that other officers considered this behavior unusual. Christopher McKee, *A Gentlemanly and Honorable Profession: The Creation of the U.S. Naval Officer Corps, 1794–1815* (Annapolis, MD: Naval Institute Press, 1991), 438–39.

74. Torrey, *Journal of the Cruise*, 86.

75. For one of these cases, see H. Baily to [Charles G. Coffin and Henry Coffin], Sept. 15, 1844, Charles G. and Henry Coffin Collection, 1829–62, Ms 152, NHA. Besides this case and two others, one from 1838 and the other from 1835, Creighton also describes an 1861 sodomy trial of a whaleship captain. Although convicted, the captain continued to protest his innocence. Creighton, *Rites and Passages*, 190–92. See also Gilje, *Liberty on the Waterfront*, 37–39.

76. Hughes, *Swearing*, 1–34. See also Allen Walker Read, "An Obscenity Symbol," *American Speech*, 9 (1934): 264–78; Edward Sagarin, *The Anatomy of Dirty Words* (New York: Lyle Stuart, 1962); Julian Sharman, *A Cursory History of Swearing* (New York: Burt Franklin, 1968; orig. pub. 1884); Jesse Sheidlower, ed., *The F Word* (New York: Random House, 1995); Montagu, *The Anatomy of Swearing*, 300–15. For the pornographic fringes of Victorian culture, see Lisa Z. Sigel, "Name Your Pleasure: The Transformation of Sexual Language in Nineteenth-Century British Pornography," *Journal of the History of Sexuality*, 9 (2000): 395–419.

77. George G. Carey, ed., *A Sailor's Songbag: An American Rebel in an English Prison, 1777–1779* (Amherst: University of Massachusetts Press, 1976), 24–25, 116.

78. Rawson, *Wicked Words*, 166. See also George Rudé, *Wilkes and Liberty: A Social Study of 1763 to 1774* (Oxford: Clarendon Press, 1962), 31–36.

79. *The Frisky Songster: Being a Select Choice of Such Songs as Are Distinguished for Their Jollity, High Taste and Humour* ... (London: Sold by the booksellers in town and country, 1776), 34–37.

80. H. L. Mencken, "American Profanity," *American Speech*, 19 (1944): 247, n. 19. See also Read, "An Obscenity Symbol," *American Speech*, 9 (1934): 264–78, which provides a history of "fuck" without ever mentioning the word.

81. *A Short Narrative of the Horrid Massacre in Boston* ... (Boston, MA: Edes and Gill, 1770), 20, 24; *The Trial of William Wemms* ... (Boston, MA: Fleeming, 1770), 106, 107; *A Fair Account of the Late Unhappy Disturbance in New England* ... (London: B. White, 1770), 8, 20.

2. The Language of Jack Tar

1. Leigh Eric Schmidt, *Hearing Things: Religion, Illusion, and the American Enlightenment* (Cambridge, MA: Harvard University Press, 2000), 15.

2. Paul A. Gilje, *Free Trade and Sailors' Rights in the War of 1812* (New York: Cambridge University Press, 2013), 85–98.

3. For other explorations of the language of Jack Tar, see J. Parry, "Sailors' English," *Cambridge Journal*, 2 (1948–49): 660–70; Isaac Land, "The Many-Tongued Hydra: Sea Talk, Maritime Culture, and Atlantic Identities, 1700–1800," *Journal of American and Comparative Cultures*, 25 (2002): 412–17; Horace Beck, *Folklore and the Sea* (Middletown, CT: Wesleyan University Press, 1973), 57–75.

4. Hester Blum, *The View from the Masthead: Maritime Imagination and Antebellum American Sea Narratives* (Chapel Hill: University of North Carolina Press, 2008), 85; Thomas Philbrick, *James Fenimore Cooper and the Development of the American Sea Fiction* (Cambridge, MA: Harvard University Press, 1961), 81–83; Hugh Egan, "Cooper and His Contemporaries," in Haskell Springer, ed., *America and the Sea: A Literary History* (Athens: University of Georgia Press, 1995), 64–82.

5. James Fenimore Cooper, *The Red Rover, a Tale*, Thomas and Marianne Philbrick, eds. (Albany: State University of New York Press, 1991; orig. pub. 1827), xx, 32–34.

6. Cooper, *The Red Rover*, 54–63, 75, 117–19.

7. Herman Melville, *Moby Dick, or the Whale* (New York: Modern Library, 1982; orig. pub. 1851), 54–69.

8. Cooper, *The Red Rover*, 164, 186.

9. Melville, *Moby Dick*, 2. Herman Melville, *Typee: A Peep at Polynesian Life during a Four Month's Residence in a Valley of the Marquesas* (New York: New American Library, 1964; orig. pub. 1846); Melville, *Omoo: A Narrative of Adventures in the South Seas*, Harrison Hayford, ed. (Evanston, IL: Northwestern University Press, 1968; orig. pub. 1847).

10. Richard Henry Dana Jr., *Two Years before the Mast: A Personal Narrative of Life at Sea*, Thomas Philbrick, ed. (New York: Penguin, 1981; orig. pub. 1840), 45; Herman Melville, *Redburn: His First Voyage, Being the Sailor-boy Confessions and Reminiscences of the Son-of-a-Gentleman in the Merchant Service*, Harold Beaver, ed. (New York: Penguin, 1976; orig. pub. 1849), 117–18. Melville's inclusion of "Son-of-a-Gentleman" in the title may well have been a play on sailor swearing and "son-of-a-bitch."

11. William Falconer, *An Universal Dictionary of the Marine ...* (London: T. Cadell, 1769). For an updated book that provides insight into this technical language, see John Harland, *Seamanship in the Age of Sail: An Account of Shiphandling of the Sailing Man-of-War 1600–1860, Based on Contemporary Sources* (Annapolis, MD: Naval Institute Press, 1984).

12. Hershel Parker, *Herman Melville: A Biography, Volume I, 1819–1851* (Baltimore, MD: Johns Hopkins University Press, 1996).

13. These comments are based on the definitions and derivations of these terms in the *Oxford English Dictionary*, s. v. "Jack" and "tar."

14. *London Weekly Journal or British Gazetteer*, April 27, 1723; *London Daily Post*, August 22, 1726; *London Daily Post and General Advertiser*, May 19, 1740; *London Champion or Evening Advertiser*, October 31, 1741.

15. Tobias Smollett, *The Adventures of Roderick Random*, James G. Basker, et al., eds. (Athens: University of Georgia Press, 2012; orig. pub. 1748), 23, 24; Philbrick, *James Fenimore Cooper*, 6–7, 81–83.

16. For recent discussions of the British maritime empire in the eighteenth century, see David Armitage, *The Ideological Origins of the British Empire* (Cambridge: Cambridge University Press, 2000); Eliga H. Gould, *The Persistence of Empire: British Political Culture in the Age of the American Revolution* (Chapel Hill: University of North Carolina Press, 2000); Anthony Pagden, *Lords of All the World: Ideologies of Empire in Spain, Britain and France, c. 1500 –c. 1800* (New Haven, CT: Yale University Press, 1995). On the development of British national identity, see Linda Colley, *Britons: Forging the Nation, 1707–1837* (New Haven, CT: Yale University Press, 1992); Isaac Land, *War, Nationalism, and the British Sailor, 1750–1850* (New York: Palgrave Macmillan, 2009).

17. [Isaac Bickerstaff], *Thomas and Sally; or the Sailor's Return…* (Dublin: Sarah Cotter, [1761], 21–23.

18. Thomas Rowlandson, "Sailors Drinking the Tunbridge Waters", 1815, The Lewis Walpole Library, Yale University, New Haven, Connecticut; Thomas Tegg, "Jack in a White Squall, Amongst Breakers – on the Lee Shore of St. Catherine's," 1811, Reproduction Number: LC-USZ62-20409, LC; "The Last Jig, or, Adieu to Old England," Thomas Rowlandson and Thomas Tegg, 1818, Anne S. K. Brown Military Collection, Brown University Library, Providence, Rhode Island. In addition, the National Maritime Museum, Greenwich, UK has many of these prints available for viewing on its Web site. See http://collections.rmg.co.uk/collections.html#!csearch;searchTerm=sailor_caricatures.

19. Charles Dibden, *Tom Bowling* (London: 1790), broadsheet.

20. Thomas Dibden, *Songs, Naval and National, of the Late Charles Dibden; with a Memoir and Addenda* (London: John Murray, 1841), 1–2, 21, 37, 41–42, 56, 89, 247, 266, 276; Philbrick, *James Fenimore Cooper*, 7–8; Land, *War, Nationalism, and the British Sailor*, 77–97. See also Robert Fahrner, *The Theatre Career of Charles Dibden the Elder (1745–1814)* (New York: Peter Lang, 1989); Terence M. Freeman, *Dramatic Representations of British Soldiers and Sailors on the London Stage* (Lewiston, NY: Edwin Mellon Press, 1995). The image of Jack Tar remained important in British theater well into the nineteenth century. Jim Davis, "British Bravery, or Tars Triumphant: Images of the British Navy in Nautical Melodrama," *New Theatre Quarterly*, 4 (1988): 122–43.

21. *Boston Evening Post*, June 1, 1741; *Boston Chronicle*, April 9–12, 1770; *Salem Essex Gazette*, October 2–9, 1770; *Boston Massachusetts Spy*, November 22, 1771; *Newport Mercury*, January 3, 1774.

22. Adams to Jonathan Sewall [spring 1763?], Adams Papers Digital Editions, MHS; "Adams Argument for the Defense," December 3–4, 1770, ibid.

23. I explore these points further in Paul A. Gilje, *Liberty on the Waterfront: American Maritime Culture in the Age of Revolution* (Philadelphia:

University of Pennsylvania Press, 2004), 97–191; and Gilje, *Free Trade and Sailors' Rights*, 85–98.

24. *Philadelphia General Advertiser*, March 16, 1793.
25. *Philadelphia Freeman's Journal*, September 4, 1782.
26. *Philadelphia Pennsylvania Evening Post*, August 4, 1784.
27. For Jack Tar jokes about fashion, see *Savannah Georgia Gazette*, October 22, 1789; *Portsmouth New Hampshire Spy*, February 1, 1792. On other topics, see *Boston Columbian Centinel*, March 17, 1792; *Charleston Columbian Herald*, May 12, 1788; *Salem Gazette*, January 19, 1796; *Danbury (Connecticut) Republican Journal*, January 9, 1797; *Greenfield (Massachusetts) Gazette*, December 10, 1798; *Windham (Connecticut) Herald*, December 31, 1801; *Providence Phoenix*, October 15, 1803; *New York Daily Advertiser*, May 10, 1805.
28. *Haverhill (Massachusetts) Merrimack Intelligencer*, January 27, 1810. For other Jack Tar jokes involving religion, see *Catskill (New York) Packet*, September 24, 1792; *New York Diary*, January 29, 1793; *Stockbridge (Massachusetts) Western Star*, January 29, 1793; *Hudson (New York) Bee*, February 7, 1808.
29. [Isaac Bickerstaff], *Thomas and Sally: Or the Sailor's Return ...* (Philadelphia, PA: Henry Taylor, 1791). For examples of American productions, see advertisements in *New York Argus*, May 18, 1796; *Providence United States Chronicle*, November 16, 1797; *Philadelphia Gazette of the United States*, April 4, 1799; *Boston Columbian Centinal*, March 12, 1800; *Baltimore Federal Gazette*, May 30, 1807; *Charleston City Gazette*, April 20, 1808.
30. J. C. Cross, *The Purse; or, Benevolent Tar ...* (Dublin: R. Cowley, 1794), 10; Cross, *The Purse; or, Benevolent Tar ...* (Boston, MA: W. Pelham, 1797), 8–9. For advertisements of the production under the title *The Purse; or American Tar*, see *New York American Minerva*, February 18, 1795; *Boston Mercury*, October 30, 1795; *Charleston Gazette and Daily Advertiser*, February 17, 1796; *Baltimore Federal Gazette*, March 2, 1796; *New York Diary*, August 29, 1797; *New York Commercial Advertiser*, January 26, 1798; *New York Daily Advertiser*, April 15, 1799; *Boston Massachusetts Mercury*, December 30, 1800.
31. Washington Irving, *Letters of Jonathan Oldstyle, Gent....*, Bruce I. Granger and Martha Hartzog, eds. (Boston, MA: Twaine Publishers, 1977), 10. There is no extant copy of the play. It was advertised in *New York American Citizen*, November 24, 1802. See also Robert J. Allison, *The Crescent Obscured: The United States and the Muslim World, 1776–1815* (Chicago, IL: University of Chicago Press, 1995), 187–88. For another British musical with a maritime theme that played in both London and New York, see Samuel James Arnold, *The Shipwreck: A Comic Opera in Two Acts* (New York: D. Longworth, 1805).
32. *New York Daily Advertiser*, June 29, 1787; *Philadelphia Pennsylvania Packet*, June 28, 1787.
33. *Elizabethtown New Jersey Journal*, November 8, 1786; *Philadelphia Independent Gazetteer*, July 10, 1789.

34. *Charleston Morning Post*, March 14, 1787; *Newburyport Massachusetts Impartial Herald*, January 17, 1794.

35. *Concord (New Hampshire) Mirrour*, April 28, 1794; *Philadelphia Independent Gazatteer*, November 8, 1794; *New York Columbian Centinel*, November 1, 1794.

36. This news item has both the Tom Bowling and Tom Bowline spellings. *Boston Columbian Centinel*, November 5, 1796.

37. *Boston Independent Chronicle*, October 27, 1800.

38. Gilje, *Free Trade and Sailors' Rights*, 174–89.

39. Alexander Hamilton, et al., *The Federalist Papers*, Clinton Rossiter, ed. (New York: New American Library, 1961); *The Anti-Federalist Papers and the Constitutional Convention Debates*, Ralph Ketchum, ed. (New York: New American Library, 1986); Bernard Bailyn, *The Ideological Origins of the American Revolution* (Cambridge, MA: Harvard University Press, 1967), 1–54; David S. Shields, *Civil Tongues and Polite Letters in British America* (Chapel Hill: University of North Carolina Press, 1997), 262–66; Eran Shalev, "Ancient Masks, American Fathers: Classical Pseudonyms during the American Revolution and Early Republic," *JER*, 23 (Summer 2003), 173–206.

40. John Dickinson, *Letters from a Farmer in Pennsylvania, to the Inhabitants of the British Colonies* (Boston, MA: John Mein, 1768); Samuel Seabury, *Free Thoughts on the Proceedings of the Continental Congress ...* (New York: James Rivington, 1774); J. Hector St. John de Crevecoeur, *Letters from an American Farmer and Sketches of Eighteenth-Century America*, Albert E. Stone, ed. (New York: Penguin, reprint edition, 1981).

41. Paul A. Gilje, "Mechanics in New York City in the Era of the Constitution," in Robert Goler, ed., *Federal New York: A Symposium* (New York: Fraunces Tavern Museum, 1990), 20–26; Howard B. Rock, *Artisans of the New Republic: The Tradesman of New York City in the Age of Jefferson* (New York: New York University Press, 1979).

42. Caroline Moseley, "Henry D. Thoreau and His Favorite Popular Song," *Journal of Popular Culture*, 12 (1979): 624–29.

43. *New York American*, November 27, 1832; *Philadelphia Public Ledger*, March 6, 1840.

44. *Albany Argus*, June 14, 1844. For additional Jack Tar jokes, see *Boston New England Palladium*, January 9, 1816; *Portland Gazette*, July 2, 1816; *Boston Idiot*, April 4, September 12, 1818; *Cherry-Valley (New York) Gazette*, November 26, 1818; *Portsmouth New-Hampshire Gazette*, September 27, 1819, March 25, 1834; *Woodstock (Vermont) Observer*, January 25, 1820; *Amherst (New Hampshire) Hillsboro Telegraph*, March 11, 1820; *Baltimore Patriot*, February 20, 1821; *Dedham (Massachusetts) Village Register*, June 14, 1822; *New Haven Columbian Register*, May 3, 1823, February 27, 1836; *Salem Gazette*, July 30, 1824; *Alexandria (Virginia) Gazette*, January 8, 1825, October 4, 1848; *Bennington Vermont Gazette*, November 22, 1825; *Providence Literary Cadet*, July 1, 1826; *Norwich (Connecticut) Courier*, August 8, 1827; *Portland Weekly Eastern Argus*, July 5, 1830; *Brattleboro (Vermont) Messenger*, May 25, 1833; *Barre (Massachusetts) Farmers Gazette*,

August 8, 1834; *Baltimore Gazette*, October 11, 1834; *Hartford Times*, September 2, 1837; *New Orleans Times Picayune*, September 21, 1839, January 15, 1843; *Charleston Courier*, February 2, 1841; *Schenectady Cabinet*, March 28, 1843; *New London Morning News*, June 27, 1845; *Manchester (New Hampshire) Telescope*, July 28, 1849.

45. *Salem Gazette*, October 2, 1829. See also *Keene New Hampshire Sentinel*, July 6, 1827; *Providence Patriot*, February 10, 1830; *Baltimore Gazette*, February 14, 1833; *Concord New-Hampshire Patriot*, February 23, 1835; *Philadelphia Public Ledger*, November 17, 1836; *Baltimore Sun*, September 26, 1838; *Portsmouth New-Hampshire Gazette*, September 3, 1844, August 31, 1847; *Charleston Southern Patriot*, December 10, 1844; *New Orleans Times Picayune*, October 18, 1846; *Gloucester (Massachusetts) Telegraph*, August 26, 1848.

46. William S. Cardell, *Story of Jack Halyard, the Sailor Boy, or The Virtuous Family: Designed for American Children in Families and Schools* (New York: J. Seymour, 1825).

47. *New York People's Friend*, July 27, 1807; *Hudson (New York) Balance*, April 12, 1808; *Middletown (Connecticut) American Sentinel*, May 4, 1825; *New York American*, May 18, 1827; *Salem Gazette*, April 3, 1828. Ned Buntline began publishing sea tales in 1844. See "The White Squall," *Western Literary Magazine*, 4 (January 1844): 85–87; "Running the Blockade," *The Knickerbocker* 24 (October 1844): 319–25. On Ned Buntline, see Peter G. Buckley, "The Case against Ned Buntline: The 'Words, Signs, and Gestures' of Popular Authorship," *Prospects*, 13 (1988): 249–72; Jay Monaghan, *The Great Rascal: The Life and Adventures of Ned Buntline* (Boston, MA: Little, Brown and Company, 1951).

48. *St. Augustine Florida Herald*, June 2, 1838.

49. *Boston Daily Atlas*, November 6, 1844. See also *New Haven Connecticut Herald*, September 23, 1817; *Boston Patriot*, March 19, 1819; *Hallowell (Maine) American Advocate*, March 27, 1819; *Charleston Courier*, August 8, 1820, February 6, 1836; *Charleston City Gazette*, October 12, 1822; *Boston Independent Chronicle*, April 2, 1823; *Boston Commercial Gazette*, April 5, 1824; *Salem Gazette*, April 16, 1824; *Nantucket Enquirer*, September 8, 1832; *Portsmouth (New Hampshire) Journal*, July 19, 1834; *New York Evening Post*, November 3, 1834, March 24, 31, 1836; *Brattleboro Vermont Phoenix*, August 14, 1835; *Sing-Sing (New York) Hudson River Chronicle*, February 6, 1838; *Baltimore Sun*, May 23, 1838; *New York Spectator*, April 16, 1840; *Boston Daily Atlas*, November 6, 1844; *Milwaukee Sentinel*, October 30, 1848.

50. See, for example, Gilje, *Liberty on the Waterfront*. For an excellent appraisal of these sailor narratives, see Myra C. Glenn, *Jack Tar's Story: The Autobiographies and Memoirs of Sailors in Antebellum America* (New York: Cambridge University Press, 2010). For sailor narratives that rely heavily on Jack Tar's language, see Horace Lane, *The Wandering Boy, or Careless Sailor* ... (Skaneateles , NY: Luther Pratt, 1839); George Little, *Life on the Ocean; or Twenty Years at Sea* ... (Baltimore, MD: Armstrong and Berry, 1843); [Henry James Mercier], *Life in a Man of War, or Scenes in*

"*Old Ironsides*" ... (Philadelphia, PA: L. R. Bailey, 1841); William Meacham Murrell, *Cruise of the Frigate Columbia Around the World* ... (Boston, MA: Benjamin B. Mussey, 1840).

51. Lane, *The Wandering Boy*, 68–70, 89, 105, 108; Samuel Leech, *A Voice from the Main Deck: Being a Record of the Thirty Years' Adventures of Samuel Leech*, Michael J. Crawford, ed. (Annapolis, MD: Naval Institute Press, 1999; orig. pub. 1843), 111, 197.

52. George Edward Clark, *Seven Years of a Sailor's Life* (Boston, MA: Adams & Co., 1867), 161.

53. [Josiah Cobb], *A Green Hand's First Cruise, Roughed out from the Log-Book of Memory*, ..., 2 vols. (Baltimore, MD: Cushing & Brother, 1841), 1: 147.

54. *Life of Father Taylor: The Sailor Preacher* (Boston, MA: The Boston Port and Seamen's Aid Society, 1904), lxix, 25–26, lxxi.

55. Leech, *A Voice from the Main Deck*, 110.

56. See, for example, J. Ross Browne, *Etchings of a Whaling Cruise* ... (New York: Harper & Brothers, 1846), 17, 177, 214, 264, 457, 460. See also Clark, *Seven Years a Sailor's Life*.

57. Tiphys Aegyptus, *The Navy's Friend, or Reminiscences of the Navy* ... (Baltimore, MD: Printed for the Author, 1843).

58. Gurdon L. Allyn, *The Old Sailor's Story* ... (Norwich, CT: G. Wilcox, 1879), 23.

59. Christopher Hawkins, *The Adventures of Christopher Hawkins* ... (New York: Privately Printed, 1864), 21–22. For other examples, see Joseph Bates, *The Autobiography of Elder Joseph Bates* ... (Battle Creek, MI: Steam Press, 1868); Joseph G. Clark, *Lights and Shadows of Sailor Life* ... (Boston, MA: Benjamin B. Mussey, 1848); Ebenezer Fox, *The Adventures of Ebenezer Fox in the Revolutionary War...* (Boston, MA: Charles Fox, 1848); Roland Gould, *The Life of Gould, an Ex-Man-of-War's-Man* ... (Claremont, NH: Claremont Manufacturing Company, 1867); Jacob Hazen, *Five Years before the Mast* ..., 2nd ed. (Philadelphia, PA: William P. Hazard, 1854); Charles Herbert, *A Relic of the Revolution* ... (Boston, MA: Charles H. Pierce, 1847); John Hoxse, *The Yankee Tar* ... (Northampton, MA: John Metcalf, 1840); William McNally, *vils and Abuses in the Naval and Merchant Service Exposed* ... (Boston, MA: Cassady and March, 1839); Francis Allyn Olmsted, *Incidents of a Whaling Voyage* ... (New York: D. Appleton, 1841); Moses Smith, *Naval Scenes in the Last War* ... (Boston, MA: Gleason Publishing Hall, 1846); William Torrey, *Torrey's Narrative* ... (Boston, MA: A. J. Wright, 1848).

60. *Humorous and Diverting Dialogues, between Monsieur Baboon, a French Dancing-Master (but lately come over) and Jack Tar, an English Sailor* (London: C. Corbet, 1755), 2–3, 8–9.

61. *New York Evening Post*, March 24, 1836.

62. *New York Evening Post*, March 31, 1838.

63. Cooper, *Red Rover*, 36; William Leggett, *Naval Stories* (New York: G. & C. & H. Carvill, 1834), 21, 119, 167.

64. Olaudah Equiano, *The Interesting Narrative of the Life of Olaudah Equiano*, Robert J. Allison, ed. (Boston, MA: Bedford St. Martin's, 1995; orig. pub. 1789), 66, 85.

65. Frederick Douglass worked as a ship caulker on the Baltimore waterfront and disguised himself as a sailor when he escaped to freedom. In all likelihood he knew how to sound like a sailor. See Frederick Douglass, *Life and Times of Frederick Douglass* ..., rev. ed. (Boston, MA: DeWolfe. Fiske & Co. 1892), 246–47.

66. Venture Smith, *A Narrative of the Life and Adventures of Venture, a Native of Africa* ... (New London, CT: C. Holt, 1798).

67. Philip M. Hamer, "Great Britain, the United States and the Negro Seamen Acts, 1822–1848," *Journal of Southern History*, 1 (1935): 3–28; W. Jeffrey Bolster, *Black Jacks: African American Seamen in the Age of Sail* (Cambridge, MA: Harvard University Press, 1997), 190–214.

68. *New York Emancipator*, March 9, 1843. See also the discussion in Gilje, *Free Trade and Sailors' Rights*, 331–35.

69. *Boston Emancipator and Republican*, March 4, 1842.

70. A. G. Gardner to F. S. Allen, Dec., 29, 1844, Folder 3, Box 41, subgroup 3, Series F, Swift and Allen Collection, Ms 5, NBWM.

71. Caleb Foote, ed., "Reminiscences of the Revolution. Prison Letters of Caleb Foot: Born 1750; Died 1787," *EIHC*, 26 (1889): 97–98.

72. For correspondence written by seamen, see "Letters between Jacob W. Ball and Mary Timbrell Ball," 1822–31, Ball Family Papers, Ms 2958.413, N-YHS; Business Records Collection, Ms 56, NBWM; Continental Army and Navy Letters, MbHS; "Undelivered Letters," Boxes 73 and 74, Cory Family Papers, Ms 80, NBWM; George Dennison, Letter to Father, 1814, Colls. 1966, Misc. Box 94/16, MeHS; John Edgar to his mother, Mary, 1804, Dr. Arthur Bining Collection, HSP; Box 1, Nathan Gallup Fish Papers, 1826–65, Coll. 252, Mystic; Chauncy Fitch Letters, 1839–40, Ms N-151, MHS; Garnder Family Papers, AAS; Gardner Family Papers, Ms 87, NHA; Samuel Gatchell Papers, 1844–46, Ms 1988, MdHS; Letters of Moses Gray, Gray Family Papers, 1742–1904, MHS; Gregory Family Papers, PEM; Hammond Family Papers, Ms 46, NBWM; Cornelius Albert Lee Letters, Donel O'Brien Collection, Ms 273, NHA; John Palmer Papers, 1776–86, Coll. 53, Mystic. See also John Remington Congdon, Journal, 1840, Ms 82–240, RIHS; Simeon Crowell, "Commonplace Book of Simeon Crowell," 1818–46, Ms, MHS.; Jacob Reeves Papers, 1809–35, Ms, MHS; Nathan Coleman and Elizabeth Hodgdon Letters, 1842–44, Sanborn Family Papers, 1785–1875, MHS; John D. Symonds, Letters, Symonds Family Papers, Ms O.144, PEM. See also Thomas Smith, "Revolutionary Letter from Thomas Smith, Forton Prison, 1780," *EIHC*, 41 (1905): 227; George Thompson, "Diary of George Thompson of Newburyport, Kept at Forton Prison, England, 1777–81," *EIHC*, 76 (1940): 221–42; Joseph, Valpey Jr., *Journal of Joseph Valpey, Jr., of Salem, November 1813–April 1815: With Other Papers Relating to His Experience in Dartmoor Prison* (no place: Michigan Society of Colonial Wars, 1922).

3. The Logbook of Memory

1. James Fenimore Cooper, *The Pilot: A Tale of the Sea* (New York: G. P. Putnam's Sons, n.d.; orig. pub. 1823).
2. Jonathan D. Spence, *The Memory Palace of Matteo Ricci* (New York: Penguin, 1983).
3. *New Orleans Daily Picayune*, June 1, 1843.
4. Log of the *Barbarita*, kept by Joseph P. Clifford, 1830, PPL. See also Log of the *Polly*, kept by John Baker, 1804–05, Log 1804A B4, PEM; Log of the *St. Paul*, kept by Augustus Hamblet, 1839–42, Log 656, PEM.
5. J. Fenimore Cooper, ed., *Ned Myers; or Life before the Mast*, William S. Dudley, intro. and notes (Annapolis, MD: Naval Institute Press, 1989; orig. pub. 1843), 278. See also Myra C. Glenn, *Jack Tar's Story: The Autobiographies and Memoirs of Sailors in Antebellum America* (Cambridge: Cambridge University Press, 2010), 19–20.
6. Hester Blum, "Before and after the Mast: James Fenimore Cooper and *Ned Myers*," in Paul A. Gilje and William Pencak, eds., *Pirates, Jack Tar, and Memory: New Directions in American Maritime History* (Mystic, CT: Mystic Seaport, 2007), 126–27; Blum, *The View from the Masthead: Maritime Imagination and Antebellum American Sea Narratives* (Chapel Hill: University of North Carolina Press, 2008), 94, 102–06, 114.
7. James Atkinson, *Epitome of the Art of Navigation …* (London: William Mount and Thomas Page, 1744), 266.
8. Stuart C. Sherman, *The Voice of the Whalemen: With an Account of the Nicholson Whaling Collection* (Providence, RI: Providence Public Library, 1965), 26–27.
9. Sherman, *The Voice of the Whalemen*, 25–31.
10. Atkinson, *Epitome of the Art of Navigation …*, ix, 265–66. Earlier editions of this book did not include this detailed information on the logbook. See also John Hamilton Moore, *The Practical Navigator and Seaman's New Daily Assistant …*, 3rd ed. (London: B. Law, 1776), 153–95.
11. "The History of Naval Logbooks," The National Maritime Museum, Greenwich, UK, Web site, accessed June 1, 2012. http://www.rmg.co.uk/about/partnerships-and-initiatives/cliwoc/the-history-of-naval-logbooks.
12. R. Liddel, *The Seaman's New Vade Mecum: Containing a Practical Essay on Naval Book-Keeping …* (London: G. G. and J. Robinson, 1794), 214–15.
13. United States, *Extract from the Naval Regulations, Issued by Command of the President of the United States of America, January 25, 1802* (New York: Prior and Dunning, 1810).
14. The sailing master was a special officer responsible for the navigation of a warship. He was a warrant officer whose commission was below a lieutenant. United States, *Rules, Regulations, and Instructions for the Naval Service of the United States …* (Washington, DC: E. De Krafft, 1818), 42–43, 72, 76, 85, 119.
15. *U.S. Statutes at Large* 1 (1790), 55–65, 133. For similar reference to logbooks in British regulations, see Charles Abbot, *A Treatise of the Law Relative to Merchant Ships and Seamen …* (Philadelphia, PA: James Humphries, 1802), 319, 320, 329; James Allen Park, *A System of the Law*

of Marine Insurances ... (Philadelphia, PA: Joseph Crukshank, 1789), 66, 67, 346.

16. Nathaniel Bowditch, *The New American Practical Navigator* ... (Newburyport, MA: Edmund Blunt, 1802), 273–301.

17. Richard Henry Dana Jr., *The Seaman's Friend* (Delmar, NY: Scholars' Facsimiles, 1979; orig. pub. 1851), 145, 200.

18. Log of the *Stonington*, kept by Alanson Fournier, 1846–47, Log 335, Mystic. See also Log of the *Chilo*, kept by G. I. Day, 1846–47, Log 1846C, PEM.

19. "Depositions Concerning the Brig *Nereus*," ca. 1835, Folder 5, Box 1, Rogers Family Papers, Ms 87, PEM.

20. Log of the *Africa*, kept by Samuel Tillinghast, 1750, Vault A #36B, Shelf 24, NHS.

21. Log of the *Agnes*, kept by William Brown, 1808, Log 1808A, PEM.

22. Log of the *Neva*, 1818–20, Log 1818 N2, PEM.

23. Log of the *Stork*, 1751–52, Folder 1, Box 25, Stuyvesant-Rutherfurd Papers, Ms 605, N-YHS.

24. Log of the *Acastus*, kept by Francis A. Burnham, 1817, Barker-Edes-Noyes Papers, Ms N-1800, MHS.

25. Log of the *Catherine*, kept by Ebenezer William Sage, 1809, Ebenezer William Sage Papers, Ms N-856, MHS. Calculating longitude was a complicated process that relied on dead reckoning and other navigational information, as well as the use of navigational tables in manuals. For an eighteenth-century explanation of these calculations, see Atkinson, *Epitome of the Art of Navigation*, 93. See also Donald Launer, *Navigation Through the Ages* (Dobbs Ferry, NY: Sheridan House, 2009). For a discussion of the development of the chronometer to determine longitude, see Dava Sobel, *Longitude: The Story of a Lone Genius Who Solved the Greatest Scientific Problem of His Time* (New York: Penguin, 1995). Although a workable chronometer to aid in determining longitude was built by 1761, it was so expensive that most ships continued to navigate without one until well into the nineteenth century.

26. See, for example, Log of the *Hannah and Elizabeth*, kept by Robert Emery, 1798–99, Logbook 024, MM.

27. Log of the *Henry Eubank*, 1834, Log 688, Mystic.

28. Log of the *Tartar*, 1817–18, kept by William A. Rogers, Log 1817 T4, PEM.

29. This study is based on the examination of more than 250 logbooks and journals, which represents only a small percentage of the total available in archives. See the appendix for a discussion of the logbook research.

30. Log of the *Lotos*, kept by Thomas Wilson Ross, 1832, Log 1832 L4, PEM.

31. Log of the *Dispatch Packet*, kept by Edward Norris, 1820–21, typescript, Norris Ms, MHS.

32. Log of the *Prince Ferdinand*, kept by William Bedlow, 1759, BV Bedlow, Ms 877, N-YHS.

33. Log of the *Adventure*, kept by Francis Boardman, 1776, Log 1774A, PEM.

34. Log of the *John*, kept by David Chever, 1812–13, Log 1812J B5, PEM.

35. Dana Jr., *The Seaman's Friend*, 145, 200.

36. Log of the *Agnes*, kept by William Brown, 1808, Log 1808A, PEM.

37. *Jamestown (New York) Journal*, February 10, 1841.
38. Log of the *Acastus*, 1817, kept by Francis A. Burnham, Barker-Edes-Noyes Papers, Ms N-1800, MHS; Log of the *Laurel*, kept by Francis A. Burnham, 1817, Barker-Edes-Noyes Papers, Ms N-1800, MHS; Log of the *Three Sisters*, 1820, kept by Francis A. Burnham, 1818–19, Barker-Edes-Noyes Papers, Ms N-1800, MHS; Log of the *Fenwick*, kept by Francis A. Burnham, 1822, Barker-Edes-Noyes Papers, Ms N-1800, MHS.
39. Log of the *Edward*, 1811, kept by Enos Field, Field Howe Papers, Ms N-1220, MHS; Log of *Nuestra Senora de Pezla*, kept by Enos Field, 1816, Field-Howe Papers, Ms N-1220, MHS.
40. Log of the *China*, 1832–35, ODHS Log 880A, NBWM. See also Log of the *Neva*, 1818–20, Log 1818 N2, PEM; Log of the *Success*, kept by Joseph Crowell 1750–52, Folder 1, Box 25, Stuyvesant-Ruthurford Papers, Ms 605, N-YHS.
41. Log of the *Mary*, 1820–21, Log 22, Mystic; Log of the *Commodore Perry*, 1821–22, Log 22, Mystic; Log of the *Commodore Perry*, 1822–23, Log 22, Mystic; Log of the *Commodore Perry*, 1823, Log 22, Mystic.
42. Log of the *Ann*, 1776, Log 1776A, PEM; Log of the *Three Sisters*, 1789–90, Log 1776A, PEM.
43. Log of the *America*, 1824–25, Log 1824A, PEM.
44. Log of the *Hawke*, kept by Thomas Nicolson, 1778, Thomas Nicolson Navigation and Logbooks, 1766–1813, Folder 3, Ms N-590, MHS.
45. Daniel Vickers with Vince Walsh, *Young Men and the Sea: Yankee Seafarers in the Age of Sail* (New Haven, CT: Yale University Press, 2005), 96–130, 214–51; Paul A. Gilje, *Liberty on the Waterfront: American Maritime Culture in the Age of Revolution* (Philadelphia: University of Pennsylvania Press, 2004), 24–32.
46. See, for example, the scribbling in Log of the *Ontario*, [kept by Murray Mason], 1824–25, Naval History Society Collection, Logbooks, Ontario, Ms 439, N-YHS; Log of the *Sandwich*, kept by Micajah Coffin, 1762–63, PPL.
47. For a log/journal that later was used as a scrapbook by the family, see Log of the *Porpoise*, kept by James Freeman Curtis, 1821–22, Curtis-Stevenson Family Papers, Ms N-288, MHS. See also Log of the *Wilson*, 1816, BV Wilson, Ms 2846, N-YHS.
48. Log of the *Hannah and Elizabeth*, kept by Robert Emery, 1798–99, Logbook 024, MM.
49. Log of the *Prince Ferdinand*, kept by William Bedlow, 1759, BV Bedlow, Ms 877, N-YHS.
50. Log of the *Betty*, kept by Lot Stetson, 1772, Ms S-801, MHS.
51. Log of the *Prince Ferdinand*, kept by William Bedlow, 1759, BV Bedlow, Ms 877, N-YHS.
52. Log of the *Sally*, 1792, Vault A, #28, Shelf 4, NHS.
53. Log of the *St. Paul*, kept by Augustus Hamblet, 1839–42, Log 656, PEM.
54. Log of the *William and Henry*, 1788–90, Log 1788W, PEM; Log of the *Grand Turk*, 1792–93, Log 1788W, PEM.
55. Log of the *Reaper*, kept by Benjamin Neal, 1837–39, Log 1837 R3, PEM.
56. Log of the *Recovery*, kept by Benjamin Daniels, 1816–17, MHS.

57. Log of the *Prudent*, kept by Holton J. Breed, 1804–06, Log 1804 P3, PEM.

58. Log of *Remembergrace*, kept by Thomas Nicolson, 1769, Thomas Nicolson Navigation and Logbooks, 1766–1813, Folder 2, Ms N-590, MHS. For other impressments mentioned in a logbook, see Log of the *Susanna*, 1805–06, Log 1805S O5, PEM.

59. Log of the *Industry*, 1766–67, Vault A #34, Shelf 24, NHS.

60. Log of the *Mercury*, 1800, Log 835, Mystic.

61. Log of the *Prudent*, kept by Holton J. Breed, 1804–06, Log 1804 P3, PEM.

62. Log of the *Reaper*, kept by Benjamin Neal, 1837–39, Log 1837 R3, PEM. See also Log of the *Triumph*, kept by Abner Lothrop, 1791, ODHS Log 875, NBWM; Log of the *Action*, kept by Enos Field, 1813, Field-Howe Papers, Ms N-1220, MHS; Log of the *Ann*, kept by Ebenezer H. Mix, 1817–18, Msc. Stack, CHS; Log of the *Ann and Hope*, kept by Benjamin Carter, 1799–1800, Ms 828, RIHS; Log of the *Cicero*, kept by Ebenezer Nye, 1827, Log 429, Mystic.

63. Log of the *America*, kept by James Cheever, 1812–13, Log 1812 A2, PEM.

64. For navigational and mathematical calculations, see Log of the *John and William*, 1751, Folder 1, Box 25, Stuyvesant-Rutherfurd Papers, Ms 605, N-YHS; Log of the *Paulina*, 1834–36, Ser. 1, Vol. 26, Maritime Records, Coll. 949, MeHS; Log of the *Polly*, 1767–68, kept by Thomas Nicolson, Thomas Nicolson Navigation and Logbooks, 1766–1813, Folder 2, Ms N-590, MHS; Log of the *Sandwich*, kept by Micajah Coffin, 1762–63, PPL: Log of the *Three Sisters*, 1789–90, Log 1776A, PEM; Log of the *Action*, kept by Enos Field, 1813, Field-Howe Papers, Ms N-1220, MHS; Log of the *Betty*, kept by Lot Stetson, 1772, Ms S-801, MHS.

65. Log of the *Matsey*, kept by Nathaniel K. Helme, 1793, Vault A, #38, Shelf 24, NHS. For a book that was mainly a navigational workbook, but that also had a few pages devoted to logging a short voyage, see Samuel Clarke, Navigational Problems … with a log of a Voyage from Boston to Antigua January 2, 1775 – February 26, 1775, Box 57, Vol. 113, Perry-Clarke Ms, MHS.

66. Log of the *Morrison*, kept by J. Wiley, 1838, Log 992, Mystic.

67. Log of the *Addison*, kept by Moses Smith, 1834–37, PPL.

68. Log of the *Exchange*, 1764, Logbook 283, MM.

69. Log of the *Prudent*, kept by Holton J. Breed, 1804–06, Log 1804 P3, PEM.

70. Log of the *Nancy*, 1811, kept by Seth Barlow, ODHS Log 196, NBWM.

71. Log of the *Industry*, kept by William Bedlow, 1769, BV Bedlow, Ms 877, N-YHS.

72. Log of the *Kingston*, kept by Thomas Nicolson, 1784, Thomas Nicolson Navigation and Logbooks, 1766–1813, Ms N-590, MHS.

73. Log of the *Nancy*, kept by Seth Barlow, 1811, ODHS Log 196, NBWM.

74. Log of the *Union*, kept by Peter Pease, 1769–70, ODHS Log 458D, NBWM. See also Log of the *Vaughan*, kept by Francis Boardman, 1767, Log 1767 V3 B24, PEM.; Log of the *Three Sisters*, 1789–90, Log 1776A, PEM; Log of the *General Wolfe*, 1767–69, Log 1767L, PEM.

75. Log of the *Ann and Hope*, kept by Benjamin Carter, 1798–99, Ms 828, RIHS; Log of the *Ann and Hope*, kept by Benjamin Carter, 1799–1800, Ms

828, RIHS; Log of the *Ann and Hope*, kept by Benjamin Carter, 1800, Ms 828, RIHS.

76. Log of the *Catherine*, kept by William E. Leeds, 1843–44, Log 940, Mystic; Log of the *Ann Parry*, 1845–48, kept by Ezra Goodnough and John Joplin, Log 656 1845A, PEM.

77. Alexandra Johnson, *A Brief History of Diaries: From Pepys to Blogs* (London: Hesperus Press, 2011).

78. Samuel Pepys, *The Diary of Samuel Pepys. A New and Complete Transcription*, Robert Latham and William Matthews, eds., 11 vols. (Berkeley: University of California Press, 1970–); William Maclay, *Journal of William Maclay, United States Senator from Pennsylvania, 1789–1791* (Washington, DC: U.S. Congress, Senate, 1998).

79. Steven E. Kagle, *American Diary Literature, 1620–1799* (Boston, MA: Twayne Publishers, 1979); Kagle, *Early Nineteenth-Century American Diary Literature* (Boston, MA: Twayne Publishers, 1986).

80. Log of the *Nancy*, 1785–86, PPL.

81. Log of the *Albion*, 1829–30, PPL; Log of the *Elizabeth*, 1769–74, MM.

82. Log of the *Eliza*, kept by Eleazer Elderkin, 1796–98, CHS. See also Log of the *Shark*, kept by A. A. Adee, 1826–27, Vault A #1337 Shelf 28, NHS; Log of the *Vincennes*, kept by James Alden, 1838–42, LC; Log of the *Constitution*, kept by Lucius M. Mason, 1844, Logbook 128, MM; Log of the *Trumbull*, kept by Henry Bowers, 1810–13, Log 828, Mystic; Log of the *Amelia*, kept by D. C. Powers, 1849–50, Log 510, Mystic; Log of the *Emiline*, kept by Washington Fosdick, 1843–44, ODHS Log 147 NBWM; Log of the *Shark*, kept by A. A. Adee, 1826–27, Vault A #1337 Shelf 28, NHS; Log of the *Portsmouth*, kept by William Weaver, 1848–49, Diary of William Weaver, N-YHS; Log of the *Relief*, kept by William Clarke, 1833–39, Log 1838V, PEM; Log of the *Peacock*, kept by Thomas J. Harris, 1824–27, LC.

83. Log of the *Eliza*, kept by Eleazer Elderkin, 1796–98, CHS. See also Log of the *Shark*, kept by A. A. Adee, 1826–27, Vault A #1337 Shelf 28, NHS.

84. John Remington Congdon, Journal, 1840, Ship *Albion*, Ms 82–240, RIHS; Journal of Cynthia S. Congdon 1841–45 in John Remington Congdon Papers, Ms 82–240, RIHS.

85. Kagle, *American Diary Literature*, 114–21; Charles Herbert, *A Relic of the Revolution ...* (Boston, MA: Charles H. Pierce, 1847).

86. Log of the *General Hancock*, [1778], Hoadley Coll. Box 19, 34162, CHS. For other sea journals during wartime, see Log of the *Nonesuch*, 1812, Series 8D, Reel 49, Peter Force Collection, LC; Log of the *Pilgrim*, kept by Josiah Bartlett, 1781–82, microfilm, Bartlett Ms, MHS; Log of the *Polly*, kept by Jeduthan Upton, typescript, MHS; Log of the *Revenge*, kept by John Palmer, 1777–78, Folder 12, Vol. 5, John Palmer Papers, 1776–86, Coll. 53, Mystic; Log of the *Serapis*, kept by Beaumont Groube, 1778–80, in John S. Barnes, *The Logs of the Serapis, Alliance, Ariel, Under the Command of John Paul Jones, 1779–1780 ...* (New York: Navy History Society by DeVinne Press, 1911); Log of the *Superior*, kept by James A. Dudley, 1814, microfilm, Dudley Ms, MHS; Log of the *John*, kept by David Chever, 1812–13, Log 1812 J B5, PEM.

87. Log of the *Polly*, kept by Jeduthan Upton, 1812–13, typescript, MHS.
88. Log of the *Dolly*, kept by Sam Winchester, 1809–10, Ms 917, MdHS.
89. Log of the *Peacock*, kept by Thomas J. Harris, 1824–27, LC.
90. Log of the *Equality*, kept by Louis Brantz, 1793–94, series 8D, Reel #31, Peter Force Collection, LC.
91. Log of the *Talma*, 1833, Log 968, Mystic.
92. Log of the *Vesper*, kept by Alfred Terry, 1846–48, Log 955, Mystic.
93. Log of the *Herald*, kept by Thomas Delano, 1817–19, PPL. See also Log of the *Trumbull*, kept by Henry Bowers, 1810–13, Log 828, Mystic.
94. Log of the *President*, kept by Alexander S. Wadsworth, 1805, Ser. 1, Vol. 18, Maritime Records, Coll. 949, MeHS; Log of the *Constitution*, kept by Alexander S. Wadsworth, 1811, Ser. 1, Vol. 19, Maritime Records, Coll. 949, MeHS. See also Log of the *Hornet*, kept by Horatio Nelson Cady, 1825–26, Cady Ms, LC; Log of the *Merrimack*, kept by Joseph Brown, Log 1799M, PEM; Log of the *Ontario* [kept by Murray Mason], 1824–25, Naval History Society Collection, Logbooks, Ontario, Ms 439, N-YHS; Log of the *Peacock*, kept by Thomas J. Harris, 1824–27, LC; Log of the *Portsmouth*, kept by William Weaver, 1848–49, Diary of William Weaver, N-YHS; Log of the *Serapis*, kept by Beaumont Groube, 1778–80, in Barnes, *The Logs of the Serapis*....
95. Log of the *Porpoise*, kept by James Freeman Curtis, 1821–22, Curtis-Stevenson Papers, Ms N-288, MHS.
96. Log of the *Porpoise*, 1838–40, Ms Coll. BV Log Books, N-YHS.
97. Log of the *St. Louis*, kept by James L. Henderson, Series 8D, Reel 42, Peter Force Collection, LC.
98. Log of the *Atahalpa*, kept by Ralph Haskins, 1800–03, Beinecke; Log of the *Eliza Haily*, kept by James Babcock, 1809, CHS; Log of the *Flying Fish*, kept by Richard Gatewood, 1815, Logbook 097, MM; Log of the *Logan*, kept by Thomas Handsayd Cabot, 1834, microfilm roll 118, Vol. 1, Lee Family Papers, MHS; Log of the *Susanna*, 1805–06, Log 1805S O5, PEM.
99. Log of the *John G. Coster*, kept by Thomas W. Abbott, 1845–46, MHS. See also the Log of the *Congress*, kept by William White, 1815, PEM; Log of the *Thomas Russell*, kept by Samuel Curson, 1798–99, MHS.
100. Log of the *Ann and Hope*, kept by Benjamin Carter, 1798–99, Ms 828, RIHS; Log of the *Ann and Hope*, kept by Benjamin Carter, 1799–1800, Ms 828, RIHS; Log of the *Ann and Hope*, kept by Benjamin Carter, 1800, Ms 828, RIHS; Log of the *Atlantic*, kept by Theodore Lewis, 1835–37, Log 822, Mystic. See also the Log of the *Shark*, kept by A. A. Adee, 1826–27, Vault A #1337 Shelf 28, NHS.
101. John Adams, February 13, 1778 – April 1, 1778, Diary of John Adams, Adams Papers Digital Editions, MHS.
102. Log of the *Rialto*, kept by George Denham, 1849, Log 1849, Mystic.
103. Log of the *Alexander Coffin*, kept by A. B. Mayhew, 1849–50, PPL. See also the Log of the *Amelia*, kept by D. C. Powers, 1849–50, Log 510, Mystic.
104. Blum, *The View from the Masthead*, 26–32.
105. Gilje, *Liberty on the Waterfront*, 24–25.
106. Log of the *Peacock*, kept by Thomas J. Harris, 1824–27, LC.

107. Log of the *Cavalier*, kept by William H. Wilson, 1848–50, Log 18, Mystic. However, it was in published memoirs that common seamen expressed more fully their demand for the protection of their rights as citizens. Gilje, *Liberty on the Waterfront*, 245–49.

108. Log of the *La Plata*, 1848–50, Log 1847 W3 B15, PEM.

109. See, for example, the love poetry in Log of the *Betsy*, kept by John Palmer, 1785–86, Folder 17, Vol. 10, John Palmer Papers, 1776–86, Coll. 53, Mystic.

110. Log of the *Halcyon*, kept by William George Bailey, 1843–48, Log 988, Mystic.

111. Log of the *Bengal*, kept by William Silver, 1832–35, Log 1832 B3, PEM.

112. Log of the *Cavalier*, kept by William H. Wilson, 1848–50, Log 18, Mystic.

113. Log of the *Constitution*, kept by Lucius M. Mason, 1844, Logbook 128, MM.

114. Log of the *Bengal*, kept by William Silver, 1832–35, Log 1832 B3, PEM.

115. Log of the *Polly*, kept by John Baker, 1804–05, Log 1804A B4, PEM.

116. Log of the *Arab*, kept by Ephraim Harding, 1842–45, ODHS Log 435A, NBWM.

117. Journal of Cynthia S. Congdon 1841–45 in John Remington Congdon Papers, Ms 82–240, RIHS.

118. Haskell Springer, "The Captain's Wife at Sea," in Margaret S. Creighton and Lisa Norling, eds., *Iron Men, Wooden Women: Gender and Seafaring in the Atlantic World, 1700–1920* (Baltimore, MD: Johns Hopkins University Press, 1996), 97–98.

119. Mary Brewster, *"She Was a Sister Sailor": The Whaling Journals of Mary Brewster, 1845–1851*, Joan Druett, ed. (Mystic, CT: Mystic Seaport Museum, 1992); Martha Smith Brewer Brown, *She Went A-Whaling: The Journal of Martha Smith Brewer Brown ...*, Anne Mackay, ed. (Orient, NY: Oyster Ponds Historical Society, 1993); Mary Chipman Lawrence, *The Captain's Best Mate: The Journal of Mary Chipman Lawrence on the Whaler Addison, 1856–1860*, Stanton Garner, ed. (Hanover, NH: Published for Brown University Press by University Press of New England, 1966). See also David Cordingly, *Women Sailors and Sailors' Women: An Untold Maritime Story* (New York: Random House, 2001); Druett, *Hen Frigates: Wives of Merchant Captains under Sail* (New York: Simon & Schuster, 1998); Druett, "Those Female Journals," *Log of Mystic Seaport*, 40 (1989): 115–25; Lisa Norling, *Captain Ahab Had a Wife: New England Women and the Whalefishery, 1720–1870* (Chapel Hill: University of North Carolina Press, 2000).

120. Quoted in Blum, *The View from the Masthead*, 80.

121. Richard Henry Dana Jr., *Two Years before the Mast: A Personal Narrative of Life at Sea*, Thomas Philbrick, ed. (New York: Penguin, 1981; orig. pub. 1840), 37–38.

122. James Fenimore Cooper, *The Red Rover, a Tale*, Thomas and Marianne Philbrick, eds. (Albany: State University Press of New York, 1991; orig. pub. 1827), 290; Thomas Philbrick, *James Fenimore Cooper and*

the Development of American Sea Fiction (Cambridge, MA: Harvard University Press, 1961), 77–83.

123. Dana Jr., *Two Years before the Mast*, 37–38.
124. Nathaniel Ames, *A Mariner's Sketches* (Providence, RI: Cory, Marshall and Hammond, 1830); Ames, *Nautical Reminiscences* (Providence, RI: Marshall, 1832); Ames, *An Old Sailor's Yarns* (New York: George Dearborn, 1835).
125. Thomas Farel Heffernan, *Stove by a Whale: Owen Chase and the Essex* (Hanover, NH: Wesleyan University Press, 1981); Nathaniel Philbrick and Thomas Philbrick, eds., *The Loss of the Ship Essex Sunk by a Whale* (New York: Penguin, 2000); Nathaniel Philbrick, *In the Heart of the Sea: The Tragedy of the Whaleship Essex* (New York: Viking, 2000).
126. *Lives and Confessions of John Williams, Francis Frederick, John R. Rog, and Peter Peterson* ... (Boston, MA: J. T. Buckingham, 1819). See also *A Report of the Trial of Samuel Tulley and John Dalton ... for Piracy* ... (Boston, MA: J. Belcher, 1812); *A Sketch of the Life and Confessions of Thos. J. Winslow, One of the Pirates* ... (New York: Isaac Chaunay, 1832) [This last pamphlet was found in PEM, although it is not listed in the online catalog. Winslow is a misspelling of Wansley]; Joeph Baker, *The Confessions of Joseph Baker ... For Murder and Piracy* ... (Philadelphia, PA: Folwell, [1800]).
127. See, for example, June Namias, *White Captives: Gender and Ethnicity on the American Frontier* (Chapel Hill: University of North Carolina Press, 1993). For non-Native American captivity see Paul Baepler, ed., *White Slaves, African Masters: American Barbary Captivity Narratives* (Chicago, IL: University of Chicago Press, 1999); Linda Colley, *Captives: Britain, Empire, and the World, 1600–1850* (New York: Random House, 2002); Lawrence A. Peskin, *Captives and Countrymen: Barbary Slavery and the American Public, 1785–1816* (Baltimore, MD: Johns Hopkins University Press, 2009); Lisa Voight, *Writing Captivity in the Early Modern Atlantic: Circulations of Knowledge and Authority in the Iberian and English Imperial Worlds* (Chapel Hill: University of North Carolina Press, 2009).
128. William Lay and Cyrus M. Hussey, *A Narrative of the Mutiny on Board the Whaleship Globe* (New London: William Lay and C. M. Hussey, 1828).
129. John Foss, *A Journal of the Captivity and Sufferings of John Foss: Several Years a Prisoner in Algiers* ... (Newburyport, MA: A. March, [1798]); William Ray, *Horrors of Slavery: Or the American Tars in Tripoli* ... (Troy, NY: Oliver Lyon, 1808). See also Thomas Nicholson, *An Affecting Narrative of the Captivity of Thomas Nicholson* ... (Boston, MA: H. Trumbull, 1816). For another captivity narrative of an American held in the Muslim world on the Arabian coast, see Daniel Saunders Jr., *A Journal of the Travels and Sufferings of Daniel Saunders* ... (Salem, MA: Thomas C. Cushing, 1794).
130. John Blatchford, *Narrative of the Remarkable Occurrences in the Life of John Blatchford* ... (New London, CT: T. Green, 1788); Joshua Davis, *A Narrative of Joshua Davis* ... (Baltimore, MD: B. Edes, 1811).

131. Charles Andrews, *The Prisoners' Memoirs, or Dartmoor Prison* ... (New York: Printed for the Author, 1815); *A Narrative of the Capture of the United States' Brig Vixen* ... (New York: The Office of the War, 1813); R. S. Coffin, *A Concise Narrative of the Barbarous Treatment*... (Danville, VT: Ebenezer Eaton, 1816); Ebenezer Fox, *The Adventures of Ebenezer Fox in the Revolutionary War* ... (Boston, MA: Charles Fox, 1848); James M'Lean, *Seventeen Years' History of the Life and Sufferings of James M'Lean* ... (Hartford, CT: B & J. Russell, 1814); Joshua Penny, *The Life and Adventures of Joshua Penny* ... (New York: Alden Spooner, 1815); Israel R. Potter, *Life and Remarkable Adventures of Israel Potter* ... (Providence, RI: J. Howard, 1824); Andrew Sherburne, *Memoirs of Andrew Sherburne* ... (Utica, NY: William Williams, 1828). See also Robert C. Doyle, *Voices of Captivity: Interpreting the American POW Narrative* (Lawrence: University Press of Kansas, 1994).
132. Dana Jr., *Two Years before the Mast*, 17, 38.
133. Dana Jr., *Two Years before the Mast*, 37–42, 43–59, 70–71, 94–95.
134. Dana Jr., *Two Years before the Mast*, 335, 53–56.
135. Dana Jr. *Two Years before the Mast*, 44–47, 462, 20.
136. Glenn, *Jack Tar's Story.*
137. Besides the works cited later, these seamen narratives included Tiphys Aegyptus, *The Navy's Friend, or Reminiscences of the Navy* ... (Baltimore, MD: Printed for the Author, 1843); Gurdon L. Allyn, *The Old Sailor's Story*... (Norwich, CT: G. Wilcox, 1879); Joseph Bates, *The Autobiography of Elder Joseph Bates* ... (Battle Creek, MI: Steam Press, 1868); J. Ross Browne, *Etchings of a Whaling Cruise* ... (New York: Harper & Brothers, 1846); George Edward Clark, *Seven Years a Sailor's Life* (Boston, MA: Adams & Co., 1867); Joseph G. Clark, *Lights and Shadows of Sailor Life* ... (Boston, MA: Benjamin B. Mussey, 1848); Elijah Cobb, *Elijah Cobb, 1768–1848, A Cape Cod Skipper*, forward by Ralph D. Paine (New Haven, CT: Yale University Press, 1925); John Elliott, *The Reformed: An Old Sailor's Legacy* (Boston, MA: Usher and Strickland, 1841); Roland Gould, *The Life of Gould, an Ex-Man-of-War's-Man* ... (Claremont, NH: Claremont Manufacturing Company, 1867); Christopher Hawkins, *The Adventures of Christopher Hawkins* ... (New York: Privately Printed, 1864); Nathaniel Hawthorne, ed., *The Yarn of a Yankee Privateer*, Clifford Smyth, intro. (New York: Funk and Wagnalls, 1926; orig. pub. 1846); Herbert, *A Relic of the Revolution*; John Hoxse, *The Yankee Tar* ... (Northampton, MA: John Metcalf, 1840); William M. Bryant, *The Old Sailor: A Thrilling Narrative of the Life and Adventures of Elias Hutchins* ... (Biddeford, ME: Eastern Journal, 1853); Nicholas Peter Isaacs, *Twenty Years before the Mast* ... (New York: J. P. Beckworth, 1845); Horace Lane, *The Wandering Boy, or Careless Sailor* ... (Skaneateles, NY: Luther Pratt, 1839); Samuel Leech, *A Voice from the Main Deck: Being a Record of the Thirty Years' Adventures of Samuel Leech*, Michael J. Crawford, ed. (Annapolis, MD: Naval Institute Press, 1999; orig. pub. 1843); George Little, *Life on the Ocean; or Twenty Years at Sea* ... (Baltimore, MD: Armstrong & Berry, 1843); Alfred Lorraine, *The Helm, the Sword, and the Cross: A Life Narrative* (Cincinnati,

OH: Poe and Hitchcock, 1862); William McNally, *Evils and Abuses in the Naval and Merchant Service Exposed* ... (Boston, MA: Cassady and March, 1839); [Henry James Mercier], *Life in a Man of War, or Scenes in "Old Ironsides"* ... (Philadelphia, PA: L. R. Bailey, 1841); Francis Allyn Olmsted, *Incidents of a Whaling Voyage* ... (New York: D. Appleton, 1841); Solomon H. Sanborn, *An Exposition of Official Tyranny in the United States Navy* (New York: no pub., 1841); Elijah Shaw, *Short Sketch, of the Life of Elijah Shaw, Who Served for Twenty-Two Years in the Navy* ... (Rochester, NY: Strong & Dawson, 1843); Moses Smith, *Naval Scenes in the Last War* ... (Boston, MA: Gleason Publishing Hall, 1846); F. P. Torrey, *Journal of the Cruise of the United States Ship Ohio* ... (Boston, MA: Samuel N. Dickinson, 1841); William Torrey, *Torrey's Narrative* ... (Boston, MA: A. J. Wright, 1848).

138. George Lightcraft, *Scraps from the Log Book of George Lightcraft* ... (Syracuse, NY: Hall & Dickinson, 1847).

139. [Josiah Cobb], *A Green Hand's First Cruise, Roughed out from the Log-Book of Memory* ..., 2 vols. (Baltimore, MD: Cushing & Brother, 1841), 1: iii–iv.

140. Lightcraft, *Scraps from the Log Book*, 59–61, 75–76.

141. Jacob Hazen, *Five Years before the Mast* ..., 2nd. Ed. (Philadelphia, PA: William P. Hazard, 1854), 57–62, 92–97.

142. Charles Nordhoff, *Man-of-War-Life: A Boy's Experience in the United States Navy* ..., John B. Hattendorf, intro. (Annapolis, MD: Naval Institute Press, 1985; orig. pub. 1855); J. Fenimore Cooper, ed., *Ned Myers; or, A Life before the Mast*, William S. Dudley, intro. (Annapolis, MD: Naval Institute Press, 1989; orig. pub. 1843).

143. Hazen, *Five Years before the Mast*, 95, 412.

144. William Meacham Murrell, *Cruise of the Frigate Columbia around the World* ... (Boston, MA: Benjamin B. Mussey, 1840), 48–54. Quotation, ibid., 51. On travel literature, see Alfred Bendixen and Judith Hamera, eds., *The Cambridge Companion to American Travel Writing* (Cambridge: Cambridge University Press, 2009).

145. Stephen Carl Arch, *After Franklin: The Emergence of Autobiography in Post-Revolutionary America, 1780–1830* (Hanover, NH: University Press of New England, 2001).

146. Herman Melville, *Typee: A Peep at Polynesian Life during a Residence in a Valley of the Marquesas* (New York: New American Library, 1964; orig. pub., 1846); Melville, *Omoo: A Narrative of Adventures in the South Seas*, Harrison Hayford, et al., eds. (Evanston, IL: Northwestern University Press, 1968; orig. pub. 1847).

147. Herman Melville, *Redburn: His First Voyage, Being the Sailor-boy Confessions and Reminiscences of the Son-of-a-Gentleman in the Merchant Service*, Harold Beaver, ed. (New York: Penguin, 1976; orig. pub. 1849); Melville, *White-Jacket, or The World in a Man-of-War*, Alfred Kazin, intro. (New York: New American Library, 1979; orig. pub. 1850). Quotation, ibid., 408.

148. Herman Melville, *Moby Dick, or the Whale* (New York: Modern Library, 1982; orig. pub. 1851), 744–49, 806–25. Quotation, ibid., 749.

4. Spinning Yarns

1. On the special role of yarn spinning in maritime culture, see Ann Fabian, *The Unvarnished Truth: Personal Narratives in Nineteenth-Century America* (Berkeley: University of California Press, 2000), 43–45; Eric W. Sager, *Seafaring Labour: The Merchant Marine of Atlantic Canada, 1820–1914* (Montreal: McGill-Queen's University Press, 1989), 231–33; Knut Weibust, *Deep Sea Sailors: A Study in Maritime Ethnology*, 2nd ed. (Stockholm: Nordiska Museets, 1976), 135–46; Hester Blum, *The View from the Masthead: Maritime Imagination and Antebellum American Sea Narratives* (Chapel Hill: University of North Carolina Press, 2008), 69; Marcus Rediker, *Outlaws of the Atlantic: Sailors, Pirates, and Motely Crews in the Age of Sail* (Boston, MA: Beacon Press, 2014), 9–29; Paul A. Gilje, *Liberty on the Waterfront: American Maritime Culture in the Age of Revolution* (Philadelphia: University of Pennsylvania Press, 2004), 81–82.

2. *Oxford English Dictionary*, s.v. "yarn." William Shakespeare used the metaphor of "mingled yarn" in reference to the course of one's life. This usage is different from the sailor metaphor for telling stories, but may have contributed to the popularity of the phrase "spinning yarns" for writers in the early nineteenth century when Shakespeare was often played on stage. See William Shakespeare, *All's Well that Ends Well*, Act 4, scene 3: "The web of our life is of a mingled yarn, good and / ill together: our virtues would be proud, if our / faults whipped them not; and our crimes would / despair, if they were not cherished by our virtues."

3. James Hardy Vaux, *Memoirs of James Hardy Vaux, Written by Himself*, 2 vols. (London: W. Clowes, 1819), 2: 173–74, 226. During the 1840s a flash culture developed in the United States that centered more on the publication of salacious material. See Patricia Cline Cohen, Timothy Gilfoyle, and Helen Lefkowitz Horowitz, *The Flash Press: Sporting Male Weeklies in 1840s New York* (Chicago, IL: University of Chicago Press, 2008).

4. William Falconer, *An Universal Dictionary of the Marine...* (London: T. Cadell, 1769), 295.

5. Richard Henry Dana Jr., *Two Years before the Mast: A Personal Narrative of Life at Sea*, Thomas Philbrick, ed. (New York: Penguin, 1981; orig. pub. 1840), 54. For references to making spun-yarn on ships, see Log of the *Adventure*, kept by Francis Boardman, 1776, Log 1774A, PEM; Log of the *Hind*, kept by Francis Boardman, 1784, Log 1774A, PEM; Log of the *Three Sisters*, 1789–90, Log 1776A, PEM.

6. For American magazines reprinting sailor yarns from British sources, see "Greenwich Hospital," *The Atheneum; or, Spirit of the English Magazines*, 1 (September 15, 1823): 488–89; "Greenwich Hospital, an Old Sailor," ibid., 1 (May 1, 1824): 99–104; Humphrey Felt, "Sketches of Society: Character-High Strikes," ibid., 1 (May 15, 1824): 188–90; "Greenwich Hospital," ibid., 1 (September 1, 1824): 425–29; "Greenwich Hospital: Their Majesties the King and Queen of the Sandwich," ibid. (September 15, 1824): 464–68; "Greenwich Hospital: the Barge's Crew," ibid., 1 (November 15, 1824): 159–62; "The Doomed Man," *The Museum of Foreign Literature, Science, and Art*, 3

(November 1, 1823): 440–46; "Greenwich Hospital: the Barge's Crew: from the London Literary Gazette, an Old Sailor," *The New-England Galaxy and United States Literary Advertiser*, 7 (November 5, 1824): 369. For newspapers printing sailor yarns from British sources, see *Salem Gazette*, October 3, 1823; *Boston Traveler*, August 5, 1825; *Edwardsville (Illinois) Spectator*, October 29, 1825; *Philadelphia Inquirer*, November 13, 1829.

7. "Greenwich Hospital," *The Atheneum; or, Spirit of the English Magazines*, 1 (September 15, 1823): 488–89.

8. "A Melee. Cornwallis's Retreat; with the First of June. - A Gallay ..." *The Museum of Foreign Literature, Science, and Arts*, 8 (June 1826): 496–97.

9. "A Melee. Cornwallis's Retreat; with the First of June. –A Gallay ..." *The Museum of Foreign Literature, Science, and Arts*, 8 (June 1826): 494.

10. Dana Jr. *Two Years before the Mast*, 74–75. See also Jason Berger, "Antebellum Fantasies of the Common Sailor; Or, Enjoying the Knowing Jack Tar," *Criticism*, 51 (2009): 29–61.

11. *The Critic*, 17 (April 8, 1820): 143–53.

12. "Original Nautical Tales: Forecastle Yarns," *The New York Mirror*, 12 (August 9, 1834): 42.

13. Samuel Leech, *A Voice from the Main Deck: Being a Record of the Thirty Years' Adventures of Samuel Leech*, Michael J. Crawford, ed. (Annapolis, MD: Naval Institute Press, 1999; orig. pub. 1843), 174–75.

14. [Benjamin Waterhouse], *A Journal of a Young Man of Massachusetts ...* (Lexington, KY: Worsley & Smith, 1816), 129–31. This account was actually written by Amos G. Babcock and edited by Waterhouse. See Henry R. Viets, "A Journal of a Young Man of Massachusetts ... Written by Himself, Boston: 1816 and a Note on the Author," *Yale Journal of Biology and Science*, 12 (1940): 605–22.

15. Alexander Hamilton Heysham, "The Messenger; or, A Yarn upon the Lee Booms – A Sea Story," *Lady's Book* (June 1831): 293–98.

16. "Original Nautical Tales: The Haunted Brig," *The New-York Mirror*, 11 (May 17, 1834): 361.

17. William Leggett, *Tales and Sketches by a Country Schoolmaster* (New York: J. & J. Harper, 1829), 205–18; Leggett, *Naval Stories* (New York: G. & C. & H. Carvell, 1834).

18. "Literary Notices," *The Ladies Companion ...*, 1 (August 1834): 202.

19. Leggett, *Naval Stories*, 61–86. For background on Leggett, see Richard Hofstadter, "William Leggett, Spokesman of Jacksonian Democracy," *Political Science Quarterly*, 58 (1943): 581–94); Sean Wilentz, *The Rise of American Democracy: Jefferson to Lincoln* (New York: Norton, 2005), 422–24; Jeffrey Sklansky, "William Leggett and the Melodrama of the Market," in Michael Zakim and Gary J. Kornblith, eds., *Capitalism Takes Command: The Social Transformation of Nineteenth-Century America* (Chicago, IL: University of Chicago Press, 2012), 199–221.

20. Leggett, *Naval Stories*, 61.

21. "Original Nautical Tales: Forecastle Yarns," *The New-York Mirror*, 12 (August 9, 1834): 42.

22. "A Piratical Sketch," *The Huntress*, 2 (June 2, 1838): 1.

23. E. C. Wines, *Two Years and a Half in the Navy: Or, Journal of a Cruise in the Mediterranean and Levant* ... (Philadelphia, PA: Carey & Lea, 1832), 68.

24. Leech, *A Voice from the Main Deck*, 174–75.

25. William Reynolds, *The Private Journal of William Reynolds: United States Exploring Expedition, 1828–1842*, Nathaniel Philbrick and Thomas Philbrick, eds. (New York: Penguin, 2004), 51.

26. Nathaniel Ames, *An Old Sailor's Yarns* (New York: Dearborn, 1835).

27. Log of the *Hannibal*, kept by Nathaniel Sexton Morgan, 1849–50, Log 862, Mystic.

28. Log of the *La Plata*, 1848–50, Log 1847 W3 B15, PEM.

29. Log of the *Relief*, kept by William Clarke, 1833–39, Log 1838V, PEM.

30. Edward Cutbush, *Observations on the Means of Preserving the Health of Soldiers and Sailors* ... (Philadelphia, PA: Thomas Dobson, 1808), 127–28.

31. [Josiah Cobb], *A Green Hand's First Cruise, Roughed out from the Log-Book of Memory* ..., 2 vols. (Baltimore, MD: Cushing & Brother, 1841), 2: 83–84, 95.

32. George Little, *Life on the Ocean; or Twenty Years at Sea* ... (Baltimore, MD: Armstrong & Berry, 1843); Little, *The American Cruiser: A Tale of the Last War* (Boston, MA: W. J. Reynolds and Company, 1847); J. Ross Browne, *Etchings of a Whaling Cruise* ... (New York: Harper & Brothers, 1846); Log of the *Ohio*, kept by Hugh Calhoun, 1847–48, MHS.

33. Gilje, *Liberty on the Waterfront*; Daniel Vickers with Vince Walsh, *Young Men and the Sea: Yankee Seafarers in the Age of Sail* (New Haven, CT: Yale University Press, 2005).

34. Little, *Life on the Ocean*, 90–91, 104, 123–27, 135, 139–43, 164–67, 171–73, 175–76, 298.

35. Little, *The American Cruiser*, 122. See also ibid., 105–09, 134–39, 171–73, 218–26, 286–94.

36. Leech, *A Voice from the Main Deck*, 174–75.

37. Browne, *Etchings of a Whaling Cruise*, 79–97.

38. [Henry James Mercier], *Life in a Man of War, or Scenes in "Old Ironsides"* ... (Philadelphia, PA: L. R. Bailey, 1841), 48–49.

39. [Waterhouse], *A Journal of a Young Man of Massachusetts*, 129.

40. Browne, *Etchings of a Whaling Cruise*, 79–97.

41. [Mercier], *Life in a Man-of-War*, 55–59.

42. [Cobb], *A Green Hand's First Cruise*, 2: 83–84, 302; [Waterhouse], *A Journal of a Young Man of Massachusetts*, 129; Charles Tyng, *Before the Wind: The Memoir of an American Sea Captain, 1808–1833*, Susan Fels, ed. (New York: Penguin, 1999), 20, 57.

43. George Edward Clark, *Seven Years a Sailor's Life* (Boston, MA: Adams & Company, 1867), 306–07.

44. [Mercier], *Life in a Man-of-War*, 54.

45. Charles Nordhoff, *Man-of-War-Life: A Boy's Experience in the United States Navy* ..., John B. Hattendorf, intro. (Annapolis, MD: Naval Institute Press, 1985; orig. pub. 1855), 93–100.

46. Log of the *Ohio*, kept by Hugh Calhoun, 1847–48, MHS.

47. Browne, *Etchings of a Whaling Cruise*, 165–66, 170–82, 195. There is a children's book version of John Tabor's ride that skips over the alcohol issue and portrays Tabor as a young sailor unhappy about going to sea and he begins the ride from a ship. Edward C. Day, *John Tabor's Ride* (New York: Knopf, 1989).

48. Blum, *The View from the Masthead*; Myra C. Glenn, *Jack Tar's Story: The Autobiographies and Memoirs of Sailors in Antebellum America* (New York: Cambridge University Press, 2010).

49. John Blatchford, *Narrative of the Remarkable Occurrences, in the Life of John Blatchford* ... (New London, CT: T. Green, 1788); Owen Chase, "Narrative of the Most Extraordinary and Distressing Shipwreck of the Whale-Ship Essex ... " in Thomas Farel Heffernan, *Stove by a Whale: Owen Chase and the Essex* (Middletown, CT: Wesleyan University Press, 1981), 13–76; Ebenezer Fox, *The Adventures of Ebenezer Fox in the Revolutionary War...* (Boston, MA: Charles Fox, 1848).

50. Sarah J. Purcell, "John Blatchford's New America: Sailors. Print Culture, and Post-Colonial American Identity," in Paul A. Gilje and William Pencak, eds., *Pirates, Jack Tar, and Memory: New Directions in American Maritime History* (Mystic, CT: Mystic Seaport, 2007), 76.

51. Blatchford, *Narrative of the Remarkable Occurrences*. For quotations, see ibid., title page, 15, 16, 22.

52. Although this story can be interpreted as an example of a sailor's willingness to sail under any flag during the Revolutionary War in an effort just to survive, it can also be seen as an assertion of an American national identity because Blatchford's narrative always had his return home as its ultimate goal and it demonstrated to a broad national readership the sacrifices common seamen made in the struggle for independence. See. Gilje, *Liberty on the Waterfront*, 97–99; Purcell, "John Blatchford's New America: Sailors," in Gilje and Pencak, eds., *Pirates, Jack Tar, and Memory*, 73–93.

53. On the Revolutionary War, see Barnabas Downs Jr., *A Brief and Remarkable Narrative of the Life and Extreme Sufferings* ... Boston, MA: E. Russell, 1786); Nathaniel Fanning, *Narrative of the Adventures of Nathaniel Fanning* ... (New York: Printed for the Author, 1806); Israel R. Potter, *Life and Adventured of Israel Potter* ... (Providence, RI: J. Howard, 1824); Andrew Sherburne, *Memoirs of Andrew Sherburne* ... (Utica, NY: William Williams, 1828). On Barbary captivity, see John Foss, *A Journal of the Captivity and Sufferings of John Foss: Several Years a Prisoner in Algiers* ... (Newburyport, MA: A. March, [1798]); William Ray, *Horrors of Slavery; or the American Tars in Tripoli* ... (Troy, NY: Oliver Lyon, 1808). On the War of 1812, see Charles Andrews, *The Prisoners' Memoirs, or Dartmoor Prison* ... (New York: Printed for the Author, 1815); R. S. Coffin, *A Concise Narrative of the Barbarous Treatment* ... (Danville, VT: Ebenezer Eaton, 1816); [Charles Calvert Egerton], *The Journal of the Unfortunate Prisoner* ... (Baltimore, MD: Printed for the Author, 1813); Joshua Penny, *The Life and Adventures of Joshua Penny* ... (New York: Alden Spooner, 1815); [Waterhouse], *A Journal of a Young Man of Massachusetts*. See also Paul A. Gilje, *Free Trade and Sailors' Rights in the War of 1812* (New York: Cambridge University Press, 2013), 185–86.

54. Heffernan, *Stove by a Whale: Owen Chase and the Essex*, 70–71. See also Nathaniel Philbrick, *In the Heart of the Sea: The Tragedy of the Whaleship Essex* (New York: Viking, 2000).

55. Samuel Swett, *An Interesting Narrative of the Loss of the Ship Milo ...* (Newburyport, MA: William B. Allen, 1814); Charles H. Barnard, *A Narrative of the Sufferings of Capt. Charles H. Barnard ...* (New York: J. Lindon, 1829); James Riley *An Authentic Narrative of the Loss of the American Brig Commerce ...* (Hartford, CT: Printed for the Author, 1817); William Lay and Cyrus M. Hussey, *A Narrative of the Mutiny on Board the Whaleship Globe* (New London, CT: William Lay and C. M. Hussey, 1828); Barnabas Lincoln, *Narrative of the Capture, and Sufferings and Escape of Capt. Barnabas Lincoln and His Crew ...* (Boston, MA: Ezra Lincoln, 1822). On Riley, see also the discussion in Robert J. Allison, *The Crescent Obscured: The United States and the Muslim World, 1776–1815* (Chicago, IL: University of Chicago Press, 1995), 207–25.

56. Olaudah Equiano, *The Interesting Narrative of the Life of Olaudah Equiano, Written by Himself*, Robert J. Allison, ed. (Boston, MA: Bedford/ St. Martin's, 1995; orig. pub. 1789); Venture Smith, *A Narrative of the Life and Adventures of Venture, a Native of Africa ...* (New London, CT: C. Holt, 1798). See Vincent Carretta, *Equiano, the African: Biography of a Self-Made Man* (Athens: University of Georgia Press, 2005).

57. Robert Adams, *The Narrative of Robert Adams, an American Sailor, Who Was Wrecked on the Western Coast of Africa ...* (Boston, MA: Wells and Lilly, 1817). For another story by a black sailor, see Smith, *A Narrative of the Life and Adventures*.

58. Fox, *The Adventures of Ebenezer Fox*.

59. Tiphys Aegyptus, *The Navy's Friend, or Reminiscences of the Navy ...* (Baltimore, MD: Printed for the Author, 1843), 11, 15, 45, 43.

60. James Fenimore Cooper, ed., *Ned Myers, a Life before the Mast*, William S. Dudley, intro. (Annapolis, MD: Naval Institute Press, 1989; orig. pub. 1843), 73. On the collaboration, see Blum, *View from the Masthead*, 92–102; Blum, "Before and after the Mast: James Fenimore Cooper and Ned Myers," in Gilje and Pencak, eds., *Pirates, Jack Tar and Memory*, 115–34; Glenn, *Jack Tar's Story*, 19–20.

61. Ned Buntline, "Ned Buntline's Life-Yarn: An 'Ower True Talk,'" *Knickerbocker*, 26 (November 1845): 432–42. Quotations, ibid., 434, 439. See also Buntline, "Ned Buntline's Life Yarn," *Knickerbocker*, 27 (January 1846): 35–40; Buntline, *Ned Buntline's Life-Yarn* (New York: Garrett, 1849); Buntline, *The Last of the Buccaneers: A Yarn of the Eighteenth Century* (New York: G. Garrett, [1856]). For a list of works by Ned Buntline, see Jay Monaghan, *The Great Rascal: The Life and Adventures of Ned Buntline* (Boston, MA: Little, Brown and Company, 1952), 321–33.

62. Mark Valentine, "Mark Twain's Novels and Ned Buntline's Wildcat Literature," *Mark Twain Journal*, 48 (2010): 29–48; Peter G. Buckley, "The Case against Ned Buntline: The 'Words, Signs, and Gestures' of Popular Authorship," *Prospects*, 13 (1988): 249–72. Monaghan, *The Great Rascal*. Buntline even included the word "yarn" in one of his titles about urban life.

See *The Wheel of Misfortune, Or, the Victims of Lottery and Policy Dealers a Yarn from the Web of New York Life* (New York: Garrett, [1853]).

63. David S. Reynolds, *Beneath the American Renaissance: The Subversive Imagination in the Age of Emerson and Melville* (New York: Knopf, 1988), 275–308. Quotation from Melville, ibid., 278. For Melville and the Astor Place riot, see Buckley, "The Case against Ned Buntline."

64. Herman Melville, *White-Jacket, or the World in a Man-of-War*, Alfred Kazan, intro. (New York: New American Library, 1979; orig. pub. 1850), 11, 21, 103, 317–24; Melville, *Redburn: His First Voyage, Being the Sailor-boy Confessions and Reminiscences of the Son-of-a-Gentleman in the Merchant Service*, Harold Beaver, ed. (New York: Penguin, 1976; orig. pub. 1849), 107–08. See also Hershel Parker, *Herman Melville: A Biography, Volume I, 1819–1851* (Baltimore, MD: Johns Hopkins University Press, 1996), 194.

65. *Typee: A Peep at Polynesian Life during a Four Month Residence in a Valley in the Marquesas* (New York: New American Library, 1964; orig. pub. 1846); Parker, *Herman Melville*, 231, 354; Wallace E. Bezanson, "Herman Melville: Uncommon Common Sailor," in John Bryant and Robert Milder, eds., *Melville's Evermoving Dawn: Centennial Essays* (Kent, OH: Kent State University Press, 1997), 33, 39.

66. Herman Melville, *Israel Potter: His Fifty Years of Exile*, Harrison Hayford, et al., eds. (Evanston, IL: Northwestern University Press, 1982), 84, 161. Potter dictated his narrative to printer Henry Trumbull, who then published it in 1824. See "Melville's Basic Source" in ibid., 277–85. A facsimile of *Life and Remarkable Adventures of Israel Potter ...* (Providence, RI: Henry Trumbull, 1824) can be found in ibid., 286–394. See also David Chacko and Alexander Kulcsar, "Israel Potter: Genesis of a Legend," *WMQ*, 3rd ser., 61 (1984): 365–89.

67. J. N. Reynolds, "Mocha Dick: or the White Whale of the Pacific: A Leaf from a Manuscript," *Knickerbocker*, 13 (May 1839): 377–91, quotation on 384; Heffernan, *Stove by a Whale: Owen Chase and the Essex*; Herman Melville, *Moby Dick, or the Whale* (New York: Modern Library, 1982; orig. pub. 1851).

5. Songs of the Sailorman

1. Herman Melville, *Billy Budd, Sailor and Other Stories*, Harold Beaver, ed. (New York: Penguin, 1967; orig. pub. 1924), 321–32.

2. Samuel Leech, *A Voice from the Main Deck: Being a Record of the Thirty Years' Adventures of Samuel Leech*, Michael J. Crawford, ed. (Annapolis, MD: Naval Institute Press, 1999; orig. pub. 1843), 41–43.

3. See, for example, Folder 5, Box 1 – poems, love letters, and song lyrics from 1776, John Palmer Papers, 1776–86, Coll. 53, Mystic; Log of the *Vaughan*, kept by Francis Boardman, 1767, Log 1767V3 B24, NBWM; Log of the *General Wolfe*, 1767–69, Log 1767 L, PEM; Log of the *Three Sisters*, 1789–90, Log 1776A, PEM; Log of the *Polly*, kept by John Baker, 1804–05, Log 1804A B4, PEM; Charles P. Clinton, Journal, 1802–06, WA Ms 9, Beinecke; *Bengal*, kept by William Silver, 1832–35, Log 1832 B3, PEM; Log of the *Tusker*, 1840, Box 1, MH 32, Papers of Isaac W. Baker, PEM.

4. George G. Carey, ed., *A Sailor's Songbag: An American Rebel in an English Prison, 1777–1779* (Amherst: University of Massachusetts, 1976). See also Journal of Alden White, Vol. 4, Box 74, Series W, Sub-series 25, Alden White Papers, Biographical Collection, Ms 64, NBWM.

5. [Josiah Cobb], *A Green Hand's First Cruise, Roughed out from the Log-Book of Memory* ..., 2 vols. (Baltimore, MD: Cushing & Brother, 1841), 2: 165.

6. Roy Palmer, ed., *The Oxford Book of Sea Songs* (Oxford: Oxford University Press, 1986), xv–xvii.

7. Palmer, ed., *The Oxford Book of Sea Songs*, 1–2.

8. Stan Hugill emphasizes the difference between the art song and the folk song. Stan Hugill, *Shanties and Sailors' Songs* (New York: Frederick A. Praeger, 1969), 6–12. For the argument that the distinction between art songs and folk songs is an artificial construct, see Matthew Gelbart, *The Invention of "Folk Music" and "Art Music": Emerging Categories from Ossian to Wagner* (Cambridge: Cambridge University Press, 2007).

9. Palmer, ed., *The Oxford Book of Sea Songs*, 2–4, 8–10; Eric Nebeker, "The Heyday of the Broadside Ballad," *English Ballad Broadside Collection*, UCSB, http://ebba.english.ucsb.edu/page/heyday-of-the-broadside-ballad accessed December 11, 2013.

10. *The Sailor's Departure from his Dearest Love* (1681–84), EBBA ID: 21824, Magdalene College Pepys 4.162, UCSB, http://ebba.english.ucsb.edu accessed December 11, 2013. For similar ballads, see *A Dainty New Ditty of a Saylor and His Love* ... (1684–86), EBBA ID: 21819, Magdalene College Pepys 4.157, ibid.; *The Undaunted Marriner* ... (1664–1703), EBBA ID: 22188, Magdalene College Pepys 5.364, ibid.; *Loyal Constancy* ... (1672–96), EBBA ID: 30770, British Library Roxburghe 2.320–321, ibid.; *The Green-Sickness Grief* ... (1663–74?), EBBA ID: 31833, University of Glasgow Library Euing 125, ibid.; *The Jealous Lover* ... (1683–1703?), EBBA ID: 22191, Magdalene College Pepys 5.367, ibid.; *The Seaman's Adieu to His Dear* ... (1624–80?), EBBA ID: 30428, British Library Roxburghe 3.106–07, ibid.; *The Two Lymas Lovers* ... (1685–88), EBBA ID: 21828, Magdalene College Pepys 4.166 ibid.; Palmer, ed., *The Oxford Book of Sea Songs*, 38–64. For a sailor returning to his love, see *A Pleasant New Song betwixt a Saylor and His Love* ... (1691–84), EBBA ID: 21818, Magdalene College Pepys 4.156, ibid.

11. *The Perjured Sayler* (1693), EBBA ID: 22195, Magdalene College Pepys 5.371, UCSB, http://ebba.english.ucsb.edu accessed December 11, 2013. See also *The Cruel Lover: or, The False-Hearted Saylor* ... (1664–1703), EBBA ID: 22196, Magdalene College Pepys 5.372, ibid.; *An Excellent New Song, Call'd Nelly's Constancy, or Her Unkind Lover* ... (1690–1700?) EBBA ID: 22052, Magdalene College Pepys 5.217, ibid.

12. *The Laundry-Maids Lamentation for the Loss of Her Seaman* ... (1677–96), EBBA ID: 21826, Magdalene College Pepys 4.164, UCSB, http://ebba.english.ucsb.edu accessed December 17, 2013.

13. *The She-Mariners Misfortune* ... (1664–1703?), EBBA ID: 21849, Magdalene College Pepys 4.187, UCSB, http://ebba.english.ucsb.edu accessed December 17, 2013.

14. *The Maiden Sailor* ... (1693), EBBA ID: 22190, Magdalene College Pepys 5.366, UCSB, http://ebba.english.ucsb.edu accessed December 17, 2013.

15. *The Bristol Bridegroom* ... (1728–63), EBBA ID: 31374, British Library Roxburghe 3.859, UCSB, http://ebba.english.ucsb.edu accessed December 17, 2013. See also *An Excellent New Song, Called Billy's Answer to Phillis's Complaint* ... (1696), EBBA ID: 22177, Magdalene College Pepys 5.350, ibid.; *An Admirable New Northern Story* ... (1684), EBBA ID: 20255, Magdalene College Pepys 1.534–535, ibid. See also Dianne Dugaw, "Female Sailors Bold: Transvestite Heroines and Markers of Gender and Class," in Margaret S. Creighton and Lisa Norling, eds., *Iron Men, Wooden Women: Gender and Seafaring in the Atlantic World, 1700–1900* (Baltimore, MD: Johns Hopkins University Press, 1996), 34–54.

16. *Love without Blemish. Or, the Unfortunate Couple* ... (1681–84), EBBA ID: 21346, Magdalene College Pepys 3.331, UCSB, http://ebba.english.ucsb.edu accessed December 17, 2013; *The Two Unfortunate Lovers* ... (1685–88), EBBA ID: 21365, Magdalene College Pepys 3.350, ibid.

17. *The Benjamin's Lamentation for Their Sad Loss at Sea* ... (1684–95), EBBA ID: 21862, Magdalene College Pepys 4.200, UCSB, http://ebba.english.ucsb.edu accessed December 17, 2013. See also Palmer, ed., *The Oxford Book of Sea Songs*, 44–47, 64–66.

18. Linda Colley, *Captives: Britain, Empire and the World, 1600–1850* (New York: Random House, 2002), 82–84.

19. Stuart M. Frank, *The Book of Pirate Songs* (Sharon, MA: The Kendall Whaling Museum, 1998), 2–47. Quotations, ibid., 15, 27, 41.

20. *An Excellent New Song, Entitled a Hot Engagement between a French Privateer and an English Fire-Ship* (1691), EBBA ID: 22208, Magdalene College Pepys 5.386, UCSB, http://ebba.english.ucsb.edu accessed December 11, 2013. See also Palmer, ed., *The Oxford Book of Sea Songs*, 62–64.

21. *Buxom Joan of Lymas's Love to a Jolly Tar* ... (1672–96?), EBBA ID: 22185, Magdalene College Pepys 5.361, UCSB, http://ebba.english.ucsb.edu accessed December 11, 2013.

22. *A Jobb for a Journeyman-Shoomaker, with a Kind-Hearted Seamans Wife* ... (1671–1702?), EBBA ID: 21842, Magdalene College Pepys 4.180, UCSB, http://ebba.english.ucsb.edu accessed December 11, 2013.

23. *The Seamens Wives Frolick oer a Punch Bowl* ... (1685–88), EBBA ID: 21846, Magdalene College Pepys 4.184, UCSB, http://ebba.english.ucsb.edu accessed December 11, 2013. For a response in defense of seamen's wives, see *The Seamens Wives Vindication, Or, An Answer to the Pretended Frolick, Which Was Said to Be by Them over a Bowl of PUNCH* ... (1685–88), EBBA ID: 21847, Magdalene College Pepys 4.185, ibid.

24. *A Warning for Married Women* ... (1650?), EBBA ID: 30338, British Library Roxburghe 1.502, UCSB, http://ebba.english.ucsb.edu accessed December 17, 2013.

25. *A Farewell to Graves-end...* (1671–1702?), EBBA ID: 30876, British Library Roxburghe 4.3, UCSB, http://ebba.english.ucsb.edu accessed December 17, 2013.

26. *The Seaman's Frolick: Or, a Cooler for the Captain* ... (1680–82), EBBA ID: 21875, Magdalene College Pepys 4.213, UCSB, http://ebba.english.ucsb .edu accessed December 11, 2013.

27. *The Mothers Kindness, Conquer'd by her Daughters Vindication of Valient and Renowned Seamen* ... (1675–96), EBBA ID: 21874, Magdalene College Pepys 4.212, UCSB, http://ebba.english.ucsb.edu accessed December 11, 2013. See also *The Praise of Saylors Is Here Set Forth* ... (1681–84), EBBA ID: 21859, Magdalene College Pepys 4.197, ibid.; *Saylors for My Money* ... (1630), EBBA ID: 20197, Magdalene College Pepys 1.420–421, ibid.; *The Boatswain's Call* ... (1675–96?), EBBA ID: 21868, Magdalene College Pepys 4.206, ibid.

28. *Neptune's Raging Fury* ... (1684–86), EBBA ID: 21863, Magdalene College Pepys 4.201, UCSB, http://ebba.english.ucsb.edu accessed December 11, 2013. See also *The Praise of Sailors Is Here Set Forth* ... (1681–84), EBBA ID: 21859, Magdalene College Pepys 4.197, ibid.; *Saylors for My Money* ... (1630), EBBA ID: 20197, Magdalene College Pepys 1.420–421, ibid.; *The Boatswain's Call* ... (1675–96?), EBBA ID: 21868, Magdalene College Pepys 4.206, ibid.; *The Sea-man's Compass* ... (1623–61?), EBBA ID: 31990, University of Glasgow Library Euing 325, ibid.; *The Jovial Mariner...* (1664–88?), EBBA ID: 32976, University of Glasgow Library Crawford 544, ibid.; Palmer, ed., *The Oxford Book of Sea Songs*, 4–5, 21–24, 27–29, 33–36.

29. *The Dover Lovers...* (1690–1700), EBBA ID: 22187, Magdalene College Pepys 5.363, UCSB, http://ebba.english.ucsb.edu accessed December 17, 2013; *The Undaunted Marriner* ... (1669–73), EBBA ID: 22188, Magdalene College Pepys 5.364, ibid.; *The Couragious Seaman* ... (1690), EBBA ID: 21872, Magdalene College Pepys 4.210, ibid.

30. *The Seaman's Loyal Love* ... (1692), EBBA ID: 21879, Magdalene College Pepys 4.217, UCSB, http://ebba.english.ucsb.edu accessed December 17, 2013.

31. *The Undaunted Seaman* ... (1675–96), EBBA ID: 21873, Magdalene College Pepys 4.211, UCSB, http://ebba.english.ucsb.edu accessed December 17, 2013.

32. *The Protestant Seaman's Resolution To Fight for King William* ... (1690), EBBA ID: 21870, Magdalene College Pepys 4.208, UCSB, http://ebba .english.ucsb.edu accessed December 17, 2013. See also *The Boatswains Call* ... (1675–96?), EBBA ID: 21868, Magdalene College Pepys 4.206, *ibid.*; *The Protestant Courage...* (1671–1702), EBBA ID: 21871, Magdalene College Pepys 4.209, *ibid.*; *The English-mans Valour...* (1660–85), EBBA ID: 31813, University of Glasgow Library Euing 107, *ibid.*; Palmer, ed., *The Oxford Book of Sea Songs*, 29–30, 56–57.

33. *The Sea-Martyrs* ... (1691), EBBA ID: 22198, Magdalene College Pepys 5.375, UCSB, http://ebba.english.ucsb.edu accessed December 17, 2013. See also Palmer, ed., *The Oxford Book of Sea Songs*, 6–7, 58–62, 70–72, 80–82.

34. Palmer, ed., *The Oxford Book of Sea Songs*, 8–11, 66–68, 30–33. See also ibid., 13–17, 24–29, 41–44, 50–53.

35. Richard Baker and Antony Miall, *Everyman's Book of Sea Songs* (London: J. M. Dent & Sons, Ltd, 1982), 17–21, 29–32.

36. Leech, *A Voice from the Main Deck*, 19.
37. Baker and Miall, *Everyman's Book of Sea Songs*, 125–28.
38. Palmer, ed., *The Oxford Book of Sea Songs*, 93–94, 96–97, 122–24.
39. *The Gosport Tragedy...* (1728–63), EBBA ID: 31213, British Library Roxburghe 3.510–511, UCSB, http://ebba.english.ucsb.edu accessed December 17, 2013. Palmer, ed., *The Oxford Book of Sea Songs*, 126–29, 101–02.
40. *Two Excellent New Songs...* (1740?), EBBA ID: 31089, British Library Roxburghe 3.386, UCSB, http://ebba.english.ucsb.edu accessed December 17, 2013.
41. *The Breath of Life...* (1763–75?), EBBA ID: 31440, British Library Roxburghe 3.722–723, UCSB, http://ebba.english.ucsb.edu accessed December 17, 2013.
42. Log of the *Union*, kept by Peter Pease, 1770–71, ODHS Log 458D, NBWM; Log of the *Herald*, kept by Thomas Delano, 1817–19, PPL.
43. Clare A. Lyons, *Sex among the Rabble: An Intimate History of Gender and Power in the Age of Revolution, Philadelphia, 1730–1830* (Chapel Hill: University of North Carolina Press, 2006), 130, 155–56. For other American prerevolutionary sources, see Log of the *Vaughan*, kept by Francis Boardman, 1767, Log 1767V3 B24, PEM; Log of the *General Wolfe*, 1767–69, Log 1767 L, PEM.
44. A DVD collection of colonial and revolutionary sea songs has three songs that mention John Paul Jones. One is a recent translation of a contemporary Dutch song. The other two do not have a clear date for their origin. The collection also includes a song about privateersman Abraham Whipple. *Colonial and Revolutionary War Sea Songs and Chantey, Sung at Seaport '76* by Cliff Haslam and John Millar, CD, Smithsonian Folkways Archive. See also Palmer, ed., *The Oxford Book of Sea Songs*, 141–43. For a broadside with a privateering song featuring John Manly, see *Manly: A Favorite New Song* in NBWM. See also Log of the *Boston*, kept by Samuel Tucker, 1778, Log 1778B B2, PEM.
45. Folder 5, Box 1, John Palmer Papers, 1776–86, Coll. 53, Mystic.
46. Joshua Davis, *A Narrative of Joshua Davis ...* (Baltimore, MD: B. Edes, 1811), 35–37. See also Paul A. Gilje, *Liberty on the Waterfront: American Maritime Culture in the Age of Revolution* (Philadelphia: University of Pennsylvania Press, 2004), 129.
47. Christopher Hawkins, *The Adventures of Christopher Hawkins ...* (New York: Privately Printed, 1864), 62–64.
48. Albert Greene, *Recollections of the Jersey Prison-Ship ...* (Providence, RI: H. H. Brown, 1829). See also John van Dyke, "Narrative of Confinement in the Jersey Prison Ship by John Van Dyke, Captain in Lamb's Regiment, NYSA." *Historical Magazine*, 7 (May 1863): 148–49; Charles Herbert, *A Relic of the Revolution ...* (Boston, MA: Charles H. Pierce, 1847), 50.
49. Folder 5, Box 1, John Palmer Papers, 1776–86, Coll. 53, Mystic.
50. Carey, ed., *A Sailor's Songbag*, 110–11. See also ibid., 120–21.
51. Carey, ed., *A Sailor's Songbag*, 56–57, 42–43. See also ibid., 58–64.
52. Carey, ed., *A Sailor's Songbag*, 67–68. See also ibid., 96–97, 130, 152–53.
53. Carey, ed., *A Sailor's Songbag*, 132–33. See also ibid., 37, 40–41, 44–49, 65–68, 74–79, 84–89, 100–01, 106–09, 136–37, 140–41, 144–45, 150–51.

54. Carey, ed., *A Sailor's Songbag*, 128–29. For "fuck," see 24–25, 116. See also 24–31, 50–51, 80–81, 90–95, 98–99, 102–04, 112–13, 116–19, 122–29, 142–43, 147–49. For general background, see Gilje, *Liberty on the Waterfront*, 97–129.

55. Thomas Dibden, *Songs, Naval and National, of the Late Charles Dibden; with a Memoir and Addenda* (London: John Murray, 1841), 58–59.

56. Baker and Miall, *Everyman's Book of Sea Songs*, 3–10. For a book full of Dibden's maritime music, see Dibden, *Songs, Naval and National, of the Late Charles Dibden*.

57. Palmer, ed., *The Oxford Book of Sea Songs*, 168–69, 174–75. For similar songs, see ibid., 162–64, 171–73, 176–77; Baker and Miall, *Everyman's Book of Sea Songs*, 129–38.

58. Palmer, ed., *The Oxford Book of Sea Songs*, 164–65, 66–68, 172–73.

59. *The Political Harmonist* ... (London: T. Williams, 1797), 35–36. Bethany R. Mowry, "Labor, Lyrics and the Land-Sea Link: The Functions of Sea Songs and Shanties in the Anglo-American Atlantic, 1760–1815," unpublished manuscript; Isaac Land, *War, Nationalism and the British Sailor, 1750–1850* (London: Palgrave, 2009), 106. For the larger English context, see E. P. Thompson, *The Making of the English Working Class* (New York: Pantheon, 1963).

60. For a contrasting argument, see Robert D. Madison, "Hymns, Chanteys and Sea Songs," in Haskell Springer, ed. *America and the Sea: A Literary History* (Athens: University of Georgia Press, 1995), 99–108.

61. The song in question was not identified, but it was "Jack at Greenwich." *New Haven Connecticut Herald*, June 11, 1805.

62. *The Festival of Mirth, and American Tar's Delight* ... (New York: Thomas B. Jansen, 1800), 10–11, 46–48. A few entries did mention Dibden by name. See ibid., 49. See also *The Sailor's Medley: A Collection of the Most Admired Sea and Other Songs* (Philadelphia, PA: Matthew Carey, 1800); *The Syren: A Choice Collection of Sea Hunting, and Other Songs* (Philadelphia, PA: Matthew Carey, 1800); *The Nautical Songster or Seaman's Companion* ... (Baltimore, MD: Henry S. Keatinge, 1798). For sheet music, see Charles Dibden, *The Lucky Escape* (Philadelphia, PA: Carr & Rice, [1794]); Dibden, *The Token* (Philadelphia, PA: Carr, [1794]); Dibden, *Twas in the Good Ship Rover; or the Greenwich Pensioner* (Philadelphia, PA: Carr, [1794]); James Cobb, *The Capture: A Favorite Song in the Pirates Composed by S. Storace* (Philadelphia, PA: Carr, [1793]); Cobb, *Lullaby – A Favorite Ballad in the Comic Opera of the Pirates* (Philadelphia, PA: Carr, [1793]); Cobb, *A Sailor Lov'd a Lass, Composed for the Cherokee by S. Storace* (Philadelphia, PA: Carr, [1796]); Prince Hoare, *The Sailor Boy* (Philadelphia, PA: Carr, 1793); [William Reeve], *When Seated with Sal: A Favorite Sea Song Sung by Mr. Harwood in the Purse, or Benevolent Tar* (Philadelphia, PA: Carr, [1795]); Steven Storace, *The Shipwrecked Seaman's Ghost* (Philadelphia, PA: Carr, 1793). See also [Isaac Bickerstaff], *Thomas and Sally: Or, the Sailor's Return* ... (Philadelphia, PA: Henry Taylor, 1791); Richard Cumberland, *The Sailor's Daughter: A Comedy in*

Five Acts (New York: David Longworth, 1804); J. C. Cross, *Songs in the Purse; or, Benevolent Tar, A Musical Drama in One Act. As Performed at the New Theatre, Philadelphia* (Philadelphia, PA: Wrigley and Berriman, 1794).

63. Charles Dibden, *Poor Tom Bowling* [sheet music] (Philadelphia, PA: Carr, [1794]). *Charleston Morning Post*, March 12, 1787; *Philadelphia Independent Gazetteer*, October 12, 1789; *Philadelphia Federal Gazette*, July 1, 1790; *Philadelphia General Advertiser*, January 31, 1793; *Hartford American Mercury*, October 12, 1795; *Portland Gazette*, January 13, 1806.

64. *The Cabin-Boy and Forecastle Sailor's Delight ...* (New York: S. A. Burtus, 1817), 27–28.

65. Susanna Rowson, *New Song ... The Sailor's Landlady* (Philadelphia, PA: M. Carey, [1794]). For a more sentimentalized view of the sailor, see Rowson, *The Little Sailor Boy. A Ballad ...* (Philadelphia, PA: Carr, [1798]).

66. Susanna Rowson, *Truxton's Victory: A Naval Patriotic Song* ([Boston, MA: Thomas and Andrews, 1799]); Rowson, *Huzza for the Constellation* (Philadelphia, PA: J. Carr, [1799]); Rowson, *Captain Truxton or "Huzza" for the Constellation* (New York: J. Hewett, [1799]). See Marion Rust, *Prodigal Daughters: Susanna Rowson's Early American Women* (Chapel Hill: University of North Carolina Press, 2008).

67. *Boston Price-Current*, November 2, 1797; *Philadelphia Gazette*, September 18, 1797; *Boston Massachusetts Mercury*, November 3, 1797; *New York Daily Advertiser*, May 30, 1798; *New-York Gazette*, June 1, 1798. See also Paul A. Gilje, *Free Trade and Sailors' Rights in the War of 1812* (New York: Cambridge University Press, 2013), 85–98; Liam Riordan, "'O Dear What Can the Matter Be?' The Urban Early Republic and the Politics of Popular Songs in Benjamin Carr's *Federal Overture*," *JER*, 31 (2011): 179–227.

68. Robert J. Allison, *The Crescent Obscured: The United States and the Muslim World, 1776–1815* (Chicago: Chicago University Press, 1995), 187–206.

69. *Washington, D. C., National Intelligencer*, July 20, 1807.

70. *New York Public Advertiser*, July 9, 1807.

71. *The American Republican Harmonist ...* (Philadelphia, PA: William Duane, 1803), 1, 10, 21, 24, 53–54, 61, 68, 73, 90, 102, 103, 122–23. Quotations ibid., 21, 53–54.

72. These lines appear under the heading "poetry," but because there are several stanzas all with the same refrain at the end, in all probability the lines were meant to be sung. Other songs in newspapers at this time appeared under the heading of poetry. *Hallowell, Massachusetts [Maine], American Advocate*, November 1, 1810.

73. Log of the *Ann and Hope*, kept by Benjamin Carter, 1799–1800, Ms 828, RIHS; Log of the *Boston*, kept by Samuel Tucker, 1778, Log 1778B B2, PEM.

74. The songs in this book were copied down by both Charles P. Clinton and Ebenezer Clinton, apparently a relative on the same ship. It is not always clear which Clinton copied which song. Clinton, Journal, 1802–06, WA Ms 9, Beinecke.

75. Joshua Gott, Commonplace Book, 1781–1807, PEM.

76. Log of the *Prudent*, kept by Holton J. Breed, 1804–06, Log 1804 P3, PEM.

77. Although the log is dated before the Embargo of 1807, this song and others were written at the end of the log and must have been added after Baker's return from the voyage chronicled in the log. Log of the *Polly*, kept by John Baker, 1804–05, Log 1804A B4, PEM.

78. William Ray, *Horrors of Slavery: or the American Tars in Tripoli ...* (Troy, NY: Oliver Lyon, 1808), 149. See also Gilje, *Liberty on the Waterfront*, 151–56.

79. Some of the material in this source may just be poetry. But the label and context of Waller's famous poem suggest that it was intended to be sung. Log of the *Polly*, kept by John Baker, 1804–05, Log 1804A B4, PEM; *Scots Magazine, and Edinburgh Literary Miscellany, Being General*, 66 (1804): 776; John D. Ross, ed., *Celebrated Songs of Scotland: From King James V. to Henry Scott Riddell* (New York: William Pagan, Jr., & Son, 1887), 304–06.

80. Log of the *Three Sisters*, 1789–90, Log 1776A, PEM. The *Salem Gazette* reference was not found. But the same article appeared in *Boston Massachusetts Centinel*, January 6, 1790. See also Luminarium: Anthology of English Literature, Web site, "A Song," by Lord Rochester, http://www.luminarium .org/eightlit/rochester/phillis.htm, accessed January 13, 2014; Dibden, *Songs, Naval and National, of the Late Charles Dibden*, 6–7, 305–06.

81. Clinton, Journal, 1802–06, WA Ms 9, Beinecke; *Hood Triumphant* (London: J. Evans, 1793).

82. Clinton, Journal, 1802–06, WA Ms 9, Beinecke. The dating of *The Rochester Lass* remains conjectural. It was published in London without a clear date. It was also published in the United States in 1805, after Clinton went to sea. *The Rochester Lass*, broadside (London: Pitts, n.d.); *Tom Tuff, Decatur's Victory, James Irwin, The Rochester Lass. As Sure as a Gun* (Philadelphia, PA: s.n. 1805?).

83. Clinton, Journal, 1802–06, WA Ms 9, Beinecke; John Ashton, *Real Sailor-Songs* (London: Leadenhall Press, 1891), 70–71.

84. Clinton, Journal, 1802–06, WA Ms 9, Beinecke; *Spicer's Pocket Companion* (Northampton, MA?: A Wright?, 1800?), 53–54; Dibden, *Songs, Naval and National*, 315–17.

85. Clinton, Journal, 1802–06, WA Ms 9, Beinecke.

86. For good general surveys of the War of 1812, see Donald R. Hickey, *The War of 1812: A Forgotten Conflict*, Bicentennial edition (Champaign: University of Illinois Press, 2012); J. C. A. Stagg, *The War of 1812: Conflict for a Continent* (New York: Cambridge University Press, 2012). For the naval conflict, see Kevin D. McCranie, *Utmost Gallantry: The U.S. and Royal Navies at Sea in the War of 1812* (Annapolis, MD: Naval Institute Press, 2011); William M. Fowler, *Jack Tars and Commodores: The American Navy, 1783–1815* (Boston, MA: Houghton Mifflin, 1984).

87. *Charleston City Gazette*, September 21, 1812.

88. *New York Evening Post*, January 8, 1813.

89. *New York Statesman*, September 4, 1812; William Dunlap, *Yankee Chronology; or, Huzza for the Constitution! ...* (New York: D. Longworth, 1812). Dunlap even felt compelled to explain that the line had really referred to the "felicity of the cultivators of the soil in this country" to obscure its

obvious prediction of military victories on land. For the song, see Dunlap, *Yankee Chronology*, 9–12. Quotation, ibid., 12.

90. *The Naval Songster, or the Sailor's Pocket Companion* (Boston, MA: Coverly, 1813), 3–7.

91. *New York Columbian*, December 12, 1812; *Philadelphia Poulson's American Daily Advertiser*, October 6, 1812; *New York Columbian*, November 4, 1812; *Boston Gazette*, February 22, 1813; *Boston Daily Advertiser*, March 18, 1813; *Boston New England Palladium*, April 30, 1813; *Albany Gazette*, May 31, 1813; *Philadelphia Democratic Press*, August 27, 1813; *Providence Rhode Island American*, September 10, 1813; *New York Columbian*, November 29, 1813.

92. "The Lads of Columbia," *New York Columbian*, September 12, 1812; "Ye Tars of Columbia," *Newark (New Jersey) Centinel of Freedom*, September 15, 1812; "Hull's Victory ..." *Hallowell, Massachusetts [Maine], American Advocate*, September 17, 1812; "The Yankee Sea Fight," *Charleston, The Investigator*, September 25, 1812; "Good Ship Columbia," *Boston Gazette*, October 1, 1812; "A Song – Written in '76," *Burlington Vermont Centinel*, October 29, 1812; "Constitution and Guerriere," *Raleigh Star*, October 30, 1812; "Sea Song," *Chillicothe (Ohio) Supporter*, November 7, 1812; "The American Tars on Shore," *Baltimore American and Commercial Advertiser*, December 11, 1812; "Yankee Tars," *New York Columbian*, December 14, 1812; "Yankee Frolics," *New York Gazette*, February 19, 1813; "The Battle of Lake Erie," *Philadelphia Voice of the Nation*, October 5, 1813; "Columbian Tars Fight Victorious," ibid., November 9, 1813; "Bainbridge's Tid-Rel-I," *Elizabethtown New Jersey Journal*, February 15, 1814; "Sea Song," *Clinton Ohio Register*, May 10, 1814; "Saturday Night at Sea," *Goshen (New York) Orange County Gazette*, August 16, 1814; *The Naval Songster* (1813). For additional songsters, see *The Naval Songster, Containing a Collection of the Best Selected Naval Songs ...* (Frederick Town, MD: Bartgis, 1814); Edward C. Holland, *Odes, Naval Songs, and Other Occasional Poems* (Charleston, SC: J. Hoff, 1813).

93. *The Naval Songster* (1814), 31–32. See also ibid., 9, 19–21, 25–29.

94. *Goshen (New York) Orange County Gazette*, August 16, 1814.

95. Holland, *Odes, Naval Songs*, 22–23.

96. *The Naval Songster* (1814), 50–55. For other War of 1812 naval versions, see *New York Western Star*, March 13, 1813; *Washington, D. C. Daily National Intelligencer*, May 29, 1813. For early antecedents, see *A New Ballad of King John and the Abbott of Canterbury ...* (1672–85?), EBBA ID: 31305, British Library Roxburghe 3.883, UCSB, http://ebba.english.ucsb.edu accessed January 8, 2014. For the British lineage, see William Chappell, *Ballad Literature and Popular Music of the Olden Time*, 2 vols. (London: 1855–59), 1: 348–53. For examples of a colonial appearance of the song, see *Philadelphia American Weekly Mercury*, December 6–14, 1733; *Williamsburg Virginia Gazette*, February 11, 1737. For an example of its use in Revolutionary politics, see *Baltimore Maryland Journal*, July 26, 1775. For examples of its use in the early republic, see *Boston Massachusetts Gazette*, November 30, 1787; *New York Commercial Advertiser*, August 4, 1798.

97. R. S. Coffin, *A Concise Narrative of the Barbarous Treatment* ... (Danville, VT: Ebenezer Eaton, 1816), 23–24.

98. *Narrative of the Capture of the United States' Brig Vixen* ... (New York: Office of "The War," 1813), 18–19; Joshua Penny, *The Life and Adventures of Joshua Penny* ... (New York: Alden Spooner, 1815), 29–30; Benjamin F. Palmer, *The Diary of Benjamin F. Palmer, Privateersman* ... (n. p.: Acorn Club, 1914), 14–15, 23, 57, 63.

99. [Cobb], *A Green Hand's First Cruise*, 1: 155–61.

100. Journal of Alden White, Vol. 4, Box 74, Series W, Sub-series 25, Alden White Papers, Biographical Collection, Ms 64, NBWM.

101. [Benjamin Waterhouse], *A Journal of a Young Man of Massachusetts* ... (Lexington, KY: Worsley & Smith, 1816), 123; *The Impressment of an American Sailor Boy*, Broadside, N-YHS.

102. [Cobb], *A Green Hand's First Cruise*, 2: 165–66; Charles Andrews, *The Prisoner's Memoirs, or Dartmoor Prison* ... (New York: For the Author, 1815).

103. Andrews, *The Prisoner's Memoirs, or Dartmoor Prison*, 93, 96–104, 154–61. For expanded treatments of Dartmoor, see Gilje, *Liberty on the Waterfront*, 178–91; Gilje, *Free Trade and Sailors' Rights*, 262–75.

104. Gilje, *Free Trade and Sailors' Rights*, 199–214. For a collection of naval patriotic songs, see Robert W. Neeser, ed., *American Naval Songs and Ballads* (New Haven, CT: Yale University Press, 1938).

105. [Waterhouse], *A Journal of a Young Man of Massachusetts*, 81.

106. Several writers have looked back on the 1815 to 1860 period not only as the halcyon days of the age of sail, but also the great age of the sailor song. See Stan Hugill, *Shanties and Sailors' Songs*, 1–66; Hugill, *Shanties from the Seven Seas: Shipboard Work-Songs and Songs Used as Work-Songs from the Great Days of Sail* (Mystic, CT: Mystic Seaport Museum, 1994), 12, 35; Joanna C. Colcord, *Songs of American Sailormen* (New York: Norton, 1938), 17–22. See also Terry L. Kinsey, *Songs of the Sea* (London: Robert Hale, 1989), 11–44.

107. Richard Henry Dana Jr., *Two Years before the Mast: A Personal Narrative of Life at Sea*, Thomas Philbrick, ed. (New York: Penguin, 1981; orig. pub. 1840), 342–43; Hugill, *Shanties from the Seven Seas*, 1–23. For the use of shanties, see J. Ross Browne, *Etchings of a Whaling Cruise* ... (New York: Harper & Brothers, 1846), 133–34; Joseph G. Clark, *Lights and Shadows of Sailor Life* ... (Boston, MA: Benjamin B. Mussey, 1848), 271; Log of the *John G. Coster*, kept by Thomas W. Abbot, MHS; Augustus Alvey Adee to Amelia (his wife), Dec. 24, 1840, Folder 1, Box 1, Adee Family Papers, LC. On the historical background of the shanty, see Hugill, *Shanties and Sailor Songs*, 1–66. Shanties can also be found in Frederick J. Davis and Ferris Tozer, *Sailors' Songs or "Chanties"* (London: Boosley & Co., [1906]); William Main Doerflinger, *Songs of the Sailor and Lumberman*, rev. ed. (New York: MacMillan, 1972); orig. pub. 1951); Stuart M. Frank, "Ballads and Songs of the Whale-Hunters, 1825–1895: From the Manuscripts in the Kendall Museum" (PhD diss., Brown University, 1985); Frederick Pease Harlow, *Chanteying Aboard American Ships* (Barre, MA: Barre Publishing,

1962); Robert Lloyd Webb, "'Make Some Noise Boys!' Deepwater Sea Chanteys," *Aquashpere*, 16 (1982–83): 18–24.

108. Gilje, *Liberty on the Waterfront*, 66–94; Carl C. Cutler, *Greyhounds of the Sea: The Story of the American Clipper Ship*, 3rd ed. (Annapolis, MD: Naval Institute Press, 1984; orig. pub. 1930).

109. Dana Jr., *Two Years before the Mast*, 193–94, 342–43, 346–48.

110. Roger D. Abrahams, *Deep Water, Shallow the Shore Three Essays on Shantying in the West Indies* (Austin: University of Texas Press, 1974); W. Jeffrey Bolster, *Black Jacks: African American Seamen in the Age of Sail* (Cambridge, MA: Harvard University Press, 1997); David S. Cecelski, *The Waterman's Song: Slavery and Freedom in Maritime North Carolina* (Chapel Hill: University of North Carolina Press, 2001).

111. Augustus Alvey Adee to Amelia (his wife), Dec. 24, 1840, Folder 1, Box 1, Adee Family Papers, LC.

112. Hugill, *Shanties from the Seven Seas*, 5, 18, 43–48, 115–22, 140–45, 215–32, 299–95; Hugill, *Shanties and Sailors' Songs*, 122–24; Palmer, ed., *The Oxford Book of Sea Songs*, 124–25; Baker and Miall, *Everyman's Book of Sea Songs*, 156–59.

113. For a sample of such comments, see Hugill, *Shanties from the Seven Seas*, 135, 138, 140, 156, 158, 165, 182.

114. Hugill, *Shanties from the Seven Seas*, 137–40.

115. Colcord, *Songs of American Sailormen*, 49–50, 78.; Hugill, *Shanties from the Seven Seas*, 109–10, 202–07.

116. Hugill, *Shanties from the Seven Seas*, 283–85. See also ibid., 176–78, 241–44, 305–06, 402–06.

117. Hugill, *Shanties from the Seven Seas*, 341–43.

118. Colcord, *Songs of American Sailormen*, 42.

119. Hugill, *Shanties from the Seven Seas*, 218–22, 241–44, 254–55.

120. Hugill, *Shanties from the Seven Seas*, 139–45, 215–16, 323–26, 366–69; Colcord, *Songs of American Sailormen*, 83.

121. Hugill, *Shanties from the Seven Seas*, 74–82, 139–44.

122. Log of the *Herald*, kept by Thomas Delano, 1817–19, PPL. See also Gale Huntington, *Songs the Whalemen Sang* (Barre, MA: Barre Publishers, 1964), 100–02. Huntington compiled 175 songs from more than seventy logbooks and journals and thus provides a wonderful source for the forebitter. Twenty-five of the songs are not from the 1815 to 1861 period. Of the remaining 150 songs more than a third were sentimentally romantic and another 29 sentimentally described ships and the sea. Only nine could be considered bawdy – in the broadest sense. Some commentators define forebitters as unsentimental. See Kinsey, *Songs of the Sea*, 120. The analysis in this chapter defines forecastle songs as those songs found in journals and logbooks. Huntington thus provides a good guide for the nature of the forecastle song. In addition I have examined logbook and journals myself. See also the forecastle songs in Colcord, *Songs of American Sailormen*, 125–207; and Hugill, *Shanties and Sailor Songs*, 208–32.

123. Perhaps even more of these lyrics would have survived had not some censor, maybe the sailor himself or a relative, not cut out what might have

been offending passages. The bottom of the page with the lines just cited has been sliced out, and whole sections were removed from a songbook written aboard the *Cortes* in 1847. See also Log of the *Herald*, kept by Thomas Delano, 1817–19, PPL; Huntington, *Songs the Whalemen Sang*, 185–86, 190–92, 263–64. For drinking, see ibid., 203–04. For abuse of sailors at sea, see ibid., 15–17, 47–49. See also Colcord, *Songs of American Sailormen*, 136–40, 156–57, 168–69, 176–77, 180–82, 185–86; Hugill, *Shanties and Sailor Songs*, 208–26, 230–33.

124. Stuart M. Frank, *Oooh, You New York Girls! The Urban Pastorale in Ballads and Songs about Sailors Ashore in the Big City* (Sharon, MA: Kendall Whaling Museum, 1996), 11–19.

125. Jon W. Finson, *The Voices that Are Gone: Themes in Nineteenth-Century American Popular Song* (New York: Oxford University Press, 1994).

126. Huntington, *Songs the Whalemen Sang*, 99–100, 62–63, 119–22.

127. Huntington, *Songs the Whalemen Sang*, 63–64, 11–15, 17–27, 30–32, 34–38, 42–46, 68–70, 96–98.

128. Colcord, *Songs of American Sailormen*, 126–33; Huntington, *Songs the Whalemen Sang*, 161–62, 160, 170, 278–79.

129. [Henry James Mercier], *Life in a Man-of-War, or Scenes in "Old Ironsides"* ... (Philadelphia, PA: L. R. Bailey, 1841), 223–25.

130. Herman Melville, *Redburn: His First Voyage, Being the Sailor-boy Confessions and Reminiscences of the Son-of-a-Gentleman in the Merchant Service*, Harold Beaver, ed. (New York: Penguin, 1976; orig. pub. 1849), 264; Dana Jr., *Two Years before the Mast*, 367.

131. George Little, *Life on the Ocean; or Twenty Years at Sea* ... (Baltimore, MD: Armstrong & Berry, 1843), 172.

132. Frank, *The Book of Pirate Songs*, 80–81, 85–89; Huntington, *Songs the Whalemen Sang*, 74–81.

133. Log of the *Herald*, and other vessels, kept by Thomas Delano, 1817–19, PPL; Huntington, *Songs the Whalemen Sang*, 103–05, 111–12. See also Caroline Moseley, "Images of Young Women in Nineteenth-Century Songs of the Sea," *Log of Mystic Seaport*, 35 (1984): 132–39.

134. [Mercier], *Life in a Man-of-War*, 206–07.

135. Huntington, *Songs the Whalemen Sang*, 232–61; Dibden, *Songs, Naval and National*, 3.

136. Dana Jr., *Two Years before the Mast*, 347.

137. *Baltimore Gazette and Daily Advertiser*, June 4, 1830.

138. *New York Evening Post*, January 4, 1830.

139. *New York Evening Post*, August 13, 1840.

140. John Gay, *Poems on Several Occasions* ..., 2 vols., (London: S. Crowder, C. Ware, ND t. Payne, 1771), 108.

141. Paul A. Gilje, *The Road to Mobocracy: Popular Disorder in New York City, 1763–1834* (Chapel Hill: University of North Carolina Press, 1987), 247; New York *National Advocate*, October 29, 1817; *Philadelphia Inquirer*, October 10, 1829.

142. Epes Sargent, *Songs of the Sea* (Boston, MA: J. Munroe, 1847), 51.

143. Caroline Moseley, "Henry D. Thoreau and His Favorite Popular Song," *Journal of Popular Culture*, 12 (1979): 624–29. See also *New York American*, November 21, 1832; *New York Evening Post*, May 19, 1837, September 24, 1844; *Pittsfield (Massachusetts) Sun*, September 5, 1839; *Salem Register*, September 6, 1841; *Dedham (Massachusetts) Norfolk Democrat*, March 29, 1844; *Boston Courier*, November 4, 1844; *Gloucester (Massachusetts) Telegraph*, January 26, 1846.

6. The Pirates Own Book

1. *New Orleans Times-Picayune*, July 3, 1841.
2. For the print revolution, see Eve Tanor Bannet, *Transatlantic Stories and the History of Reading, 1720–1810: Migrant Fictions* (Cambridge: Cambridge University Press, 2011); Roger Chartier, *The Order of Books: Readers, Authors, and Libraries in Europe between the Fourteenth and Eighteenth Centuries*, Lydia G. Cochrane, trans. (Stanford, CA: Stanford University Press, 1994); Chartier, "Texts, Printing, Readings," in Lynn Hunt, ed., *The New Cultural History* (Berkeley: University of California Press, 1989), 154–75; Robert Darnton, "First Steps Toward a History of Reading," in *The Kiss of Lamourette: Reflections in Cultural History* (New York: Norton, 1990), 154–87; William J. Gilmore, *Reading Becomes a Necessity of Life: Material Cultural Life in Rural New England, 1780–1835* (Knoxville: University of Tennessee Press, 1989); Robert A. Gross and Mary Kelley, eds., *An Extensive Republic: Print, Culture, and Society in the New Nation* (Chapel Hill: University of North Carolina Press, 2010); David D. Hall, *Cultures of Print: Essays in the History of the Book* (Amherst: University of Massachusetts Press, 1996); David Paul Nord, *Faith in Reading: Religious Publishing and the Birth of Mass Media in America* (New York: Oxford University Press, 2004); Rosalind Remer, *Printers and Men of Capital: Philadelphia Book Publishers in the New Republic* (Philadelphia: University of Pennsylvania Press, 1996); Ronald J. Zboray, *A Fictive People: Antebellum Economic Development and the American Reading Public* (New York: Oxford University Press, 1993).
3. *The Pirates Own Book, or Authentic Narratives of the Lives, Exploits, and Executions of the Most Celebrated Sea Robbers* ... (Salem, MA: Marine Research Society, 1924; orig. pub. 1837). Charles Johnson, *A General History of the Pyrates, from Their First Rise and Settlement in the Island of Providence, to the Present Time* ..., 2nd ed. (London: T. Warner, 1724). For much of the twentieth century this work was misattributed to Daniel Defoe. Michael Winship, "Pirates, Shipwrecks, and Comic Almanacs: Charles Ellms Packages Books in Nineteenth-Century America," *Printing History*, 9 (2011): 3–16.
4. Hester Blum, *The View from the Masthead: Maritime Imagination and Antebellum American Sea Narratives* (Chapel Hill: University of North Carolina Press, 2008), 28–29; Harry R. Skallerup, *Books Afloat and Ashore: A History of Books, Libraries, and Reading among Seamen during*

the Age of Sail (Hamden, CT: Archon Book, 1974), 22, 205. Examination of seaman protection certificates suggests a slightly lower literacy rate before 1820. See Ira Dye, "Early American Merchant Seafarers," *Proceedings of the American Philosophical Society*, 120 (1976): 340–44.

5. On the importance of reading as an experience that expanded one's world, see Mary K. Kupiec Cayton, "The Expanding World of Jacob Norton: Reading, Revivalism, and the Construction of the 'Second Great Awakening' in New England, 1787–1804," *JER*, 26 (2006): 221–48; Gilmore, *Reading Becomes a Necessity of Life.*

6. Andrew Sherburne, *Memoirs of Andrew Sherburne* ... (Utica, NY: William Williams, 1828), 86; Charles Herbert, *A Relic of the Revolution* ... (Boston, MA: Charles H. Pierce, 1847), 31, 57, 64, 100, 105–06, 118, 126, 146, 153, 169, 174, 185, 190.

7. Richard Henry Dana Jr. to Edmund T. Dana, et al., March 13, 1835, Box 7, Dana Family Papers, I, 1835–1840, MHS; Dana Jr., *Two Years before the Mast: A Personal Narrative of Life at Sea*, Thomas Philbrick, ed. (New York: Penguin, 1981; orig. pub. 1840), 225–26.

8. Herman Melville, *Redburn: His First Voyage, Being the Sailor-boy Confessions and Reminiscences of the Son-of-a-Gentleman in the Merchant Service*, Harold Beaver, ed. (New York: Penguin, 1976; orig. pub. 1849), 140–43.

9. Blum, *The View from the Masthead*, 19–32; Skallerup, *Books Afloat and Ashore*, 205.

10. Quoted in Skallerup, *Books Afloat and Ashore*, 80.

11. Melville, *Redburn*, 140–43. For the books mentioned, see Adam Smith, *An Inquiry into the Nature and Causes of the Wealth of Nations*, Edwin Cannan, ed. (New York: Modern Library, 1994; orig. pub. 1776); Susanna Rowson, *Charlotte Temple: Authoritative Text, Contexts, Criticism*, Marion Rust, ed. (New York: Norton, 2011; orig. pub. 1791); George Walker, *Three Spaniards, a Romance* (London: S. Low, 1800). *Delirium Tremors* may be J. Root, *The Horrors of Delirium Tremors* (New York: J. Adams, 1844), Charles Stuart Tripler, *Remarks on Delirium Tremens* (New York: J. Seymor, 1827), or another book.

12. Herman Melville, *White-Jacket, or The World in a Man-of-War*, Alfred Kazin, intro. (New York: New American Library, 1979; orig. pub. 1850), 169–71; Paul A. Gilje, *Liberty on the Waterfront: American Maritime Culture in the Age of Revolution* (Philadelphia: University of Pennsylvania Press, 2004), 213; Owen Chase, "Narrative of the Most Extraordinary and Distressing Shipwreck of the Whaleship *Essex*, ... " in Thomas Heffernan, *Stove by a Whale: Owen Chase and the Essex* (Middleton, CT: Wesleyan University Press, 1981), 13–76; Herman Melville, *Moby Dick, or the Whale* (New York: Modern Library, 1982; orig. pub. 1851). For Melville reading about the *Essex*, see Hershel Parker, *Herman Melville: A Biography, Volume I, 1819–1851* (Baltimore, MD: Johns Hopkins University Press, 1996), 199. Not all of the works Melville mentioned can be identified. Nichola Machiavelli, *The Art of War* was originally published in 1521 and has been republished countless times, including *The Art of War in Seven*

Books by Nicholas Machivell ... (Albany, NY: Henry C. Southwick, 1815). John Locke's essays could refer to a collection of his essays or his "Essay on Human Understanding," of which there were countless editions. Thomas Moore's *Loves of the Angels* was probably Thomas Moore, *The Loves of the Angels, a Poem* (London: Longman, Hurst, Rees, Orme, and Brown, 1823).

13. *Alexandria (Virginia) Gazette*, January 9, 1843. See also Skallerup, *Books Afloat and Ashore*, 209; New Bedford Port Society Records, *Twelfth Annual Report* (1842), NBWM.

14. See, for example, the advertisements in the following: *Newburyport (Massachusetts) Herald*, April 21, 1837; *New Haven Columbian Register*, May 6, 1837; *Norfolk (Connecticut) Advertiser*, May 20, 1837; *Charleston Courier*, May 22, 1837; *Philadelphia National Gazette*, June 6, 1837; *Kalamazoo (Michigan) Gazette*, June 24, 1837; *Baltimore Sun*, July 8, 1837; *St. Louis Daily Commercial Bulletin*, August 29, 1837; *Columbus Ohio Statesman*, September 11, 1837.

15. For a discussion of how publishers rearranged material in books on both sides of the Atlantic, see Bannet, *Transatlantic Stories and the History of Reading*.

16. *The Pirates Own Book, or Authentic Narratives of the Lives, Exploits, and Executions of the Most Celebrated Sea Robbers* ... (Boston, MA: Thomas Groom, 1837). The 1837 edition was republished in 1924. All page citations are to the 1924 edition. See *The Pirates Own Book* (1924), 102.

17. *The Pirates Own Book, or Authentic Narratives of the Lives, Exploits, and Executions of the Most Celebrated Sea Robbers* ... ([Philadelphia, PA]: Thomas Cowperthwait & Co., 1839). Johnson, *A General History of the Pyrates*. For Kidd and Benavides, see *The Pirates Own Book* (1924), 171–200. On illustrations, see Georgia B. Barnhill, "Transformations in Pictorial Printing," in Gross and Kelley, eds., *An Extensive Republic*, 422–40.

18. *The History of the Pirates, Containing the Lives of Those Noted Pirate Captains* ... (Haverill, MA: Thomas Carey, 1825); *The History of the Pirates, Containing the Lives of Those Noted Pirate Captains* ... (Hartford, CT: Henry Benton, 1829); *The History of the Lives and Bloody Exploits of the Most Noted Pirates* ... (Hartford, CT: Silas Andrus & Son, 1836). There was also an 1850 edition of this work: *The History of the Bloody Exploits of the Most Noted Pirates* ... (Hartford, CT: Silas Andrus & Son, 1850).

19. *A Report of the Trial of Pedro Gilbert, Bernardo De Soto, Francisco Ruiz,* ... (Boston, MA: Russell, Odiorne & Metcalf, 1834); *Trial of the Twelve Spanish Pirates on the Schooner Panda, A Guinea Slaver* ... (Boston, MA: Lemuel Gulliver, 1834); *Supplement to the Report of the Trial of the Spanish Pirates with Confessions on Protests Written by Them in Prison* ... (Boston, MA: Lemuel Gulliver, 1835).

20. For examples, see A. Solis, *Dying Confession [of] Pirates, viz. Collins, Furtado, and Palacha* ... ([Boston, MA: no pub., 1794]); *The Interesting Trials of the Pirates for the Murder of William Little, Captain of the Ship American Eagle* (Newburyport, MA: Herald Press, [1797]); Joseph Baker, *The Confessions of Joseph Baker ... for Murder and Piracy* ... ([Philadelphia, PA]: Folwell,

[1800]); John Soren, *The Narrative of Mr. John Soren ... Piratically Captured on the High Seas* ... (Boston, MA: no pub., 1800); William Wheland, *A Narrative of the Horrid Murder & Piracy* ... (Philadelphia, PA: Folwell, [1800]); John Fillmore, *A Narration of the Captivity of John Fillmore* ... (Suffield, CT: Gray, 1802); Charles Johnson, *The History of Blackbeard & Roche, Two Noted Pyrates* (Salem, MA: Cushing, 1802); *Lives and Confessions of John Williams, Francis Frederick, John R. Rog, and Peter Peterson,* ... (Boston, MA: J. T. Buckingham, 1819); *The Pirates. A Brief Account of the Horrid Massacre of the Captain, Mate, and Supercargo of the Schooner Plattsburg* ... (Boston, MA: H. Trumbull, 1819); *The Pirates. A Brief Account of the Horrid Murder of the Captain and Mate of a Buenos Ayrean Prize Schooner* ... (Boston, MA: H. Trumbull, [1820]); Aaron Smith, *The Atrocities of the Pirates* ... (New York: Robert Lowry, 1824); Lucretia Parker, *Piratical Barbarity or the Female Captive* ... (New York: S. Walker for G. Parker, 1825); *Dying Declaration of Nicholas Fernandez* ... ([New York: George Lambert], 1830); *A Sketch of the Life and Confessions of Thos. J. Winslow, One of the Pirates* ... (New York: Isaac Chidsay, 1832); *A Report of the Trial of Pedro Gilbert.*

21. *The Pirates Own Book* (1924), 364–407; Barnabas Lincoln, *Narrative of the Capture, and Sufferings and Escape of Capt. Barnabas Lincoln and His Crew* ... (Boston, MA: Ezra Lincoln, 1822).

22. Johnson, *A General History of the Pyrates*, 157; "Pirates and Piracy from the Earliest Ages. No. I.: Pirates of the Classical and Mediaeval," *The Museum of Foreign Literature, Science, and Art*, 25 (October 1834): 341; *The Pirates Own Book* (1924), 2, 418–23.

23. Lieutenant Murray, *Fanny Campbell, the Female Pirate Captain: A Tale of the Revolution* (Boston, MA: F. Gleason, 1845). Quotation, ibid., 54. The first edition in 1844 did not have the illustration. Lieutenant Murray, *Fanny Campbell, the Female Pirate Captain: A Tale of the Revolution* (New York: Samuel French, 1844).

24. Lincoln, *Narrative of the Capture, and Sufferings*, 8–10.

25. See, for example, comments in George Little, *Life on the Ocean; or Twenty Years at Sea* ... (Baltimore, MD: Armstrong & Berry, 1843), 350, 365.

26. Some scholars view sea robbers as a would-be proletariat rejecting the authority of the quarterdeck and commercial capitalism. Perhaps this egalitarian message attracted sailors. But this assumption overstates the case. Although there is some evidence to substantiate the argument for the relative equality aboard pirate ships, few seamen embraced the outlaw lifestyle For pirates as proletariat, see Marcus Rediker, *Between the Devil and the Deep Blue Sea: Merchant Seamen, Pirates, and the Anglo-American Maritime World, 1700–1750* (New York: Cambridge University Press, 1987); Rediker, "'Under the Banner of King Death': The Social World of Anglo-American Pirates, 1716–1726," *WMQ*, 3rd ser., 38 (1981): 203–27; Rediker, *Villains of All Nations: Atlantic Pirates in the Golden Age* (Boston, MA: Beacon Press, 2004). For a corrective to this view, see David Cordingly, *Under the Black Flag: The Romance and the Reality of Life among the Pirates* (New York: Random House, 1996). See also Crystal Williams, "Nascent

Socialists or Resourceful Criminals? A Reconsideration of Transatlantic Piracy, 1690–1726," in Paul A. Gilje and William Pencak, eds., *Pirates, Jack Tar, and Memory: New Directions in American Maritime History* (Mystic, CT: Mystic Seaport, 2007), 31–50; and Guy Chet, *The Ocean Is a Wilderness: Atlantic Piracy and the Limits of State Authority, 1688–1856* (Amherst: University of Massachusetts Press, 2014).

27. Thomas Philbrick, *James Fenimore Cooper and the Development of the American Sea Fiction* (Cambridge, MA: Harvard University Press, 1961), 88–89; Joseph Gibbs, *Dead Men Tell No Tales: The Lives and Legends of the Pirate Charles Gibbs* (Columbia: University of South Carolina Press, 2007); David J. Starkey, "Voluntaries and Sea Robbers: A Review of Academic Literature on Privateering, Corsairing, Buccaneering and Piracy," *Mariner's Mirror*, 97 (2011): 127–47; Jerome Garitee, *The Republic's Private Navy: The American Privateering Business as Practiced by Baltimore during the War of 1812* (Middletown, CT: Wesleyan University Press, 1977), 224–29; David Head, "Slave Smuggling by Foreign Privateers: The Illegal Slave Trade and the Geopolitics of the Early Republic," *JER*, 33 (2013), 433–62; Head, "Sailing for Spanish America: The Atlantic Geopolitics of Foreign Privateering from the United States in the Early Republic" (PhD diss., State University of New York, Buffalo, 2010).

28. William Bligh, *A Narrative of the Mutiny, on Board His Britannic Majesty's Ship Bounty; and the Subsequent Voyage of Part of the Crew ...* (Philadelphia, PA: William Spotswood, 1790); Sir John Barrow, *A Description of Pitcairn's Island and Its Inhabitants with an Authentic Account of the Mutiny of the Ship Bounty, and of the Subsequent Fortunes of the Mutineers* (New York: Harper & Brothers, 1838); *Theatre, Holliday-Street. First Appearance in this Theatre of Monsieur Gouffe ... the Entertainments to Conclude with the Melo Drama of Pitcairn's Island, or the Mutiny on the Bounty* (Baltimore, MD: J. Robinson, [1832]). For references to the *Bounty*, see Stanton Garner, ed., *The Captain's Best Mate: The Journal of Mary Chipman Lawrence on the Whaler Addison, 1856–1860* (Providence, RI: Brown University Press, 1966), 68; Little, *Life on the Ocean*, 132; William Torrey, *Torrey's Narrative ...* (Boston, MA: A. J. Wright, 1848), 101–02; Herman Melville, *Omoo: A Narrative of Adventures in the South Seas*, Harrison Hayford, et al., eds. (Evanston, IL: Northwestern University Press, 1968; orig. pub. 1847), 66–67.

29. *The Trial of Richard Parker, Complete; President of the Delegates, for Mutiny, &C. On Board the Sandwich, and Others of His Majesty's Ships, at the Nore, in May, 1797...* (Boston, MA: Samuel Etheridge, for William T. Clap, 1797); *The Tryal, Last Dying Words, Speech and Confession of Richard Parker (Alias Admiral Parker) Late President of the Mutinous Fleet ...* ([New York?: no pub., 1797?]). For a sample of newspaper articles on the mutiny of the British fleet, see *New York Diary*, August 7, 1797; *Philadelphia Gazette*, August 10, 1797; *Salem Gazette*, September 22, 1797; *New York The War*, July 4, 1812; *Philadelphia Inquirer*, June 30, 1833. For a sample of newspaper articles on the *Hermione*, see *New York Gazette*, November 18, 1797; *Baltimore Federal Gazette*, March 17, 1798; *Philadelphia Gazette*, August 12, 1799; *New York Daily Advertiser*,

March 12, 1800; *Washington, D. C., National Intelligencer*, September 8, 1802; *Boston The Democrat*, May 21, 1806; *Worcester (Massachusetts) National Aegis*, October 3, 1838.

30. [James Fenimore Cooper], *The Cruise of the Somers* ... (New York: J. Winchester, 1844); Alexander Slidell Mackenzie, *Case of the Somers' Mutiny: Defence of Alexander Slidell Mackenzie, Commander of the U.S. Brig Somers, before the Court Martial Held at the Navy Yard, Brooklyn* (New York: Tribune Office, 1843).

31. *The Pirates. A Brief Account of the Horrid Massacre; Lives and Confessions of John Williams; an Address to the Spectator of the Awful Execution of the Pirates in Boston, February 19, 1819* (Boston, MA: Boston Society for the Moral and Religious Instruction of the Poor, U. Crocker, 1819).

32. William Lay and Cyrus M. Hussey, *A Narrative of the Mutiny on Board the Whaleship Globe* (New London, CT: William Lay and C. M. Hussey, 1828); William Comstock, *The Life of Samuel Comstock, the Terrible Whaleman Containing an Account of the Mutiny, and Massacre of the Officers of the Ship Globe, of Nantucket* ... (Boston, MA: James Fisher, 1840); Hiram Paulding, *Journal of a Cruise of the United States Schooner Dolphin* ... (New York: G. & C. & H. Carvill, 1831).

33. *The History of the Bloody Exploits of the Most Noted Pirates*, 285–92; *A Sketch of the Life and Confessions of Thos. J. Winslow, One of the Pirates*; Gibbs, *Dead Men Tell No Tales*.

34. Lincoln, *Narrative of the Capture, and Sufferings*, 106.

35. Parker, *Piratical Barbarity or the Female Captive*, 11–13, 22.

36. *A Sketch of the Life and Confessions of Thos. J. Winslow*, iii.

37. *The Pirates. A Brief Account of the Horrid Massacre*, 6–7, 24.

38. William McNally, *Evils and Abuses in the Naval and Merchant Service Exposed* ... (Boston, MA: Cassady and March, 1839), 71–72; Dana Jr., *Two Years before the Mast*, 153, 466.

39. Paul A. Gilje, *Free Trade and Sailors' Rights in the War of 1812* (New York: Cambridge University Press, 2013), 185–89.

40. For accounts written about the Revolutionary War experience, see Thomas Andros, *The Old Jersey Captive* ... (Boston, MA: William Pierce, 1833); Joshua Davis, *A Narrative of Joshua Davis* ... (Baltimore, MD: B. Edes, 1811); Albert Greene, *Recollections of the Jersey Prison-Ship* ... (Providence, RI: H. H. Brown, 1829); Nathaniel Fanning, *Narrative of the Adventures of Nathaniel Fanning* ... (New York: Printed for the Author, 1806); Ebenezer Fox, *The Adventures of Ebenezer Fox in the Revolutionary War...* (Boston, MA: Charles Fox, 1848); Christopher Hawkins, *The Adventures of Christopher Hawkins* ... (New York: Privately Printed, 1864); Herbert, *A Relic of the Revolution*; Sherburne, *Memoirs of Andrew Sherburne*. For accounts written about the War of 1812 experience, see Charles Andrews, *The Prisoners' Memoirs, or Dartmoor Prison* ... (New York: Printed for the Author, 1815); Charles H. Barnard, *A Narrative of the Sufferings of Capt. Charles H. Barnard* ... (New York: J. Lindon, 1829); [Josiah Cobb], *A Green Hand's First Cruise, Roughed out from the Log-Book of Memory* ..., 2 vols. (Baltimore, MD: Cushing & Brother, 1841); R. S. Coffin, *A Concise Narrative*

of the Barbarous Treatment ... (Danville, VT: Ebenezer Eaton, 1816); James Fenimore Cooper, ed., *Ned Myers, a Life before the Mast*, William S. Dudley, intro. (Annapolis, MD: Naval Institute Press, 1989; orig. pub. 1843); James Durand, *James Durand: Able Seaman of 1812* ..., George S. Brooks, ed. (New Haven, CT: Yale University Press, 1926; orig. pub. 1820); [Charles Calvert Egerton], *The Journal of the Unfortunate Prisoner* ... (Baltimore, MD: Printed for the Author, 1813); Joshua Penny, *The Life and Adventures of Joshua Penny* ... (New York: Alden Spooner, 1815); Moses Smith, *Naval Scenes in the Last War* ... (Boston, MA: Gleason Publishing Hall, 1846); [Benjamin Waterhouse], *A Journal of a Young Man of Massachusetts* ... (Lexington, KY: Worsley & Smith, 1816). See also Francis D. Cogliano, *American Maritime Prisoners in the Revolutionary War: The Captivity of William Russell* (Annapolis, MD: Naval Institute Press, 2001); Sheldon S. Cohen, *Yankee Sailors in British Gaols: Prisoners of War at Forton and Mill, 1777–1783* (Newark: University of Delaware Press, 1995); Edwin G. Burrows, *Forgotten Patriots: The Untold Story of American Prisoners during the Revolutionary War* (New York: Basic Books, 2008).

41. Linda Colley, *Captives: Britain, Empire, and the World, 1600–1850* (New York: Random House, 2002), 88–89.

42. Robert Adams, *The Narrative of Robert Adams, an American Sailor, Who Was Wrecked on the Western Coast of Africa* (Boston, MA: Wells and Lilly 1817); *Humanity in Algiers: Or the Story of Azem by an American, Late Slave in Algiers* (Troy , NY: Moffitt, 1801); [Mathew Carey], *A Short Account of Algiers* ... (Philadelphia, PA: J. Parker for M. Carey. 1794); Jonathan Cowdery, *American Captives in Tripoli* ..., 2nd ed. (Boston, MA: Bucher and Armstrong, 1806); John Foss, *A Journal of the Captivity and Sufferings of John Foss: Several Years a Prisoner in Algiers* ... (Newburyport, MA: A. March, [1798]); Thomas Nicholson, *An Affecting Narrative of the Captivity and Sufferings of Thomas Nicholson* ... (Boston, MA: H. Trumbull, 1816); Susanna Rowson, *Slaves in Algiers* ... (Philadelphia, PA: Wrigley and Berrian, 1794); Elijah Shaw, *Short Sketch, of the Life of Elijah Shaw, Who Served for Twenty-Two Years in the Navy* ... (Rochester, NY: Strong & Dawson, 1843); James Wilson Stevens, *An Historical and Geographical Account of Algiers* ... (Philadelphia, PA: Hogan & M'Elroy, 1797); Raynor Taylor, *The American Captive's Emancipation: Written by a Tar* (Philadelphia, PA: G. E. Blake, 1805); Royall Tyler, *The Algerine Captive* ... (Walpole, NH: David Carlisle Jr., 1797); John Willcock, *The Voyages and Adventures of John Willcock, Mariner* ... (Philadelphia, PA: George Gibson, 1798).

43. Paul Baepler, "The Barbary Captivity Narrative in American Culture," *Early American Literature*, 39 (2004): 217–46; Robert J. Allison, *The Crescent Obscured: The United States and the Muslim World, 1776–1815* (Chicago, IL: Chicago University Press, 1995); Blum, *The View from the Masthead*, 46–70.

44. Foss, *A Journal of the Captivity and Sufferings of John Ross* ..., [2].

45. James Riley, *Authentic Narrative of the Loss of the American Brig Commerce* ... (Hartford, CT: Printed for the Author, 1817); Allison, *The Crescent Obscured*, 207–25.

46. Charles Ellms, *Shipwrecks and Disasters at Sea, or Historical Narratives of the Most Noted Calamities and Providential Deliverances from Fire and Famine on the Ocean. With a Sketch of the Various Expedients for Preserving the Life of Mariners by the Aid of Life Boats, Life Preservers, &c.* (Boston, MA: S. N. Dickinson, 1836).

47. *Shipwrecks and Disasters at Sea, or Historical Narratives of the Most Noted Calamities and Providential Deliverances which Have Resulted from Maritime Enterprise with a Sketch of Various Expedients for Preserving the Lives of Mariners* (Edinburgh: George Ramsey, 1812).

48. Archibald Duncan, *The Mariner's Chronicle; Being a Collection of the Most Interesting Narratives of Shipwrecks, Fires, Famines, and Other Calamities Incident to a Life of Maritime Enterprise; with Authentic Particulars of the Extraordinary Adventures and Sufferings of the Crews, Their Reception and Treatment on Distant Shores; and a Concise Description of the Country, Customs, and Manners of the Inhabitants: Including an Account of the Deliverance of the Survivors. By Archibald Duncan, Esq. Late of the Royal Navy. In Four Volumes.* Vol. I[-IV] (Philadelphia, PA: James Humphreys, 1806).

49. Archibald Duncan, *The Mariner's Chronicle; Being a Collection of the Most Interesting Narratives of Shipwrecks, Fires, Famines, and Other Calamities Incident to a Life of Maritime Enterprise; with Authentic Particulars of the Extraordinary Adventures and Sufferings of the Crews, Their Reception and Treatment on Distant Shores; and a Concise Description of the Country, Customs, and Manners of the Inhabitants: Including an Account of the Deliverance of the Survivors. By Archibald Duncan, Esq. Late of the Royal Navy. In Four Volumes.* Vol. I[–IV] (Philadelphia, PA: Thomas Desilver, 1810); *The Mariner's Chronicle: Containing Narratives of the Most Remarkable Disasters at Sea, such as Shipwrecks, Storms, Fires, Famines[,] also Naval Engagements, Piratical Adventures, Incidents of Discovery, and Other Extraordinary and Interesting Occurrences* (New Haven, CT: George W. Gorton, 1834); *The Mariner's Chronicle: Containing Narratives of the Most Remarkable Disasters at Sea, such as Shipwrecks, Storms, Fires, Famines[,] also Naval Engagements, Piratical Adventures, Incidents of Discovery, and Other Extraordinary and Interesting Occurrences* (New Haven, CT: George W. Gorton, 1835). Subsequent citations for Duncan, *The Mariner's Chronicle* are from the 1806 edition.

50. In addition to the anthologies cited earlier see *God's Wonders in the Great Deep, Recorded in Several Wonderful and Amazing Accounts Sailors, Who Have Met with Unexpected Deliverances* ... (Newburyport, MA: Allen for Thomas & Whipple, 1805); *Remarkable Shipwrecks, or A Collection of Interesting Accounts of Naval Disasters with Many Particulars of the Extraordinary Adventures and Sufferings of the Crews* ... (Hartford, CT: Andrus and Starr, 1813); William Allen, *Accounts of Shipwreck, and Other Disasters at Sea* ... (Brunswick, ME: Joseph Griffen, 1823); *Ben Boatswain's Yarns, or Tales of the Ocean* (New York: Murphy, 184?); Edward Pelham, *Narrative of the Adventures, Sufferings, and Deliverance of Eight English Seamen, Left by Accident in Greenland, in the Year 1630. To Which Is Added,*

the Loss of the Lady Holbert Packet, Adventures of Four Russian Sailors, and the Loss of the Ship Litchfield (Philadelphia, PA: Bennett and Walton, 1812), 4; Cyrus Redding, *A History of Shipwrecks and Disasters at Sea, from the Most Authentic Sources*, 2 vols. (London: Whitaker, Treacher & Co., 1833); R. Thomas, *Interesting and Authentic Narratives of the Most Remarkable Shipwrecks, Famines, Calamities, Providential Deliveries, and Lamentable Disasters on the Sea* ... (Boston, MA: Shepard, Oliver and Co., 1835).

51. Duncan, *Mariner's Chronicle*, 1:5–8, 210, 262, 285–87; Ellms, *Shipwrecks and Disasters at Sea*, 59–60, 208; Thomas, *Interesting and Authentic Narratives of the Most Remarkable Shipwrecks*, 39–40, 113.

52. Ellms, *Shipwrecks and Disasters at Sea*, 13–51; Thomas, *Interesting and Authentic Narratives of the Most Remarkable Shipwrecks*, 323–25, 295–98; Lay and Hussey, *A Narrative of the Mutiny on Board the Whaleship Globe*; Ann Saunders, *Narrative of the Shipwreck and Sufferings of Miss Ann Saunders* ... (Providence, RI: Z. S. Crossmon, 1827). For other single ship-wreck publications, see Adams, *The Narrative of Robert Adams; An Elegy on the Death of Captain Valentine*, ... (no place: Broadside, [1801]); Barnard, *A Narrative of the Sufferings of Capt. Charles H. Barnard*; Chase, "Narrative of the most Extraordinary and Distressing Shipwreck of the Whaleship Essex, ..." in Heffernan, *Stove by a Whale*, 13–76; Jonathan Dickenson, *The Remarkable Deliverance of Robert Barrow* ... (Dover, NH: Eliphant Lad, 1793); Barnabas Downs Jr., *A Brief and Remarkable Narrative of the Life and Extreme Sufferings* ... ([Boston, MA]: E. Russell, 1786); Jean Gaspard Dubois-Fantalle, *The Shipwreck and Adventures of Monsieur Viaud ..., trans. from the French by Mrs. Griffith* ... (Dover, NH: Samuel Bragg Jr., 1799); George Keate, *An Account of the Pelew Islands* ... (Philadelphia, PA: Joseph Crukshank, 1789); Henry Larcom, "Captain Larcom's Narrative," *Hartford Connecticut Courant*, August 15, 1810; Edward Pelham, *Narrative of the Adventures, Sufferings, and Deliverance of Eight English Seamen, Left by Accident in Greenland, in the Year 1630* ... (Philadelphia, PA: Bennett and Walton, 1812); Daniel Saunders Jr., *A Journal of the Travels and Sufferings of Daniel Saunders* ... (Salem, MA: Thomas C. Cushing, 1794); Benjamin Stout, *Narrative of the Loss of the Ship Hercules* ... (New York: James Chevalier, [1798]); Samuel Swett, *An Interesting Narrative of the Loss of the Ship Milo* ... (Newburyport, MA: William B. Allen, 1814).

53. [Cobb], *A Green Hand's First Cruise*, 1:15–16.

54. Jacob A. Hazen, *Five Years before the Mast* ..., 2nd ed. (Philadelphia, PA: William P. Hazard, 1854), 19.

55. Winship, "Pirates, Shipwrecks, and Comic Almanacs," *Printing History*, 9 (2011): 15–16.

56. *The Tragical cale[ndar] and Pirates Own Almanac, 1846* (Baltimore, MD: J. B. Keller, 1846).

57. Baepler, "The Barbary Captivity Narratives in American Culture," *Early American Literature*, 39 (2004): 217–46.

58. Melville, *Redburn*, 97; Herman Melville, *Israel Potter: His Fifty Years of Exile*, Harrison Hayford et al., eds. (Evanston, IL: Northwestern University Press, 1982); Melville, *Moby Dick*.

59. Edgar Allan Poe, *The Narrative of Gordon Pym of Nantucket*, Harold Beaver, ed. (New York: Penguin, 1975; orig. pub. 1838).

60. Joyce Appleby, *Inheriting the Revolution: The First Generation of Americans* (Cambridge, MA: Harvard University Press, 2000), 165.

61. Log of the *Prudent*, kept by Holton J. Breed, 1804–06, Log 1804 P3, PEM.

62. Dana Jr., *Two Years before the Mast*, 282.

63. Blum, *The View from the Masthead*, 20–25; Log of the *Charles W. Morgan*, kept by James C. Osborn, 1841–45, Log 143, Mystic.

64. J. Ross Browne, *Etchings of a Whaling Cruise* …(New York: Harper & Brothers, 1846), 110–11. "Lady Dacre's Diary of a Chaperon" is probably *Recollection of a Chaperon*, Lady Dacre, ed., 3 vols. (London: Richard Bentley, 1833). The Songster's Own Book has not been identified. There were many versions of books called "A Complete Letter Writer" in circulation at the time. Most were "how-to" instruction manuals showing the proper form of writing different letters.

65. Blum, *The View from the Masthead*, 20–24; Parker, *Herman Melville*, 231–33, 268–73. See also [Henry James Mercier], *Life in a Man of War, or Scenes in "Old Ironsides"* … (Philadelphia, PA: L. R. Bailey, 1841), 105–09.

66. Cathy N. Davidson, "The Novel as Subversive Activity: Women Reading, Women Writing," in Alfred F. Young, ed., *Beyond the American Revolution: Explorations in the History of American Radicalism* (DeKalb: Northern Illinois University, 1993), 286.

67. Cathy N. Davidson, *Revolution and the Word: The Rise of the Novel in America* (New York: Oxford University Press, 1986); Davidson, "The Novel as Subversive Activity," in Young, ed., *Beyond the American Revolution*, 283–316. See also Nancy Armstrong, *Desire and Domestic Fiction: A Political History of the Novel* (New York: Oxford University Press, 1987); Karen A. Weyler, *Intricate Relations: Sexual and Economic Desire in American Fiction, 1789–1814* (Iowa City: University of Iowa Press, 2004); Ruth Perry, *Novel Relations: The Transformations of Kinship in English Literature and Culture, 1748–1818* (Cambridge: Cambridge University Press, 2004).

68. March 2, 1850, John K. Barker, Journal of a Voyage from Boston, Mass, Towards San Francisco, Upper California in the ship *Hanibal*, Geo. H, Willis, Master, 1849–50, May-Winship-Barker-Archibald Papers, 1775–1922, MHS; Richard Henry Dana Jr. to Edmund T. Dana et al., March 1 and 20, 1835, Box 7, Dana Family Papers, I, 1835–1840, MHS.

69. Daniel Defoe, *The Life and Adventures of Robinson Crusoe*, Angus Ross, ed. (New York: Penguin, 1965; orig. pub. 1719).

70. *Narrative of the Capture of the United States' Brig Vixen* … (New York: Office of "The War," 1813), 15; [Cobb], *A Green Hand's First Cruise*, 2: 6–7; Penny, *The Life and Adventures of Joshua Penny*, 31–35; Browne, *Etchings of a Whaling Cruise*, 207.

71. Bannet, *Transatlantic Stories and the History of Reading*, 25–45; Charles Ellms, *Robinson Crusoe's Own Book: Or, The Voice of Adventure, from the Civilized Man Cut off from His Fellows* … (Boston, MA: Joshua V. Pierce,

1843). See also Christopher Hill, "Robinson Crusoe," *History Workshop Journal*, 10 (1980): 6–24.

72. Daniel Defoe, *The Life, Adventures, and Piracies of the Famous Captain Singleton*, reprint of 1840 edition, Sir Walter Scott, ed. (New York: AMS Press, 1973; orig. pub. 1720).

73. William Falconer, *The Shipwreck: A Poem, in Three Cantos, by a Sailor* (London: A Millar, 1762); Duncan, *The Mariner's Chronicle*, [5].

74. Lord Byron, *The Corsair, a Tale* (Boston, MA: West & Blake, 1814); Walter Scott, *The Pirate* (Edinburgh: Archibald Constable, 1822).

75. James Fenimore Cooper, *The Red Rover, a Tale*, Thomas and Marianne Philbrick, eds. (Albany: State University of New York Press, 1991; orig. pub. 1827).

76. Blum, *The View from the Masthead*, 36. James Fenimore Cooper, *History of the Navy of the United States*, 2nd ed., 2 vols. (Philadelphia, PA: Lea and Blanchard, 1840); Cooper, *Red Rover*; Cooper, *The Pilot: A Tale of the Sea* (New York: G. P. Putnam's Sons, no date; orig. pub. 1823); *The Water Witch: or the Skimmer of the Seas, a Tale* (Philadelphia, PA: Carey and Lea, 1831). For men at sea reading *The Red Rover*, see Hazen, *Five Years before the Mast*, 61; [J. S. Henshaw], *Around the World: A Narrative of a Voyage in the East India Squadron ...*, 2 vols. (New York: Charles S. Francis, 1840), 1: 16, 157–58.

77. Parker, *Herman Melville*, 232; Captain [Frederick] Marryat, *Poor Jack* (London: George Rutlege and Sons, [1840]).

78. [Mercier], *Life in a Man of War*, 95–96; Captain [Frederick] Marryat, *Mr. Midshipman Easy* (New York: Penguin, 1982; orig. pub. 1836).

79. Joseph C. Hart, *Miriam Coffin, or The Whale-Fishermen*, Edward Halsey Foster, forward (New York: Garrett Press, 1969; orig. pub. 1834), 32.

80. J. Ross Browne to Dana, Nov. 9, 1846, Box 10, 1845–48, Dana Family Papers, I, 1835–40, MHS.

81. Hazen, *Five Years before the Mast*; George Edward Clark, *Seven Years a Sailor's Life* (Boston, MA: Adams & Co., 1867); Nicholas Peter Isaacs, *Twenty Years before the Mast ...* (New York: J. P. Beckworth, 1845); Little, *Life on the Ocean*; Samuel Leech, *A Voice from the Main Deck: Being a Record of the Thirty Years' Adventures of Samuel Leech*, Michael J. Crawford, ed. (Annapolis, MD: Naval Institute Press, 1999; orig. pub. 1843); Cooper, ed., *Ned Myers*.

82. James Fenimore Cooper, *The Pathfinder: Or, The Inland Sea*, 2 vols. (Philadelphia, PA: Lea and Blanchard, 1840); Cooper, *Mercedes of Castile, or, the Voyage to Cathay*, 2 vols. (Philadelphia, PA: Lea and Blanchard, 1840); Cooper, *Homeward Bound, or The Chase a Tale of the Sea* (Philadelphia, PA: Carey, Lea & Blanchard, 1838). See also Philbrick, *James Fenimore Cooper*; Alan Taylor, *William Cooper's Town: Power and Persuasion on the Frontier of the Early American Republic* (New York: Knopf, 1995).

83. Washington Irving, *Bracebridge Hall, or The Humorists a Medley* (New York: C. S. Van Winkle, 1822); Samuel Warren, *Ten Thousand a-Year* (Edinburgh: W. Blackwood and Sons, 1841); Micahel Steig, "Subversive Grotesque in Samuel Warren's Ten Thousand a-Year," *Nineteenth-Century Fiction*, 24 (1969): 154–68.

84. A. D. Harvey, "George Walker and the Anti-Revolutionary," *Novel, Review of English Studies,* new series, 28 (1977): 290–300.

85. Edward Bulwer-Lytton, *Pelham, or Adventures of a Gentleman* (Philadelphia, PA: J. B. Lipponcot, 1883); J. W. Oakley, "The Reform of Honor in Bulwer's Pelham," *Nineteenth-Century Literature,* 47 (1992): 49–71.

86. Andrew Monnickendau, "The Good, Brave-Hearted Lady: Christian Isobel Johnstone and National Tales," *Atlantis,* 20 (1998): 133–47.

87. Blum, *The View from the Masthead,* 20; Andrew Cayton, *Love in the Time of Revolution: Transatlantic Literary Radicalism and Historical Change, 1793–1818* (Chapel Hill: University of North Carolina Press, 2013).

88. Cooper, ed., *Ned Myers,* 241; Simeon Crowell, "Commonplace Book of Simeon Crowell," 1818–46, Ms, MHS. Paine explained his deism in *The Age of Reason* published in 1794. Charles Herbert read *The American Crisis* as a prisoner of war during the Revolution; Herbert, *A Relic of the Revolution,* 79.

89. Cordelia Stark, *The Female Wanderer: An Interesting Tale Founded on Fact, Written by Herself* (no place: Printed for the Proprietor, 1824).

90. *Sailor's Magazine,* 19 (May 1847): 262; New Bedford Port Society, *Twelfth Annual Report* (New Bedford, 1842): 7.

91. *Sailor's Magazine,* 13 (September 1840): 19.

92. Patricia Cline Cohen, Timothy J. Gilfoyle, and Helen Lefkowitz Horowitz, *The Flash Press: Sporting Male Weeklies in 1840s New York* (Chicago, IL: University of Chicago Press, 2008).

93. Herbert, *A Relic of the Revolution,* 28, 31, 49, 64, 118, 122, 146, 153, 169, 174, 185, 190. Quotation, ibid., 190.

94. [Waterhouse], *A Journal of a Young Man of Massachusetts,* 86, 185–86. See also Perez Drinkwater Jr., "Sailing Problems & Examples, Account of Imprisonment in Dartmoor, Feb. 1815," Ser. 6, Vol. 1, Maritime Records, Coll. 949, MeHS; Log of the *Polly,* kept by Jeduthan Upton, 1812–13, typescript, MHS; Benjamin F. Palmer, *The Diary of Benjamin F. Palmer, Privateersman ...* (n. p.: Acorn Club, 1914), 140; [Egerton], *The Journal of an Unfortunate Prisoner,* 12, 39–40, 50; *Narrative of the Capture of the United States' Brig Vixen,* 25–27.

95. E. Norman Flayderman, *Scrimshaw and Scimshanders: Whales and Whalemen* (New Milford, CT: N. Flayderman & Co., Inc., 1972).

96. Dana Jr., *Two Years before the Mast,* 332–33. See also [Mercier], *Life in a Man of War,* 229–30; Log of the *La Plata,* 1848–50, Log 1847 W3 B15, PEM.

97. Blum, *The View from the Masthead,* 204–05, n. 54. Edward Gibbon, *The History of the Decline and Fall of the Roman Empire,* Vol. 1 (London: W. Strahan, 1776); George Bancroft, *A History of the United States, from the Discovery of the American Continent to the Present Time,* 10 vols. (Boston, MA: Charles Bowen, 1834–78).

98. McNally, *Evils and Abuses of the Naval Merchant Service,* 160.

99. Martin Brückner, *The Geographic Revolution in Early America: Maps, Literacy, and National Identity* (Chapel Hill: University of North Carolina Press, 2006).

100. Michael J. Quin, *A Steam Voyage down the Danube with Sketches of Hungary, Wallachia, Servia, Turkey, &c.*, 2nd ed., rev. and corr. (London: R. Bentley, 1835). "Travels in Egypt and Nubia Felix" cannot be clearly identified. Frederik Ludvig Norden, *Travels in Egypt and Nubia. By Frederick Lewis Norden. F.r.s. Captain of the Danish Navy ...* (London: Lockyer Davis and Charles Reymers, 1757) may have been too old by the 1840s. There are some other books with similar titles published in the nineteenth century. See also Dona Brown, "Travel Books," in Gross and Kelley, eds., *An Extensive Republic*, 449–58; Alfred Bendixen and Judith Hamera, eds., *The Cambridge Companion to American Travel Writing* (Cambridge: Cambridge University Press, 2009).

101. Benjamin Morrell Jr., *A Narrative of Four Voyages, to the South Sea ...* (New York: J & J. Harper, 1832). See also Skallerup, *Books Afloat and Ashore*, 79.

102. Nathaniel Bowditch, *The New Practical Navigator ...* (Newburyport, MA: Edmund M. Blunt, 1802). See also John Hamilton Moore, *The New Practical Navigator ...* (Newburyport, MA: Edmund M. Blunt, 1799); George Baron, *Exhibition of the Genuine Principles of Common Navigation ...* (New York: Sage and Clough, 1803). See also Jordan D. Marché, II, "Restoring a 'Public Standard' to Accuracy: Authority, Social Class, and Utility in the American Almanac Controversy, 1814–1818," *JER* (1998): 693–710.

103. Lawrence Furlong, *The American Coast Pilot ...*, 1st ed. (Newburyport, MA: Blunt and March, 1796); *The American Pilot: Containing the Navigation of the Sea-Coast of North America ...* (Boston, MA: William Norman, 1803). An earlier version was John Norman, *The American Pilot, Containing the Navigation of the Sea Coasts of North America ...* (Boston, MA: John Norman, 1791). See also John Malham, *The Naval Gazateer, or Seaman's Guide, Containing a Full and Accurate Account ... of the Several Coasts of the Countries and Islands in the Known World ...* (Boston, MA: W. Spotswood and J. Nancrede, 1797).

104. Samuel Buckner, *The American Sailor: A Treatise on Practical Seamanship ...* (Newburyport, MA: Peter Edes, 1790); John Clerk, *A System of Seamanship and Naval Tactics ...* (Philadelphia, PA: Dobson, 1799); Darcy Lever, *The Young Sea Officer's Sheet Anchor, or, a Key to the Leading of Rigging and to Practical Seamanship* (New York: Edward W. Sweetman, 1963; orig. pub. 1819); Thomas Truxton, *Remarks, Instructions, and Examples Relating to the Latitude and Longitude ...* (Philadelphia, PA: T. Dobson, 1794).

105. William Falconer, *An Universal Dictionary of the Marine ...* (London: T. Cadell, 1769); [William Duane], *The Mariner's Dictionary, or American Seaman's Vocabulary of Technical Terms ...* (Washington, DC: Duane, 1805).

106. Log of the *Bengal*, kept by Ira A. Pollard, 1832–35, PPL. See also Log of the *Niger*, kept by John Perry, 1844–47, PPL.

107. Richard Henry Dana Jr., *The Seaman's Friend* (Delmar, NY: Scholars' Facsimiles, 1979; orig. pub. 1851).

108. Oliver Goldsmith, *An History of the Earth and Animated Nature*, 8 vols. (London: J. Nourse, 1774). For the popular nature of this work, see

D. Graham Burnett, *Trying Leviathan: The Nineteenth-Century New York Case that Put the Whale on Trial and Challenged the Order of Nature* (Princeton, NJ: Princeton University Press, 2007), 80–83.

109. [Mercier], *Life in a Man of War*, 107.

110. John Mason Good, *The Book of Nature*, 3 vols. (London: Longman, Rees, Orme, Brown, and Green, 1826).

111. Richard Reece, *The Lady's Medical Guide: Being a Popular Treatise on the Causes, Prevention, and Mode of Treatment* ... (Philadelphia, PA: Carey, Lea, and Blanchard, 1833); Mary E. Fissell, "Hairy Women and Naked Truths: Gender and the Politics of Knowledge in 'Aristotle's Masterpiece,' " *WMQ*, 3rd ser., 60 (2003): 43–74.

112. This publication may be an eight-page poem: *The Duty of a Husband: Or, the Lady's Answer to the Duty of a Wife* ([London]: no pub., [1707?]).

113. *The Gentleman's Pocket Library* ... (Boston, MA: W. Spotswood, 1794).

114. William A. Allcott, *The Young Man's Guide*, 12th ed. (Boston, MA: Perkins and Marvin, 1838; orig. pub. 1835); Blum, *The View from the Masthead*, 20–24.

115. On general reform efforts to influence the reading of Americans, see Nord, *Faith in Reading*.

116. Herbert, *A Relic of the Revolution*, 114.

117. Sherburne, *Memoirs of Andrew Sherburne*, 162.

118. Log of *Eliza*, kept by Eleazer Elderkin, 1796–98, CHS.

119. Crowell, "Commonplace Book," Ms, MHS.

120. Cooper, ed., *Ned Myers*, 206.

121. *Narrative of the Capture of the United States' Brig Vixen*, 16. See also Log of the *Arab*, kept by Samuel W. Chase, 1842–45, Ser. 1, Vol. 1 Maritime Records, Coll. 949, MeHS; Log of the *Catherine*, kept by William E. Leeds, 1843–44, Log 940, Mystic; Log of the *Relief*, kept by William Clarke, 1833–39, Log 1838V, PEM; Log of the *Hull*, kept by Augustus Hamblet, 1838–39, Log 656, PEM.

122. Log of the *Ann Parry*, 1845–48, kept by Ezra Goodnough and John Joplin, Log 656 1845A, PEM. *Oxford English Dictionary*, s. v. "Fiddler's Green."

123. Little, *Life on the Ocean*, 87, 93–94.

124. [George Jones], *Sketches of Naval Life, with Notices of Men, Manners and Scenery* ..., 2 vols. (New Haven, CT: Hezekiah Hone, 1829), 2: 237.

125. Cooper, ed., *Ned Myers*, 263–72. For reference to another sailor occasionally reading the Bible, see Leech, *A Voice from the Main Deck*, 64.

126. Hester Blum, "Before and after the Mast: James Fenimore Cooper and *Ned Myers*," in Gilje and Pencak, eds., *Pirates, Jack Tar, and Memory*, 115–34.

127. Cooper, ed., *Ned Myers*, 263–72.

128. *Annual Report of the Board of Directors of the Boston Seamen's Friend Society*, vols. 18, 19, 20, PEM; Nord, *Faith in Reading*, 86, 151.

129. Nord, *Faith in Reading*. See also Hugh H. Davis, "The American Seaman's Friend Society and the American Sailor, 1828–1838," *American Neptune*, 39 (1979): 45–57; Stuart M. Frank, "The Seamen's Friend," *Log of Mystic Seaport*, 29 (1977): 52–58; Eugene T. Jackman, "Efforts Made before 1825 to Ameliorate the Lot of the American Seaman: With Emphasis on His Moral

Regeneration," *American Neptune*, 24 (1964): 109–18; Roald Kverndal, *Seamen's Missions: Their Origin and Early Growth: A Contribution to the History of the Church Maritime* (Pasadena, CA: William Carey Library, 1986); George Sydney Webster, *The Seamen's Friend: A Sketch of the American Seamen's Friend Society* ... (New York: American Seamen's Friend Society, 1932).

130. Cooper, ed., *Ned Myers*, 263–72; *Boston Recorder*, May 16, 1844; Nord, *Faith in Reading*, 127; Blum, *The View from the Masthead*, 30. John Hoxse quoted Flavel in his reminiscence of his years at sea. John Hoxse, *The Yankee Tar* ... (Northampton, MA: John Metcalf, 1840), 157–200; John Bunyan, *The Pilgrim's Progress*, W. R. Owens, ed. (New York: Oxford University Press, 2003; orig. pub. 1678); Richard Baxter, *A Call to the Unconverted* ... (Boston, MA: T. Bedlington, 1818; orig. pub., 1658); Baxter, *The Saint's Everlasting Rest* ... (Philadelphia, PA: Jonathan Pounder, 1817; orig. pub. 1650); Joseph Alleine, *An Alarm to the Unconverted Sinners* ... (London: T. N. Longman and T. Wiche, 1797; orig. pub. 1671); John Flavel, *The Touchstone of Sincerity* ... (Boston, MA: E. Bellamy, 1818; orig. pub. 1679); Philip Doddridge, *The Rise and Progress of Religion in the Soul* ... (London: J. Waugh, 1745).

131. Nathan Hatch, *Democratization of American Christianity* (New Haven, CT: Yale University Press, 1989), 146; Cooper, ed., *Ned Myers*, 264–65. For examples of pocket-sized hymnals printed for sailors, see Joshua Leavitt, *Seamen's Devotional Assistant, and Mariners' Hymns* ...(New York: Sleight & Robinson, 1830); Leavitt, *Seamen's Devotional Assistant, and Mariners' Hymns* ... (New York: William Van Norden, Printer, 1836).

132. Cooper, ed., *Ned Myers*, 264–65; *Christian Herald and Seaman's Magazine*, 1–11 (March 1816–November 1824).

133. *Sailors' Magazine*, 1 (April 1829): 245–48; ibid., 10 (November 1837): 73–74; ibid., 3 (May 1831): 280–81; Nathaniel Ames, *Nautical Reminiscences* (Providence, RI: William Marshall, 1832), 47–48.

134. Cooper, ed., *Ned Myers*, 265.

135. Quoted in Nord, *Faith in Reading*, 119.

136. *Dialogue between Two Seamen after a Storm* (Boston, MA: Lincoln and Edmands, 1813); *Dialogue between Two Seamen after a Storm* (Hartford, CT: Hartford Evangelical Tract Society, 1816). For the earlier British publication see *The Seaman's Confidence: Dialogue between Two Seamen after a Storm* (Banbury: T. Cheyney, [1800]). On how to read the Bible, see Nord, 123–24.

137. Quoted in Nord, *Faith in Reading*, 56, 115–17.

138. Allison, *The Crescent Obscured*, 207–25.

7. Tar-Stained Images

1. For the importance of the tarpaulin hats, see Richard Henry Dana Jr., *Two Years before the Mast: A Personal Narrative of Life at Sea*, Thomas Philbrick, ed. (New York: Penguin, 1981; orig. pub. 1840), 40, 116, 134, 304–05, 365.

2. On the importance of tar to the maritime world, see Mikko Airakinen, "Tar Production in Colonial America," *Environment and History*, 2 (1996): 115–25. On tar's role in the sailor's clothing, see Dana Jr., *Two Years before the Mast*, 304, 365; Theodore Fay, "A Series of Familiar Letters from Abroad," *New York Mirror*, 11 (April 26, 1834): 340; Margaret S. Creighton, *Dogwatch and Liberty Days: Seafaring Life in the Nineteenth Century* (Salem, MA: Peabody Museum of Salem, 1982), 4–5.

3. On the importance of images as historical evidence, see Peter Burke, *Eyewitnessing: The Uses of Images as Historical Evidence* (Ithaca, NY: Cornell University Press, 2001).

4. In some instances, eighteenth-century depictions of the Sailor's Farewell are about officers and not common seamen. See J. Simon "Sailor's Farewell," 1787, PAF4031, NMM. For an image of Nelson and common seamen, see Richard Westall, "Nelson in Conflict with a Spanish Launch, 3 July 1797," 1806, BHC2908, NMM.

5. For further discussion of these developments, see Paul A. Gilje, *Free Trade and Sailors' Rights in the War of 1812* (New York: Cambridge University Press, 2013); Gilje, *Liberty on the Waterfront: American Maritime Culture in the Age of Revolution* (Philadelphia: University of Pennsylvania Press, 2004).

6. "The Bostonians Paying the Excise-man or Tarring & Feathering," PC 1 – 5232B, LC; "Bostonians in Distress," PC 1 – 5241, LC. See Richard L. Bushman, "Caricature and Satire in Old and New England before the American Revolution," *Proceedings of the Massachusetts Historical Society*, 3rd ser., 88 (1976): 19–34.

7. Thomas Tegg, "Jack in a White Squall, amongst Breakers – on the Lee Shore of St. Catherine's," 1811, PAF3862, NMM. The National Maritime Museum, Greenwich, UK, has many of these prints available for viewing on its Web site. See http://collections.rmg.co.uk/collections.html#!csearch;searchTerm=sailor_caricatures.

8. George M. Roberts Woodward, "Sailors in Argument," PAF3775, NMM. For a similar view, see S. W. Fores, "Nautical Politeness or British Sailors Perusing the Dispatches from Cadiz," PAF4167, NMM; Thomas Sutherland, "A Scene on the Main Deck of a Line of Battle Ship in Harbour," 1820, PAH7339, NMM; Thomas Tegg, "Equity or a Sailor's Prayer before Battle. Anecdote of the Battle of Trafalgar," PAF3761, NMM; Thomas Rowlandson et al., "The Welch Sailor's Mistake or Tars in Conversation," PAF3757, NMM; Robert Laurie and James Whittle, "A Sailors Life in a Calm," 1803, PAD0172, NMM; George Cruikshank after Lieut. John Sheringham, "In Irons for Getting Drunk: From a Sailor's Progress," 1818, PAD0157, NMM.

9. John Rafael Smith, "Sailors in a Fight," 1798, PAH7352, NMM; Smith, "Sailors in a Storm," 1798, PAH7353, NMM; Smith, "Sailors in Port," 1798, PAH7355, NMM; Smith, "A Sailor's Return in Peace' to His Family," 1798, PAH7354, NMM.

10. Gilje, *Free Trade and Sailors' Rights*, 178–79; *New York Mercantile Advertiser*, January 26, 1806.

11. *Springfield, Massachusetts, Hampshire Federalist*, February 11, 1806.

12. James Akin, "A Bug-a-boo to frighten John Bull, or the Wright mode for kicking up a Bubbery ... " [1806], Charles Peirce Collection, AAS. See also Maureen O'Brien Quimby, "The Political Art of James Akin," *Winterthur Portfolio*, 7 (1972): 59–112.

13. James Akin, "The Bloody Arena," [1806], Charles Peirce Collection, AAS. For additional background, see Gilje, *Free Trade and Sailors' Rights*, 153, 179–80.

14. S. W. Fores, "Balance of Justice," March 3, 1802, PAF3882, NMM.

15. Benjamin Dearborn patented large scales used in warehouses along the wharves. The reference to the scales would therefore be familiar to anyone in a port city. *Philadelphia Poulson's American Daily Advertiser*, December 24, 1801; *Baltimore Federal Gazette*, May 4, 1802 (note: this advertisement has an illustration); *Charleston South-Carolina State-Gazette*, August 17, 1802 (note: this advertisement has an illustration); *Washington, D. C., National Intelligencer*, October 4, 1802; *Boston Independent Chronicle*, May 21, 1804; *Richmond Enquirer*, December 20, 1804.

16. *New York Daily Advertiser*, April 28, 1806.

17. *New York Republican Watch-Tower*, April 29, May 2, 1806.

18. *New York Mercantile Advertiser*, April 29, 1806. See also *Trial of Capt. Henry Whitby, for the Murder of John Pierce ...* (New York: Gould, Banks, and Gould, 1812).

19. *New York Daily Advertiser*, April 28, 1806.

20. *New Haven Connecticut Journal*, May 1, 1806.

21. *New York Commercial Advertiser*, April 30, 1806.

22. In the eighteenth century a waist jacket could refer to a vest-like inner jacket, or to the waist-length jacket worn by sailors and working men. The sailor's jacket was sometimes referred to as a monkey jacket. Linda Baumgarten, *What Clothes Reveal: The Language of Clothing in Colonial and Federal America, The Colonial Williamsburg Collection* (New Haven, CT: Yale University Press, 2002), 125–26.

23. Dumas Malone, *Jefferson and the Rights of Man* (Boston, MA: Little, Brown and Company, 1951), 27–32; Merrill D. Peterson, *Thomas Jefferson and the New Nation: A Biography* (New York: Oxford University Press, 1970), 310–14.

24. For images depicting press gangs with cudgels, see J. Barlow, "Manning the Navy," 1790, PAD4732, 1800ca., NMM; W. Humphrey, "The Liberty of the Subject," 1779, PAG8527, NMM; "The Neglected Tar," PAD4772, NMM; Thomas Rowlandson, "The Press Gang," PAF5935, NMM.

25. Akin, "The Bloody Arena" [1806], Charles Peirce Collection, AAS. Translated by Kyle Harper, Classics and Letters Department, University of Oklahoma.

26. Lorraine Welling Lanmon, "American Caricature in the English Tradition: The Personal and Political Satires of William Charles," *Winterthur Portfolio*, 11 (1976): 1–51. See also Alan Nevins and Frank Weitenkampf, *A Century of Political Cartoons: Caricature in the United States from 1800 to 1900* (New York: Charles Scribner's Sons, 1944), 24–25.

27. There are several definitions in the *Oxford English Dictionary* that could apply to the term "scud" in this print, including "hurried movement," dirt

or refuse, a light or sudden wind, and the ocean foam sprayed by the wind. Given the nautical context of the reference, the last definition is probably most appropriate. None of the terms would be complimentary to the editor's comments. *Oxford English Dictionary* s. v. "scud."

28. Lanmon, "American Caricature in the English Tradition," *Winterthur Portfolio*, 11 (1976): 1–51.

29. James Akin, "The Sailors Glee" (Newburyport, MA: James Akin, 1805), Charles Peirce Collection, AAS. Compare this picture with Thomas Rowlandson, "The Last Jog or Adieu to Old England," 1818, PAG8630, NMM; and Rowlandson, "Wapping," 1807, PAF3823, NMM.

30. A similar if less pronounced development occurred in Great Britain. See, for example, Thomas Rowlandson, "The Sailor," PAF5937, NMM; Thomas Potter Cook, [A Sailor], BHC2631, NMM.

31. Because this painting represented the sailor as a symbol of the nation at the end of the War of 1812, I selected it for the cover of *Free Trade and Sailors' Rights*. The painting is part of the private collection of Nicholas S. West.

32. "A Brother Cruiser," "The Boatswain's Mate," *Naval Magazine*, 1 (November 1836): [516]–21; *The Family Magazine; or, Monthly Abstract of General Knowledge* (1837): 41–43; Fitch W. Taylor, *A Voyage Round the World, and Visits to Various Foreign Countries in the United States Frigate Columbia …*, 2nd ed., 2 vols. (New Haven, CT: H. Mansfield, 1842), 1: 17. The same article without the illustration appeared in the Philadelphia *Public Ledger*, November 16, 1836.

33. American Seamen's Friend Society Certificate, Mystic. Illustration appears in Gilje, *Liberty on the Waterfront*, 225.

34. Edward Hazen, *The Panorama of the Professions …* (Philadelphia, PA: Uriah Hunt, 1836), 103.

35. "The Times," 1840, Edward Williams Clay, Reproduction Number PC/US-1837.C619, LC.

36. "Decatur's Conflict with the Algerine at Tripoli. Reuben James Interposing His Head to Save the Life of His Commander, August 1804," copy after Alonzo Chappel, National Archives Identifier 513331, Local Identifier 30-N-31(105), Series: Historical Photograph Files, compiled 1896–1963, Record Group 30: Records of the Bureau of Public Roads, 1892–1972, NA; "Death of Captain Lawrence. 'Don't Give Up the Ship,' June 1813," copy of engraving by H. B. Hall after Alonzo Chappel, circa 1856, National Archives Identifier 531087, Local Identifier 111-SC-96966, Record Group 111: Records of the Office of the Chief Signal Officer, 1860–1985, NA. See also Barbara J. Mitnick and David Meschutt, *The Portraits and History Paintings of Alonzo Chappel* (Chadds Ford, PA: Brandywine River Museum, 1992).

37. Hawser Martingdale, *Tales of the Ocean, and Essays for the Forecastle …* (New York: John Slater, 1840).

38. These illustrations appear in James Fenimore Cooper, *The Red Rover, a Tale*, Thomas and Marianne Philbrick, eds. (Albany: State University of New York Press, 1991; orig. pub. 1827), Plate XIII and Plate XVI.

39. W. Jeffrey Bolster, *Black Jacks: African American Seamen in the Age of Sail* (Cambridge, MA: Harvard University Press, 1997). See also Harold D. Langley,

"The Negro in the Navy and the Merchant Service, 1798–1860," *Journal of Negro History*, 52 (1967): 273–86.

40. Thomas Tegg, "A Milling Match between Decks," 1818, PC 1- 11981, LC.

41. George Cruikshank, "Mr. B. on the Middle Watch," 1835, PAD0162, NMM; Cruikshank, "Lacing in Style, 1819, PAG8634, NMM.

42. David Wilkie, "Billy Waters," ca. 1815, ZBA2427, NMM; unknown, Billy Waters, ca. 1820, ZBA2698, NMM.

43. See illustrations in Bolster, *Black Jacks*, following page 112. For a discussion of black images in this period, see Barbara Lacey, "Visual Images of Blacks in Early American Imprints," *WMQ*, 3rd ser., 53 (1996): 137–80.

44. Journal of William Alfred Allen (1840), NBWM; "Sketch of three sailors, one drinking, two smoking," Unsigned, ca. 1840, PEM. These illustrations appear in Gilje, *Liberty on the Waterfront*, 31, 257.

45. Log of the *Tartar*, kept by David M. Bryant, 1815–16, Log 1815P B6, PEM.

46. Log of the *Clara Bell*, kept by Robert Weir, 1855–58, Log 164, Mystic.

47. Log of the *Alexander Coffin*, kept by A. B. Matthew, 1849–50, PPL; Log of the *Niger*, kept by John Perry, 1844–47, PPL.

48. Kenneth R. Martin, *Whalemen's Paintings and Drawings: Selections from the Kendall Whaling Museum Collection* (Sharon, MA: The Kendall Whaling Museum, 1983), 107.

49. Martin, *Whalemen's Paintings and Drawings*, 102.

50. Log of the *Amelia*, kept by D. C. Powers, 1849–50, Log 510, Mystic.

51. For examples of ship pictures found in logbooks and journals, see Log of the *Ohio*, kept by Hugh Calhoun, 1847–48, MHS; Log of the *Hunter*, kept by John Child, 1810–15, MHS; Thomas Nicolson, "Thomas Nicolson Navigation and Logbooks, 1766–1813," Ms N-590, MHS; Log of the *Catherine*, kept by Ebenezer William Sage, 1809, Ebenezer William Sage Papers, Ms N-856, MHS; Log of the *Constitution*, kept by Lucius M. Mason, Logbook 128, 1844, MM; Log of the *La Plata*, 1848–50, Log 1847 W3 B15, PEM; Log of the *Lotos*, kept by Thomas Wilson Ross, 1832, Log 1832 L4, PEM; Joshua Gott, Commonplace Book, 1781–1807, PEM; Log of the *Richmond*, kept by Charles F. Morton, 1844–47, NBFPL; Log of the *Bengal*, kept by Ira A. Pollard, 1832–35, PPL; Log of the *Mayflower*, kept by Roland Swain, 1827–30, PPL; Log of the *Nancy*, kept by Seth Barlow, 1811, ODHS Log 196, NBWM; Log of the *Arab*, kept by Ephraim Harding, 1842–45, ODHS Log 435A, NBWM; Log of the *Euphrates*, 1842–46, ODHS Log 864, NBWM; Log of the *Condor*, 1839–41, Log 445, NBWM; Log of the *Emiline*, kept by Washington Fosdick, 1843–44, ODHS Log 147, NBWM. For a set of published ship portraits from logbooks and journals, see Martin, *Whalemen's Paintings and Drawings*, 95–121.

52. Log of the *Arab*, kept by Ephraim Harding, 1842–45, ODHS Log 435A, NBWM.

53. Log of the *Niger*, 1844–47, kept by John Perry, PPL. For several published portraits of whaling and published ship portraits from logbooks and journals, see Martin, *Whalemen's Paintings and Drawings*, 13–34. Some of the more detailed and lifelike of these drawings were made after 1860, which is beyond the date considered in this study. See also Michael P. Dyer, "An

Interpretive Analysis of Illustrations in American Whaling Narratives, 1836–1927," *New England Journal of History*, 53 (1996): 57–77; Dan Bouk and D. Graham Burnett, "Knowledge of Leviathan: Charles W. Morgan Anatomizes His Whale," *JER*, 28 (2008): 433–66.

54. Logs kept by Nicholas Pocock, 1741–1821, MM.
55. Log of the *Edward*, 1849, kept by Francis Barrett, NHA; Log of the *Samuel and Thomas*, 1847, kept by Joseph Bogart, NBWM. These illustrations appear in Gilje, *Liberty on the Waterfront*, 67, 84.
56. Log of the *Chilo*, kept by Sargent S. Day, 1846–47, Log 1846C, PEM.
57. Martin, *Whalemen's Paintings and Drawings*, 51. Martin has a number of work pictures in his book, but almost all of them were drawn after 1860. Ibid., 35–52.
58. Log of the *Tartar*, kept by David M. Bryant, 1815–16, Log 1815P B6, PEM; Log of the *Clara Bell*, kept by Robert Weir, 1855–58, Log 164, Mystic.
59. D. Graham Burnett, *Trying Leviathan: The Nineteenth-Century New York Case that Put the Whale on Trial and Challenged the Order of Nature* (Princeton, NJ: Princeton University Press, 2007), 125–28.
60. Log of the *Emiline*, kept by Washington Fosdick, 1843–44, ODHS Log 147, NBWM; Martin, *Whalemen's Paintings and Drawings*, 74–94.
61. Log of the *Vincennes*, kept by Joseph G. Clark, 1838–42, LC.
62. Log of the *Neva*, 1818–20, Log 1818 N2, PEM; Log of the *Constitution*, kept by Lucius M. Mason, 1844, Logbook 128, MM; Martin, *Whalemen's Paintings and Drawings*, 55, 64; Log of the *Shark*, kept by A. A. Adee, 1826–27, Vault A #1337 Shelf 28, NHS.
63. Log of the *Arab*, kept by Ephraim Harding, 1842–45, ODHS Log 435A, NBWM; Log of the *Three Sisters*, 1789–90, Log 1776A, PEM; Log of the *Shark*, kept by A. A. Adee, 1826–27, Vault A #1337 Shelf 28, NHS; Log of the *America*, 1824, Log 1824A PEM; Log of the *Three Sisters*, 1821, kept by Francis A. Burnham, Barker-Edes-Noyes Papers, Ms N-1800, MHS; Log of the *Emiline*, kept by Washington Fosdick, 1843–44, ODHS Log 147, NBWM; Log of the *Arab*, kept by Ephraim Harding, 1842–45, ODHS Log 435A, NBWM; Log of the *Alexander Coffin*, kept by A. B. Mahew, 1849–50, PPL.
64. Ned Buntline, "Ned Buntline's Life-Yarn: An 'Ower True Talk," *Knickerbocker*, 26 (November 1845): 437.
65. Captain Lawrence Furlong, *The American Coast Pilot* ..., 1st ed. (Newburyport, MA: Blunt and March, 1796); Captain Lawrence Furlong, *The American Coast Pilot* ..., 2nd ed. (Newburyport, MA: Blunt, 1798). This work underwent many editions in the nineteenth century and quickly became known as *Blunt's American Coast Pilot*. For a book that had some charts, see John Norman, *The American Pilot Containing the Navigation of the Sea Coasts of North America* ... (Boston, MA: John Norman, 1791). Interestingly this work contained only fourteen charts that covered large areas and might have been difficult to use in navigation. The book also included profiles.
66. Lawrence C. Wroth, *The Way of a Ship: An Essay in the Literature of Navigation Science* (Portland, ME: Southworth-Anthoensen Press, 1937), 39–43. See also John Blake, *The Sea Chart: The Illustrated History of Nautical Maps and Navigational Charts* (Annapolis, MD: Naval Institute Press, 2004).

67. Martin, *Whalemen's Paintings and Drawings*, 130–31, color image opposite page 29; Log of the *Hippomenes*, 1825, BV Wilson, George, Ms 2856, N-YHS; Log of the *George Washington*, kept by William Henry Allen, 1800, Huntington Library; Log of the *Angler*, 1809–10, Log 1809 A, PEM. See also Log of the *Catherine*, kept by Ebenezer William Sage, 1809, Ebenezer William Sage Papers, Ms N-856, MHS; Log of the *Vesper*, kept by Alfred Terry, 1846–48, Log 955, Mystic; "When I am far Away", NBWM. Several of these illustrations appear in Gilje, *Liberty on the Waterfront*, 40, 49, 64.

68. Log of the *Tartar*, kept by David M. Bryant, 1815–16, Log 1815P B6, PEM.

69. Log of the *Wilson*, 1816, BV Wilson, Ms 2856, N-YHS.

70. R. S. Coffin, *A Concise Narrative of the Barbarous Treatment* ... (Danville, VT: Ebenezer Eaton, 1816), 9.

71. Charles Andrews, *The Prisoner's Memoirs, or Dartmoor Prison* ... (New York: For the Author, 1815), 211; ([Josiah Cobb], *A Green Hand's First Cruise, Roughed out from the Log-Book of Memory* ..., 2 vols. (Baltimore, MD: Cushing & Brother, 1841), 2: 221–23; Perez Drinkwater Jr. "Sailing Problems & Examples, Account of Imprisonment in Dartmoor, Feb, 1815," Ser. 6, Vol. 1, Maritime Records, Coll. 949, MeHS.

72. Stuart M. Frank, *Dictionary of Scrimshaw Artists* (Mystic, CT: Mystic Seaport Museum, 1991); Martha Lawrence, *Scrimshaw: The Whaler's Legacy* (Atglen, PA: Schiffer, 1993); Nina Hellman and Norman Brouwer, *A Mariner's Fancy: The Whaleman's Art of Scrimshaw* (Seattle: South Street Seaport Museum with the University of Washington Press, 1992); E. Norman Flayderman, *Scrimshaw and Scimshanders: Whales and Whalemen* (New Milford, CT: N. Flayderman, 1972); Richard C. Malley, *Graven by the Fishermen Themselves: Scrimshaw in Mystic Seaport Museum* (Mystic, CT: Mystic Seaport Museum, 1983); Charles R. Meyer, *Whaling and the Art of Scrimshaw* (New York: David McKay, 1976).

73. Lawrence, *Scrimshaw*, 22. See also ibid., 33, 72, 124, 132.

74. For examples, see Hellman and Brouwer, *A Mariner's Fancy*, 28–29, 55; Malley, *Graven by the Fishermen Themselves*, Plate I opposite page 80; Flayderman, *Scrimshaw and Scimshanders*, 2, 24, 25, 56, 71, 73, 84, 93, 107, 216; Lawrence, *Scrimshaw*, 36, 37, 40, 75, 133, 136, 137.

75. Hellman and Brouwer, *A Mariner's Fancy*, 36, 37, 39; Malley, *Graven by the Fishermen Themselves*, 56, Plate I, opposite page 80; Lawrence, *Scrimshaw*, 18–19, 126, 127, 128, 134, 135.

76. Malley, *Graven by the Fishermen Themselves*, 52.

77. Abel Bowen, *The Naval Monument, Containing Official and Other Accounts of All the Battles Fought Between the Navies of the United States and Great Britain during the Late War* ... (Boston, MA: A. Brown, 1816). Malley, *Graven by the Fishermen Themselves*, 72, Plate II, opposite page 81; Flayderman, *Scrimshaw and Scimshanders*, 58, 65, 74; Lawrence, *Scrimshaw*, 135.

78. Lawrence, *Scrimshaw*, 69, 73–74; Malley, *Graven by the Fishermen Themselves*, 66; Flayderman, *Scrimshaw and Scimshanders*, 76–79.

79. Malley, *Graven by the Fishermen Themselves*, 59–63; Hellman and Brouwer, *A Mariner's Fancy*, 24, 31, 38, 39, 40, 42, 43, 46, 47; Flayderman, *Scrimshaw*

and Scimshanders, 60, 67–69; Lawrence, *Scrimshaw*, 38, 54, 55, 56, 57, 68, 124, 125.

80. Malley, *Graven by the Fishermen Themselves*, 54–59; Hellman and Brouwer, *A Mariner's Fancy*, 40, 48; Flayderman, *Scrimshaw and Scimshanders*, 31, 60, 65–67; Lawrence, *Scrimshaw*, 46–47, 65, 69, 70, 126, 132.

81. Lawrence, *Scrimshaw*, 83. See also Malley, *Graven by the Fishermen Themselves*, 63–65.

82. Hellman and Brouwer, *A Mariner's Fancy*, 46, 48, 49; Flayderman, *Scrimshaw and Scimshanders*, 66.

83. Hinsdale Collection, NBWM; Flayderman, *Scrimshaw and Scimshanders*, 70; Gilje, Liberty on the Waterfront, 258.

84. For examples of tusk scrimshaw, see Hellman and Brouwer, *A Mariner's Fancy*, 69–73; Flayderman, *Scrimshaw and Scimshanders*, 30–31, 242; Lawrence, *Scrimshaw*, 53–55.

85. Quoted in Lawrence, *Scrimshaw*, 166.

86. Malley, *Graven by the Fishermen Themselves*, 85–90; Hellman and Brouwer, *A Mariner's Fancy*, 66; Flayderman, *Scrimshaw and Scimshanders*, 162–73; Lawrence, *Scrimshaw*, 45, 50, 76, 78, 166–70, 174.

87. Hellman and Brouwer, *A Mariner's Fancy*, 9, 14–17, 24–25, 67–68; Flayderman, *Scrimshaw and Scimshanders*, 174–242; Lawrence, *Scrimshaw*, 43, 58–63, 93–119, 139–65.

88. J. Welles Henderson and Rodney P. Carlisle, *Marine Art and Antiques: Jack Tar, a Sailor's Life, 1750–1910* (Woodbridge, UK: J. Antique Collectors' Club, 1999), 106–29; Flayderman, *Scrimshaw and Scimshanders*, 243–93; Ewart C. Freeston, *Prisoner-of-War Ship Models, 1775–1825* (Annapolis, MD: Naval Institute Press, 1973).

89. Charles Tyng, *Before the Wind: The Memoir of an American Sea Captain, 1808–1833*, Susan Fels, ed. (New York: Penguin, 1999), 48–49.

90. Ira Dye, "Early American Seafarers," *Proceedings of the American Philosophical Society*, 120 (1976): 353–58; Dye, "The Tattoos of Early American Seafarers, 1796–1818," *Proceedings of the American Philosophical Society*, 133 (1989): 520–54; Simon P. Newman, *Embodied History: The Lives of the Poor in Early Philadelphia* (Philadelphia: University of Pennsylvania Press, 2003), 104–24; Newman, "Reading the Bodies of Early American Seafarers," *WMQ*, 3rd ser., 55 (1998): 59–82; B. R. Burg, "Sailors and Tattoos in the Early American Steam Navy: Evidence from the Diary of Philip C. Van Buskirk, 1884–89," *International Journal of Maritime History*, 6 (1994): 161–74; Burg, "Tattoo Designs and Locations in the Old U. S. Navy," *Journal of American Culture*, 18 (1995): 69–75.

Epilogue: The Sea Chest

1. Herman Melville, *Moby Dick, or the Whale* (New York: Modern Library, 1982; orig. pub. 1851), 9–15.

2. Charles Tyng, *Before the Wind: The Memoir of an American Sea Captain, 1808–1833*, Susan Fels, ed. (New York: Penguin, 1999), 15.

3. Samuel Smith to Rebecca Smith, Oct. 25, 1841, Box 73, Series S, Sub-series 20, Business Records Collection, Ms 56, NBWM.

4. Mystic Seaport has a collection of sea chests; two of the smallest of these have measurements of H 12¾" × W 31½" × D 13¾" and H 13¼" × W 34¾" × D 12". Two of the largest sea chests measured H 2½" × W 47" × D 23½" and H 22¼" × W 42½" × D 23¼". Two sea chests of average size were H 16" × W 44½" × D 19" and H 12¾" × W 31½" × D 13¾". This information was provided by Chris White, collections manager at G. W. Blunt White Library Mystic Seaport. Thanks, too, for the assistance of Paul O'Pecko, vice president, collections and research, director, G. W. Blunt White Library, Mystic Seaport.

5. Examinations of the use of material culture in studying the early republic include Richard L. Bushman, *The Refinement of America: Persons, Houses, Cities* (New York: Knopf, 1992); David Jaffe, *A New Nation of Goods: The Material Culture of Early America* (Philadelphia: University of Pennsylvania Press, 2010); Kariann Akemi Yokota, *Unbecoming British: How Revolutionary America Became a Postcolonial Nation* (New York: Oxford University Press, 2011).

6. J. Welles Henderson and Rodney P. Carlisle, *Marine Art and Antiques: Jack Tar – A Sailor's Life, 1750–1910* (Woodbridge, Suffolk, UK: Antique Collectors' Club, 1999), 122.

7. Herman Melville, *Redburn: His First Voyage, Being the Sailor-boy Confessions and Reminiscences of the Son-of-a-Gentleman in the Merchant Service*, Harold Beaver, ed. (New York: Penguin, 1976; orig. pub. 1849), 69.

8. Albert Greene, *Recollections of the Jersey Prison-Ship …* (Providence, RI: H. H. Brown, 1829), 57.

9. Log of the *Ohio*, kept by Hugh Calhoun, 1847–48, MHS; Log of the *Hull*, kept by Augustus Hamblet, 1839–42, Log 656, PEM; Richard Henry Dana Jr. to Edmund T. Dana, et al., March 1 and 20, 1835, Box 7, Dana Family Papers, I, 1835–40, MHS; Knut Weibust, *Deep Sea Sailors: A Study in Maritime Ethnology*, 2nd ed. (Stockholm: Nordiska Museets, 1976), 108–09. In some instances this overhauling of sea chests took place on Saturday. George Little, *Life on the Ocean; or Twenty Years at Sea …* (Baltimore, MD: Armstrong & Berry, 1843), 68–69.

10. Alfred M. Lorraine, *The Helm, the Sword, and the Cross: A Life Narrative* (Cincinnati, OH: Poe & Hitchcock, 1862), 58–60.

11. William McNally, *Evils and Abuses of the Naval Merchant Service, Exposed …* (Boston, MA: Cassady and March, 1839), 197–201.

12. Joseph G. Clark, *Lights and Shadows of Sailor Life …* (Boston, MA: Benjamin B. Mussey, 1848), 257–59; McNally, *Evils and Abuses of the Naval Merchant Service*, 21; *Harbinger*, Ship Records, 1842–61, Agent Owners Accounts, Vol. 1, Box 63, Series F, Sub-series 1, Cory Family Papers, Ms 80, NBWM; Accounts of the Ship *Gratitude*, 1841–42, Vol. 38, Box 20, sub-group 3, Series C, Sub-series 2, Swift and Allen Collection, Ms 5, NBWM; Bark *Mars*, Accounts & Crew Cash Book, 1842–45, NBFPL; Log of the *Cicero*, kept by Ebenezer Nye, 1827, Log 429, Mystic; Bark *Mars*, Accounts & Crew Cash Book, 1842–45, NBFPL; Richard Henry Dana Jr., *Two Years*

before the Mast: A Personal Narrative of Life at Sea, Thomas Philbrick, ed. (New York: Penguin, 1981; orig. pub. 1840), 78–79.

13. Little, *Life on the Ocean*, 89.

14. John Hoxse, *The Yankee Tar* ... (Northampton, MA: John Metcalf, 1840), 33.

15. James Fenimore Cooper, ed., *Ned Myers; or, A Life before the Mast*, William S. Dudley, intro. (Annapolis, MD: Naval Institute Press, 1989; orig. pub. 1843), 25, 35, 155, 271.

16. Dana Jr., *Two Years before the Mast*, 134.

17. Tyng, *Before the Wind*, 15.

18. Dana Jr., *Two Years before the Mast*, 365.

19. Harold D. Langely, "Warren Opie's Uniform at Winterthur," *Winterthur Portfolio*, 38 (2003): 131–42; Henderson and Carlisle, *Marine Art and Antiques*, 109. For descriptions of naval outfits in the nineteenth century, see [George Jones], *Sketches of Naval Life, With Notices of Men, Manners and Scenery* ..., 2 vols. (New Haven, CT: Hezekiah Hone, 1829), 1: 10–11, 108, 190.

20. Christopher Hawkins, *The Adventures of Christopher Hawkins* ... (New York: Privately Printed, 1864), 24.

21. For accounts indicating the types of clothing sailors purchased, see *Harbinger*, Ship Records, 1842–61, Agent Owners Accounts, Vol. 1, Box 63, Series F, Sub-series 1, Cory Family Papers, Ms 80, NBWM; Accounts of the Ship *Gratitude*, 1841–42, Vol. 38, Box 20, subgroup 3, Series C, Sub-series 2, Swift and Allen Collection, Ms 5, NBWM; Bark *Mars*, Accounts & Crew Cash Book, 1842–45, NBFPL; Log of the *Cicero*, kept by Ebenezer Nye, 1827, Log 429, Mystic. For a description of a sailor's kit in 1845, see Charles Nordhoff, *Man-of-War-Life: A Boy's Experience in the United States Navy* ..., John B. Hattendorf, intro. (Annapolis, MD: Naval Institute Press, 1985; orig. pub. 1855), 25.

22. Kathleen M. Brown, *Foul Bodies: Cleanliness in Early America* (New Haven, CT: Yale University Press, 2009), 103–04; Beverly Lemire, *Dress, Culture and Commerce: The English Clothing Trade before the Factory, 1600–1800* (New York: St. Martin's Press, 1997), 9–22.

23. Michael Zakim, *Ready-Made Democracy: A History of Men's Dress in the American Republic, 1760–1860* (Chicago, IL: University of Chicago Press, 2003), 44.

24. Stephen Allen, "Memoirs of Stephen Allen (1767–1852): Sometime Mayor of New York ...", John Travis, ed., typescript, NYHS.

25. Linda Baumgarten, *What Clothes Reveal: The Language of Clothing in Colonial and Federal America, The Colonial Williamsburg Collection* (New Haven, CT: Yale University Press, 2002), 125–26.

26. *Williamsburg Virginia Gazette*, July 22, 1773; Brown, *Foul Bodies*, 26–28.

27. Samuel Leech, *A Voice from the Main Deck: Being a Record of the Thirty Years' Adventures of Samuel Leech*, Michael J. Crawford, ed. (Annapolis, MD: Naval Institute Press, 1999; orig. pub. 1843), 129; Tyng, *Before the Wind*, 50–51.

28. David Proctor, *Music of the Sea* (London: HMSO in association with the National Maritime Museum, 1992), 33–88.

29. James Akin, "The Sailors Glee" (Newburyport, MA: James Akin, 1805), Charles Peirce Collection, AAS.

30. *Albany Gazette*, September 13, 1804.

31. Charles Herbert, *A Relic of the Revolution* ... (Boston, MA: Charles H. Pierce, 1847), 15–16.

32. Leech, *A Voice from the Main Deck*, 105.

33. Dana Jr., *Two Years before the Mast*, 223, 225, 249, 262–63, 330, 348, 401, 412, 480. Harry R. Skallerup, *Books Afloat and Ashore: A History of Books, Libraries, and Reading among Seamen during the Age of Sail* (Hamden, CT: Archon Book, 1974), 207.

34. Tyng, *Before the Wind*, 15.

35. Henderson and Carlisle, *Marine Art and Antiques*, 106–29.

36. William Bell Clark, et al., eds., Vols. 1–, *Naval Documents of the American Revolution* (Washington, DC: U.S. Government, 1976–), 11: 288.

37. John Foss, *A Journal of the Captivity and Sufferings of John Foss* ... (Newburyport, MA: A. March, [1798]), 6.

38. William Fairgrave to Wm. B. Preston, Sec. of U.S. Navy, Box 353, Naval Records Collection, RG 45, NA.

39. Little, *Life on the Ocean*, 120–21; Accounts of the Ship *Gratitude*, 1841–42, Vol. 38, Box 20, subgroup 3, Series C, Sub-series 2, Swift and Allen Collection, Ms 5, NBWM; Ledgers, Payments to Officers and Crews, 1823–25, Edward Carrington Papers, RIHS.

40. Thomas Dibden, *Songs, Naval and National, of the Late Charles Dibden; with a Memoir and Addenda* (London: John Murray, 1841), 77–78.

41. Paul A. Gilje, *Liberty on the Waterfront: American Maritime Culture in the Age of Revolution* (Philadelphia: University of Pennsylvania Press, 2004), 21–22.

42. John D. Symonds to Ebenezer Symonds, January 20, 1822, Symonds Family Papers, Ms O.144, PEM.

43. Little, *Life on the Ocean*, 181.

44. Thomas Gregory to Joseph Gregory, Oct. 2, 1821, Gregory Family Papers, PEM.

45. Gelston to Sec. of Treasury, Nov. 1, 1815, Correspondence with Sec. of Treasury, July–Dec. 1815, Folder 6, Box 6, David Gelston Papers, Coll. 170, Mystic.

46. Ebenezer Clinton, "Remarks," June 4, 1805, Beinecke.

47. William Reynolds, *The Private Journal of William Reynolds: United States Exploring Expedition, 1838–1842*, Nathaniel Philbrick and Thomas Philbrick, eds. (New York: Penguin, 2004), 25, 86, 173.

48. Log of the *Relief*, kept by William Clarke, 1833–39, Log 1838V, PEM.

49. Melville, *Moby Dick*, 314–31.

50. Melville, *Moby Dick*, 684–91, 825.

Bibliography of Primary Sources

Logbooks

Acastus, kept by Francis A. Burnham, 1817, Barker-Edes-Noyes Papers, Ms N-1800, MHS.

Action, kept by Enos Field, 1813, Field-Howe Papers, Ms N-1220, MHS.

Addison, kept by Moses Smith, 1834–37, PPL.

Adventure, kept by Francis Boardman, 1776, Log 1774A, PEM.

Africa, kept by Samuel Tillinghast, 1750, Vault A #36B, Shelf 24, NHS.

Agnes, kept by William Brown, 1808, Log 1808A, PEM.

Albion, 1829–30, PPL.

Alert, kept by Edward H. Faucon, 1833–34, Faucon Ms, MHS.

Alert, 1836, Dana Family Papers, I, Box 389, MHS.

Alexander Coffin, kept by Daniel Jenkins, 1832–35, PPL.

Alexander Coffin, kept by A. B. Mahew, 1849–50, PPL.

Alfred, 1812, Log 1812A3, PEM.

Amelia, kept by D. C. Powers, 1849–50, Log 510, Mystic.

America, kept by James Cheever, 1812–13, Log 1812 A2, PEM.

America, 1824–25, Log 1824A, PEM.

Angler, 1809–10, Log 1809A, PEM.

Ann, 1776, Log 177A, PEM.

Ann, kept by Ebenezer H. Mix, 1817–18, Msc. Stack, CHS.

Ann and Hope, kept by Daniel Arnold, 1798–1800, Ms 828, RIHS.

Ann and Hope, kept by Benjamin Carter, 1798–99, Ms 828, RIHS.

Ann and Hope, kept by Benjamin Carter, 1799–1800, Ms 828, RIHS.

Ann and Hope, kept by Benjamin Carter, 1800, Ms 828, RIHS.

Ann Parry, kept by Ezra Goodnough and John Joplin, 1845–48, Log 656 1845A, PEM.

Apollo, kept by John Upton, 1819–20, Log 936, PEM.

Arab, kept by Ephraim Harding, 1842–45, ODHS Log 435A, NBWM.

Arab, kept by Samuel W. Chase, 1842–45, Ser. 1, Vol 1, Maritime Records, Coll. 949, MeHS.

Arabella, 1830–31, PPL.

Atahalpa, kept by Ralph Haskins, 1800–03, Western American Collection, Beinecke.

Atlantic, kept by Theodore Lewis, 1835–37, Log 822, Mystic.

Atlas, 1813, MHS.

Averich Heishen, kept by George De Wolf, 1839, ODHS Log 638, NBWM.

Balance, kept by Melatiah Davis, 1833–37, PPL.

Barbarita, kept by Joseph P. Clifford, 1830, PPL.

Belvidere, kept by Jared Gardner, 1849, AAS.

Bengal, kept by William Silver, 1832–35, Log 1832 B3, PEM.

Bengal, 1832–35, Log 1832B B10, PEM.

Bengal, kept by Ira A. Pollard, 1832–35, PPL.

Betsy, kept by John Palmer, 1785–86, Folder 17, Vol. 10, John Palmer Papers, Coll. 53, Mystic.

Betsy, kept by Thomas Cutts, 1787–98, Ms N-1077 (Tall), MHS.

Betty, kept by Lot Stetson, 1772, Ms S-801, MHS.

Boston, kept by Samuel Tucker, 1778, Log 1778B B2, PEM.

Brandywine, kept by Henry Knox Thatcher, 1839–41, Folder 1, Box 1, Henry Knox Thatcher Papers, Ms 795, John Hay Library, Brown University.

Buckskin, 1812, Log 1812B BJ, PEM.

Catherine, kept by Ebenezer William Sage, 1809, Ebenezer William Sage Papers, Ms N-856, MHS.

Catherine, kept by William E. Leeds, 1843–44, Log 940, Mystic.

Cavalier, kept by William H. Wilson, 1848–50, Log 18, Mystic.

Ceres, 1783, Thomas Nicolson Navigation and Logbooks, 1766–1813, Folder 5, Ms N-590, MHS.

Chalcedon, kept by Edward H. Faucon, 1831–33, Faucon Ms, MHS.

Charles, kept by William Bedlow, 1759, BV Bedlow, Ms 877, N-YHS.

Charles Phelps, kept by Silas Fitch, 1842–44, Log 142, Mystic.

Charles W. Morgan, kept by James C. Osborn, 1841–45, Log 143, Mystic.

Charlotte, 1847–48, Coll. 238, Vol. 22, Mystic.

Charming Nancy, 1775–76, NYH-S.

Chesapeake, kept by Alexander S. Wadsworth, 1811, Maritime Records, Coll. 949, MeHS.

Chilo, kept by G. I. Day, 1846–47, Log 1846C, PEM.

China, 1832–35, ODHS Log 880A, NBWM.

China, 1837–38, ODHS Log 880B, NBWM.

Cicero, kept by Ebenezer Nye, 1827, Log 429, Mystic.

Commodore Perry, 1821–22, Log 22, Mystic.

Commodore Perry, 1822–23, Log 22, Mystic.

Commodore Perry, 1823, Log 22, Mystic.

Concord, kept by Nathaniel Appleton, 1799–1802, Log 1799C, PEM.

Condor, 1839–41, ODHS Log 445, NBWM.

Congress, 1815, kept by William White, Log 930, PEM.

Congress, 1815, kept by Jacob Crowinshield, Log 929, PEM.

Constitution, kept by Lucius M. Mason, 1844, Logbook 128, MM.

Constitution, kept by Alexander S. Wadsworth, 1811, Maritime Records, Coll. 949, MeHS.

Count D'Estainge, 1783–84, Folder 16, Vol. 6, John Palmer Papers, Coll. 53, Mystic.

Delphi, 1840–43, Log 947, Mystic.

Dispatch Packet, kept by Edward Norris, 1820–21, typescript, Norris Ms, MHS.

Dolly, kept by Sam Winchester, 1809–10, Ms 917, MdHS.

Doris, 1807–08, Log 82, PEM.

Duke of Cumberland, 1758–59, MHS.

Economy, 1827–28, Log 878, Mystic.

Edmund, 1780–81, N-YHS.

Edward, 1811, kept by Enos Fields, Field Howe Papers, Ms N-1200, MHS.

Edward, 1849, kept by Francis Barrett, NHA.

Effort, 1827–28, Log 241, PEM.

Eliza, kept by Eleazer Elderkin, 1796–98, CHS.

Eliza Adams, kept by Ephraim Harding, 1846–48, ODHS Log 435B, NBWM.

Eliza Haily, kept by James Babcock, 1809, CHS.

Elizabeth, 1769–74, MM.

Elizabeth, 1782, Log 1782E2 B2, PEM.

Emiline, kept by Washington Fosdick, 1843–44, ODHS Log 147, NBWM.

Equality, kept by Louis Brantz, 1793–94, series 8D, Reel #31, Peter Force Collection, LC.

Equator, 1839–41, ODHS Log 211, NBWM.

Essex, 1809–11, microfilm, Baury Ms, MHS.

Euphrates, 1842–46, ODHS Log 864, NBWM.

Exchange, 1764, Logbook 283, MM.

Fairplay, kept by John Palmer, 1779, Folder 14, Vol. 6, John Palmer Papers, Coll. 53, Mystic.

Fenwick, kept by Francis A. Burnham, 1822, Barker-Edes-Noyes Papers, Ms N-1800, MHS.

Flying Fish, kept by Richard Gatewood, 1815, Logbook 097, MM.

Franklin, 1821–24, Series 8D, Reel 87, Peter Force Collection, LC.

General Hancock, [1778], Hoadley Coll. Box 19, 34162, CHS.

General Wolfe, 1767–69, Log 1767 L, PEM.

George, kept by Josiah Bartlet Peel, 1821, Log 154, PEM.

Georgia, kept by Grovnor Gates, 1832–33, Log 1022, Mystic.

George Washington, kept by William Henry Allen, 1800, Huntington.

Gloucester, 1782–83, Log 1782 G2, PEM.

Grand Turk, 1792–93, Log 1788W, PEM.

Grand Turk, kept by Holton J. Breed, 1813–14, Log 924, PEM.

Halcyon, kept by William George Bailey, 1843–48, Log 988, Mystic.

Hannah and Elizabeth, kept by Robert Emery, 1798–99, Logbook 024, MM.

Hannibal, kept by Nathaniel Sexton Morgan, 1849–50, Log 862, Mystic.

Hawke, kept by Thomas Nicolson, 1778, Thomas Nicolson Navigation and Logbooks, 1766–1813, Folder 3, Ms N-590, MHS.

Hecla, 1841–44, Log 934, Mystic.

Henrietta, 1811, kept by Enos Field, 1813, Field-Howe Papers, Ms N-1220, MHS.

Henry Eubank, 1834, Log 688, Mystic.

Herald, kept by Thomas Delano, 1817–18, PPL.

Herald, kept by Thomas Delano, April 15–June 30, 1819, PPL.

Herald, kept by Thomas Delano, September 1–October 18, 1819, PPL.

Herald, 1828–29, PPL.

Hind, kept by Francis Boardman, 1784, Log 1774A, PEM.

Hippomenes, 1825, Ms 2846, BV Wilson, George, N-YHS.

Hornet, kept by Horatio Nelson Cady, 1825–26, Cady Ms, LC.

Hull, kept by Augustus Hamblet, 1838–39, Log 656, PEM.

Hunter, kept by John Child, 1810–15, MHS.

Industry, kept by William Bedlow, 1769, BV Bedlow, Ms 877, N-YHS.

Industry, 1766–67, Vault A #34, Shelf 24, NHS.

Israel, 1841–42, Log 90, Mystic.

Jamestown, kept by Henry Knox Thatcher, 1851–52, Folder 2, Box 1, Henry Knox Thatcher Papers, Ms 795, John Hay Library, Brown University.

John, kept by David Chever, 1812–13, Log 1812J B5, PEM.

John Adams, 1802–03, Log 227, Mystic.

John and William, 1751, Folder 1, Box 25, Ms 605, Stuyvesant-Rutherfurd Papers, N-YHS.

John G. Coster, kept by Thomas W. Abbott, 1845–46, MHS.

Joseph Starbuck, kept by Sanford Wilber, 1838–42, Log 228, NHA.

Juno, 1766, PPL.

Kingston, kept by Thomas Nicolson, 1784, Thomas Nicolson Navigation and Logbooks, 1766–1813, Ms. N-590, MHS.

La Plata, 1848–50, Log 1847 W3 B15, PEM.

Laurel, kept by Francis A. Burnham, 1817, Barker-Edes-Noyes Papers, Ms N-1800, MHS.

Liberty, 1774–76, MHS.

Lilly, kept by Thomas Cottrell, 1784–95, Vault A, #1448, Shelf 28, NHS.

Lilly, 1812, Ser. 1, Vol. 33, Maritime Records, Coll. 949, MeHS.

Little Rebecca, kept by John Palmer, 1779, Folder 14, Vol. 6, John Palmer Papers, Coll. 53, Mystic.

Lively, 1783–84, Log 1782 G2, PEM.

Logan, kept by Thomas Handsayd Cabot, 1834, microfilm roll 118, Vol. 1, Lee Family Papers, MHS.

Lotos, kept by Thomas Wilson Ross, 1832, Log 1832 L4, PEM.

Manufacturer, kept by John Taber, 1756, ODHS 0509 279, NBWM.

Martha, 1836–38, PPL.

Martha, kept by John D. Taber, 1838–41, PPL.

Mary, 1820–21, Log 22, Mystic.

Massachusetts, 1777, AAS.

Matsey, kept by Nath. K. Helme, 1793, Vault A, #38, Shelf 24, NHS.

Mayflower, kept by Roland Swain, 1827–30, PPL.

Mercury, 1800, Log 835, Mystic.

Merrimack, kept by Joseph Brown, 1799, Log 1799M, PEM.

Minerva, kept by Nicholas Pocock, 1776, MM.

Morrison, kept by J. Wiley, 1838, Log 992, Mystic.

Nancy, 1785–86, PPL.

Nancy, kept by Seth Barlow, 1811, ODHS Log 196, NBWM.

Nelle, kept by Peter Pease, 1769, ODHS Log 458A, NBWM.

Neva, 1818–20, Log 1818 N2, PEM.

New Jersey, kept by John M. Whitall, 1827–28, Mystic.

Niger, 1844–47, kept by John Perry, PPL.

Nonesuch, 1812, Series 8D, Reel 49, Peter Force Collection, LC.

Norwich, 1754–56, MM.

Nuestra Senora de Pezla, kept by Enos Field, 1816, Field-Howe Papers, Ms N-1220, MHS.

Ohio, kept by Hugh Calhoun, 1847–48, MHS.

O'Cain, kept by Francis A. Burnham, 1818–19, Barker-Edes-Noyes Papers, Ms N-1800, MHS.

Olive Branch, kept by Holton J. Breed, 1806, Log 1804P3, PEM.

Ontario, [kept by Murray Mason], 1824–25, Naval History Society Collection, Logbooks, Ontario, Ms 439, N-YHS.

Otter, kept by Samuel Fergerson, 1809–11, Western American Collection, Beinecke.

Palestine, kept by Larkin Turner, 1832, Vol. 14, Larkin Turner Papers, Mystic.

Palestine, 1839–41, Log 1839P2 O5 PEM.

Patty, kept by John M. Stillman, 1802, AAS.

Paulina, 1834–36, ser., 1, Vol. 26, Maritime Records, Coll. 949, MeHS.

Peacock, kept by Thomas J. Harris, 1824–27, LC.

Perseverance, 1800–01, Log 1800P, PEM.

Phenix, 1818–1819, Log 143, PEM.

Pilgrim, kept by Josiah Bartlett, 1781–82, microfilm, Bartlett Ms, MHS.

Pilgrim, kept by Edward H. Faucon, 1834–35, Faucon Ms, MHS.

Pliant, kept by Edward H. Faucon, 1829–31, Faucon Ms, MHS.

Polley, kept by Samuel Atkins, 1774–75, PPL.

Polly, kept by John Baker, 1804–05, Log 1804A B4, PEM.

Polly, kept by Jeduthan Upton, 1812–13, typescript, MHS.

Polly, kept by Thomas Nicolson, 1767–68, Thomas Nicolson Navigation and Logbooks, 1766–1813, Folder 2, Ms N-590, MHS.

Porpoise, 1838–40, Ms Coll. BV Log Books, N-YHS.

Porpoise, kept by James Freeman Curtis, 1821–22, Curtis-Stevenson Family Papers, Ms N-288, MHS.

Portsmouth, kept by William Weaver, 1848–49, Diary of William Weaver, N-YHS.

President, kept by Alexander S. Wadsworth, 1805, Ser. 1, Vol. 18, Maritime Records, Coll. 949, MeHS.

President, 1811, Ser. 1, Vol. 19, Maritime Records, Coll. 949, MeHS.

President Adams, kept by Joseph Ward, 1809, AAS.

Prince Ferdinand, kept by William Bedlow, 1759, BV Bedlow, Ms 877, N-YHS.

Prudent, kept by Holton J. Breed, 1804–06, Log 1804 P3, PEM.

Ranger, 1778–80, MM.

Ranger, 1794, Marblehead Historical Society.

Ready Money, kept by John Palmer, 1785, Folder 18, Vol. 11, John Palmer Papers, Coll. 53, Mystic.

Reaper, kept by Benjamin Neal, 1837–39, Log 1837 R3, PEM.

Recovery, kept by Benjamin Daniels, 1816–17, MHS.

Relief, kept by William Clarke, 1833–39, Log 1838V, PEM.

Remembergrace, kept by Thomas Nicolson, 1769, Thomas Nicolson Navigation and Logbooks, 1766–1813, Folder 2, Ms N-590, MHS.

Retrieve, 1776, Maritime Records, Coll. 949, MeHS.

Revenge, kept by John Palmer, 1777–78, Folder 12, Vol. 5, John Palmer Papers, Coll. 53, Mystic.

Revenge, kept by John Palmer, 1778, Folder 13, Vol. 6, John Palmer Papers, Coll. 53, Mystic.

Reward, 1807–08, Log 1807R, PEM.

Rialto, kept by George Denham, 1849, Log 1849, Mystic.

Richmond, kept by Charles F. Morton, 1844–47, NBFPL.

Russell, 1820–22, PPL.

Sabina, kept by Henry Green, 1849–50, Log 754, Mystic.

Sally, 1792, Vault A, #28, Shelf 4, NHS.

Sandwich, kept by Micajah Coffin, 1762–63, PPL.

Santiago, 1846, Coll. 238, Vol. 21, William Goddard Papers, Mystic.

Saratoga, 1813, Vault A #1917 Shelf 28, NHS.

Serapis, kept by Beaumont Groube, 1779–80, in John S. Barnes, *The Logs of the Serapis, Alliance, Ariel, under the Command of John Paul Jones, 1779–1780* ... (New York: Navy History Society by DeVinne Press, 1911).

Shark, kept by A. A. Adee, 1826–27, Vault A #1337 Shelf 28, NHS.

Sharon, 1841–45, *Abstract from a Journal Kept Aboard of the Ship Sharon* ... (Providence, RI: Paul C. Nicholson, 1953).

Sheffield, 1849–50, Log 351, Mystic.

Splendid, kept by William W. Gifford, ODHS Log 469, NBWM.

Squirrel, kept by Peter Pease, 1769, ODHS Log 458B, NBWM.

St. Louis, kept by James L. Henderson, [1831] Series 8D, Reel 42, Peter Force Collection, LC.

St. Paul, kept by Augustus Hamblet, 1839–42, Log 656, PEM.

Stonington, kept by G. W. Hamley, 1843–45, Log 335, Mystic.

Stonington, kept by Alanson Fiournier, 1846–47, Log 335, Mystic.

Stork, 1751–52, Folder 1, Box 25, Ms 605, Stuyvesant-Rutherfurd Papers, N-YHS.

Success, 1754–56, MM.

Success, kept by Joseph Crowell, 1750–52, Folder 1, Box 25, Ms 605, Stuyvesant-Rutherfurd Papers, N-YHS.

Superior, kept by James A. Dudley, 1814, microfilm, Dudley Ms, MHS.

Susanna, 1805–06, Log 1805S O5, PEM.

Sweden, kept by Benjamin Daily, 1849, Log 395, Mystic.

Swift, 1812, Vault A #1919 Shelf 28, NHS.

Talma, 1833, Log 968, Mystic.

Tartar, kept by David M. Bryant, 1815–16, Log 1815P B6, PEM.

Tartar, kept by William A. Rogers, 1817–18, Log 1817 T4, PEM.

Thomas Russell, kept by Samuel Curson, 1798–99, MHS.

Three Sisters, 1788–89, Derby-Peabody Papers, Box I, MHS.

Three Sisters, 1789–90, Log 1776A, PEM.

Three Sisters, 1820, kept by Francis A. Burnham, 1818–19, Barker-Edes-Noyes Papers, Ms N-1800, MHS.

Three Sisters, 1820–21, kept by Francis A. Burnham, 1818–19, Barker-Edes-Noyes Papers, Ms N-1800, MHS.

Tom, 1812, Vault A #1922 Shelf 28, NHS.

Triumph, kept by Abner Lothrop, 1791, ODHS Log 875, NBWM.

Trumbull, kept by Henry Bowers, 1810–13, Log 828, Mystic.

Tuscaloosa, kept by George DeWolfe, 1840–44, ODHS Log 640, NBWM.

Tusker, 1840, Box 1, MH 32, Papers of Isaac W. Baker, PEM.

Tyrannicide, kept by John Fiske, 1776–77, AAS.

Union, kept by Peter Pease, 1769–70, ODHS Log 458D, NBWM.

Union, 1780, Thomas Nicolson Navigation and Logbooks, 1766–1813, Folder 5, Ms N-590, MHS.

Valentine, 1812, Vol. 1, Box ½, Stephen B. Chace Papers, Mystic.

Vancouver, kept by Ebenezer Clinton, Western American Collection, Beinecke.

Vaughan, kept by Francis Boardman, 1767, Log 1767V3 B24, PEM.

Venus, 1782, Thomas Nicolson Navigation and Logbooks, 1766–1813, Folder 7, Ms N-590, MHS.

Venus, 1782–83, Thomas Nicolson Navigation and Logbooks, 1766–1813, Folder 5, Ms N-590, MHS.

Vesper, kept by Alfred Terry, 1846–48, Log 955, Mystic.

Vincennes, kept by Peter Myers, 1828–29, Log 630, Mystic.

Vincennes, 1833–39, PEM.

Vincennes, kept by James Alden, 1838–42, LC.

Vincennes, kept by Joseph G. Clark, 1838–42, LC.

Wasp, 1782, kept by John Fairbanks, Coll. 1411, MeHS.

Weymouth, 1823, Log 507, Mystic.

William, kept by William Bedlow, 1761, BV Bedlow, Ms 877, N-YHS.

William, 1769, kept by Thomas Nicolson, 1769, Thomas Nicolson Navigation and Logbooks, 1766–1813, Folder 3, Ms N-590, MHS.

William, 1770, kept by Thomas Nicolson, 1769, Thomas Nicolson Navigation and Logbooks, 1766–1813, Folder 3, Ms N-590, MHS.

William, 1771, kept by Thomas Nicolson, 1769, Thomas Nicolson Navigation and Logbooks, 1766–1813, Folder 3, Ms N-590, MHS.

William, 1783–84, kept by Thomas Nicolson, 1769, Thomas Nicolson Navigation and Logbooks, 1766–1813, Folder 6, Ms N-590, MHS.

William and Henry, 1788–90, Log 1788W, PEM.

William Hamilton, 1834–37, kept by Richard Lee, Ms S-727, MHS.

Wilson, 1816, Ms 2846, BV Wilson, N-YHS.

Young Teazer, 1813, Ser. 1, Vol. 41, Maritime Records, Coll. 949, MeHS.

Manuscripts

Adams Papers Digital Editions, MHS.

Adee Family Papers, LC.

Allen, Stephen, "Memoirs of Stephen Allen (1767–1852): Sometime Mayor of New York …," John Travis, ed., typescript, NYHS.

Ball Family Papers, Ms 2958.413, N-YHS.

Bark *Mars*, Accounts & Crew Cash Book, 1842–45, NBFPL.

Bining, Dr. Arthur, Collection, HSP.

Biographical Collection, MS 64, NBWM.

Brooklyn (ship) Ms., Manuscript Legal Documents, 1846–48, relating to the case of *John C. Dunford, Cooper v. Samuel Jeffrey*, Master of the *Brooklyn*, Mystic.

Business Records Collection, Ms 56, NBWM.

Carrington, Edward, Papers, Ledgers, Payments to Officers and Crews, 1823–25, RIHS.

Clinton, Ebenezer, June 4, 1805, "Remarks," Western Americana Collection, Beinecke.

Clinton, Charles P., Journal, 1802–06, WA Ms 9, Western Americana Collection, Beinecke.

Coffin, Charles G. and Henry, Collection, 1829–62, Ms 152, NHA.

Congdon, John Remington, Papers, Ms 82–240, RIHS.

Continental Army and Navy Letters, MbHS.

Cory Family Papers, Ms 80, NBWM.

Crowell, Simeon, "Commonplace Book of Simeon Crowell," 1818–46, Ms, MHS.

Dana Family Papers, MHS.

Dana Legal Papers, AAS.

Dunlap, Andrew Papers, PEM.

Fish, Nathan Gallup, Collection 252, Box 1, Mystic.

Fitch, Chauncy, Letters, 1839–40, Ms N-151, MHS.

Gardner Family Papers, AAS.

Gardner Family Papers, Ms 87, NHA.

Gatchell, Samuel, Papers, 1844–46, Ms 1988, MdHS.

Gelston, David, Papers Coll. 170, Box 6, Mystic.

Gott, Joshua, Commonplace Book, 1781–1807, PEM.

Gray Family Papers, Letters of Moses Gray, 1742–1904, MHS.

Gregory Family Papers, PEM.

Hammond Family Papers, Ms 46, NBWM.

Maritime Records, Perez Drinkwater Jr., "Sailing Problems & Examples, Account of Imprisonment in Dartmoor, Feb, 1815," Ser. 6, Vol. 1, Coll. 949, MeHS.

May-Winship – Barker-Archibald Papers, John K. Barker, Journal of a Voyage from Boston, Mass, Towards San Francisco, Upper California in the ship *Hanibal*, Geo. H, Willis, Master, 1849–1850, 1775–1922, MHS.

Misc. Coll., Colls. 1966, Misc. Box 94/16. MeHS.

Naval Records Collection, RG 45, NA.

New Bedford Port Society Records, NBWM.

Nicolson, Thomas, "Thomas Nicolson Navigation and Logbooks, 1766–1813," Ms N-590, MHS.

O'Brien, Donel Collection, Cornelius Albert Lee Letters, Ms 273, NHA.

Perry-Clarke Ms, MHS.

Palmer, John, Papers, 1776–86, Coll. 53, Mystic.

Reeves, Jacob, Papers, 1809–35, MHS.

Rogers Family Papers, Ms 87, PEM.

Sanborn Family Papers, Nathan Coleman and Elizabeth Hodgdon Letters, 1842–44, 1785–1875, MHS.

Swift and Allen Collection, Ms 5, NBWM.
Symonds Family Papers, 1822–37, Ms O.144, PEM.
White, Alden, Papers, Biographical Collection, MS 64, NBWM.

Newspapers

Albany Argus, June 14, 1844.
Albany Gazette, September 13, 1804, May 31, 1813.
Albany Wisconsin Chief, December 25, 1849.
Alexandria (Virginia) Gazette, January 8, 1825, January 9, 1843, October 4, 1848.
Amherst (New Hampshire) Hillsboro Telegraph, March 11, 1820.
Baltimore American and Commercial Advertiser, December 10, 1812.
Baltimore Federal Gazette, March 2, 1796, March 17, 1798, May 4, 1802, April 30, 1808, March 19, 1811.
Baltimore Gazette, February 14, 1833, October 11, 1834.
Baltimore Gazette and Daily Advertiser, June 4, 1830.
Baltimore Maryland Journal, July 26, 1775.
Baltimore Patriot, February 20, 1820.
Baltimore Sun, July 8, 1837, May 23, September 26, 1838.
Barre (Massachusetts) Farmers Gazette, August 8, 1834.
Bennington Vermont Gazette, November 22, 1822.
Boston American Traveller, May 6, 1837.
Boston Chronicle, April 9–12, 1770.
Boston Columbian Centinel, March 17, 1792, November 5, 1796, March 12, 1800.
Boston Commercial Gazette, April 5, 1824.
Boston Courier, November 4, 1844.
Boston Daily Advertiser and Repertory, March 18, 1813.
Boston Daily Atlas, November 6, 1844.
Boston Emancipator and Republican, March 4, 1842.
Boston Evening Post, March 23, 1765.
Boston Gazette, October 1, 1812, February 22, 1813.
Boston Idiot, April 4, September 12, 1818.
Boston Independent Chronicle, October 27, 1800, May 21, 1804, April 2, 1823.
Boston Daily Atlas, November 6, 1844.
Boston Massachusetts Gazette, November 30, 1787.
Boston Massachusetts Mercury, November 3, 1797, December 30, 1800.
Boston Massachusetts Spy, November 22, 1771.
Boston Mercury, October 30, 1795.
Boston New England Palladium, April 30, 1813, January 9, 1816.
Boston Patriot, March 18, 1819.
Boston Price-Current, November 2, 1797.
Boston Recorder, May 16, 1844.
Boston The Democrat, May 21, 1806.
Boston Traveler, August 5, 1825.
Brattleboro (Vermont) Messenger, May 25, 1833.
Brattleboro Vermont Phoenix, August 14, 1835.
Burlington Vermont Centinel, October 29, 1812.

Catskill (New York) Packet, September 24, 1792.

Charleston City Gazette, April 20, 1808, September 21, 1812, October 12, 1822.

Charleston Columbian Herald, May 12, 1798.

Charleston Courier, August 8, 1820, February 6, 1836, May 22, 1837, February 2, 1841.

Charleston Gazette and Daily Advertiser, February 17, 1796.

Charleston Morning Post, March 14, 1787.

Charleston South-Carolina State-Gazette, August 17, 1802.

Charleston Southern Patriot, December 10, 1844.

Charleston The Investigator, September 25, 1812.

Cherry-Valley (New York) Gazette, November 26, 1818.

Chillicothe (Ohio) Supporter, November 7, 1812.

Clinton Ohio Register, May 10, 1814.

Columbus Ohio Statesman, September 11, 1837.

Concord (New Hampshire) Mirrour, April 28, 1794.

Concord New-Hampshire Patriot, February 23, 1835.

Concord New-Hampshire Patriot and State Gazette, May 17, 1824.

Danbury (Connecticut) Republican Journal, January 9, 1797.

Dedham (Massachusetts) Norfolk Democrat, March 29, 1844.

Dedham (Massachusetts) Village Register, June 14, 1822.

Edwardsville (Illinois) Spectator, October 29, 1825.

Elizabethtown New Jersey Journal, November 8, 1786, February 15, 1814.

Gloucester (Massachusetts) Telegraph, January 26, 1846, August 26, 1848.

Goshen (New York) Orange County Gazette, August 16, 1814.

Greenfield Massachusetts) Gazette, December 10, 1798.

Hallowell (Massachusetts [Maine]), American Advocate, November 1, 1810, September 17, 1812, March 27, 1819.

Hartford American Mercury, October 12, 1795.

Hartford Times, September 2, 1837.

Haverhill (Massachusetts) Merrimack Intelligencer, January 27, 1810.

Hudson (New York) Balance, April 12, 1808.

Hudson (New York) Bee, February 7, 1808.

Jamestown (New York) Journal, February 10, 1841.

Kalamazoo (Michigan) Gazette, June 24, 1837.

Keene New Hampshire Sentinel, July 6, 1827, August 31, 1837.

London Champion or Evening Advertiser, October 31, 1741.

London Daily Post, August 22, 1726.

London Daily Post and General Advertiser, May 19, 1740.

London Weekly Journal or British Gazetteer, April 27, 1723.

Manchester (New Hampshire) Telescope, July 28, 1849.

Middletown (Connecticut) American Sentinel, May 4, 1825.

Milwaukee Sentinel, October 30, 1848.

Nantucket Enquirer, September 8, 1832.

New Haven Columbian Register, May 3, 1823, February 27, 1836, May 6, 1837.

New Haven Connecticut Herald, June 11, 1805, September 23, 1817.

New Haven Connecticut Journal, May 1, 1806.

New London Morning News, June 27, 1845.

New Orleans Times Picayune, September 21, 1839, July 3, 1841, January 15, June 1, 1843, October 18, 1846.

New York American, May 18, 1827, November 12, 27, 1832.

New York American Citizen, July 13, 1810.

New York American Minerva, February 18, 1795.

New York Argus, May 18, 1796.

New York Columbian, April 5, 1811, September 12, 1812, November 24, 1812, December 14, 1812, November 29, 1813.

New York Columbian Centinel, November 1, 1794.

New York Commercial Advertiser, January 26, August 4, 1798, April 30, 1806.

New York Daily Advertiser, June 28, 1787, May 30, 1798, March 12, 1800, May 10, 1805, April 28, 1806.

New York Diary, January 29, 1793, August 7, 29, 1797.

New York Emancipator, March 9, 1843.

New York Evening Post, January 8, 1813, January 4, 1830, March 24, 31, November 3, 1834, May 19, 1837, August 13, 1840, September 24, 1844.

New York Gazette, November 18, 1797, June 1, 1798, February 19, 1813.

New York Mercantile Advertiser, April 29, 1806.

New York National Advocate, October 29, 1817.

New York People's Friend, July 27, 1807.

New York Public Advertiser, July 9, 1807.

New York Republican Watch-Tower, June, 1, 1805, April 29, 1806, May 2, 1806.

New York Spectator, April 16, 1840.

New York Statesman, September 4, 1812.

New York The War, July 4, 1812.

Newark (New Jersey) Centinel of Freedom, September 15, 1812.

Newburyport (Massachusetts) Herald, April 21, 1837.

Newburyport (Massachusetts) Impartial Herald, January 17, 1794.

Newport Mercury, January 3, 1774, January 23, 1798.

Norfolk (Connecticut) Advertiser, May 20, 1837.

Norwich (Connecticut) Courier, August 8, 1827.

Philadelphia American Weekly Mercury, December 14, 1733.

Philadelphia Daily Advertiser, October 6, 1812.

Philadelphia Democratic Press, August 22, 1813.

Philadelphia Federal Gazette, July 1, 1790.

Philadelphia Freeman's Journal, September 4, 1782.

Philadelphia Gazette, August 10, September 18, 1797, August 12, 1799.

Philadelphia Gazette of the United States, April 4, 1799.

Philadelphia General Advertiser, January 31, 1793, March 16, 1793.

Philadelphia Independent Gazatteer, July 10, 1789, October 12, 1789, November 8, 1794.

Philadelphia Inquirer, October 10, 1829, November 13, 1829, June 30, 1833.

Philadelphia National Gazette, June 6, 1837.

Philadelphia Pennsylvania Evening Post, August 4, 1784.

Philadelphia Pennsylvania Packet, June 28, 1787.

Philadelphia Poulson's American Daily Advertiser, December 24, 1801.

Philadelphia Public Ledger, November 17, 1836, March 6, 1840.
Philadelphia Voice of the Nation, October 5, 1813, November 9, 1813.
Pittsfield (Massachusetts) Sun, September 5, 1839.
Portland Gazette, June 13, 1806, July 2, 1816.
Portland Weekly Eastern Argus, July 5, 1830.
Portsmouth (New Hampshire) Journal, July 19, 1834.
Portsmouth New-Hampshire Gazette, September 27, 1819, March 25, 1834, September 3, 1844, August 31, 1847.
Portsmouth New Hampshire Spy, February 1, 1792.
Providence Gazette, April 23, 1803.
Providence Patriot, February 10, 1830.
Providence Phoenix, October 15, 1803.
Providence Literary Cadet, July 1, 1826.
Providence Rhode Island American, September 10, 1813.
Providence United States Chronicle, November 16, 1796.
Raleigh Star, October 30, 1812.
Richmond Enquirer, December 20, 1804.
Salem Essex Gazette, October 2–9, 1770.
Salem Essex Registery, February 20, 1811.
Salem Gazette, January 19, 1796, September 22, 1797, October 3, 1823, April 16, July 30, 1824, April 3, 1828, October 2, 1829.
Salem Register, September 6, 1841.
Savannah Georgia Gazette, October 22, 1789.
Schenectady Cabinet, March 28, 1843.
Sing-Sing (New York) Hudson River Chronicle, February 6, 1836.
St. Augustine Florida Herald, June 2, 1838.
St. Louis Daily Commercial Bulletin, August 29, 1837.
Stockbridge (Massachusetts) Western Star, January 29, 1793.
Trenton Federalist, April 15, 1811.
Washington, D. C., National Intelligencer, September 8, October 4, 1802, July 20, 1807.
Williamsburg Virginia Gazette, February 11, 1739, July 23, 1773.
Wilmington (Delaware) American Watchman, November 18, 1809, May 5, 1811.
Windham (Connecticut) Herald, December 31, 1801.
Woodstock (Vermont) Observer, January 25, 1820.
Worcester (Massachusetts) National Aegis, October 3, 1838.

Magazines

Felt, Humphrey, "Sketches of Society: Character-High Strikes, *The Atheneum; or, Spirit of the English Magazines*, 1 (May 15, 1824): 188–90.
"Greenwich Hospital," *The Atheneum; or, Spirit of the English Magazines*, 1 (September 15, 1823): 488–89.
"Greenwich Hospital, an Old Sailor," *The Atheneum; or, Spirit of the English Magazines*, 1 (May 1, 1824): 99–104.
"Greenwich Hospital," *The Atheneum; or, Spirit of the English Magazines*, 1 (September 1, 1824): 425–29.

"Greenwich Hospital: Their Majesties the King and Queen of the Sandwich," *The Atheneum; or, Spirit of the English Magazines* (September 15, 1824): 464–68.

"Greenwich Hospital: the Barge's Crew," *The Atheneum; or, Spirit of the English Magazine*, 1 (November 15, 1824): 159–62.

Christian Herald and Seaman's Magazine, 1–11 (March 1816–November 1824).

The Critic, 17 (April 8, 1820): 143–53.

Berger, Jason, "Antebellum Fantasies of the Common Sailor; Or, Enjoying the Knowing Jack Tar," *Criticism*, 51 (2009): 29–61.

Dyke, John Van, "Narrative of Confinement in the Jersey Prison Ship by John Van Dyke, Captain in Lamb's Regiment, NYSA." *Historical Magazine*, 7 (May 1863): 148–49.

"A Piratical Sketch," *The Huntress*, 2 (June 2, 1838): 1.

Buntline, Ned, "Ned Buntline's Life-Yarn: An 'Ower True Talk," *The Knickerbocker*, 26 (November 1845): 432–42.

Buntline, Ned, "Ned Buntline's Life Yarn," *The Knickerbocker*, 27 (January 1846): 35–40.

Buntline, Ned, "Running the Blockade," *The Knickerbocker* 24 (October 1844): 319–25.

Reynolds, J. N. "Mocha Dick: or the White Whale of the Pacific: A Leaf from a Manuscript, *The Knickerbocker*, 13 (May 1839): 377–91.

Heysham, Alexander Hamilton, "The Messenger; or, A Yarn Upon the Lee Booms – A Sea Story, *Lady's Book* (June 1831): 293–98.

"Literary Notices," *The Ladies Companion ...*, 1 (August 1834): 202.

"Original Nautical Tales: The Haunted Brig," *The New-York Mirror*, 11 (May 17, 1834): 361.

The New York Mirror, 12 (August 9, 1834): 42.

"The Doomed Man," *The Museum of Foreign Literature, Science, and Art*, 3 (November 1, 1823): 440–46.

"A Melee. Cornwallis's Retreat; with the First of June. –A Gallay ..." *The Museum of Foreign Literature, Science, and Arts*, 8 (June 1826): 496–97.

"Pirates and Piracy from the Earliest Ages. No. I.: Pirates of the Classical and Mediaeval," *The Museum of Foreign Literature, Science, and Art*, 25 (October 1834): 337–43.

"Greenwich Hospital: the Barge's Crew: from the London Literary Gazette, an Old Sailor," *The New-England Galaxy and United States Literary Advertiser*, 7 (November 5, 1824).

Sailor's Magazine, Vols. 1–22 (1828–50).

Scots Magazine, and Edinburgh Literary Miscellany, Being General, 66 (1804).

Buntline, Ned, "The White Squall," *Western Literary Magazine*, 4 (January 1844): 86–87.

Printed Material

Abbot, Ariel, *The Mariner's Manual: A Sermon Preached in Beverly on Lord's Day, March 4, 1804* (Salem, MA: Joshua Cushing, 1804).

Abbot, Charles, *A Treatise of the Law Relative to Merchant Ships and Seamen ...* (Philadelphia, PA: James Humphries, 1802).

Adams, Robert, *The Narrative of Robert Adams, an American Sailor, Who Was Wrecked on the Western Coast of Africa* ... (Boston, MA: Wells and Lilly, 1817).

Aegyptus, Tiphys, *The Navy's Friend, or Reminiscences of the Navy* ... (Baltimore, MD: Printed for the Author, 1843).

Alcott, Louisa May, *Little Women*, James Prunier, ill. (New York: Viking, 1996; orig. pub. 1868–69).

Allcott, William A., *The Young Man's Guide*, 12th ed., (Boston, MA: Perkins and Marvin, 1838; orig. pub. 1835).

Alleine, Joseph, *An Alarm to the Unconverted Sinners* ... (London: T. N. Longman and T. Wiche, 1797; orig. pub. 1671).

Allen, William, *Accounts of Shipwreck, and Other Disasters at Sea* ... (Brunswick, ME: Joseph Griffen, 1823).

Allyn, Gurdon L., *The Old Sailor's Story* ... (Norwich, CT: G. Wilcox, 1879).

Ames, Nathaniel, *A Mariner's Sketches* (Providence, RI: Cory, Marshall and Hammond, 1830).

    Nautical Reminiscences (Providence, RI: Marshall, 1832).

    An Old Sailor's Yarns (New York: George Dearborn, 1835).

Andrews, Charles, *The Prisoners' Memoirs, or Dartmoor Prison* ... (New York: Printed for the Author, 1815).

Andros, Thomas, *The Old Jersey Captive* ... (Boston, MA: William Pierce, 1833).

Anon., *An Address to the Spectator of the Awful Execution of the Pirates in Boston, February 19, 1819* (Boston, MA: Boston Society for the Moral and Religious Instruction of the Poor: U. Crocker, 1819).

    The American Pilot: Containing the Navigation of the Sea-Coast of North America ... (Boston, MA: William Norman, 1803).

    The American Republican Harmonist ... (Philadelphia, PA: William Duane, 1803).

    The Anti-Federalist Papers and the Constitutional Convention Debates, Ralph Ketchum, ed. (New York: New American Library, 1986).

    Ben Boatswain's Yarns, or Tales of the Ocean (New York: Murphy, 184?).

    The Cabin-Boy and Forecastle Sailor's Delight ... (New York: S. A. Burtus, 1817).

    Captain James Who Was Hung and Gibbeted in England, for Starving to Death His Cabin Boy (Newburyport: Broadside, 1800).

    A Christian Exhortation to Sailors, and Persons Engaged in a Seafaring Life (New York: Samuel Wood & Sons, 1817).

    A Circumstantial Narrative of the Loss of the Haswell ... (Springfield, MA: Drins and Russell, 1786).

    Dartmoor Massacre (Pittsfield, MA: Allen, 1815).

    Dialogue between Two Seamen after a Storm (Boston, MA: Lincoln and Edmands, 1813).

    Dialogue between Two Seamen after a Storm (Hartford, CT: Hudson, Hartford Evangelical Tract Society, 1816).

    The Duty of a Husband: Or, the Lady's Answer to the Duty of a Wife (London: 1707).

    Dying Declaration of Nicholas Fernandez ... (New York: George Lambert, 1830).

An Elegy on the Death of Captain Valantine, ... (Broadside, 1801).

A Fair Account of the Late Unhappy Disturbance in New England (London: B. White, 1770).

The Festival of Mirth, and American Tar's Delight (New York: Thomas B. Jones, 1800).

The Frisky Songster: Being a Select Choice of such Songs as are Distinguished for Their Jollity, High Taste and Humour ... (London, 1776).

A Full and Particular Account of the Trial of Franciso Dos Santos ... (New York, 1806).

The Gentleman's Pocket Library ... (Boston, MA: W. Spotswood, 1794).

God's Wonders in the Great Deep, Recorded in Several Wonderful and Amazing Accounts Sailors, Who Have Met with Unexpected Deliverances ... (Newburyport, MA: Allen for Thomas & Whipple, 1805).

The History of the Bloody Exploits of the Most Noted Pirates ... (Hartford, CT: Silas Andrus & Son, 1850).

The History of the Lives and Bloody Exploits of the Most Noted Pirates ... (Hartford, CT: Silas Andrus & Son, 1836).

The History of the Pirates, Containing the Lives of Those Noted Pirate Captains ... (Hartford, CT: Henry Benton, 1829).

The History of the Pirates, Containing the Lives of Those Noted Pirate Captains ... (Haverill, MA: Thomas Carey, 1825).

Horrid Massacre at Dartmoor Prison (Broadside, 1815).

Humanity in Algiers: Or the Story of Azea by an American, Late Slave in Algiers (Troy, NY: Moffitt, 1801).

Humorous and Diverting Dialogues, between Monsieur Baboon, a French Dancing-Master (but lately come over:) and Jack Tar, an English Sailor (London: C. Corbet: 1755).

Impressed Seamen from Salem (Salem, MA: Broadside, March 30, 1815).

The Impressment of an American Sailor Boy, Broadside, N-YHS.

The Interesting Trials of the Pirates for the Murder of William Little, Captain of the Ship American Eagle (Newburyport, MA: Herald Press, 1797).

The Life, Adventures, and Piracies of Captain Singleton, reprint of the 1840 ed., Sir Walter Scott, ed. (New York: AMS Press, 1973; orig. pub. 1720).

Life of Father Taylor: The Sailor Preacher (Boston, MA: The Boston Port and Seamen's Aid Society, 1904).

Lives and Confessions of John Williams, Francis Frederick, John R. Rog, and Peter Peterson, ... (Boston, MA: J. T. Buckingham, 1819).

Manly: A Favorite New Song (no place: no pub., n.d.), in NBWM.

The Mariner's Chronicle: Containing Narratives of the Most Remarkable Disasters at Sea, Such as Shipwrecks, Storms, Fires, Famines, also Naval Engagements, Piratical Adventures, Incidents of Discover, and Other Extraordinary and Interesting Occurrences (New Haven, CT: George W. Gorton, 1834).

The Mariner's Chronicle: Containing Narratives of the Most Remarkable Disasters at Sea, Such as Shipwrecks, Storms, Fires, Famines, also Naval Engagements, Piratical Adventures, Incidents of Discover, and Other Extraordinary and Interesting Occurrences (New Haven, CT: George W. Gorton, 1835).

The Mariners' Church (New York, 1818).

A Narrative of the Capture of the United States' Brig Vixen ... (New York: The Office of *The War*, 1813).

Narratives of Shipwrecks, Fires, Famines, and Other Calamities Incident to a Life of Maritime Enterprise; with Authentic Particulars of the Extraordinary Adventures and Sufferings of the Crews, Their Reception and Treatment on Distant Shores; and a Concise Description of the Country, Customs, and Manners of the Inhabitants: Including an Account of the Deliverance of the Survivors. By Archibald Duncan, Esq. Late of the Royal Navy. In Four Volumes, Vol. I–IV (Philadelphia, PA: Thomas Desilver, 1810).

The Nautical Songster or Seaman's Companion ... (Baltimore, MD: Henry S. Keatinge, 1798).

The Naval Chaplain, Exhibiting a View of American Efforts to Benefit Seamen (Boston, MA: T. R. Marvin, 1831).

The Naval Songster, or the Sailor's Pocket Companion (Boston, MA: Coverly, 1813).

The Naval Songster, Containing a Collection of the Best Selected Naval Songs ... (Frederick Town, MD: Bartgis, 1814).

Patriotic Medley: Being a Choice Collection of Patriotic, Sentimental, Hunting, and Sea Songs ... (New York: Jacob Johnkin, 1800).

The Pirates. A Brief Account of the Horrid Massacre of the Captain, Mate, and Supercargo of the Schooner Plattsburg ... (Boston, MA: H. Trumbull, 1819).

The Pirates. A Brief Account of the Horrid Murder of the Captain and Mate of a Buenos Ayrean Prize Schooner... (Boston, MA: H. Trumbull, 1820).

The Pirates Own Book, or Authentic Narratives of the Lives, Exploits, and Executions of the Most Celebrated Sea Robbers ... (Boston, MA: Thomas Groom, 1837).

The Pirates Own Book, or Authentic Narratives of the Lives, Exploits, and Executions of the Most Celebrated Sea Robbers (Salem, MA: Marine Research Society 1924; orig. pub. Boston, 1837).

The Pirates Own Book, or Authentic Narratives of the Lives, Exploits, and Executions of the Most Celebrated Sea Robbers. With Historical Sketches of the Joassamee, Spanish, Ladrone, West India, Malay, and Algerian Pirates (Philadelphia, PA: Thomas Cowperthwait & Co., 1839).

The Political Harmonist ... (London: T. Williams, 1797).

Remarkable Shipwrecks, or A Collection of Interesting Accounts of Naval Disasters with Many Particulars of the Extraordinary Adventures and Sufferings of the Crews ... (Hartford, CT: Andrus and Starr, 1813).

A Report of the Trial of Pedro Gilbert, Bernardo De Soto, Francisco Ruiz, ... (Boston, MA: Russell, Odiorne & Metcalf, 1834).

A Report of the Trial of Samuel Tulley and John Dalton ... *for Piracy* ... (Boston, MA: J. Belcher, 1812).

The Rochester Lass, broadside (London: Pitts, n.d.).

The Sailor's Medley: A Collection of the Most Admired Sea and Other Songs ... (Philadelphia, PA: Matthew Carey, 1800).

The Seaman's Confidence: Dialogue between Two Seamen after a Storm (Banbury, UK: T. Cheyney, 1800).

Shipwrecks and Disasters at Sea, or Historical Narratives of the Most Noted Calamities and Providential Deliverances which Have Resulted from

Maritime Enterprise with a Sketch of Various Expedients for Preserving the Lives of Mariners (Edinburgh: George Ramsey, 1812).

A Short Narrative of the Horrid Massacre in Boston ... (Boston, MA: Edes and Gill, 1770).

A Sketch of the Life and Confessions of Thos. Winslow, One of the Pirates ... (New York: Isaac Chaunay, 1832).

Supplement to the Report of the Trial of the Spanish Pirates with Confessions on Protests Written by Them in Prison ... (Boston, MA: Lemuel Gulliver, 1835).

The Syren: A Choice Collection of Sea Hunting, and Other Songs ... (Philadelphia, PA: Matthew Carey, 1800)

Theatre, Holliday-Street. First Appearance in this Theatre of Monsieur ... the Entertainments to Conclude with the Melo Drama of Pitcairn's Island, or the Mutiny on the Bounty (Baltimore, MD: J. Robinson, 1832).

The Tragical Calendar and Pirates Own Almanac, 1846 (Baltimore, MD: J. B. Keller, 1846).

Trial of Capt. Henry Whitby, for the Murder of John Pierce ... (New York: Gould, Banks, and Gould, 1812).

Trial of the Twelve Spanish Pirates on the Schooner Panda, a Guinea Slaver ... (Boston, MA: Lemuel Gulliver, 1834).

The Trial of William Wemms ... (Boston, MA: Fleeming, 1770).

A True Account of the Loss of the Ship Columbia, Exeter, lately Commanded by Isaac Chauncey (Portsmouth, NH: Broadside, 1792).

The Tryal, Last Dying Words, Speech and Confession of Richard Parker, (Alias Admiral Parker) Late President of the Mutinous Fleet (New York, 1797).

Tom Tuff, Decatur's Victory, The Rochester Lass. As Sure as a Gun (Philadelphia, PA, 1805).

Arnold, Samuel James, *The Shipwreck: A Comic Opera in Two Acts* (New York: D. Longworth, 1805).

Atkinson, James, *Epitome of the Art of Navigation* ... (London: William Mount and Thomas Page, 1744).

Baker, Joseph, *The Confessions of Joseph Baker ... for Murder and Piracy* ... (Philadelphia, PA: Folwell, 1800).

Bancroft, George, *A History of the United States, from the Discovery of the American Continent to the Present Time*, 10 vols. (Boston, MA: Charles Bowen, 1834–78).

Barnard, Charles H., *A Narrative of the Sufferings of Capt. Charles H. Barnard* ... (New York: J. Lindon, 1829).

Barney, Mary, ed., *Biographical Memoir of the Late Joshua Barney* ... (Boston, MA: Gray and Bowen, 1832).

Baron, George, *Exhibition of the Genuine Principles of Common Navigation* ... (New York: Sage and Clough, 1803).

Barrow, Sir John, *A Description of Pitcairn's Island and Its Inhabitants with an Authentic Account of the Mutiny of the Ship Bounty, and of the Subsequent Fortunes of the Mutineers* (New York: Harper & Brothers, 1838).

Bates, Joseph, *The Autobiography of Elder Joseph Bates* ... (Battle Creek, MI: Steam Press, 1868).

Baxter, Richard, *A Call to the Unconverted* ... (Boston, MA: T. Bedlington, 1818; orig. pub., 1658).
   The Saint's Everlasting Rest ... (Philadelphia, PA: Jonathan Pounder, 1817; orig. pub. 1650).
Bickerstaff, Isaac, *Thomas and Sally; or the Sailor's Return* ... (Dublin: Sarah Cotter, 1761).
   Thomas and Sally: Or the Sailor's Return ... (Philadelphia, PA: Henry Taylor, 1791).
Blatchford, John, *Narrative of the Remarkable Occurrences in the Life of John Blatchford* ... (New London, CT: T. Green, 1788).
Bligh, William, *A Narrative of the Mutiny, on Board His Britannic Majesty's Ship Bounty; and the Subsequent Voyage of Part of the Crew* ... (Philadelphia, PA: William Spotswood, 1790).
Boston Seaman's Friend Society, *Annual Report of the Board of Directors of the Boston Seamen's Friend Society*, Vols 1–21 (Boston, MA: T. R. Marvin, 1829–40).
Boston Society for the Religious and Moral Improvement of Seamen, *Address to Masters of Vessels on the Objects of the Boston Society for the Religious and Moral Improvement of Seamen* (Boston, MA: John Eliot, 1812).
   Address to a Master of a Vessel, Intended to Accompany a Book of Prayers for the Use of Seamen (Boston, MA: Eliot, 1815).
   The First Annual Report of the Executive Committee of the Boston Society for the Religious and Moral Improvement of Seamen (Boston, MA: Broadside, 1813).
   Handsome Jack: Or an Example for Sailors, no. V (Boston, MA: Eliot, 1815).
   Prayers Social and Private, To Be Used at Sea (Boston, MA: John Eliot, 1815).
   A Sailor's Tribute of Gratitude to Two Virtuous Women, No. II (Boston, MA: John Eliot, 1812).
Boston Society for the Religious and Moral Improvement of Seamen, *The Sailor's Life Boat, Tract No IX* (Boston, MA: John Eliot, 1816).
Bowditch, Nathaniel, *The New American Practical Navigator* ... (Newburyport, MA: Edmund M. Blunt, 1802).
Bradford, Gamaliel, *The Seaman's Friend* (Boston, MA: The Boston Society for the Religious and Moral Improvement of Seamen, 1817).
Brazier, John *The Duty and Privilege of an Active Benevolence, Address Delivered before the Seamen's Widow and Orphan Association* ... (Salem, MA: Essex Register Office, 1836).
Brewster, Mary, *"She Was a Sister Sailor": The Whaling Journals of Mary Brewster, 1845–1851*, Joan Druett, ed. (Mystic, CT: Mystic Seaport Museum, 1992).
Bromley, J. S., *The Manning of the Royal Navy: Selected Public Pamphlets, 1693–1873* (London: The Navy Records Society, 1974).
Brown, Andrew, *A Sermon on the Dangers of a Seafaring Life* ... (Boston, MA: Belknap and Hall, 1793).
Brown, Martha Smith Brewer, *She Went A-Whaling: The Journal of Martha Smith Brewer Brown* ..., Anne Mackay, ed. (Orient, NY: Oyster Ponds Historical Society, 1993).

Browne, J. Ross, *Etchings of a Whaling Cruise* ... (New York: Harper & Brothers, 1846).

Bryant, William M. *The Old Sailor: A Thrilling Narrative of Elias Hutchins* ... (Biddeford, ME: Eastern Journal, 1853).

Buckner, Samuel, *The American Sailor: A Treatise on Practical Seamanship* ... (Newburyport, MA: Peter Edes, 1790).

Bulwer-Lytton, Edward, *Pelham, or Adventures of a Gentleman* (Philadelphia, PA: J. B. Lipponcot, 1832).

Buntline, Ned, *Ned Buntline's Life-Yarn* (New York: Garrett, 1849).

   The Wheel of Misfortune, Or, the Victims of Lottery and Policy Dealers a Yarn from the Web of New York Life (New York: Garrett, ca. 1853).

Bunyan, John, *The Pilgrim's Progress*, W. R. Owens, ed. (New York: Oxford University Press, 2003; orig. pub. 1678).

Burrington, George *A Voyage to New South Wales, with a Description of the Country* ... (Philadelphia, PA: Thomas Dobson, 1796).

Butts, I. R., *Laws of the Sea: The Rights of Seamen, the Coaster's & Fisherman's Guide* ... (Boston, MA: I. R. Butts, 1854).

Byron, Lord, *The Corsair, a Tale* (Boston, MA: West & Blake, 1814).

Cardell, William S., *Story of Jack Halyard, the Sailor Boy, or The Virtuous Family: Designed for American Children in Families and Schools* (New York: J. Seymour, 1825).

Carey, George G., ed., *A Sailor's Songbag: An American Rebel in an English Prison, 1777–1779* (Amherst: University of Massachusetts Press, 1976).

Carey, Mathew, *A Short Account of Algiers* ... (Philadelphia, PA: J. Parker for M. Carey. 1794).

Carpenter, Jonathan, *Jonathan Carpenter's Journal: Being the Diary of a Revolutionary War Solder and Pioneer Settler of Vermont*, Miriam and Wes Herwig, eds. (Randolph Carter, VT: A Greenhills Book, 1994).

Chapin, Stephen, *A Sermon Addressed to Mariners, North Yarmouth, State of Maine* ... (Portland, ME: Thomas Todd, 1821).

Chase, Owen, "Narrative of the Most Extraordinary and Distressing Shipwreck of the Whaleship Essex, ... " in Thomas Heffernan, *Stove by a Whale: Owen Chase and the Essex* (Middleton, CT: Wesleyan University Press, 1981), 15–96.

Clark, George Edward, *Seven Years a Sailor's Life* (Boston, MA: Adams & Co., 1867).

Clark, Joseph G., *Lights and Shadows of Sailor Life,* ... (Boston, MA: Benjamin B. Mussey, 1848).

Clark, William Bell, et al., eds., *Naval Documents of the American Revolution* ..., Vols 1– (Washington, DC: U.S. Government Printing Office, 1964–).

Claypoole, John, "John Claypoole's Memorandum-Book," Charles Francis Jenkins, ed., *Pennsylvania Magazine of History and Biography*, 16 (1892): 178–90.

Clerk, John, *A System of Seamanship and Naval Tactics* ... (Philadelphia, PA: Dobson, 1799).

Cleveland, Richard, *A Narrative of Voyages and Commercial Enterprises* (London: Edward Moxon, 1842).

Cobb, James, *The Capture: A Favorite Song in the Pirates Composed by S. Storace* (Philadelphia, PA: Carr, 1793).

Lullaby – A Favorite Ballad in the Comic Opera of the Pirates (Philadelphia, PA: Carr, 1793).

A Sailor Lov'd a Lass, Composed for the Cherokee (Philadelphia, PA: Carr, 1796).

Cobb, Josiah, *A Green Hand's First Cruise, Roughed out from the Log-Book of Memory...*, 2 vols. (Baltimore, MD: Cushing & Brother, 1841).

Cobb, Elijah, *Elijah Cobb, 1768–1848, A Cape Cod Skipper*, Ralph D. Paine, foreword (New Haven, CT: Yale University Press, 1925).

Coffin, R. S., *A Concise Narrative of the Barbarous Treatment ...* (Danville, VT: Ebenezer Eaton, 1816).

Comstock, William, *The Life of Samuel Comstock, the Terrible Whaleman Containing an Account of the Mutiny, and Massacre of the Officers of the Ship Globe, of Nantucket ...* (Boston, MA: James Fisher, 1840).

Cooper, James Fenimore, *The Cruise of the Somers ...* (New York: J. Winchester, 1844).

History of the Navy of the United States, 2nd ed., 2 vols. (Philadelphia, PA: Lea and Blanchard, 1840).

Homeward Bound, or The Chase a Tale of the Sea (Philadelphia, PA: Carey, Lea & Blanchard, 1838).

ed., *Ned Myers, A Life before the Mast*, William S. Dudley, intro. (Annapolis, MD: Naval Institute Press, 1989; orig. pub. 1843).

The Pilot: A Tale of the Sea (New York: G. P. Putnam's Sons, n.d.; orig. pub. 1823).

The Red Rover, a Tale, Thomas and Marianne Philbrick, eds. (Albany: State University of New York Press, 1991; orig. pub. 1827).

The Water Witch: or the Skimmer of the Seas, a Tale (Philadelphia, PA: Carey and Lea, 1831).

The Wing-and Wing, or Le Few-Foullet, a Tale, Thomas Philbrick, ed. (New York: Henry Holt, 1998; orig. pub. 1842).

Cowdery, Jonathan, *American Captives in Tripoli ...*, 2nd ed. (Boston, MA: Bucher and Armstrong, 1806).

Crawford, Michael, ed., *The Autobiography of a Yankee Mariner: Christopher Prince and the American Revolution* (Washington, DC: Brassey's, 2002).

Crocker, Hannah Mather, *The School of Reform, or Seamen's Safe Pilot to the Cape of Good Hope* (Boston, MA: John Eliot, 1816).

Cross, J. C., *The Purse; or, Benevolent Tar ...* (London: R. Cowley, 1794).

Cross, J. C., *The Purse; or, Benevolent Tar ...* (Boston, MA: W. Pelham, 1797).

Cumberland, Richard, *The Sailor's Daughter: A Comedy in Five Acts* (New York: David Longworth, 1804).

Cutbush, Edward, *Observations on the Means of Preserving the Health of Soldiers and Sailors ...* (Philadelphia, PA: Thomas Dobson, 1808).

Dana, Jr., Richard Henry, *Cruelty to Seamen, Being the Case of Nichols and Couch* (Berkeley, CA: no pub., 1937; orig. pub. 1839).

The Seaman's Friend (Delmar, NY: Scholars' Facsimiles, 1979; orig. pub. 1851).

Two Years before the Mast: A Personal Narrative of Life at Sea, Thomas Philbrick, ed. (New York: Penguin, 1981; orig. pub. 1840).

Davis, Frederick J. and Ferris Tozer, *Sailor Songs or Chanties* (London: Boosley & Co., 1906).

Davis, Joshua, *A Narrative of Joshua Davis* ... (Baltimore, MD: B. Edes, 1811).

de Crevecoeur, J. Hector St. John, *Letters from an American Farmer and Sketches of 18th-Century America* (New York: Penguin, reprint edition, 1981).

Defoe, Daniel, *The Life and Adventures of Robinson Crusoe*, Angus Ross, ed. (New York: Penguin, 1965; orig. pub. 1719).

The Life, and Adventures, and Piracies of the Famous Captain Singleton, reprint of 1840 edition, Sir Walter Scott, ed. (New York: AMS Press, 1973; orig. pub. 1720).

Moll Flanders, an Authoritative Text: Backgrounds and Sources; Criticism, Edward Kelly, ed. (New York: Norton, 1973; orig. pub. 1722).

Dibden, Charles, *The Lucky Escape* (Philadelphia, PA: Carr & Rice, 1794).

Tom Bowling (London: 1790).

Poor Tom Bowling [sheet music] (Philadelphia, PA: Carr, 1794).

The Token (Philadelphia, PA: Carr, 1794).

Twas the Good Ship Rover; or the Greenwich Pensioner (Philadelphia, PA: Carr, 1794).

Dibden, Thomas, *Songs, Naval and National, of the Late Charles Dibden; with a Memoir and Addenda* (London: John Murray, 1841).

Dickenson, Jonathan, *The Remarkable Deliverance of Robert Barrow* ... (Dover, NH: Eliphant Lad, 1793).

Dickinson, John, *Letter from a Pennsylvania Farmer, to the Inhabitants of the British Colonies* (Boston, MA: John Mein, 1768).

Doddridge, Philip, *The Rise and Progress of Religion in the Soul* ... (London: J. Waugh, 1745).

Doerflinger, William Main, *Songs of the Sailor and Lumberman*, rev. ed. (New York: MacMillan, 1972; orig. pub. 1951).

Douglass, Frederick, *Life and Times of Frederick Douglass* ... rev. ed. (Boston, MA: DeWolfe. Fiske & Co. 1892).

Downs, Barnabas, Jr., *A Brief and Remarkable Narrative of the Life and Extreme Sufferings* ... (Boston, MA: E. Russell, 1786).

Duane, William, *The Mariner's Dictionary, or American Seaman's Vocabulary of Technical Terms* ... (Washington, DC: Duane, 1805).

Dubois-Fantalle, Jean Gaspard, *The Shipwreck and Adventures of Monsieur Viaud ...*, trans. from the French by Mrs. Griffith ... (Dover, NH: Samuel Bragg Jr., 1799).

Duncan, Archibald, *The Mariner's Chronicle; being a Collection of the Most Interesting Narratives of Shipwrecks, Fires, Famines, and Other Calamities Incident to a Life of Maritime Enterprise; with Authentic Particulars of the Extraordinary Adventures and Sufferings of the Crews, Their Reception and Treatment on Distant Shores; and a Concise Description of the Country, Customs, and Manners of the Inhabitants: Including an Account of the Deliverance of the Survivors. By Archibald Duncan, Esq. Late of the Royal Navy. In Four Volumes.* Vol. I–IV (Philadelphia, PA: James Humphreys, 1806).

The Mariner's Chronicle; Being a Collection of the Most Interesting Narratives of Shipwrecks, Fires, Famines, and Other Calamities Incident to a Life of Maritime Enterprise; with Authentic Particulars of the Extraordinary Adventures and Sufferings of the Crews, Their Reception and Treatment on Distant Shores; and a Concise Description of the Country, Customs, and Manners of the Inhabitants: Including an Account of the Deliverance of the Survivors. By Archibald Duncan, Esq. Late of the Royal Navy. In Four Volumes. Vol. I–IV (Philadelphia, PA: Thomas Desilver, 1810).

Dunlap, William, *Yankee Chronology; or, Huzza for the Constitution!* ... (New York: D. Longworth, 1812).

Durand, James, *James Durand: Able Seaman of 1812* ..., George S. Brooks, ed. (New Haven, CT: Yale University Press, 1926; orig. pub. 1820).

Egerton, Charles Calvert, *The Journal of the Unfortunate Prisoner* ... (Baltimore, MD: Printed for the Author, 1813).

Elliott, John, *The Reformed: An Old Sailor's Legacy* (Boston, MA: Usher and Strickland, 1841).

Ellms, Charles, *Robinson Crusoe's Own Book: Or, The Voice of Adventure, from the Civilized Man Cut off from His Fellows* ... (Boston, MA: Joshua V. Pierce, 1843).

Shipwrecks and Disasters at Sea, or Historical Narratives of the Most Noted Calamities and Providential Deliverances from Fire and Famine on the Ocean. With a Sketch of the Various Expedients for Preserving the Life of Mariners By the Aid of Life Boats, Life Preservers, &c. (Boston, MA: S. N. Dickinson, 1836).

Emerson, Joseph, *A Chart for Seamen: Exhibited in a Sermon Preached in Beverly* ... (Salem, MA: John Cushing, 1804).

Equiano, Olaudah, *The Interesting Narrative of the Life of Olaudah Equiano*, Robert J. Allison, ed. (Boston, MA: Bedford St. Martin's, 1995; orig. pub. 1789).

Falconer, William, *The Shipwreck: A Poem, in Three Cantos, by a Sailor* (London: A Millar, 1762).

An Universal Dictionary of the Marine ... (London: T. Cadell, 1769).

Fanning, Nathaniel, *Fanning's Narrative: Being the Memoirs* ..., John S. Barnes, ed. (New York: Naval History Society, 1912; orig. pub. 1806).

Narrative of the Adventures of Nathaniel Fanning ... (New York: Printed for the Author, 1806).

Fielding, Henry, *Tom Jones, an Authoritative Text: Contemporary Reactions; Criticism*, Sheridan Warner Baker, ed. (New York: Norton, 1973; orig. pub. 1749).

Fillmore, John, *A Narration of the Captivity of John Fillmore* ... (Suffield, CT: Gray, 1802).

Flavel, John, *Navigation Spiritualized; or a New Compass for Seamen* ... (Newburyport, MA: Edmund Blunt, 1796; orig. pub. 1664).

The Touchstone of Sincerity ... (Boston, MA: E. Bellamy, 1818; orig. pub. 1679).

Foote, Caleb, ed., "Reminiscences of the Revolution. Prison Letters of Caleb Foot: Born 1750; Died 1787," *EIHC*, 26 (1889): 90–122.

Fordyce, William Mavor, *Historical Account of the Celebrated Voyages, Travels, and Discoveries, from the Time of Columbus to the Present Period*, 14 vols. (Philadelphia, PA: Samuel F. Bradford, 1802).

Foss, John, *A Journal of the Captivity and Sufferings of John Foss: Several Years a Prisoner in Algiers* ... (Newburyport, MA: A. March, 1798).

Fox, Ebenezer, *The Adventures of Ebenezer Fox in the Revolutionary War* ... (Boston, MA: Charles Fox, 1848).

Freneau, Philip, *Some Account of the Capture of the Ship Aurora* (New York: M. F. Mansfield and E. A. Wessels, 1899).

Furlong, Lawrence, *The American Coast Pilot* ..., 1st ed. (Newburyport, MA: Blunt and March, 1796).

Gay, John, *Black Eyed Susan's Garland. Composed of Four Excellent New Songs...* (Worcester, UK: s.n., 1770?).

Gibbon, Edward, *The History of the Decline and Fall of the Roman Empire*, Vol. 1 (London: W. Strahan, 1776).

Goldsmith, Oliver, *An History of the Earth and Animated Nature*, 8 vols. (London: J. Nourse, 1774).

Good, John Mason, *The Book of Nature*, 3 vols. (London: Longman, Rees, Orme, Brown, and Green, 1826).

Gould, Roland, *The Life of Gould, an Ex-Man-of-War's-Man* ... (Claremont, NH: Claremont Manufacturing Co., 1867).

Greene Albert, *Recollections of the Jersey Prison-Ship* ... (Providence, RI: H. H. Brown, 1829).

Griffon, Edmund Dorr, *The Claims of Seamen: A Sermon Preached* ... (New York: J. Seymour, 1819).

Griffon, John, *Anecdotes of a Sailor* (Hartford, CT: Hartford Evangelical Tract Society, 1816).

Grose, Francis, *A Classical Dictionary of the Vulgar Tongue* (London: S. Hooper, 1785).

Hamilton, Alexander, et al., *The Federalist Papers*, Clinton Rossiter, ed. (New York: New American Library, 1961).

Harlow, Frederick Pease, *Chanteying aboard American Ships* (Barre, MA: Barre Publishing, 1962).

Hart, Joseph C., *Miriam Coffin, or The Whale-Fishermen*, Edward Halsey Foster, foreword (New York: Garrett Press, 1969; orig. pub. 1834).

Hawkins, Christopher, *The Adventures of Christopher Hawkins* ... (New York: Privately Printed, 1864).

Hawthorne, Nathaniel, *The Scarlet Letter* (New York: Vintage, 1990; orig. pub. 1850).

ed., *The Yarn of a Yankee Privateer*, Clifford Smyth, introduction (New York: Funk and Wagnalls, 1926; orig. pub. 1846).

Hazen, Edward, *The Panorama of the Professions* ... (Philadelphia, PA: Uriah Hunt, 1836).

Hazen, Jacob, *Five Years before the Mast* ..., 2nd ed. (Philadelphia, PA: William P. Hazard, 1854).

Henshaw, J. S., *Around the World: A Narrative of a Voyage in the East India Squadron* ..., 2 vols. (New York: Charles S. Francis, 1840).

Herbert, Charles, *A Relic of the Revolution* ... (Boston, MA: Charles H. Pierce, 1847).

Hoare, Prince, *The Sailor Boy* (Philadelphia, PA: Carr, 1793).

Holland, Edward C., *Odes, Naval Songs, and Other Occasional Poems* (Charleston, SC: J. Hoff, 1813).

Hoxse, John, *The Yankee Tar* ... (Northampton, MA: John Metcalf, 1840).

Hugill, Stan, *Shanties and Sailors' Songs* (New York: Frederick A. Praeger, 1969).
   Shanties from the Seven Seas: Shipboard Work-Songs from the Great Days of Sail (Mystic, CT: Mystic Seaport Museum, 1994).

Huntington, Gale, *Songs the Whalemen Sang* (Barre, MA: Barre Publishers, 1964).

Ingersoll, Samuel B., *Address Delivered before the Marine Bible Society of New-Haven* ... (New Haven, CT: Office of the Religious Intelligencer, 1819)

Irving, Washington, *Bracebridge Hall, or The Humorists Medley* (New York: C. S. Van Winkle, 1822).
   Letters of Jonathan Oldstyle, Gent ..., Bruce I. Granger and Martha Hartzog, eds. (Boston, MA: Twaine Publishers, 1977).

Isaacs, Nicholas Peter, *Twenty Years before the Mast* ... (New York: J. P. Beckworth, 1845).

Johnson, Charles, *A General History of the Pyrates, from Their First Rise and Settlement in the Island of Providence, to the Present Time* ..., 2nd ed. (London: T. Warner, 1724).
   The History of Blackbeard & Roche, Two Noted Pyrates (Salem, MA: Cushing, 1802).

Johnson, Ebenezer, *A Short Account of a Northwest Voyage, Performed in the Years 1796, 1797 & 1798* (Boston, MA: Printed for the Author, 1798).

Jones, George, *Sketches of Naval Life, with Notices of Men, Manners and Scenery* ..., 2 vols. (New Haven, CT: Hezekiah Hone, 1829).

Keate, George, *An Account of the Pelew Islands* ... (Philadelphia, PA: Joseph Crukshank, 1789).

Kinsey, Terry L., *Songs of the Sea* (London: Robert Hale, 1989).

Lane, Horace, *The Wandering Boy, or Careless Sailor* ... (Skaneateles, NY: Luther Pratt, 1839).

Larcom, Henry, "Captain Larcom's Narrative," *Hartford Connecticut Courant*, August 15, 1810.

Lawrence, Mary Chipman, *The Captain's Best Mate: The Journal of Mary Chipman Lawrence on the Whaler Addison, 1856–1860*, Stanton Garner, ed. (Hanover, NH: Published for Brown University Press by University Press of New England, 1966).

Lay, William and Cyrus M. Hussey, *A Narrative of the Mutiny on Board the Whaleship Globe* (New London, CT: William Lay and C. M. Hussey, 1828).

Leavitt, Joshua, *Seaman's Devotional Assistant, and Mariner Hymns* ... (New York: Sleight and Robinson, 1830).
   Seamen's Devotional Assistant, and Mariners' Hymns ... (New York: William Van Norden, Printer, 1836).

Leech, Samuel, *A Voice from the Main Deck: Being a Record of the Thirty Years' Adventures of Samuel Leech*, Michael J. Crawford, ed. (Annapolis, MD: Naval Institute Press, 1999; orig. pub. 1843).

Leggett, William, *Naval Stories* (New York: G. & C. & H. Carvill, 1834).

Tales and Sketches by a Country Schoolmaster (New York: J. & J. Harper, 1829).

Lever, Darcy, *The Young Sea Officer's Sheet Anchor, or a Key to the Leading of Rigging and to Practical Seamanship* (New York: Edward W. Sweetman, 1963; orig. pub. 1819).

Liddel, R., *The Seaman's New Vade Mecum: Containing a Practical Essay on Naval Book-Keeping ...* (London: G.G. and J. Robinson, 1794).

Lightcraft, George, *Scraps from the Log Book, of George Lightcraft ...* (Syracuse, NY: Hall & Dickinson, 1847).

Lincoln, Barnabas, *Narrative of the Capture, and Sufferings and Escape of Capt. Barnabas Lincoln and His Crew ...* (Boston, MA: Ezra Lincoln, 1822).

Little, George, *The American Cruiser: A Tale of the Last War* (Boston, MA: W. J. Reynolds and Co., 1847).

Life on the Ocean; or Twenty Years at Sea ... (Baltimore, MD: Armstrong & Berry, 1843.)

Lorraine, Alfred, *The Helm, the Sword, and the Cross: A Life Narrative* (Cincinnati, OH: Poe and Hitchcock, 1862).

Mackenzie, Alexander Slidell, *Case of the Somers' Mutiny Defence of Alexander Slidell Mackenzie, Commander of the U.S. Brig Somers, before the Court Martial Held at the Navy Yard, Brooklyn* (New York: Tribune Office, 1843).

Maclay, William, *Journal of William Maclay, United States Senator from Pennsylvania, 1789–1791* (Washington, DC: U.S. Congress, Senate, 1998).

Macy, Obed, *The History of Nantucket ...* (Boston, MA: Hilliard, Gray, and Co., 1835).

Malham, John, *The Naval Gazateer, or Seaman's Guide, Containing a Full and Accurate Account ... of the Several Coasts of the Countries and Islands in the Known World ...* (Boston, MA: W. Spotswood and J. Nancrede, 1797).

Marine Bible Society Charleston, South Carolina, *First Annual Report of the Marine Bible Society ...* (Charleston, SC: W. P. Young, 1819).

Marine Bible Society of New York, *Constitution of the Marine Bible Society of New York ...* (New York: J. Seymour, 1817).

Report of the Marine Bible Society of New-York, at Their First Anniversary Meeting, April 21, 1817 (New York: J. Seymour, 1817).

The Third Annual Report of the Marine Bible Society of New-York ... (New York: J. Seymour, 1819).

Mark, Richard, *The Shipmates: An Evening Conversation; being a Supplement to the Tract Intitled, Conversation in a Boat* (Hartford, CT: Hartford Evangelical Tract Society, 1818).

Marryat, Captain Frederick, *Mr. Midshipman Easy* (New York: Penguin, 1982; orig. pub. 1836).

Poor Jack (London: George Rutledge and Sons, 1840).

Martingdale, Hawser, *Tales of the Ocean, and Essays for the Forecastle ...* (New York: John Slater, 1840).

Mavor, William Fordyce, *Historical Account of the Celebrated Voyages, Travels, and Discoveries* ... 14 vols. (Philadelphia, PA: Samuel F. Bradford, 1802).

M'Lean, James, *Seventeen Years History of the Life and Sufferings of James M'Lean* ... (Hartford, CT: B. J. Russell, 1814).

McNally, William, *Evils and Abuses in the Naval and Merchant Service Exposed* ... (Boston, MA: Cassady and March, 1839).

Melish, John, *A Description of Dartmoor Prison with an Account of the Massacre* ... (Philadelphia, PA: for the author, 1815).

Melville, Herman, *Billy Budd, Sailor and Other Stories*, Harold Beaver, ed. (New York: Penguin, 1967; orig. pub. 1924).

Moby Dick, or the Whale (New York: Modern Library, 1982; orig. pub. 1851).

Omoo: A Narrative of Adventures in the South Seas, Harrison Hayford, ed. (Evanston, IL: 1968; orig. pub. 1847).

Redburn: His First Voyage, being the Sailor-boy Confessions and Reminiscences of the Son-of-a-Gentleman in the Merchant Service, Harold Beaver, ed. (New York: Penguin, 1976; orig. pub. 1849).

Typee: A Peep at Polynesian Life during a Four Month's Residence in a Valley of the Marquesas (New York, 1964; orig. pub. 1846).

White-Jacket, or The World in a Man-of-War, Alfred Kazin, introduction (New York: New American Library, 1979; orig. pub. 1850).

Mercier, Henry James, *Life in a Man of War, or Scenes in "Old Ironsides"* ... (Philadelphia, PA: L. R. Bailey, 1841).

Miltmore, William, *Seamen's Farewell: A Discourse Preached at Falmouth* ... (Portland, ME: M'Kown, 1811).

Moore, John Hamilton, *The Practical Navigator and Seaman's New Daily Assistant* ..., 3rd ed. (London: B. Law, 1776).

The New Practical Navigator ... (Newburyport, MA: Edmund M. Blunt, 1799).

Morrell, Abby Jane, *Narrative of a Voyage to the Ethiopic and South Atlantic, Indian Ocean, Chinese Sea, North and South Pacific Ocean in the Years 1829, 1830, 1831* (New York: J. J. Harper, 1833).

Morrell, Benjamin, Jr., *A Narrative of Four Voyages, to the South* ... (New York: J. & J. Harper, 1832).

Murray, Lieutenant, *Fanny Campbell, the Female Pirate Captain: A Tale of the Revolution* (New York: Samuel French, 1844).

Fanny Campbell, the Female Pirate Captain: A Tale of the Revolution (Boston, MA: F. Gleason, 1845).

Murrell, William Meacham, *Cruise of the Frigate Columbia around the World* ... (Boston, MA: Benjamin B. Mussey, 1840).

Neese, Robert W., ed., *American Naval Songs and Ballads* (New Haven, CT: Yale University Press, 1938).

New Bedford Port Society, *Twelfth Annual Report* (New Bedford, MA: 1842).

Nicholson, Thomas, *An Affecting Narrative of the Captivity and Sufferings of Thomas Nicholson* ... (Boston, MA: H. Trumbull, 1816).

Norden, Frederik Ludvig, *Travels in Egypt and Nubia. By Frederick Lewis Norden. F.r.s. Captain of the Danish Navy* ... (London: Lockyer Davis and Charles Reymers, 1757).

Nordhoff, Charles, *Man-of-War-Life: A Boy's Experience in the United States Navy* ..., John B. Hattendorf, intro. (Annapolis, MD: Naval Institute Press, 1985; orig. pub. 1855).

Norman, John, *The American Pilot, Containing the Navigation of the Sea Coasts of North America* ... (Boston, MA: John Norman, 1791).

Olmsted, Francis Allyn, *Incidents of a Whaling Voyage* ... (New York: D. Appleton, 1841).

Palmer, Benjamin F., *The Diary of Benjamin F. Palmer, Privateersman* ... (n. p.: Acorn Club, 1914).

Palmer, Roy, ed., *The Oxford Book of Sea Songs* (Oxford: Oxford University Press, 1986).

Park, James Allen, *A System of the Law of Marine Insurances* ... (London: reprinted in Philadelphia, PA: Joseph Crukshank, 1789).

Parker, Lucretia, *Piratical Barbarity or the Female Captive* ... (New York: S. Walker for G. Parker, 1825).

Paulding, Hiram, *Journal of a Cruise of the United States Schooner Dolphin* ... (New-York: G. & C. & H. Carvill, 1831).

Pelham, Edward, *Narrative of the Adventures, Sufferings, and Deliverance of Eight English Seamen, Left by Accident in Greenland, in the Year 1630* ... (Philadelphia, PA: Bennett and Walton, 1812).

Penny, Joshua, *The Life and Adventures of Joshua Penny* ... (New York: Alden Spooner, 1815).

Pepys, Samuel, *The Diary of Samuel Pepys. A New and Complete Transcription*, Robert Latham and William Matthews, eds., 9 vols. (Berkeley, University of California Press, 1970).

Pierce, Nathaniel, "Journal of Nathaniel Pierce of Newburyport, Kept at Dartmoor Prison, 1814–1815," *EIHC*, 73 (1937): 24–59.

Poe, Edgar Allan, *The Narrative of Gordon Pym of Nantucket*, Harold Beaver, ed. (New York: Penguin, 1975; orig. pub. 1838).

Potter, Israel R., *Life and Adventures of Israel Potter* ... (Providence, RI: J. Howard, 1824).

Purse, John C., *Songs in the Purse; or, Benevolent Tar, a Musical Drama in One Act. As Performed at the New Theatre, Philadelphia* (Philadelphia, PA: Wrigley and Berriman, 1794).

Quin, Michael J., *A Steam Voyage down the Danube with Sketches of Hungary, Wallachia, Servia, Turkey, &c.*, 2nd ed., rev. and corr. (London: R. Bentley, 1835).

Ray, William, *Horrors of Slavery; or the American Tars in Tripoli* ... (Troy, NY: Oliver Lyon, 1808).

Redding, Cyrus, *A History of Shipwrecks and Disasters at Sea, from the Most Authentic Sources*, 2 vols. (London: Whitaker, Treacher & co., 1833).

Reece, Richard, *The Lady's Medical Guide: Being a Popular Treatise on the Causes, Prevention, and Mode of Treatment* ... (Philadelphia, PA: Carey, Lea, and Blanchard, 1833).

Reeve, William, *When Seated with Sal: A Favorite Sea Song Sung by Mr. Harwood in the Purse, or Benevolent Tar* (Philadelphia, PA: Carr, 1795).

Reynolds, J. N., *Address, on the Subject of a Surveying and Exploring Expedition to the Pacific Ocean* ... (New York: Harper & Brothers, 1836).

Reynolds, William, *The Private Journal of William Reynolds: United States Exploring Expedition, 838–1842,* Nathaniel Philbrick and Thomas Philbrick, eds. (New York: Penguin, 2004).

Rhodes, John, *The Sufferings of John Rhodes* ... (New York: Cotton and Foreman, 1798).

Riley, James, *An Authentic Narrative of the American Brig Commerce* ... (Hartford, CT: Printed for the Author, 1817).

Roberts, Edmund, *Embassy to the Eastern Courts of Cochin-China, Siam, and Muscat* ... (New York: Harper & Brothers, 1837).

Romeyn, John B., *A Sermon Delivered in the Middle Dutch Church ... for the Benefit of the New-York Marine Missionary Society* (New York: J. Seymour, 1819).

Rowson, Susanna, *Captain Truxton or "Huzza" for the Constellation* (New York: Hewett for Carrs, 1799).

Huzza for the Constellation (Philadelphia, PA: B. Carr, 1799).

The Little Sailor Boy. A Ballad (Philadelphia, PA: Carr, 1798).

New Song ... The Sailors's Landlady, (Philadelphia, PA: M. Carey, 1794).

Slaves in Algiers ... (Philadelphia, PA: Wrigley and Berrian, 1794).

Truxton's Victory: A Naval Patriotic Song (Boston, MA: Thomas and Andrews, 1799).

Ruschenberger, William Samuel Waithman, *Three Years in the Pacific: Including Notices of Brazil, Chile, Bolivia, and Peru* (Philadelphia, PA: Carey, Lea & Blanchard, 1834).

Russell, William, "Journal of William Russell (1776–1782)," in Ralph D. Payne, *The Ships and Sailors of Old Salem: The Record of a Brilliant Era of American Achievement* (New York: The Outing Publishing Company, 1909), 118–74.

Ryther, John, *The Seaman's Preacher: Consisting of Nine Short and Plain Discourses on Jonah's Voyage Addressed to Seamen* (Cambridge: William Hilliard, 1806).

Sanborn, Solomon H., *An Exposition of Official Tyranny in the United States Navy* (New York: no pub., 1841).

Saunders, Ann, *Narrative of the Shipwreck and Sufferings of Miss Ann Saunders* ... (Providence, RI: Z. S. Crossman, 1827).

Saunders, Daniel, Jr., *A Journal of the Travels and Sufferings of Daniel Saunders* ... (Salem, MA: Thomas C. Cushing, 1794).

Scott, Walter, *The Pirate* (Edinburgh: Archibald Constable, 1822).

Seabury, Samuel, *Free Thoughts on the Proceedings of the Continental Congress* ... (New York: James Rivington, 1774).

Seamen's Aid Society, *Ninth Annual Report of the Seaman's Aid Society of the City of Boston* (Boston, MA: S. N. Dickinson, 1842).

Shaw, Elijah, *Short Sketch, of the Life of Elijah Shaw, Who Served for Twenty-Two Years in the Navy* ... (Rochester, NY: Strong & Dawson, 1843).

Sherburne, Andrew, *Memoirs of Andrew Sherburne* ... (Utica, NY: William Williams, 1828).

Smith, Aaron, *The Atrocities of the Pirates* ... (New York: Robert Lowry, 1824).

Smith, Moses, *Naval Scenes in the Last War* ... (Boston, MA: Gleason Publishing Hall, 1846).

Smith, Thomas, "Revolutionary Letter from Thomas Smith, Forton Prison, 1780," *EIHC*, 41 (1905): 227.

Smith, Venture, *A Narrative of the Life and Adventures of Venture, A Native of Africa* ... (New London, CT: C. Holt, 1798).

Smollett, Tobias, *The Adventures of Roderick Random*, James G. Basker, et al., eds. (Athens: University of Georgia Press, 2012; orig. pub. 1748).

Solis, A., *Dying Confession of Pirates, viz. Collins, Furtado, and Palacha* ... (Boston, MA: no pub., 1794).

Soren, John. *The Narrative of Mr. John Soren ... Piratically Captured on the High Seas* ... (Boston, MA: no pub., 1800).

Stafford, Ward, *Important to Seamen, Extracts for a Report Entitled New Missionary Field* (New York: no pub., 1817).

  New Missionary Field: A Report to the Female Missionary Society for the Poor ... (New York: J. Seymour, 1817).

Stark, Cordelia, *The Female Wanderer: An Interesting Tale Founded on Fact, Written by Herself* (no place: Printed for the Proprietor, 1824).

Stedman, Ebenezer, *Catalogue of Sea-Books, Charts, Pilots for Sale by Ebenezer Stedman, at the Newburyport Bookstore* (Newburyport, MA: Broadside, 1804).

Steven, James Wilson, *An Historical and Geographical Account of Algiers* ... (Philadelphia, PA: Hogan & M'Elroy, 1797).

Stewart, C. S., *A Visit to the South Sea, in the U.S. Ship Vincennes* ..., 2 vols. (New York: John P. Haven, 1831).

Storace, Steven, *The Shipwrecked Seaman's Ghost* (Philadelphia, PA: Carr, 1793).

Stout, Benjamin, *Narrative of the Loss of the Ship Hercules* ... (New York: James Chevalier, 1798).

Sullivan, William, *Sea Life: or What May or May Not Be Done, and What Ought to be Done By Ship-Owners, Ship Masters, Mates and Seamen* (Boston, MA: James B. Dow, 1837).

Swett, Samuel, *An Interesting Narrative of the Loss of the Ship Milo* ... (Newburyport, MA: William B. Allan, 1814).

Taylor, Fitch W., *The Broad Pennant: or A Cruise in the United States Flag Ship of the Gulf Squadron* ... (New York: Leavitt, Trow & Co., 1848).

  A Voyage Round the World, and Visits to Various Foreign Countries in the United States Frigate Columbia ..., 2 vols. (New Haven, CT: H. Mansfield, 1856).

Taylor, Raynor, *The American Captive's Emancipation: Written by a Tar* (Philadelphia, PA: G. E. Blake, 1805).

Thoreau, Henry David, *Cape Cod* (New York: Penguin, 1987; orig. pub. 1865).

Thomas, R., *Interesting and Authentic Narratives of the Most Remarkable Shipwrecks, Famines, Calamities, Providential Deliveries, and Lamentable Disasters on the Sea* ... (Boston, MA: Shepard, Oliver and Co., 1835).

Thompson, George, "Diary of George Thompson of Newburyport, Kept at Forton Prison, England, 1777–81," *EIHC*, 76 (1940): 221–42.

Torrey, F. P., *Journal of the Cruise of the United States Ship Ohio* ... (Boston, MA: Samuel N. Dickinson, 1841).

Torrey, William, *Torrey's Narrative* ... (Boston, MA: A. J. Wright, 1848).

Trotter, Thomas, *Medicina Nautica: An Essay on the Diseases of Seamen* ... (London: T. Cadell, Jun. and W. Davies, 1797).

Observations on the Scurvy ... (Philadelphia, PA: John Parker, 1793).

Truair, John, *Call from the Ocean, Or an Appeal to the Patriot and the Christian in Behalf of Seamen* (New York: John Gray, 1826).

Truxton, Thomas, *Remarks, Instructions, and Examples Relating to the Latitude and Longitude* ... (Philadelphia, PA: T. Dobson, 1794).

Tyler, Royall, *The Algerine Captive* ... (Walpole, NH: David Carlisle Jr., 1797).

Tyng, Charles, *Before the Wind: The Memoir of an American Sea Captain, 1808–1833*, Susan Fels, ed. (New York: Penguin 1999).

United States, *Extract from the Naval Regulations, Issued by Command of the President of the United States of America January 25, 1802* (New York: Prior and Dunning, 1810).

Rules, Regulations, and Instructions for the Naval Service of the United States ... (Washington, DC: E. De Krafft, 1818).

U.S. Statutes at Large 1 (1790).

University of California, Santa Barbara, English Broadside Ballad Archive, online.

Valpey, Joseph, Jr., *Journal of Joseph Valpey, Jr., of Salem, November 1813–April 1815: With Other Papers Relating to His Experience in Dartmoor Prison* (no place: Michigan Society of Colonial Wars, 1922).

Vaux, James Hardy, *Memoirs of James Hardy Vaux, Written by Himself* (London: W. Clowes, 1819).

Waddell, John Hunter, *The Dartmoor Massacre* (Boston, MA: no pub., 1815).

Wallis, Mary Davis, *Life in Feejee, or Five Years among Cannibals* (no place: William Heatth, 1851).

Warren, Samuel, *Ten Thousand a-Year* (Edinburgh: W. Blackwood and Sons, 1841).

Warriner, Francis, *Cruise of the United States Frigate Potomac Round the World, during the Years 1831–34* ... (New York: Leavitt, Lord & co., 1835).

Waterhouse, Benjamin, *A Journal of a Young Man of Massachusetts* ... (Lexington, KY: Worsley & Smith, 1816).

Wheland, William, *A Narrative of the Horrid Murder & Piracy* ... (Philadelphia, PA: Folwell, 1800).

Widger, William, "The Diary of William Widger of Marblehead, Kept at Mill Prison, England, 1781, *EIHC*, 73 (1937), 311–47 and ibid., 74 (1938), 22–23, 48, 142–58.

Willcock, John, *The Voyages and Adventures of John Willcock, Mariner* ... (Philadelphia, PA: George Gibson, 1798).

Williams, William, *Mr. Penrose: The Journal of Penrose, Seaman*, David Howard Dickason, ed. (Bloomington: Indiana University Press, 1969; orig. pub. 1815).

Wines, E. C., *Two Years and a Half in the Navy: Or, Journal of a Cruise in the Mediterranean and Levant* ... (Philadelphia, PA: Carey & Lea, 1832).

Index